Frontier Democracy

Frontier Democracy examines the debates over state constitutions in the antebellum Northwest (Indiana, Illinois, Iowa, Michigan, Minnesota, Ohio, and Wisconsin) from the 1820s through the 1850s. This is a book about conversations: in particular, the fights and negotiations over the core ideals in the constitutions that brought these frontier communities to life. Silvana R. Siddali argues that the northwestern debates over representation and citizenship reveal two profound commitments: the first, to fair deliberation, and the second, to ethical principles based on republicanism, Christianity, and science. Some of these ideas succeeded brilliantly: within forty years, the region became an economic and demographic success story. However, some failed tragically: racial hatred prevailed everywhere in the region, in spite of reformers' passionate arguments for justice, and resulted in disfranchisement and even exclusion for nonwhite northwesterners that lasted for generations.

Silvana R. Siddali is Associate Professor of History at Saint Louis University.

Frontier Democracy

Constitutional Conventions in the Old Northwest

SILVANA R. SIDDALI
Saint Louis University

CAMBRIDGE
UNIVERSITY PRESS

CAMBRIDGE
UNIVERSITY PRESS

32 Avenue of the Americas, New York, NY 10013-2473, USA

Cambridge University Press is part of the University of Cambridge.

It furthers the University's mission by disseminating knowledge in the pursuit of education, learning, and research at the highest international levels of excellence.

www.cambridge.org
Information on this title: www.cambridge.org/9781107090767

First published 2016

Printed in the United States of America

A catalog record for this publication is available from the British Library.

Library of Congress Cataloging in Publication Data
Siddali, Silvana R., author.
Frontier democracy : constitutional conventions in the Old Northwest / Silvana R. Siddali.
pages cm
Includes bibliographical references and index.
ISBN 978-1-107-09076-7 (hardback)
1. Constitutional conventions – Northwest, Old – History – 19th century.
2. Northwest, Old – Politics and government – 19th century. 3. Northwest, Old – Social conditions – 19th century. I. Title.
KF4530.S55 2015
342.77'024209034–dc23 2015025686

ISBN 978-1-107-09076-7 Hardback

In loving memory of my parents

Contents

Permissions

For parts of Chapter 7:

Portions adapted from "'Principle, Interest, and Patriotism all Combine': The Fight over Iowa's Capital City," by Silvana R. Siddali, *Annals of Iowa* 64 (Spring 2005): 111–38. Used with the permission of the publisher.

For parts of Chapter 10:

Copyright by the Western History Association. Reprinted by permission. The article first appeared as Silvana R. Siddali, "Regulating the Jackals of the Monetary World: Banking and Constitutional Reform in the Antebellum Northwest," *Western Historical Quarterly* 44 (Winter 2013): 389–409.

Illustrations

FIGURES

TABLES

MAPS

Acknowledgments

So many archivists, colleagues, family members, friends, funding agencies, institutions, and librarians have helped me with this project that I may never be able to thank them all properly, but I know what a great debt I owe to all of them. I should begin with my late mentor, William Gienapp, who inspired my abiding fascination with the antebellum era. To this day, I miss his encouragement, his support, and his understanding of awkward nineteenth-century humor. God rest his soul. I'm also grateful to dear friends from graduate school, who remained staunch allies throughout the vagaries of storming the Academy. To name just a few: Andy Coopersmith, Christine Dee, Yonatan Eyal, Libra Hilde, Susan Hunt, Pearl Ponce, Corinna Treitel, Mike Vorenberg, and Eva Sheppard Wolfe. Most of these friends read drafts of various chapters, and all of them supplied moral support. Chandra Manning deserves her own special thank you for taking the time to read my manuscript at the busiest possible moment in her career. Chandra is always a great inspiration and a reminder of all the reasons I love history.

In its early stages this book received funding from Illinois State University. I'd like to thank my friends and colleagues in the History Department there, especially Kyle Ciani, Ray Clemens, Linda Clemmons, Michal Ditzian, John Freed, Alan Lessoff, Patrice Olsen, and Lou Perez, all of whom read and critiqued early drafts.

I am grateful for generous funding from the Bentley Historical Library at the University of Michigan, the Gilder-Lehrman Institute, the State Historical Society of Iowa, the Lilly Library at Indiana University, the Mercantile Library at the University of Missouri-St. Louis, the National Endowment for the Humanities, and the Newberry Library in Chicago.

One of the greatest pleasures of a historian's life is to work with archivists and librarians. I am deeply grateful to all of the many kind and helpful people who worked with me at the Abraham Lincoln Presidential Library;

the Allen County, Indiana, Public Library; the Bentley Historical Library; the Chicago Historical Society; the Clements Library at the University of Michigan (particularly Barbara deWolfe); the Gilcrease Museum Archives; the Indiana State Archives; the Indiana State Historical Society; the Indiana State Library; the Indiana State Museum and Historic Sites; the Indiana Supreme Court; the Iowa State Historical Society in Des Moines and in Iowa City; the Kent State University Archives; the Library of Congress Manuscripts Division; the Mercantile Library in St. Louis, Missouri (especially Charlie Brown); the Minnesota Historical Society; the Missouri Historical Society (especially Dennis Northcott), the National Archives; the New York Public Library Manuscripts and Rare Books Divisions; the Oberlin College Archives; the Ohio State Historical Society; the Pius XII Library at Saint Louis University; the Regenstein Library at the University of Chicago, the Western Historical Manuscripts Collection at the University of Missouri; and the State Historical Society of Wisconsin. It would be impossible to thank individually every person who worked with me at these marvelous institutions, but I hope they know how grateful I am.

Saint Louis University has supported this work with funding for research travel, time off from teaching, and, perhaps most valuable of all, with outstanding graduate research assistants: Brian Forbes, Rob Haulton, Mike Karp, Aleksey Kazakevich, Chris Schnell, and Cindy Stachecki. I should single out Chris Schnell in particular because he served for two patient and long-suffering years, and his expertise in antebellum legal history was especially valuable throughout the final stages of writing. Chris Pudlowski and Kelly Goersch: You are always so patient, knowledgeable, and encouraging. I couldn't do my job without you. At Saint Louis University, I also received the Summer Research Award, several grants from the Mellon Fund, and the President's Research Fund, without which this book would have taken many more years to finish. Colleagues at SLU, particularly those who participated in the faculty seminars, have been very helpful in reading (far too many) drafts. Thanks especially to Flannery Burke, Phil Gavitt, Lorri Glover, Torrie Hester, Ben Looker, Emily Lutenski, Matt Mancini, Nathaniel Millett, Hal Parker, Jen Popiel, Michal Rozbicki, Mark Ruff, Damian Smith, and Katrina Thompson. I'm especially grateful to Damian, a Medievalist, for reading the entire manuscript and giving me the benefit of his incisive scholarly mind and his precise British prose.

Speaking of which: As a member of the British American Nineteenth Century Historians, I have been able to draw on a great fund of knowledge, friendship, and good cheer. I would especially like to thank Richard Carwardine, who has been kind enough to mentor me since Bill Gienapp's early passing. Dave Brown, Chris Clark, Martin Crawford, Susan-Mary Grant, Don Ratcliffe, and Rob Cook commentated conference papers and provided valuable critiques.

I must also thank good friends and colleagues in my own field who were generous with their time and their expertise. Dennis Boman critiqued the delegates chapter and provided nineteenth-century encouragement and wit;

Nathan Jérémie-Brink, David Brodnax Sr., Deborah Cohen, Anna-Lisa Grace Cox, Jim Huston (who has always been unfailingly kind and generous), Stacey Robertson, Jim Simeone, and Dana Weiner have all been terrific colleagues. Stacey was kind enough to read and commentate the chapter on wives at a very busy time in her life. Anders Walker read and critiqued the three legal history chapters. Thank you for all your helpful advice. Of course all errors remain my own responsibility. I'd also like to thank the anonymous reviewers, whose comments helped improve the book beyond measure. Warm thanks to Deborah Gershenowitz and to Dana Bricken for all their patience and help. I am so grateful for your faith in this project. Thanks also to Nishanthini Vetrivel and to Susan Thornton.

Thanks as always to Patrick McAllister, my steadfast companion. Finally, to my family, my great love and everlasting appreciation: Wolff, Chris, Raphael, Mary, Steve, Gita, Erica, John, Jim, and Laura.

Introduction

In January 1851, delegates to the Colored Citizens League gathered in Columbus, Ohio, to protest their disenfranchisement in the state constitution. Although these women and men had been meeting annually for several years, the 1851 convention was of special significance. The league had timed their meeting to coincide with the Ohio state constitutional convention, which – even at that moment – was considering whether to grant suffrage to black men. Representatives from the league met with delegates from the constitutional convention to present their demands for justice and equality. Declaring that their "social, political, and religious rights [were] at the mercy of the [Ohio] law-makers," the league delegates now insisted that the convention grant equal voting rights to black men. They received a sympathetic hearing from several of the more reform-minded members of the constitutional convention, but their efforts failed: The 1851 Ohio state constitution retained the word "white" in its list of voter qualifications. Yet the members of the league had insisted on (and won) a meeting with the convention delegates, a concession that suggests that they were able to participate in the conversation about reforming their state government. More to the point, it also suggests that they believed in the power of democratic deliberation to change society, in spite of the fact that they had been forcibly excluded from the constitution-building project.[1]

How do citizens in a racially and politically diverse frontier democracy talk to each other about framing governments and defining rights? What happens when those citizens – in spite of the profound differences that drive them apart – agree on the core ethical principles of democratic self-government? *Frontier Democracy* explores the creation of constitutional democracies in new political communities. More specifically, this book investigates the building of state

[1] *Minutes of the State Convention of the Colored Citizens of Ohio, Convened at Columbus, Jan. 15th, 16th, 17th, and 18th, 1851* (Columbus, OH: 1851), 1: 266.

constitutions in the antebellum Northwest (Indiana, Illinois, Iowa, Michigan, Minnesota, Ohio, and Wisconsin) from the 1820s through the 1850s. Even so, *Frontier Democracy* is primarily a book about conversations rather than about foundational documents: in particular, the fights and negotiations over the core ideals in the constitutions that brought these new communities to life.

To put these ideas into perspective, it may be instructive to contemplate an 1847 petition from a group of angry Illinois citizens. Upon hearing, to their dismay, that the Illinois constitutional convention had refused to talk about a provision excluding black people from the state, the petitioners complained that this decision "stifled their voices." The resolution not to act on black exclusion negated the "will of the people" and, worst of all, promoted the destruction of good society and the peace of the community. The petitioners declared that they had no other remedy than to place their demands before the "convention of the people." The only way to ensure that their rights would be respected – in this case, to live in a segregated society – was to inscribe that privilege into the state constitution.[2] In the long run the Illinois petitioners prevailed. The constitutional convention reconsidered its earlier decision and permitted Illinois citizens to vote on the question of black persons' exclusion from Illinois. The result was a resounding victory for the petitioners: 60,585 voted for exclusion, and 15,903 against. The situation in Ohio was only slightly more propitious. The state had already dismantled some of the black laws the year before the convention met but did not grant full political equality to black men (at least on paper) until the 1880s. Although the delegates to the 1850 Ohio state constitution did not debate an exclusion provision, their convention votes on the black suffrage provision were similarly depressing: thirteen for black suffrage, and seventy-five against.[3]

Both the Ohio antiprejudice activists and the Illinois proexclusion petitioners believed that they had to address a constitutional body in order to establish the kind of society they wanted. This paradox exposes a thorny question – indeed, a dilemma that all northwestern delegates confronted. Was the process of building a democratic constitution morally neutral? That is: Could such conversations and negotiations (at least in theory) accommodate both

[2] Illinois Constitutional Convention, *Journal of the Convention, Assembled at Springfield ... for the Purpose of Altering, Amending, or Revising the Constitution of ... Illinois* (Springfield: Lanphier & Walker, 1847), 95–96. The petition was signed by H. J. Grimsley and five other unnamed people. H. J. Grimsley was probably Harrison J. Grimsley, active in antiabolition vigilante posses, who had married Eliza Todd (Mary Todd Lincoln's cousin) in 1842. The state constitutional convention had decided the day before, on June 25, 1847, to table a proposal for such a provision. For the convention discussion, see Arthur Charles Cole, ed., *The Constitutional Debates of 1847*, vol. 14 of Collections of the Illinois State Historical Library (Springfield: Illinois State Historical Library, 1919), 228.

[3] For votes on black exclusion and disenfranchisement, see Table 8.2, Chapter 8. For information on black exclusion laws and constitutional convention provisions, see Leslie A. Schwalm, *Emancipation's Diaspora: Race and Reconstruction in the Upper Midwest* (Chapel Hill: University of North Carolina Press, 2009), chap. 1.

those people fighting for their rights and those people battling for a segregated society? Antebellum delegates would not have considered that a legitimate question. Each side argued that the other misinterpreted the foundational principles of American constitutionalism or, worse, deliberately twisted those principles for selfish and destructive ends. While the process of constitution building was under way, the delegates had to allow all members of society to have a say; constitutional conventions had been intentionally designed that way. And some outsiders would make powerful ethical arguments that explicitly framed the constitution-making project as a moral enterprise. Yet the end product (the state constitution and any referendum questions left open for a public vote) could only be ratified by legitimate voters, most of whom consistently denied rights to the outsiders. If a society inscribed racial injustice in its written constitution, then that constitution would shape laws, judicial decisions, and economic arrangements for generations. Could such a society be considered democratic and republican, even by the standards antebellum northwesterners set up for themselves? While I hope this question has been settled, at least in philosophy and law, for modern Americans, it was still open to question in the antebellum Northwest.

The antebellum Northwest provides an opportunity to watch people strive to build new governments in a hectic, pressured, hopeful, violent new region: in some ways a great laboratory in which both traditional and innovative ideas were tested to their limits. I chose to write about a region I call the "Northwest," an area slightly larger than the Old Northwest and somewhat smaller than the new Midwest. That way I could study the idea of constitutionalism in a region nominally (though not in practice) free of slavery, a region that represented the working out of American democracy, and one whose government was based on an ordinance that enshrined many rights. The original Northwest Territory comprised the present-day states of Illinois, Indiana, Michigan, Ohio, and Wisconsin, as well as part of what is today Minnesota. I have included Iowa (Map 1), as a state bordering on the Mississippi, and as one of the agriculturally most important free states in the Great Lakes and Upper Mississippi region. I have excluded states such as Kansas and Nebraska because both were part of the bitter controversies over slavery, and both entered the Union during or after the Civil War.

During those contentious years (the 1820s through the late 1850s) every state in the nation attempted to revise its constitution, and nearly two-thirds of them succeeded.[4] Historians usually observe that the great age of state constitutional revision was triggered, in large part, by the economic panics that plagued the antebellum era. Citizens throughout the nation were trying to balance legislative power with political, economic, and cultural aims, and in order

[4] For an extremely useful and detailed discussion of state constitutional conventions in a national context, see John J. Dinan, *The American State Constitutional Tradition* (Lawrence: University Press of Kansas, 2009), 7–28.

MAP 1. The Old Northwest with Iowa.

to achieve lasting changes, they had to rewrite (not just amend) their state charters. My book examines one region – the fastest-growing and economically most vibrant in the nation – in an effort to search for deeper reasons for this era of fervent constitutionalism. This book suggests that the process of building and revising state constitutions during those fractious decades represented a profound moral struggle. If the constitutional deliberations, both inside and outside the convention halls, were the arena for that struggle, then the specific subjects under debate (black people's rights, banks and paper money, married women's property rights, the power of the legislature, and the authority of the judiciary) were the objectives at stake. Those topics were vitally important to all northwesterners. For many of the people living in the region, the outcomes of the convention debates represented the difference between a decent, worthwhile, prosperous life and a corrupt, degraded, impoverished existence. After all, the new state constitutions would frame governments, delineate rights, clarify the state's physical boundaries, and empower all the branches of government. The newly elected delegates who traveled to their state capitals to undertake this challenge believed that so long as they followed the basic constitutional principles and paid attention to the popular will they would be able to acquit themselves honorably. But they soon found that writing democratic charters for new communities in a diverse region entailed insuperable challenges.

The colonial charters of Virginia (1606) and Connecticut (1662) swept away Indian possessions by extending the western boundaries to the Mississippi River, thus granting ownership of all lands to the colonial proprietors. Five other states claimed lands in the western continent.[5] Throughout the eighteenth century, British and French explorers and fur traders set up trade relationships with the people who lived in the Northwest: the Ojibwa and Huron in the Great Lakes region, the Miami and Kickapoo farther south near the Mississippi, and the Leni Lenape, Shawnee, and Wyandotte in the Ohio Country. Illegal settlements caused serious problems with the Native people already living in the region, to a degree that forced the British government to pass an ordinance in 1763 forbidding settlement west of the Ohio River – a law that was essentially ignored. By the early 1780s, before the Treaty of Paris settled the land claims west of Pennsylvania in 1783, thousands of Americans had already begun to move across the Appalachian Mountains into the Northwest, northward into Vermont and Maine, and southward to Arkansas and Texas. Meanwhile, the British and French retained control in military forts, and French voyageurs who had intermarried with Indian women founded families of about four thousand métis people in Wisconsin and Minnesota.[6]

The western lands claimed by the seven states created serious rivalries with those five states without land claims (Delaware, Maryland, New Jersey, Pennsylvania, and Rhode Island.) Delaware, Maryland, and New Jersey at first refused to ratify the Articles of Confederation government until the larger states agreed to give up their lands to the public domain. As a concession to states that did not hold land, and in order to ensure ratification, these landholding states ceded their claims on the territory to the federal government: New York in 1782, Virginia in 1784, Massachusetts and Connecticut in 1786. Virginia and Connecticut reserved the land of two areas to use as compensation to military veterans: the Virginia Military District and the Connecticut Western Reserve. As a result the majority of the territory became public land owned by

[5] The following states had western land claims: Connecticut, Georgia, Massachusetts, New York, North Carolina, South Carolina, and Virginia.

[6] Beverley W. Bond, *The Civilization of the Old Northwest: A Study of Political, Social, and Economic Developments, 1788–1812* (New York: MacMillan, 1934), 3. See also, Andrew Cayton, *Contact Points: American Frontiers from the Mohawk Valley to the Mississippi, 1760–1830* (Chapel Hill: University of North Carolina Press, 1998).

the U.S. government. Thomas Jefferson crafted a series of land ordinances to cope with these disputes and to facilitate white settlement. The 1784 ordinance allowed for orderly settlement but encouraged large-scale land speculation, essentially a way to ensure that the country would be settled quickly and to create revenue for a nearly bankrupt national government. This ordinance established the grid pattern, established future self-government (that is, rejected the idea of colonial relationships for the new territories), and attempted two radical innovations: prohibition of slavery and free lands for settlers (ultimately dropped from subsequent iterations of the ordinance.) The 1785 ordinance decreed that the region would eventually be subdivided into three to five states; townships would be six miles square, subdivided into thirty-six sections of 640 acres. That amounted to four family farms and one lot for schools. The grid pattern, the disregard for individual topographical features or even the presence of timber and water, and the minimum purchase requirement of 640 acres and hard money made it more difficult for individual settlers to obtain land and encouraged large-scale speculators.[7]

Two years later, the articles government passed Jefferson's 1787 Northwest Ordinance, which set up stages of development from territory to statehood. The Northwest Territory (then known as the Territory Northwest of the River Ohio) was to write its own legal code and appoint local magistrates. By 1803, a year after Ohio joined the Union, Congress assigned the rest of the Old Northwest to the Indiana Territory, which was later subdivided. The resulting territories were renamed and reconfigured with the growing population. When settlement had proceeded to the point where five hundred families had acquired a fifty-acre freehold, the inhabitants elected their own territorial legislature and a congressional (nonvoting) delegate. The third stage, at which point the territory was presumably ready to assume the burdens and responsibilities of self-governance, occurred when the number of white inhabitants had reached sixty thousand. The territory now began the process of electing delegates to a state constitutional convention. The territorial legislature passed an enabling act, which empowered the legislature to set up elections and to assemble the machinery of constitution building. The first three territories to achieve statehood (Ohio in 1802, Indiana in 1816, and Illinois in 1818) moved quickly and copied the majority of the constitutional provisions from older states: Kentucky, Virginia, and New York. Those three conventions were able to finish their work in three to four weeks in spite of bitter divisions over slavery, black people's civic rights, and battles over the gubernatorial veto.[8]

[7] For public land policy development and Anglo-American settlement in the Northwest see Paul W. Gates, *History of Public Land Law Development* (Washington, DC: U.S. Government Printing Office, 1968), 33–86; see also, Malcolm Rohrbough, *Land Office Business: The Settlement and Administration of American Public Lands, 1789–1837* (New York: Oxford University Press, 1968).

[8] Nicole Etcheson, *Emerging Midwest: Upland Southerners and the Political Culture of the Old Northwest, 1787–1861* (Bloomington: Indiana University Press, 1996), explains that by the 1840s sectional differences had become muted, though she argues that they flared up again

Within two decades, as thousands of people migrated into these states from the South, from the mid-Atlantic, and from New England, the people living in these three states began to talk about the need to revise their first constitutions. Meanwhile, inhabitants in the new territories started the process toward statehood. By the late 1840s the region had changed dramatically. Northwestern citizens demanded fundamental constitutional reform: not just minor problem-solving amendments, but a radical transformation that weakened state legislatures, rendered political offices elective, did away with grand juries, and strengthened the power of the people to influence their representatives. By that point, swift western expansion, two catastrophic economic crises, and sharpening sectional divisions rendered constitution building a much more difficult task. While the first territorial conventions took three or four weeks, the conventions from 1835 through 1857 took much longer – some as long as six months. During this period of intense democratic reform, state constitutional conventions throughout the nation made significant democratizing changes in the structure of government. And they were usually successful. This was especially true in the antebellum Northwest, where state constitutional revision shortened legislative sessions and rendered annual sessions biennial, deprived lawmaking bodies of the authority to pass economic legislation, and instituted popular vetoes over economic legislation, such as the state assembly's right to charter private corporations.

By 1850, about 5 million people lived in the Ohio River Valley, the Great Lakes region, and the area west of the Mississippi River north of Missouri. By comparison, the total U.S. population was about 23 million. Within a decade, the upper Midwest expanded to nearly 7 million inhabitants and was home to a quarter of the U.S. population.[9] In the United States, 2,244,000 (9.7 percent) were foreign born in 1850. In the Middle West, the percentage was somewhat higher (about 12 percent), or 500,000.[10] The farther north the state, and the newer the state, the higher the percentage of foreign born. Those included Canadians and European immigrants from the German states, as well as from Scandinavia, Ireland, England, Wales, and Scotland. Historians have also frequently commented on the sectional nature of the population changes, particularly when "Yankees" from New England began to move into upper Illinois

during the Civil War era. For further discussion and the national context on regional migration to the west, see Christopher Clark, *Social Change in America: From the Revolution through the Civil War* (Chicago: Ivan R. Dee, 2006), 149–151.

9 Robert P. Swierenga, "The Settlement of the Old Northwest: Ethnic Pluralism in a Featureless Plain," *Journal of the Early Republic* 9 (Spring 1989): 86.

10 Richard Sisson, Christian Zacher, Andrew Cayton, eds., *The American Midwest: An Interpretive Encyclopedia* (Bloomington, IN: 2007), 180; Swierenga, "The Settlement of the Old Northwest: Ethnic Pluralism in a Featureless Plain," 73–105; Richard K. Vedder, "Migration and the Old Northwest," *Essays in Nineteenth Century American Economic History: The Old Northwest*, ed. David C. Klingaman and Richard K. Vedder (Athens: Ohio University Press, 1997), 161.

and Indiana. New Englanders had always lived in the Western Reserve of Ohio and antislavery Quakers had been populating eastern counties along what was then the Ohio-Virginia border. Nicole Etcheson's *Emerging Midwest* traces the cultural divide between the two groups but also explains that the conflicts became muted in the early nineteenth century, a conclusion that is borne out by the research for this book. For the purposes of building their constitutions, and resolving conflicts in democratic self-governance, the delegates and their constituencies forged political alliances on the most controversial issues. By the late 1840s through the late 1850s, the time when every state in the region held constitutional conventions to create or revise its charter, the states' populations had spread northward and westward to their present-day borders, and political divisions became more important than demographic or sectional ones. Delegates were aware of and occasionally referred to the intensifying sectional conflict. But other than antiprejudice or antislavery comments, most delegates were wary of discussing contemporary political events in the conventions.

Frontier Democracy picks up the story at the moment the northwestern states were beginning to push their way into the national polity and economy. These territories and states were not merely interested in joining the Union. They declared themselves to be equal in every political, economic, and cultural arena. This book examines the eleven northwestern conventions that occurred during the antebellum era, roughly from 1835 to 1857. Although the constitutions formed by the first three conventions (Ohio 1802, Indiana 1816, and Illinois 1818) laid the foundation for the later constitutions, these charters were primarily copied from older southern and eastern state constitutions and were therefore less innovative than the constitutions written after 1830.

State	First Constitution	Failed Attempts	Revised Constitutions
Illinois	1818	1824 (voters rejected the call for a convention)	1848*
Indiana	1816		1851*
Iowa	1846*	1844*	1857*
Michigan	1835*		1850*
Minnesota	1857*		
Ohio	1802		1851*
Wisconsin	1848*	1846*	

* This book discusses the conventions marked with an asterisk.

Two nonnegotiable requirements framed the delegates' work: They had to abide by parliamentary procedures, and they had to carry out the mandates of the U.S. Constitution and the Northwest Ordinance in their work. Even so, there was still plenty of room for all sorts of popular intrusions. This book argues that the conversations within and outside the convention halls reveal two crucial aspects of democratic self-governance. First, in spite of obstinate antebellum cultural attitudes toward nonwhite people, northwesterners did not flinch from painful subjects even when overwhelming majorities supported a predictable outcome. Therefore, people who were deliberately excluded from participating in their own governments could and often did join in the ongoing conversations. They may have lost every battle in the struggle for equality, but they maintained a presence in all conversations. The radical reformers – who must have known how slim their chances were of reforming northwestern society – chose to stand on the foundational frameworks (religion, scientific reason, and revolutionary ideology) in their arguments. As a result, and in small and hesitant ways, I suggest, they were able to change the terms of the debate. *Frontier Democracy* explores how the undergirding frameworks – republicanism, Christianity, and reason – fared in the debates over self-government during the most contentious and economically challenging decades of the nineteenth century. Some of these ideas succeeded brilliantly: Within forty years, the region became an economic success story, as well as the geographic and demographic center of the nation. And some failed tragically: Racial hatred prevailed everywhere in the region, in spite of reformers' passionate arguments for justice, and resulted in disfranchisement and even exclusion for nonwhite northwesterners that lasted for generations.

No matter how frustrating or painful some of these conversations may have become, however, northwesterners remained deeply committed to seeing them through. They loved talking to one another about the kind of government they wanted: specifically, how they envisioned and defined justice and democracy on an antebellum frontier. As these people – black, white, Indian, migrants from the New England and southern states, European immigrants, men and women – argued over their new governments, they discovered that they had to rethink everything they had believed about democracy, rights, and justice: indeed, what it meant to be an American citizen. They debated every aspect of their political, economic, and private lives, including the citizenship of black people and Indians; the placement of important state and local boundaries, as well as transportation and civic projects such as canals, railroads, colleges, and courthouses; married women's property rights; the role of the judiciary; and economic problems and institutions including banks, debts, and paper money.

Most of the delegates who took up these subjects in the conventions would have shared an agreement that constitutions should be both ethical and rational. Even in a society that revered popular sovereignty and took great care to engrave it in the foundational charters, ethics and reason had to remain the pillars that supported the work. The constant back and forth in those conversations – between foundational principles and unwritten prejudices, between convention delegates and their constituencies – forms the core narrative here. Underlying deeply held beliefs embraced all their conversations, even while the delegates fought so bitterly and (at the same time) attempted to compromise with one another. The origin of these ideas and theoretical frameworks can be traced to the core sources for nineteenth-century American thought: Scripture, Greek and Roman classical writers, and the eighteenth- and nineteenth-century political and philosophical thinkers, whom the college-educated delegates would have studied as young men. Those included Enlightenment authors (chiefly John Locke and Montesquieu), as well as Scottish Enlightenment thinkers including William Paley and Thomas Reid. The lawyer delegates would have been deeply familiar with English legal theorist William Blackstone, and American legal commentators such as Joseph Story and Chancellor James Kent. The citizens living in the region, even those who had not been educated beyond basic literacy, were aware of and persuaded by a worldview that combined Christianity, democracy, reason, and history. These people experienced little trouble, in the abstract, imagining a divinely created universe in which Christianity and nature created a perfect democratic body of law. The purpose of constitutions was to frame governments and delineate rights, but constitutions also had a higher purpose as well: to reflect and support ethics and reason, and to create a just, law-abiding, and moral polity.

How would this best be achieved? For antebellum Americans, that had to be done through written agreements. They wanted to be able to read a physical document that set forth these negotiations in ink on paper, so that they could decide for themselves whether their rights, and the rights of their communities, were being respected. Yet there was an awkward contradiction in the notion that constitutions could frame out agreements based on immutable principles and, at the same time, abide by local customs and conditions. In most northwestern minds, that conflict could give rise to political disagreements, but it certainly did not imply a criticism of popular sovereignty. Such a suggestion that would have been considered unpatriotic and even heretical in the early nineteenth century. Antebellum Americans firmly believed that the very process of constitution building (which would have included the deliberations, the public discussions, and the final act of ratification) was in itself an elevating process, and would have beneficial effects on all participants. Yet they were able to mold these principles into a framework that supported discrimination and segregation. Modern readers are probably less shocked by the notion that popular sovereignty is neither inherently moral nor even reasonable, especially when they confront the relentless race prejudice and resulting discrimination against and disfranchisement of nonwhite persons.

That logical and ethical paradox is precisely what this book explores. Northwesterners struggled to resolve their conflicts through the medium of public and private conversations. This analysis concerns itself with these conversations, therefore, rather than with the largely predictable outcomes. In an effort to trace the development of northwestern opinions on constitutional matters, the individual chapters delve into the philosophical, spiritual, and political roots of those opinions. That in itself is a difficult task and requires some speculation, since the speakers were not always careful to harmonize their political opinions or personal feelings with their own ideals. Yet as their letters, speeches, and newspaper editorials reveal, northwesterners understood these ideas as part of a unified whole, and they took seriously the notion that they would have to (and would be able to) construct a government that harmonized with those frameworks. Local needs, alongside time-honored social, religious, and cultural traditions, had to remain at the forefront of this work. If their goal was to set up a just democratic government, then they would have to allow room for many nonlegal customs and rules, including unwritten laws about a respectable family life or, more problematically, what nineteenth-century American reformers called "the laws of prejudice." All sorts of rules could serve as laws, such as, for example, the laws of nature or the axioms of mathematics. Other laws were agreed upon in formal political votes in assemblies and constitutional conventions. Those were usually reported in newspapers. Still others were recorded for posterity in the journals of constitutional or reform conventions. Judicial verdicts could act as laws if they affected subsequent economic or social arrangements. Powerful social prejudices became laws when they deprived persons of their legal and constitutional rights. This concatenation of written and unwritten laws, colliding as it did just at the moment the northwestern communities were writing their own governing charters, created a nearly insoluble logical and moral dilemma, one that reached into every area of the human experience.

Northwesterners' concerns reveal how they thought about the human condition, and about law and justice. In my research, I used a rough-and-ready heuristic to discover the topics of most burning interest to the convention delegates and to their constituencies: Simply, which questions took up the most space in convention debates? Which ones inspired the most commentary in popular petitions, letters, and newspaper editorials? And finally, which ones ignited the most inflammatory rhetoric inside and outside the convention halls? Those three categories overlapped, but were not identical. For example, the convention delegates debated black people's rights at immense length, but the home front largely avoided that question. For their part, the citizens were deeply engaged with the location of state and county capitals, and state and county boundaries, but the delegates in most states usually disposed of such issues in committee meetings. It may be worth explaining that some crucial aspects of democratic governance will not be extensively discussed here – not because I did not consider them important, but simply because they were rarely raised in the conventions or in the public discussions. Because the core theme explored in this book is the way people talked to one another about democratic governance, I decided to focus on the subjects that agitated the delegates and the citizens. That does not mean that the delegates ignored, or dismissed, such subjects as education, internal improvements, taxation, or constitutional amendment procedure. Most of those questions, however, were settled in the committees, and neither the delegates nor the public expressed strong views on them.

The danger of a thematic arrangement is that it can mislead the reader into imagining a well-organized and coherent process. The delegates followed parliamentary procedure, and they worked from a set agenda, but their conversations often devolved into angry rants, and they frequently dragged in irrelevant subjects. The rhetorical style of the conversations and the emotional and even physical outbursts are, I believe, a crucial factor in understanding how antebellum Americans worked and fought with each other and how they built their governments. Therefore, the book begins by presenting the delegates as they arrived in the state capitals to start their work in the conventions. Their daily lives and the demands they faced forced them to confront an onslaught of private and political pressures that shaped both the constitutions and their future careers. Indeed, the pressure became an important part of the story. Specifically, the delegates felt that they had to leave the most controversial topics to popular referenda in order to prevent a wholesale rejection of their constitutions. In this way popular sovereignty (for good or ill) became the final arbiter of such crucial questions as black people's rights. Since all popular votes disenfranchised or excluded black people from the northwestern states, these odious restrictions became part of the state constitutional tradition in the Middle West and had far-reaching consequences for many generations of black people living in the region.

From there, the fundamental ideas and frameworks the delegates and their constituencies relied upon when they talked about democratic constitutional government are introduced. The next three chapters explain emerging interpretations about law: criticism of the common law, the relative power of legislatures and fears of their corruption and incompetence, and, finally, the move toward elective judiciaries and ideas about grassroots judicial review. The following two chapters place these conversations on the physical landscape and show how northwesterners "constitutionalized" ideas about land, property rights, and the physical state. Chapters 8 and 9 introduce the people whose rights were most under contention: people who were neither white nor male. Finally, Chapter 10 describes the fights over economic institutions and laws.

This book's title may conjure outdated ideas of egalitarian white men introducing democracy to an uncivilized wilderness, but the book's purpose and conclusions are nearly opposite. It may no longer be necessary to revisit the debates over Frederick Jackson Turner's frontier thesis. Most historians agree that both constitutionalism and democracy arrived before white settlers.[11] More to the point, conversations over the meaning of constitutionalism and democracy ignited a bitter and often quite exasperating battle that had to be fought out to a conclusion, whether the people who possessed the power and

[11] The historian Donald J. Ratcliffe argues persuasively that politics had already become "thoroughly democratized" in Ohio (and by extension, in the region) by the early nineteenth century. Donald J. Ratcliffe, *Party Spirit in a Frontier Republic: Democratic Politics in Ohio 1793–1821* (Columbus: Ohio State University, 1998), 12. For further discussion of the elimination of property qualifications in state constitutions, see also Dinan, *American State Constitutional Tradition*, 145–148.

the vote wanted to participate in that battle or not. This book attempts to get to the core of that painful dilemma. In many of these states it would take another century and a half before black people and Indians possessed the rights promised to them by the undergirding philosophy that, ideally, was supposed to guide the building of constitutions. Black people living in Illinois did not have the vote until 1870; the last vestige of Ohio black laws remained on the books until 1866, when Congress passed the Civil Rights Act. This book proposes that these debates function as a description of human moral struggles and not as a triumphalist or exceptionalist narrative. My own commitment to and faith in the idea of constitutional democracy will, I suppose, become clear throughout the coming chapters. Even if one contemplates the tragic failure of a human conflict over rights, the history of any confused, contradictory, morally fraught debate is always instructive in its own right. What is perhaps more hopeful is the notion that human beings, even at their most limited, can and often do strive for moral, rational, and just self-government. The degree to which northwesterners were able to accomplish those aims is uncertain. The combatants refused to allow popular sovereignty to reign without a moral or rational challenge. Certainly the most vital questions of human rights were never resolved during the antebellum decades and in some cases would take another century to come to fruition.

1

Delegates

FIGURE 1.1. Stephen Hempstead (1812–1883) served as a Democrat in the 1846 Iowa constitutional convention, and later became governor of the state of Iowa, 1850–1854. "Daguerreotype of Stephen Hempstead and daughter Olivia [#1450], circa 1850." *Source*: Unknown daguerreotype artist. Courtesy of the State Historical Society of Iowa, Des Moines.

Late in the evening on October 20, 1850, thirty-six year old farmer Oliver P. Davis sat "all alone" in his Indianapolis hotel room writing to his wife. Oliver had arrived in the state capital less than two weeks ago to serve as a delegate to the constitutional convention, and he already missed his family desperately. "To tell the honest truth," Oliver confessed to Eliza, "I am really homesick. I would give any thing to be with you today and see our little children." The Davis family owned a large farm in Vermillion County, close to the Illinois border, about seventy-five miles west of Indianapolis. That was too far to allow Oliver to visit his family more than a few times while the convention was in session. The separation from his wife, who was expecting another baby in January, left him anxious. As did most of his colleagues in the convention, Oliver Davis found the opportunity to help build his state's constitution both deeply interesting and profoundly irksome. And like most of the men he was learning to know in Indianapolis, he remained there, despite intense personal pressures and loneliness, until the task was accomplished. From 1802 through 1857, young white farmers, merchants, and lawyers gathered in constitutional conventions throughout the Great Lakes region.[1] They left their families, their crops, and their businesses to take a hand in crafting the constitutions that would frame their governments and define their rights. Most of them thought they would return home in a few weeks: Their task, after all, was simply to hammer together a basic document that met the requirements of the U.S. Constitution and the Northwest Ordinance and could pass a popular referendum. What they experienced, instead, was a grueling crash course in democratic deliberation.[2]

These delegates arrived in their state capitals prepared to work hard and to make a name for themselves. Most had a competent grasp of the fundamental principles of republican constitutionalism and parliamentary procedure.[3] What

[1] Judging from contemporary biographical references, about a third of the delegates had some local political experience. It is difficult to determine precisely how many served in the territorial or state legislatures. County histories and biographical dictionaries chronicled the lives of notable men, but many convention delegates (at least those who chose not to continue their political careers) have been lost to history. It has not been possible to compile detailed biographical information on the convention delegates. All but one of the conventions (Wisconsin 1848) published schedules containing the names, addresses, ages, and professions of the delegates. I have been able to find census information for many of the delegates in the 1850 and 1860 federal census returns. Census and genealogical databases provided some information on educational backgrounds, pre- and postconvention political careers, Civil War era military service, relative standing in their communities, but those data are not available for every delegate and must therefore be taken as speculative. See Tables 1.3a and 1.3b.

[2] Oliver Davis to Eliza Davis, October 20, 1850, Oliver Davis Papers, Indiana State Archives, Indianapolis.

[3] Data were drawn from the 1850 Federal Census, as well as contemporary biographical encyclopedias such as Appleton's, Arthur Cole's biographical sketches for Illinois delegates, Milo Milton Quaife's biographical sketches for Wisconsin delegates, as well as county histories, and state "Bar and Bench" biographical collections. All of this information is incomplete and must be interpreted

they did not fully appreciate, at least until they confronted their peers and rivals in the conventions, was the difficulty or even the necessity of building a functioning deliberative body. Tackling the creation of such a body – a separate living entity with its own ethos and personality – forced everything into the open: not just individual achievement, but also community welfare; not only political negotiations and differences, but a deep contemplation of how constitutions affected every aspect of their private and public lives. This chapter explores the relationships brought to life by these conventions: first, the delegates' unwilling, inadvertent, and sometimes even violent effort to build a deliberative body, and second, the delegates' fractured and highly volatile relationship with their constituencies, friends, families, and, perhaps most problematic of all, the people at the fringes of their political communities.

In the early 1840s, when he was still in his twenties, having recently arrived in Indiana from New Hampshire, Oliver Davis had read and practiced law for a few years. That meant that he had rather more legal education than many of his colleagues, whose youth, lack of political experience, and rough-and-ready relationship with their constituencies would exert a profound influence on the state constitutions they helped to build. As these men argued with one another over their new governments they discovered that they had to rethink everything they had believed about democracy, rights, and justice: indeed, what it meant to be an American citizen. They debated such burning issues as the citizenship of black people and Indians; the placement of important transportation and civic projects such as colleges, courthouses, canals, and railroads; married women's property rights; the role of the judiciary and grand juries in administering justice; and, spurring them on through every topic, the catastrophic economic problems that plagued their region during the 1820s through the 1850s.

All of those matters had to be worked out quickly and efficiently. No one could leave his farm, store, or office for long. Nothing would be worse than

with caution. Because so many delegates were lost to history (for example, I found detailed biographical information on only 51 of 162 Illinois delegates) the percentages of political experience and education and age may be somewhat inaccurate, but they resemble the patterns found in other northwestern states. I assume that the information for those conventions that compiled age, profession (Indiana, Ohio, both Iowa conventions), and political party affiliation (not found in Indiana) is reliable. Seventh Census of the United States, 1850 (National Archives Microfilm Publication M432, 1009 rolls), Records of the Bureau of the Census, Record Group 29, National Archives and Records Administration, Washington, DC (accessed using Ancestry.com); James Grant Wilson and John Fiske, eds., *Appletons' Cyclopedia of American Biography*, 6 vols. (New York: 1887–89); Arthur Charles Cole, ed., *The Constitutional Debates of 1847*, vol. 14 of *Collections of the Illinois State Historical Library* (Springfield: Illinois State Historical Library, 1919); Milo Milton Quaife, ed., *The Convention of 1846*, vol. 27 of *Publications of the State Historical Society of Wisconsin* (Madison: State Historical Society of Wisconsin, 1919); John M. Palmer, *The Bench and Bar of Illinois: Historical and Reminiscent*, 2 vols. (Chicago, 1899); Parker McCobb Reed, *The Bench and Bar of Wisconsin: History and Biography* (Milwaukee, 1882); Charles W. Taylor, *Biographical Sketches and Review of the Bench and Bar of Indiana....* (Indianapolis, 1895); *Bench and Bar of Iowa* (Chicago: American Biographical, 1901).

wasting an entire harvesting season in convention, only to have the charter fail in the popular vote or be dismissed in Congress. Yet these men had thrown their hats into the delegate races believing that they could accomplish their task before the harvest was ready to gather, or, at the latest, by the time the winter court sessions began. They had no reason to think otherwise; all of the earliest northwestern conventions (those that met before 1820) had been able to finish their work within three weeks. Theophilus Crawford, a member of the 1844 Iowa convention, wrote to his father in Vermont that he had been at Iowa City for three weeks and hoped to be home "in about one week more." His convention would take another five months to finish its labors.[4] The world had changed since the first white people settled in the region. Massive population growth, combined with the struggle to build a transportation, communication, and civic infrastructure, created problems that constitutional convention delegates would find nearly overwhelming. These men would have to find a way to make sense of those changes, with all the frustrating, difficult work that entailed.

The delegates coped with daunting challenges: First, they would have to contend with articulate, competitive opponents inside the convention. That was hard enough, particularly when those adversaries were more experienced, were better educated, or had more powerful backing from a majority political party. But that was not the worst. These men, many of whom were politically inexperienced, faced a steady onslaught of criticism, demands, petitions, and letters from outside the convention. These assaults came from their constituencies, the opposing partisan press, and from people excluded from the democratic processes (such as black people, Indians, and women activists) who refused to be silenced. In their effort to make sense of these pressures, the northwestern delegates, perhaps inadvertently, created a highly responsive constitutionalism that gave a prominent place to the public will.

The delegates had brushed up on the rules of parliamentary procedure, which, most believed, ought to be enough to keep the conventions operating efficiently. The younger, less-experienced men probably did not intend to make stirring speeches in the convention, but all must have expected to deliberate in the committee meetings. They would have defined deliberation as the process of winning over opponents through bracing oratory, through indisputable evidence, and, if all else failed, through political machinations such as back-room caucus deals. The lawyers would have had some experience making arguments and attempting to sway opinions. Even those who had never spoken in public would have negotiated business deals or real estate transactions. As active, hard-working young men unused to sitting in airless rooms for eight to ten

[4] Theophilus Crawford to Theophilus Crawford, October 27, 1844, Crawford Family Papers, State Historical Society of Iowa, Des Moines. Unfortunately the younger Crawford would discover that his convention (Iowa 1844) did waste its time: The voters rejected the constitution decisively, because of fights over the state boundaries.

hours a day, the delegates hoped, at best, to acquit themselves honorably, to make notable speeches (if they were so inclined), and to abide by the tenets laid down for them through national and state laws.

Yet if we define democratic deliberation as the full panoply of the private, public, and political conversations that bring constitutions to life, we find, then as now, a complicated undertaking. Successful and ethical deliberation involves the self-creation of a principled body: one that follows rules of procedure, enjoins civility, prevents the discussion from becoming bogged down in minutiae, and, above all, negotiates fair resolutions to internal conflicts. Such a body also requires access to the information it needs to do its job, and, if it is to be a democratic body, an efficient means of communicating its decisions to, and hearing the wishes of the community. Further, democratic deliberative bodies have physical requirements. The polity must be sufficiently developed (both in population as well as in transportation and civic infrastructure) to warrant the expense of a convention. Such a body must be large enough to represent people geographically, yet not so large as to be more expensive than the community could afford or to become hopelessly impractical. Perhaps most challenging of all, somehow these delegates had to represent both their communities and their political parties. In the case of the antebellum Northwest, that meant electing one or two delegates for each county, which by the 1840s and 1850s, could amount to upward of 150 men. Therefore, the towns in which the northwestern conventions met had to be able to accommodate the delegates in hotels and boarding houses, feed them in restaurants, furnish them with libraries and reading rooms, provide newspapers that could report their doings, and amuse or enlighten them. In short, a deliberative body was a luxury and required a developed civic, political, and cultural infrastructure, yet one that these states had to find a way to finance.

The ethical and rational requirements of fair deliberation demanded that the constitutional project, fraught as it was with political and local fights, had to be fair. After all, democratic constitutions are the result of conversations about good government and rights. Their very existence implies a willingness to negotiate and to abide by the resulting agreements.[5] Otherwise, why commit to such an expensive, time-consuming, and physically arduous effort? If the outcome were perceived to be unfair, or if the provisions went against the popular will, then all the delegates' hard work would be lost in the single popular vote that either ratified or scuttled the constitution. Therefore, throughout these conversations, the urgent transparency of the process in the Northwest facilitated an aggressive (and often effective) intrusion of the popular will.[6]

[5] See Arabella Lyon, *Deliberative Acts: Democracy, Rhetoric, and Rights* (University Park: Pennsylvania State University Press, 2013) for the theory of performative deliberation. See Christian Kock and Lisa S. Villadsen, eds., *Rhetorical Citizenship and Public Deliberation* (University Park: Pennsylvania State University Press, 2012), who argue that participation and deliberation are actually constitutive of citizenship.

[6] According to Maurizio Passerin d'Entrèves, Edmund Burke explained that parliament was a deliberative body, not just a collection of people who disagreed with one another. Maurizio

Black people and women activists – who would certainly never have been permitted to serve as delegates – refused to be excluded from these discussions. They participated in the deliberations through parallel reform conferences that met while several of the constitutional conventions were in session.[7] At least four African American conventions met in Ohio just before, during, and after the 1850 constitutional convention; two more met in Indiana. At least three women's rights conventions met in both Ohio and Indiana as well.[8] One of these conventions became nationally renowned. In Akron, Ohio, shortly after the convention finished its labors, Sojourner Truth gave her famous "Aren't I A Woman?" speech at the national Women's Convention in May 1851.[9] The women and men who

Passerin d'Entrèves, "Political Legitimacy and Democratic Deliberation" in *Democracy as Public Deliberation* (Manchester, UK: Manchester University Press, 2002), 1. Stephen Macedo, ed., in *Deliberative Politics: Essays on Democracy and Disagreement* (New York: Oxford University Press,1999), 3–4, argues that today moral decisions are taken away from citizens by the courts, so citizen role is sidelined; instead, emphasis is on individual rights. He describes a secular, scientific basis of argument that "unfairly silences the religious voice in our politics." I argue in Chapter 2 that in antebellum conventions, Christianity worked alongside and through science. In their essay "Democratic Disagreement" in *Deliberative Politics*, 243–79, Amy Gutmann and Dennis Thompson posit six basic moral principles, which, according to the editor, Macedo, cover a "broad swath of moral conflicts that should not be usurped by the courts" nor resolved by "interest group bargaining" (p. 5). See also, Seyla Benhabib, "Deliberative Rationality and Models of Democratic Legitimacy," *Constellations: An International Journal of Critical and Democratic Theory* 1, no. 1 (Dec. 1994): 26–52. On self-control, see Daniel Bell's essay "Democratic Deliberation: The Problem of Implementation," in *Deliberative Politics*, 73, where Bell explains that deliberation can often intensify conflicts. Sharon R. Krause explores the role of emotions in *Civil Passions: Moral Sentiment and Democratic Deliberation* (Princeton, NJ: Princeton University Press, 2008), where she is especially concerned with the role of moral formation and its influence on deliberation. Guido Pincione and Fernando R. Tesón in *Rational Choice and Deliberation: A Theory of Discourse Failure* (Cambridge: Cambridge University Press, 2006) have an excellent historiographic note at the beginning of chapter 1.

7 In Indiana, the Congregational Friends called a meeting at Greensboro, Henry County, in January 1851. The convention held October 14–15, 1851, at Dublin adopted resolutions for political, social, and financial rights for women. "State Convention of the People of Color of the State of Indiana," August 9, 1851, in Philip S. Foner and George E. Walker, eds., *Proceedings of the Black State Conventions, 1840–1865* (Philadelphia, PA: Temple University Press, 1979), 1: 176–77; "Minutes and Address of the State Convention of the Colored Citizens of Ohio, Convened at Columbus, January 10th, 11th, 12th, & 13th, 1849," in *Proceedings of the Black State Conventions*, 1: 218–40; "Minutes of the State Convention, of the Colored Citizens of Ohio, Convened at Columbus, January 9th, 10th, 11th, and 12th, 1850," in *Proceedings of the Black State Conventions*, 1: 241–56; "Minutes of the State Convention, of the Colored Citizens of Ohio, Convened at Columbus, Jan. 15th, 16th, 17th, and 18th, 1851," in *Proceedings of the Black State Conventions*, 1: 257–73.

8 Thomas D. Hamm, *The Anti-Slavery Movement in Henry County, Indiana*, 2nd ed. (New Castle, IN: Henry County Historical Society, 1987), 21, 23–25, 73; Thomas D. Hamm, *God's Government Begun: The Society for Universal Inquiry and Reform, 1842–1846* (Bloomington: Indiana University Press, 1995), 111–12, 217–18; Inez Haynes Irwin, *Angels and Amazons: A Hundred Years of American Women* (Garden City, NY: Doubleday, Doran, 1933), 91–92.

9 Nell Irvin Painter, *Sojourner Truth: A Life, a Symbol* (New York: W. W. Norton, 1996), 121. See also, Robert W. Audretsch, ed., *The Salem, Ohio, 1850 Women's Rights Convention Proceedings*

participated in the activist conventions spoke for a focused and united community that agreed on most fundamental goals and aims. They argued over strategy and discussed the precise wording of resolutions, but rarely differed over the need to fight for citizenship rights and equal education.

By contrast, the delegates for the state constitutional conventions represented the full range of political attitudes within their own communities. A few constitutional convention delegates represented radical reformers in their states, even though those people were a small (if highly vocal) minority. For the rest – the Jacksonian Democrat majority, the Free Soilers, and the chronically outnumbered Whigs – the elections betrayed a "politics as usual" attitude on the part of political wire workers. Constitutional reform provided rich opportunities for local political parties. It is likely that party caucuses chose most of the delegates, with or without their consent.[10] When territorial or state legislatures called for delegate elections, therefore, a political free-for-all ensued, and chicanery played a prominent role. In the Minnesota delegate elections for both parties, for example, hundreds of illegal ballots were cast in St. Paul, and "while the election board were at dinner certain rowdies known as the Swan River Blues took possession of the ballot box and threw it into the Mississippi river."[11] In Michigan, two opposing candidates for the 1835 convention became embroiled in an altercation on election day and candidate Mark Howard called his rival Edward Mundy "a traitor to his country" because of his accommodating stance on the Michigan boundary dispute. An eyewitness testified that "Mundy answered him, Howard kept at it," and Mundy then gave Howard "a single kick against ... said Howard's nether parts."[12] Mundy won the election. They need hardly have exerted themselves, however; there were few surprises in the outcome of that election or most of the others.[13]

At first glance these contests resulted in precisely the sort of body one would have predicted: a group of successful, well-educated white husbands and fathers in the prime of life, most of them Democrats and almost all of them Christians. The election outcomes, taken across all the states, show us who was considered the best possible person to help craft a young state's founding charter – indeed, to speak for the community, if we also study the delegates who attended the reform conventions. For that reason, political parties and leaders ran the

(Salem, OH: Salem Area Bicentennial Committee and Salem Public Library, 1976); and Indiana Woman's Suffrage Association, Record Book 1851–1886, folder 1, Indiana Historical Society, Indianapolis.

10 In Wisconsin, for example, party caucuses nominated the convention delegates. Robert C. Nesbit, *Wisconsin: A History*, 2nd ed. (Madison: University of Wisconsin Press, 2004), 214–16.

11 William D. Green, *Peculiar Imbalance: The Fall and Rise of Racial Equality in Early Minnesota* (St. Paul: Minnesota Historical Society Press, 2007), 83; William Anderson, "The Constitution of Minnesota," *Minnesota Law Review* 5, no. 6 (May 1921): 407–35.

12 "Sworn testimony by Leonard Stillson," November 10, 1836, Edward Mundy Papers, Bentley Historical Library, University of Michigan, Ann Arbor.

13 Logan Esarey claims that there was very little voter turnout. Logan Esarey, *A History of Indiana from Its Exploration to 1850*, 2nd ed. (Indianapolis, IN: B. F. Bowen, 1918), 1: 514.

delegate elections as political contests: usually in the same way and often at the same time as their state assembly or township elections. Undoubtedly most northwesterners understood the technical difference between state legislators and constitutional convention delegates. As future chapters will show, northwesterners placed greater confidence in, and had more respect for delegates than for their lawmakers. But the fact that the delegate and legislative elections were often carried out in the same place and time, and used the same rules for numerical representation, blurred the line between political representative and convention delegate. For example, because Illinois delegate election laws mandated an equal number of delegates and legislators, the 1847 convention was a huge, unwieldy body composed of 162 men.[14] The 1850 Indiana convention called for fifty delegates from senatorial districts and one hundred from House districts.[15] As a result northwesterners frequently wrote to their convention delegates, expecting them to behave as legislators, and the delegates often obliged with constitutional provisions that resembled legal code.

Party affiliations in conventions mirrored northwestern politics accurately. Democrats dominated almost all of the convention, just as they dominated state political offices (Table 1.1a outlines party affiliations, and Table 1.1b lists statewide election results). In many communities local party caucuses instructed the winners how to handle contentious issues. In its nominating conventions, for example, the Iowa Democratic Party instructed all candidates for the 1846 convention to vote against banks.[16] Whigs – always bitterly aware of their numerical minority, and always insisting that party politics ought to have no influence on the delegate elections or the constitutional deliberations – were sometimes able to negotiate or logroll for a slightly better showing. For example, districts that could not afford elections negotiated the number of delegates for each party. In Marion County, Indiana, local Whigs offered to divide the ticket evenly and "make no contest," but the Democrats, no doubt convinced they would win a majority in any case, refused.[17] In Ohio, where Democratic voters outnumbered Whigs by 1.5 to 1, the Whig *Scioto Gazette* plaintively compared the constitutional delegates to potential dictators, finding it "rather strange that decisions made for the whole state, were only in the hands of few."[18] A Whig Minnesota newspaper editor also denounced party influence

[14] Janet Cornelius, *The History of Constitution-Making in Illinois* (Urbana: University of Illinois Press, 1969), 29. See also, Robert S. Friedman and Sybil L. Stokes, "The Role of Constitution-Maker as Representative," *Midwest Journal of Political Science* 9, no. 2 (1965): 143–66.

[15] Esarey, *History of Indiana*, 1: 515.

[16] Howard Hall Preston, *History of Banking in Iowa* (Iowa City: State Historical Society of Iowa, 1922), 42; Benjamin F. Shambaugh, *History of the Constitutions of Iowa* (Des Moines: Historical Department of Iowa, 1902), 291–92.

[17] Esarey, *History of Indiana*, 1: 515. Indiana Whigs managed to negotiate for fusion tickets in other counties.

[18] *Scioto Gazette* (Chillicothe, OH), March 3, 1850.

TABLE 1.1A. *Political affiliation of convention delegates*

Party	Illinois (1847)	Indiana (1850)	Iowa (1844)	Iowa (1846)	Iowa (1857)	Michigan (1835)	Michigan (1850)	Ohio (1850)	Minnesota Democrats (1857)	Minnesota Republicans (1857)	Wisconsin (1846)	Wisconsin (1848)
Democrat	91	107	51	22	15	Unknown (large Dem. majority)[a]	79	64	59	–	103	46
Whig	71	52	21	10	–		21	41	–	–	18	23
Free Soil	–	1	–	–	–	–	–	3	–	–	–	–
Republican	–	–	–	–	21	–	–	–	–	55	–	–
Other	–	4	–	–	–	–	–	–	–	–	3	–

[a] The 1835 Michigan convention did not publish votes. No precise record of party affiliation exists, but the convention was "overwhelmingly Democratic," according to Harold M. Dorr, *The Michigan Constitutional Conventions of 1835–36: Debates and Proceedings* (Ann Arbor: 1940), 17.

TABLE 1.1B. *State election results*

Illinois votes, 1844–1848[a]
Presidential

Election of 1844	Candidates	Electoral vote	Popular vote
Democrat	James K. Polk	9	58,795
Whig	Henry Clay	0	45,854
Liberty	James G. Birney	0	3,469
Election of 1848	Candidates	Electoral vote	Popular vote
Democrat	Lewis Cass	9	55,952
Whig	Zachary Taylor	0	52,853
Free Soil	Martin Van Buren	0	15,702
Whig	Henry Clay	0	89

Votes for convention delegates

Convention of 1847	Votes cast	Number of delegates elected
Democrats	86,293	91
Whigs	47,747	71
Liberty	2,901	0
Other/Unknown	37,805	–

Indiana votes, 1844–1848[b]
Presidential

Election of 1848	Candidates	Electoral vote	Popular vote
Democrat	Lewis Cass	12	74,745
Whig	Zachary Taylor	0	69,907
Free Soil	Martin Van Buren	0	8,100
Election of 1852	Candidates	Electoral vote	Popular vote
Democrat	Franklin Pierce	13	95,340
Whig	Winfield Scott	0	80,901
Liberty	John Hale	0	6,929

Votes for convention delegates

Convention of 1850–51	Votes cast	Number of delegates elected
Democrats	56,011	107
Whigs	37,696	52
Free Soil	436	0
Other/Unknown	38,013	4

(*continued*)

TABLE 1.1B *(continued)*

Iowa votes Iowa presidential votes 1848–1860[c]				
	Presidential candidate	**Political party**	**Iowa electoral vote**	**Iowa popular vote**
Election of 1848	Lewis Cass	Democratic	4	11,238
	Zachary Taylor	Whig	0	9,930
	Martin Van Buren	Free Soil	0	1,103
Election of 1852	Franklin Pierce	Democratic	4	17,763
	Winfield Scott	Whig	0	15,856
	John Hale	Free Soil	0	1,606
Election of 1856	John Fremont	Republican	4	45,073
	James Buchanan	Democratic	0	37,568
	Millard Fillmore	American	0	9,669
Election of 1860	Abraham Lincoln	Republican	4	70,302
	Stephen Douglas	Democratic	0	55,639
	John Bell	Constitutional Union	0	1,763
	John Breckenridge	Southern Democrat	0	1,035

[a] Atlas of U.S. Presidential Elections, http://uselectionatlas.org/RESULTS/ (accessed October 11, 2011); NARA, U.S. Historical Election Results, http://www.archives.gov/federal-register/electoral-college/votes/votes_by_state.html (accessed October 11, 2011); Theodore Calvin Pease, *Illinois Election Returns, 1818–1848* (Springfield: Illinois State Historical Society, 1923), 437–463.

[b] Atlas of U.S. Presidential Elections, http://uselectionatlas.org/RESULTS/ (accessed October 9, 2011), NARA, U.S. Historical Election Results, http://www.archives.gov/federal-register/electoral-college/votes/votes_by_state.html (accessed October 10, 2011). Dorothy Riker and Gayle Thornbrough, *Indiana Election Returns, 1816–1851*, Indiana Historical Collections, Volume XL (Indiana Historical Bureau, 1960), 379–387.

[c] Atlas of U.S. Presidential Elections, http://uselectionatlas.org/RESULTS/ (accessed October 14, 2011), NARA, U.S. Historical Election Results, http://www.archives.gov/federal-register/electoral-college/votes/votes_by_state.html (accessed October 14, 2011).

in the delegate election. Like most Whigs, however, he aligned himself with democratic principles, deprecating "all anti-democratic feeling." Whigs were constantly irritated by the Democratic insistence on dominating every conversation with reference to the "dear people." One candidate bitterly complained to a friend that his rival "thinks if he cries out *Dimmecrat! Dimmecrat!!* he can do anything."[19]

Somewhat separate from party affiliations, local reform-minded communities nominated passionate, highly motivated activists. In areas settled by

[19] *Milwaukee Courier*, May 21, 1845; Andrew E. Elmore to Moses M. Strong, September 25, 1846, Moses M. Strong Papers, Wisconsin Historical Society, Madison. Elmore was elected to the convention; M. J. Bonee was defeated.

New Englanders, such as the Western Reserve in Ohio, the reform candidates won the elections and would provide an important counterpoint to traditional antibank and anti–black rights views in the conventions.[20] The Indiana, Ohio, and Wisconsin conventions included several articulate radicals: socialists, Fourierists, Harmonists, and antislavery Quakers. Scottish-born Robert Dale Owen, already famous through his writing and political career, served in the 1850–51 Indiana convention and would work tirelessly for married women's property rights. As a socialist reformer and pro–birth control activist, it was rather surprising that he was able to gain a seat in Indiana, but as a Jacksonian Democrat he had distinguished himself in public service, both in the state legislature and in Congress.[21] Ceresco, a Fourierist Phalanx in Wisconsin, sent Warren Chase, who would battle mightily for African American and Indian rights in the 1848 Wisconsin convention. Ohio's William Savery Bates was elected by his antislavery, pro–black rights Quaker community. Norton Strange Townshend (Figure 1.2), a well-known activist who had participated in the World Anti-Slavery Conference in England in 1840, fought hard for equal rights for Ohio's black citizens and for women's civil and property rights, as did his wife, Margaret Bailey Townshend (Figure 1.3).[22]

The abolitionist Jacob Lybrand threw in his hat for the 1846 Wisconsin convention. His radical views kept him out, but he still wrote long letters to the delegates demanding rights for black people.[23] Robert Huston Milroy – whose father, Samuel, had served in the 1816 Indiana convention – announced his candidacy for the Indiana 1850 constitutional convention in thirty pages of closely covered foolscap outlining his ideas for the new constitution.[24] A Protestant missionary, the Reverend Stephen R. Riggs, who lived with and evangelized to the Dakota in Minnesota for twenty years, became deeply interested in the formation of the new state government. "It seems to me," he told his friend Martin McLeod, who later became a delegate, that Minnesota "in laying her platform

[20] Speaking at the thirty-fifth anniversary of the Indiana 1850–51 convention, the former delegate William S. Holman, for example, explained that party spirit was "hushed," and that "citizens unknown in politics but eminent in other pursuits were called for." William Steele Holman, *The Constitutional Convention of Indiana of 1850-'51: The Reforms It Accomplished* … (Washington, DC, 1886), 4.

[21] Robert Dale Owen, *Threading My Way, Twenty-seven Years of Autobiography* (London, 1874).

[22] For biography of Norton Strange Townshend see, *History of Lorain County, Ohio, with Illustrations and Biographical Sketches of Some of Its Prominent Men and Pioneers* (Philadelphia: 1879), 131–32. See also Frederick J. Blue and Robert McCormick, "Norton S. Townshend: A Reformer for All Seasons," in Jeffrey P. Brown and Andrew R. L. Cayton, eds., *The Pursuit of Public Power: Political Culture in Ohio: 1787–1861* (Kent, OH: Kent State University Press, 1994), 144–154.

[23] Jacob Lybrand to Delegates of Constitutional Convention, October 17, 1846, Constitution file, Wisconsin Historical Society, Madison. Lybrand's petition was read into the record and laid on the table.

[24] Robert Huston Milroy Papers, [1850?], Constitution collection, Indiana Historical Society, Indianapolis.

FIGURE 1.2. Norton Strange Townshend (1815–1895). Townshend served as a delegate to the 1850 Ohio constitutional convention, where he battled for the rights of black people and for married women's property rights. He was a physician, who later served in the House of Representatives in Congress (1851–1853) and as medical inspector for the U.S. Army during the Civil War.

Source: Unknown daguerreotype artist. Courtesy of the Clements Library, University of Michigan.

of human rights *should* take a step in advance of anything hitherto existing." Riggs told McLeod that if he had been a citizen of an organized county he would be "almost tempted to try to be a member of the convention."[25]

The evidence from delegate biographies suggests that convention delegates emerged from a narrow pool: men at the beginning of their careers, without much political experience, but with a great deal of community backing as

25 Stephen R. Riggs to Martin McLeod, February 27, 1857, Martin McLeod Papers, Minnesota Historical Society, St. Paul.

FIGURE 1.3. Margaret Bailey Townshend (1823–1912) grew up orphaned and impoverished, but worked hard to educate herself and her sisters. She taught mathematics at the Esther Institute at Columbus, Ohio, and maintained a strong interest in the rights of African Americans and in women's suffrage throughout her life.
Source: Unknown daguerreotype artist. Courtesy of the Clements Library, University of Michigan.

prosperous, well-educated, and well-respected citizens. On the other hand, if no one volunteered, parties chose candidates without bothering to obtain their consent. Iowa candidate A. Rawson told William Penn Clarke that he had no desire to be a delegate to the convention, was absent throughout most of the campaign, and still lost by only eighty-two votes; he laughingly admitted that as a result the election had been conducted "as to make it an agreeable pastime for all and a source of regret to none."[26]

[26] A. Rawson to William Penn Clarke, July 22, 1850, William Penn Clarke Papers, State Historical Society of Iowa, Des Moines.

Meanwhile, as the candidates stepped forward to throw their hats into the ring for the convention, the larger territorial or state towns also entered the fray. As soon as any northwestern territorial or legislative assembly passed the law calling for a state constitutional convention, the announcement launched frantic activity in the state capitals or any larger town accessible via water or horseback. Hotels, boarding houses, theaters, special schools for the deaf or blind or asylums for the insane, and fraternal organizations such as the Masons or the Odd Fellows competed feverishly for the business and the ear of the delegates. Local widows vied to rent rooms to them. Some efforts at catering to the delegates could poke gentle fun at their debates: The *Illinois State Register* carried an advertisement inviting "friends of both sexes" to a "Bank! or No Bank! Ice Cream Saloon," which operated out of a room in the State House. No doubt the convention delegates would "find it very *cooling*, after a *warm* debate about the future interests of the Sucker state."[27]

Civic deliberations required impressive surroundings: prestige, sufficient and respectable accommodations, and accessibility. The Illinois delegates traveled by stage coach through Galena or Jacksonville to Springfield. Ohio delegates journeying to Columbus could travel via the National Road or the Ohio and Erie Canal. If the citizens of a democracy demanded equal geographic representation, then those people had to be able to travel to a centrally located town; and that town had to offer amenities such as hotels, libraries, public records, and, above all, communication via newspapers and telegraphs. Finally, the hall had to be big enough to accommodate a good cross section of the polity. If the assembly rooms were available, most of the conventions met in the hall of representatives; if not, then they rented some other large room proffered by a local group, such as the Masonic Brotherhood. The convention would be a significant source of income and prestige for any town, and the delegates would presumably be open to the influence of local boosters, institutions, and political wire workers.

The lawyers might already have been familiar with their state capitals; the farmers from distant counties no doubt found these cities imposing. Indianapolis had already become a center of commerce by 1850. The National Road had reached the city in 1827, bringing migrants and goods from the eastern states. Visitors admired the beautiful capitol, modeled after the Parthenon. By 1850 the town boasted several stylish hotels, theaters, bookstores, newspapers, and – most exciting for those delegates who had never before seen a locomotive – a railroad station.[28] (The delegates took a field trip to the depot.) Columbus, Ohio, also possessed a railway depot, and major Ohio cities had for several decades been connected via the National Road and several turnpikes to the

[27] *Illinois State Register* (Springfield), July 20, 1847.

[28] Jeffrey Tenuth, *Indianapolis: A Circle City History* (Charleston, SC: Arcadia, 2004), 34. Although the National Road was finished in 1824, the Center Canal was hopelessly stalled by 1850. The depot was finished in 1847.

eastern states, routes for stage coaches and freight wagons.[29] By the late 1840s many of the delegates could use the new roads or canals to reach the capital cities. Springfield, Illinois, had recently finished its pale sandstone capitol, and "a hundred new buildings" downtown had arrived within the past decade.[30] Some delegates found themselves in close company of free black people for the first time in their lives. Those who had not previously met or worked with free black people wrote home expressing their bemusement at having their firewood and water fetched or their boots polished by a black person.[31]

When the time came to leave, the delegates closed their offices, turned their farms over to their wives, or their legal or medical practices to colleagues, and said good-bye to their children. Once arrived at the state capital each man had to find a boarding house or hotel. Ohio delegate James Loudon complained to his wife about his hotel, which was too far from the hall and rather expensive. "The board – or, as members of the convention term it the *tariff* will be high about $8 dollars per week," he told her – and since the delegates were being paid only two dollars per day, that barely allowed Loudon to pay for his lodging and meals, let alone send home anything to his family.[32] Most delegates received from two to four dollars per day, which had to pay for accommodations and meals, and – for the less prosperous among them – still leave enough to support their families. Depending on their affluence, then, some tried to share rooms or even beds with other delegates. Oliver Davis, one of the most prosperous men in Vermillion County, was able to afford a room in the beautiful Bates Hotel, but after the convention dragged on for months even he had to move to a boarding house. Oliver Davis was fortunate; his hotel – one of the most expensive in the city – was just three blocks from the state capitol. Many of the less prosperous members boarded at the homes of local widows, such as Mrs. Nowland, who was well known and well liked and had rented rooms to state legislators since 1822.[33]

A keen sense of excitement pervaded the air as the delegates unpacked their valises, found their way to the convention hall, met their colleagues, and tried to size up the men with whom they would argue and work in the coming weeks. They felt hopeful and enthusiastic. Indiana delegate John Barron Niles told

29 Charles Chester Cole, *A Fragile Capital: Identity and the Early Years of Columbus, Ohio* (Columbus: Ohio State University Press, 2001), 49–50.

30 Paul M. Angle, *"Here I Have Lived," A History of Lincoln's Springfield, 1821–1865* (Springfield, IL: Abraham Lincoln Association, 1935), 90–95.

31 For example, Oliver Davis often wrote to Eliza expressing his surprise that he was being served by a young black man. Oliver Davis to Eliza Davis, December 3 and December 12, 1850, Oliver Davis Papers, Indiana State Archives, Indianapolis.

32 James Loudon to Elizabeth Loudon, December [2?], 1850, DeWitt Clinton Loudon papers, Ohio Historical Society, Columbus. Loudon was a prosperous farmer, who owned about twelve thousand dollars worth of property in Brown County, Ohio, and had seven children at the time of the convention.

33 Berry Sulgrove, *History of Indianapolis and Marion County, Indiana* (Philadelphia: 1884), 51–52.

his wife that the convention was "made up mainly of honest men, who wish to do their duty faithfully."[34] His colleague Alvin Hovey (Figure 1.4) who at twenty-nine was one of the youngest in the convention, would spend the rest of his time in Indianapolis obsessed with impressing his colleagues and constantly measuring himself against his rivals. As he settled into his seat he told his Mary that he found "many men of talent in the convention – few able speakers but a great many good *thinkers*."[35] Illinois judge David Davis (Figure 1.5) was inclined to think that this body would "make a good Constitution – There were about eighty of the members on hand this morning." From their appearance he supposed they "generally had good health."[36] Indeed, Davis told his wife, Sarah, that everyone he had met so far believed that the convention was "comprise[d of] the best body of men, that have ever assembled in the State."[37]

Davis may have been right, if we define "best" as respectable, prosperous, rising "men of parts." These were well-educated white men who had already made something of themselves in the new West.[38] Members of the African American and women's rights conventions that met in tandem with the constitutional conventions possessed similar qualities. Biographical information for these activists is scarce, but the available evidence suggests that they were well-educated and prominent members of their communities. Many of the delegates to Colored Citizens Conventions in Ohio and Indiana, for example, were physicians, teachers, and ministers, including the Reverend James Overall, a well-known "conductor" of the Indiana Underground Railroad, and the Reverend Spencer Turner, another Indiana minister, who risked his own freedom when he allowed himself to be sold into slavery in Kentucky a few years later, in order to protest the state's oppressive black exclusion laws.[39] The 1850 Ohio Women's Suffrage meeting included L. Maria Giddings, daughter of the antislavery politician Joshua Giddings, and Betsy Mix Cowles, a famous educator, writer, and abolitionist who had been educated at Oberlin.[40]

[34] John Barron Niles to Mary Niles and family, October 19, 1850, Niles MSS, Lilly Library, Indiana University, Bloomington.

[35] Alvin Hovey to Mary Ann Hovey, October 18, 1850, Hovey MSS, Lilly Library, Indiana University, Bloomington.

[36] David Davis to unknown, June 19, 1847, David Davis Papers, Chicago History Museum.

[37] David Davis to Sarah Davis, June 25, 1847, David Davis Papers, Chicago History Museum.

[38] Peter S. Onuf, "Early State Legislatures," in Joel H. Silbey, ed., *Encyclopedia of the American Legislative System* (New York: Scribner, 1994), 1: 194. David Alan Johnson collected data on individual delegates in three western states (California, Oregon, and Nevada). He notes that while many delegates were lawyers, these men also "collected" professions in the Hofstadter "Jacksonian Men" sense. The same is true for farmers, who reported other jobs on their biographical chart resumes. Some were full-time lawyers but many more split their time among other endeavors in this prespecialization period. David Alan Johnson, *Founding the Far West: California, Oregon, and Nevada, 1840–1890* (Berkeley: University of California Press, 1992), 104. I am mainly interested in the political behavior of delegates inside the conventions.

[39] For further discussion on Roberts, see Chapter 7.

[40] Audretsch, *The Salem, Ohio, 1850 Women's Rights Convention*, 21, 22. There were also members of both the Hayes and Tilden families present at the convention (p. 21). Cowles's obituary

FIGURE 1.4. Alvin Hovey (1821–1891) served as a delegate to the 1850 Indiana constitutional convention. Four years later he was appointed to the Indiana Supreme Court; he served as a general during the Civil War and became governor of Indiana (1889–1891). *Source*: Unknown photographer. Courtesy of the Indiana Supreme Court.

The members of the state constitutional conventions in the antebellum Northwest have not enthralled modern historians, perhaps because these men personified old-fashioned characters striding across the western landscapes – men like Frederick Jackson Turner's heroic white pioneers of American democracy.[41] Their early twentieth-century biographers, particularly those of

called her an "ardent advocate of all true reforms, and a woman of singular independence and vigor of mind." *The Revolution* (New York), October 12, 1871. See also, Stacey Robertson, *Betsy Mix Cowles: Champion of Equality* (Boulder, CO: Westview Press, 2014).

41 This is true of all early histories of state constitutions, whether in a regional or national context. For example, Willi Paul Adams explains that Massachusetts delegates were essentially the same people as in the assembly, and while he discusses how they were elected generally, he does not discuss them further. Willi Paul Adams, *The First American Constitutions: Republican Ideology and the Making of the State Constitutions in the Revolutionary Era*, trans. Rita Kimber and Robert Kimber, expanded ed. (Lanham, MD: Rowman & Littlefield, 2001), 31. Gordon Wood did not mention delegates in *The Creation of the American Republic 1776–1787* (Chapel Hill: University of North Carolina Press, 1969); neither did Don E. Fehrenbacher in *Constitutions and Constitutionalism in the Slaveholding South* (Athens: University of Georgia Press, 1989) as well as *Sectional Crisis and Southern Constitutionalism* (Baton Rouge: Louisiana State University Press, 1989). Stephanie D. Moussalli discussed delegates in "Florida's Frontier Constitution: The Statehood, Banking and Slavery Controversies." *Florida*

FIGURE 1.5. David Davis (1815–1886) and Sarah Walker Davis (1814–1879) lived in Bloomington, Illinois. David Davis served as a delegate to the 1847 Illinois constitutional convention and later became a supreme court justice (1862–1872).
"Wedding portrait of David and Sarah Davis, circa 1838."
Source: Unknown tintype artist. Courtesy of the Abraham Lincoln Presidential Library.

the "founders day" school, wrote essays on their achievements that took on tinges of hagiography. The farmer delegates must have known that their names would go down in county histories, which in those days, and until at least the early twentieth century, became the repositories of civic pride. The county founders, and the many men who went on to fight for the Union Armies in the Civil War were the ones whose careers and achievements have been remembered. Like many of his colleagues, for example, Oliver Davis had made a grand success of himself. He exported hundreds of tons of wheat and corn to a starving Ireland and served two terms in the Indiana House of Representatives. He had left New Hampshire with nothing more than fifty cents in his coat pockets, which he freely shared with a "jolly dentist," who, in turn, taught him how to extract teeth. That profession quickly gave way to a study of the law, and by the time he was in his late twenties, Davis had started a thriving farm, founded

Historical Quarterly 74, no. 4 (April 1996): 423–39. Hannah Rosen explored delegate biographies in *Terror in the Heart of Freedom: Citizenship, Sexual Violence, and the Meaning of Race in the Postemancipation South* (Chapel Hill: University of North Carolina Press, 2009).

a community (later called Opedee, in honor of his initials), and married his Eliza just three years prior to the convention.[42] Unfortunately the more obscure men have been forgotten. For those men we have incomplete information, and not all of it is reliable. The overall picture is consistent enough, however, to give us a sense of the personality of the collective body of northwestern convention delegates.[43] In addition to the 1850 (and in a few cases the 1860) censuses, we have biographical details from late nineteenth-century county histories, as well as "bench and bar" anthologies and obituaries. Therefore, we have information for the more active and prosperous among these men, primarily for those who persisted in the state. Men who left the Northwest for the gold rush, for example, were not usually recorded in county histories.[44]

The most trustworthy details on the delegates appear in decorative biographical charts produced by convention printers, which showed their ages, party affiliations, marital status, home counties, and temporary residences. These graphic tables allowed the delegates to gain a sense of the political and professional makeup of their body, and to find one another for committee meetings, caucuses, or private conversations. Printers embellished these charts with fancy scrolls and imposing fonts; Indiana's was lavishly turned out on pink silk. Indiana also included witticisms and personal declarations such as, for several single men, "candidate for matrimony," or, as one proud father announced, he had "three Democrat daughters and three Whig sons."[45] If we

[42] Joseph P. Elliott, *Biographical and Historical Record of Vermillion County, Indiana* (Chicago: 1888), 260–1.

[43] The 1810 and 1820 census information is sparse and contains no wealth or age data. The extant evidence suggests that these men were politically experienced and more prosperous than the delegates who served after 1840. I did not include the 1835 Michigan convention delegates because there is no information available on them other than their names. The U.S. Census did not begin including information on value of real estate until the 1850 census and did not include data on value of personal wealth until the 1860 census. Therefore, for a rough idea of the relative economic standing of delegates in their communities, I studied the 1850 census information for value of real estate.

[44] Most political historians concentrate on the voting records of national legislators. Joel Silbey and Allan Bogue have studied voting records in Congress; Heather Cox Richardson examined relationships between Republicans during the Civil War era. The primary concern of these historians was with identifying radicals and conservatives or establishing the loyalty and stability of party affiliations. Joel H. Silbey, ed., *The United States Congress in a Partisan Political Nation, 1841–1896*, 3 vols. (Brooklyn, NY: Carlson, 1991); Allan G. Bogue, *The Earnest Men: Republicans of the Civil War Senate* (Ithaca, NY: Cornell University Press, 1981); and Heather Cox Richardson, *The Greatest Nation of the Earth: Republican Economic Policies during the Civil War* (Cambridge, MA: Harvard University Press, 1997).

[45] By contrast, state legislatures only published the names and counties of their members in their journals. The pink silk chart is in the collections of the Indiana State Historical Society. Many of the state historical societies collected letters of delegates. Not every convention published its debates, but historians have collected newspaper editorials that recreate the debates in those conventions, see: Arthur Charles Cole, ed., *The Constitutional Debates of 1847*, vol. 14 of *Collections of the Illinois State Historical Library* (Springfield: Illinois State Historical Library, 1919) (hereafter Illinois 1847); Milo Milton Quaife, ed., *The Convention of 1846*, vol. 27 of

take all of the northwestern constitutional convention delegates from 1835 through 1857 together as an aggregate, we find a homogenous body: white married men with small children, almost all of them landowners, Christian, well educated, reasonably prosperous, and well respected in their communities. They consisted of 1,170 people in the antebellum northwestern territorial and state conventions.

At least 90 percent of the delegates had a high social and economic standing in their communities. Examination of delegate biographies and census data within states, and then within their home counties, reveals that the pattern held true across the region. The delegates in the newer, more northern states (Michigan, Wisconsin, and Minnesota) lived in communities that were markedly less affluent than those in the older states (Ohio, Illinois, and Indiana.) The U.S. Census did not begin collecting data on the value of real estate until 1850. The reported data are speculative at best, since that information was self-reported and did not account for the quality of or improvements on the land. Even so, most of the delegates owned enough real estate to be recognized as successful farmers. For the wealth analysis of this study, I chose Illinois, Indiana, Ohio, and Wisconsin and studied the census reports for 1850 for all of the counties.[46] Yet even a cursory comparison can give us a picture of the relative standing of these men within their own conventions. The evidence suggests that most northwestern delegates across the region (at least 40 percent) were at least of average wealth; almost none was below average, and about 30 percent were significantly wealthier than their fellow county citizens.[47] A few outstripped all of their neighbors, and were among the wealthiest men in the region, reporting upward of $100,000 in real estate.[48]

Three of the 1847 Illinois convention delegates were not reported in the census, but aside from those three people, none owned an estate worth less than $1,000.[49] In Illinois there was greater variation of real estate property than in

Publications of the State Historical Society of Wisconsin (Madison: State Historical Society of Wisconsin, 1919) (hereafter Wisconsin 1846); and Harold M. Dorr, ed., *The Michigan Constitutional Conventions of 1835–1836: Debates and Proceedings* (Ann Arbor: University of Michigan Press, 1940) (hereafter Michigan 1835). All of the other conventions published detailed journals containing most of the speeches and all of the votes and resolutions.

46 I chose these four states because I wanted to compare an older, more eastern, more prosperous state (Ohio) with a younger, more western, less economically developed state (Wisconsin.) I chose Illinois and Indiana because both states represent more or less equal southern and northern in-migration and are representative of the "middle period" of northwestern settlement and development. This also allowed me to study states that had fairly complete agricultural data.

47 About five or six delegates from each convention were missing from the census reports.

48 Indiana, like Illinois, was settled in the 1810s but had a more developed transportation infrastructure. Data on the so-called poor delegates is incomplete and possibly misleading. Of 150 Indiana delegates 41 were middling, 27 wealthy, and 38 extremely wealthy.

49 In Illinois, we had census and biographical information for 51of 162 delegates. Of them, 3 were "poor," that is, owned almost no real estate, or considerably less than other families in their communities; 10 were "middling," meaning that their real estate was worth about the same as

the more northern or newer states.[50] Indiana delegates were far more prosperous than their Illinois brethren. Forty-one of 150 were of "middling" wealth in comparison to their county neighbors, 27 were affluent, and 38 (slightly more than 25 percent) were extremely wealthy. For example, Allen Hamilton was by far one of the wealthiest men in the Northwest, with $110,000 in real estate. It is difficult to distinguish precisely how many of the Indiana delegates either were poor (at least in terms of landownership) or refused to report their real estate holdings, but about 14 of the delegates either reported no information (for example, Samuel McKinzey, who was a contractor, or Robert M. Evans, an attorney who owned no land).

Ohio was an older and more economically established state, so the delegates in the lowest economic tier (about one-third) owned between three thousand and five thousand acres, which was still average for their counties. Another third owned between eight thousand and ten thousand acres (significantly wealthier than average) and slightly more than a third owned an immense amount of property.[51] Twenty-two men owned significantly more than anyone else in the state, upward of eight thousand to thirty-six thousand acres. In the 1846 Wisconsin convention an appreciably higher percentage of the delegates owned more than their county neighbors: 43 of 124 (nearly 35 percent) were conspicuously wealthy. A. H. Smith owned $150,000 in 1850. Several of these men became much wealthier within a decade. Ten years later, A. H. Smith owned $2.7 million in land.[52] What does information about landholdings tell us about our delegates? Without more detailed biographical information, it is dangerous to speculate, but clearly, northwesterners admired and wanted to be represented by the men who had made something of themselves.

While it may not be surprising that the northwestern convention delegates were among the more prosperous members of their community, it is worth pointing out that they had achieved their social standing at a relatively early age.[53] For example, when Iowan Stephen Hempstead became a delegate to the 1844 constitutional convention at thirty-four, he had already served in

their county neighbors'; 13 were considerably wealthier; and 9 were far above all others in their communities.

[50] George W. Akin of Franklin County owned $3,000 worth of real estate and was the wealthiest man in Franklin, while Peter Green, who owned $10,000, was about in the middle in Clay County. Similarly, Andrew McCallen only owned about $800 worth of real estate, but was about average in Shawneetown.

[51] In the Ohio 1850 convention, 8 of the delegates were poor, 15 middling, 21 wealthy, 22 elite, and for 23 we had insufficient data to judge.

[52] As a younger state, all of whose delegates were born elsewhere, Wisconsin nevertheless remained true to the established pattern: Of the delegates 21 were in the "poor" category (though this category is misleading because it may represent people for whom there is little or no evidence), 13 were middling, 22 wealthy, and 43 were extremely wealthy in comparison to their communities. Yet in Wisconsin almost no one would have been considered wealthy by Indiana or Ohio standards.

[53] Compared to relative ages in the Northwest. See the table in the Introduction.

the territorial legislature, and had been elected as legislative council president (Figure 1.1). His colleagues in all of the conventions were younger than legislators in their own states, and a great deal younger than delegates to coeval eastern or southern constitutional conventions. Across all conventions, both the mean and median age was 39.5, which was at least a year or two younger than the age of the average northwestern legislator. In Ohio, for example, in contrast to the average thirty-nine-year-old convention delegates, the average age of legislators was forty-three, with state senators typically about a year older than representatives.[54] Compared to constitutional convention delegates from other states, northwesterners who served in their state conventions were significantly younger. The mean and median ages of eastern and southern state delegates were 47.2 and 47.3, respectively.[55] In most northwestern conventions, Democrats were two to three years younger, and less experienced, than either Whigs or Republicans, most of whom had cut their political teeth in New England or the Mid-Atlantic states.[56] The younger and farther north the territory, the younger and less experienced the delegates. This is particularly true in Wisconsin and Minnesota, the two newest Great Lakes states, whose delegates were in their thirties. (See Tables 1.2a–1.2b.) These were also the only two states that had mixed-race delegates, for instance, Wisconsin's Joseph Rolette and Henry Bailly, both of whom had Indian ancestry.[57]

Information about political experience could only be gleaned from Illinois, Wisconsin, and Minnesota, which were the only three states that kept detailed biographical records from before and after the conventions. (See Tables 1.3a and 1.3b.) About a third of the Illinois and Wisconsin delegates took to their conventions some local (town or county) political experience. Most of those were county commissioners, an office inherited from southern states, which controlled local business such as internal improvement contracts. Forty percent of Illinois delegates also had state political experience, including a term or two in the state legislature, or served in the judiciary. Only five men in all four conventions combined had national experience, and of those, two were elected as convention president. Illinois, as the oldest state of the three, also had the most experienced men; Wisconsin and Minnesota, as newer states, had the least. In fact, nearly two-thirds of all men in Minnesota had no experience at all. Minnesota split into two conventions (Republican and Democratic), and the Democratic convention had even less experience than their Republican opponents.

[54] David M. Gold, *Democracy in Session: A History of the Ohio General Assembly* (Athens: Ohio University Press, 2009), 50.

[55] According to Peter S. Onuf, they were about forty or forty-one. Onuf, "The Origins and Early Development of State Legislatures," *Encyclopedia of the American Legislative System*, 1: 194.

[56] Minnesota and Wisconsin state histories contain further information about delegates

[57] Today's average legislator is closer to sixty, a little older for Democrats and senators. This is also true of Congress. Still, these ages have to be seen in context: In 1840, 78.3 percent of northwesterners were below the age of twenty-nine.

TABLE 1.2A. *Age distribution of Northwest convention delegates*

Age	Illinois (1847)	Indiana (1816)	Indiana (1850)	Iowa (1844)	Iowa (1846)	Iowa (1857)	Michigan (1850)	Minnesota (1857)	Ohio (1850)	Wisconsin (1846)
21–25	–	–	2	–	3	–	1	5	3	3
26–30	19	3	15	10	3	7	4	11	5	14
31–35	29	8	14	13	10	4	11	15	12	24
36–40	38	5	27	21	5	7	21	10	18	29
41–45	30	9	29	15	5	6	27	9	23	13
46–50	24	5	22	3	2	7	19	3	20	12
51–55	12	2	14	4	2	3	12	4	15	6
56–60	5	2	11	4	1	1	4	–	7	7
61–65	5	1	1	1	–	–	–	–	4	2
66–70	1	–	4	1	1	–	–	–	3	3
71–75	–	1	1	–	–	–	–	–	–	–
76–80	–	–	–	–	–	–	–	–	–	–
Unknown	–	7	6	–	–	–	1	1	–	–
Mean	38	35.6	42.7	39.7	37.7	40.8	41.6	35.6	45.5	38.4
Median	40	41	43	38	35.5	40	42	35	44	37

TABLE 1.2B. *Ages of non-Northwest convention delegates*

Mean and median ages of convention delegates outside the Northwest			
Calculation	**Kentucky (1849)**	**New York (1846)**	**Massachusetts (1853)**
Mean	45	47.3	49.5
Median	44	48	50

In Illinois, nearly 66 percent of the delegates had no political experience; about 34 percent had some county- or state-level experience, and none had held national office. About a third of Minnesota's and Wisconsin's delegates had some political experience, all of it local. As a result, parliamentary procedure often went out the window. The presidents of the conventions rarely intervened, except when asked about points of order. That meant that explosive topics intruded constantly and that the floor of the convention often resembled a raucous mob scene. This circumstance annoyed the more experienced delegates, who complained bitterly in their letters home about the chaos, but it also kept controversial topics alive.[58]

Because the delegates' educational background was reconstructed from biographies and county histories, those data are skewed toward the more successful and well-known men of their time. Even so, judging from extant and anecdotal data, all delegates were fully literate, and many had taught school for two or three years in their late teens. Every delegate must have had at least a common school education, or a near-equivalent for those who had been privately tutored at home. Nearly 90 percent in both Wisconsin and Illinois (for whom we have educational information) had attended high school or an academy. At least half of the delegates for whom we have biographical data attended college. The lawyers, preachers, and physicians obviously also had some professional training, if not in college, then through an apprenticeship. Once again, however, the farther north the convention, the less well educated the delegates. According to a contemporary observer, who compared Wisconsin delegates to the founding fathers, "some of them had never seen the inside of a college, and most of them could have carried their private libraries on their backs."[59]

Many historians of the Midwest have commented on the dual migration streams that carried white settlers into the region. People from Kentucky and

[58] For example, see Michael Les Benedict and John F. Winkler, eds., *The History of Ohio Law* (Athens: Ohio University Press, 2004), 53, for a discussion on James Loudon and other sympathetic delegates jumping into the convention's deliberations to talk about black suffrage.

[59] Alexander M. Thomson, *A Political History of Wisconsin*, 2nd ed. (Milwaukee: C. N. Caspar Co., 1902), 74. During the 1850 Indiana debates a delegate looked up Cato and Livy in the Indiana State Library for his speech. *Report of the Debates and Proceedings of the Convention for the Revision of the Constitution of the State of Indiana. 1850* (Indianapolis, 1850), 1: 474 (hereafter Indiana 1850).

TABLE 1.3A. *Political experience before the constitutional conventions – Illinois, Wisconsin, Minnesota*

State and year	Local gov't.	State gov't. (legis., admin., or judge)	Congress/ fed. gov't	Governor or lt. gov.	State Supreme Court	Ran for state office and lost	Military Service (Black Hawk War et. al)	Nat'l party conv. or presid. elector	Const. conv. of another state	None or unknown
Illinois (1847)	34%	39%	4%	1% (2 men)	1% (1 man)	6%	14%	2%	.06% (1 man)	35%
Wisconsin (1847–48)	36%	19%	–	–	–	–	–	–	–	51%
Minnesota (1857)	7%	29%	2% (1 man)	–	–	–	2% (1 man)	–	–	67%

TABLE 1.3B. *Political experience after the constitutional conventions – Illinois, Wisconsin, Minnesota*

State and year	Local gov't.	State gov't. (admin. or judicial)	Governor or lt. gov.	State legis.	State Supreme Court	Congress, fed gov't, or U.S. Supreme Court	Ran for state office and lost	Ran for fed. office and lost	Civil War military service	None or unknown
Illinois (1847)	25%	21%	2% (one became lt. gov. of Oregon)	29%	2% (one went to Oregon)	15%	2%	5%	6%	39%
Wisconsin (1847–48)	38%	14%	4%	42%	4%	6%	3%	6%	17%	25%
Minnesota (1857)	–	5%	5%	16%	2% (1 man)	2% (1 man)	–	–	13%	67%

Virginia, and to a lesser degree, Maryland and Tennessee, settled in the southern counties of Illinois and Indiana.[60] New Englanders arrived about a decade later and moved into the northern tiers of those states. Connecticut settlers had populated the Ohio Western Reserve since the eighteenth century. Although the U.S. Census did not report nativity data until 1850, it was possible to determine nativity for all but one hundred of the delegates from every convention except the 1835 Michigan convention. The data reveal that by the time of the great era of state constitutional revisions in the 1840s and 1850s, the settlement streams had evened out. The two states in the Northwest with the greatest sectional difference, Illinois and Indiana, also showed the greatest homogeneity by 1850. For example, 26 percent of the delegates to the 1816 Indiana convention hailed from New England and the Mid-Atlantic states, and 60 percent from southern slave states. In the 1850 convention those percentages had equalized: 50 percent from northern states, 69 percent from the South. In Illinois the evening-out process was even more striking. In the 1818 Illinois convention 28 percent were from New England and the Mid-Atlantic states, and 54 percent from southern states. Ten percent migrated from within the Northwest. By 1848, 46 percent were from New England plus the Northwest and 47 percent from the South. (See Tables 1.4a–1.4c.)

The proportion of free-state to slave-state northwesterners increased significantly by 1857. In Iowa, for example, 68 percent of the delegates were from free states and 39 percent from the South. The difference was even greater in the 1850 Ohio convention, where 70 percent of the delegates were from the North and 17 percent from the South. This book does not claim that the delegates' place of birth had a strong influence in their votes or speeches. Most of the delegates across all the conventions held before 1857 were Democrats, and almost all of them held similar cultural beliefs about black people and paper money, regardless of their birthplace. Therefore, the votes and outcomes were far more likely to be influenced by other factors, such as political allegiance or local commitments.

Taken together, these details provide a portrait of an active, conscientious, ambitious, and somewhat inexperienced body. All of these men (and the people who staffed the parallel activist conventions as well) had spent their early years gathering work and business experience. Two-thirds were farmers or merchants, not lawyers. Tables 1.5a–1.5b show the top five professions of convention delegates, in the Northwest and, by way of comparison, in sample states from New England, the Southwest, and the Mid-Atlantic. Three-quarters of these men were engaged in skilled trades, including – besides farmers and lawyers – census takers, surveyors, clergymen, printers

[60] Nicole Etcheson, *Emerging Midwest: Upland Southerners and the Political Culture of the Old Northwest, 1787–1861* (Bloomington: Indiana University Press, 1996), explains that by the 1840s sectional differences had become muted, though she argues that they flared up again during the Civil War era.

TABLE 1.4A. *Delegate count: all percentages based on number of nativities found (indicated in parentheses in the delegate count table; fractional percentages rounded up from .5 and higher so the percentage totals for each convention range from 99 percent to 101 percent)*

State convention year	Delegate count (nativity identified)
Illinois 1818	33 (29)
Illinois 1847	162
Indiana 1816	43 (42)
Indiana 1850	150
Iowa 1844	72
Iowa 1846	32
Iowa 1857	36
Michigan 1835[a]	91 (0)
Michigan 1850	100
Minnesota Republican 1857	58
Minnesota Democrat 1857	55 (54)
Ohio 1802	35
Ohio 1850	110
Wisconsin 1846	124 (122)
Wisconsin 1848	69 (68)
Total	1170 (1070)

[a] I did not attempt to identify nativities for these delegates.

or newspaper editors, millers, and pork packers. As we shall see in future chapters, the lawyers dominated all of the convention and committee debates on the judiciary, but the farmers and merchants were more vocal on economic problems.

Deliberative bodies – particularly those composed of inexperienced and highly opinionated members – require a venerable moderator, preferably one with some knowledge of the rules of decorum, and, in antebellum western territories and states, someone with enough wisdom, age, and dignity to rein in the inevitable political flare-ups. The first order of business in all of the conventions was to elect the president. Several of the convention presidents had parents who had lived through or even been active in the revolutionary era.[61] Every one of the northwestern convention presidents was well known, well educated, politically experienced, and considerably older than the average delegate. Illinois delegate David Davis believed that Judge Logan had "more influence in the body than anyone else," in spite of the fact that like Davis, he was a

[61] Zadoc Casey's father, an Irish immigrant who moved to North Carolina in the 1780s, fought in the Revolutionary War under Francis Marion. John Reynolds, *The Pioneer History of Illinois* (Chicago: 1887), 413–14. Edward Tiffin, the president of the first Ohio constitutional convention, served in the Revolutionary War. Linden F. Edwards, "Governor Edward Tiffin: Pioneer Doctor," *Ohio History* 56 (October 1947): 349–61.

TABLE 1.4B. *Delegate nativity*

	AL	CT	DE	GA	IL	IN	KY	ME	MD	MA	MI	MN	MO	NH	NJ	NY	NC	OH	PA	RI	SC	TN	VA	VT	WDC	WI	Eng	Can	Ger	Hol	Ire	Jam	Lux	Nor	Scot	Swe	Swis
IL 18[a]		1			2		7		2	1					1	1		1	4		1	1	4								2						
IL 47		4	1	1	8	1	29	2	6	8				4	2	24	9	7	13	1	2	13	16	6					1		1				3		
IN 16[b]		2	1				7		5						2		1		6		1		11								5						1
IN 50		2	1			13	22		7	4				1	1	16	10	17	19		4	7	19	1							3				3		
IA 44		1			1	1	8	1		1				1	1	9	6	8	13			1	11	6					1		1				1		
IA 46	1	4					6		1							2	3	5	2				4	4													
IA 57		3				2	4	2	1	1					1	7		7	3			1	4														
MI 50		10						2		13	1			5	2	43	1	2	3				1	8			1	5			2				1		
MN R 57						1		4		5				10	1	10	1	4	6	1			2	6			1	1	2		1				1	1	
MN D 57[c]		1			1		2	4	1	1	1	2	2		2	11		6	5				1	1		1	1	5	1	1	3		1				
OH 02		2							5	3				1	3	1			7				9				2				2						
OH 50		11	2	1			3		4	5				2	1	9		30	25			1	8	2	1		3		1		1						
WI 46[d]		8			1		4	1	1	8				2	4	46			6	1	1	1	2	23			2		3		7	1					
WI 48[e]		9					4	1	1	7				2	1	24		2	2				1	7					1		5			1			

[a] Nativity of four delegates undetermined/unknown. Percentage based on total of 29.
[b] Nativity of one delegate undetermined/unknown. Percentage based on total of 42.
[c] Nativity of one delegate undetermined/unknown. Percentage based on total of 54.
[d] Nativity of two delegates undetermined/unknown. Percentage based on total of 122.
[e] Nativity of one delegate undetermined/unknown. Percentage based on total of 68.

TABLE 1.4C. *Percentage delegate nativity by U.S. region*

Delegates from New England

New England	CT	ME	MA	NH	RI	VT	Total region	Percentage of total
IL 18	1		1				2	7
IL 47	4	2	8	4	1	6	25	15
IN 16	2						2	5
IN 50	2		4	1		1	8	5
IA 44	1	1	1	1		6	10	14
IA 46	4					4	8	25
IA 57	3	2	1				6	17
MI 50	10	2	13	5		8	38	38
MN R 57		4	5	10	1	6	26	45
MN D 57	1	4	1			1	7	13
OH 02	2		3	1			6	17
OH 50	11		5	2		2	20	18
WI 46	8	1	8	2	1	23	43	35
WI 48	9	1	7	2		7	26	38
Total							245	23

Delegates from the Mid-Atlantic states

Mid-Atlantic	DE	NJ	NY	PA	Total region	Percentage of total
IL 18		1	1	4	6	21
IL 47	1	2	24	13	40	25
IN 16	1	2		6	9	21
IN 50	1	1	16	19	37	25
IA 44		1	9	13	23	32
IA 46			2	2	4	13
IA 57		1	7	3	11	31
MI 50		2	43	3	48	48
MN R 57		1	10	6	17	29
MN D 57		2	11	5	18	33
OH 02		3	1	7	11	31
OH 50	2	1	9	25	37	34
WI 46		4	46	6	56	46
WI 48		1	24	2	27	40
Total					344	32

Delegates from Upper South states

Upper South	KY	MD	MO	VA	WDC	Total region	Percentage of total
IL 18	7	3		4		14	48
IL 47	29	6		16		51	32
IN 16	7	5		11		23	55
IN 50	22	7		19		48	32
IA 44	8			11		19	26
IA 46	6	1		4		11	34
IA 57	4	1		4		9	25
MI 50				1		1	1
MN R 57				2		2	4
MN D 57	2	1	2	1		6	11
OH 02		5		9		14	40
OH 50	3	4		8	1	16	15
WI 46	4	1		2		7	6
WI 48	4	1		1		6	9
Total						227	21

Delegates from southeastern states

Southeast	GA	NC	SC	Total region	Percentage of total
IL 18			1	1	3
IL 47	1	9	2	12	7
IN 16		1	1	2	5
IN 50		10	4	14	9
IA 44		6		6	8
IA 46		3		3	9
IA 57				0	0
MI 50		1		1	1
MN R 57		1		1	2
MN D 57				0	0
OH 02				0	0
OH 50	1			1	1
WI 46			1	1	1
WI 48				0	0
Total				40	4

(*continued*)

TABLE 1.4C (*continued*)

Delegates from southwestern states				
Southwest	**AL**	**TN**	**Total region**	**Percentage of total**
IL 18		1	1	3
IL 47		13	13	8
IN 16			0	0
IN 50		7	7	5
IA 44		1	1	1
IA 46	1		1	3
IA 57		1	1	3
MI 50			0	0
MN R 57			0	0
MN D 57			0	0
OH 02			0	0
OH 50		1	1	1
WI 46		1	1	1
WI 48			0	0
Total			26	2

Delegates from northwestern states and territories								
Northwest	**IL**	**IN**	**MI**	**MN**	**OH**	**WI**	**Total Region**	**Percentage of total**
IL 18	2				1		3	10
IL 47	8	1			7		16	10
IN 16							0	0
IN 50		13			17		30	20
IA 44	1	1			8		10	14
IA 46					5		5	16
IA 57		2			7		9	25
MI 50			1		2		3	3
MN R 57		1			4		5	9
MN D 57	1		1	2	6	1	11	20
OH 02							0	0
OH 50					30		30	27
WI 46	1						1	1
WI 48					2		2	3
Total							125	12

Foreign-born delegates

Foreign	Eng	Can	Ger	Hol	Ire	Jam	Lux	Nor	Scot	Swed	Swiss	Total foreign	Percentage of total
IL 18					2							2	7
IL 47			1		1				3			5	3
IN 16					5						1	6	14
IN 50					3				3			6	4
IA 44			1		1				1			3	4
IA 46												0	0
IA 57												0	0
MI 50	1	5			2				1			9	9
MN R 57	1	1	2		1				1	1		7	12
MN D 57	1	5	1	1	3		1					12	22
OH 02	2				2							4	11
OH 50	3		1		1							5	5
WI 46	2		3		7	1						13	11
WI 48			1		5			1				7	10
Total												79	7

Sources: Illinois 1818: Richard V. Carpenter, "The Illinois Constitutional Convention of 1818," *Journal of the Illinois State Historical Society* 6, no. 3 (Oct. 1894): 327–53.

Illinois: Arthur Charles Cole, ed. *The Constitutional Debates of 1847*, vol. 14 of *Collections of the Illinois State Historical Library* (Springfield: Illinois State Historical Library, 1919), Delegate Chart.

Indiana 1816: "Members of the Indiana's 1816 Constitutional Convention," at http://www.in.gov/history/2484.htm; Indiana Legislative Bureau, "Members of the Indiana Constitutional Convention of 1816," *Indiana Magazine of History* 26, no. 2 (June 1930): 147–51.

Indiana 1850: Delegate Chart.

Iowa 1844: Benjamin F. Shambaugh, ed., *Fragments of the Debates of the Iowa Constitutional Conventions of 1844 and 1846* … (Iowa City: State Historical Society of Iowa, 1900), 408–10.

Iowa 1846: Benjamin F. Shambaugh, ed., *Fragments of the Debates of the Iowa Constitutional Conventions of 1844 and 1846* … (Iowa City: State Historical Society of Iowa, 1900), 413–14.

(*continued*)

TABLE 1.4C (*continued*)

Iowa 1857: W. Blair Lord, *The Debates of the Constitutional Convention; of the State of Iowa, Assembled at Iowa City, Monday, January 19, 1857 ...* (Davenport, IA, 1857), 1:4.
Michigan 1835: Christopher J. Carl, ed., *Michigan Manual 2009–2010* (Landing, MI: Legislative Service Bureau, 2010), I-3.
Michigan 1850: Christopher J. Carl, ed., *Michigan Manual 2009–2010* (Landing, MI: Legislative Service Bureau, 2010), II-4; *Report of the Proceedings and Debates in the Convention to Revise the Constitution of State of Michigan, 1850* (Lansing, MI, 1850), v–vi.
Minnesota 1857 Republican: Delegate Chart.
Minnesota 1857 Democrat: Minnesota Legislative Reference Library query at http://www.leg.state.mn.us/legdb/results.aspx?search=const; 1860 U.S. Census Returns for Minnesota.
Ohio 1802: Fred J. Milligan, *Ohio's Founding Fathers* (Lincoln NE: iUniverse, 2003).
Ohio 1850: J. V. Smith, *Report of the Debates and Proceedings of the Convention for the Revision of the Constitution of the State of Ohio, 1850–51* (Columbus, OH, 1851), 1:3–5.
Wisconsin 1846: Delegate Chart.
Wisconsin 1848: H. A. Tenney and David Atwood, *Memorial record of the fathers of Wisconsin, containing sketches of the lives and careers of the members of the constitutional conventions of 1846 and 1847–8* (Madison, WI, 1880).

staunch Whig.[62] He had already served in the legislature for five years, and the convention delegates considered him a man of "uncommon intellectual vigor – great nervousness of maner [sic] & unsurpassed quickness."[63] At fifty-one, Indiana convention president Zadoc Casey, whom delegate John Niles called "an honest tanner from Sawinac" was – like all convention presidents – considerably older than the average delegate.[64] All had territorial or state experience, several had held national office, and most were lawyers. Several of the convention presidents later became governors of their states. Davis told his wife that he thought Newton Cloud (who served as convention president after Judge Logan) was a "Methodist Preacher [and] fair man" and in spite of having been "caucused in by the Loco's" would probably run the convention well.[65]

After the president accepted the delegates' credentials, he immediately had to begin arranging the committees, a highly politicized and fractious process. Davis told his wife Sarah that there had been "a great deal of dissatisfaction in the arrangement of [the] committees."[66] The conventions set up twelve to fifteen standing committees, which debated the principal constitutional sections: the powers and duties of the governor and the state legislature; the elective

[62] David Davis to unknown, June 19, 1847, David Davis Papers, Chicago History Museum; James Loudon to Elizabeth Loudon, May 19, 1850, Dewitt Clinton Loudon Papers, Ohio Historical Society, Columbus.

[63] David Davis to Sarah Davis, June 25, 1847, David Davis Papers, Chicago Historical Museum.

[64] John Barron Niles to Mary Niles and family, October 19, 1850, Niles MSS, Lilly Library, Indiana University, Bloomington.

[65] David Davis to unknown, June 7, 1847, David Davis Papers, Chicago History Museum.

[66] David Davis to Sarah Davis, June 25, 1847, David Davis Papers, Chicago History Museum. The *Scioto Gazette* (Chillicothe, OH), for example, complained that William Medill, the Ohio convention president, was biased on committee appointments, May 14, 1850.

TABLE 1.5A. *Top five professions of convention delegates (Northwest)*

Profession	Illinois (1847)	Indiana (1850)	Iowa (1844)	Iowa (1846)	Iowa (1857)	Michigan (1850)	Minnesota (1857)	Ohio (1850)	Wisconsin (1846)
Lawyer	54	41	10	7	15	22	13	43	26
Farmer	75	64	41	13	12	48	19	38	70
Merchant	9	12	4	5	2	11	8	8	6
Physician	12	18	6	4	1	6	2	8	3
Mechanic	5	1	3	1	0	1	1	0	1
Other	22	15	8	1	10	12	23	20	19
Total	*177*	*154*	*72*	*32*	*38*	*100*	*61*	*111*	*124*

Top five professions of convention delegates by percentage (Northwest)

Profession	Illinois (1847)	Indiana (1850)	Iowa (1844)	Iowa (1846)	Iowa (1857)	Michigan (1850)	Minnesota (1857)	Ohio (1850)	Wisconsin (1846)
Lawyer	30.5	26.6	13.9	21.9	39.5	22	21.3	38.7	20
Farmer	42.4	41.6	57	40.6	31.6	48	31.1	34.2	56.5
Merchant	5	7.8	5.6	15.6	5.3	11	13.1	7.2	4.8
Physician	6.7	11.7	8.3	12.5	2.6	6	3.3	7.2	2.4
Mechanic	2.8	0.6	4.2	3.1	0	1	1.6	0	0.8
Other	12.4	9.7	11.1	3.1	26.3	12	37.7	18	15.3

TABLE 1.5B. *Professions of delegates outside Old Northwest*

Top five professions

Profession	Kentucky (1849)	New York (1846)[a]	Massachusetts (1853)
Lawyer	42	45	73
Farmer	37	50	128
Merchant	1	14	65
Physician	9	8	18
Mechanic	2	4	11
Other	6	13	125
Total	98	134	417

Top five professions by percentage

Profession	Kentucky (1849)	New York (1846)	Massachusetts (1853)
Lawyer	43	34	17.5
Farmer	38	37	30.7
Merchant	1	10	15.6
Physician	9	6	4.3
Mechanic	2	3	2.6
Other	6	10	30

[a] Some delegates held multiple jobs.

franchise; citizenship; the judiciary, education, constitutional amendments, and revision; and economic issues such as banks and taxation. Others could be called into existence or consolidated as the convention saw fit. Standing committees were supposed to be at least geographically representative; in the 1847 Illinois convention, for example, every standing committee had to include two members from each county. The presidents made little effort to balance political affiliations of committees. Virtually all of the standing committee members in the Michigan 1835 convention, for example, were Democrats.[67]

Ambitious delegates who put themselves forward usually managed to join their desired committees. Illinoisan John Palmer asked to serve on the education committee and was granted his request. Unfortunately he would continually serve as an arbiter for the three men battling to chair the committee.[68] John Barron Niles told his wife that when his convention president appointed the committees, "he did not seem to know that there was any such man as me in the convention," but evidently, after he voiced his concerns, the president obliged and Niles served on more committees "than any other one in the convention & [had] a better chance to influence the character of the new

[67] Michigan 1835, 192.

[68] John M. Palmer, *Personal Recollections of John M. Palmer: The Story of an Earnest Life* (Cincinnati, OH: Robert Clarke Co., 1901), 1: 43.

constitution."[69] Presidents also studied the professional backgrounds of delegates. Ohio delegate Jacob Green observed that thirteen men known for their legal experience and knowledge had been appointed to the committee on the judiciary.[70] This was true of the Michigan 1835 convention as well; all the men on the judiciary committee were lawyers, and there was one judge.

Committees were the engines that drove the constitution-building effort. Members chose their own chair, and usually worked by cutting, pasting, revising, and arguing over printed copies of their own part of the constitution. They must have fought hard over some issues. Many of the convention journals contain dissenting or minority reports. Ohio delegate John Larwill told his brother that the majority of the committee on banking and currency had agreed on the report, but none of the Democrats were in favor. He felt so strongly about it that he offered a minority report, convinced that "many of the best Democrats in Convention" agreed with him.[71] Although the real work of the convention was done in the committee meetings, unfortunately no committees preserved minutes of their work. Certainly the work was less visible, more frustrating, and likely to earn far less praise and gratitude from their constituencies than the grandiloquent speeches on the floor of the convention.[72]

For those who took no part in the showy work of making speeches in the convention as a whole, hashing out provisions in committee rooms was tedious work, particularly for energetic young men accustomed to working out of doors or riding a circuit. Most conventions met six days per week, from nine to noon, adjourned for two hours, and convened again until four or five, and sometimes late into the evening. In the 1835 Michigan convention the committee to organize the constitutional debates worked "night and day," according to committee member Edward Ellis.[73] The long sessions left little time for committee work, which occurred in the evenings, during lunch breaks, on weekends, and occasionally when members prevailed on the convention to take a few hours off from deliberating in the main body.

[69] John Barron Niles to Mary Niles and family, October 19, 1850, Niles MSS, Lilly Library, Indiana University, Bloomington.

[70] J. V. Smith, *Report of the Debates and Proceedings of the Convention for the Revision of the Constitution of the State of Ohio, 1850–1851* (Columbus, OH, 1851), 1: 66–67 (hereafter Ohio 1850).

[71] John Larwill to Joseph Larwill, June 30, 1850, Larwill Family Papers, Ohio Historical Society, Columbus. The Committee on Banking was actually staffed by Whig Elias Florence, Democrat John Larwill, Robert Leech (political affiliation unknown), Daniel Peck (political affiliation unknown), M. H. Mitchell (political affiliation unknown), E. C. Roll (political affiliation unknown), and the Whig John Milton Williams. If the Committee on Banking and Currency was indeed primarily composed of Whigs, then that would be surprising, considering that the convention president, William Medill, was a staunch Democrat.

[72] Tim Groseclose and David C. King, "Committee Theories Reconsidered," in Lawrence C. Dodd and Bruce I. Oppenheimer, eds., *Congress Reconsidered*, 7th ed. (Washington, DC: CQ Press, 2000).

[73] Michigan 1835, 25.

In the midst of all the hard work, there were also parties and outings. The capital cities turned themselves out to entertain or enlighten the delegates, and local politicians took advantage of opportunities to strengthen political connections. In Springfield, Illinois, Abraham Lincoln invited about twenty of the convention delegates to his house – but there were "no ladies present, not even Mrs. Lincoln." Lincoln's friend David Davis had attended, but he told Sarah that an "exclusive party of gentlemen never looks well – what say you?"[74] A few Indiana delegates took a fascinating trip to see the new locomotive in Indianapolis. Others attended exhibitions and recitals set up by local institutions for the blind or the deaf who hoped for permanent provisions by the state. Oliver Davis promised his little boy that he would bring him a "Verry Pretty" wagon, made by "a great many Poor Blind Boys and Girls."[75] The Indiana delegates also attended a recital at the Deaf and Dumb Asylum, which must have impressed them deeply. Many of them wrote home about a Miss Orchard, a young lady who had learned a form of sign language.[76] The delegates were also honored by the visits of famous guests. According to the *Cincinnati Daily Enquirer*, Amin Bey visited the Ohio constitutional convention and made flattering remarks about the proceedings. Horace Greeley visited the Iowa 1857 convention (as well as the Kansas constitutional convention the year before). Supreme Court Justice John McLean, famed for his Free Soil views, visited the Illinois convention on June 8, 1847.[77]

Party politics – particularly as organized by the overwhelming Democratic majority – functioned well to build important committees, push through agendas, and rally votes for provisions. Both parties met in caucuses throughout the conventions, beginning with the selection of delegates, convention officers, printers, and even local teenagers, who served as messenger boys. In the 1847 Illinois convention, Hezekiah Wead observed that the Whigs, headed by Stephen T. Logan of Sangamon County, "attempted to rally, and embarrass the proceedings of the Convention by obtaining from that body a decision" on the power to set salaries for officers and members (virtually the only real spoils available to the convention.)[78] Political enmities also made delegates cautious

[74] David Davis to Sarah Davis, June 19, 1847, David Davis Papers, Chicago History Museum.

[75] Oliver P. Davis to unknown, February 2, 1851, Oliver P. Davis Papers, Indiana State Archives, Indianapolis.

[76] Alvin Hovey to Mary Ann Hovey, December 18, 1850, Hovey Mss., Lilly Library, Indiana University, Bloomington.

[77] *Cincinnati (OH) Daily Enquirer*, December 13, 1850; W. Blair Lord, *The Debates of the Constitutional Convention; of the State of Iowa, Assembled at Iowa City, Monday, January 19, 1857* (Davenport, IA, 1857), 1: 220–21 (hereafter, Iowa 1857); *Journal of the Convention, Assembled at Springfield, June 7, 1847, ... for the Purpose of Altering, Amending, or Revising the Constitution of the State of Illinois* (Springfield, IL, 1847), 12. Seven years later Supreme Court Justice John McLean later voiced the dissenting opinion in the *Dred Scott* case.

[78] Hezekiah Wead manuscript diary, June 9, 1847, Abraham Lincoln Presidential Library, Springfield, IL.

and at least in one case kept a delegate working through the terrifying cholera epidemic in Ohio. elegate John Larwill told his brother once again (as he did nearly every day throughout the convention) that he was desperate to get back to his family for at least two weeks, but he was afraid to give his "enemies any advantage" during his absence. Evidently some of his political enemies were casting aspersions, saying that his health rendered him unsuited for his "present or any other public office," an allegation that he feared augured poorly for his future political career.[79]

In spite of their majority, the Democrats were internally divided, so for both parties, troublesome issues required sensitive coordination. Larwill intended to "call the Democratic portion of the Committee on banking & the currency together this evening with a view to get them to agree ... before the 4th of July." Wisconsin Democratic delegate John Y. Smith recalled that "a large and powerful party" (also Democrats) organized for the purpose of putting down an enemy faction, had already been "thoroughly organized and drilled" before the convention had even begun. Because the territory was about to achieve statehood, there were many (as Smith phrased it) "ducks in the wind," by which he meant, opportunities for political patronage.[80]

Antebellum men, particularly those with political ambitions, enjoyed hearing and making a good speech.[81] Most of the delegates would have known how to present pieces they had learned by heart, or how to defend a resolution in a debating club. Those who had at least basic literacy education, either in common schools or through tutors, would have been deeply familiar with textbooks such as the *Columbian Orator*. The *Orator* stressed speaking loud enough to be heard, pronouncing words clearly, assuming appropriate poses, and harmonizing the tone, emphasis, tempo, and gestures with the spoken words. Orators were to express themselves with warmth and naturalness (that is, to refrain from theatrical tones or gestures) and to fill the hall with their voices, but without becoming harsh or shrill.[82]

[79] John Larwill to Joseph Larwill, July 2, 1850, Larwill Papers, Ohio Historical Society, Columbus.

[80] John Y. Smith to Henry Dodge, March 5, 1856, John Y. Smith Letters, Wisconsin Historical Society, Madison.

[81] Nancy Isenberg observed that constitutional and other conventions were visual, theatrical spectacles. Nancy Isenberg, *Sex and Citizenship in Antebellum America* (Chapel Hill: University of North Carolina Press, 1998), 15–16.

[82] On the power of language to uplift and reform, see: James Perrin Warren, *Culture of Eloquence: Oratory and Reform in Antebellum America* (1999; repr., University Park: Pennsylvania State University Press, 2004). Allen C. Guelzo, in *Lincoln and Douglas: The Debates That Defined America* (New York: Simon & Schuster, 2008), 94–95, discusses the basic textbooks used by orators but notes that these manuals espoused a style of debate that was more akin to "political declamation" than "intelligent persuasion." Carolyn Eastman, in *A Nation of Speechifiers: Making an American Republic after the Revolution* (Chicago: University of Chicago Press, 2008), 21–22, explains that millions of these schoolbooks reached even distant rural areas. She is talking about the northeast, but with Cincinnati as a major publishing center, the schoolbooks would certainly have been sold in the Northwest as well. She also

For many, delivering a public address in the convention became an exhilarating adventure. The temptation to make a name for oneself, to impress one's colleagues, as well as one's constituents, family, and party officials, compelled those who had political ambitions. But that could only be achieved with the aid of long, well-crafted speeches studded with classical allusions or references to European events. Men able or willing to indulge themselves in that fashion were in a minority. Only a small percentage of the delegates made most of the speeches, and of those, most were practicing lawyers. Oliver Davis, who had given up his law office, never addressed the Indiana 1850 convention. By contrast, his colleague Alvin Hovey, an active lawyer with young children and a similar background, became passionately enthralled with oratory – particularly his own.[83] The speeches within the convention hall were intended as public addresses, whose principal aim was to persuade political opponents, and as compositions to be printed and widely distributed. The more experienced delegates wrote and revised their speeches, then presented them in the convention, gave their handwritten notes to the stenographer, or hoped (often vainly) that the newspaper men recording the convention's doings would report their remarks accurately.[84] They could also have their speeches printed at a job printer to mail to their constituencies, to party leaders, as well as to friends, family members, and neighbors.

Those delegates with the drive and oratorical training endeavored to dominate the conventions. They were usually successful. The rest were impressed, bored, or frustrated. Among the ambitious speakers there was certainly, as Hovey put it, a "scramble" to obtain the floor. He told Mary (somewhat disingenuously) that he had thus far taken "but little part in the proceedings," castigating his colleagues as "very vain and feeble men ... fond of hearing themselves talk though they speak to but little purpose, their main aim being to have their names published in the papers." Although he vehemently denied following their example, and claimed a determination only to speak when he had "something worthy of being heard," the convention record disproves his asseverations.[85] Hovey liked nothing better than to hear his own voice. He became miserable if Mary reacted with anything less than strong enthusiasm

comments on the modern duality of oratory and rhetoric. See also, also Todd F. McDorman and David M. Timmerman, eds., *Rhetoric and Democracy: Pedagogical and Political Practices* (East Lansing: Michigan State University Press, 2008), 11.

83 There is no record that Oliver Davis ever spoke, while Alvin Hovey spoke at least fifty times.

84 Several manuscript files, such as Indiana delegate Robert Milroy's manuscript collection, contain drafts of speeches – some cut and pasted or crossed out. Alvin Hovey's files do not contain drafts of speeches, but he must have written them out because he frequently sent home printed pamphlet versions.

85 Alvin Hovey to Mary Ann Hovey, October 18, 1850, Hovey MSS, Lilly Library, Indiana University, Bloomington. This analysis interleaves his letter to his wife with his convention speech. He made this speech on October 24, 1850. For the full text, see Indiana 1850, 1: 204–7. He wrote to Mary about it on October 27, 1850.

or if he felt ignored by his colleagues or in the press. In the long run his determination paid off. By the end of his career, he had served as a general during the Civil War, later become governor of Indiana, and finally been elected to the U.S. Senate.

Ambitious delegates like Hovey stretched their wings in the convention and experienced intense satisfaction with their first successful speeches. Alvin sent Mary a newspaper that contained some of his remarks on the grand jury question. As always he asked for her applause. It was the first great speech of his life, and judging from the convention journal, it was a polished, erudite, well-paced work – one that defended the grand jury system in true conservative Whig fashion. When he rose to speak he had, at first, felt "greatly embarrassed."[86] He began by confessing his diffidence at the prospect of addressing "such a learned body."[87] Within a few moments, however, his nervousness left him, and he felt that he had never in his life been "as complete master of [his] voice, thoughts and gestures as then," nor been so "completely satisfied" with himself, expressing an "earnest fervid passion" and making "the hall ... ring like a trumpet."[88] He assured his colleagues of his stern duty toward his constituents, likening his task to that of a "sentinel guarding the besieged city of the state of Indiana."[89] Hovey captivated his audience with powerful imagery: prison walls, the blood of the innocent, and stained ermine robes. Then he collected himself and talked more quietly: It was easier to tear down than to build up again. Destroy any part of the system, and once it was demolished, "the whole superstructure must feel the shock." As did many Whigs, Hovey resorted to democratic slogans to win over his opponents and began with simple, straightforward oratorical devices, defining the term and then redefining it to suit his arguments. "What is a Grand Jury – Of what is it composed? Is it composed of lawyers and doctors of clergymen and justices of the peace? No: it is composed of the very bone and sinew of the county of the farmer, the mechanic, the merchant." The rest of that long speech (which must have taken at least two hours) then dismantled counterarguments, and finally parsed the existing legislation and precedent. He ended by saying very simply that those who sent him to the convention wanted the "good now, and all that [was] untested left to the future."[90]

Writing to Mary a few evenings later, Hovey was positive that the entire convention body had remained "as still and as attentive as though they were listening to the voice of a *real orator*." He expatiated in this vein for several more pages, finally telling Mary that former governor, David Wallace, now serving as a delegate, called him "one of the ten finest speakers in the state."

86 Alvin Hovey to Mary Ann Hovey, October 27, 1850, Hovey MSS, Lilly Library, Indiana University, Bloomington.

87 Indiana 1850, 1: 204.

88 Alvin Hovey to Mary Ann Hovey, October 27, 1850, Hovey MSS, Lilly Library, Indiana University, Bloomington.

89 Indiana 1850, 1: 206.

90 Indiana 1850, 1: 205, 207.

Several others had taken him by the hand and complimented him "in the most glowing terms." His only disappointment was that his beloved Mary had not been present. He admitted shamefacedly that she would probably call him "too vain," but if she had heard him, he was sure, she would be "too vain also."[91]

Words were the delegates' principal stock in trade. This was especially true of men who earned their living as attorneys. Granted, some delegates were making the first public speeches they had ever made in their lives; others became so enamored of the sound of their own voices that their colleagues were forced to pass rules governing the length and number of times a man was to be permitted to speak on a topic. Meanwhile, their colleagues, particularly those uninterested in speaking in the committee of the whole, were becoming heartily bored. Some ignored the proceedings, read papers, wrote to their families and business contacts, or, as Niles frequently did, ambled about the room to visit colleagues. Indiana delegate George Tague sarcastically told one of his associates that he could not quite follow his arguments because he had been attempting to "read a little" in his newspaper.[92] That particular problem became so severe that many of the conventions prohibited the practice of reading newspapers in the convention hall – generally to little effect. The 1850 Michigan convention passed such a provision, but when Isaac Willard quipped, "unless long and dull speeches are made," the motion was laid on the table.[93] In the Indiana 1850 convention, George Moore raised a humorous resolution to silence delegates who talked out of turn, and to criticize those who left the hall to "roam and swagger about." In response, John Pettit added a friendly amendment "to throw a hammer at their heads," which provoked a round of laughter.[94]

In spite of (or perhaps because of) the intense effort at regulating the work of the convention, these proceedings often devolved into noisy, chaotic, disorganized messes. It could take weeks to learn and build a proper convention culture. The veteran delegates had trouble reining in their younger and less experienced colleagues. Some of the noise was due to logistical challenges: Most legislatures had not appropriated enough funds to pay for the long convention sessions, so several of the conventions were forced to work in large, uncarpeted rooms unsuited to deliberation, and the sounds of chairs and tables scraping on the floors often drowned out speakers.[95] The halls became scenes of hilarity, anger,

[91] Alvin Hovey to Mary, October 27, 1850, Hovey MSS, Lilly Library, Indiana University, Bloomington.

[92] Indiana 1850, 1: 633.

[93] *Report of the Proceedings and Debates in the Convention to Revise the Constitution of the State of Michigan, 1850* (Lansing: 1850), 104 (hereafter, Michigan 1850). For similar views, see also Indiana 1850, 2: 1131, 1160–62, 1342.

[94] Charles Kettleborough, *Constitution Making in Indiana: A Source Book of Constitutional Documents with Historical Introduction and Critical Notes* (Indianapolis: Indiana Historical Commission, 1916), 1: 234. Indiana 1850, 2: 1827.

[95] Robert Dykstra mentions the "freshly plastered, but carpetless chamber," in *Bright Radical Star: Black Freedom and White Supremacy on the Hawkeye Frontier* (Cambridge, MA: Harvard University Press, 1993; repr., Ames: Iowa State University Press, 1997), 47.

childish pranks, and astonishing rudeness, sometimes to the point of fisticuffs. Someone became so drunk in the 1846 Wisconsin convention that the delegates were moved to protest his "discourteous interruptions."[96] A few weeks later, in the same convention, Moses Strong threw his cane at an opponent. Though the cane failed to strike its target (it hit an intervening column instead), Strong apologized to the convention for his breach of decorum. His opponent felt similarly obligated, but added a cutting rider that he was apologizing to everyone *except* Strong.[97] Some of the fights became ugly. Reporting on the 1847 Illinois convention, the *St. Louis Republican* described sparring between Judge Walter B. Scates and Dr. Daniel H. Whitney that became so obscene that the paper refused to reprint it, explaining that such language was rarely heard even in "lecture[s] on obstetrics or among the rude jests of a dissecting room."[98]

Several disagreements escalated into physical violence. When the two delegates from Jo Daviess County attempted to settle their fight in a duel, their colleagues forcibly intervened. A few days later, Irish-born William Grimshaw (Figure 1.6), who considered such displays unseemly, helped to engineer a constitutional provision that would render it impossible for anyone who had ever fought a duel to assume public office.[99] Alvin Hovey, who seemed to be especially sensitive to slights, warned his wife that she would no doubt read an account in the newspapers "of a little affair" that had transpired the day before. While making a motion Hovey had spoken harshly of his opponents. In response, Mr. Kent called him a "Low Coward" within the hearing of several delegates. Hovey walked around to Kent's seat and asked him to repeat the insult. Kent obliged, and Hovey "struck him in the face." He told his wife later that the convention exonerated him; the published record only explains that "considerable confusion" occurred.[100]

During one long debate Indiana delegate John Niles left his seat and wandered over to visit a colleague, the cheerful Dr. Foster, on the other side of the hall. Niles (who, judging by his letters home, which he usually wrote during the debates, was easily distracted from the proceedings) recounted several unprofessional pranks that occurred in the convention. He told his wife that "a good many funny things" happened. ormer governor Wallace, "a large & good natured man," who was standing in the open space in front of the clerk's desk "where every body could see him ... rose up ... [and] when one of the reporters took his chair, ... set back & rolled over on the floor."[101] During a discussion

96 Wisconsin 1846, 366. The delegate was not identified in the journal record.

97 Wisconsin 1846, 558.

98 *St. Louis Republican*, August 20, 1847. See also, Hezekiah Wead manuscript diary, 22–24, Abraham Lincoln Presidential Library, Springfield, IL.

99 Illinois 1847, 870.

100 Alvin Hovey to Mary Ann Hovey, January 25, 1851, Hovey MSS, Lilly Library, Indiana University, Bloomington. This incident was reported in Indiana 1850, 2: 1822.

101 John Barron Niles to Mary Niles, November 3, 1850, Niles MSS, Lilly Library, Indiana University, Bloomington.

FIGURE 1.6. William Grimshaw (1813–1895), Whig delegate to the 1847 Illinois convention, was born in Ireland. He later became a Republican and served as trustee and director of many charitable and educational institutions.
Source: Unknown daguerreotype artist. Courtesy of William A. Grimshaw Grote.

about the rights of married women, several of the "rogues in the convention" presented "two simple minded old men – one of them a Dutchman" and forced them to make speeches, much to the hilarity of the convention. Niles thought that the convention had been acting like "a class of school boys." He also observed that there were many ladies in the lobbies, and the "whole concern ... resolved into a kind of roar."[102]

But the jokes could become seriously disruptive, and many letters home complained about the uncontrolled rabble that deliberated in the conventions. David Davis told his wife "that the ever lasting subject of banks [was] still rife in the Convention." He found it impossible even to determine whether the convention's work would be worth the expense, and the excitement had become "unwholesome" to him.[103] Many of the delegates had been cooped up with their colleagues, who (according to one irritated Michigan citizen) talked

[102] John Barron Niles to unknown, November 15, 1850, Niles MSS, Lilly Library, Indiana University, Bloomington.

[103] David Davis to Sarah Davis, August 8, 1847, David Davis Papers, Chicago History Museum. See also David Davis to unknown, August 2, 1846, David Davis Papers, Chicago History Museum, which describes a fight that occurred between Thompson Campbell, who had a

too much and "constitutioned" too little, and they were growing increasingly irritable.[104]

Because capital city newspapers reported the debates in great detail, the constituents at home had a fairly clear picture of what was going on in the conventions – which were, after all, costing them at least two dollars per day per delegate. If deliberation was meant to animate, express, and support democracy, then such speeches required an efficient and transparent stream of information to the public. Capital city newspapers admirably served that function. Their reports on the convention were in turn copied in local county papers, and judging by frequent mentions of reportage in the delegates' private correspondence, the public read them eagerly. Indiana delegate Daniel Kelso declared that at least 70 percent of Indiana's citizens followed the debates with "a more intense interest than was felt during the time of the adoption of our first Constitution."[105] David Davis had directed the editors of the Springfield newspapers to send their daily editions to his father-in-law while the convention was in session, because he wanted him to see what was going on. In the Michigan 1850 convention, delegate Isaac Crary was positive that every head of every family read his newspapers from "the first to the third page."[106]

Public opinion functioned as the single most relentless driving force behind the delegate votes. That was particularly true of any controversial topic. Although some of the delegates voted their consciences and dared to contravene their constituents' expressed wishes, many declined to do so. They did not care to see their work destroyed in the final ratification vote, and more to the point, they believed their task was to represent the popular will. Some delegates simply refused to vote on controversial provisions, regardless of their political inclinations, until they had a clear indication of what their constituencies wanted. Michigan delegate Russell Briggs told his colleagues that his "only object was to vote so as to be approved by his constituents."[107] Allen Hamilton frequently asked friends and neighbors for their opinions on controversial subjects such as black civil liberties.[108] Some even traveled home to collect public opinion on controversial topics. According to Wisconsin delegate Benjamin Hunkins, two-thirds of the delegates had gone home to obtain their constituents' opinion on banking.[109]

reputation for being sharp and witty, and O. C. Pratt. Both were arrested. See also Hezekiah Wead manuscript diary, 22–24, Abraham Lincoln Presidential Library, Springfield, IL.

104 William A. Richmond to Alpheus Felch, August 31, 1850, Alpheus Felch Papers, Bentley Historical Library, University of Michigan, Ann Arbor. See also Daniel Kelso's observations about the moblike nature of the 1850 Indiana Convention. Indiana 1850, 2: 1123.

105 Indiana 1850, 1: 52; 117, 737. Kelso mentioned that every newspaper in the state would publish the convention debates. Indiana 1850, 2: 1733.

106 Michigan 1850, 173.

107 Michigan 1835, 141, 150.

108 These letters are described in detail in Chapter 8.

109 Wisconsin 1846, 691.

The delegates used the media to influence public opinion or even launch a discussion supporting a provision. When asked to adjourn, Michigan 1835 convention delegate Crary refused because he wanted his constituents to know that they were at work. His colleague Mr. Briggs told his colleagues that his "only object was to vote so as to be approved by his constituents."[110] When delegates felt they lacked political experience and expertise on such challenging topics as economic or legal questions, some indicated that they could not move forward unless they knew precisely what their constituents wanted, and they used their local newspapers as tools to discover public opinion. A delegate to the 1850 Ohio convention told his brother that he would call a caucus of the Democrats on the Committee on Banking. He hoped to publish the report before he left so that it would "call fourth an expression of the democratic papers before it is acted on in convention."[111] In the 1850 Indiana convention, the vote on the legislature's right to grant a charter to the state bank had to be delayed because many desired to "hear from constituents" and it would take a few days to gather their opinions.[112]

Publicity was the heart and soul of democratic deliberation. Because these men met in the capital city, usually in the halls of government, and because they were laying the groundwork of self-governance for at least a generation of future citizens, many felt that it was vital to preserve a record of their debates. This was not merely to support personal or political aspirations. It is unlikely that all of them cherished dreams of achieving political office. By way of contrast, few state legislators bothered to have their speeches printed privately. Legislative journals contained only records of votes and roll calls and only preserved minority and other reports. They only identified the names and counties of the members (not their political affiliations, marital status, or other personal details). Capital city newspapers rarely published more than legislative excerpts or votes. Yet many of the conventions voted to publish their complete deliberations in hard-bound journals. These immense books, which often ran to two volumes, contained the votes, speeches, most of the petitions, the supporting documents or letters, as well as a great deal of personal information about the men who formed the constitutions. They were meant to constitute a part of the historic record of the state. In the 1857 Iowa convention, for example, the delegates voted to place copies in the state library.[113]

Not every convention could afford such an expensive undertaking. All of the conventions that met before 1850 (the 1847 Illinois, the 1835 Michigan, the 1844 and 1846 Iowa, and the 1846 Wisconsin conventions) had to content themselves with publishing only votes and resolutions in convention journals

[110] Michigan 1835, 141, 150.
[111] John Larwill to Joseph Larwill, June 27, 1850, Larwill Family Papers, Ohio Historical Society, Columbus.
[112] Indiana 1850, 1: 220.
[113] Iowa 1857, 2: 1026.

and left it to the capital city newspapers to publish their speeches. These newspapers reported on the convention debates exhaustively, and their editorials and excerpts were copied in papers around the state. Delegates in most conventions were granted an allowance of up to twenty copies of the capital city newspaper so that they could mail them home for their constituents' responses. Several conventions voted to pay fifty dollars to newspapers to print the constitution in full.[114] If some protested the cost, others declared that they were making history and the expense was worthwhile to preserve a detailed record. In the 1850 Ohio convention, for example, delegate Sawyer feared that "their extreme anxiety to protect the public treasury might induce them to stint themselves." But he wanted so much to "perpetuate the fact by one volume in his own library throughout all time that he was a member of the Convention that framed a good Constitution for the State of Ohio." He thought every member should have a copy of the deliberations, and one should go to "every literary institution in the State, to each county in the State and a copy or more to every State in the Union and to the United States in order that the libraries of Congress and of the States should have a copy." And the convention ought to "print 15 per cent of the ... copies in the German language."[115]

The Indiana delegates decided to preserve not only the speeches, but also their portraits in recognition of a historically significant moment, so they commissioned daguerreotypes made by a prominent photographer. Alvin Hovey mentioned to Mary that these daguerreotypes would be preserved in a "large frame, to be hung up on the state library." Although he protested that he "did not much like to do it as it appeared a little vain," when "older and more notable men" seemed to think otherwise, he consented. Because Hovey found the daguerreotypist a superior artist, and "as he offered to take an additional one for each member at a reduced price" he thought he would send one home.[116] But the picture disappointed Mary, who thought Alvin looked less handsome with his "whiskers cut off."[117]

None of the delegates would have dreamed of closing the convention deliberations to visitors or keeping their votes secret; indeed, many made a serious effort and bore significant expense to assure that their constituencies knew what they were about. Whether through political ambition or a genuine desire to fulfill their constituencies' wishes, the delegates ensured that their speeches and votes remained entirely transparent. And the people carried on their side of the conversation with zest, not only responding to the delegates' questions, but hammering in with demands, criticisms, praise, and sometimes even ire. The

[114] Michigan 1850, 173.

[115] Ohio 1850, 1: 33. Kettleborough, *Constitution Making in Indiana*, 2: 644. The Indiana convention paid nearly nine thousand dollars in printing and binding expenses.

[116] Alvin Hovey to Mary Ann Hovey, November 20, 1850, Hovey MSS, Lilly Library, Indiana University, Bloomington.

[117] Alvin Hovey to Mary Ann Hovey, December 13, 1850, Hovey MSS, Lilly Library, Indiana University, Bloomington.

barrage of news copied from the capital papers kept the convention's doings front and center. Partisan organs used the convention debates and votes to push their agendas. The voters insisted that their ideas and demands be taken seriously. In this way the deliberations traveled outside the convention halls to include a wide variety of participants, both citizens and the disfranchised. News reached home within two or three weeks, in letters and in speeches, resolutions, and editorials copied from the capital newspaper. Meanwhile the delegates were at their labors long enough to allow an interchange of ideas.[118]

The *Milwaukee Courier* published a warning editorial on the elected judiciary question stating explicitly that if the delegates were not sufficiently instructed, then the people ought to "take special care" to make these men understand what they wanted, and to express their wishes in a fashion "too clear to be disobeyed."[119] In the 1850 Michigan convention, Alvord mocked his colleagues, always fearful of the "mighty power of the press," and when people talked about "the dear people," it was always "buncombe."[120] Henry O'Connor wrote an incensed letter to Iowa delegate William Clarke, demanding to know what in "the name of sense & reason can have induced the convention to leave the Supreme Court as at present constituted." Making it clear that the entire judicial body was to represent the people's wishes, he added as a sharp postscript: "You (I mean the convention) must have misunderstood the people."[121] If that was the case, the voters could hardly be blamed. They thrust their way into constitutional conventions through letters, newspaper editorials, and petitions. And if they became too dissatisfied with their delegates' convention votes, they held local indignation meetings.[122] Some delegates received a sharp scolding, both from newspapers and from irate voters. A Wisconsin newspaper trumpeted that every delegate "may rest assured of the fact, that if the people do not award him ... praise, that they will inflict upon him the lash of censure."[123]

For their part, the constituents of both parties used the time-honored method of signature gathering to drive their will into the center of the convention deliberations. Long pasted-together scrolls bearing hundreds of names were not mere sentiments or declarations of philosophies, however: They were demands for action.[124] The voters from Racine, Wisconsin, explicitly drew the

[118] Indiana 1850, 1: 52. Daniel Kelso explained that publishing the debates in the capital city newspapers would enable delegates to mail the editions home to their local papers. Indiana 1850, 1: 117.

[119] *Milwaukee Courier*, August 26, 1846.

[120] Michigan 1850, 258.

[121] Henry O'Connor to William Penn Clarke, February 18, 1857, William Penn Clarke Papers, State Historical Society of Iowa, Des Moines.

[122] Arabella Lyon discusses remonstrations as a crucial part of democratic deliberation in *Deliberative Acts*, 36–38.

[123] *The Milwaukee Courier*, September 23, 1846.

[124] Susan Zaeske sees petitions as actions too. See Susan Zaeske, *Signatures of Citizenship: Petitioning, Antislavery, and Women's Political Identity* (Chapel Hill: University of North Carolina Press, 2003).

line between abstract principles and concrete results. These people told the 1848 Wisconsin convention that they wanted a fair and broad homestead policy. "The undersigned would represent to your honorable Body that a mere recognition of the principle will not meet their wishes. Insted of a shadow, the undersigned want a substantial provision on the subject."[125]

Unsuccessful petitions were not preserved. For example, none of the petitions asking for black suffrage and residence rights survived, though many of the petitions in Ohio were at least read into the journal record. Judging from the extant documents, however, the most frequent subject for petitions pertained to land issues: homestead exemptions, county boundaries, and redistricting court circuits. In the 1846 Wisconsin convention, for example, exemption became a highly charged issue. According to a newspaper covering the convention, "friends in different sections of the territory" were making their will known so that their delegates would be informed of public opinion. "If the will of every man, woman, and child from the Lake to the River could be heard, it would sound as the voice of strong men compared to an infant's cry, and would strike as a death knell upon the ear of the cold hearted oppressor." The writer was so convinced that this "universal sentiment" was so strongly in its favor that "however obnoxious the constitution may be made upon other points," the charter would be ratified "by an almost unanimous vote."[126]

Those hapless delegates who disappointed their constituencies could expect to be fired. When Judge Vance of Butler County voted against the legislature's right to repeal bank charters in the 1850 Ohio convention, the citizens held an "indignation meeting" demanding his resignation.[127] In the 1850 Indiana convention, delegate Charles Brookbank warned that "indignation meetings" would utter a "sharp reproof from the yeomanry."[128] His colleague Allen Hamilton received a letter from one of his constituents complaining that there was "little progress & too much talking" and threatening that the constitution

[125] Letters from electors of Racine to Constitutional Convention, 1847–48, Horace A. Tenney Papers, Wisconsin Historical Society, Madison. Petitions were not listed individually in the following conventions: Ohio 1802, Indiana 1816, Illinois 1818, Illinois 1847, Iowa 1844 and 1846, Michigan 1835 conventions. The other conventions did mention petitions in their journals, but comparison to newspaper editorials suggests that the record is incomplete. (This would include the Wisconsin 1848 convention; the Indiana, Michigan, and Ohio 1850 conventions; and both of the Minnesota 1857 conventions.)

[126] Milo Milton Quaife, ed., *The Struggle over Ratification 1846–1847*, vol. 28 of *Publications of the State Historical Society of Wisconsin* (Madison: State Historical Society of Wisconsin, 1920), 130–31. This editorial, titled, "The Exemption," appeared in the *Madison Wisconsin Democrat* on October 31, 1846. See also Quaife, *Struggle over Ratification*, 144–45, for an editorial titled, "Strictures upon Marshall M. Strong," *Madison Wisconsin Democrat*, December 12, 1846.

[127] James Loudon to unknown, January 16, 1851, Dewitt Clinton Loudon Papers, Ohio Historical Society, Columbus.

[128] Indiana 1850, 1: 924.

would be "*unmade* by the people in a very short time."[129] In Wisconsin, John Tweedy received an angry letter from Rufus King sharply condemning the banking committee's "preposterous" report. Everyone he had met considered the banking provisions both absurd and impracticable. If the convention dared to "engraft such principles?? upon the Constitution," he warned, the charter would be "emphatically d____d by the people."[130]

"No!" was the strongest weapon the voters wielded. The messiness of these deliberations was only partly due to powerful political divisions or inexperience. Indeed, the chaos reveals how strongly the delegates believed that the public should weigh in, and at the same time, how much they feared that the public *would* weigh in. In an aggressive speech against black suffrage he made in the 1846 Wisconsin convention, Moses Strong told his colleagues that if they allowed black men to vote, the constitution would not receive fifty votes. In that case, the people would wage "war to the knife, and the knife to the hilt" to defeat the constitution.[131] Judd agreed, explaining that submitting the provision on black suffrage to a popular vote (rather than either providing or prohibiting black suffrage in the constitution) would "quiet excitement," both inside the convention and among the voters.[132] In contrast, his colleague Burchard was far more cautious. He thought his colleagues, whether for or against black suffrage, would not want their votes known to the people – and therefore recommended that the subject be referred for a popular vote.[133] Morgan L. Martin, a delegate in the 1848 Wisconsin convention, explained that the principal object of the convention had been to draft a "popular" constitution, and this could only be accomplished by "allowing the people to fight over such questions of policy among themselves."[134] Most northwestern constitutions were submitted to a popular vote for ratification, and many included separate referenda on black rights, corporate privileges, and constitutional amending procedures.

Meanwhile, inside the conventions, the time began to drag. The delegates suffered because of the long absence from their wives and children, and their businesses or farms needed their urgent attention. Some become painfully disillusioned. Ohio delegate John Larwill wrote to his wife and brother nearly

[129] Edgerton to Allen Hamilton, January 9, 1851, Allen Hamilton Papers, Indiana Historical Society, Indianapolis.

[130] Rufus King to John Hubbard Tweedy, October 17, 1846, John Hubbard Tweedy Papers, Wisconsin Historical Society, Madison. Rufus King was currently serving in the New York state constitutional convention.

[131] Wisconsin 1846, 121. The phrase "war to the knife and the knife to the hilt" has a long history and would become a famous battle cry during the Kansas troubles in the mid-1850s. According to the *London Quarterly Review*, July 1816, this slogan of ancient Sparta was popularized during the battle of Saragossa and was defined as mortal hand-to-hand combat.

[132] Wisconsin 1846, 241.

[133] Wisconsin 1846, 222.

[134] Reuben G. Thwaites, "Narrative of Morgan L. Martin, in an Interview with the Editor," in *Collections of the State Historical Society of Wisconsin* (Madison, WI: 1888), 11: 409.

every day, commenting in each letter on the prospect of adjournment and his terror of the cholera epidemic currently raging through the city.[135] John B. Niles complained to his wife that the convention chamber was "very unhealthy" but hoped by using great care to be able to remain well. By then the cholera had disappeared in Indiana, but he no longer liked "the spirit of the convention" as well as when he had first arrived. He still found "excellent & honest men" among his colleagues, but also many who were "ignorant & prejudiced."[136] One of Allen Hamilton's neighbors, responding to Hamilton's complaint that he had to consume his "hours and days in listening to endless and unprofitable speeches," observed that the convention's progress was indeed imperceptible, and the people were beginning to lose patience. It was growing cold and their long speeches would soon, he hoped, "freeze in their mouths."[137] In the 1847 Illinois convention Onslow Peters declared that he made "no speeches on this subject for home consumption," while Walter Scates (who actually addressed the convention more often than any other delegate) raked over his colleagues for making endless "speeches for Buncombe," or deploying "the weapon called sarcasm."[138] There must have been great temptation toward "speaking for Buncombe" because for more than half of these men, this would be the first (and for some, perhaps the only) time they saw their names in print. One Indiana delegate observed wryly that the "intellectual forces of this body" had become "pretty well exhausted," and that some gentlemen were now suggesting that the convention was "chiefly composed of such animals as are usually called jassacks."[139] Voters protested that the ceaseless oratory was an abuse of the deliberative process. Such speeches fooled few of their audiences, in the convention or at home. Demagoguery reaped mockery inside the conventions, criticism in opposition newspapers, and angry letters from the voters. And yet for delegates like Alvin Hovey, who yearned for fame, any lack of attention was a pillory. Hovey was bitterly disappointed that "apparently the *Whig* doesn't know the convention is doing anything because there is nothing about it in the paper."[140]

The concatenation of pressures became almost unbearable for many of the delegates. It was difficult to cope with their loneliness, the mounting cost of the convention, the chronic (and occasionally quite hostile) demands of their constituencies, and the criticism – some of it unfair – that often appeared in

135 John Larwill to Joseph Larwill, June 25, 1850, Larwill Family Papers, Ohio Historical Society, Columbus.

136 John Barron Niles to Mary Niles, November 20, 1850, Niles MSS, Lilly Library, Indiana University, Bloomington.

137 I. Benoit to Allen Hamilton, December 6, 1850, Hamilton Family Papers, Indiana State Library, Indianapolis.

138 Illinois 1847, 27, 30, 39.

139 Indiana 1850, 2: 1106.

140 Alvin Hovey to Mary Ann Hovey, November 6, 1850, Hovey MSS, Lilly Library, Indiana University, Bloomington.

the newspapers. In spite of those internal and external pressures, the delegates had to craft a complicated document that would meet all the demands of a government that was both democratic and republican and would also establish and protect rights and duties of citizens. The conventions dragged on, month after weary month, far beyond the time that any of the delegates had expected. Michigan delegate Dr. Henry Alvord lost patience. He chided his colleagues for their fear of the "mighty power of the press." It was time to move on. Complaining that they had already been working too long, he was positive that everyone was desperate to go home. In response his colleague Isaac Crary sighed. He yearned to leave Detroit but at the same time realized how painfully hard it would be to arrive at home – the profound relief, only to have to "pack up and return to the capitol" then waste more time figuring out "where we are" and, finally, pick up the threads again. Another delegate voted against a temporary adjournment because he would have to ride two hundred miles in the burning sun, which was not worthwhile for a four-day visit.[141] Alvin Hovey visited home in early January and had a long and difficult trip back to Indianapolis. He was heartily tired of this extended absence from home and law office. "So far as money [was] concerned," he thought he would be "greatly a looser in coming here atall."[142] A reporter for the *St. Louis Republican* made fun of the Illinois delegates – whom they called "double refined servants of the people" – sitting together seven to eight hours a day, in ninety-degree weather. "If they do not labor earnestly in the service of those whom they represent, I freely bear witness that they at least perspire."[143] By mid-August 1847, Illinois delegate Hezekiah Wead recorded in his diary that the convention was "anxious to get home" because the farmers did not want to miss their opportunity "to put in their full crop." A week later he observed that many were talking about their "desire to return to their families."[144]

These conventions were expensive, and they became more costly day by day. Allen Hamilton received a letter from one of his constituents telling him to hurry up "& come home." Evidently the majority of the delegates had "forgotten that their pay [came] from the taxpayers." There was one thing certain: "it will learn [us] who to send again."[145] After six, seven, sometimes eight months of deliberation, the delegates were eager to be done, and the voters equally eager to have them finish. This was particularly urgent in the territories that were trying to become states, where a go-ahead, energetic Democratic Party was pushing for early admission. But even in the older states, the mounting cost

[141] Michigan 1850, 258–60.

[142] Alvin Hovey to Mary Ann Hovey, January 16, 185[1], Hovey MSS, Lilly Library, Indiana University, Bloomington.

[143] *St. Louis Republican*, August 17, 1847.

[144] Hezekiah Wead manuscript diary, August 19 and August 24, 1847, Abraham Lincoln Presidential Library, Springfield, IL.

[145] John H. Browning to Allen Hamilton, November 30, 1850. Allen Hamilton Papers, Indiana State Library, Indianapolis.

of these "two dollar a day men" frustrated the voters. "If the Constitutional Convention continues to make itself as *interesting* as it has thus far – I think next year we can tumble it, and the Locofoco party together overboard."[146]

Because both the hall rental and the delegates' pay were reckoned by the day, the cost of the conventions was directly related to the time they spent and became an important factor in the chronic demand for adjournment that began to beleaguer the proceedings. The Indiana Legislature had appropriated forty thousand dollars for the convention, and by the time they adjourned, the cost had mounted to more than eighty thousand dollars.[147] Michigan delegate DeWitt Clinton Walker talked about the "petty larceny of stealing from the State for our own convenience and our own interest even a single day of that time for which we are employed and paid to work for the people." He soon became carried away with his metaphors, declaiming that the convention had been appointed "to stop the leaks, to diminish the freight, and to put new spars into the ship of State, and not to scuttle and sink the vessel."[148] They were facing the double pressure of wasting money in convention and missing their families, as well as having chores and business that simply could no longer be put off. Worse still, as one Michigan delegate pointed out, the "sickly season" was approaching and it had become "positively crucial to finish."[149]

Deliberation might have been interesting; or it might have been tiresome. These conversations might have helped catapult some men's political careers or convince them never to run for office again. But the convention work also required stringent personal sacrifices. Some delegates withstood the strain and remained at their duties more conscientiously than others. Indiana delegate William Thomas observed that his colleague Dr. Helm planned to leave for his home the following morning to be gone a week or ten days, in order to take his wife and daughters back with him. "About thirty of the members are absent all of the time on leave," he told his wife, Polly, "but I feel an unwillingness to do so while my own and the health of my family does not require it. Custom does not always make right. And when a man undertakes to serve the public he has something else to do besides gratifying his own inclination particularly if it is to be done at public expense."[150] Oliver Davis had to miss some of the most important moments in his family's life; he was in Indianapolis for Christmas,

146 John Greiner to Thomas Ewing, December 20, 1850, Thomas Ewing Family Papers, Library of Congress, Washington, DC.

147 Appropriations reported in Indiana 1850, 1: 26. Cost is in Kettleborough, *Constitution Making in Indiana*, 2: 642–45.

148 Michigan 1850, 258–60.

149 Michigan 1850, 258–60. For a study of the strains experienced by families of U.S. Congressmen see Rosemarie Zagarri, "The Family Factor: Congressmen, Turnover, and the Burden of Public Service in the Early American Republic." *Journal of the Early Republic* 33 (Summer 2013): 283–316.

150 William Winans Thomas to Polly Thomas, October 31, 1850, William W. Thomas Papers, Indiana Historical Society, Indianapolis.

and a month later, he was absent during the birth of his second daughter. He wrote to his wife congratulating her and suggested she name their baby after Andrew Jackson's wife, because, as he observed, Andrew Jackson Davis would not be a "verry pretty name for a Girl."[151] And some of the delegates experienced irreparable personal losses and heartbreak. When thirty-six-year-old Indiana delegate Walter Beach lost his beloved wife suddenly, he was "overwhelmed with sorrow," and the convention adjourned in respect.[152] Yet Beach returned to the convention to finish his work. Another delegate even gave his life to the labor of building a constitution. James Vanbenthusen, who at seventy-two was by far the oldest member of the Indiana convention, fell ill with cholera – and in spite of extreme discomfort, remained in his seat working until the day before he died.[153]

The delegates expressed intense yearning for the company of their wives, children, and friends. Illinois delegate David Davis told Sarah that he trusted the convention would be finished by early August because "but few members [had] their wives" with them.[154] When Sarah was slow in responding, he was "rendered so unhappy" that he "could not write." Meanwhile, whenever he was not physically in the convention or in committee meetings, his time was "wholly occupied in answering business letters" because his office at home was closed.[155] Hovey wrote several letters to Mary complaining of his loneliness and increasing melancholy, especially when she or their children were ill. Only duty compelled him to remain in Indianapolis.[156] He longed for the "noise and prattle" of his "little ones" and the "smiles and kindness" of his Mary to cheer and comfort him.[157] His colleague Niles was also greatly concerned about his wife's health and told her that if she became ill, she should telegraph him immediately. He could hardly express his anxiety to get home. "When I once get out of this scrape," he assured them, "I shan't be caught in the like again soon. I shall value home more than ever before if I am so [fortunate] as to get home well and to find you all so."[158]

The delegates' wives and children missed them too. Some found the burden of running the family farm or business increasingly hard to bear. Mary Hovey

[151] Oliver P. Davis to Eliza Davis, December 25, 1850 and January 8, 1851, Oliver P. Davis Papers, Indiana State Archives, Indianapolis. Oliver and Eliza named their daughter Alice. She later became a published poet and author.

[152] Indiana 1850, 2: 1458.

[153] See obituary, Indiana 1850, 1: 491. The convention paid for Vanbenthusen's funeral expenses. Kettleborough, *Constitution Making in Indiana*, 2: 645.

[154] David Davis to Sarah Davis, June 19, 1847, David Davis Papers, Chicago History Museum.

[155] David Davis to Sarah Davis, June 25, 1847, David Davis Family Papers, Abraham Lincoln Presidential Library, Springfield, IL.

[156] Alvin Hovey to Mary Ann Hovey, October 18, 1850, Hovey MSS, Lilly Library, Indiana University, Bloomington.

[157] Alvin Hovey to Mary Ann Hovey, December 18, 1850, Hovey MSS, Lilly Library, Indiana University, Bloomington.

[158] John Barron Niles to Mary Niles, November 3, 1850, Niles MSS, Lilly Library, Indiana University, Bloomington. Niles would go on to serve two terms in the Indiana Senate, in 1865

experienced terrible longing for Alvin and often begged him to let her join him in Indianapolis, but he worried about the possible risk to her and Charley's health. There had been both a smallpox and a cholera scare within the past year. He told her to cheer up and gently reminded her of "the happy hours of their courtship" and the day he spilled wine on her dress in the sugar tree grove.[159] William Thomas became concerned about the burden on his family. He told his wife, Polly, that their work was still moving along slowly and he feared would continue to do so "for several long weeks yet." He realized that his absence would mean that "cares and anxieties" must fall on Polly for some time.[160] Polly and her son, Buel, missed him dreadfully, however, and she agreed that the convention was moving along too slowly. "I think so," she told him, "quite [too] slow for me ... if you have to be gone till late in January." His all-too-brief visit home had spoiled her, though, and now she could not sleep without him.[161]

James Loudon thought of his boys "fifty times every one of these hot days." He missed them all terribly and felt that he ought to be with them but recognized that he was "in for this abominable job" and remained determined not to disgrace his family or constituents. But he promised to try to go home on July 11, because that anniversary was far more important to him than the "4th of the month." He told Elizabeth how much he loved and valued her after twenty-four years of marriage. Attempting unsuccessfully to hide his pride, he also told her that a fellow Ohio delegate "affects to think that Clint is a very smart fellow or rather the making of such an one – He told me one day that I ought to be proud of such a son."[162] Indiana delegate John Barron Niles told his children that he was pleased by a recent letter, which contained a handwritten newspaper; it was "just what [he] wanted to see."[163]

Nevertheless, most of the delegates and their wives remained committed to their duty. Mary Niles, more robust than Mary Hovey, admitted that although her husband was "very much needed," she believed that he was doing more good where he was than if he were at home "and if so, *all right*, I am content."[164] A Minnesota miller named Thomas Bolles who served in the 1857

and 1867. For similar views, see also M. M. Noel to John G. Davis, December 9, 1850, John G. Davis Papers, Indiana Historical Society, Indianapolis.

159 Alvin Hovey to Mary Ann Hovey, December 7, 1850, Hovey MSS, Lilly Library, Indiana University, Bloomington.

160 William W. Thomas to Polly Thomas, October 31, 1850, William W. Thomas Papers, Indiana State Library, Indianapolis.

161 Polly Thomas and Buel Thomas to William W. Thomas, December 6, 1850, William W. Thomas Papers, Indiana State Library, Indianapolis. They would have to wait five more weeks; the convention would not finish until February 10, 1851.

162 James Loudon to Elizabeth Loudon, June 27, 1850, DeWitt Clinton Loudon papers, Ohio Historical Society, Columbus. James had married Elizabeth on July 11, 1826.

163 John Barron Niles to William, Henry, and Mary Niles, October 10, 1850, Niles MSS, Lilly Library, Indiana University, Bloomington.

164 Mary Niles to John Barron Niles, January 19, 1851, Lilly Library, Indiana University, Bloomington.

Republican convention confessed to his colleagues that he was "really needing his time at home" but wanted to be proud of the constitution.[165] Polly Thomas wrote a grimly humorous P.S. to her husband, William, telling him that because this was the "last sheet of paper in the house and the envelopes [were] all used up," he would simply "have to come home."[166] In his answer, William reassured Polly that there seemed to be a general determination to bring the business to a close. Several delegates had already left for home, and more would leave in the following week. He felt "extremely anxious to be at home" with her, and if he could reconcile it with his sense of duty, he would leave immediately. They would both have to "await the time as patiently as may be."[167]

Over the coming months the delegates would have to struggle painfully to craft their charters, working through insufferable tedium and long nights, sometimes with men they had come to detest. But many would form fast friendships too. Ohio delegate James Loudon told his wife, after returning to the convention from a flying visit home, that his friends there appeared as glad to see him as though he had been "to California or some other far off place."[168] The work that lay ahead of the delegates would require intense concentration and long hours, but for many it was worth the sacrifice. Loudon, for example, who at fifty-four was one of the oldest delegates in the Ohio convention, had served two terms in the State House and the State Senate twenty years earlier. Although by the time he was finished with his work on the constitution he was determined never to involve himself in politics again, during the Civil War he decided to come out of retirement to serve in the Ohio State Senate.[169] Roughly 30 percent of the delegates went on to prestigious political or judicial careers: some into Congress, some even to the gubernatorial chair in their home states. Many of these men would serve as senior officers in the Civil War. Although some were lost to obscurity, most of them left behind at least an honorable mention in their county histories. In the months ahead, as the delegates struggled to frame their constitutions, they would have to reconcile their deepest beliefs about good government with their responsibilities to their friends, families, and constituencies at home.

[165] T. F. Andrews, *Debates and Proceedings of the Constitutional Convention for the Territory of Minnesota, to Form a State Constitution Preparatory to Its Admission into the Union as a State* (St. Paul, MN: 1858), 156.

[166] Polly Thomas to William W. Thomas, January 3, 1851, William W. Thomas Papers, Indiana State Library, Indianapolis.

[167] William W. Thomas to Polly Thomas and Children, February 1, 1851, William W. Thomas Papers, Indiana State Library, Indianapolis. James Loudon expressed exactly the same sentiment, in James Loudon to Elizabeth Loudon, May 19, 1850, DeWitt Clinton Loudon papers, Ohio Historical Society, Columbus.

[168] James Loudon to Elizabeth Loudon, January 16, 1851, DeWitt Clinton Loudon Papers, Ohio Historical Society, Columbus.

[169] *The History of Brown County, Ohio …* (Chicago, 1883), 359.

2

Constitutions

In 1811 Dennis Pennington (Figure 2.1), a "sturdy, honest, and strenuous" stonemason from Virginia, built a foursquare capitol for his new hometown of Corydon, Indiana Territory. Local farmers harnessed teams of oxen to haul the blue limestone from a nearby quarry and split the stone so that it would break into flat plates; these Pennington saved to dress the two-foot-thick walls. The ground floor consisted of an open hall with a raised dais to accommodate the speaker of the territorial legislature – who happened to be Pennington himself. An affable, brisk, powerfully built man with little formal education but a shrewd grasp of politics, Pennington had already become the heart and soul of Corydon's public affairs.[1] As a speaker of the territorial legislature and a well-known census enumerator, he easily won a seat as delegate to the convention in 1816, in spite of his strong antislavery stance.[2] Hardworking, driven by a stubborn ambition, a sharp politician and negotiator, and a skilled builder, he was still powerful enough in his seventies to challenge a political opponent half his age to a wrestling match (an offer that was declined).[3] Pennington literally built the civic life of Corydon. In erecting his stone capitol, he took calculated risks: It would take the new state legislature a long time to pay him for his work. Still, he must have experienced profound satisfaction when he met his fellow constitutional convention delegates inside his own building during that oppressively hot July in 1816.[4]

1 Matilda Gresham, *Life of Walter Quintin Gresham, 1832–1895* (Chicago: Rand, McNally, 1919), 23–34; John W. Ray, "A Recollection of Dennis Pennington," *Indiana Quarterly Magazine of History* 3, no. 1 (Mar. 1907): 26–30.

2 Logan Esarey, *History of Indiana from Its Exploration to 1922*, ed. John Iglehart (Dayton, OH: Dayton Historical, 1922), 1: 244.

3 Merrill Moores, "Indiana in 1816," *Indiana Magazine of History* 12, no. 3 (Sept. 1916): 271–80.

4 The Indiana 1816 convention was not elected along political party lines. According to James H. Madison, "all but nine" of the forty-three delegates were originally from below the Mason-Dixon line. James H. Madison, *The Indiana Way: A State History* (Bloomington: Indiana University Press, 1986), 51. Pennington and his wife, Elizabeth, had been committed to

FIGURE 2.1. Dennis Pennington (1776–1854) served as a delegate to the 1816 Indiana constitutional convention. He also served as speaker of the Indiana Territory and later in the Indiana State House of Representatives and Senate for many terms.
Source: Unknown photographer. Courtesy of the Indiana State Museum and Historic Sites.

This chapter explores how constitutional convention delegates such as Pennington – men who had invested their wealth and energy in their communities and who were learning how to frame and run their own governments – talked about the abstract principles that would guide their work in the conventions. The delegates used metaphors and allegories to help them manage the physically and intellectually arduous task they confronted in their conventions. These metaphors were not precisely (or not only) rhetorical tools, though, but moral and rational frameworks for their governments. The delegates traveled to their territorial and state capitals well prepared, or so they thought: armed with copies of the U.S. and other state constitutions, memoranda containing mandates from their local political organizations, and petitions bearing hundreds of signatures from their constituents. But these

antislavery principles since they were first married in Kentucky; and in spite of the fact that he was outnumbered by proslavery delegates, he managed to force through a constitutional provision that upheld the Northwest Ordinance's ban on slavery.

delegates soon discovered that the process of constitution building was much harder than simply adapting the federal and state constitutions for their own use and inscribing political agendas in their charters. As they encountered opposition in their committees and on the floor of the convention hall, the delegates realized that they would have to confront their own fundamental beliefs in much greater depth and with a sharper critical eye than they expected. In order to answer their articulate, often hostile political opponents, the delegates would have to base their arguments on an unshakable foundation. Specifically, they had to force the opposition to acknowledge the nonnegotiable political, philosophical, and, for most, Christian truths that underlay their arguments. That was the only way to disarm major disagreements. Their arguments had to harmonize with the important philosophical and religious beliefs that were sacred to them and to their opponents. The process of framing their state constitutions, therefore, required delegates to found their convention speeches in a unified conception of governance that balanced republican constitutionalism, Christian ethics, and plain logic – that is, in a worldview in which justice, goodness, and common sense supported and amplified one another. Most of them believed that this task lay within their reach precisely because they believed that Christianity, reason, and American constitutionalism formed a single harmonious whole that supported the popular will. The reality was much messier, of course.[5] Whether these frameworks can be harmonized is not the main question here, but rather, how the delegates and their diverse communities tried to make sense of the constitution-building project, and how they defined these concepts – concepts that formed the tools with which these people sought to persuade one another.

At the same time, the delegates' great dilemma was that they believed in the sovereignty of the popular will. True, Whigs and Democrats differed on the extent to which the people's wishes ought to be consulted. Yet those political questions were far more fraught, and far more difficult to categorize, than this summary suggests. The traditional pillars of antebellum constitutionalism were meant to support popular sovereignty. At the same time, the delegates also knew that the people they represented were far from perfect. In the months ahead the delegates occasionally deplored their constituents' selfishness, their susceptibility to the wiles of demagogues, and their readiness to fling themselves headlong into risky ventures. Therefore, the delegates had to find a way to balance a harmonious worldview against the idiosyncrasy and unpredictability of an unchained popular will. They also had to set community welfare against raw individual striving. Should constitutions guide and inspire citizens – or should the governing bodies, such as legislatures and courts,

[5] This was true from the founding era. James Q. Whitman explains that revolutionary-era lawyers, lawmakers, constitutional delegates, and political theorists attempted to harmonize conflicting philosophies in "Why Did the Revolutionary Lawyers Confuse Custom and Reason?" *University of Chicago Law Review* 58, no. 4 (Autumn, 1991): 1321–68.

confer authority on the people? If so, how much? And should the constitutions that framed these bodies stand like temples (or churches) to that triad of principles – republicanism, Christian ethics, and logic – or should they remain changeable, flexible, and responsive to contemporary needs? This chapter, and future chapters, will examine how the delegates and their constituents actually defined terms such as "republican" and "democratic." This requires some caution. Although the delegates must have had a grasp of the fundamental meaning of such terms, they rarely defined of any of them explicitly. Perhaps they believed that everyone would have agreed on the same basic sense of these words, or that the meaning was so clear that the words did not require definition. Their attempts to define and redefine these terms reveal that in practice these ideas were expressed in completely new ways.

The delegates had inherited their definition of republican from traditional sources: Those who were originally from the New England and Mid-Atlantic states would have learned the history of the American Revolution through their common school textbooks, and those from the southern states would have read history and political economy with their tutors or in their academies. All of them would have memorized the important documents of American political history. The college-educated would likely have studied the *Federalist Papers*, and the lawyers would certainly have a good grasp of constitutional theory and history, as well as political theory.[6] The outcomes of the debates, however, suggest that the classical ideas about republicanism had to give way to a concatenation of pressures that included a driving popular will and the delegates' personal commitments.[7]

As the delegates strove to resolve the fundamental dilemmas of democratic governance, they employed allegories, metaphors, and logic – rhetorical tools most had learned as schoolboys – to flesh out abstract principles about good government. When the delegates talked about framing their foundational documents, they were literally setting their hands to the task: cutting and pasting printed constitutions, hammering out compromises in committee meetings, and sitting up late in their rented rooms composing speeches. Figures of speech that evoked architecture or history helped them to balance the tangible and abstract facets of their work. And because these metaphors were so influential and evocative, they shaped, illustrated, and, occasionally, also endangered the work of building democratic state constitutions.

Most scholars of nineteenth-century state constitutions have framed their discussion either as a comparison to the U.S. Constitution or else as a criticism of the pragmatic, perhaps even provincial nature of state constitutions, which

[6] For a discussion of delegate education, see Chapter 1. For explanation of lawyers' education, see Chapter 5.

[7] Laura Scalia has studied the commitment to popular sovereignty in state constitutions. She finds a powerful consensus across American state constitutional conventions, even across party allegiances, in *America's Jeffersonian Experiment* (DeKalb: Northern Illinois University Press, 1999).

were often encumbered by detailed provisions that might better have been left to state legislatures. Even so, historians of state constitutions start with the idea that all such charters had to be based on the U.S. Constitution, and that those delegates in the Great Lakes region also had to take the Northwest Ordinance as their pattern. Therefore, any innovations or local adjustments are deemed to fall into two categories: At worst, they are seen as cumbersome reflections of political agendas, and at best, as sensible accommodations that respected popular will and completed the U.S. Constitution. Adherence to traditional American structures of governance (a tripartite government, a bicameral legislature, and the inclusion of a bill of rights), they agreed, was mandated and therefore not subject to experimentation. All intrusions by the popular will can be explained away by dominant party politics: in this case, brash Jacksonian democracy, mitigated by a flurry of Whiggish and radical reform.[8] While this analysis is still valid, the framing of northwestern democracy required more than just formulaic (if reverential) adherence to revolutionary ideology or traditional constitutionalism. Delegates had to work out of the role of popular will – chaotic, irrepressible, energetic – in bringing to life a constitutional system in which history, religion, and science constituted a coherent ethical system of democratic governance. Later on we will see how this tension worked in specific topical discussions: for example, the bitter fights over banks, over black people's citizenship, and over married women's property rights. Here we begin with the theoretical underpinnings, and explore how the delegates used

[8] Donald S. Lutz has explained that state constitutions complete the "unfinished work" of the federal charter, in "The United States Constitution as an Incomplete Text," *Annals of the American Academy of Political Science* 496 (Mar. 1988): 23, 26. See also, Donald S. Lutz, "From Covenant to Constitution in American Political Thought" *Publius* 10, no. 4 (Autumn 1980): 101–2; Willi Paul Adams, *The First American Constitutions: Republican Ideology and the Making of the State Constitutions in the Revolutionary Era*, trans. Rita Kimber and Robert Kimber (Chapel Hill: University of North Carolina Press, 1980); G. Alan Tarr, *Understanding State Constitutions* (Princeton, NJ: Princeton University Press, 1998), 94–135; Peter S. Onuf, "State Politics and Republican Virtue: Religion, Education, and Morality in Early American Federalism," and Morton J. Horwitz, "Republican Origins of Constitutionalism," both in Paul Finkelman and Stephen E. Gottlieb, eds. *Toward a Usable Past: Liberty under State Constitutions* (Athens: University of Georgia Press, 1991), 91–116, 148–53; Christian G. Fritz, *American Sovereigns: The People and America's Constitutional Tradition before the Civil War* (Cambridge: Cambridge University Press, 2008), 246–76; John Dinan, *The American State Constitutional Tradition* (Lawrence: University Press of Kansas, 2006); and Don E. Fehrenbacher, *Sectional Crisis and Southern Constitutionalism* (Baton Rouge: Louisiana State University Press, 1980). For the relationship of the Northwest Ordinance to the U.S. Constitution and to state constitutions in the Northwest, see also Peter S. Onuf, "From Constitution to Higher Law: The Reinterpretation of the Northwest Ordinance," *Ohio History* 94 (1985): 5–33; James E. Davis, "'New Aspects of Men and New Forms of Society': The Old Northwest, 1790–1820," *Journal of the Illinois State Historical Society* 69, no. 3 (Aug. 1976): 164–72; James H. Madison, "The Northwest Ordinance and Constitutional Development in Indiana," *The International Journal of Social Education* 2, no. 1 (Spring 1987): 16–29.

(and often misunderstood) these concepts, in building the northwestern notion of republicanism.

The convention delegates were not just framing governments and delineating rights: They were shaping a brand new iteration of the American political ideal, a government that would be at once more rational, more ethical, and more democratic than the charters of the states they had left when they migrated to the West. In short, they sought to craft institutions that were more faithful to the underlying principles they had learned in school and at church. As they packed their shirts and left last-minute instructions to their wives or their employees, these citizens had to make sense of the confusing mixture of abstract ideas and practical questions as they shaped a republican constitution that would resolve pressing economic and political problems.

Perhaps it was for this reason that northwestern convention delegates frequently referred to their constitutions as buildings, homes, temples, or palladia of liberty.[9] The metaphors they used to talk about the kind of state they wanted for themselves and for their children functioned as oratorical tools to illustrate or to persuade. For this reason, "building" was the era's single most commonly used metaphor for the constitutions being framed. Similarly, personages, incidents, and slogans from the revolutionary era became models for the project of a western democratic republic that reaffirmed the founding generation's principles. Those images and stories, however, were more than beautiful metaphors. They also wielded a power and force of their own. They reminded listeners of their revolutionary heritage, of their shared Christian faith, of irreducible political axioms that functioned as sacred truths, and of the simple logic of a democracy built by near-equals.

Nineteenth-century orators used metaphors to clothe abstract ideas and make them accessible to ordinary listeners.[10] Figures of speech served to democratize, motivate, and ennoble political ideas. As schoolboys – whether in Vermont or

[9] "Palladium," which meant "safeguard," appeared frequently in political speeches throughout the nation, particularly in the context of a need to protect civil liberties. In political oratory, the phrase "palladium of liberties" was based on the classical allusion to Pallas Athene, whose image was supposed to safeguard or protect the city of Athens. See, for example, H. Fowler, *Report of the Debates and Proceedings of the Convention for the Revision of the Constitution of the State of Indiana* (Indianapolis, IN: 1850), 1: 155 (hereafter, Indiana 1850); R. Sutton, *Report of the Debates and Proceedings of the Convention for the Revision of the Constitution of the State of Kentucky, 1849* (Frankfort, KY: 1849), 184; *Journal of the Proceedings of the Convention of the State of Louisiana ...* (New Orleans, LA: 1845), 100; *Journal of the Constitutional Convention of the Commonwealth of Massachusetts ...* (Boston: 1853), 774; John Agg, *Proceedings and Debates of the Convention of the Commonwealth of Pennsylvania to Propose Amendments to the Constitution ...* (Harrisburg, PA: 1837), 1: 510; J. V. Smith, *Report of the Debates and Proceedings of the Convention for the Revision of the Constitution of the State of Ohio, 1850–1851* (Columbus, OH: 1850), 1: 75 (hereafter Ohio 1850).

[10] See, for example, T. N. Talfourd, "Pulpit Oratory," *London Magazine*, February 1821, quoted in Samuel Austin Allibone, *A Critical Dictionary of English Literature and British and American Authors ...* (Philadelphia, 1899), 1: 766. For the eighteenth-century context, see Carroll C. Arnold, "Early Constitutional Rhetoric in Pennsylvania," in *American Rhetoric: Context*

Virginia – the delegates had memorized passages from the *Columbian Orator* and learned how to use metaphors to strengthen their arguments. The *Orator* extolled the "strength and vivacity" of the figures that adorned classical oratory: rhetorical forms such as allegory and metaphor, which, according to still another popular textbook, "enrich[ed] language, and render[ed] it more copious."[11] Later, as young men, the delegates heard or read political speeches and sermons freely adorned by metaphors.[12] And when the time came to write persuasive convention speeches – perhaps the first public addresses they had ever given in their lives – they relied on familiar figures and concepts to clarify theoretical ideas.

Although these men would soon become involved in raucous fights over such thorny topics as banks and votes for black men, they also had a great deal in common. Most were literate, God-fearing Protestants, deeply interested in politics. They agreed on the importance of fostering advancement in science and technology, particularly in communication, transportation, and agriculture. As most literate Americans did, they read widely in newspapers, travel journals, political almanacs, historical works, Shakespeare, the Bible, and, for those who had been educated in academies and colleges, classical texts by Euclid for mathematics, Archimedes for science, and Cicero for law and rhetoric.[13] At the same time, sectional disagreements caused strife: Many still clung to

and Criticism, ed. Thomas W. Benson (Carbondale: Southern Illinois University Press, 1989), 131–200. For metaphors, see James Darsey, *The Prophetic Tradition and Radical Rhetoric in America* (New York: New York University Press, 1997), 35–60; and Kenneth Cmiel, *Democratic Eloquence: The Fight over Popular Speech in Nineteenth-Century America* (New York: William Morrow, 1990), 55–93.

[11] Caleb Bingham, *The Columbian Orator: Containing a Variety of Original and Selected Pieces Together with Rules Calculated to Improve Youth and Others in the Ornamentation and Useful Art of Eloquence* (Boston: 1817), 11. Bingham also encouraged young orators to imitate these metaphors with facial expressions. For example, when speaking of fire, or burning, the eyes were to sparkle. Bingham, *Columbian Orator*, 22. See also, Nan Johnson, *Nineteenth Century Rhetoric in North America* (Carbondale: Southern Illinois University Press, 1991), 251–55. For a discussion of imagery in the rhetoric of early Ohio, see Andrew R. L. Cayton, "Language Gives Way to Feelings": Rhetoric, Republicanism, and Religion in Jeffersonain Ohio," in Jeffrey P. Brown and Andrew R. L. Cayton, eds., *The Pursuit of Public Power: Political Culture in Ohio, 1787–1861* (Kent, Ohio, and London: Kent State University Press, 1994), 31–48.

[12] Many mid-nineteenth-century textbooks on homiletics refer to scriptural parables, and particularly to the frequent use of metaphors in the New Testament. See, for example, Samuel Drew's 1828 commentary on George Whitefield's sermons, in *Sermons on Important Subjects by the Rev. George Whitefield ...* (London, 1828), 546–47. Whitefield cautioned against dismissing biblical exhortations as "mere metaphors" lest the hearers "interpret themselves out of their salvation." See also, "Essay on the Second Death," *Evangelical Magazine and Gospel Advocate* 1, no. 35 (August 28, 1830): 273. For modern discussions of rhetoric, especially metaphors and figures of speech, in nineteenth-century oratory, see Arnold, "Early Constitutional Rhetoric in Pennsylvania," in *American Rhetoric: Context and Criticism*; Cmiel, *Democratic Eloquence: The Fight over Popular Speech in Nineteenth Century America*, 23–54; Darsey, *The Prophetic Tradition and Radical Rhetoric in America*, 1–14.

[13] See Carl J. Richard, *The Golden Age of the Classics in America: Greece, Rome, and the Antebellum United States* (Cambridge, MA: Harvard University Press, 2009). For the popularity of the

the convictions they had carried from their birthplaces. New Englanders had settled in the northern-tier counties of their territories and arrived with strong antislavery and, often, probank beliefs. Upland southerners were more tolerant of slavery; until the mid-1820s, some even strove to install human bondage in their new northwestern states.[14] They rigorously opposed any suggestion of political equality for black men. Social reformers, both those who were from the East and those whose roots lay across the Atlantic, introduced radical ideas about property ownership, racial equality, and even marriage to the convention debates. Therefore those four strands (political, historical, religious, and scientific) shaped the delegates' thinking about their constitution-making project, a particularly challenging undertaking in a diverse frontier society that lacked political or law enforcement infrastructure and was wracked by economic instability. Still, the Northwest was an active, go-ahead, market-oriented society that promoted a liberal insistence on individual rights and limitless opportunities for white men. At the same time, however, delegates always had to keep in mind that they were responsible for shoring up community welfare, and that this would mean finding a way to restrain their constituencies' selfish impulses.

Was it the work of a constitution to build a palladium to restrain those impulses? Most northwesterners would have disliked that notion. Human impulses fluctuated with the changing times, and a constitution should not be built to last forever. As one delegate told his wife, "What we are doing, of course, is not permanent but will have to be rewritten every few years to meet changing conditions. I will say that the constitution should be rewritten every 40 years."[15] A Milwaukee newspaper explained that their state constitutions, like their homes, ought to be "framed [for] the present condition of society and the necessities of our citizens."[16] For Wisconsin delegate Alexander Randall, the constitution was not the finished structure, but the foundation for the state that would be built on its base. Once the constitution was in place it served as a safeguard, a support, and a future source of strength for the people, who in their wisdom and through their hard work would build the state. Randall explained that as the "great embodiment of the will of the people" and the source of legislative, judicial, and executive power, the constitution formed the foundation of laws and state institutions. "We fall back upon it when we seek our rights in courts of justice – we lean upon it as the bulwark of our political

works of William Shakespeare, see *Lawrence Levine, Highbrow/Lowbrow: The Emergence of Cultural Hierarchy in America* (Cambridge, MA: Harvard University Press, 1990). S. Alexander Rippa, *Education in a Free Society: An American History*, 8th ed. (New York: Longman, 1997), 65–67. Arthur M. Cohen, *The Shaping of American Higher Education: Emergence and Growth of the Contemporary System* (San Francisco: Jossey-Bass, 1998), 73–83.

14 For example, in 1824, proslavery citizens in Illinois attempted to revise the state constitution to permit slavery. See James Simeone, *Democracy and Slavery in Frontier Illinois: the Bottomland Republic* (De Kalb: Northern Illinois University Press, 2000).

15 Unsigned letter, January 1851, George Wayman Papers, Indiana State Library, Indianapolis.

16 *Milwaukee Courier*, October 28, 1846.

and civil strength – all our hopes are centered in it, and must be, so long as it stands the great general law of our young vigorous state."[17] Indiana delegate John Barron Niles declared that the last thing he wanted to do – wildly mixing his metaphors – was to "destroy our civil fabric or mar its fair proportions." Echoing the popular antebellum "log cabin" political slogans, he declared that it would be wrong to "tear down the humble dwelling in which I find shelter and which is still my home until a better had been provided," simply to construct a more comfortable edifice.[18]

Other northwesterners believed that the government had to fit its citizens properly, and so constitutions should grow organically – perhaps like a new skin, or like a tailored garment that was cut and then altered to suit the changing circumstances of the wearer or the future needs of his children.[19] In a sermon he preached in Illinois in 1852, the Reverend Henry G. Weston explained that no one ever had wisdom enough intentionally to create an entirely new and permanent form of government. Every successful government grew "naturally from the people embraced in it, and adapt[ed] itself to them." No government could be "first formed with all its parts, and then put into operation, ... as you [would] build a house and then put a family in it." A good government, rather, was "like the surface covering of a man's body, formed upon that body, growing out of it, and with it, and forming a part of it, and not first made and then the body put into it." These charters had to be flexible, organic, responsive to current needs, and attuned to popular sovereignty: in other words, modern. Such a constitution would focus on, and represent, local and changing conditions; in this metaphor, Weston appeared to suggest that a constitution should be a living creature. Criticizing the revolutionary French statesmen who had "formed constitutions for every conceivable state of society," for example, he declared that not one of those charters could ever "have an hour of healthy life."[20] A writer for the *Western Monthly Magazine* even likened these foundational principles to conception and birth. He believed that the principles

[17] Milo M. Quaife, ed., *The Convention of 1846*, vol. 27 of *Publications of the State Historical Society of Wisconsin* (Madison: State Historical Society of Wisconsin, 1919), 165 (hereafter Wisconsin 1846). See also, Michael J. McManus, *Political Abolitionism in Wisconsin, 1840–1861* (Kent, OH: Kent State University Press, 1998), 28. Randall entered the convention as a diehard Democrat. He made strong anti–black suffrage speeches in the convention but became one of the few delegates who voted for black suffrage. Randall eventually joined the Republican Party.

[18] Indiana 1850, 1: 182. I found no references to buildings, or building parts, in the New York, Pennsylvania, Massachusetts, or Kentucky state constitutional convention journals. However, delegates at the Virginia 1830–31 convention used this metaphor quite often.

[19] *Wisconsin Argus* (Madison), November 11, 1845.

[20] Henry G. Weston, *Our Obligations to God: A Discourse, Delivered in Peoria, Illinois, on Thanksgiving Day, November 25, 1852* (Peoria, IL: 1852), 12. Weston was born in Lynn, Massachusetts, and was educated at Brown University. It is difficult to reconstruct his political leanings, but his father published the mildly antislavery Baptist journal the *Christian Watchman* in Boston from 1831 to 1842.

of the Declaration of Independence had "led to our existence," and the U.S. Constitution "provided the ligaments that tied us together."[21] The constitution had to be built to a human scale and serve a human function. Democracy had to be built on the ground, carried out in real life, and remain adaptive to individual needs.

The task at hand, however, was constrained by restrictions and parameters, some of which the delegates embraced enthusiastically (the U.S. Constitution's guarantee of republican government for all states) and others that chafed them (for those who wanted to introduce slavery into their state, the Northwest Ordinance).[22] No new state could have entered the Union from the northwestern territories with a constitution that conflicted with congressional, presidential, or national goals. The northwestern states fulfilled an important political function for free-state factions in Congress, who wanted to create as many states as possible from the area governed by the Northwest Ordinance in order to balance new slave states entering the Union from the southwestern territories. Disputes over new state boundaries endangered political alliances in Congress, so if the northwestern territories wanted to join the Union, they would have to accept congressional restrictions. For example, Iowa had to wait for two more years for statehood because of a dispute over the boundary with Missouri. Their 1844 constitution failed because Iowans refused to agree to a constricted state boundary, mandated by the House of Representatives.[23] When Michigan requested statehood, voters had to accept an unpleasant compromise on their southern boundary because President Andrew Jackson refused to alienate the Ohio congressional delegation and so awarded disputed water rights to Ohio.[24]

These men would now have to sort out the differences between their current political commitments and the ideals they were striving to make real. Political differences and geographic rivalries ensured lively debates. Those delegates who had been put forward by their political party went to the capital city with powerful agendas. Democrats, particularly the "hard money" variety, promised

[21] "Duties of American Citizens," *Western Monthly Magazine*, April 1837.

[22] U.S. Const. art. 4, sec. 4; Northwest Ordinance, art. 4.

[23] Eric Biber has called this process the "price of admission," meaning that territories had to negotiate their entry into the Union by conforming to fundamental principles, negotiating the release of valuable lands or other advantages, or, perhaps most important, contributing to the majority party's national program. Eric Biber, "The Price of Admission, Causes, Effects, and Patterns of Conditions Imposed on States Entering the Union," *American Journal of Legal History* 46, no. 2 (April 2004): 119–208. The first three states to be carved out of the Northwest Territory (Ohio 1802, Indiana 1816, and Illinois 1818) sparked political debates in Congress, specifically over the addition of new free states, which had to be balanced by new slave states. That precedent had been set by the addition of Mississippi (1817), which balanced Indiana, and Alabama (1819), which entered shortly after Illinois. Missouri and Maine joined in 1821 and 1820, respectively. Arkansas would be partnered with Michigan (1836 and 1837), and Florida with Iowa (1845 and 1846).

[24] Peter S. Onuf, "The Toledo War and American Federalism." *Northwest Ohio Quarterly* 59 (1987): 135–52.

to wage war on banks. Whigs had vowed to battle against such newfangled democratic innovations as an elected, rather than appointed judiciary. Those with a radical tinge to their politics would fight for the political rights of black men. The delegates believed that principles and politics would be harmonious, or at least easy to reconcile. Certainly the partisan newspapers linked the two explicitly. Locofoco (hard-line Democrat) newspapers proclaimed that a truly democratic constitution, for example, would get rid of state-controlled banks because they were dangerous, aristocratic, antirepublican institutions. For Whigs, however, the problem of identifying principles with political goals was trickier, at least in part because their party name was not as readily synonymous with their political platforms. Moreover, because Whigs were in a minority in conventions before 1850, Whig-controlled newspapers always complained about political influences on constitutions.[25] In Ohio, for example, rival newspapers battled over whether the constitution should be politically motivated. The *Cincinnati Daily Dispatch* proclaimed that party qualifications were of far less importance than "soundness of head and honesty of heart."[26] The Whig *Scioto Gazette* did not want a "Party Constitution!" The editor proclaimed that it was wrong to drag in party affiliation. Paradoxically, the paper also declaimed that a good constitution should be "a living argument against all the oppressions of the world," which it could not resist defining as "the wickedness of slavery." In the Ohio convention, Whig Samson Mason declared, "All [the people] want is a good constitution, a republican constitution, a democratic Constitution, a whig constitution."[27]

In American political philosophy, the phrase "frequent recurrence to first principles" enjoyed a long history in older state constitutions' bills of rights, such as those of Virginia and Massachusetts, as a way of exhorting citizens to remain alert to the potential corruptions of governing power.[28] The authors of the *Federalist Papers* based their defense of the Constitution, especially in its separation of the branches of government, on Montesquieu's *Spirit of the Laws*.[29] Although Montesquieu specifically referred to the division of powers as the most important first principle, Alexander Hamilton and James Madison

[25] The Republican Party capitalized on the identification with republican principles, especially in the later conventions (Iowa and Minnesota in 1857). This was not lost on Democrats, especially in the sharply politicized twin conventions in Minnesota, where Democrats barely even mentioned republican principles (only twice in their convention) and even then, only in connection with European immigrants' desire for a republican government.

[26] *Scioto Gazette* (Chillicothe, OH), March 6, 1850 and May 6, 1850; *Cincinnati Daily Dispatch*, April 1, 1850.

[27] Ohio 1850, 1: 648.

[28] Edward J. Erler, *The American Polity: Essays on the Theory and Practice of Constitutional Government* (New York: Taylor & Francis, 1991), 2.

[29] Charles de Secondat, Baron de Montesquieu, *The Spirit of the Laws*, trans. and ed. Anne M. Cohler, Basia Carolyn Miller, and Harold Samuel Stone (New York: Cambridge University Press, 1989), xxv, xxvii; Mark H. Waddicor, *Montesquieu and the Philosophy of Natural of Law* (The Hague: Martinus Nijhoff, 1970).

expanded the notion to include all representative structures.[30] Their version survived in eighteenth-century state constitutions and subsequently entered into the American political canon as a general rule to preserve the people's liberties by reverting to foundational tenets. State charters placed the responsibility for keeping this process active squarely on the shoulders of the citizens. Otherwise, powerful, dangerous entities could develop and grow to independent strength. For Democrats, those included banks and corporations, and for Whigs, democratic delusions and temporary fads.[31]

From the 1820s through the 1850s – the great age of American state constitutional revision – delegates believed it was their duty to imitate, and perhaps even perfect, what their founding fathers had created. They were so deeply familiar with the story of the origin of their republic that they had only to remind one another of a name, a battle, a political slogan, or a place in the revolutionary era in order to rally everyone to elemental truths.[32] Every history schoolbook recounted the story of the Philadelphia convention; most also contained the founding documents, including the U.S. Constitution, the Bill of Rights, the Declaration of Independence, and George Washington's Farewell Address. The delegates referred to these documents, and more specifically, to the underlying ideologies that had produced them, as *First Principles*. For those who launched propositions, *First Principles* remained the best way to smooth over agitation, and for those who opposed them, to draw the fractious back to consensus. The phrase rarely referred to abstract theories – indeed, many delegates scoffed at discussions that veered too far from the concrete or the practical. Democrats, in particular, had little use for high-flown sentiments, even in their most altisonant declarations of love of democracy or liberty. More to the point, therefore, the phrase was nearly always paired with a word, name, incident, or slogan referring to the period of the American Revolution. All manner of historic incidents, personages, battles, debates, words, speeches, and even revolutionary-era slogans could be pressed into service as metaphorical shorthand for republican government. One had only to mention "taxation without representation" in order to caution one's opponents not to exclude voters.[33]

30 Alexander Hamilton, *Federalist* 31, quoted in Quentin P. Taylor, ed., *The Essential Federalist: A New Reading of the Federalist Papers* (Madison, WI: Madison House, 1998), 28. See also, Thomas S. Engeman, Edward J. Erler, and Thomas B. Hofeller, eds., *The Federalist Concordance* (Chicago: University of Chicago Press, 1988).

31 The Illinois 1818 and 1848 and the Wisconsin 1848 constitutions all contained provisions that explicitly exhorted citizens to revert to first principles. Illinois Const. of 1818, art. VIII, sec. 18; Illinois Const. of 1848, art. XIII, sec. 19; Wisconsin Const. of 1848, art. I, sec. 22.

32 Hugh Morrison discusses the application of neoclassical architecture to many other activities in *Early American Architecture, from the First Colonial Settlements to the National Period* (New York: Oxford University Press, 1952), 572. See the last chapter, "Toward a National Style."

33 This worked for both conservative Democrats and antislavery Whigs and Republicans. Democrats used the phrase to fight against taxes on bonds, and Whigs and Republicans to fight for the rights of free black people.

Similarly, in the 1850 Indiana convention, a reference to "the illustrious Washington" encapsulated the principle of limiting political office terms.[34] All of these elements together created a constitutional landscape. The references to first principles were not mere rhetorical flourishes. The terrain of revolutionary first principles included ideas, people, and places and reminded the delegates strongly of the physical state they were trying to create: a place that included contradictory and sometimes frightening elements, including cities and wildernesses, legitimate citizens and undesirable people, virtues and faults, political friends and enemies, words and deeds.

The philosophical concept of *First Principles* was originally derived from Aristotle, who defined the phrase "first principles" (*archai*) as origins, causes, or fundamental elements and propositions.[35] *Archai* could not be reduced to other elements and had to be understood in order to master the whole body of knowledge. Such facts or axioms were foundational; more to the point, they were self-evidently rational, because they could be proven by concrete evidence. First principles, in learning, were those foundational facts and skills that would provide the students with a basis upon which to build advanced knowledge of the subject. In mathematics, for example, first principles were axiomatic, commonsense propositions.[36] Therefore, the titles of most early nineteenth-century school texts on scientific or mathematical subjects began with the phrase "first principles in," for example, *First Principles of Natural Philosophy*, *Chemistry*, or *Geography*. Similarly, political principles, or problems of governance, could also be derived from fundamental logical propositions.[37]

[34] Indiana 1850, 1: 334.

[35] Terence Irwin, *Aristotle's First Principles* (New York: Oxford University Press, 1988), 3. Aristotle defined *archai* as first principles, which must be grasped by an inborn faculty (*nous*) as the "starting point of knowledge." Johannes Morsink describes this as "processes of perception and memory, which together yield the constituents of experience, experience being a series of memories of perceptions of the same kind of object," in "The Mandate of Topics 1, 2" *Apeiron: A Journal for Ancient Philosophy and Science* 16, no. 2 (Dec. 1982): 102–28.

[36] The historian John Mikhail has discussed the Scottish Common Sense origins of American law, in his "Scottish Common Sense and Nineteenth-Century, American Law: A Critical Appraisal," *Law & History Review* 26, no. 1 (Spring 2008): 167–75. See also, Mark Noll, *America's God: From Jonathan Edwards to Abraham Lincoln* (New York: Oxford University Press, 2002), 6. See also Daniel Walker Howe, *Making the American Self: Jonathan Edwards to Abraham Lincoln* (New York: Oxford University Press, 2009) 57–63.

[37] Aristotle's principles were mentioned in Indiana 1850, 2: 1871, for example, In a speech by Mr. March opposing the grand jury system, though he agreed with principles, argued that Aristotle distorted the facts to support it. He wanted a "plain common sense system" to replace the "cobwebs." See also, Thomas Paine, *Dissertation on First Principles of Government* (London, 1795). Textbooks published during this period include James Renwick, *First Principles of Natural Philosophy, Being a Familiar Introduction to the Study of that Science …* (New York: 1842); Benjamin Silliman, *First Principles of Chemistry for the use of Colleges and Schools* (Philadelphia: 1850); and George Clinton Whitlock, *Elements of Mathematics, or, First Principles of Arithmetic, Algebra, Geometry, Trigonometry, and the Differential and Integral Calculus* (New York: 1838).

In 1776 John Adams had expanded the idea of *First Principles* to include commonsense axioms, derived from the people themselves, who knew best how to safeguard their well-being. In his *Thoughts on Government*, Adams insisted that American governments incorporate "popular Principles and Maxims" in order to "secure the welfare of the people."[38] Alexander Hamilton had explained that this new American political philosophy led to scientific approaches to constitution making.[39] In 1788 Hamilton used this precept in the thirty-first *Federalist*, explaining that governments needed revenue in order to function. In the Ohio 1850 convention, Democrat D. P. Leadbetter took both Adams and Hamilton at their word in a speech about money invested in taxing bonds. Declaring that the government had the right to tax profits, and that exempting bonds was an unfair and unequal tax on the "laboring community," Leadbetter pointedly adverted to the "no taxation without representation" revolutionary slogan. "We have been gravely reminded," he told his colleagues, "that we should frequently recur to ... those great leading ... elementary principles upon which the broad foundations of the government were laid, and upon which it must ever remain, if you would give it strength or durability." If anything were to threaten "this great and splendid fabric," then nothing could save it from "tottering to its fall but a speedy return, extending justice and equality to all, as it was originally designed."[40]

For antebellum Americans, the progression from commonsense maxims to scientific principles, and, through those, to good government developed along a natural, logical path. In education and philosophy, first principles were derived from natural laws, originating in, and proven through, a detached scientific reliance on information gained through the senses. For this reason, nature personified (through God's divine gift, creation) was still the best authority on truth. Knowledge of principles applied to reason would deduce the moral laws governing ethical, political, economic, and constitutional systems.[41] According to an article in the *Democratic Review*, nature was able to "maintain everything she had created." It followed rationally that it was only under complete civil liberty and recognition of individual independence that natural sciences could be applied to, and in turn would illuminate, the best possible government on earth: a government that "left its people free to progress."[42] In a speech on married women's property rights, for example, Indiana 1850 convention delegate Thomas W. Gibson referred to mathematical axioms, such as a straight line between two points, as the best way to assess the validity of "axioms in political and moral science." To his mind, granting married women control over

38 John Adams quoted in Fritz, *American Sovereigns*, 31.

39 Taylor, ed., *Essential Federalist*, 28.

40 Ohio 1850, 2: 738–39.

41 There were several references to Cicero in convention speeches throughout the nation, especially in the Massachusetts and New York conventions, but references to other classical authors were rare.

42 "The Reciprocal Influence of the Physical Sciences and of Free Political Institutions," *United States Magazine and Democratic Review* 18, no. 91 (Jan. 1846): 3–17.

their own property was as sensible as solving a mathematical sum, because it was both rational and just.[43] As a rhetorical tactic, *First Principles* encountered few enemies. The delegates found it relatively easy to establish their logic and force.[44] At the same time, because so many believed that the American founding had been divinely ordained, the constitutional ethos forced the delegates to engage in a serious discussion of integrity, morality, and Christian ethics. *First Principles*, functioning as revolutionary symbols and metaphors, did not exist in a secular constitutional vacuum. They had to interact and correspond with deeply held religious beliefs. The providential democratic republic, therefore, lived in harmony with revealed truth.[45]

For antebellum northwesterners, *First Principles* arose out of both history and faith. Before the delegates ever began their constitution-making task, the Northwest Ordinance had ordained that because "religion, morality, and knowledge" were necessary to "good government and the happiness of mankind" they would "forever be encouraged" in the northwestern territories. Shortly after Indiana achieved statehood, one local newspaper went so far as to propose a nation "governed by no other laws than those in [the] blessed book." The Bible was "so complete a system, that nothing can be added to it, or taken from it."[46] State constitutions, especially those crafted during the decades when evangelical Protestant revivals and itinerant preachers influenced northwestern culture, enshrined the ordinance's moral imperative by inserting the phrase "and to countenance and encourage the principles of humanity, honesty, industry and morality" in their preambles.[47]

43 Indiana 1850, 1: 479. See, for example, Susan K. Carpenter, "'Conspicuously Enlightened Policy': Criminal Justice in Indiana," in *History of Indiana Law*. ed. David J. Bodenhamer and Randall T. Shepard (Athens: Ohio University Press, 2006), 125.

44 The 1818 Illinois constitution contained the phrase "That the general, great, and essential principles of liberty and free government may be recognized and unalterably established, we declare (rights)." Illinois Const. of 1818, art. VIII.

45 Democrats and Whigs defined morality differently. While this book does not argue that Democrats and Whigs arrived at a consensus on the idea of morality or ethics, in general they did agree that good governments based their foundational charters on both moral and rational precepts. Although it has been impossible to determine the religious commitments of most of the delegates, the frequent scriptural quotations and references to religious teachings imply that delegates at least considered Christian teachings to be an unanswerable argument. Daniel Walker Howe has explained, for example, that "Whig rhetoric emphasized 'morality' and 'duty' rather than 'rights.'" See *Political Culture of the American Whigs* (Chicago: University of Chicago Press, 1984), 21, 34. By contrast, Jean Harvey Baker focused on education as a principal source of moral formation, but she also explains that Democrats feared political power over individual rights as the prime source of evil and corruption. *Affairs of Party: The Political Culture of Northern Democrats in the Mid-Nineteenth Century* (New York: Fordham University Press, 1998), 27–33, 116.

46 W. H Farner, J. A. Williamson, J. C. Savery, Polk County Constitutional Committee, untitled broadside, July 22, 1857, Iowa Constitution vertical file, State Historical Society of Iowa, Iowa City; *Indiana Intelligencer* (Charlestown), [n.d.]1821.

47 Indiana Const. of 1816, art. IX, sec. 1.

A republican government based on Christian faith could be either redemptive or aspirational – though probably not both. That is, such a government could either redeem citizens from monarchial oppressions (such as "aristocratic" corporations with banking powers) or, on the other hand, inspire legislators to reach for progressive, enlightened, liberal reforms (such as temperance or voting rights for black men). Political allegiances often determined how the delegates would interpret the role of Christianity in influencing their constitutions. Democrats believed that government should be purified of aristocratic or outdated elements and fought bitterly against the idea that their constitution should function as an instrument for morality – for example, in prohibiting the sale of alcohol. Whigs, on the other hand, believed that a moral government ought to guide, enlighten, and sometimes even lead the people in reform (for example, in removing racially discriminatory provisions). Both viewpoints, however, centered on the idea of morality as an essential component of good government. Democratic physician William F. Sherrod, speaking in the Indiana 1850 convention, used scriptural language to rebuke the state assembly. "If there ever was a State under the canopy of Heaven cursed by too much legislation it is the State of Indiana."[48] Reducing the number of men in the House, he declared, would not only reduce the size and cost of government; it would also draw out the "best character" of the men elected to office, because the people would select only the most virtuous men among them.[49]

On the other hand, Ohio Whig delegate Edward Archbold attempted (unsuccessfully) to insert an amendment exhorting citizens to recur frequently to first principles, because, he believed – pessimistic, as most Whigs – that the fallibility of human beings made such an admonition necessary. Quoting James Madison, Archbold observed that because men were not angels, they needed government. Therefore, a good constitution would "provide for the moral polity of our government by returning it to its original functions." Indeed, it would be "morally sublime in this endeavor to restore government to its original functions." In his speech, Archbold worried about the Democratic Party's political spoils system, which he likened to a wild, dangerously burgeoning landscape. Party spirit had risen to a "fearful height" and had caused a "broad stream of corruption to flow through the length and breadth of the land." It was time, therefore, to return to the "pure and simple standard of seventy six, and to take away these enormous encouragements to corruption."[50] For Ohio Whig Simeon Nash, good government served as an instrument for redemption. Good

[48] The phrase "under the canopy of heaven" occurs in both the Old and the New Testament and was frequently heard in antebellum sermons. See, for example, "He spread a cloud for a covering," Ps. 105: 39 (King James Bible); "Moses stood bareheaded in the hail under the canopy of heaven," Exodus 9: 33, or Acts 21:3–6, Paul praying "under the canopy of heaven."

[49] Indiana 1850, 1: 268.

[50] Ohio 1850, 2: 333. See also, David M. Gold, *Democracy in Session: A History of the Ohio General Assembly* (Athens: Ohio University Press, 2009), 56–57. Edward Archbold later became a Republican. Joseph P. Smith, ed., *History of the Republican Party in Ohio* (Chicago, 1898), 1: 191.

government was meant to serve higher ends. Indeed, the best governments served the "great interests of humanity," even before the masses were ready for them, and so should bring about the "intellectual and moral improvement of a people." Nash believed that any government that refused to "regard the elevation of the individual and the masses above all other duties" was doomed to failure.[51] Such governments were purely pragmatic and so would eventually succumb to the selfish desires of corrupt political ends.

Was a constitution based on Christian justice, and free of flaws, within reach? Those delegates whose religious convictions arose from a faith in millennial perfectionism were sure that it was. At the same time, most also believed in a strict separation of church and state. Moreover, there were several free thinkers among the northwestern delegates, such as Indiana's Oliver Davis, as well as utopianists such as Robert Dale Owen. As a result, even though Protestants probably constituted a significant majority in the conventions, the delegates struggled to achieve consensus about the best way to incorporate Christian justice or morality in their constitutions. For some, their faith in God could be forward-thinking and reformist. For example, Iowa's radical Whig Horace Clark based his arguments against race discrimination on the declaration that "Nature's God" forbade it.[52] On the other hand, if based on an Old Testament retributive or exigent interpretation, Christianity did not require political or social equality; nor did it interfere in established hierarchies or traditional family arrangements. Conservative Indiana delegate the Reverend Oliver P. Badger excoriated his colleague Robert Dale Owen, whose marriage contract had been written on socialist principles. "Sir, tell it not in Indiana," Badger thundered; "publish it not in the streets of this beautiful city, that the learned and the elite ones of the land are the votaries of a system which is rife with mischief to the best and holiest interests of society," a system (socialism) that he believed would conflict with the "teachings of the laws of nature and of nature's God."[53]

That phrase – "laws of Nature and of Nature's God" – appeared in many convention speeches by members of both parties, who took it directly from the Declaration of Independence, though evidently they did not explicitly derive that phrase from natural law principles. College-educated delegates may have studied classical natural law, but there is no evidence that any of them ever quoted Aristotle or Cicero in that context, and it is highly unlikely that any of them ever read Aquinas. They were certainly familiar with the writings

[51] Ohio 1850, 2: 333–35. Simeon Nash was originally from Massachusetts. He was a lawyer, had served in the Ohio Senate, and later became a Judge. Sylvester Nash, *The Nash Family; or Records of the Descendants of Thomas Nash ...* (Hartford, CT: 1853), 277–79.

[52] W. Blair Lord, *The Debates of the Constitutional Convention; of the State of Iowa, Assembled at Iowa City, Monday, January 19, 1857* (Davenport, IA: 1857), 2: 715 (hereafter Iowa 1857).

[53] Indiana 1850, 2: 1159–60. This reference is to 2 Sam. 1: 20 (KJB), "Tell it not in Gath," which translates as an exhortation to refrain from spreading scandalous gossip. The Reverend Oliver P. Badger was a pastor in the Christian Church, Putnam County, east-central Indiana. Jesse W. Weik, *Weik's History of Putnam County Indiana* (Indianapolis, IN: B. F. Bowen & Co., 1910), 755–56.

of John Locke, and some may have read European natural law philosophers such as Vattel, Grotius, and Burlamaqui, but there are no references to any of those works in the northwestern conventions. Meanwhile, their constituents cobbled together a rough-and-ready natural law theory from foundational revolutionary-era documents, but they allied these ideas with Christianity and common law, and not with classical or European sources. Even so, the specific phrase "laws of Nature and of Nature's God" enjoyed a wide currency in political speeches and sermons throughout the early national era. In their debates over constitutional rights, antebellum Americans casually linked conceptions of natural law, natural rights, and the laws of "nature's God," laws that demanded that the individual citizen contribute to the good of the community. Only those delegates who had the benefit of a college education would have understood the distinctions in meaning; for most, the phrase provided a convenient bridge from nature, through religion, to science, and from all those to correct ideas about government.

Both Democrats and Whigs used the whole phrase "laws of Nature and of Nature's God" in their arguments; both defined it as a body of observable, fundamental laws, set in place by Divine Providence for the benefit of humankind. Still, "laws of nature" arguments were mostly employed by reformers who wanted to extend rights to nonwhite people, while a reference to "Nature's God" more often was made by delegates arguing for keeping social hierarchies intact.[54] For example, in a debate over the death penalty, arguing for capital punishment, conservative Ohio Whig Samson Mason explained that "there is no other safety to society; ... the only method by which we can insure that peace, protection, and enjoyment of life and happiness that man has ever devised." He was particularly disgusted by the new pseudosciences, which he believed had led the faithful astray. The alleged "science of phrenology or infidelity in any of their various developments" had never, and would never furnish anyone with a remedy for social or physical ills. He warned his more progressive colleagues to take care how they adopted these "new lights," which would only bewilder and mislead. He implored his fellow delegates to follow the tenets established in the Old Testament. "We have the law of nature and of nature's God, ... and the law of defence to uphold us in the doctrine of taking the murderer's life."[55] Similarly, conservative Democrat Charles Reemelin invoked nature's God when arguing against treatment of corporations as individuals. Corporations, he believed, should be nothing more than the creatures of the law, which was all that gave them breath. On the other hand, "natural persons" derived their rights "from Nature's God. Their rights are inalienable."[56]

[54] See Chapter 7 for a detailed discussion.

[55] Ohio 1850, 2: 33.

[56] Ohio 1850, 2: 198. Charles Reemelin (né Carl Rümelin) emigrated from Germany and later became a leading light in the Republican Party in Ohio. Charles Reemelin, *Life of Charles Reemelin* (Cincinnati, OH, 1892).

Both men were referring to the legacy of the revolutionary forebears, the idea that human beings could write their own documents framing governmental structures, limiting and distributing power, recognizing and shielding rights. The *First Principles* were the original ideas laid down by the founders, together with the creation story of the revolution and now being bequeathed to a new generation. Nineteenth-century Americans understood the world as a part of growing, developing, dynamic nature, created for their use, prosperity, and instruction by the Divine Author.[57]

Antebellum northwestern political rhetoric frequently linked the sacred to the political realm.[58] A group of Iowa 1857 convention delegates published a broadside exhorting voters to ratify their work because it had shaken off the temporal and risen to the celestial. "The organic law is the highest in a State. To it all laws passed by the Legislature must be subordinate. There is a sacredness about it which should not be invaded by partisan feeling and prejudices."[59] Sacredness was therefore in direct conflict with politics. In order to remove any possible taint of politics, the signers urged ratification, precisely because the constitution was a compromise document that had the approval of *both* parties. In this way they suggested that the constitution rose above party considerations and embodied precepts to which all could agree. In American political speeches and pamphlets, the word "sacred" frequently came into play in discussions about honor, duty, family ties, and obligations. Its chronically repeated use sometimes tempted speakers to use the word "sacred" in a sarcastic manner, to mock foolish stock beliefs and political shibboleths. For example, Michigan delegate John D. Pierce argued that the convention had a perfect right to repeal corporate charters, in spite of the fact that the state assembly may have ratified them. No matter how "burdensome and oppressive and productive of evil corporations may become," his Whig opponents had pronounced them "sacred," and "not to be touched." If that were true – if the constitution could not repeal charters – then, he believed, there would be no remedy left "but the last resort of oppressed people: revolution by physical force."[60]

57 Walter H. Conser Jr., *God and the Natural World, Religion and Science in Antebellum America* (Columbia: University of South Carolina Press, 1993), 25.

58 Robert E. Shalhope commented on the link between Christian goodness and virtue, in "In Search of the Elusive Republic," review of *Republicanism and Bourgeois Radicalism: Political Ideology in Late Eighteenth-Century England and America*, by Isaac Kramnick, *Reviews in American History* 19, no. 4 (Dec. 1991): 468–73.

59 W. H Farner, J. A. Williamson, J. C. Savery, Polk County Constitutional Committee, untitled broadside, July 22, 1857, Iowa Constitution vertical file, State Historical Society of Iowa, Iowa City.

60 *Report of the Proceedings and Debates in the Convention to Revise the Constitution of State of Michigan, 1850* (Lansing, MI: 1850), 588 (hereafter Michigan 1850); John Pierce was a strict New England Congregationalist minister who founded both the homestead exemption and Michigan's educational system in the 1850 convention. See Charles O. Hoyt and R. Clyde Ford, *John D. Pierce, Founder of the Michigan School System: A Study of Education in the Northwest* (Ypsilanti, MI, 1905).

The recurrent use of the word "sacred" in so many contexts also blurred the boundaries among reverence for historical heroes, Divine Providence, and natural laws. Antebellum American political speeches referred to rights as sacred, marriage as sacred, civic duties as sacred. At the same time, during those years, utopian societies had infiltrated northwestern culture, and even if they could not challenge the prevailing Protestant faith, their mere presence indicated potential destabilization. When those "new lights," as Ohio's Samson Mason had called them, stormed the doctrinal ground previously occupied by traditional churches, then they veered dangerously close to heresy. They threatened established (and hitherto dependable) practices, and they raised the knotty problem of coping with abstractions. For example, if natural law was an abstraction, and if phrenological principles were also abstractions, then how was one to determine the validity of either?

State constitutional conventions throughout the nation, since revolutionary days, debated this problem of the validity and practicality of abstractions, accusing one another either of creating meaningless daydreams or, in opposition, of resorting to a coarse expediency. The nineteenth-century word "visionary" was in fact a term of opprobrium; it was used to disparage an idea as speculative, fanciful, and unrealistic. Abstractions had to have a "practical use," a statement often heard in the earlier eastern and southern state constitutional conventions.[61] Such discussions often arose when the delegates debated the constitutional preambles, precisely because the words taken from the Declaration of Independence could be marshaled for both radical and conservative ends. For example, in debates over black men's rights, radicals focused on the phrase "all men are created equal," and the conservatives (in supporting the idea of popular sovereignty) on the citizens' right to alter their government. Delegates who dismissed conceptual approaches to constitution making sometimes sneered at those who based their arguments on principles, rather than pragmatism, arguing that such philosophizing had no place in a convention whose first concern was to finish the order of business and save their constituents' money. Impatience with abstractions should in no way be construed as a dismissal of metaphysics or as an embrace of Hobbesian utilitarianism. Nineteenth-century Americans were appalled at what they considered an expedient, immoral, corrupt worldview.[62]

The core debate between constitutional conservatives and reformers rested in their understanding of abstract principles: Should they be articulated as specific, limited, carefully defined constitutional provisions, or should they be left open and free, to spread their protection over the widest possible population?

[61] James A. Henretta, "The Rise and Decline of 'Democratic-Republicanism': Political Rights in New York and the Several States, 1800–1915," in *Toward a Usable Past*, 50.

[62] Daniel T. Rodgers, *Contested Truths, Keywords in American Politics Since Independence* (New York: Basic Books, 1987; repr., Cambridge, MA: Harvard University Press, 1998), 32–35. Although several convention delegates cited Jeremy Bentham's ideas about legal reform, they considered him to be in grave error in his philosophy. See, for example, Ohio 1850, 1: 634.

Conservative Democrats mistrusted general, undefined principles, considering them dangerous abstractions. Yet conservatives would later fight bitterly against any effort to codify common law principles, particularly when they supported time-honored ideas about women's natural role in the family.[63] By contrast, reform-minded Whigs believed that leaving principles open-ended was the only way to achieve broad Christian justice. But conservative Democrats based their interpretation of Christian justice on the Old Testament. In the Wisconsin 1846 convention Stoddard Judd dismissed humanitarian ideals. Theory could be piled up "line upon line and precept upon precept until it becomes mountain high," but "a little plain practical common sense" had more power to persuade him "than all of it from top to bottom." Similarly, Democrat Alexander Williams Randall contemptuously dismissed abstract principles that had been "chosen from the ten thousand loose doctrines, creeds, dogmas, and delusions by which in this progressive age we are all surrounded."[64] It was hardly surprising, then, that in response to these ultraisms, speeches in nearly every constitutional convention throughout this period contained scriptural quotations – until one delegate caustically observed, "we have had plenty of preaching, but not enough prayer."[65]

In a debate over black people's rights, however, Indiana Free Soiler Isaac Kinley argued that just because society had not yet reached perfection, that did not mean that the underlying ideal was not true. The specific question was whether the constitution should advert to the "natural equality of man" in its bill of rights, which he said had been attacked "because 1. it is not true, and 2. it is true only in the abstract." He reminded his listeners that "all first principles" were abstractions. Indeed, he explicitly linked religion, law, and science in his understanding of theoretical basis: "Christianity is founded upon an abstraction. Government, law, science, all [are] based upon abstractions." And that glorious abstraction – Christianity – which, he said was the center of "all that civilizes and happifies," indeed, of all conceptions of human liberty, should therefore occupy a "prominent place in the Constitution of a people." Perhaps it was true that the government had not reached the perfection of all its doctrines. Was it not true that in practice, principles of Christianity and of law were often violated? Did that mean that "sin" had the power to weaken "principles of the gospel or deny the power of justice?" Surely no one would argue that because their government did not write laws that defended the "whole idea of the natural equality man ... therefore the principle [was] unsound?"[66]

[63] For a discussion of codification, see Chapter 3. For common law rule of coverture, see Chapter 9.

[64] Wisconsin 1846, 166.

[65] See, for example, Michigan 1850, 224; Ohio 1850, 2: 31; Indiana 1850, 1: 420; Iowa 1857, 2: 948.

[66] Indiana 1850, 1: 964. Isaac Kinley was elected to the convention on a "fusion" ticket composed of moderate Democrats, Free Soil Whigs, abolitionists, and prohibitionists, but he was the only one of all the Henry County delegates who actually espoused these radical reform ideas. George

The harmony between the revealed political truths (told in parables and metaphors) and the evidence of historical events (such as the obvious success of the American Revolution) associated the founding generation with divinely organized nature. American democracy was ordained by God, and therefore ultimately rational because observably successful. The American democratic republic had been established through the revolutionary generation's sacrifice, acting out God's providential design. So the world of laws, government, nature, and religion included not only the rich, abundant nature in which they chose to make their new homes. It was also capable of being interpreted scientifically, by discerning and identifying principles, understanding underlying irreducible axioms, and observing the effects of God's and nature's laws on human societies.[67] A few years after Illinois achieved statehood, the *Edwardsville Spectator* wondered whether constitutional law was like "chemistry, always in a state of progressive improvement, and still open for new discoveries?" The editor suggested, with a tinge of gentle irony, that the "*great constitutional lawyers* of the day" might be able to answer that question.[68] Scientific discoveries would take government to a state of perfection, but that depended on two forms of investigation: first, by observing the past, and, second, by experimenting and using the resulting observations to perfect the government for the future. Therefore, metaphors that reminded people of the revolutionary generation could be used to inspire reform and perfection, particularly when employed to remove old outdated aristocratic accretions.[69]

Antebellum Americans enthusiastically studied scientific treatises and explorations. Western journals, like their eastern counterparts, teemed with articles on astronomy, geology, "ethnological philosophy" (cultural anthropology), natural philosophy, and botany.[70] Illinois literary and travel magazines

Hazzard, *Hazzard's History of Henry County, Indiana, 1822–1906* (New Castle, IN, 1906), 2: 975.

[67] See Conser, *God and the Natural World.* Hugh Slotten argues that the professionalization and dissemination of scientific education grew out of a culture of Whiggery, but I find that Jacksonian Democrats used the same scientific language when talking about the science of good government. Hugh R. Slotten, "Science, Education, and Antebellum Reform, the Case of Alexander Dallas Bache," *History of Education Quarterly* 31, no. 3 (Autumn 1991): 323–42. See also, Noll, *America's God*; Theodore Dwight Bozeman, *Protestants in an Age of Science: The Baconian Ideal and Antebellum American Religious Thought* (Chapel Hill: University of North Carolina Press, 1977); and George M. Marsden, "Everyone One's Own Interpreter? The Bible, Science, and Authority in Mid-Nineteenth Century America," in *The Bible in America: Essays in Cultural History*, eds., Nathan O. Hatch and Mark Noll (New York: Oxford University Press, 1982), 79–100.

[68] Emphasis in the original. *Edwardsville* [IL] *Spectator*, February 13, 1821.

[69] "Reciprocal Influence of the Physical Sciences," 13.

[70] See Donald Zochert, "Science and the Common Man in Ante-Bellum America," *Isis* 65, no. 4 (Dec. 1974): 448–73; George H. Daniels, *American Science in the Age of Jackson* (New York: Columbia University Press, 1968); Dorothy Ross, *The Origins of American Social Science* (Cambridge: Cambridge University Press, 1991), 22–52 (chap. 2, "The American Exceptionalist Vision").

abounded with anthropological, geographic, and scientific explorations of "natural philosophy" (natural history), along with frequent asseverations of the curiosity of the Western mind.[71] Westerners' fascination with technology, scientific discoveries, and cultural explorations was allied with their desire to participate equally in the modern world.[72] Young Americans were educated for republicanism through science; observations in natural history would train their young minds in rational observation; therefore, scientific schoolbooks often contained simple experiments.[73] This was true for both men and women: *Godey's Lady's Book*, *Peterson's*, and the Ohio *Ladies' Repository and Gatherings of the West* contained dozens of scientific and anthropological studies.[74] *Godey's* masthead declared that the magazine was dedicated to "domestic science," and the publication frequently contained articles on the marvels of practical science including "physics, chemistry, and mechanics."[75]

In order to benefit humanity, however, all scientific and political advancements had to be tailored to fit the people they were meant to serve.[76] For one young Indianan, therefore, the notion of government as science always had to be related to changing circumstances. Eighteen-year-old George Augustus Bicknell, who would later become an Indiana congressman and a professor of law at Indiana University, doubted that the best possible government could be devised "as one might follow a rule in mathematics" that would hold good under every possible combination of circumstances. Mathematics, he explained, was "founded on incontrovertible physical fact," but government

[71] See for example, "Geology or Scripture?" *Hesperian, a Western Quarterly Illustrated Magazine* 1, no. 2 (Aug.–Oct. 1834): 55–60.

[72] Joyce Appleby has observed that "science became the lodestar for those who thought they were at the dawn of a new age" in *Liberalism and Republicanism in the Historical Imagination* (Cambridge, MA: Harvard University Press, 1992), 337. See also Daniel J. Elazar, "Constitution-Making: The Preeminently Political Act," in Keith G. Banting and Richard Simeon, eds. *Redesigning the State: The Politics of Constitutional Change*, (Toronto: University of Toronto Press, 1985), 232 and quoted in Tarr, *Understanding State Constitutions*, 11n19; and Robert V. Bruce, *The Launching of American Science, 1846–1876* (New York: Knopf, 1987).

[73] Katherine Pandora, "The Children's Republic of Science in the Antebellum Literature of Samuel Griswold Goodrich and Jacob Abbott," *Osiris* 24, no. 1 (2009): 75–98. Pandora argues that "a prime objective of indigenous authors writing for American children was educating the young so they would be ready to assume their republican responsibilities" (p. 75).

[74] *The Ladies' Repository and Gatherings of the West: A Monthly Periodical Devoted to Literature and Religion* was published in Cincinnati from 1841 to 1848 and edited by the Reverend Leonidas Lent Hamline, a Methodist bishop who was instrumental in helping to divide the Methodist Church during the sectional crisis. Joanna Hawke, "Leonidas Lent Hamline," *American National Biography Online* (Feb. 2000), http://www.anb.org/articles/08/08-00613.html (accessed June 2, 2014).

[75] *Godey's Lady's Book* 2 (May 1831): 230. The same issue contained an article on the history of insects (p. 255). See also: Jan Pilditch, "'Fashionable Female Studies': The Popular Dissemination of Science in *Godey's Lady's Book*, 1830–60," *Australasian Journal of American Studies* 24, no. 1 (July 2005): 20–37; and Elizabeth B. Keeney, *The Botanizers: Amateur Scientists in Nineteenth-Century America* (Chapel Hill: University of North Carolina Press, 1992), 36.

[76] Daniels, *American Science in the Age of Jackson*, 20–26.

"upon a computation of probabilities." The first depended upon absolute certainty, and the other on moral certainty. He believed that "that government is best which best suits the circumstances and situation of its subjects."[77] Thus a perfect government was not based upon a mathematical formula but rather consisted of a political experiment, which could shift and change to suit the requirements of the citizens.

Politics could harmonize with an interest in the natural sciences, so long as experimentation and progress always accorded with popular will. John A. O'Sullivan, editor of the *Democratic Review*, introduced the first issue of his journal and laid out its fundamental commitment to democratic republicanism. In a detailed discussion of experimentation in American politics and government, O'Sullivan asserted that the natural world was the best model for changes, which should be neither too rash nor too slow. He explicitly condemned "all precipitate radical changes in social institutions." Nature was still the best guide – and metaphor – for political progress, because "she accomplishes her most mighty results of the good and beautiful by the silent and slow operation of great principles, without the convulsions of too rapid action."[78] On the other hand, it was equally important to be on the guard against "that specious sophistry" that perpetuated old evils by appealing to blind veneration for the "wisdom of our fathers." Neither inertia nor fear of the untried ought to prevent modern Americans from trying experiments, because, after all, the American Revolution had been an experiment of "gigantic boldness." Indeed, every step in the "onward march of improvement by the human race" had been an experiment; and the present was "most emphatically an age of experiments."

Jacksonian Democrats – who dominated the northwestern state constitutional conventions – held as a basic tenet of their political faith that rational political experiments had to lead toward an expansion of democracy. Innovations in self-government, they argued, should not burden the people with frivolous legislation or precipitous social transformations. The *Review* laid out a path for the correct action of political experimentation: Lawmakers ought to seek out every opportunity to simplify the action of government, to curtail its "hundred giant arms," and to substitute instead the "healthful action of the free voluntary principle," in which public opinion and will could be brought to bear directly on the political institutions. It would be impossible to go wrong in this direction; it was only necessary "to be cautious not to go too fast."[79] Thomas Prentice Kettell, a political economist and journalist who wrote widely on political science, took over the editorship of the *Democratic Review*

[77] *Edwardsville* (IL) *Spectator*, February 13, 1821; George Augustus Bicknell manuscript diary, Bicknell MSS, Lilly Library, Indiana University, Bloomington.

[78] Slotten, "Science, Education, and Antebellum Reform," 323–42.

[79] John L. O'Sullivan, "Introduction: The Democratic Principle – the Importance of Its Assertion and Application to Our Political System and Literature," *United States Magazine and Democratic Review* 1, no. 1 (Oct.–Dec. 1837): 9.

in 1846. As a strong supporter of Jacksonian democracy, Kettell frequently wrote on constitutional reform throughout the mid-1840s, primarily to support the call for the revision of the New York state constitution. According to the modern science of government, Kettell explained, the purpose of a constitution was to operate as a guarantee both against legislative encroachment on the rights of the people, and, at the same time, against the political caprices of the people themselves. Scientific progress, he explained, took place in two ways: by experimentation, and through observation of the results. A constitution was the working out of legislative experiments and would therefore require regular observation and "repairs" to keep it responsive to a wide range of interests.[80]

In the Northwest, Ohio politician Clement Vallandigham, another diehard Jacksonian, likened the Ohio state constitution to a mechanical instrument.[81] He rose in the Ohio Assembly to urge passage of a bill that would let the residents decide whether they wished to revise their constitution. A constitutional convention provided "a way for resolving again into its original elements the machinery of our state government, for the purpose of its reorganization by those from whose hands it came [the people], and whose creature it is." The progress of constitutional science, as shown in the development of American state constitutions, had already "amazed the civilized world." Still, he was careful to admonish his listeners not to forget the past. Experimentation was the "great laboratory of politics," but its results had to be carried into practice by reforms, or they were of no value.[82] Using mathematical, mechanical, and scientific principles of good government – a rational worldview that observed, experimented, corrected, and recorded political progress – could lead to greater perfection, creating more just, equal, better functioning government. Such a constitution would be based on both rational and progressive principles, without becoming infatuated with novelties. The northwestern convention speeches contained hundreds of examples of delegates decrying the idea of political experiments; many of the criticisms were aimed at the problem of "engrafting" an experimental provision in the constitution, when it ought to be properly tried as legislation instead.[83]

Conservatives of both parties agreed, but they insisted that such advances had to be used to bring about a more democratic society, one that fulfilled

[80] Thomas Prentice Kettell, "Constitutional Reform," *United States Magazine and Democratic Review* 13, no. 66 (Dec. 1843): 563–76. This article was widely reprinted in pamphlet form. See also, Arthur A. Ekirch Jr., "Democracy and Laissez Faire: The New York State Constitution of 1846," *Journal of Libertarian Studies* 1, no. 4 (1977): 319–23.

[81] Vallandigham would gain notoriety during the Civil War by being exiled to the Confederacy for his Copperhead speeches.

[82] Clement Vallandigham, *Remarks of Mr. Vallandigham, of Columbiana, on the Bill to Provide for Ascertaining the Will of the People upon the Question of Calling a Convention to Amend the Constitution of the State …* (Columbus, OH: 1847), 5, 11.

[83] For negative connotations of "experiment," see, for example, Michigan 1850, 54 and 101; for positive, Michigan 1850, 209.

the original intentions of the founders. On the whole, antebellum Americans mistrusted the notion that scientific truths could be deduced through experiments, unless those experiments were based on direct observation or religious teachings.[84] If anything, experiments should teach by experience – usually in the form of cautionary tales. For example, in 1853, the Whig *North American Review* published one bitterly critical review of John C. Calhoun's radical works, and another of the French Revolution's headlong rush into a republican government.[85] Both Democrats and Whigs worried about legislative experimentation that could become time-consuming, cumbersome, and expensive, whether carried out in constitutional or legislative acts. The staunch Democrat *New Constitution* complained that Ohio's legislature had "done little else, since the state organization, but legislate. – No state in the Union, of the same age, can exhibit such a huge pile of statutory laws, with so much that has been tried upon experiment – and so much that has been repealed."[86]

When lawmakers resorted to trial and error, trying haphazard solutions for the sake of novelty, or (worst of all) launching radical "ultra" laws that threatened existing hierarchies, then the word "innovation" became a term of opprobrium. State constitutions throughout the country were innovating: They were becoming more democratic, discarding property qualifications, rendering offices elective, and permitting immigrants to vote before naturalization. That was fine; American state constitutions were supposed to translate the American democratic republic into a local context. But where did reform end and dangerous novelty begin? Northwestern convention speeches expressed intense anxiety about innovation, which they feared threatened to subvert the will of the people. Writing a constitution was a precarious business because in forming their new political communities, they would almost certainly have to try fresh solutions. And yet, if the "building" metaphor was the principal figure of speech for creating a constitution, then it made sense that their charter had to be built on a permanent landscape. For antebellum convention delegates, the physical and theoretical state were both founded on the popular will, and both were embellished with shrines to democracy and liberty. The Whig *Scioto Gazette* exhorted its readers, "Look at this time-honoured instrument! – the monument of our fathers' virtue and wisdom! – wonder at it, and worship them."[87] In other words, written constitutions were more sacred, and therefore harder to amend, than statutes, which could be repealed or changed by succeeding

[84] Daniels, *American Science in the Age of Jackson*, 156.

[85] Unsigned review of *The Works of John C. Calhoun*, vol. 1, *A Disquisition on Government and a Discourse on the Constitution and Government of the United States*, by John C. Calhoun, ed. Richard K. Cralle, *North American Review* 76, no. 159 (April 1853): 473–507; "Travellers in France," *North American Review* 76, no. 159 (April 1853): 397–428.

[86] "Constitutional Reform – Excessive Legislation," *New Constitution* (Columbus, OH), June 9, 1849, 96. See also, Reed W. Smith, *Samuel Medary and the Crisis: Testing the Limits of Press Freedom* (Columbus: Ohio State University Press, 1995), 49.

[87] The *Scioto Gazette* (Chillicothe, OH), March 3, 1850.

legislatures. The Whig *Illinois Monthly Magazine* observed that "Land-Marks are permanent," explained the difference between permanent principles and frequently changed municipal regulations.[88] And an Iowa Whig editorial in the *Bloomington Herald*, titled "Progression," chided Democrats for being zealots for innovation, insisting that the Iowa convention delegates "pay some regard to the provisions of the Constitutions within their reach and not rely too much upon their own invention." The *Herald* regretted the "spirit of innovation" that seemed bent upon "breaking down all ancient landmarks and treating with contempt the opinions of those who have gone before us." Observing sardonically that it may be idle to raise a voice against the "progressive ... spirit of the age," the paper's editors confessed to a "reverence for the laws and institutions of our forefathers, [and] that we are guilty of believing the views of such men as Washington, Jay, Hamilton, and Madison upon the subject of government to be more worthy of respect than the opinions of those great moderns" such as Thomas Dorr, who had by now become the very embodiment of radical innovation because he had usurped the state constitutional process in Rhode Island in the name of radical democracy.[89]

Every northwesterner, whether conservative or radical, Democrat or Whig, believed (or at least conceded) that the best way to approach constitutional reform was to submit all changes to the judgment of the people. Democrats believed that popular will would subject all proposals for reform to a rigorous scrutiny. Whigs were perhaps not entirely convinced but knew that the voters could easily reject the constitution if they thought it transgressed the popular will.[90] Ohio Whig delegate John L. Green explained that innovation

88 James Hall, "Notes on Illinois: Laws," *Illinois Monthly Magazine* 2, no. 18 (Mar. 1832): 241.

89 Benjamin F. Shambaugh, ed., *Fragments of the Debates of the Iowa Constitutional Conventions of 1844 and 1846 along with Press Comments and Other Materials* ... (Iowa City: State Historical Society of Iowa, 1900), 385–87 (hereafter Iowa 1846), quoting the *Bloomington* [IA] *Herald*, May 15, 1846. Thomas Dorr tried to start a rebellion in Rhode Island.

90 None of the first three state constitutions (Ohio 1802, Indiana 1816, Illinois 1818) was submitted for a popular vote for ratification; Willi Paul Adams explains that most early state constitutions were not: *First American State Constitutions*, 67–77. The early framers worried that a popular vote on the state constitution would create a chaotic situation, and that a convention body was sovereign and had the right to draft a constitution without popular ratification. That belief retained legitimacy in the antebellum southern states, and in territories and states dominated by southern migrants. See, for example, Chris Childers who explains this process as a failure of popular sovereignty, in *Failure of Popular Sovereignty: Slavery, Manifest Destiny, and the Radicalization of Southern Politics* (Lawrence: University Press of Kansas, 2012). See also, Nicole Etcheson, *Bleeding Kansas: Contested Liberty in the Civil War Era* (Lawrence: University Press of Kansas, 2004), 141–48. On the other hand, G. Alan Tarr has explained that after the 1820s it became "standard practice" to submit state constitutions to popular ratification, suggesting that the situation in Kansas was motivated by radical proslavery activism. Tarr, *Understanding State Constitutions*, 30n.1. In the Northwest, after the first three, all but one of the state constitutions were submitted to popular vote. The 1846 Iowa constitution went to Congress without popular ratification, but the voters were so angry about the congressionally defined boundaries of the state that they later rejected the state constitution and delayed statehood for two more years.

had to be based on popular will, but with wisdom and restraint. True reform, he explained, had but one enemy: "her own friends." Some reforms were necessary, but that did not mean "destroying everything and starting *de novo*. All other foes must sooner or later fall before the expression of the popular Will, provided it be urged with sincerity and temper." He deplored intemperate reforms. "Let us coolly calmly and philosophically survey the ground before us – not entertaining propositions merely because they are reforms in name, but look at the thing itself."[91] By contrast, the Whig *Illinois Monthly* did not appear to be very distraught over the prospect of the "often anomalous, and sometimes absurd" experiments of new state constitutions. First, experiments often embraced beneficial improvements, which advanced political science; and second, inevitably the people would correct their errors by further experimentation.[92] The delegates would have to decide whether they were in accord with, or in advance of, public opinion; whether constitutions were meant to perfect existing constitutions and laws, or to create entirely new structures of self-governance.

New and valuable theories were all very well in their place and would certainly conduce to the benefit of the state. But moderate Democrat Alexander W. Randall believed that innovations should never outrun the will of the people. Indeed, "if your theories are good and have a beneficial practical tendency it is fit and proper that they ... lead and direct public opinion, that they temper and mold that opinion." Advocacy was fine, but legislation required more prudence. "You may reason and theorize in advance but you cannot legislate in advance of the great public will." Statute laws (and, more to the point, constitutional provisions) should "ever be up even with the settled public will, but never beyond it." His chief argument was that abstract principles, or "fancies," could do more harm than good. "The knowledge of men's rights, interests, and duties, which ... in fancy dreams have come across our minds is [a] poor foundation upon which to build the civil and political hopes of men."[93] On the contrary, the Warsaw, Illinois, *Temperance Crusader* published an editorial in 1854 protesting against "unwise and injurious legislation," which the editor defined as laws that did not "keep pace with the wants and the lights of the times." But when had legislation ever kept pace with the wants and the lights of the times? The reformer was always in advance of his age, because he perceived "wants which others do not, he has lights where others have not." It might take another fifty or a hundred years before anyone listened, but by then "general unanimity and irresistible outside pressure [would] literally compel the enactment of the necessary law."[94]

[91] Ohio 1850, 2: 72. Green was a lawyer, later judge of common pleas, and became a Republican in the late 1850s. *Ohio Law Bulletin* 66 (1921): 782.

[92] James Hall, *Sketches of History, Life, and Manners in the West* (Philadelphia, 1835), 2: 154. See also, "Reform," *Illinois Monthly Magazine* 2, no. 16 (Jan. 1832): 177–85.

[93] Wisconsin 1846, 164–66.

[94] "Unwise and Injurious Legislation," *Temperance Crusader, A Campaign Paper Devoted to the Legal Prohibition of the Liquor Traffic* (Warsaw, IL), March 15, 1854, in Everett D. Graff Collection of Western Americana, Newberry Library, Chicago.

As political writers watched these new northwestern states experiment – as though in a giant laboratory – with political innovations, they believed they were witnessing the inevitable democratic progress in American constitutional science. This idea crossed party lines: The editor of the Whig *Illinois Monthly Magazine* observed that any departures from long-established traditions had always occurred gradually, and always tended "toward democracy."[95] Similarly, in an article titled "The Fear of Innovation," Democrat Samuel Medary encouraged innovative thinking in constitutional reform: The Whiggish "dread of innovation," he declared, had ever been a "stumbling block in the way of reform and of progress." Such fears were "idle in a republic where the people [possessed] the inherent power to right all wrongs."[96]

For antebellum midwesterners, then, history, religion, science, and politics – as the constitutive elements of democratic civic engagement – created a moral and rational worldview that served both ethical and practical goals: ends that included prosperity, commercial success, civil rights and equality for white men, participation in the world economy and in the greatness of the nation; maintenance of the social and racial order; and healthy, happy families. Because they lived in a new, undeveloped society, westerners were beginning to loosen many basic political concepts, including the definitions of citizenship and of property rights. Yet these men were hardly revolutionary. They did not believe that they needed to be, even though they were in the midst of precipitous changes, both in their own lives and in national politics. They were aware of threats to national unity as sectional fissures appeared around them, so some of them grasped at profoundly traditional definitions of good government. And one of the most important concepts they had to redefine for themselves was the idea of a republic.[97]

But that was precisely the problem: A republic was hardly stable. Indeed, the birth of new republics could entail scenes of revolutionary conflagration. True, the delegates may not have resembled the self-sacrificing state builders of the previous generation, nor the European hotheads attempting to overthrow monarchies or establish republics. And they may have become extremely individualistic. But they were not ready to jettison all the principles inherited from

[95] Hall, "Notes on Illinois: Laws," 241.

[96] Iowa 1846, 326; Samuel Medary, "The Fear of Innovation," *New Constitution* (Columbus, OH), May 5, 1849, 7.

[97] The historian Robert Shalhope explained that they were "committed to harmony, order, and communal well-being ... while actively creating an aggressive, individualistic, liberal one." Robert E. Shalhope, *The Roots of Democracy: American Thought and Culture, 1760–1800* (Lanham, MD: Rowman & Littlefield, 1990), 138. For Peter Onuf, Americans were seeking "private interest and enterprise, not self-denial and sacrifice." Peter S. Onuf, "Liberty, Development, Union: Visions of the West in the 1780s," *William and Mary Quarterly* 43, no. 2 (April 1986): 203. Steven Watts points out that the scholars of the early republic have identified the "tension in American political culture between republican ideals and increasingly self-interested social and economic behavior," which created a "volatile, fractured republican culture." Steven Watts, review of *The Lost Soul of American Politics: Virtue, Self-Interest, and the Foundations of Liberalism*, by John P. Diggins, *American Quarterly* 37, no. 2 (Summer

their revolutionary forebears. It is possible to see within their contradictions and disputes the emergence of a new definition of republican philosophy that supported both community welfare and individual striving. The metaphors still worked, but it was their inherent contradictions, and not their harmonious blending, that was at the forefront when the delegates attempted to define and realize their idea of a democratic republic. In their convention speeches, the delegates used the word "republican" hundreds of times. As was true of most other theoretical or philosophical principles, the speakers rarely bothered to define the term. By the 1820s, the political philosophy of republicanism had already undergone dramatic changes – from a creed that mistrusted mobs and sought to enshrine political hierarchies, to a much more egalitarian attitude that focused on a freedom from governmental restraint.[98] Judging from the context of the most common usages, most delegates understood that the term "republican" referred to a representative government elected by the people, whose powers and interests were carefully separated – a government that refrained from catering to a privileged class and that depended on plain, hard-working, productive people. Most Jacksonians would also have felt deeply persuaded by John Taylor of Caroline's definition of republicanism as "the right of the people to create … and influence their own government."[99] The delegates took care to inscribe these new principles of republicanism into many of their constitutions. Explicit exhortations to the separation of powers appeared in the constitutions of Indiana, Iowa, Michigan, and Minnesota, and reminders to revert to First Principles appeared in the Illinois and Ohio charters.[100]

1985): 295. According to the historian Willi Paul Adams, this classical republicanism was superseded by an "individualistic, competitive, and market-oriented allegedly Lockean liberalism." Adams, *First American Constitutions*, 303.

98 College-educated northwestern convention delegates likely read the sources of classical republicanism, including John Locke, Harrington, Montesquieu, and William Blackstone. Classical republicanism emphasized civic virtue: the notion that property ownership conferred a stake in society and encouraged political participation. Republicanism also frequently warned against the dangers of corruption, a notion that Jacksonian Democrats translated as a fear of aristocratic (in this case, corporate) domination of the popular will. For a helpful discussion of the historiography, see Daniel T. Rodgers, "Republicanism: Career of a Concept," *Journal of American History* 79, no. 1 (1992): 13–14 and Roger E. Shalhope, "Toward a Republican Synthesis: The Emergence of an Understanding of Republicanism in American Historiography," *William and Mary Quarterly* 3rd ser., 29, no. 1 (1972): 49–80, as well as Roger E. Shalhope, "Republicanism and Early American Historiography," *William and Mary Quarterly* 3rd ser., 39, no. 2. (1982): 3–26. For definitions of republicanism in the antebellum era, see Drew R. McCoy, *The Elusive Republic: Political Economy in Jeffersonian America* (Chapel Hill: University of North Carolina Press, 1996) and Lance Banning, *The Jeffersonian Persuasion: Evolution of a Party Ideology* (Ithaca, NY: Cornell University Press, 1980); for shifts in attitudes, see James T. Kloppenberg, *The Virtues of Liberalism* (New York: Oxford University Press, 1998), 59–69.

99 This definition appears in John Taylor, *New Views of the Constitution of the United States* (Washington, DC: 1823), 227.

100 I searched through all of the northwestern convention journals for both the words "republican" and "republicanism." "Republican" as an adjective (*not* referring to the political party) occurs

The process of reworking republican government was by no means inherently logical or coherent, and it often involved internal contradictions, as well as self-serving and even irrational accommodations to political ends. As a slogan, republicanism (or its broader analogue, *First Principles*) embodied both democratic consensus and virtuous government, but these ideas were also frequently pressed into service as trump cards in a variety of disputes. Therefore, sometimes their definitions of republicanism were ironic or downright unconstitutional. The delegates were passionately involved with the project of defining, building, and protecting republican government in their states. The pivot around which this redefinition turned was a rational and ethical engagement with popular will. For diehard Jacksonian Democrats, popular will was always the best – perhaps the only – measure by which to judge the legitimacy of any political act. Whigs feared that the popular will could easily be led astray by delusions. Nevertheless, antebellum western constitutions enshrined basic concepts in their charters that were directly derived from classical republicanism.[101] In essence, they were struggling mightily with the contradictory efforts to respect and restrain the popular will in their redefinition of republicanism. At the same time, they were fully aware that they lived in a complicated society. Convention delegates frequently observed that their society was fractured by the same kinds of divisions that were threatening national unity. New Englanders and southerners who had migrated into the Northwest were kin to the men who were now fighting in Congress over the expansion of slavery into the western territories, over the rights of European immigrants and free black people, and over the rights and powers of banking corporations.[102]

Ohio governor Duncan McArthur's 1830 inaugural speech to the state legislature can serve as an illustration of the transition from the early national republican ideas to the rough, disorderly, inherently contradictory republican ideas of the western states. McArthur was an old-style Democratic Republican and a tough campaigner who had distinguished himself as a soldier in the Ohio River Valley in 1812. Now as the newly elected governor of Ohio he reminded the legislature that the federal and the Ohio state constitutions were already

on average about 70 times in each convention. I found fewer than a half-dozen mentions of republicanism. And one of those was used pejoratively – i.e., criticizing the Jacobin republicanism of the French Revolution.

101 Joyce Appleby defined the objects of country opposition as "public debt, standing armies, executive influence, government by money." Joyce Appleby, "Republicanism in Old and New Contexts," *William and Mary Quarterly* 3rd ser., 43, no. 1 (Jan. 1986): 24. I argue that Jacksonian Democrats saw themselves as the new revolutionary generation and the corrupt new corporations seeking to assume individual status and to purchase political influence (and so generating debt and therefore, by extension, Whigs) as the new aristocracy.

102 In 1857 Frank Moore reprinted many important American speeches in which the subject of republican government was discussed intensively. For example, see New York senator DeWitt Clinton's 1803 speech "Navigation of the Mississippi." Frank Moore, *American Eloquence: A Collection of Speeches and Addresses by the most Eminent Orators of America* (New York, 1857), 1: 567–76.

well equipped to protect the people's rights, which comprised the "essential principles of a republican government." In return, the people's civil obligations were to guard "purity of morals, love of country and a just respect for religion." Then he dropped a strong hint to the Ohio legislatures not to overreach themselves. "It would seem, therefore, that but little legislation of a general nature would be necessary, where so much is provided for by the Constitution."[103] McArthur believed that the principal goal of republican government was to safeguard rights, reputation, and property, and that in return, the people owed personal moral purity and patriotism. In order to keep this compact firmly in place, the legislatures ought to be careful not to tinker too much.

Because they were not in rebellion, these men did not leave behind that plethora of pamphlet literature or manifestos that characterized the American (or European) revolutionary periods. One must seek their definition of the philosophy in challenges and rebukes. For that reason, they often used the term "republican" in an adversarial manner, which may be somewhat deceptive. We must pick our way carefully through their disputes to arrive at a picture of what they thought republican meant from what they explicitly felt it did not mean. And because the delegates rarely used the word "republicanism," it is likely that they thought the adjective "republican" described specific (and explicit) forms of government and rights, and not a unified political philosophy. This particular problem – the confusions and lack of clarity about a fundamental political theory – can be difficult to understand and explain, since the explanations rest on a contradictory or even an incomplete understanding. But confusions can be a rich source of information about shifting ideologies. As people begin to confront their fundamental ideas about human life and rights (particularly true of delegates writing or revising their foundational charters) either they must find a way to reconcile intellectual and moral conflicts, or they must resign themselves to changing their minds. In the long run, the most stubborn delegates did neither. Instead, they left the hardest decisions (those that forced moral questions against expedient ones, for example) to the voters themselves.[104]

[103] Manuscript speech, "Duncan McArthur, to the Ohio state legislature, upon his election to the Governorship," December 18, 1830, Duncan Macarthur Papers, Library of Congress, Washington, DC; James Grant Wilson and John Fiske, eds., *Appleton's Cyclopaedia of American Biography* (New York, 1887–89), 4: 72–73.

[104] This book argues that while there were clear divisions between the views of Democrats and Whigs, or between people loosely identified as conservatives or reformers, the views more often overlapped or conflicted internally. Two valuable books explore the fundamental differences in American intellectual history, and both of them categorize the views of constitutional convention delegates. For example, Rush Welter divides the opponents as conservative Democrats versus Liberal Whigs, in *The Mind of America, 1820–1860* (New York: Columbia University Press, 1975). Welter does explain that Whigs had democratized their party platforms to such a degree that they had become virtually indistinguishable from the Democratic aims (p. 444). By contrast, Laura Scalia distinguishes delegates as supportive of property ownership or advocating reform, in *America's Jeffersonian Experiment*. In the northwestern constitutional

Meanwhile, some of their definitions of such concepts as republicanism betrayed a lack of familiarity with political philosophy. For example, in 1847, George Akin, an Illinois Democrat originally from Tennessee, offered a resolution banning Reverend Hale from ever holding another prayer in the convention, because the latter had denounced the war with Mexico as unjust. Proclaiming that such declarations "ought not to be tolerated, more especially in a republican government" (and incidentally unbecoming a minister of the Gospel), Akin felt that Hale's sermon set a bad example "before the young and rising generation." The resolution failed, eighty-two to thirty-six.[105] In the Wisconsin 1848 convention, Whig lawyer Orsamus Cole's definition of republicanism flatly contradicted the new Jacksonian definitions. Instead of basing the government on the will of the people, he asserted that neither the executive nor the legislative department of the government acted as the "agents of the popular will." Instead, he believed that it was often necessary to "resist and restrain the popular will" in order to "compel it to act with more mature deliberation than it might in a moment of excitement if it had the immediate control of its own agents." History had shown examples of "democracies running mad" and might again. He knew these sentiments were unpopular and might be "regarded as anti-republican," but he could not help but believe that this was the "right spirit and genius of government."[106]

Some delegates deliberately turned the term "republican" on its head, using the ironic contrast to highlight or strengthen their argument – a rhetorical ploy that no doubt further served to obfuscate the classical definition of the term. In the 1857 Iowa convention, Democrat Jonathan C. Hall argued for governmental support of popular education and a meritocracy but did so using aristocratic terms. "The aristocracy of intellect is the only aristocracy to which I will ever subscribe and it is one which I will forever worship." More to the point, if Iowa required "tyranny and despotism in order to give that aristocracy a fair field," then that is what it should have. In referring to the "aristocracy" of intellect, Hall was in fact arguing for a meritocracy. He believed that the safety and perpetuity of republican institutions depended solely on the intellect, because that was the only way to "perfect and develop" republican institutions. Indeed, the "very existence of the government itself" depended upon the intelligence of the people.[107] Where Hall believed that government ought to play a central

conventions, however, these categories are less useful. Both Democrats and Whigs feared corrupt corporations (a subject explained in Chapter 10) and members of both parties feared the popular disapproval of constitutions, and therefore either tacitly or enthusiastically left important decisions to a popular vote.

105 Arthur Charles Cole, ed., *The Constitutional Debates of 1847*, vol. 14 of *Collections of the Illinois State Historical Library* (Springfield: Illinois State Historical Library, 1919), 167.

106 *Journal of the Convention to form a Constitution for the State of Wisconsin, with a Sketch of the Debates begun and held at Madison, on the fifteenth day of December, 1847* (Madison, WI: 1848), 57 (hereafter Wisconsin 1848).

107 Iowa 1857, 2: 822; Indiana 1850, 1: 78.

role in developing the western character (and so supporting republican institutions), Wisconsin's Orsamus Cole went further in stating that the government ought to prevent popular will from "running mad."[108]

Conservative delegates still clung to classical republicanism's suspicion of popular mobs. But moderates found such fears offensive. In Ohio's 1850 convention, moderate Whig Horace D. Clark argued against the allegation that the honesty and virtue of the people would only move to the fore if their delusions were restrained by conservatism. He argued for longer terms of office, defending the virtue of the people against his opponents' claim that only short terms would restrain their selfish impulses. He considered this a "gross libel upon the honesty and virtue of the people." Because the masses loved justice and order, it was "only because they will tolerate neither disorder or injustice that order and justice prevail."[109] In the long run, as we shall see, these ambiguous and sometimes even contradictory definitions of "republican" would find their way into the final drafts of the state constitutions, particularly in controversial topics such as black people's civic rights or the rights of corporations to print paper money.

Meanwhile, in spite of conservative caution most convention delegates believed in the principle of popular sovereignty: that all governing authority ought to be based entirely upon the people's goodwill and support. As early as 1802, the first Ohio constitution had proclaimed that because "every free republican government [had been] founded on their sole authority, and organized for the great purpose of protecting their rights and liberties and securing their independence; to effect these ends, they have at all times a complete power to alter, reform, or abolish their government whenever they deem it necessary." And in 1846 a Milwaukee Democratic newspaper reminded delegates that they were required to carry out "the wishes of the peoples by whom they were elected." The constitution had to be made for the benefit of the people, whose best interests had to be served, because the constitution should not be created for individuals, but for the community.[110]

Still, contradictions and conflicts of opinion remained a vital part of the republican process. Popular will was diverse and had to be expressed, respected, and (according to Whigs) contained. In the Indiana 1850 convention, Biddle explained that the state had been "made up from year to year of minds taken from every section of the Union, and every part of the world." Inevitably, among men "educated under every form of government upon earth," conflicts of opinion in legislation would arise, at least until "they should all become wholehearted Hoosiers." Therefore, the only object of legislation was to "give form and expression to the opinions of the people, and … the oftener they could get that expression, the nearer they would approach to a perfect republican

108 Wisconsin 1848, 57.
109 Ohio 1850, 1: 718.
110 *Milwaukee Courier*, August 26, 1846.

government."[111] The people, at least once they had become thorough Hoosiers, were naturally and inherently good.

Becoming republican, unlike becoming a Hoosier, a Sucker, or a Buckeye, was not simply a matter of moving to the Northwest. To understand the state constitution, it was "indispensably necessary," according to the constitutional law theorist Daniel Raymond, "to have a republican heart." No amount of intellect or education would "ever enable either a nullifier or an aristocrat to understand it any more than talents and learning will enable an infidel to understand the Bible."[112] Republican ideals represented an emotional, optimistic appeal to the highest sentiments, perhaps even an essentially northwestern approach to representative government. Democrat lawyer and archaeologist Caleb Atwater, in the section entitled "Remarks on the Constitution of Ohio," complained about the powers of the legislature, which he felt amounted to a betrayal of the people. "Without more restraints on the law making power," he warned, the Ohio constitution could not endure. The republican form of government could only last "while the people [were] in love with it." Take from it the affections of the people and "like a mist in a clear morning" it would be gone in an hour.[113] For all these reasons, republicanism could easily become both passionate and, if great care were not taken, even irrational; as we shall see in future chapters, republicanism (and democratic self-government) had to be based on popular sentiment as well as the more principled triad of Christianity, reason, and history, and could therefore become subject to the vagaries of unwritten, nonlegal standards and rules.

Republican passions burned so bright that they could ignite patriotism; if uncontrolled, however, they could threaten the welfare of minority political opponents. Some Democrat delegates worried about a strong central government. A constitution would be no safeguard against tyranny unless the rights of minorities were explicitly protected. In Indiana's 1850 convention, Howe explained that although there was a great deal of talk about liberty and equality, was it not possible that a majority in a republic could "inflict as much injustice and oppression upon the minority as a despot on his throne upon his subjects?" He defined tyranny as the action of "supreme power without or in defiance of Constitutional limits." It made no difference who exercised this power, whether a "despot on his throne or … a triumphant majority of the people in defiance of their own Constitution." Linking state government to national concerns, Howe believed that abolition fanaticism (in this case, honoring the constitutional protections of the rights of free black people moving from one state to another) had already subjected the United States to widespread "denunciation abroad." Europeans justly accused Americans of "constantly sacrificing the rights of minorities and individuals through an unjust

[111] Indiana 1850, 1: 95.

[112] Daniel Raymond, *The Elements of Constitutional Law* (Cincinnati, OH: 1845), 47.

[113] Caleb Atwater, *History of the State of Ohio, Natural and Civil* (Cincinnati, OH: 1838), 172.

exercise of power by the majority." The tendency of the people of all republican governments, he explained, "especially the American," was to adopt "opinions and measures."[114] Similarly, in the Michigan 1850 convention, Democratic delegate Calvin Britain decried "ultra republican fanaticism" as "zeal which is not according to knowledge" and which forgot the "divine injunction to be subject to the higher powers, for the powers that be are ordained of God." While he supported the cause of temperance, he simply did not believe that it ought to be in the constitution.[115] Britain hoped to save the constitution from ultrarepublican fanaticism by submitting it as a separate question "for the consideration of the people."[116]

A republic might be turbulent and at times dangerous to established practices, but that only served to purify it of unhealthy humors. In an Independence Day speech, Chicago lawyer Henry Brown dared his listeners to trust their futures to a republic, in spite of the fact that the democratic passions that ruled the American heart might create temporary disturbances. "Under a despotic government, every thing is smooth and quiet upon the surface, while a sea of black and bitter waters roll beneath." In a republic, on the other hand, "every obnoxious thing" was constantly striving to rise to the surface. A republic, therefore, was "like a mountain torrent; if it is not forever pure, it is forever rolling." The great state of Illinois had to place its trust in the free exchange of ideas, and in the native intelligence of men who had been educated in American history, who had ennobled and enlightened their understanding of the world by rational scientific observation, and who followed the teachings of Christianity.[117]

In their task of building good constitutions, then, convention delegates relied on three frames of reference: historical origin narratives, Christianity, and rational scientific observation. All three were ways of attaining knowledge about and interpreting the world around them. The delegates' duty was to try to fit their ideas of ethics, good government, morality, and common sense into a constitutional framework. They had arrived at their conventions

[114] Indiana 1850, 1: 439–40. Howe was referring to the reciprocity clause conferring equal rights on black people. Although he did not explicitly say so, Howe may have been referencing Alexis De Tocqueville's *Democracy in America*, which had by now appeared in an English translation. Alexis de Tocqueville, *Democracy in America*, ed. and trans., Henry Reeve (London, 1835–40). For a discussion of Tocqueville's notion of the "tyranny of the majority," see Alexis de Tocqueville, *Democracy in America*, ed. and trans., Harvey Mansfield and Delba Winthrop (Chicago: University of Chicago Press, 2000), lii–lviii.

[115] The phrase "zeal which is not according to knowledge" is probably adapted from Romans 10: 2 (KJB) and would have appeared in many sermons around this time. It meant "ignorant enthusiasm" and was often used to criticize those who took on popular fads without properly submitting their ideas to God.

[116] Michigan 1850, 403.

[117] Henry Brown, *An Oration, Delivered at Chicago, Illinois, on the Fourth of July, 1846* (Chicago, 1846), 17. Henry Brown was an abolitionist judge in Illinois. John M. Palmer, ed. *The Bench and Bar of Illinois, Historical and Reminiscent* (Chicago, 1899), 2: 617.

convinced that they were equal to this mission, but they reckoned without the more unpredictable and impulsive nature of the popular will. And so, antebellum westerners' positive, hopeful, energetic outlook centered (with God's providence and aid) on the human beings who worked so hard to create their own country. This worldview took from history the certitude that the best possible government on earth had been bequeathed to them by the revolutionary generation. From religion it took the notion that the republic was a divine gift from God. And from science this worldview acquired the belief that their political structures, and their inner sense of ethos, were directly based on and harmonious with nature. In this go-ahead, vigorous age, democracy was imbued with all these ways of understanding the world.[118] All of these frameworks lived on a continuous moral and intellectual landscape, but they formed neither a closed system nor an entirely coherent worldview. And so they could accommodate widely divergent political ideas. Delegates argued about how far to extend abstract ideas and what counted as legitimate evidence, but because this worldview extended far into the distant past, through the hopeful present, and into a glorious future, all could find a home in this western landscape.[119]

[118] See: Nathan O. Hatch, *The Democratization of American Christianity* (New Haven, CT: Yale University Press, 1989); Conser, *God and the Natural World*; Darsey, *Prophetic Tradition*; and Paul E. Johnson, *A Shopkeeper's Millennium, Society and Revivals in Rochester, New York, 1815–1837*, rev. ed. (New York: Hill & Wang, 2004).

[119] Most constitutions included two statements, first, that they were grateful to Almighty God, and second, that education and scientific study ought to be encouraged by the legislature.

3

Laws

"We may talk about Democracy as much as we please & the people governing themselves," a St. Louis surveyor told Lucius Lyon, who had served as a Democratic delegate to the 1835 Michigan constitutional convention. "This is all *right* in the *abstract* & *true* in *theory*," the surveyor admitted. The stark reality, however, was that regardless of what the people may have wanted, party leaders would always run the show. Worse: If any hapless candidate launched himself against the dominant political party it would be as impossible for that man to succeed "as if the masses were opposed to him."[1] This problem crossed political party lines: An Indiana Whig was equally incensed to observe how demagogues talked about "a free country and freedom of speech and conscience," while political ostracism remained "perfectly cruel and unrelenting" – so cruel, in fact, that he felt able to compare the treatment of Indiana Whigs to the sufferings of free black people in his state.[2]

Most northwesterners would have agreed that party caucuses controlled both candidates and issues, but they trusted that the deliberations of constitutional conventions would rise above sordid political machinations. Put plainly, political parties set policy and doled out spoils, and constitutions provided the ethical framework that kept these behind-the-scenes processes in line. They did so in two ways: by separating the powers of governance according to a rhetoric

[1] Capt. William S. Brown to Lucius Lyon, October 20, 1849, Lucius Lyon Papers, Clements Library, University of Michigan, Ann Arbor. Lyon had served as a delegate to Michigan's first constitutional convention in 1835, and after statehood as a congressman and senator from Michigan. Lyon was a Democrat.

[2] David McDonald to Henry Smith Lane, January 17, 1852, Henry Smith Lane Mss, Lilly Library, Indiana University, Bloomington. For a similar view, see also Henry G. Weston, *Our Obligations to God: A Discourse, Delivered in Peoria, Illinois, on Thanksgiving Day, November 25, 1852* (Peoria, 1852), 5. Weston believed that Christians had relinquished their faith in God's government on earth to "party machinery," which forced voters to elect men chosen by caucus, rather than in accordance with the will of the people.

of first principles, and by formally expressing the will of the sovereign people. At best, the whole concern functioned as a machine that performed the practical work of ostensibly catering to the people's will and (actually) carrying out the dominant party's program. Political power, as managed by parties, was the oil that kept the gears turning smoothly. Even so, most northwesterners – who had few illusions about the might and moral compass of organized political parties – trusted that their constitutional conventions would, in the long run, direct the energy of the process along ethical channels.[3] Northwesterners certainly believed that constitutions would enshrine principles, but they also saw quite clearly that no principle could prosper without the life-giving force of political power. More problematic, the convention delegates, whose job it was to distribute political power, would have to figure out a way to accomplish that in a confusing and disorganized legal landscape. All sorts of codes contended for dominance in the conventions: common law, statutes, social customs, and biblical commandments. Somehow these had to be reconciled and inscribed in the state constitutions, a challenging process that always triggered intense political fights.

Yet perhaps the relationship between constitutionalism and political power was not quite as fraught as that description implies. Constitutional conventions possessed the authority, the mandate, and the moral force to build an ethical foundation for organic law. More to the point, most northwesterners (at least, the Jacksonian Democrats among them) believed that politics and foundational principles were reasonably well aligned. After all, the Democratic Party held sway throughout the region, at least until the mid-1850s. That meant that "The Democracy" (a nickname for both party members and sweeping, if undefined, principles of popular government) would easily achieve their goals: economizing on state government and strengthening popular sovereignty. The constitutional conventions were to address both of these aims by severely cutting back both the sessions and the power of legislatures, particularly in deficit spending. Democrats also demanded a shift from an appointed to an elected judiciary. That said, throughout the era of constitutional revision, particularly in the Northwest, the Whig delegates agreed with most of those aims and principles. In fact, during the elections for the 1847 Wisconsin convention, the Whigs managed to beat the Democrats to the punch by publishing their platform first – a platform that contained all of the Democratic planks, including an elected judiciary, shorter legislative sessions, and strong antibanking laws. The Democrats bitterly accused the Whigs of stealing their thunder and playing to

3 For cynical attitudes toward political power, see Glenn C. Altschuler and Stuart M. Blumin, *Rude Republic: Americans and Their Politics in the Nineteenth Century* (Princeton, NJ: Princeton University Press, 2000). For a contrasting view on politics as central to nineteenth-century public culture, see William E. Gienapp, "'Politics Seem to Enter into Everything': Political Culture in the North, 1840–1860," in Stephen E. Maizlish and John J. Kushma, eds., *Essays on American Antebellum Politics, 1840–1860* (College Station: Texas A&M University Press, 1982), 15–69.

the voters, but they still won a two-thirds majority in the convention.[4] In any case, as they deliberated, the northwestern convention delegates would have to find ways of understanding, harnessing, and wielding power: both as the force that enabled the political machine to run, and as the expression of popular will.

Northwesterners defined political power in two principal ways: as a scientific force and as an ethical imperative that functioned to achieve the aims of democratic governance. But forces and imperatives could be subverted by selfish, undemocratic entities. The states convening constitutional conventions after 1830 – whether they were building the first charters for new territories or revising the constitutions of established states – all confronted similar crises: economic panics, legislative incompetence or even corruption, and rapid growth of the electorate that outstripped every effort to keep pace with the organization of the government and the judiciary. The conventions based their efforts to resolve these problems on four overlapping frameworks of governance: the embattled English common law tradition, American constitutionalism, scientific approaches to self-governance, and ethical or moral foundations, particularly Protestant Christianity.[5] Northwesterners believed that these frameworks were part of a harmonious, rational system that linked God's creation, the founding of America, and human reason.[6] Granted, the English common law tradition came in for severe criticisms during this era, so one cannot assume consensus on all of these elements. But the notion that law should be based on both moral and rational grounds undergirded both the convention and public assumptions about good government.

Convention delegates who had attended college (probably at least a quarter of them) would have learned the fundamental principles of the Baconian scientific method: that is, the direct observation of nature through one's senses, classifying and recording of one's observations, and from there deduction of general principles. Antebellum Americans were deeply interested in scientific studies of weather, soil, and geology and experienced little difficulty in transferring the skills and methods of scientific observation and classification to other fields of human endeavor, such as law and governance. That

4 Jack Stark, *The Wisconsin State Constitution: A Reference Guide* (Westport, CT: Greenwood Press, 1997), 4–5.

5 Howard Schweber suggests a similar basis for legal science, which he calls "Protestant Baconianism." In his view, the four characteristics of Protestant Baconianism are "a commitment to natural theology, the doctrine that the study of nature proved religious truths; a commitment to a limited form of inductivism that defined science as fundamentally an exercise in taxonomy; a belief in a grand synthesis that bound all forms of knowledge together in a system of analogies; and a claim that science was a public undertaking that would produce moral and political uplift." Howard Schweber, "The 'Science' of Legal Science: The Model of the Natural Sciences in Nineteenth-Century American Legal Education," *Law and History Review* 17, no. 3 (Fall 1999): 423–24.

6 George H. Daniels, *American Science in the Age of Jackson* (Tuscaloosa: University of Alabama Press, 1994), 48, 190; Mark A. Noll, *America's God: From Jonathan Edwards to Abraham Lincoln* (New York: Oxford University Press, 2002), 288.

made sense to nineteenth-century Americans, who believed that all moral, ethical, and intellectual knowledge could be analogized in a harmonious, unified system. Moreover, academy- and college-educated delegates would certainly have read the works of some of the Enlightenment philosophers, particularly Scottish Common Sense thinkers such as Thomas Reid and Dugald Stewart, both of whom were immensely popular and whose works were emphasized in American college curricula.[7] True, most of the northwestern constituents would not have had the benefit of a university education, but these ideas nevertheless formed a highly popular and persuasive worldview that helped literate northwesterners make sense of their political and public lives.[8] Essentially, they believed that an innate moral faculty enabled human beings to perceive, distinguish, and choose right from wrong, rational from unreasonable, and good from evil. Thomas Reid – whose work was profoundly influential in American law and science – expressed a worldview that would have been highly congenial to Jacksonian Democrats, particularly those living in the northwestern territories. Explaining that the "knowledge that is necessary to all, must be attainable by all," Reid declared that any rational person could, therefore, expect "from the analogy of nature" that a knowledge of morals was equally "necessary to all men."[9] That faculty, common to all human beings, would enable them to lead virtuous lives and would guide them to make good laws for their communities. This notion that a study of nature could yield insights into religion, and that direct observation of human societies could reveal correct and just laws, was entirely compatible with democratic doctrine. After

[7] Toni Vogel Carey, Howard Schweber, and Sylvia Hoffert explain that the Common Sense philosophers were required reading in every American college, and, more to the point, that their ideas constituted the dominant worldview in antebellum America. Toni Vogel Carey, "Scotland and Harvard Yard: The Dominance and Decline of Common Sense" (paper presented at the Princeton Theological Seminary Bicentennial Celebration, Scottish Common Sense Philosophy and the Natural Law Tradition in America, Princeton, NJ, September, 6–9, 2012); Schweber, "The 'Science' of Legal Science," 430, 444; Sylvia D. Hoffert, *When Hens Crow: The Woman's Rights Movement in Antebellum America* (Bloomington: Indiana University Press, 1995), 46–47.

[8] Susanna Blumenthal locates the notion of an innate moral faculty specifically in the Scottish Enlightenment, whereas John Mikhail locates it more generally in Enlightenment or even Western philosophical tradition. The literature on the influence of Scottish Enlightenment philosophy is immense. See: Susanna L. Blumenthal, "The Mind of a Moral Agent: Scottish Common Sense and the Problem of Responsibility in Nineteenth-Century American Law," and "Metaphysics, Moral Sense, and the Pragmatism of the Law," both in "Forum: Consciousness and Culpability on Trial," *Law and History Review* 26, no. 1 (Spring 2008): 99–159, 177–85; and John Mikhail, "Scottish Common Sense and Nineteenth-Century American Law: A Critical Appraisal," in "Forum: Consciousness and Culpability on Trial," *Law and History Review* 26, no. 1 (Spring 2008): 167–75.

[9] Thomas Reid, *Essays on the Intellectual Powers of Man*, ed. Derek Brookes (1785; repr. University Park: Penn State University Press, 2002), 554, quoted in Daniel N. Robinson, "James Wilson and Natural Rights Constitutionalism: The Influence of the Scottish Enlightenment," *Natural Law, Natural Rights, and American Constitutionalism*, http://www.nlnrac.org/ (accessed October 2, 2014).

all, any person who could observe nature, society, or even one's fellow human beings would be able to make judgments and express opinions.

It would be a mistake to view this worldview about the nature of law and political power as a well-thought-out, consciously constructed system. Their fundamental cosmology, which centered on nature's God, whose providential goodness had been proven beyond doubt through the brilliant success of the American founding, worked well with the principles of Jacksonian democracy and popular sovereignty.[10] Yet northwesterners interpreted these ideas in a rough-and-ready manner, cobbling together a wide variety of philosophies and methods of reasoning. Where the previous chapter explained the fundamental philosophical and religious frameworks for democratic self-governance, this chapter focuses on the way northwesterners tried to make sense of both law and power from within a patchwork of ethics, reason, and politics. Still, according to most of the people addressing the problem of governance and justice in their constitutions, both law and power were part of the same well-balanced system and ought to be in perfect harmony with revealed faith.

Whether they admitted it to themselves or not, however, the delegates and their constituencies experienced serious dilemmas when they attempted to draw logical conclusions about self-government and justice from scientific observations. If all persons had similar innate abilities to perceive and to reason, alongside an inborn ability to judge right from wrong, then how would one cope with the notion of individual free will? What explained the sharp political divisions (even within parties) that plagued the Northwest?

The end purpose of constitutional convention debates about the frame of government and the rights of the people had to revolve around the correct distribution of power. On a more pragmatic level, one had to find a way to keep political power out of the hands of one's opponents. When pressed, most northwesterners appeared strangely reluctant to address the idea of political power directly. Yet they still talked about power (in a general sense) all the time: as a force of nature that could be quantified, controlled, and then wielded to do good, and as a moral energy, channeled through legitimate authority, such as state governors, legislators, or judges, to allow political communities to govern themselves. Most would have agreed that power ought to be wielded to achieve both prosperity and freedom for political communities. In the wrong hands, of course, power could be exercised in the service of greed, oppression, and corruption. Political power, if directed through parties, constitutions, courts, and legislatures, would determine the future economic and political direction of the state and would control all questions of rights and governance.

[10] James Q. Whitman explains that revolutionary-era lawyers, lawmakers, constitutional delegates, and political theorists were cobbling together disparate and incongruent philosophies. James Q. Whitman, "Why Did the Revolutionary Lawyers Confuse Custom and Reason?" *University of Chicago Law Review* 58, no. 4 (Fall 1991): 1321–68.

At the same time both the delegates and their constituencies also understood that popular sovereignty – the people's will – had to remain the driving force that channeled political power. Managing these two ill-suited teams, in a politically divided and swiftly growing region, was a Herculean task. Moreover, although the practical aims of the Whig and Democratic Party platforms overlapped a great deal, there were fundamental differences in the underlying philosophies about political power. Democrats wanted to exercise power through popular sovereignty, while Whigs (and after 1854, Republicans) wanted to do so through more centralized state control. True, all political parties had to base their definitions of power on the same fundamental ethical and legal frameworks, but they argued over the best way to distribute and harness that power in the service of a prosperous and free community. It all began with an inherited, "unwritten" system of English common law whose foundations rested on time-honored tradition, but was now in conflict with a new system – a scientific, rational set of laws that had been published, and could therefore be read and judged, by the citizens of the antebellum Northwest. Power that could not be "read" (in the sense of printed party platforms, statutes, or published court decisions) could not be properly allocated. The notion of a scientific government framed according to the dictates and maxims of reason had a long history in American government, one that the antebellum northwestern delegates shared with the framers of the U.S. Constitution. What was different now was a new habit of mind: the enthusiastic popular participation in science, and the growing rejection of English common law tradition and precedent.[11]

Before General Arthur St. Clair moved into the Northwest Territory in 1785 to take up his autocratic rule, the Illinois and Miami lived in the region, trading with a few hundred French habitants and English fur traders and coping with the unlawful squatters who trespassed on their lands. As a result of the inevitable conflicts over land, St. Clair decided to demolish Indian land rights and in 1789 negotiated an illegal treaty with some members of the Iroquois, Wyandot, Delaware, Ottawa, Chippewa, Potawatomi, and Sauk, which forced them off their lands and delivered their property to federal and territorial government rule.[12] By then the

[11] Michael Kammen observed that the eighteenth-century American idea about government as a type of machine "had its origins in Newtonian science." *A Machine that Would Go of Itself: The Constitution in American Culture* 3rd ed., (New Brunswick, NJ: Transaction, 2009), 17, 59, 88. On the relationship between rising faith in the scientific nature of law and the reaction to codification, see Morton J. Horwitz, *The Transformation of American Law, 1780–1860* (Cambridge, MA: Harvard University Press, 1977), 257; see also, Perry Miller, *The Life of the Mind in America from the Revolution to the Civil War* (New York: Harcourt, Brace & World, 1965), 99–121.

[12] Richard White, *The Middle Ground: Indians, Empires, and Republics in the Great Lakes Region, 1650–1815* (1991; repr., New York: Cambridge University Press, 2011); Eric Hinderaker, *Elusive Empires: Constructing Colonialism in the Ohio Valley, 1673–1800* (New York: Cambridge University Press, 1997); Laurence M. Hauptman, *Conspiracy of Interests: Iroquois Dispossession and the Rise of New York State* (Syracuse, NY: Syracuse University Press, 1999); Kevin Patrick Kopper, "Arthur St. Clair and the Struggle for Power in the Old Northwest, 1763–1803" (PhD

Continental Congress had already established the common law via the Northwest Ordinance. In 1795, St. Clair and the federally appointed territorial judges passed laws formally adopting the common law of England, to remain in force through the entire Northwest Territory.[13] Indeed, every American colony, and later, every new state except Louisiana, passed reception statutes: laws that explicitly adopted English common law and delineated how much English precedent would become law.[14] The Northwest Territory adopted the Virginia reception statute of 1776, which declared that the common law would be followed "until repealed by legislative authority," verbatim.[15] The problem was that the American colonies, and later territories and states, inherited English common law without the underlying English court system and tried to set it up in a new context – a cultural and geographic milieu that (particularly in the newer western territories) had come to life without an established civic infrastructure, and without a clear social hierarchy.[16]

Most Americans understood the common law as a series of "unwritten" English judicial decisions, separate from and often in conflict with the statutes passed by their legislative assemblies. Still, they revered the foundational principles of English common law, which protected the right to private property as the basis of civilized society. Any citizens had the right to dispute infringements

diss., Kent State University, 2005); Gregory Evans Dowd, "Little Turtle and the Origins of a Great Native American Debate," *Northwest Ohio Quarterly* 74, no. 1 (Winter 2002): 5–21; Andrew R. L. Cayton, "Land, Power, and Reputation: The Cultural Dimension of Politics in the Ohio Country," *William & Mary Quarterly* 3rd ser., 47, no. 2 (April 1990): 266–86; Jeffrey P. Brown, "Arthur St. Clair and the Northwest Territory," *Northwest Ohio Quarterly* 59, no. 3 (Summer 1987): 75–90; Peter S. Onuf, "From Constitution to Higher Law: the Reinterpretation of the Northwest Ordinance," *Ohio History* 94 (Winter–Spring 1985): 5–33. Cayton argues that the creation of territorywide political structures paralleled U.S. government.

13 Andrew R. L. Cayton, *The Frontier Republic: Ideology and Politics in the Ohio Country, 1780–1825* (Kent, OH: Kent State University Press, 1986), 98–99.

14 See Kunal M. Parker, *Common Law, History, and Democracy in America, 1790–1900: Legal Thought before Modernism* (New York: Cambridge University Press, 2011), 117–67 (chapter titled, "Time as Spirit: Common Law Thought in the Early Nineteenth Century"). Parker defines codification as the "actualization of the people's spirit" (p. 131).

15 Theodore Clavin Pease, ed., *The Laws of the Northwest Territory, 1788–1800*, vol. 17 of *Collections of the Illinois State Historical Library* (Springfield: Illinois State Historical Library, 1925), 253. Reception statute of Virginia, May 1776: "And be it further ordained, That the common law of England, all statutes or acts of Parliament made in aid of the common law prior to the fourth year of the reign of King James the first, and which are of a general nature, not local to that kingdom, together with the several acts of the General Assembly of this colony now in force, so far as the same may consist with several ordinances, declarations, and resolutions of the General Convention, shall be the rule of decision, and shall be considered as in full force, until the same shall be altered by the legislative power of this colony." "An Ordinance to Enable the Present Magistrates and Officers to Continue the Administration of Justice, and for Settling the General Mode of Proceedings in Criminal and Other Cases till the same can be more amply provided for" (May 1776), Sec. 6, in William Waller Hening, *Hening's Statutes at Large* (Richmond, VA: 1821), 9: 127.

16 For the transatlantic relationship of the adoption and interpretation of common law in the American colonies, see Mary Sarah Bilder, *The Transatlantic Constitution: Colonial Legal Culture and the Empire* (Cambridge, MA: Harvard University Press, 2004).

on that property in a court of law. Further, individuals retained the right to make contracts with whomever they pleased (within reasonable restrictions that respected community welfare), and they expected that those contracts would be honored.[17] Courtroom adversaries were to be treated equally, and the lawyers' pleadings (formal documents they filed in court in order to institute or respond to a lawsuit) had to follow specific, time-honored patterns.[18] Judicial decisions had to follow prior judgments, even though (at the same time) judges always adapted their opinions to current circumstances. Common law judges and lawyers were part of a trained body of literate men who understood and respected the established procedures of pleading. Common law, therefore, was meant to be both reasonable and knowable, based on the straightforward notion that like cases should be treated alike. As such, for many Americans, common law harmonized nicely with the dictates of mathematical and scientific analogies.

Meanwhile, however, custom had already lost a great deal of its explanatory force in early nineteenth-century America.[19] Antebellum Americans certainly believed that custom restrained an irrepressible selfish popular will, but most no longer adhered to the notion that tradition, all by itself (that is, without a supporting foundation in the popular will), functioned as a repository for truth.[20] This was especially evident in reform speeches and conventions. For example, in the 1852 women's rights convention held in Dublin, Indiana, one of the speakers declared that the mere fact that the rule of coverture was "time-honored" was insufficient justification for its continued existence.[21]

Published law reports, alongside legal treatises and commentaries, certainly helped to clarify prior judicial decisions. But they were still judge-made law: Such laws were not subject to the popular oversight. In the early years of the republic American judges and lawyers relied on the eighteenth-century English legal theorist William Blackstone's *Commentaries* as the basis for understanding and expounding the principles of common law.[22] In 1803, St. George Tucker updated Blackstone, whom he already considered outdated,

[17] Note, "The Anti-Discrimination Principle in the Common Law," *Harvard Law Review* 102, no. 8 (June 1989): 1993. Maxwell Bloomfield also says that the common law promoted an "aggressive individualism," in *American Lawyers in a Changing Society, 1776–1876* (Cambridge, MA: Harvard University Press, 1976), 138.

[18] Lawrence M. Friedman, *A History of American Law*, rev. 3rd ed. (New York: Simon & Schuster, 2005), 50–51. Friedman stresses the importance of written codes in colonial America.

[19] See Charles L. Barzun, "Common Sense and Legal Science," *Virginia Law Review* 90, no. 4 (June 2004): 1051–92.

[20] Christian G. Fritz, *American Sovereigns: The People and America's Constitutional Tradition Before the Civil War* (New York: Cambridge University Press, 2008), 290, 400; Donald S. Lutz, *Popular Consent and Popular Control: Whig Political Theory in the Early State Constitutions* (Baton Rouge: Louisiana State University Press, 1980), 38.

[21] Indiana Woman's Suffrage Association, Record Book 1851–1886, folder 1, Indiana Historical Society, Indianapolis.

[22] Kunal M. Parker, "Historicising Blackstone's *Commentaries on the Laws of England*," in Angela Fernandez and Markus D. Dubber, eds., *Law Books in Action: Essays on the Anglo-American Legal Treatise* (Portland, OR: Hart, 2012), 26–27.

for the American context.[23] After 1826, lawyers eagerly adopted New York chancellor James Kent's magisterial four-volume adaptation of the English common law. Kent's *Commentaries on American Law*, published from 1826 through 1830 – though firmly entrenched in the English common law tradition – were immensely popular and went through at least twelve editions until 1841.[24] Kent's commentaries supplemented and expanded common law for American courts in two important ways: first, by adapting elements of Roman law (essentially, the European civil law tradition) wherever precedents were missing or unsuitable for the American context, and, perhaps more important, by instituting the practice of publishing all judicial opinions in reports rather than leaving some as oral opinions, abstracted only in digests.[25]

The American commentaries rendered English common law both accessible and comprehensible. Lawyers and legal scholars (and as we shall see, any literate citizens interested in the study or practice of law) had long complained about the "unwritten" and obscure nature of English common law precedent.[26] American lawyers who might have been able to obtain copies of Blackstone or Kent had a harder time finding detailed information on common law cases. This was particularly true for lawyers working far from centers of publication, such as New York, Philadelphia, or Cincinnati, or far from state capital libraries.[27] The Northwest Ordinance had decreed that territorial assemblies would draw upon such statutes as they needed from older eastern states, primarily Virginia and Pennsylvania.[28] But it was almost impossible to harmonize common law and the adopted statutes with the new lawsuits over property boundaries, debts, and slander (the most common bases for suits in the region). The

[23] According to Philip Girard, even English legal philosophers began to consider Blackstone outdated, almost from the moment his *Commentaries* were published. Philip Girard, "'Of Institutes and Treatises': Blackstone's *Commentaries*, Kent's *Commentaries*, and Murdoch's *Epitome of the Laws of Nova Scotia*," in *Law Books in Action*, 43–62.

[24] Carl F. Stychin, "The Commentaries of Chancellor James Kent and the Development of an American Common Law," *American Journal of Legal History* 37, no. 4 (Oct. 1993): 443.

[25] Bloomfield, *American Lawyers in a Changing Society*, 78.

[26] Gary L. McDowell, *The Language of Law and the Foundations of American Constitutionalism* (New York: Cambridge University Press, 2010), 76, 212.

[27] Barbara A. Terzian, "Ohio's Constitutional Conventions and Constitutions," in Michael Les Benedict and John F. Winkler, eds., *The History of Ohio Law* (Athens: Ohio University Press, 2004), 1: 40–57; Elizabeth Gaspar Brown, "Frontier Justice: Wayne County, 1796–1836," *American Journal of Legal History* 16, no. 2 (April 1972), 139.

[28] Sec. 5: "The governor and judges, or a majority of them, shall adopt and publish in the district such laws of the original States, criminal and civil, as may be necessary and best suited to the circumstances of the district, and report them to Congress from time to time: which laws shall be in force in the district until the organization of the General Assembly therein, unless disapproved of by Congress; but afterwards the Legislature shall have authority to alter them as they shall think fit." Northwest Ordinance, July 13, 1787; (National Archives Microfilm Publication M332, roll 9); Miscellaneous Papers of the Continental Congress, 1774–1789; Records of the Continental and Confederation Congresses and the Constitutional Convention, 1774–1789, Record Group 360; National Archives and Records Administration, Washington, DC.

judges lacked published law reports that would guide their decisions, and even if they had access to such reports, they often had no idea how to apply English precedent.[29] Local conditions were far too complicated and confused. Worse, common law was of no use in researching or resolving conflicting land claims made by citizens of foreign nations such as France and England.[30] Therefore, as the northwestern territories attained statehood, many of the legislatures repealed their reception statutes within a year or two after adoption.[31] The Ohio legislature, for example, had passed a reception statute in 1805, but immediately repealed it in 1806; the Michigan territorial assembly passed and repealed its reception statute in 1810, a quarter of a century before applying for statehood. By 1846 the Michigan legislature had adopted its own criminal code, a significant step away from relying simply on the English common law of crimes, though most of the crimes did echo those in England.[32] In 1819, the first Illinois legislature, like those of most of the other northwestern territories, adopted English law, but at the same time permitted the courts to modify and update laws "until repealed by legislative authority."[33]

That by no means solved the problem. To begin with, a chronic shortage of both published legal materials and experienced judges plagued the Northwest Territory throughout the settlement era – from the turn of the nineteenth century until Minnesota entered the Union in 1858. The lawyers who had been trained in eastern or southern law schools might have had a battered copy of Blackstone's and Kent's *Commentaries* or, if they were more prosperous, bound volumes of legal reports and digests from their home states. Others sent away for volumes, usually through a family member back east or a friendly merchant traveling to New York or Philadelphia on a buying trip. The scope of a law

[29] St. Clair and the territorial judges fought bitterly over the question of whether they could make their own laws or had only the power to adopt and publish existing ones. Andrew R. L. Cayton, "Law and Authority in the Northwest Territory," in *History of Ohio Law*, 1: 24–27.

[30] Louis Pelzer, "The Private Land Claims of the Old Northwest Territory," *Iowa Journal of History and Politics* 12, no. 3 (July 1914): 373–93. Conflicting foreign land claims are discussed in Burke Aaron Hinsdale, *The Old Northwest: With a View of the Thirteen Colonies as Constituted by the Royal Charters* (1888; repr., New York, 1891), 1: 41–46, 90, 176.

[31] James W. Gordon, *Lawyers in Politics: Mid-Nineteenth Century Kentucky as a Case Study* (New York: Garland, 1990); William T. Utter, "Ohio and the English Common Law," *The Mississippi Valley Historical Review* 16 no. 3 (Dec. 1929): 321–33; John M. Goodenow, *Historical Sketches of the Principles and Maxims of American Jurisprudence, in Contrast with the Doctrines of the English Common Law on the Subject of Crimes and Punishments* (Steubenville, OH, 1819), vi.

[32] Paul Finkelman and Martin J. Hershock, eds., *The History of Michigan Law* (Athens: Ohio University Press, 2006), 9.

[33] "An Act declaring what Laws are in force in this State," (February 4, 1819) *Laws Passed by the First General Assembly of the State of Illinois* (1819), 1. Beverley W. Bond, *The Civilization of the Old Northwest: A Study of Political, Social, and Economic Development, 1788–1812* (1934; repr., Freeport, NY: Books for Libraries Press, 1970). Jeffersonian Republican aversion to concentrated power is discussed in Cayton, "Law and Authority in the Northwest Territory," *History of Ohio Law*, 1: 310–31; and Utter, "Ohio and the English Common Law," 321–33.

library was also an important factor when young lawyers chose a mentor.[34] Lawyers and judges who lived close enough to a capital city with a mercantile and law library might have had access to published statutes or law reports, but circuit-riding judges – who would have had to travel on horseback to the more remote districts – might not have been able to consult the volumes they needed to arrive at their decisions. And if they encountered "novel" problems, according to Ohio Supreme Court Judge Jacob Burnet, then the judges were often forced to "legislate remedies."[35] Before statehood, that was illegal in any case. Although the Northwest Ordinance established a system of governance that blurred the boundaries among the functions of government, it did not permit lawmakers or judges to write new laws. The English common law provided the foundation for the way Americans understood their legal system, but it could not be transplanted wholesale to the Northwest. The resulting muddle would require the combined forces of lawmakers, judges, constitutional convention delegates, and citizens to resolve.

Technically the convention delegates were supposed to be framing their governments, distributing power, and enshrining rights. They had to take into account the U.S. Constitution, the Northwest Ordinance, and common law, alongside statute laws and state constitutional provisions they had inherited from the older states. In practice, however, the convention and committee deliberations also had to respond to an enthusiastic and often quite irascible public will. As has been observed in an earlier chapter, the delegates confronted an immense amount of both internal and external pressure, in addition to coping with the personal exigencies of their families, businesses, farms, and law offices. The main problem was that northwesterners, inside and outside the conventions, inside and outside the circle of civic participation, did not distinguish between public and private law. Constitutional conventions often found themselves pressed into service as legislative bodies. As such they were sometimes in conflict with the legislatures that had called them into being. After all, legislatures sometimes created or altered other branches of government. Meanwhile, judges ruled on cases that then became custom and law. And all of these legal structures had to respect and include the nonlegal systems as well. Those included religious beliefs, social customs and prejudices, shifting ideas about race and the roles of married women, and new ideas about economic relationships.[36]

[34] See Mark E. Steiner, *An Honest Calling: The Law Practice of Abraham Lincoln* (DeKalb: Northern Illinois University Press, 2006), 45–46. Steiner discusses that Lincoln and his law partner William H. Herndon most likely subscribed to a service that provided "American reprints of English legal treatises" in serial form: That is, they received a portion of a treatise in uncovered pamphlet form through the mail. Presumably when they had received the entire treatise they would have it covered locally and thus save on shipping costs.

[35] Jacob Burnet, *Notes on the Early Settlement of the North-Western Territory* (New York: 1847), 304–6.

[36] Historians of nineteenth-century American legal history usually separate the development of public and private law. That is, they study constitutional conventions and legislative bodies

In the antebellum United States, the rise of popular sovereignty and the pervasive Jacksonian democracy engendered a sense that literate citizens ought to be able to judge for themselves whether a law was constitutional, whether a judicial decision was correct, and whether a legal pleading had been followed accurately.[37] Antebellum Americans, particularly those living in new territories and states, talked a great deal about what they considered the old-fashioned common law. At its heart, this discussion was an examination of the scientific, rational, and "readable" nature of law. Americans considered common law rulings "unwritten" and therefore "unreadable." Even so, the common law still depended on and functioned through official documents. Writs – judicial orders that directed jailers, lawyers, sheriffs, or even other courts to perform some action – would allow a case to proceed. For example, a writ of Mandamus required an inferior court or government agency to perform (or refrain from performing) an action within its realm of authority. Other writs could correct an error, such as a writ of habeas corpus, which required that the body of the prisoner be taken before the court and the captor provide proof of his authority to hold the prisoner. Writs further supported the idea that law should be predictable and reliable.[38] Lawyers were required to file written pleadings – standard forms that set forth the points of dispute between the two parties, in a correct manner such that both parties would know precisely what was at issue and how to formulate a defense.[39] The standard

primarily as constitutional or legislative history, and focus on private law in terms of economic questions, especially as the law developed from judicial decisions and from the gradual reshaping of American common law. See, Horwitz, *Transformation of American Law*; for the development from English to American common law, see William E. Nelson, *Americanization of Common Law: The Impact of Legal Change in Massachusetts Society, 1760–1830* (Athens: Georgia University Press, 1994); for impact of judicial decisions on common law to "release [economic] energy," see Willard Hurst, *Law and the Conditions of Freedom in the Nineteenth Century United States* (Madison: University of Wisconsin Press, 1956; repr., Madison: University of Wisconsin Press, 1984.) While legal historians have accepted a dichotomous view of American law, the difference between the rights and disputes of citizens (private law) and those that directly involve the government (public law), Kermit Hall "seeks to show the relationship among them" as they have been "shaped by legal institutions" and as they have become part of the "legal culture." Kermit L. Hall, *The Magic Mirror: Law in American History* (New York: Oxford University Press, 1989), 7–8.

37 A writ is a nonnegotiable legal instrument, essentially a "rule" or "principle," issued by a monarch. See Bernadette Meyler, "Towards a Common Law Originalism," *Stanford Law Review* 59, no. 3 (Dec., 2006): 551–600; Howard Pashman, "The People's Property Law: A Step toward Building a New Legal Order in Revolutionary New York," *Law and History Review* 31, no. 3 (August 2013): 587–626; Horwitz, *The Transformation of American Law*; James R. Stoner, *Common Law and Liberal Theory: Coke, Hobbes, and the Origins of American Constitutionalism* (Lawrence: University Press of Kansas, 1992). For criticisms of Blackstone's theoretical weaknesses and sources, see Michael Lobban, "Blackstone and the Science of Law," *The Historical Journal* 30, no. 2 (June 1987): 311–35.

38 Kenneth W. Dam, "Legal Institutions, Legal Origins, and Governance," (working paper, John M. Olin Law & Economics Working Paper No. 303, 2nd Ser., University of Chicago Law School, 2006).

39 Michael Moffitt gives a helpful definition of the history and role of pleadings, in "Pleadings in the Age of Settlement," *Indiana Law Journal* 80, no. 3 (Summer 2005): 727–77.

forms of both writs and pleadings, in both common law and equity courts, were available to lawyers through handbooks and learned by example during their apprenticeships. Although guidebooks promising to render "every man his own lawyer" had been popular in England and America since the middle of the eighteenth century, such books were less useful in the antebellum Northwest, where complicated real estate deals and disputes over debts required consultations with experts.

Moreover, there were two types of common law operating in the Northwest. The inherited English common law functioned in the realm of philosophy. That is, those northwesterners who revered the traditional common law restraints on governmental intrusion into contracts, and its protections of private property, also linked English common law precedent directly to the Christian Bible. By contrast, those men who argued for codification of common law – turning precedent into statutes – used English common law as a type of "straw man," which they set up against a rational democratic popular will. Both of those arguments disregarded (though probably only as a rhetorical device) the development of American common law, created by American courts.[40]

That conundrum gave rise to a paradox: The very precision and predictability of the written forms of pleadings and writs appeared to render the common law accessible and fair. At the same time, since the 1750s, American legal scholars including James Wilson and the Litchfield Law School professor James Gould had praised the common law for its flexibility and its adaptability to the American context. And that very adaptability, paradoxically, was due to the "unwritten" nature of common law. No law or constitution could address every local circumstance; judges would have to be able to resolve particular disputes between individual citizens. Some form of unwritten law was necessary to counteract harsh, inflexible statutes.[41] Both Story and Kent pointed out the flexibility inherent in both common law and chancery courts, though both agreed that equity courts afforded far more discretion than common law precedents.[42] According to Judge Joseph Story, a widely respected authority often quoted by both Democrats and Whigs, that flexibility formed the principal

[40] Modern legal historians focus on American common law in their research, tracing the evolution of legal doctrines through judicial decisions. Horwitz, *Transformation of American Law*; Nelson, *Americanization of Common Law*; Hurst, *Law and the Conditions of Freedom*. See also, Robert A. Ferguson, *Law and Letters in American Culture* (Cambridge, MA: Harvard University Press, 1984), 11. Ferguson repeats (from Boorstin's introduction to a modern edition of the *Commentaries*) the view that Blackstone stands second only to the Bible in importance in providing "literary and intellectual influence on the history of American institutions."

[41] The eighteenth-century law professor James Gould, for example, and other contemporary legal scholars explicitly stated that unwritten laws were necessary to counterbalance harsh/inflexible statute laws. See Ellen Holmes Pearson, *Remaking Custom: Law and Identity in the Early American Republic* (Charlottesville: University of Virginia Press, 2011); and Parker, *Common Law: History and Democracy in America*.

[42] John Theodore Horton talks about both Story and Kent in *James Kent: A Study in Conservatism 1763–1847* (1939; reprint, Union, NJ: Lawbook Exchange, 2000), 203.

justification for continuing to base American laws on the English common law. The colonies had adopted the general principles of common law but always suited its edicts to their "times and needs."[43] The common law, Story explained, was far more flexible than legislative law; an individual judge could study the local facts of a case, particularly in commercial transactions, and reach a finely grained, just decision. By contrast, lawmaking bodies – who only met annually or biannually – addressed broader issues, generally only after they had become urgent. Both Story and Kent asserted the necessity of common law as a "safe guide" when legislatures simply did not possess the maneuverability to handle economic or demographic challenges, and when the new territories had not yet been able to establish functioning legal and judicial bodies.[44]

According to both Story and Kent, the common law was particularly useful to new societies: It was amenable to translation into new contexts precisely because it was based on what Story called "universal truths."[45] This point about universal truths became a crucial turning point in arguments on both sides: that is, both for repealing common law, as well as for retaining it (albeit in an updated and rationalized form.) Many antebellum Americans, especially those who lacked the traditional faith in custom as a framework for just laws, began to express stringent criticisms of English common law. Those who found it arbitrary, outdated, and unsuitable to the American legal system felt that the English tradition had little relevance for a modern democracy. In their analysis, whether aggressive or defensive, commentators often casually conflated American common law (which had developed through judicial decisions) with inherited English common law. American legal scholars such as Hugh Swinton Legaré, for example, found the common law's flexibility disturbingly whimsical and even antidemocratic and condemned it as a "mass of irregularities and inconsistencies." Legaré explicitly denied that the common law rested on "immutable principles," or that it had been "deduced immediately from the rules of natural justice."[46] According to the widely shared ideas about scientific reasoning, correct principles were to be deduced from direct observation. This callous rejection of custom as a foundational justification

[43] See Morris L. Cohen, "The Common Law in the American Legal System: The Challenge of Conceptual Research," *Law Library Journal* 81, no. 1 (Winter 1989): 13–32; and William B. Stoebuck, "Reception of English Common Law in the American Colonies," *William & Mary Law Review* 10, no. 2 (Winter 1968): 393–426.

[44] See Lord Irvine's discussion of Kent in, Alexander Andrew Mackay Irvine, *Human Rights, Constitutional Law, and the Development of the English Legal System* (Portland, OR: Hart, 2003), 213.

[45] R. Kent Newmyer explains in depth Joseph Story's commitment to what he calls "universalism," which he defines as the notion that universal truths undergirded both the common and statute laws. R. Kent Newmyer, *Supreme Court Justice Joseph Story: Statesman of the Old Republic* (Chapel Hill: University of North Carolina Press, 1985), 183–4.

[46] Quoted in Michael H. Hoeflich, "Law and Geometry: Legal Science from Leibniz to Langdell," in Steve Sheppard, ed., *The History of Legal Education in the United States: Commentaries and Primary Sources* (Pasadena, CA: Salem Press, 1999), 2: 596–601.

angered conservative northwestern Whigs such as Indiana delegate Othniel Clark, who believed that there were "many truths embodied in the common law, which existed far anterior to the common law itself," and it was wrong to "overthrow these truths, and reject them" for no better reason than the fact that "the experience of ages [had] sanctioned" them.[47]

At the same time, paradoxically, antebellum Americans believed that immutable principles were derived from divine creation, and that Christianity and common law were deeply interwoven. That link between Christianity and common law provided a firmer basis for faith in the common law than either custom or tradition could offer. For example, in defense of the common law tradition, conservative delegates frequently referred to the Old and New Testament injunction that man and wife should become one flesh. There were other biblical references as well: for example, in the fact that neither the New Testament nor the common law sanctioned bloodshed (in arguments against capital punishment.) Indiana delegate John Barron Niles found a poignant link between Christianity and common law in the time-honored judge's charge that it was better to let ninety-nine guilty men go free than to allow one innocent man to suffer.[48] The notion that common law and Christianity were interlinked had already taken hold among many American legal theorists such as Simon Greenleaf, James Kent, Joseph Story, and Washington Van Hamm. Simon Greenleaf's *Testimony to the Harmony of Christianity, Science, and Law*, published in 1834, went so far as to assert that the "Christian religion is part of our common law, with the very texture of which it is interwoven."[49] Ohio lawyer Washington Van Hamm (a Virginia-born and -educated lawyer), who became famous through his powerful defense of the common law and his outspoken opposition to the codification movement, declared that if any statute or common law were to contravene the Ten Commandments, he would "cheerfully admit that our laws should be so altered as to conform to this great code of Divine Law."[50] According to Joseph Story, the study of law ought to be exactly like biblical exegesis. Any "minister of religion" had to study the Bible in the original Greek and Hebrew; any theologian had to master the commentaries and "first principles of interpretation." Specifically, this manner of interpretation combined a deep knowledge of Scripture with an understanding

47 H. Fowler, *Report of the Debates and Proceedings of the Convention for the Revision of the Constitution of the State of Indiana* (Indianapolis, IN: 1850), 1: 168 (hereafter Indiana 1850).

48 Indiana 1850, 1: 187.

49 According to Daniel Blinka, Greenleaf "laced together" religion, human science, and law. Daniel D. Blinka, "The Roots of the Modern Trial: Greenleaf's *Testimony* to the Harmony of Christianity, Science, and Law in Antebellum America," *Journal of the Early Republic* 27, no. 2 (Summer 2007): 303. For Hoffman's widely read law school lectures and their grounding in both the ethics and the science of law, see Thomas L. Shaffer, "David Hoffman's Law School Lectures, 1822–1833," *Journal of Legal Education* 32, no. 1 (1982): 127–38.

50 Richard F. Hamm, *Shaping the Eighteenth Amendment, Temperance Reform, Legal Culture, and the Polity, 1880–1920* (Chapel Hill: University of North Carolina Press, 1995), 35.

of the cultural and historic context in which Christianity arose.[51] For Story, there had never been a period in history "in which the Common Law did not recognize Christianity as lying at its foundation."[52]

The difficulty was to find a way to tie the science of law together with an appreciation for God's creation of the human faculty for observation and reasoning. Joseph Story had directly compared common law to scientific discovery and inductive experimentation. "In truth," he explained, the common law, "as a science, must be forever in progress; and no limits can be assigned to its principles or improvements." Like all human knowledge, the common law could never be "fully learned," just as the human mind could never "compass all human transactions." The "true glory" of the common law was that it was "flexible, and constantly expanding with the exigencies of society." This expansion of knowledge, through rational decisions that took into account new conditions and local circumstances, inspired advancement because it "daily present[ed] new motives for new and loftier efforts."[53] Of course that was also true of American common law. These commentators did not distinguish American from English common law, so their critique was aimed more generally at the idea of a precedent-based judicially created law. Certainly no one argued that courts should be done away with, though as Chapter 5 will reveal, northwesterners were eager to evaluate and critique all manner of legal and nonlegal codes: statute laws, constitutional provisions, judicial decisions, popular customs and traditions, and prejudices.

An Ohio Supreme Court Judge, Frederick Grimke (formerly of South Carolina, brother to the famous anti-slavery sisters, and now living in Chillicothe) was positive that intelligence, in the service of a scientific understanding of the law, would be beneficial to the "machine of government."[54] Yet for Grimke, usefulness could never be fully separated from principle: any analysis of custom, statute laws, and principle "ought always to be conjoined." One discovered what was useful by contemplating what was right, and what was right by understanding what was "truly useful."[55] In the northwest, that was precisely the crux of the debate over common law; was it indeed capable of reform and improvement? Did it reflect timeless religious truths? Or did it

[51] Joseph Story, *The Miscellaneous Writings, Literary, Critical, Juridical, and Political of Joseph Story, LL.D.* (Boston, 1835), 21.

[52] Newmyer, *Joseph Story*, 183.

[53] Story, *Miscellaneous Writings*, 526. Story was explicitly writing about the development of common law in England and America here. He observed that Americans had added "two hundred volumes" of reports in the past two decades. Daniel J. Hulsebosch explains that James Kent had a similar view, in *Constituting Empire: New York and the Transformation of Constitutionalism in the Atlantic World, 1664–1830* (Chapel Hill: University of North Carolina Press, 2005), 277.

[54] Frederick Grimke, *Consideration upon the Nature and Tendency of Free Institutions*, ed. John William Ward (Cambridge, MA: Belknap Press, 1968), 74. According to Ward, Frederick Grimke never used the accent mark in his last name, 3.

[55] Grimké, *Nature and Tendency of Free Institutions*, 469.

represent an aristocratic, hidebound, and therefore irrational system of law in the new western territories?[56] Reformers never saw this as a problem; they believed that justice to all human beings was both obedience to divine decree and reasonable. Iowa Republican delegate John Parvin explained that whenever someone acted "contrary to nature and to common law" there had to be a positive enactment because "God created man in his own image." All laws, both written and unwritten, had to conform with Divine decree. Therefore, since the "Almighty never created a slave," slavery was contrary to the "law of nature, the unwritten law, and the common law."[57] Parvin was a farmer, not a lawyer. In his youth, however, he had served as a clerk to the Bloomington, Iowa (later Muscatine) District Court, which suggests that he understood the difference between common law, statute laws, state constitutional provisions, and religious doctrine. Yet he appeared to be arguing for external constraints on the common law rooted in Christianity, science, and reason.[58]

How did northwestern convention delegates of both parties resolve this congeries of principles and methods? After considerable struggle – and not always successfully – they tried to align the sensible, natural, time-honored precepts of English common law with the development of statutes suitable for the new western territories. In 1817, Ohio Circuit Judge Benjamin Tappan, an ardent

[56] *Report of the Proceedings and Debates in the Convention to Revise the Constitution of State of Michigan, 1850* (Lansing, MI: 1850), 703 (hereafter Michigan 1850); Indiana 1850, 2: 1155. For adaptability of common law to economic needs, see Nelson, *Americanization of the Common Law*. Joseph Story makes a similar point in his report on Jeremy Bentham's letter on codification. See Jeremy Bentham and others, *Codification of the Common Law: Letter of Jeremy Bentham and Report of Judges Story, Metcalf and Others*, ed. David Dudley Field (New York: 1882). For Jacksonian descriptions of common law as aristocratic, see David M. Gold, "The General Assembly and Ohio's Constitutional Culture," in *History of Ohio Law*, 1: 95–96.

[57] W. Blair Lord, *The Debates of the Constitutional Convention; of the State of Iowa, Assembled at Iowa City, Monday, January 19, 1857* (Davenport, IA: 1857), 2: 704–5 (hereafter Iowa 1857). Parvin was a temperance activist and one of the founders of the Republican Party. Benjamin F. Gue, *History of Iowa: From the Earliest Times to the Beginning of the Twentieth Century*, vol. 4, *Iowa Biography* (New York: Century History, 1903), 209–10. On this specific point – that is, the conjunction of "what was useful" with "what was right" – legal scholars have long argued for a fundamentally instrumentalist development of American law. While constitutional and political historians are careful to describe reformers' focus on natural law arguments, I contend that northwesterners were talking about law as a whole – public law, private law, and other versions of legal and nonlegal codes. As a result, northwesterners could take into account ethical and rational frameworks alongside pragmatic economic goals. As will be discussed in Chapter 5, northwesterners used this broader worldview as a way of redefining their relationship to courts, legislatures, and one another as private citizens.

[58] In *Americanization of the Common Law*, William E. Nelson argued that the law of early Massachusetts was characterized by shared communal values, values that were then shattered by modernizing forces, immigration, diversity, and free market capitalism. Throughout the antebellum era, it is possible to find a similar shared values approach in the Northwest, which includes a faith in reason, Christianity, and science, and sometimes forced northwesterners to blur or even reconceive the boundaries between different types of written and unwritten laws.

anti-slavery Free Soiler, reasserted the centrality of English common law in the everyday actions of Ohio courts. In his opinion in *Ohio v. Lafferty*, a criminal case that indicted Lafferty for the sale of unwholesome food, Tappan explained that the common law of England had always been the law of the colonies and states of North America, "so far as it was applicable to our more free and happy habits of government." By then Ohio had already repealed its reception of English Common law (in 1805), and Tappan was making a point about Ohio law being out of tune with the rest of the Union. He defined the common law as a set of "maxims, principles, and forms of judicial proceeding, which have no written laws to prescribe them, but which, founded on the laws of nature and the dictates of reason, have by usage and custom, become interwoven with the written laws." In this way he directly linked common law jurisprudence to the notion of maxims and the laws of nature. Nature and reason were, if not identical, certainly closely interwoven. Order and civilization rested on both precedent and on a common sense set of practices and laws.[59] Because Divine Providence had ordained both the natural order of society and had imprinted the faculty of reason on human minds, there was no inherent conflict between man-made laws such as constitutions and statutes (which were never entirely separate in the minds of northwesterners) and laws based on religious faith.

Moreover, if the common law was founded on nature, then nature had placed human beings precisely where they ought to be. And because nature had been created by God, the common law therefore made perfect sense. Arguing against married women's property rights, Indiana delegate Othniel Clark explained that the "great mass of men and women are placed precisely in the condition which the common law recognizes, by the very nature of things." Therefore, through both natural and religious laws, fathers and mothers had been "compelled to unite their utmost exertions to feed, and educate, and protect their families." His opponent Robert Dale Owen (Figure 3.1), however, turned that argument on its head. While he explained that he would not go so far as to argue that God favored civil law over common law, he still believed that "the general tenor and tendency put forth by the Author of Christianity" were far more harmonious with civil law, though as a freethinker, Owen probably did not believe that law, reason, and religion had to harmonize.[60]

Some sharp lawyers exploited this idea of nature, common law, and reason as a loophole to explain almost any divergence from precedent. For example, Illinois lawyer Stephen A. Douglas mocked the unsuitability of English common law to the new western setting. "Our lawyers may have read in English books that, by the common law, all waters were deemed navigable so far as the tide extended and no further." But they should also have learned – and he was

[59] *Ohio v. Lafferty* (1817) in Benjamin Tappan, *Cases Decided in the Courts of Common Pleas in the Fifth Circuit of the State of Ohio; Commencing … 1816* (Steubenville, OH: 1831), 82–83.

[60] Indiana 1850, 1: 472, 825. For a similar argument to Owen's, see Indiana 1850, 2: 1188. For a similar argument to Othniel Clark's, see Wisconsin 1847, 581.

FIGURE 3.1. Robert Dale Owen (1801–1877) served as a delegate to the 1850 Indiana constitutional convention. Born in Scotland, son of the utopianist Robert Owen, Robert Dale Owen served in the Indiana House of Representatives and in Congress (1843–1847), and later as Minister to the Kingdoms of the Two Sicilies (1853–1858). "Owen is wearing a dark suit and bow tie. His overcoat has a quilted lining. He has whiskers along his jawline."

Source: W. H. Bass Photo Company Collection (P 0130). Courtesy of the Indiana Historical Society.

quoting Blackstone here – that the law was "founded upon reason, and where reason failed the rule ceased to exist." Therefore, if the common law contravened local truths, it was simply no longer reasonable. According to Douglas, if English common law had originated near Lake Michigan, it would not have operated, "because the tide did not flow."[61] Douglas was reinterpreting his sources to justify a highly pragmatic end; he wanted Lake Michigan to serve as a major transportation conduit, so he elided – indeed, probably deliberately – Blackstone's insistence on natural law and reason as superior to statute laws. Other politicians, of course, talked about common law in a less instrumentalist way. Perhaps these political debates over the nature and definition of different kinds of legal and nonlegal codes left the field free for men like Douglas to bend

[61] *North-Western Democrat* (Saint Anthony, MN), February 8, 1854.

the law to their own ends. For Blackstone, as for other eighteenth-century common law proponents, immemorial custom represented "natural law," in that the original writs – dating back five hundred years – provided the grounds for law. The law was founded on reason, but for literate citizens, rational understanding depended upon published reports, digests, and writs and therefore grew in response to the local context, rather than flowing from one universal source. Collecting facts from existing law and applying reason to analyze the situation at hand would yield a just, equitable, and ultimately coherent framework of statute laws and legal decisions.[62] In the American context, however, common law tradition had already been severely called into question, partly because the revolutionary generation had already jettisoned so much of English precedent, and partly because Americans rejected what they called "excessive veneration" of English common law.[63] Almost every northwestern state attempted or considered some effort at codifying common law in statutes. The Indiana, Michigan, Ohio, and Wisconsin state constitutions included a charge for law reform and set up law reform committees when they first issued the call for a new state constitution.[64]

Delegates to northwestern conventions balanced many interests as they made decisions about their state's organic law. Occasionally they revealed their underlying philosophies and commitments as they spoke of the religious or scientific reasons supporting their opinions. But as did jurists in midwestern courts, delegates rarely followed a single cause, such as a procapitalist instrumentalist agenda identified by the legal historian Morton Horwitz. Instead they attacked the issues before the convention with a variety and mixture of personal views and convictions, all of them colored by concern about meeting with their constituents' approval.[65]

Beginning in the 1820s legal reformers in Massachusetts and New York began to advocate a legal code (that is, a published set of statutes) that would take the place of common law. Massachusetts lawyer Robert Rantoul argued that the common law had its origin in "folly, barbarism, and feudality" and

[62] Lobban, "Blackstone and the Science of Law," 311–35.

[63] Norman W. Spaulding, "The Luxury of the Law: The Codification Movement and the Right to Counsel," *Fordham Law Review* 73, no. 3 (Dec. 2004): 983–96; Charles M. Cook, *The American Codification Movement: A Study of Antebellum Legal Reform* (Westport, CT: Greenwood Press, 1981), 61.

[64] For a discussion of the role of reason and Christianity in American common law, see Perry Miller, *The Life of the Mind in America from the Revolution to the Civil War* (New York: Harcourt, Brace & World, 1965), 2:159–161.

[65] For the instrumentalist view see Morton Horwitz, *The Transformation of American Law, 1780–1860* (Cambridge, MA: Harvard University Press, 1977; repr., New York: Oxford University Press, 1992). Peter Karsten has forcefully countered Horwitz's theory of economic determinism on the part of nineteenth-century jurists. Instead he identifies a judiciary of the heart, midwestern and southern jurists who favored precedent over giving in to economic change and equity over the harsh rules of common law. Peter Karsten, *Heart versus Head: Judge-Made Law in Nineteenth-Century America* (Chapel Hill: University of North Carolina, 1997).

was therefore unsuited to a modern, democratic America. Because it was based on "unwritten" precedent, common law allowed too much judicial power. The common law was explicitly not a science, he declared; nor was it even knowable. Because no one could tell what the common law was, one could not even "call it a law." For Rantoul, a legitimate law was a "rule of action," but any rule that was "unknown" could not legitimately govern any man's conduct. He mocked those who called common law "the perfection of human reason" and stated that the common law was "the perfection of Human Reason just as alcohol is the perfection of sugar." Indeed, drawing out the temperance metaphor, English common law was nothing more than "reason double distilled till what was wholesome and nutritive becomes rank poison," and that plunged "its victims into mazes of error."[66]

Opponents to codification, in their turn, ridiculed the notion that an entire body of experience could be reduced to a "pocket volume" of published legal codes.[67] In the northwestern conventions, conservative delegates explicitly denied that their constitution-building project should have any connection with codifying common law. Any codification risked enshrining common law irrevocably in the state's charter and would become difficult to amend. Iowa delegate Amos Harris, for example, explained that because judicial decisions had already set the precedent, there was nothing further required of the convention. The delegates had not gathered to "codify the decisions of the courts," nor to "place in the magna charta of this State the ipse dixit of any judge upon the bench." On the contrary: The delegates had gathered in Iowa City for a "peaceable and amiable revolution," whose sole purpose was to distribute the power of the government, and not to "go back into the cobweb and worm eaten systems that have prevailed heretofore."[68]

For Americans this was the fundamental issue: unwritten law could not be subjected to public scrutiny. More to the point, they could no longer find a rational scientific justification for privileging precedent over direct personal observation or individual conscience. Antebellum Americans insisted upon publishing their statutes, their legal decisions, and their constitutions: all of which they believed were part of one coherent system, based on both reason and the popular will. In reality, that did not mean that the common law ceased to exist. Courts quickly proceeded to create a new common law based on the interpretation of statutes. But according to a Vandalia, Illinois, newspaper.

[66] Robert Rantoul, *An Oration Delivered before the Democrats and Antimasons,... at Scituate, on the Fourth of July, 1836* (Boston: 1836), 37–38. For the historical role of reliance on reason in legal reform and codification, see Sanford H. Kadish, "The Model Penal Code's Historical Antecedents, *Rutgers Law Journal* 19 (1988): 521.

[67] Henry T. Terry, *Some Leading Principles of Anglo-American Law Expounded with a View to Its Arrangement and Codification* (Philadelphia: 1884), 636.

[68] Iowa 1857, 1: 149. I have not been able to discover Amos Harris's political affiliation. He voted for black exclusion. The phrase 'ipse dixit" means an unsupported allegation: The only proof of the statement is the fact that the person stated it.

because Americans wrote their own constitutions, they were able to establish an internally coherent frame of government: one that was answerable directly (and only) to the people – and not to some vague, unwritten, and therefore uninterpretable body of rules. By contrast, the British constitution (though England had "none to speak of," according to the editor) existed only by "inference from what a half hundred hirelings have written," in which they all contradicted one another, and were further "contradicted by daily practice in every transaction of State."[69] In essence, the written constitutions, published in newspapers and weighty multivolume convention proceedings, along with explicit legal codes, now required that the northwestern legal system be aligned with rational, consistent, public, and repeatable experiments. And it was the people who brought this machine to life through the mechanism of organized political parties that expressed the popular will.[70] If power could not be mechanized, then it would be easily subverted to irrational and immoral ends. Even so, as previously observed, neither delegates nor their constituents liked to talk explicitly about political power. As a result, they conflated the ideas of political power and law in their rhetoric. Both power and law were meant to be based on scientific, rational grounds.[71]

Political power drove the system as a positive force pulsating through an engine constructed by the people and their delegated representatives. According to the Michigan judge of the U.S. District Court Ross Wilkins, if properly taught to the youth of the region, such political mechanisms would be both simple and straightforward, like mathematical axioms or the laws of nature.[72] Wilkins directly linked the idea of the plain truths of democratic political power with the clear-cut theories of science: Students Could Be taught the basic elements of political power in precisely the same way they learned the principles of "steam and telegraphic power." Thus every student would discover for himself "how

[69] *Illinois Intelligencer* (Vandalia), July 26, 1831.

[70] Although the term "machine politics" did not exist before the early twentieth century, many British and American political commentators relied on the idea of a "political machine" to explain the function of party politics in democratic governance. See, for example, the writer and political commentator William Leggett (originally from New York, but then living in Edwardsville, Illinois), who thought that any public institution, such as a prison or post office, could – through mismanagement and corruption – become a "political machine." William Leggett, *A Collection of the Political Writings of William Leggett* (New York, 1840), 1: 245.

[71] According to Willard Hurst, American law provided for a "release of energy" by remaining relatively flexible. See James Willard Hurst, *Law and the Conditions of Freedom in the Nineteenth Century*. Morton J. Horwitz argued that American law bent to exigency, allowing for the rise of free market capitalism, the shattering of community, and resulting inequality. See Morton Horwitz, *The Transformation of American Law*. William Nelson explained that community norms collapsed after the revolution, giving rise to understandings of law that coincided with advancement of the individual, in *Americanization of Common Law*.

[72] This is discussed in detail in Chapter 2. Throughout the nation the mechanical and natural sciences, including geology, chemistry, astronomy, soil science, and optics, were being taught in academies and colleges.

simple the principle, and how plain to every comprehension" both mechanical and constitutional forces worked. This approach would "teach the sovereignty, nurture the root," and so "enlighten the power of the ballot box."[73] Similarly, the pungently Democratic *Galena Jeffersonian* stated that the Illinois democracy would "insist upon the adoption of a common platform of constitutional equality, in which all classes, creeds, sects, and conditions" (though evidently not races) would be "mutually protected." Such a constitution would advocate "plain provisions, plainly worded, so that whether declaratory or prohibitory," everyone could "easily comprehend them." The writer explained that law had to be "clearly defined, conformable to moral precepts, and designed to promote the general welfare." The *Jeffersonian* sharply contrasted clear wording with vague provisions, which were "capable of any and every construction, ... avarice, selfishness, and dishonesty" could impose upon them.[74] The northwestern delegates and their constituents knew that law had to be founded in Christianity, that it had to be capable of being studied and interpreted by any literate citizen, and that it had to follow the precepts of nature.[75] Perhaps for this very purpose, God had instilled in them a capacity for reason and an innate knowledge of right and wrong.[76]

Unless citizens possessed the capacity and right to read their laws, and unless the laws were published in a lucid and comprehensible manner, the democratic experiment would fail. Since the early years of the republic politicians had argued that an educated and responsible popular sovereignty protected the nation from revolutions. True, a rough-and-ready western republicanism was constantly boiling in the background, attempting to wrest power from their governors, legislatures, and judges. But widespread literacy would keep the process somewhat under control and would also ensure that the principles of good government would prevail. A year after the 1830 national nullification

[73] Judge Ross Wilkins, U.S. District Court of Michigan, "Fundamental Laws of the United States and the Rights and Duties of Citizens" (speech given at the dedication of the State Normal School, Ypsilanti, MI, October 5, 1852), in Document No. 6, "Annual Report of the Superintendant of Public Instruction," 84–89 (quotation on 88), in *Joint Documents of the State of Michigan, For the Year 1852* (Lansing, MI, 1853).

[74] *Jeffersonian* (Galena, IL), April 9, 1846.

[75] William Paley, *Principles of Moral and Political Philosophy*, 5th ed. (London, 1788), 2: 411, quoted in Bloomfield, *American Lawyers in a Changing Society*, 86. The Scottish philosopher John Erskine held similar views: "The interpretation of laws ought not to depend on critical learning, or the subtle distinctions of schoolmen: for they are directed to the whole body of people; and therefore ought to be construed in that sense which the words most obviously suggest to the understanding." John Erskine, "Of Laws in General," in Alexander Broadie, ed., *The Scottish Enlightenment: An Anthology* (Edinburgh, UK: Canongate Books, 1997), 612.

[76] Keith Lehrer, "Thomas Reid on Common Sense and Morals," *Journal of Scottish Philosophy* 11, no. 2 (Sept. 2013): 109–30. A cursory survey of the constitutional conventions in several other nonnorthwestern states revealed very little reliance on religious arguments. For example, the 1821 New York constitutional convention journal reveals only one reference to the Bible, *Reports of the Proceedings .... of the State of New York* (Albany: E. & E. Hosford,1821), 463.

crisis (and shortly after the violent revolt in France that overthrew Charles X), the young Indiana law student George Augustus Bicknell recorded in his diary that even though the "mass of the people" in the region were "comparatively well informed," they still experienced an occasional "Convulsion" that shook the "whole political fabric to its centre." What would happen in a place like France, among the "ignorant rabble that composed so great a portion of her population?" Clearly, the American upheavals and riots indicated a growing need for literacy among the people.[77]

This careful distinction between "written" and "unwritten" law reveals the difficulties of defining the rules by which northwesterners wanted to govern themselves. The Cincinnati judge Timothy Walker, who had founded a school of law in his hometown, edited and published the widely read *Western Law Journal*, a publication that captured regional concerns about law reform. Walker's journal was popular throughout the nation but exposed an original western point of view about codification, one that focused more explicitly on the problem of unwritten law. Walker's main issue of contention was that common law was not "written law," even though it appeared in reports, digests, and Blackstone's famous commentaries. For Walker, the glaring problem was that common law was not part of a legislative enactment and therefore eluded popular control. Like educators and newspaper editors, Walker believed that law should be "as simple, as intelligible, and as certain as possible."[78] The sheer impossibility of knowing this vast body of judicial decisions rendered common law both unreasonable and "unreadable." Specifically, it was "illegible" to the ordinary citizen because all of the reports, abridgments, and digests added up to more than a thousand volumes. Surely it would be possible to distill the principles from all this and to publish them? He did not doubt that it would be a vast labor of immense difficulty and would take the mind of an American legal genius like a Webster, a Marshall, or a Story; yet impossibility and difficulty were "not synonymous," he declared, particularly not in the go-ahead democratic Northwest.[79] That was the core problem: The people had no direct say over the common law because, as a system of canonical precedent without a foundation in, or the authority of the popular will, it could not be critiqued. For Walker, common law was nothing more than "judicial legislation" – that is, an encroachment by judges on democratically elected legislatures, and therefore

[77] George Augustus Bicknell, diary entry, December 31, 1833, manuscript diary, Bicknell MSS, Lilly Library, Indiana University, Bloomington. The Irish American law reformer William Sampson asserted that the common law system was meant for illiterates, whereas in America the people had a duty to study law and exert some control over it. Bloomfield, *American Lawyers in a Changing Society*, 77–78.

[78] Timothy Walker, "Codification, Its Practicality and Expediency: Being a Report Made to the Cincinnati Legislative Club, in 1835," *Western Law Journal* 1, no. 10 (July 1844): 433–44; Timothy Walker, "Law Reform in Ohio," *Western Law Journal* 1, no. 1 (Oct. 1843): 37 (quotation).

[79] Walker, "Law Reform in Ohio," 37.

both undemocratic and subversive of first principles.[80] Walker explained that "in the nature of things" no system of law could be complete. Once judges lost their discretion to formulate legislative solutions to every new situation, the many faults of the common law would become manifest. Given Walker's eminent judicial career, his authorship of legal treatises, and his founding role in the Cincinnati Law School, it is unlikely that he was dismissing all of English and American common law on the simple grounds that it was "unwritten" and therefore subject to judicial whim. He may have been making a populist argument, one that would appeal to a wide range of Jacksonian lawyers, but in the end, he still believed that one had to apply the dictates of reason to any analysis of the law.[81]

In opposition, conservative lawyers including Ohio's Washington Van Hamm did not want to consider the law as a purely mechanistic or architectural system. There had to be room for customs that had accrued over time and that would be responsive to local needs and feelings. Van Hamm condemned the notion that all law could be codified, precisely because the law was not a science; nor would codification ever be able to render it one.[82] For Van Hamm, the codifiers' mechanistic approach to the law was in itself irrational. Legal research could and ought to be conducted along scientific lines, yet in its present state, American law was still full of "incongruities, ... technicalities, ... fictions, and ... abuses." The average literate citizen ought not to attempt such a project, because the science of law was simply far beyond the comprehension of people who had never studied law. Codifying the common law would be like placing medical science into the hands of persons who had never studied physiology or anatomy. For all these reasons, Van Hamm explained, it was simply impossible for the law to exist without the aid of "some unwritten" law – what he called the customs, practices of the people – in addition to the "old laws, and old rulings" by judges in such an "old settled" community as Ohio, at that point the oldest state in the Northwest, at a little more than forty years of age.[83]

Michigan Territory attempted law reform in 1810, but after achieving statehood in 1835, the first legislature adopted the common law without further debate. In Illinois reform efforts came up for discussion shortly before the state

[80] Spaulding, "Luxury of the Law," 985–87.

[81] See, Thomas C. Grey, *Formalism and Pragmatism in American Law* (Leiden, Netherlands: Brill, 2014), 209.

[82] Washington Van Hamm, "Codification, Its Practicality and Expediency: In Answer to Judge Walker's Report," *Western Law Journal* 1, no. 12 (Sept. 1844): 529–42. At Walker's request, Washington Van Hamm published his response in September 1844. Van Hamm lived in Zanesville but had studied law at the University of Virginia. I have been unable to determine his political affiliation, but his opposition to codification and his tenure as president of the Young Men's Colonization Society of Muskingum County, Ohio, suggest that he was a Whig. See, *The African Repository and Colonial Journal* 11 (1835): 158.

[83] Van Hamm, "Codification, Its Practicality and Expediency," 529, 542.

legislature passed a law calling for a constitutional convention. In 1845 several petitions from Marshall and Peoria Counties demanded that the Illinois legislature repeal the common law in its entirety. The petitions went to the judiciary committee, whose members admitted that the signers were probably well intentioned, but dismissed their petitions as essentially ignorant and counter to the public good. The petitioners' "investigation of a subject with which they cannot be presumed to be very conversant has led them to conclusions inconsistent with sound policy, unsustained by reason, and incompatible with truth." The committee foresaw "incalculable" harm to society in the suggestion and declined to repeal the "benign and wise provisions of that very Common Law of which they complain."[84]

The lawyer delegates in the Illinois, Indiana, Michigan, Ohio, and Wisconsin conventions attempted to take up the problem of codifying statutes. Even though the Illinois legislature had dismissed the idea of repealing the entire body of the common law a little more than two years earlier, the 1847 constitutional convention briefly debated amending, altering, or even abolishing the common law. The committee on law reform voted to "abolish all differences between courts of chancery and common law" and then, in a sweeping motion, asked for the "abolition of all English laws now in force."[85] The committee also recommended a provision forcing the legislature to codify the law and declaring that after 1870, the common law or indeed "any English statute" would have no further force, but that provision did not survive in the 1847 state constitution.[86] If Democrats sounded the codification bugle, then they usually relied on time-honored party metaphors. For example, Samuel Hayes, the youngest member of the Illinois convention – a Democrat from Tennessee – explained that he had always "lived in" the elaborately finished, detailed, "costly edifices" of the common law. He likened the common law to a Gothic cathedral (no doubt a thinly veiled jab at the Catholic faith). But now, when he had subjected the common law to anxious scrutiny, he felt himself to be a Martin Luther, casting light on a despotic and tyrannical system. Indeed, he also compared himself to Galileo and many other famous scientists, explorers, and inventors. Hayes now wanted to revert to the "grandeur of nature" that

[84] Ferris Forman, "Report of Committee on the Judiciary," January 28, 1845, in *Reports Made to the Senate and House of Representatives of the State of Illinois, at Their Session Begun and Held at Springfield, December 2, 1844* (Springfield, IL: 1845), 187.

[85] Arthur Charles Cole, ed., *The Constitutional Debates of 1847*, vol. 14 of *Collections of the Illinois State Historical Library* (Springfield: Illinois State Historical Library, 1919), 160 (hereafter Illinois 1847). Samuel Hayes reported this to the committee of the whole, although he did not agree with the majority report.

[86] *Journal of the Convention, Assembled at Springfield, June, 7 1847 … For the Purpose of Altering, Amending, or Revising the Constitution of the State of Illinois* (Springfield IL: 1847), 309–10. Any English common law that had not been explicitly reenacted would have no force; all laws had to be published. This article was proposed by the Illinois 1847 Committee of Law Reform.

stood behind the Gothic edifice: simple, straightforward, knowable law.[87] But when he began taking English legal history back to the reign of James I, several of his colleagues indignantly protested that he had already used up his time. In the end the convention decided to leave the whole matter to the legislature.[88]

In Minnesota – on both sides of the fractured convention – the common law came in for more stringent criticism: Both Republicans and Democrats condemned it as outdated and useless. Republican delegate Thomas Wilson worried that if the constitution did not provide for a strong libel law, for example, and the legislature failed to do so, then they would be under the old "ridiculous" common law.[89] And on the Democratic side, Minnesota delegate M. E. Ames declared the common law barbaric and a feudal relic.[90] Yet the final compromise constitution (that is, the document hammered out by delegates sitting in rooms at the opposite sides of the building) contained no mention of common law or codification.[91]

In the Northwest the common law survived its assailants.[92] It would have been an unimaginably difficult task to codify all of common law into civil and criminal statutes. The infrastructure was simply not established, and the

[87] He may have been paraphrasing Blackstone here, but Blackstone was referring to an "old Gothic castle," and Hayes to a Gothic cathedral. See Paul O. Carrese, *The Cloaking of Power: Montesquieu, Blackstone, and the Rise of Judicial Activism* (Chicago: University of Chicago Press, 2003), 124–49 (chapter 6, "A Gothic and Liberal Constitution: Blackstone's Tempering of Sovereignty," quotation on 125).

[88] Illinois 1847, 890–96.

[89] T. F. Andrews, *Debates and Proceedings of the Constitutional Convention for the Territory of Minnesota, to Form a State Constitution Preparatory to Its Admission into the Union as a State* (St. Paul, MN: 1858), 91 (hereafter Minnesota 1857 Republican).

[90] Francis H. Smith, *The Debates and Proceedings of the Minnesota Constitutional Convention ...* (St. Paul, MN: 1857), 309 (hereafter Minnesota 1857 Democrat).

[91] Norman Spaulding holds that legal reformers such as David Dudley Field won a victory but one limited by a conservative bar that largely controlled the codification process. Spaulding, "Luxury of the Law," 990–91. For a more favorable view of the results of legal reform see Bloomfield, *Lawyers in a Changing Society*, 87–88.

[92] Even among proponents of codification, Charles Cook is careful to point out that men of "moderate" views predominated, men like Joseph Story, who was willing to contemplate limited codifications of well-settled common law principles in selected fields. The handful of lawyers Cook calls "radical" codifiers for the most part shared with the "moderates" the view that the actual work of codification could be safely entrusted only to commissions of legal experts. Charles M. Cook, *The American Codification Movement: A Study of Antebellum Legal Reform* (Westport, CT: Greenwood, 1981), 80–88. Norman Spaulding describes the idea of codification as a way of creating access to the law by allowing ordinary Americans to understand and use it. "A perfect legal code would require no intermediaries." Spaulding, "Luxury of the Law," 985. According to Charles Warren, the Field Code was a by-product of the "wave of democracy and reform" that had brought about the Chartist movement in England and the European revolutions of 1848. Charles Warren, *A History of the American Bar* (Boston: Little, Brown, 1911), 532. See also, Jed Handelsman Shugerman, *The People's Courts: Pursuing Judicial Independence in America* (Cambridge, MA: Harvard University Press, 2012), 100–1; and Lawrence M. Friedman, "Law Reform in Historical Perspective," *Saint Louis University Law Journal* 13, no. 3 (Spring 1969): 351–72.

codification proponents never strong or organized enough. The most serious obstacle to codification in the Northwest, however, was simply that the common law stood for and harmonized with deeply held religious beliefs. The connection between Christianity and the common law would become eminently clear in the debates over married women's property rights, but it was also evident in all conservative defenses of the common law tradition. These emerging political justifications for retaining the common law had no relation to economic (or what legal scholars call instrumentalist) motivations, but because they insisted on a broader, more holistic interpretation of the nature of law, may have created space for judges to use the law to "release energy." Meanwhile, the opponents of codification, consisting primarily of experienced and well-educated Whigs, continually hammered home the notion that the common law was based on *both* reason and divinely inspired truth. In defending grand juries, for example, Indiana Whig delegate Othniel Clark declared that the truths underlying the common law were older than the law itself.[93] His colleague Daniel Kelso (also a Whig) agreed. No competent lawyer would think of consulting the statute books until he had thoroughly educated himself in common law, which, according to Kelso, provided the "fundamentals upon which all laws were based." For Illinois Whig Thompson Campbell the common law stood as the "pride and glory of the world for ages."[94] And his colleague Patrick Ballingall went so far as to state that the common law granted citizens the right to vote.[95] In the early years of statehood the Ohio legislature had codified a few common law elements and modernized procedures, but the whole remained a patchwork.[96] Ohio detractors condemned codification as a "humbug of the first water," primarily because it would be so expensive to hire attorneys to reduce the immense details of the common law to published volumes.[97] In the 1850 Ohio convention, Leadbetter regretted the scoffing he was hearing and said that constitutional delegates, of all men, ought to respect the "old landmarks" of the law. Furthermore, there was no reason a declaration or pleading could not be written in clear language.[98]

In a lecture on lawyers' "Moral Nature and Practical Connection with Civil Society," the lawyer and minister the Reverend John T. Brooke of Cincinnati

[93] Indiana 1850, 1: 168

[94] Illinois 1847, 791.

[95] Illinois 1847, 389.

[96] Josiah Blackmore directly places the movement with Jeremy Bentham and John Mill as well as his son, John Stuart Mill, who strongly critiqued Blackstone's *Commentaries* and denied the existence of any human law that was not explicitly and "positively" proclaimed by a lawmaking body. Josiah H. Blackmore II, "Not from Zeus's Head Full-Blown: The Story of Civil Procedure in Ohio," in *History of Ohio Law*, 1: 446–47.

[97] *Daily Chronicle and Atlas* (Cincinnati, OH), June 27, 1850.

[98] J. V. Smith, *Report of the Debates and Proceedings of the Convention for the Revision of the Constitution of the State of Ohio, 1850–51* (Columbus, OH: 1851), 1: 576 (hereafter Ohio 1850).

explained why the repeal of the common law would never work in a modern commercial society. In theory, it was probably true that a simpler and more "efficient judicial machinery" ought to be feasible. No doubt an "amiable and benevolent theorist" could dream up a simple tribunal, composed of "a few upright judges," who would somehow adjudicate according to "the plain rules of equity, without ponderous formalities, and minute pleadings, or the professional conflicts of lawyers." But would such a scheme work in practical terms? Real life was far more complicated than that, and judges would find it difficult to discern immutable truths in the midst of a constantly changing legal landscape. According to Reverend Brooke, even the most honest judges would have a hard time figuring out how to decide each case without guidance of "precedents and specific rules," and their lack would make it very difficult for to "follow or apply general principles."[99]

In the long run, and in spite of the general failure of codification, the debates over the conflict between the common law and statute law forced the delegates and their constituents to take a hard look at the role of constitutions in interpreting and managing both the clarity and the consistency of northwestern law.[100] The core purpose of codification was to render the law both legible and useful to citizens: that is, to allow the people to assert sovereignty over statute laws and lawmakers. They wanted to build their legal institutions, not inherit them. At their heart these fights were not so much over English or American common law. They were battles over the moral and rational aspects of self-government. For the delegates, that meant resolving practical problems, such as the need to limit the size, scope, and power of lawmaking bodies. The delegates simply could not jettison a system that they all knew and understood (particularly the lawyers among them) and that harmonized with both Christianity and reason. Reading and understanding the law meant assuming the authority over the structure of government, and establishing the precise enumeration of rights and limitations. In that way citizens would retain control over the very distribution of power in itself. Common law reform, at its core, remained an effort to read, understand, and control the documents and the institutions that distributed power.

When northwestern convention delegates and their constituencies created and authorized lawmaking bodies, they understood that the legislators needed enough power to fulfill their functions. But every ounce of that strength had to be delegated, as a conscious and deliberate choice, by the citizens to their delegates. Citizens kept a strict watch over power and doled it out in grudging increments. Therefore, every attempt at reforming and democratizing legislative assemblies, administrative offices, judgeships, and courts always revolved around the belief that the people maintained sovereignty and delegated power.

[99] John T. Brooke quoted in, Timothy Walker, "The Morals and Utility of Lawyers," *Western Law Journal* n. s. 2, no. 1 (Oct. 1849): 3.

[100] Indiana 1850, 2: 1136.

Northwesterners may have been uncomfortable about admitting the need to claim political power for its own sake. Even so, all of them (Whigs, Democrats, Republicans, utopian reformers, black activists, Indians, and women's rights reformers) understood that power – both political and natural – was the key element in framing a government that would work for them. In nearly every state constitutional convention, both in the northwestern region and throughout the nation, the style committees proposed that the phrase "all political power is inherent in the people" be included in the preambles or at the head of the Bill of Rights.[101] All of the northwestern conventions agreed. Some version of the phrase appears in every antebellum northwestern constitution.[102] It is worth emphasizing that none of the convention journals, and none of the petitions or letters to the delegates, reveal any explicit discussion of power as an economic force, but the inference is nevertheless fairly clear.

According to Indiana lawyer Robert Milroy, power (which he did not define) was a mutually transformative force that changed both the governed and the government. For Milroy, who identified himself as a "progressive" Democrat in the 1850 convention, economic and political powers were part of a grand natural organism. These two forces – the people and their representatives in government – acted upon and shaped one another. Therefore, those in charge needed power to accomplish their aims, but power could therefore be both mutually beneficial and harmful. Power was always traded back and forth between the government and citizens. Milroy stated this proposition as a reciprocal chemical reaction: "The rulers act upon the people, and the people act upon the rulers." The forces that acted upon both rulers and the ruled included economic, material, political, and economic elements, in one grand design: "Capital, the amount of subsistence, soil, situation, domestic and foreign relations, facilities and disadvantages, existing institutions." All these elements influenced the "deliberations and policy of a nation," and through those both government and laws. In their turn, government and the laws influenced the "condition and relations of a country, and may very rapidly change its aspect, as we ourselves have seen in the United States."[103]

So long as political power was applied scientifically or mechanically, antebellum Americans (particularly Jacksonian Democrats) believed it could transform ideas into rational, wholesome improvements. Northwesterners knew that this process would begin in their own region, a view shared by many easterners and southwesterners as well. "In a few years," the *American*

101 Willi Paul Adams mentions that the eighteenth-century constitutional conventions frequently included a statement in their preambles. Willi Paul Adams, *The First American Constitutions: Republican Ideology and the Making of the State Constitutions in the Revolutionary Era* (Lanham, MD: Rowman & Littlefield, 2001), 27, 134.

102 Nelson, *Americanization of the Common Law*, 91.

103 Review of *The Government and Laws of Every Country Are the Effect, not the Cause, of the Condition of the People*, by Francis Ocane, *Western Review and Miscellaneous Magazine* 1, no. 1 (Aug. 1819): 18.

Monthly predicted, "the political power of this nation will rest in the valley of the Mississippi." Of all the western states, Illinois was the "choicest and loveliest, ... destined to be to the West what the West will be to the Union."[104] Power manifested as naturally occurring transformative elemental forces such as sunlight, steam, heat, or chemicals. Natural energy, like human will, could convert innate potential into survival or even wealth. Northwesterners gladly applied natural lessons to politics and framed political questions as scientific equations or more pragmatically as mechanical processes.[105] Frederick Grimke often referred to the machinery of the law in *Considerations upon the Nature and Tendency of Free Institutions*, a legal treatise he published in 1848. For Grimke, government functioned as a machine, but had to take into account the intangibles of "manners" (by which he meant, societal customs, traditions, and mores). This was precisely how English common law would work in the American context: It would provide the moral underpinnings for the rational mechanism of good government.[106]

So in politics, in economics, and in their daily lives, Americans understood that power was necessary to channel beneficial improvements and to control harmful forces. At the same time this process required the logical application of reason. Observing nature was the key to understanding God and would yield insights into the character of power and by extension into good government and justice. For example, American farmers were deeply interested in learning about transformative elements such as lime, which an agricultural journal described as "looser [in] nature than clay or loam, so that it has the power of improving tenacious soils mechanically," rendering them less "tough and solid." Similarly, the *Farmer's Cabinet* described how the sun, during the "season of its greatest power," invigorated plants to develop fruitfully.[107] Railroad journals often carried articles meant to advertise lands for sale to the public, which discussed improving the "productive power of soils" in their agricultural columns.[108] And an Indiana booster pamphlet extolling the virtues of Cannelton, a town in southern Indiana on the Ohio River, as a site of steam manufacturing of cotton cloth, described steam power in the same magical, effervescent terms as soil or nature. Because steam power was "created by art" it was "indefinite, perhaps we might say infinite, in its capacity for extension

[104] J. H., "The Illinois College," *American Monthly Magazine* 2, no. 1 (April 1830): 36–37. This article focused on the new Illinois College. The *Monthly* was published in Boston and Philadelphia.

[105] Academy and college science textbooks, specifically in "natural philosophy" and physics, stressed Newtonian mechanics, for example, and would have prepared a well-educated man such as Milroy to see the world as a place where law, art, science, and religion were all part of a grand system that could be understood through a system of analogies.

[106] Grimke, *Nature and Tendency of Free Institutions*, 69.

[107] Kenderton Smith, "On Mildew, Blight, or Rust: the Cause and Remedy," *The Farmer's Cabinet, and American Herd-Book* 5, no. 9 (April 15, 1841): 294.

[108] *The Illinois Central Rail-Road Company Offers for Sale over 2,400,000 Acres Selected Prairie, Farm and Wood Lands ... of the State of Illinois* (New York, 1855), 5–8.

and may go on to increase as long as human art and industry ... continue, as long as wood grows or water runs."[109]

Analogies from nature had long had explanatory power in American scientific thinking. When northwesterners were pondering the challenges of building their new governments, they freely employed analogies to machines, engines, buildings, chemical forces, and the laws of physics.[110] Such comparisons were especially poignant in law reform arguments, primarily because the speakers were so acutely aware of all of the tools those in power wielded, for good or evil. The physical voice, the act of speaking, and the give and take of democratic deliberation could be analogized as similarly transformative scientific forces. "The living speaker is a powerful engine," declared one of the delegates to the Colored Citizens' Convention in Columbus, Ohio. A man's voice and gestures could convert the energy of ideas into useful results.[111] A vote, whether expressed as a spoken word, a printed manifesto, or even a handwritten signature on a failed petition, represented an expression of will. Addressing the 1850 Ohio constitutional convention directly, the resolution demanded that they grant the right of suffrage to "*say* at the ballot-box who shall make and execute the law by which he is governed."[112]

Both black people's rights and women's rights activists frequently reverted to this notion of power as a force that could be unleashed at the service of reform, through the medium of speech. In a letter she wrote to the 1850 Salem Ohio Women's Rights Convention, a woman named R. M. M. Sanford denounced the irrational and unjust laws that prevented women from participating in democratic government. She explicitly linked political power to abstract virtues that served as a conduit for reform and framed her critique as a series of interrogatories: "Ask man," she demanded, "what it is that legislates, and he will answer justice, knowledge, common sense; what it is that speaks, and he will answer, intellect, moral power; what is it that votes, and he will reply, understanding."[113]

[109] "Calcareous Manures," *American Farmer: Monthly Magazine of Agriculture and Horticulture* 13, no. 11 (May 1858): 355; "Means of Increasing the Productive Powers of Soils," *American Railroad Journal and Advocate of Internal Improvements* 4, no. 12 (March 1835): 184–85; Hamilton Smith, *Cannelton, Perry County, Ind.: ... Its Natural Advantages as a Site for Manufacturing* (Louisville, KY: 1850), 17.

[110] George H. Daniels explains that analogy was the proper way to interpret nature: The "unknown" would correspond with the "known," and thus enable the scientist to draw conclusions based on direct observation. That is, if two entities corresponded in one way, then one might predict that they would correspond in other ways as well. Daniels, *American Science in the Age of Jackson*, 167–72.

[111] *State Convention of the Colored Citizens of Ohio, Convened at Columbus, January 10–13, 1849* (Oberlin, OH: 1849), quoted in Herbert Aptheker, ed., *A Documentary History of the Negro People in the United States* (New York: Carol, 1990), 278.

[112] *Minutes of the State Convention of the Colored Citizens of Ohio, Convened at Columbus, Jan. 15th, 16th, 17th, and 18th, 1851* (Columbus, OH: 1851), 16. Emphasis added by author.

[113] Robert W. Audretsch, ed., *The Salem, Ohio 1850 Women's Rights Convention Proceedings* (Salem, OH: Salem Area Bicentennial Committee and Salem Public Library, 1976), 33–34.

Only radical reformers were willing to address the question of acquiring political power in an unapologetic manner, though their language and metaphors reflected cultural assumptions of their own time. For example, every northwestern black rights convention held in the 1840s and 1850s declared openly that the whole point of rising up against oppression was to take hold of political power, and all of them placed the responsibility for making this effort squarely on the shoulders of the black population of the Northwest.[114] A Colored Citizens' convention in Michigan held in 1843 declared that their state's black people had become nothing more than the "passive instruments of all laws, just or unjust" and would remain so while they had no "instrumentality in [the laws'] formation."[115] By contrast, women's rights activists argued that political power ought to be used to protect the physically and economically weak. Women who spoke at the 1853 Cleveland National Women's Rights Convention dissected political power and argued that it was both a creative and a protective force, which could balance social inequalities: "The rich man's wealth is itself power and will generally secure him from danger. The poor man has no protection except in political power, and he above all others should have political power." Thus women required more political power because they possessed less physical strength: The fact that "woman is physically weaker than man is the very reason why she should have more political power than man, rather than that she should be deprived of civil influence and power altogether."[116] Evidently this writer was willing to accept a place on a pedestal and defined power as a defensive moral weapon. Similarly, in another women's rights convention, which took place in Ohio in 1851, one of the speakers declared that women's warfare lay only in the "field of thought."[117]

Every tool on a farm or in a workshop could become destructive and had to be handled with respect and care. Mechanisms and natural forces figured as beneficial elements in American civic life, but they possessed dangerous attributes as well. The historian Michael Kammen observed that eighteenth-century Americans likened the U.S. Constitution to a rational machine that transmitted power in a neutral fashion.[118] By the mid-1830s, however, when Americans throughout the nation began revising their state constitutions, the word "engine," when linked to political and constitutional questions, could take on ominous connotations. This was true of both Whig and Democrat pamphlets and newspaper editorials. For example, an anonymous excerpt from a

[114] See conventions minutes for Indiana, Michigan, and Ohio, in Philip S. Foner and George E. Walker, eds., *Proceedings of the Black State Conventions, 1840–1865* (Philadelphia: Temple University Press, 1979), vol. 1.

[115] Foner and Walker, *Proceedings of the Black State Conventions*, 1: 186.

[116] J. H., "The Illinois College," 30–39 (quotation on 36); T. C. Leland, *Proceedings of the National Women's Rights Convention held at Cleveland Ohio …* (Cleveland, OH, 1854), 28.

[117] Audretsch, *Salem, Ohio, 1850 Women's Rights Convention Proceedings*, 266.

[118] Michael Kammen, *A Machine That Would Go of Itself: the Constitution in American Culture* (New York: Knopf, 1986; repr., New Brunswick, NJ: Transaction, 2009), 17.

Whig political convention worried that unless local conditions were carefully observed and respected, the "power of taxation" might inadvertently become "a most oppressive and ruinous engine of power." Machines had to be calibrated after careful observation and experience. Similarly, Joseph Story's textbook for young people explained that the militia could become "an engine of tyranny" unless Congress maintained a tight control. Another well-known textbook stated that impeachment could become an "engine, capable of being used for political purposes." Engines were built and designed by mechanics, and anyone capable of sound understanding ought to be able to understand how they were constructed and how to use them. The problem was to find a way to balance the weight of tradition, especially one resting on immutable religious and mathematical principles, against the demands of powerful political alliances and goals. In a society that was struggling (however unsuccessfully) to rid itself of centuries of legal traditions, while entrusting both lawmakers and constitutional delegates with the task of inscribing timeless and "immutable" principles in its foundational charter, that would prove to be a daunting task.

4

Lawmakers

The moment the new Ohio state constitution was ready to go to the voters for ratification, the Democratic *Cleveland Daily Enquirer* told its readers to study it carefully: After all, it was the work of their "own hands." The people had elected the delegates and had weighed in throughout the time the convention was in session, so they could take both credit and responsibility for the work. Because all government was "entirely the contrivance of the people," it stood to reason that the people would now have to participate as equal partners in controlling the political power that had been framed out by the convention. According to the *Enquirer*, a democratic constitution resembled the terms and conditions of an "article of partnership," something easily understood by any prosperous farmer, lawyer, or businessman. Political and legal power was emphatically not a mystery; nor was it a threat. Just as one would consult a lawyer when striking a business deal, one would have to leave some transactions to the legislature. All this was simple, mathematical, and comprehensible by any literate citizen. It was unbecoming of Americans to "look away up at this subject, as though it were a star that might elude ... investigations by its immeasurable highth, nor to shade [their] eyes as though it were a sun that would dazzle [them]." Any competent northwesterner had to stare the question of political power "straight in the eye." The point was neither to become frightened of tyrannical misuses of power, nor to attempt to handle all of the business of government without help.[1]

This chapter examines that question: How did citizens and convention delegates talk about the delegation of power? Obviously some power had to be delegated, in the same way that farmers had to rely on a merchant to sell their crops or a lawyer to handle their conveyances or debt collection. But a "free,

[1] *Cleveland Daily Enquirer*, March 17, 1851. Lawrence Friedman suggests that a constitution can function as a treaty that ratifies compromises. Lawrence Friedman, *A History of American Law*, 3rd rev. ed. (New York: Touchstone, 2005), 75, 333.

independent, and sovereign people," as they often called themselves, had to delegate power in the right direction: upward from the people, not downward from the political representatives.[2] Where eighteenth-century theorists defined the political "power of attorney" as an instrument that enabled lawmakers to bind their constituencies to their agreements, antebellum Americans turned that definition on its head. The constituencies were delegating their wishes to their lawmakers and to their judges, who were obligated to fulfill the public will.[3] This belief that legislators were "agents" who carried out the popular will crossed party lines in the Northwest. For example, a staunch Whig newspaper published in Bloomington, Illinois, quoted from the Tenth Amendment, which limited the federal government's sphere of influence to expressed (that is, written) powers. But even this Whig editor made it clear that the people remained sovereign: The "whole constitutional and legislative authority" existed in them. Sovereignty could only be wielded through "agents deliberately selected to carry their expressed will into effect." What better way to describe the relationship between a legislature and a free people, than to "call it a Power of Attorney?" As a legally binding relationship, a power of attorney granted the "sole authority, given by the people, to organize and administer government ... instituted for their own safety and convenience."[4] This was precisely how contemporary legal textbooks described the power of attorney: Just like the popular consent to be governed, it was a "grant of power" that could be revoked

[2] A version of that phrase occurs in every northwestern state constitution except Minnesota's.

[3] Edmund S. Morgan, *Inventing the People: The Rise of Popular Sovereignty in England and America* (New York: Norton, 1988), 39, 215, 240. According to Christopher Terranova, under the Articles of Confederation, the members of the Continental Congress believed that delegates took instruction from their constituencies. Christopher Terranova, "The Constitutional Life of Legislative Instructions in America," *New York University Law Review* 84, no. 5 (Nov. 2009): 1331–74. Terranova also quotes John Adams, who stated that the power of attorney was delegated by the people, although he admitted that instructions were nonbinding (pp. 1339–40). Richard A. Primus states, however, that the founders understood that legislatures had to be chosen by and responsible to the people, and that rights had to be articulated in order to ensure that legislatures would not become arbitrary or tyrannical bodies. He argues that the federal Bill of Rights was explicitly meant to strengthen popular control over legislatures. As early as 1776 the North Carolina and Pennsylvania state constitutions provided for the people's right to instruct their representatives. Richard A. Primus, *The American Language of Rights* (New York: Cambridge University Press, 1999), 95–96. For similar ideas, see also, Cass R. Sunstein, *The Partial Constitution* (Cambridge, MA: Harvard University Press, 1998).

[4] *Cleveland Daily Enquirer*, March 17, 1851. The business metaphor applied only to deals between citizens, not to bargains with their state governments, which most people believed should stay out of business transactions. For example, on April 8, 1851, the *Cleveland Daily Enquirer* declared (as most Democratic newspapers did) that the state legislature should keep out of business, particularly money-printing corporations. See, for example, the Bloomington, Illinois, *Western Whig*, February 26, 1848. For a similar view, see also the speech of David S. Wilson in Benjamin F. Shambaugh, ed., *Fragments of the Debates of the Iowa Constitutional Conventions of 1844 and 1846 along with Press Comments and other Materials ...* (Iowa City: State Historical Society of Iowa, 1900), 308 (hereafter Iowa 1846).

"at any time" by the principal, so long as there were no outstanding financial obligations.[5]

The constitutional conventions were attempting to solve immediate pragmatic problems, particularly those caused by irresponsible legislatures, so they had to find a way to incorporate this power of attorney (which functioned principally as a tool to wield popular sovereignty) in constitutional reform. They did so by focusing on referenda that would place political power squarely in the hands of the voters, while relieving the delegates of the dangerous task of crafting controversial provisions. All American state constitutions included provisions that called for plebiscites on constitutional amendments or revision, and most states – indeed, most local and county governments – provided for the voters' rights to submit petitions to their governing bodies. However, the notion that voters ought to have the right to approve legislation *before* it was passed was a new invention in the northwestern states. Almost all of the western state constitutions included a provision that the state legislature had to ask the voters for permission to charter new banks.[6] Most historians locate the origin of modern American direct democratic action in South Dakota, whose constitution provided for initiative (defined as proposing statutes or constitutional amendments to a popular ballot) in 1898. Thomas Goebel explains that in the last decade of the nineteenth century, referenda became a tool of direct political engagement by the people to limit the power of "corporations and bosses."[7] The truth is, however, that western states began experimenting with direct voter participation – perhaps the most extreme illustration of popular

[5] See, for example, David Hoffman, "Construction of a Power of Attorney, and of a Deed," *The American Jurist and Law Magazine* 3 (Jan. and April 1830): 52–86; see also [Anonymous], *A Catechism of American Law, Adapted to Popular Use* (Philadelphia, 1832), 145. "Q. Is a power of attorney always revocable? A. A power of attorney is in general, from the nature of it, revocable at the pleasure of the party who gave it. But where it constitutes part of a security for money, or is necessary to give effect to such security, or where it is given for a valuable consideration, it is not revocable."

[6] None of the state constitutions in New England, the Mid-Atlantic, or the southern states contain such extreme democratic provisions. Canada did not entertain referenda until after the 1867 confederation. Most of the three national and fifty-eight provincial referenda occurred during the twentieth century and the majority were nonbinding. Tim Mowrey and Alain Pelletier, "Referendums in Canada: A Comparative Overview," *Electoral Insight* 3, no. 1 (Jan. 2001): 18–19. The United Kingdom has had only eleven referenda on national issues, all since the 1970s, and most of them related to devolution, http://www.parliament.uk/get-involved/elections/referendums-held-in-the-uk/ (accessed November 6, 2014).

[7] Thomas Goebel, "'A Case of Democratic Contagion': Direct Democracy in the American West, 1890–1920," *Pacific Historical Review* 66, no. 2 (May 1997): 213–30. The first state law permitting initiative and referendum was passed in California in 1911; today eighteen states have laws that permit direct democratic participation. There were no laws requiring submission of state constitutions to voters. Most of the northwestern state constitutions that were submitted for a direct vote passed (except for Iowa 1844, and Wisconsin 1846). For direct democracy in state constitutions in a national context, see John J. Dinan, *The American State Constitutional Tradition* (Lawrence: University Press of Kansas, 2009), 64–96.

sovereignty in American political and constitutional history – fifty years before the dawn of the Populist Movement.[8]

Democrats usually described their ideal government as a machine that could be set, with occasional calibrations, to do its work. Because a machine was governed by the laws of physics, it could be controlled by anyone who understood its inner mechanism. Indiana Democrat David Kilgore, for example, thought that once the convention established the legislature and the judiciary, the "great political machine" was completed, and every step the convention took beyond that was "wrong."[9] Whigs, by contrast, argued for a more organic interpretation.[10] The Whig *Iowa Standard* expressed doubts about this mechanistic approach. If it was true that the legislators functioned as the "agents and representatives of the people," then they had to be left free to exercise their human judgment. These men should never be "shackled by [any] power" (which the editorial left undefined, but almost certainly referred to the Democratic Party). Political party restraints would prohibit lawmakers from exercising "wise forethought and discretion" or from taking advantage of, or even anticipating, "circumstances that [would] arise" in the "natural course of things." In that case, the "agents of the people," instead of reflecting popular will and acting in harmony with natural, organic progress, would become "mere automata – moved and checked only by the constitution." Therefore, the constitution had to allow for discretion. Otherwise these agents did not "possess all the power inherent in the people."[11]

The convention delegates had to figure out a way to build their state government pragmatically and with an eye – in these difficult economic times – toward prudent management. Legislatures were expensive to begin with, and when they made unwise decisions that bankrupted their states or raised the deficit beyond the citizens' ability to repay, then the problem required an immediate structural solution. The costs of legislative assemblies were rising astronomically, in part

[8] William B. Fisch, "Constitutional Referendum in the United States of America," *The American Journal of Comparative Law* 54 (Fall 2006): 485–504. See also Joshua I. Miller, *The Rise and Fall of Democracy in Early America, 1630–1789: The Legacy for Contemporary Politics* (University Park: Pennsylvania State University Press, 1991), 9.

[9] H. Fowler, *Report of the Debates and Proceedings of the Convention for the Revision of the Constitution of the State of Indiana* (Indianapolis, IN, 1850), 1: 332 (hereafter Indiana 1850). Originally from Kentucky, Whig David Kilgore was an ardent nativist who later became a Republican. General William Harrison Kemper, *A Twentieth Century History of Delaware County, Indiana* (Chicago: Lewis Publishing Company, 1908), 1: 69. See also, Emma Lou Thornbrough, *Indiana in the Civil War Era, 1850–1880* (Indianapolis: Indiana Historical Bureau, 1965), 248.

[10] According to Daniel Walker Howe, Whigs "regarded the machine as an agent of redemption," *The Political Culture of the American Whigs* (Chicago: University of Chicago Press, 1979), 101.

[11] The *Iowa Standard* (Dubuque), February 6, 1845. The *Standard* was published at Dubuque, edited by Alonzo Pelham Wood, who eventually became a well-known historian of the Civil War. Alfred T. Andreas, *A. T. Andreas' Illustrated Historical Atlas of the State of Iowa* (Chicago: 1875), 274.

as a result of the increase in membership and the number of private laws necessary to charter corporations, which stretched the length of legislative sessions considerably. In 1830–31, the Illinois legislature cost the state $15,932.50. Eight years later, the expenditure had nearly tripled to $45,243.64. In 1841–42, the Ohio legislature cost $45,565.06.[12] These figures upset and annoyed the voters, particularly when the Indiana legislature cost the state $34,234.35 in 1848, during the same session that nearly bankrupted the state with a multimillion-dollar transportation deficit. That charge went significantly over budget.[13] By contrast, if voters hoped to economize on legislative expenses by revising their constitution, they were disappointed. For example, the Indiana state constitutional convention, held in 1850–51, racked up a stunning total: $88,280.39.[14]

Every northwestern state except Illinois, Iowa, and Minnesota began with annual legislative sessions, and every one of them changed to biennial sessions during the antebellum era. Democrats were in the majority everywhere until the early 1850s, so their aims prevailed through professional, articulate, well-organized political parties.[15] Democrats identified the delegation of political power with popular sovereignty: that is, with the people's right to instruct and, when the occasion demanded it, to override their state legislature. Historians such as Joyce Appleby, Edmund Morgan, and Stephen Griffin have questioned the existence of popular sovereignty at the end of the eighteenth century, especially if defined as the people's power to alter their own governments through revolution or through legitimate procedures of constitutional change. But even though northwesterners understood that political power was wielded through parties, and that political parties were immensely powerful, they would have taken deep umbrage at the thought that they might not be able to take and keep the reins of democratic government.[16] Moreover, because

[12] James T. B. Stapp, "Auditor's Report to the General Assembly, December 1832," in *Revised Laws of Illinois ...* (Vandalia, IL: 1833), 667; Levi Davis, "Report of the Auditor of Public Accounts, of the State of Illinois, Transmitted to Both Houses of the General Assembly, December 10, 1840," in *Laws of the State of Illinois, Passed by the Twelfth General Assembly...* (Springfield, IL: 1841), iv. John Brough, *Annual Report of the Auditor of State, to the Forty-First General Assembly* (Columbus, OH: 1842), 5.

[13] Douglas Maguire, "Report, General Fund," November 7, 1848, in *Documents of the General Assembly of Indiana at the Thirty-Third Session Commencing December 4, 1848* (Indianapolis, IN, 1849), 129–31.

[14] Jacob Piatt Dunn, *Indiana and Indianans: A History of Aboriginal and Territorial Indiana and The Century of Statehood* (Chicago: American Historical Society, 1919), 442.

[15] James A. Henretta, "The Rise and Decline of 'Democratic Republicanism': Political Rights in New York and the Several States, 1800–1915," in Paul Finkelman and Stephen E. Gottlieb, eds., *Toward a Usable Past: Liberty under State Constitutions* (1991; repr., Athens: University of Georgia Press, 2009), 70.

[16] Joyce Appleby argues that popular sovereignty had already intruded into the legislative terrain by the 1790s, in *Capitalism and a New Social Order: The Republican Vision of the 1790s* (New York: New York University Press, 1984), 85. Elsewhere she explains that despite reverence for popular sovereignty throughout the revolutionary era, the people were severely constrained as soon as the U.S. Constitution was ratified. Joyce Appleby, Lynn Hunt, and Margaret

many northwesterners believed that popular sovereignty was both modern and enlightened, they also believed that democracy possessed its own internal logic and would eventually carry along outdated hierarchies in its wake. Because people possessed an innate faculty to discern right from wrong, and just from unjust, they would – if given enough freedom – be able to perfect their system of government. The French political theorist Alexis de Tocqueville was traveling in America shortly after the July 1830 revolution that overthrew Charles X, the monarch who had reinstituted reactionary policies that overturned the reforms accomplished by the revolutionaries. As he was contemplating his experiences during his North American travels, Tocqueville asserted that all democracies tended toward more democratic reforms. Eventually equality and democracy would become perfect: In all democracies, citizens would of necessity become equal on all points.[17]

That notion of inevitable progress toward white equality was highly congenial to Jacksonian Democrats, particularly in the Northwest. The citizens and their delegates enjoyed pressing all their argumentative points to their logical extreme. They frequently reduced political and philosophical arguments to a rough-and-ready "all or nothing" statement: Either one enjoyed a perfect democracy, or one lived under a dictatorship; either all citizens had access to all rights and protections, or they were utterly oppressed. They had learned this style of argument from both Euclidean geometry (widely popular throughout antebellum America and taught in all academies) and from evangelical religion. In the language of the early nineteenth century, things "which were equal to the same thing, were equal to one another," according to Euclid and his translators: In other words, laws that governed one individual should govern any other person in the same way and according to the same rules.[18] The belief that mathematical certainties were analogous to political ones was firmly

Jacob, *Telling the Truth about History* (New York: Norton, 1994), 123. Stephen M. Griffin says popular sovereignty points toward an ideal of direct democracy that never existed, in *American Constitutionalism: From Theory to Politics* (Princeton, NJ: Princeton University Press, 1996), 26. See also, Christian G. Fritz, *American Sovereigns: The People and America's Constitutional Tradition before the Civil War* (New York: Cambridge University Press, 2007); and Morgan, *Inventing the People*, 55–77.

[17] Alexis de Tocqueville, *Democracy in America*, trans. and ed., Harvey C. Mansfield and Delba Winthrop (2000; repr., Chicago: Chicago University Press, 2002), 52–54.

[18] Lincoln was deeply interested in Euclid. See, Edward J. Kempf, *Abraham Lincoln's Philosophy of Common Sense: An Analytical Biography of a Great Mind* (New York: New York Academy of Sciences, 1965), vol. 1. Euclid's *Elements* was a popular text and several American editions were published during the period; see, for example, John Allen, ed., *Euclid's Elements of Geometry, the Six Volumes …* (Baltimore: 1822); John Playfair, ed., *Elements of Geometry: Containing the First Six Books of Euclid …* (New York: 1851); Robert Simson, ed., *Elements of Euclid, viz. the First Six Books, Together with the Eleventh and Twelfth …* (Philadelphia: 1829). For a bibliography of antebellum mathematics textbooks see *Theodore P. Hill Collection of Early American Mathematics Books*, Bancroft Library, University of California Berkeley, http://www.earlyamericanmathbooks.org/ (accessed November 6, 2014).

entrenched in American political life. Alexander Hamilton had stated this proposition in the thirty-first *Federalist*: Just as there were unalterable first principles in mathematics (he explicitly quoted Euclid) there were similar axioms in government. Second, evangelical Protestants learned that there were no half-measures in conversion and redemption. One was saved or one was damned.[19] And since reason and religion served as ideal analogies to good government, one could draw a parallel to the struggle to formulate state constitutions. In a perfect democracy, where the people possessed the greatest possible control over law and justice, there was no room for half-measures or incomplete freedoms. That habit of thought – that is, the tendency to press all arguments to their logical conclusion – created intense problems when northwesterners confronted the notion of perfect democracy and would plague the delegates in nearly every controversial topic. As a basic tenet of common law jurisprudence, and as a fundamental principle of logic, this argument would frequently confound those delegates who struggled with the confusions engendered by the mix of common law precedent, new statute laws required in the western territories and states, and their own idiosyncratic cultural beliefs. According to Tocqueville, however (and to most radical reformers in the region), democracy would in fact be a direct political consequence of what he called the "social state of the Anglo-Americans." Tocqueville implied that social equality was coterminous with political equality: Logically, there could be no middle ground.[20]

By then democratizing forces had already begun to transform the American political landscape.[21] Sean Wilentz has described the rise in voter participation, a slower but steady rise in the number of eligible voters, and the erosion of deference toward a "natural hierarchy" in American society during those years. Popular pressures for universal suffrage and removal of property qualifications grew exponentially after the Panic of 1819. Between 1812 and 1860, most states did away with property qualifications for voters; at the eve of the Civil War, only Delaware and South Carolina still included property qualifications. In the Great Lakes region, the urgent need for settlers induced constitutional delegates and legislatures to ease requirements for white men; literally nothing more was required than to be present for a few months, white, male, and older than twenty-one.

In antebellum America, attitudes toward both power and democracy had certainly changed since the founding. The older eastern and southern states were slower to adopt the new egalitarian ideas, while the constitutions of the new southwestern and northwestern states were more democratic.[22] In

[19] Nathan Hatch talks about the suddenness and emotionality of conversion. Nathan O. Hatch, *Democratization of American Christianity* (New Haven, CT: Yale University Press, 1989), 48, 105.

[20] Tocqueville, *Democracy in America*, 52–54.

[21] Sean Wilentz, *The Rise of American Democracy: Jefferson to Lincoln* (New York: Norton, 2006).

[22] The Alabama constitution in 1819 did away with all property requirements for voting, as did the Mississippi constitution in 1817 and the Florida constitution in 1838.

Massachusetts and Virginia, for example, constitutional change did little to overturn existing elite hierarchies. The only serious antebellum constitutional rebellion occurred in Rhode Island in 1842 when the radical lawyer Thomas Dorr called together a rogue constitutional convention to overthrow the Rhode Island state constitution, which was based on the original colonial charter and still mandated property qualifications for voters. The rebels intended to overturn the state's charter and write a new constitution that abolished property requirements. That fight, called the Dorr Rebellion, ended in a draw. Although Dorr was sentenced to life imprisonment, he received a gubernatorial pardon within two years, and Rhode Island a new and more egalitarian constitution by 1843.[23]

Eastern commentators often castigated the West as a lawless society, but when it came to constitutional reforms, the delegates and their constituents refrained from outright revolution. Northwesterners might have been cantankerous toward their legislatures, but most condemned the Rhode Island struggle and usually referred to it as a byword or a cautionary tale.[24] Two diehard Democrat delegates from Illinois, Albert Gallatin Caldwell and Thompson Campbell, thought the rebels had a "perfect right" to abolish the old undemocratic "federalist" government in Rhode Island but when James Davis accused him of advocating revolution, Campbell became so incensed that he nearly threw a glass of water at his opponent.[25] Few northwesterners evinced any interest in overthrowing existing governance, at least not after the 1810s and 1820s, when the earliest white settlers had wanted to depose their autocratic territorial governors. Even ardent abolitionist Ohio Quakers such as Benjamin B. Davis and William H. Hilles, both of whom would shortly become vehemently radical and, in joining a utopian community at Prairie Home in Ohio, spurn all human governments and constitutions, believed that

[23] See Erik J. Chaput, *The People's Martyr: Thomas Wilson Dorr and His 1842 Rhode Island Rebellion* (Lawrence: University Press of Kansas, 2013). Timothy M. Roberts calls the Dorr Rebellion the closest American analogue to European revolutions, in *Distant Revolutions: 1848 and the Challenge to American Exceptionalism* (Charlottesville: University of Virginia Press, 2009), 12.

[24] Indiana 1850, 1: 63–64. John Barron Niles, a Whig, stated that while he sympathized with the notion of popular sovereignty, he "deprecated" revolutions. Indiana 1850, 1: 71. In the 1844 Iowa convention, Hall and Grant both thought Dorr should be supported if his actions were in accordance with the will of the majority. Iowa 1844, 34–35. In the 1857 Iowa convention, Traer called the Dorr Rebellion "treason," but cautioned that if his colleagues did not leave the people enough power to amend their constitution, they would end with a similar rebellion. W. Blair Lord, *The Debates of the Constitutional Convention; of the State of Iowa, Assembled at Iowa City, Monday, January 19, 1857* (Davenport, IA: 1857), 1: 624 (hereafter, Iowa 1857).

[25] Arthur Charles Cole, ed., *The Constitutional Debates of 1847*, vol. 14 of *Collections of the Illinois State Historical Library* (Springfield: Illinois State Historical Library, 1919), 848–50 (hereafter Illinois 1847). Campbell set the glass of water down again. James Davis was a Democrat during the convention but soon joined the Whig Party. I found no other laudatory references to the Dorr Rebellion in any other convention.

the "tremendous conclusions & bloody revolutions in nearly every nation upon the European continent" had occurred because their governments had "insufficient restraints."[26]

Constitutional and political reform may not have escalated to violence in the West, but western communities, particularly those farther north or in isolated areas, experienced aggressive social upheavals.[27] Vigilante squatter organizations called "claims clubs" forced legitimate settlers out through extralegal means, and local gangs committed violent assaults on free black settlements.[28] Struggles against Indian communities continued throughout the 1830s and 1840s as white settlers encroached on Indian lands. Other violent eruptions occurred in Illinois: at Nauvoo, where vigilante mobs dragged the Mormon leader Joseph Smith from his prison cell and executed him; in Alton, when Elijah Lovejoy was murdered by a proslavery mob; and in Massac, when the so-called Regulator-Flathead War, a prolonged vigilante battle between citizens and lawless gangs, raged in 1846.[29] In Ohio, an unidentified African American man was lynched for allegedly raping a white woman in 1856. Michael Pfeifer found at least eighty-five lynchings (most of them white victims) in the Northwest between 1840 and 1877.[30] Convention delegates rarely mentioned such local commotions, and when they did, they condemned them as local crises of law and order, and never as an indictment of American democracy. Popular sovereignty was always difficult to balance against law and order, but a true republican government would permit upheavals to dissipate before they became revolutions.

Even while they dismissed local revolts and mob violence as isolated incidents, the northwestern convention delegates were sharply aware of what was going on in Europe.[31] After all, most of the conventions took place between

[26] Benjamin B. Davis to William H. Hilles, August 22, 1841, Valentine Nicholson Collection, Indiana Historical Society, Indianapolis. A year later both became members of the Society for Universal Inquiry and Reform, a radical abolitionist utopian community, which formed its own constitution. See also, Thomas D. Hamm, *God's Government Begun: The Society for Universal Inquiry and Reform, 1842–1846* (Bloomington: Indiana University Press, 1995), 11.

[27] Michael J. Pfeifer has described violence and vigilante gang warfare in the antebellum Southwest and Northwest. Michael J. Pfeifer, *The Roots of Rough Justice: Origins of American Lynching* (Urbana: University of Illinois Press, 2011), 14–15.

[28] Anna-Lisa Grace Cox, "'The Unjust Written Manacles for the Free': Black Codes and Their Impact on African American Settlement Patterns on the Antebellum Midwestern Frontier" (conference paper, Society for the Historians of the Early American Republic, Baltimore, MD, July 20, 2012). See also, James A. Schellenberg, "County Seat Wars: A Preliminary Analysis," *Journal of Conflict Resolution* 14, no. 3 (Sept. 1970): 345–52.

[29] The "Regulator-Flathead" violence is described in Nicole Etcheson, "Good Men and Notorious Rogues: Vigilantism in Massac County, Illinois 1846–1850," in Michael A. Bellesiles, ed., *Lethal Imagination Violence and Brutality in American History* (New York: New York University Press, 1999), 150–54.

[30] Pfeifer, *Roots of Rough Justice*, 54, map on 56.

[31] Nicole Etcheson argues in that in the Regulator-Flathead War, the vigilante violence was actually a way of establishing law and order. Etcheson, "Good Men and Notorious Rogues," 151–52.

1835 and 1857, those contentious years when European monarchies were experiencing violent convulsions. Most major American newspapers carried foreign news; for example, *Niles's Weekly Register* published a regular European column. Reading about the revolutions in their papers, Americans were moved to pity and admiration. But when the struggles became too violent, they often expressed profound horror. Whether they applauded, pitied, or condemned transatlantic revolutionary movements, the delegates adverted to European or Latin American news frequently.[32] In such speeches America's democracy always figured as a beacon of democratic self-governance, and the European troubles as cautionary tales. Representative Charles Oakley of Jackson County, Illinois, told his friends that it was necessary "for an American to visit Europe & see the operation of those monarcial governments, in order to duly appreciate our owne happy form of govt."[33]

As they compared their deliberative efforts to build their democracies to the violent upheavals in Europe, northwesterners found their own calm, orderly process far superior. They based their constitutional work on the principles learned through science, religion, and law, while Europeans struggled in the grip of irrational passions. Americans had simply "purchased" their modern transformations through taxes, and not through the shedding of blood. Indiana constitutional convention delegate Robert H. Milroy compared Indiana's constitutional convention, as an expression of a free people's "right to alter remodel & amend their form of government," with the "abortive attempts of the downtrodden nations of Europe to exercise the "same prerogative.... How different the manner and the result!" Alluding to the cost of a convention divided among the citizenry, he was able to declare that Indiana's constitutional convention "only cost 12 1/2 cts, apiece," while the Europeans paid in "blood & treason."[34] Whig William Woodbridge, a delegate to the Michigan 1835 convention, rather pitied "gallant and generous France," now struggling for democracy because the nation had not yet learned to "poise and balance herself in her new position." That process would require years. Moreover, he compared the battle over the Michigan state boundaries (which, though upsetting, remained nonviolent) to the popular uprisings in Latin America, where the people, desperate for freedom, were "drenched in human blood" but lacked "the power to be free" because they had never "learned the lessons of freedom."[35]

[32] Roberts, *Distant Revolutions*, 63–80. Timothy Roberts has explained that American attitudes toward European radical revolutions were positive at first and then became more critical as the revolutions became violent.

[33] Charles Oakley to John Logan, January 4, 1842, John Logan Papers, Abraham Lincoln Presidential Library, Springfield, IL.

[34] Robert H. Milroy, "Constitutional Convention 1850," manuscript memoir, Robert H. Milroy Papers, Indiana Historical Society, Indianapolis.

[35] Harold M. Dorr, ed., *The Michigan Constitutional Conventions of 1835–1836: Debates and Proceedings* (Ann Arbor: University of Michigan Press, 1940), 227–29 (hereafter Michigan

If we focus closely on the political and constitutional change in the Great Lakes region, we find little evidence of the violent revolutions that shook European states in 1821, 1830, and 1848. Still, according to Eric Hobsbawm, the Jacksonian democratic upheaval should be considered as part of the larger worldwide events, particularly European attempts to establish democratic self-government. For their part, the northwestern delegates expressed a profound appreciation for the universal human desire for liberty and self-government. Frederick Jackson Turner's famous frontier thesis depicted independent white pioneers propagating democracy on western soil. But democracy arrived before them in the form of a constitutional mandate to plant a republican form of government in the early years of the nineteenth century.[36] Beginning in the early 1820s ideas about egalitarianism – even socialist experiments in communal living – crossed the Atlantic with British Owenites and French Fourierists who established utopian communities in the Great Lakes. German revolutionaries fleeing political oppression after 1848 published English- and German-language newspapers extolling democratic self-governance.[37]

American state constitutional conventions had already accomplished those revisions. Indeed, some of the northwestern conventions (particularly the one held in 1847 in Wisconsin) inspired the British Chartists. In Philadelphia and New York, workingmen's movements stirred young men to fight for land in the West, but when those ideas reached the constitutional conventions held in the great interior, they became muted. In America – particularly in the Great Lakes region – social reforms always remained subject to the popular will and were rarely allowed to become radical or revolutionary.[38] By comparison, after the democratic revolutions swept across Europe, traditional conservative forces reestablished their authority through brutal reprisals or half-measure democratic elections that merely replicated existing power structures.[39] According to Hobsbawm, between 1815 and 1832, monarchies, aristocracies, and churches, as the three "pillars of conservatism," controlled the European nations and ensured that democratic revolutions would fail.[40] By comparison American nineteenth-century efforts to democratize, at least in the political realm, took place in state constitutional conventions that reformed legislative sessions and

1835). Woodbridge had worked with the French government during territorial times to settle French land titles. See Charles Lanman, *Life of William Woodbridge* (Washington, DC: 1867).

[36] See Andrew R. L. Cayton, *The Frontier Republic: Ideology and Politics in the Ohio Country, 1780–1825* (Kent, OH: Kent State University Press, 1986), 33–34; John D. Barnhart, *Valley of Democracy: The Frontier versus the Plantation in the Ohio Valley, 1775–1818* (Lincoln: University of Nebraska Press, 1953).

[37] See Jonathan Sperber, *The European Revolutions, 1841–1851*, 2nd ed. (New York: Cambridge University Press, 2005).

[38] See John F. C. Harrison, *Robert Owen and the Owenites in Britain and America: The Quest for the New Moral World* (1969; repr., New York: Routledge, 2010).

[39] W. Caleb McDaniel, *The Problem of Democracy in the Age of Slavery: Garrisonian Abolitionists and Transatlantic Reform* (Baton Rouge: Louisiana State University Press, 2013), 93–95.

[40] Eric J. Hobsbawm, *The Age of Revolution, 1789–1848* (London: Weidenfeld & Nicolson, 1962; repr. New York: Vintage Books, 1996), 74–133. See also, Roberts, *Distant Revolutions.*

rendered judiciaries elective. Such revolutions, though innovative, were never intended to be radical, at least not beyond the mandates of the U.S. Constitution and the Northwest Ordinance.

European aristocrats mistrusted the idea of written constitutions because such charters reminded monarchists of Napoleonic upheavals, when the rising middle classes demanded, in writing, that political privilege be based on wealth and property rather than on birth. The landholding aristocrats in England and Germany refused to be governed by documents.[41] The well-educated middle-class reformers published their liberal demands for equality, freedom of speech, religious toleration, and election of representatives in manifestos. They also set forth their principles in charters and constitutions. As Jacksonian Democrats watched these developments in Europe, they certainly expressed dissatisfaction with class differences, particularly those between eastern "monopolists" and western farmers, believing that they ran counter to fundamental democratic principles. Yet they believed that popular sovereignty and direct democracy could overcome these injustices. Antebellum Americans thought of monarchies as the principal symbol and bulwark of conservatism and the greatest threat to democracy. Therefore, both radical reformers, such as abolitionists and women's rights activists, and Jacksonian Democrats used "monarchial" as a term of opprobrium. European monarchies, even those who ruled over constitutional democracies, functioned as examples of uncontrollable power.

As they analyzed the European uprisings for cautionary lessons, northwesterners developed an understanding of the necessary and sufficient elements of democratic self-government. The inborn yearning of human nature to be free, and the providential gift of an abundant landscape, had to be aligned with the human ability to observe and to reason. Therefore, statutes, judicial decisions, and state constitutional provisions all had to be visible and legible: that is, printed and distributed to the voters. For northwesterners, the European struggles were a perfect example of what happened when any part of that architecture was missing. This process was so important that the region's chroniclers already saw in it a lesson for the ages. As early as 1838, for example, Caleb Atwater published an immensely popular history of Ohio, in which the rich land resembled a "perfect paradise." But the people had to remember that fruitfulness and beauty were not enough. According to Atwater, Germany was a similarly "perfect garden," but now its people were fleeing by the thousands "as they would from the direst pestilence." They immigrated to the American West to escape political persecution. Therefore, even under the best circumstances, "unless good government is maintained those who live under it may be truly miserable." A Democrat such as Atwater thought that the best way to prevent convulsions would be to reform the constitution to include more restraints on the "law making power."[42] Those restraints inevitably would be provided by the people themselves, and all constitutions had

[41] Hobsbawm, *Age of Revolution*, 13, 101.

[42] Caleb Atwater, "Remarks on the Constitution of Ohio," in *History of the State of Ohio, Natural and Civil*, 2nd ed. (Cincinnati, OH: 1838), 171–72.

to shore up the notion that popular sovereignty could be exercised in practical, real-world ways that would exert tangible controls over the state legislatures and the governors.

Modern political and constitutional theorists often use the phrase "popular sovereignty" to express legislative (and therefore popular) primacy over the other branches of government.[43] In antebellum America, especially in the Northwest, however, popular sovereignty still retained its revolutionary meaning: the notion that the people held power and delegated it in carefully controlled increments to lawmakers (and, by the 1830s, also to judges).[44] Popular sovereignty was beyond question, but northwesterners still tried to stretch the meaning as far as they could. They defined popular sovereignty not only as the power to act, but also as the power to rebuke and to repeal. According to Ohio Democrat R. P. Ranney, granting the people the right to approve and repeal legislation was exactly the same as the constitutional guarantee of fundamental civil liberties. The "great dividing line" that separated a "government of the people from a government of the few" depended precisely on this point: Would the people have a right to repeal unwholesome laws? If the people could not overturn laws that threatened their welfare, then the "much cherished declaration" that all political power was inherent in the people was "nothing but a falsehood." Worse, the belief that the people retained the right to "alter or abolish their form of government at pleasure" was "all a libel." In that case – if his colleagues in the convention would willingly "thus dissipate the popular sovereignty," then he would only ask them for one more thing: "simply, and consistently, to vote down all these sounding declarations in our bill of rights."[45]

In this specific case, the delegate was fighting for popular control over the people's right to repeal corporation charters – an issue that never failed to generate dire warnings of aristocratic elites trampling on the rights of the common man. The core point was, however, that the smallest diminution of any right threatened the total destruction of all rights. That "all-or-nothing" concept had

43 See Jed H. Shugerman, *The People's Courts: Pursuing Judicial Independence in America* (Cambridge, MA: Harvard University Press, 2012); William E. Nelson, *Marbury v. Madison: The Origins and Legacy of Judicial Review* (Lawrence: University Press of Kansas, 2000); Larry D. Kramer, *The People Themselves: Popular Constitutionalism and Judicial Review* (New York: Oxford University Press, 2004); Robert L. Clinton, *Marbury v. Madison and Judicial Review* (Lawrence: University Press of Kansas, 1989); and Christopher Wolfe, *The Rise of Modern Judicial Review: From Constitutional Interpretation to Judge-Made Law*, rev. ed. (Lanham, MD: Littlefield Adams, 1994).

44 Donald S. Lutz explicitly states that Americans did not regard popular sovereignty as experimental in nature, but rather as an idea that "stood at the very heart of their shared political consensus." Donald S. Lutz, "Patterns in the Amending of American State Constitutions," in *Constitutional Politics in the States: Contemporary Controversies and Historical Patters* (Westport, CT: Greenwood Press, 1996), 25.

45 J. V. Smith, *Report of the Debates and Proceedings of the Convention for the Revision of the Constitution of the State of Ohio, 1850–51* (Columbus, OH, 1851), 2: 480 (hereafter Ohio 1850).

a long history in American political thought and could be deployed to argue for opposite ends. For example, as early as 1776, John Adams argued against the destruction of property requirements for voting. The same reasoning that would permit propertyless men to vote, he declared, could be used to allow women and children the same privilege. "Generally speaking," he admitted, women and children had "as good judgments and as independent minds," as "destitute men." Therefore, Adams feared that it was "dangerous to open so fruitful a source of controversy and altercation" as would be opened by attempting to broaden the "qualification of voters."[46]

Clever politicians were acutely aware of this "all or nothing" form of reasoning and brought it into play to negotiate their deals. If any diminution of popular sovereignty threatened to destroy the entire fabric of self-governance, then the phrase "popular sovereignty" could serve as an ideal slogan for potentially explosive political fights. In the mid-1850s two northwestern senators – Lewis Cass from Michigan and Stephen A. Douglas from Illinois – appropriated the term "popular sovereignty" to resolve the worst sectional crisis the nation had faced. When the Kansas and Nebraska Territories requested admission to the Union, Cass and Douglas wanted to provide a justification for permitting proslavery settlers to introduce human bondage into the new western territories. Cass and Douglas wanted to grant these new states the right to choose for themselves whether they wished to enter as slave or free, in direct contravention of the Missouri Compromise line. As experienced politicians with a keen understanding of catchphrases that would play well with their constituencies, Cass and Douglas hoped to create a smooth link between a political compromise and time-honored beliefs that the people consented to give up part of their liberties in order to delegate powers to their representatives. Perhaps the senators were able to do so more easily because, just a few years earlier, popular sovereignty had already taken on a rather slippery meaning in the Northwest, particularly over the chronically divisive issues of banking and corporations.[47]

Even in their sharpest political disagreements, Whigs and Democrats never questioned the rational and ethical nature of sovereignty of the people. American voters had always possessed, and availed themselves enthusiastically of, mechanisms to petition or rebuke their legislators or their constitutional convention delegates. The U.S. Constitution guarantees the right to petition in the First Amendment.[48] The right to instruct one's representatives dated back to colonial

[46] John Adams to John Sullivan, May 26, 1776, in *The Works of John Adams, Second President of the United States, With a Life of the Author, Notes and Illustrations*, ed. Charles Francis Adams (Boston: Little Brown, 1850–1856), 9: 378.

[47] Willard Carl Klunder, *Lewis Cass and the Politics of Moderation* (Kent, OH: Kent State University Press, 1996), 32–38.

[48] See David D. Schmidt, *Citizen Lawmakers: The Ballot Initiative Revolution* (Philadelphia: Temple University Press, 1989). In *Giving Voters a Voice: the Origins of the Initiative and Referendum in America* (Columbia: University of Missouri Press, 2003), Steven L. Piott argues that in the later nineteenth century states whose legislatures were controlled by "powerful economic interests"

America. In the early days after ratification, Anti-Federalists wanted to add the right to instruct representatives to the U.S. Constitution. This right to instruct manifested in two ways: as public votes on constitutional provisions and as provisions that instituted direct democracy.[49] In the antebellum northwestern conventions, the pressure of public opinion forced delegates to leave the most controversial questions to separate referenda.[50] This was especially true in the inflammatory issue of banking corporations: State legislatures had recklessly passed private laws that chartered corporations with the power to print money, which northwesterners perceived (correctly) as one of the causes of economic collapse. In the 1844 Iowa convention, Democratic delegate Robert Lucas supported the amendment submitting banks to a popular vote. Everyone agreed, he claimed, that the people were sovereign, and they had elected him and his colleagues "to make a Constitution by which their sovereignty was to be guarded and expressed." The convention had already agreed to a radical example of direct democracy; therefore, why not render bank charters open to popular approval? Indeed, why not take it a step further and "say that the same mode should be followed to repeal?"[51] Northwestern citizens demanded – and through petitions, rebukes, and indignation meetings assumed – sovereignty over their lawmaking bodies. This process was most evident in the public and convention debates over economic legislation, but rose to the surface whenever any controversial subject – most saliently, black people's rights – came up for discussion.

The struggle to redefine popular sovereignty severely complicated the way antebellum Americans thought about the distribution of power. The driving purpose of antebellum constitutional revision, not just in the Northwest, but almost everywhere in the United States, was to remove power from governors and legislatures and to confer it on the people.[52] Yet power still had to be delegated to legislators: There was simply no other way to accomplish the important work of financing and running the state. Unfortunately antebellum northwesterners held a poor opinion of their lawmakers. Illinois judge David Davis, whose duties required him to spend a great deal of time in Springfield, expressed contempt for the state legislature. In 1844 he told his friend William

tended to want direct democracy. As most historians do, Piott locates the move toward direct democracy in free silver and Populist movements. Daniel Smith and Caroline Tolbert locate the origin of direct legislation in Switzerland. Daniel A. Smith and Caroline J. Tolbert, *Educated by Initiative: The Effects of Direct Democracy on Citizens and Political Organizations in the American States* (Ann Arbor: University of Michigan Press, 2004), 22, 58.

49 Terranova, "The Constitutional Life of Legislative Instructions in America," 1331; Kenneth Bresler, "Rediscovering the Right to Instruct Legislators," *New England Law Review* 26, no. 2 (Winter 1991): 355–94. Primus, *American Language of Rights*, 96–97.

50 John J. Dinan, in *The American State Constitutional Tradition* (Lawrence: University Press of Kansas, 2006), contains a useful discussion of referenda, initiatives, and direct democracy. See especially the chapter on amendment and revision (pp. 29–63).

51 Iowa 1844, 97.

52 G. Alan Tarr, *Understanding State Constitutions* (Princeton, NJ: Princeton University Press, 1998), 121–26.

Walker that at best, he supposed that the legislature had not done much harm, though the citizens of Springfield never inquired "whether it ha[d] ever done any good."[53] In spite of his misgivings, the following year he ran for and won a seat in the state House of Representatives, and two years later he was elected to the 1847 Illinois state constitutional convention. By that time Davis thought that the voters had already identified, and agreed to, many important reforms. He agreed with the convention president Casey Zadoc that the Illinois legislature had been a great source of evil, and if there had been only one in session for ten years, then Illinois would have been a "happy and prosperous State."[54] The new constitution would narrow down the legislature "to a small compass – 75 in the house & 25 in the Senate never to be increased. pay $2.00 – & can sit but 60 days." That cut the legislators' pay in half and sharply limited the length of time they could remain in session. Davis explained that the expenses of the last legislature had exceeded eighty thousand dollars, and even so, they had "actually done nothing useful or creditable to the State."[55] Some commentators thought their entire legislative body was so corrupt that it was beyond redemption. After returning from a three-month stay in the state capital, the Ohio judge Benjamin Tappan told his brother Lewis that he had witnessed more of the usual "folly and knavery in Legislature."[56] One of Indiana delegate Allen Hamilton's constituents was so incensed that he was sure the "Legislat[ure] the state the people and every thing els [sic]" was on the "broad Road to the Devil."[57] Similarly, David McDonald, an Indiana circuit judge, told delegate Henry Smith Lane that whenever he thought of "the doings of the present Legislature – of the barefaced and shameless cupidity and depravity of many of our public men" he could not refrain from saying, with Cato, "O Virtue! I have sought thee as a substance, and I have found thee a shadow!"[58] Meanwhile, it was up to the constitutional convention delegates, with due oversight from the

[53] David Davis to William P. Walker, March 2, 1844, David Davis Family Papers, Abraham Lincoln Presidential Library, Springfield, IL.

[54] In this letter David Davis was probably citing the convention president Zadoc Casey's opening address, quoted in Rodney O. Davis, "'The People in Miniature': The Illinois General Assembly 1818–1848," *Illinois Historical Journal* 81, no. 2 (Summer 1988), 95–96.

[55] David Davis to Wells Colton, June 25, 1847, David Davis Papers, Chicago History Museum.

[56] Benjamin Tappan to Lewis Tappan, February 28, 1849, Tappan Family Papers, Ohio Historical Society, Columbus.

[57] "CT" to Allen Hamilton, January 7, 1842, Allen Hamilton Papers, Indiana Historical Society, Indianapolis.

[58] David McDonald to Henry Smith Lane, January 17, 1852. H. S. Lane MSS, Lilly Library, Indiana University, Bloomington. McDonald was probably not quoting Cato. He may have been quoting Samuel Richardson, who quoted an unattributed epigram by an early seventeenth-century neo-Latinist, John Owen: "Gloria virtutem, corpus ut umbra sum," which Richardson translated as "Tho' glory always followeth virtue, yet it should be considered only as its shadow." For a contemporary source see, Samuel Richardson, *Clarissa* (London: 1748). It is also possible that McDonald may have been quoting Seneca, paraphrasing Cicero, not Cato, in one of Seneca's Moral Letters (79) to Lucilius on the topic of scientific discovery, translated as "Fame is the shadow of virtue; it will attend virtue even against her will."

voters and newspaper editors, to hold the moral and ethical line on the excesses of political power. The only way to accomplish that was to reframe state constitutions: that is, to rebuild their political home.

Perhaps William B. Conway, a young Iowa politician who served as territorial secretary before statehood, best expressed the northwestern loathing for a dishonest legislator.

> Let guileless children as he passes by
> Shrink from his touch and shudder at his eye
> Let lovely woman loath him with disgust
> And shun him like the reptile in the dust.
> And whilst he lives, let Infamy alone
> Claim the Bribed Legislator as her own,
> Until he dies and sinks into the grave
> To poison worms that feed upon the knave.
> There midst the storm let hideous Furies foul
> Hold nightly revels and in concert howl.
> Let hissing reptiles make that spot their home
> And be the watchful guardians of his tomb.
> And when he goes to Hell let Devils stare
> And ask him who the Devil sent him there.[59]

In spite of the fact that northwestern voters thought about and treated their convention delegates in the same way they did state legislators, they were still sure that the constitutional conventions were morally and intellectually superior bodies to legislative assemblies. David Davis told his wife, Sarah, that the convention was "composed of a better body of men" than the Illinois legislature, which was "full of drunkards," and, as far as he could tell there were none in the convention. "Speaks well – Don't it."[60] Indiana delegate Robert Milroy declared that the convention would be able to "make a greater change & have a more lasting & permanent influence upon the future laws & institutions of Indiana, and upon her future prosperity and greatness than ... a dozen legislatures, Congresses, or Presidents."[61] If state constitutions were more influential than "a dozen Presidents," then how did these men define constitutional power – especially over legislatures? Legislators could hardly strip themselves of political power. Nor were they likely to do so. Since the economic catastrophes of the 1820s and 1830s, northwestern newspapers had fired off relentless criticism of legislatures for their role in nearly bankrupting states through overspending on massive transportation networks.[62] For

[59] William B. Conway, manuscript poem, poetry clipping file, William B. Conway Collection, State Historical Society of Iowa, Iowa City.

[60] David Davis to Sarah Davis, June 19, 1847, David Davis Papers, Chicago History Museum.

[61] Robert H. Milroy, manuscript draft of a newspaper editorial, n. d. [1850?], Robert Huston Milroy Papers, Indiana Historical Society, Indianapolis.

[62] For a summary of internal improvement fiascoes in the Northwest see, John L. Larson, *Internal Improvement: National Public Works and the Promise of Popular Government in the Early United States* (Chapel Hill: University of North Carolina Press, 2001), 195–224.

example, an Iowa resident, Robert Robinson, wrote to the former state representative Laurel Summers explaining that the state legislature had "indebted the State several hundred thousand dollars in direct violation of the Constitution," and that this "*Lunatic Asylum*" was now attempting to build a multimillion-dollar internal transportation network that would almost certainly never see the light of day.[63]

The pervasive perception – though probably unjust – was that legislators were dishonest reprobates.[64] Legislators were certainly the target of relentless logrolling and lobbying efforts throughout this era and even felt forced to deal with logrollers in order to accomplish anything – a fact that the former Illinois governor Thomas Ford noted in his memoirs.[65] By the mid-1850s, when canal and railroad projects became important objects of political in-fighting, legislators throughout the Northwest did sometimes succumb to temptation.[66] When the Wisconsin legislature obtained a federal land grant worth $105,000 in 1856, there was a scramble in Madison to get a company charter and rights to a piece of the federal largesse. The LaCrosse & Milwaukee Railroad, headed by Moses Strong, who had served as a constitutional convention delegate and was now Democratic speaker of the House, and by his colleague Byron Kilbourn (a railroad promoter and Milwaukee Democrat), became embroiled in large-scale bribery to buy votes in the Wisconsin Statehouse. Strong and Kilbourn headed a political faction of the Wisconsin Democratic Party based in Milwaukee that was known derisively as the "Forty Thieves." Only after the land grant was passed by the legislature and signed into law, and the railroad company went into bankruptcy did the full drama of the scandal come to light. Strong and Kilbourn spent more than $800,000 buying the votes of fifty-nine representatives and nineteen senators. The Republican governor, Bashford, received $50,000 in bonds for his signature.[67] In 1858, shortly after Minnesota became a state, a local newspaper complained about bribery and corruption in the state legislature. Twelve Minnesota senators (nine Democrats and three Republicans) had been found guilty of taking bribes in bonds from the LaCrosse Railroad.[68] Yet it is doubtful that Davis's cynical description of drunkards or the wider northwestern condemnation of legislators as ignorant, shortsighted profligates was entirely fair or accurate. Like the convention delegates, these men were culled from the respectable, prosperous class

[63] Robert Robinson to Laurel Summers, November 30, 1857, Laurel Summers Papers, State Historical Society of Iowa, Des Moines.

[64] In his study of the Illinois General Assembly, Rodney Davis found little evidence of serious corruption; political dealings for personal gain involved "non-partisan logrolling and horse-trading." Davis, "People in Miniature," 103.

[65] Thomas Ford, *A History of Illinois, from Its Commencement as a State in 1818 to 1847* (Chicago, 1854), 91.

[66] John M. Lamb, "The Great Canal Scrip Fraud," *Magazine of Illinois* 16, no. 9 (Nov. 1977): 57–60.

[67] Mark W. Summers, *The Plundering Generation: Corruption and the Crisis of the Union, 1849–1861* (New York: Oxford University Press, 1987), 108–12.

[68] *Faribault* (MN) *Central Republican*, June 23, 1858.

of landowners, legal professionals, or merchants. Indeed, most of them were a little older and possibly more experienced than the convention delegates, as Chapter 1 explained.[69]

The specific problem with legislative sessions, besides the cost and the danger of irresponsible legislation, was that it was hard to know just how far to go to apportion power. The lawmakers had to have enough power (not only as legislators, but also as dispensers of spoils) to make the machine run well. On the other hand, too much power in the hands of agents posed terrible risks. Horace Comstock, a prosperous Michigan legislator, told Lucius Lyon that legislative power ought to be carefully defined, "allowing no monopolies" among lawmakers (meaning, no political cabals or caucuses). He also feared "unauthorized constructions of the power of rights & restraints."[70] Northwestern lawmakers had to be able to build the civic structure of the state, beyond the details that their state constitution could control, but they could not have so much power that they could derail prosperity. Delegate John Hubbard Tweedy asked one of his constituents what he thought of annual or biennial sessions; would the former be too infrequent to accomplish anything, or the latter too expensive? His neighbor thought that once their state was firmly established and the constitution had accomplished the necessary reforms, Wisconsin "could get along with a session once in two years." The main point was to ensure that all legislators, whether in the Senate or in the House, were to be held strictly to the confines of their duties: A good representative would "have nothing to do but assist in making laws." The way to accomplish this would be to elect every lawmaker (and incidentally, he thought, the governor and the president of the United States) every year. His curious phrasing – "assist in making laws" – suggested that the lawmakers were working for the people in writing statutes.[71]

Between 1818 and 1857, as a result of the two devastating financial panics of 1819 and 1837, the popular cry was for retrenchment. Every northwestern convention responded with zest by cutting back on the number and frequency of sessions, limiting the size of the house, and submitting controversial legislation to the people.[72] All of them also mandated biennial legislative

[69] Peter S. Onuf, "The Origins and Early Development of State Legislatures," in Joel H. Silbey, ed., *Encyclopedia of the American Legislative System* (New York: Charles Scribner's Sons, 1994), 1: 175–94; William G. Shade, "State Legislatures in the Nineteenth Century," in *Encyclopedia of the American Legislative System*, 1: 195–214; David M. Gold, *Democracy in Session: A History of the Ohio General Assembly* (Athens: Ohio University Press, 2009), 23, 41–42; and Summers, *Plundering Generation*, 274–75.

[70] H. H. Comstock to Lucius Lyon, May 20, 1835, Lucius Lyon Papers, William L. Clements Library, University of Michigan, Ann Arbor.

[71] E. B. Whiton to John H. Tweedy, November 4, 1846, John H. Tweedy Papers, Wisconsin Historical Society, Madison.

[72] Since the 1960s most assemblies have restored annual sessions with much institutional power restored as well. Still, state constitutions are replete with "superlegislation," in place to limit legislative power. Malcolm E. Jewell and Marcia Lynn Whicker, *Legislative Leadership in the American States* (Ann Arbor: University of Michigan Press, 1994), 33–36.

sessions.[73] But in their enthusiasm to respond to their constituents' expressed will, the delegates may have gone too far. Legislative reforms that aimed at retrenchment and at limiting the authority of legislatures could create awkward contradictions. The 1847 Illinois constitutional convention constrained the legislature so severely that the state had to mandate another convention in the middle of the Civil War in order to permit the lawmakers to appropriate enough funds to finance the war effort.[74] Similarly, the 1851 Indiana constitution severely cut back on the judiciary; that meant that the courts quickly became overloaded and cases hopelessly delayed. Indiana would not be able to resolve that problem for more than a century.[75] Essentially, the delegates faced an impossible task: constructing a constitution that required stronger governmental controls over economic institutions (such as banking corporations) while limiting the reach of elected representatives. Similarly, insisting on modernization while framing government in a preconstitutional structure similar to the Articles of Confederation, with a weak executive, a hamstrung legislature, and public control over financial issues, was probably unrealistic. It was hardly practical to mandate a legislature to modernize the state and at the same time restrict their power to enact economic laws. The legislators had transgressed the boundaries of reason (in making financially irresponsible decisions) and virtue (in granting charters and passing private laws). Therefore, if constitutions represented the will, virtue, and reason of a democratic people, then the delegates had both the right and the duty to prescribe a sphere of action for the legislature.[76] A constitutional convention, particularly in a young state struggling with a precarious economy, was an expensive undertaking. The popular willingness to bear the burden of electing and paying for conventions for the purpose of reforming (literally re-forming) the state charters revealed how deeply these people trusted in the constitutional project, and how necessary they thought it was.

Samuel Medary's prospectus for his proreform newspaper, the *New Constitution*, spoke for most Democrats in the region (indeed, most voters, whether Democrat or Whig). He laid out in bold phrases precisely what the people wanted: they now demanded nothing short of a

> total reform in our Judiciary system and the practice of our Courts; the election of ALL OFFICERS BY THE PEOPLE! No increase of the state debt, except by a vote of the people themselves. A system of common schools and of education, worthy [of] the

[73] The first four states in the region – Ohio (1802), Indiana (1816), Illinois (1818), and Michigan (1835) – began with annual legislative sessions, mostly to weaken gubernatorial power, and all revised their constitutions to biennial sessions. Every other state in the region (Iowa, Minnesota, and Wisconsin) provided for biennial legislative sessions throughout its history.

[74] Unfortunately the constitution crafted by the 1862 convention failed in the popular vote.

[75] Not until the 1970s. William P. McLauchlan, *The Indiana State Constitution* (Westport CT: Greenwood Press, 1996; repr., New York: Oxford University Press, 2011), 26–27, 30–31.

[76] James Willard Hurst has explained that "substantial interests pressed successfully for limitations written into constitutional form and supported the courts' authority to enforce the superiority

age and the state. No legislation but what the people can reform or annul, when found injurious.

According to this newspaper, a "progressing, reforming, radical spirit" was now "spreading over the civilized world." What a pity it would be if Ohio became the "*last* to partake of the regenerating spirit."[77]

The "unterrified" were hardly afraid of excitement, however. In fact, they considered conversations about political reform to be morally refreshing. Unlike European conflagrations, American revolutions could be controlled through constitutions. Political excitement, as dangerous as it might be if allowed to run wild, could – if properly channeled by conventions, parliamentary procedure, and fair deliberation – lead to proper republican reform, and, like evangelical religious fervor, to perfection. In 1840, Whig lawyer and close friend of Abraham Lincoln James C. Conkling was already advocating a thorough revision of the Illinois state constitution. He was concerned about the economic problems in the wake of the 1837 panic, as well as the ongoing disputes over internal improvements and banking. He still believed, however, that even the most challenging situations could lead to reformation. Wisdom always dictated a need "to remedy the evil and to perfect the system," and so could inspire the polity to engage in "luminous discussions upon principles." Surely such discussions would prepare Illinois citizens to construct a stronger, wiser, more modern, and more responsible state constitution. The main point was, as always, to "recur to first principles" and so to attain the "highest degree of perfection." As did any scientific experiment that posed a hypothetical question, as did any moral dilemma that forced a Christian to question his own failures and weaknesses, an economic or political problem, through elucidation of principles, worked to perfect society.[78] Constitutional reform was part of the great experiment in the transformation of modern American law.

Reforming government could be either progressive or conservative; that would depend on how one defined any one of those terms. More to the point: Antebellum Americans rarely used terms like "progressive" or "conservative" as descriptive or collective nouns. They were less interested in categorizing political views and far more concerned about correcting significant problems in governance. Even men who might in other contexts be considered "conservative" (such as those delegates who fought against black civil

of constitution over statute," in *Law and the Conditions of Freedom in the Nineteenth Century United States* (1956; repr., Madison: University of Wisconsin Press, 1984), 24.

[77] Samuel Medary, "Prospectus of the New Constitution," *New Constitution* (Columbus, OH), May 5, 1849, 1–2. This newspaper is in the collections of the Ohio Historical Society and has been digitized and made available online by Cleveland State University, Cleveland-Marshall College of Law Library, https://www.law.csuohio.edu/lawlibrary/ohioconstitution/medary (accessed November 6, 2014). See also, Barbara A. Terzian, "Ohio's Constitutions: An Historical Perspective," *Cleveland State Law Review* 51, nos. 3 and 4 (2004): 370–71.

[78] Undated manuscript draft of editorial letter. James C. Conkling to "Editor," n.d. [1840], Conkling Family Papers, Abraham Lincoln Presidential Library, Springfield, IL.

rights or against woman suffrage) would consider themselves both modern and progressive, because they believed in popular sovereignty and in equality for all white people. As a result every controversial topic that plagued these conventions – from the extension of rights to nonwhite persons to the bitter fights over banking corporations – reveals how difficult it can be to fit these battles into political categories.[79]

Nevertheless, antebellum Americans, especially those living in the western states, rarely subscribed to coherent political platforms. Western Whigs purloined many of the Jacksonian Democrats' policies, and the Democrats (not just in the West, but in the entire nation) were a bitterly divided party. Many Free Soil Democrats were more progressive on black people's rights than moderate Whigs. If we take the northwestern conventions out of the national context, then such categories, definitions, and classifications become less helpful when talking about political and constitutional reform. Second, only radicals in the northwestern conventions actively pushed for the civil rights of nonwhite persons. The fights over the franchise and property rights of nonwhite people were far more complicated: As a later chapter argues, some Democrats even agreed that black men ought to have rights, but then, like many Whigs, refused to assent to those rights. Finally, the political aspects of reform are hard to parse. Since Whigs frequently appropriated Democratic Party platforms, sometimes reform could encompass improvements that supported both progressive and conservative ideas.[80]

For most middle-of-the-road delegates who were attempting to please their constituents and their political parties, making radical changes to one's system of government – improvements that stepped to the very edge of constitutionalism – remained the province of visionary reformers. But for most antebellum Americans, even many Whigs, "modernizing" meant extending the white franchise by removing property qualifications, shortening legislative sessions, and streamlining governmental costs. Democratic reform would always become progressive and liberating – a belief shared by the members of both political parties. Those who favored strong state constitutional changes exhibited little of the reverence they felt for the U.S. Constitution. The most vocal supporters of constitutional reform expressed stringent criticisms of their

[79] For a discussion of historic and historiographic uses of categories such as "progressive" and "conservative," see Gene Wise, *American Historical Explanations: A Strategy for Grounded Inquiry*, 2nd rev. ed. (Minneapolis: University of Minnesota Press, 1980), 344. See also David S. Brown, especially his discussion of Richard Hofstadter's analysis of Jacksonian America, *Beyond the Frontier: The Midwestern Voice in American Historical Writing* (Chicago: University of Chicago Press, 2009), 106–9.

[80] See Laura J. Scalia, *America's Jeffersonian Experiment: Remaking State Constitutions, 1820–1850* (DeKalb: Northern Illinois University, 1999). Scalia contrasted pro–black rights progressives with pro–property rights conservatives; for example, she was comparing constitutional conventions and debates across regions: from the South, the Middle West, and New England.

earlier state charters, which they castigated as outdated, "rickety," and "palsied."[81] The *Rushville Jacksonian*, a vehemently Democratic Indiana paper, declared that anyone interested in constitutional reform ought to speak up and heaped contempt on those "who wish to plod along under the semi-barbarian usages of our ancestors." After all, a convention "of the people" could do no harm, because the people, in their wisdom, would "do nothing to their own injury." The *Jacksonian* was in favor of "great and RADICAL changes" in Indiana's fundamental law. The popular sovereignty revisions the editor demanded included the election of all public officers, a biennial legislature, and provisions that prohibited the legislature from borrowing money except in time of internal insurrection; and of course all such questions had to be submitted to the people.[82]

Constitutional revision could serve as a force for clarifying the purpose and purity of laws: that is, envisioning and realizing larger goals – even some goals that were in advance of the popular will. Democrats would have indignantly rejected the notion that progressive reform was the sole province of Whigs (or later, Republicans). Indiana delegate Dr. William F. Sherrod, at twenty-seven one of the youngest men in the convention and an ardent Virginia-born Democrat, impatiently demanded to know why they were even meeting. Surely there had to be "larger and more important objects" to their task than "merely to economize"? If the delegates had been sent to Indianapolis to frame the organic law "in accordance with the advanced and still progressive spirit of the age, [and] the well known wishes of the people," then surely such a constitution would enable an unfettered Indiana "to rise in her strength and beauty and take her place among the constellation of United States as a star of the first magnitude." Wild applause greeted this speech.[83]

Northwesterners loved calling together conventions, and they found many reasons to gather: to effect progress or reform, to build canals and railroads, to demand the right of suffrage, or to encourage one another to persevere in the face of discrimination.[84] They published their resolutions and demands as

[81] "Reform Convention," *New Constitution* (Columbus, OH), May 26, 1849, 55. This was a reprinted report from the *Baltimore Argus*. Samuel Medary's *e New Constitution* was dedicated to the call for revision of Ohio's constitution.

[82] "Constitutional Reform," *Rushville* [IN] *Jacksonian*, n.d., quoted in *New Constitution* (Columbus, OH), May 26, 1849, 55.

[83] Indiana 1850, 1: 268.

[84] Jean H. Baker, "Politics, Paradigms, and Public Culture," *Journal of American History* 84, no. 3 (Dec. 1997): 894–99; Donald Yacovone, "The Transformation of the Black Temperance Movement, 1827–1854: An Interpretation," *Journal Of The Early Republic* 8, no. 3 (Fall 1988): 281–97; R. J. Young, *Antebellum Black Activists: Race, Gender, and Self* (New York: Garland, 1996), 161–77; Lori D. Ginzberg, *Untidy Origins: A Story of Woman's Rights in Antebellum New York* (Chapel Hill: University of North Carolina Press, 2005), 12–13; Judith Wellman, *The Road to Seneca Falls: Elizabeth Cady Stanton and the First Woman's Rights Convention* (Urbana: University of Illinois Press, 2004), 36–63, (chapter 2, "Entering the World of Reform: Anti-Slavery and Women's Rights, 1835–1840").

pamphlets, broadsides, or petitions or in newspaper editorials. If we consider their exhortations and position statements as manifestos, then black activists' demands for political rights, or women's declarations of equality were all examples of a coeval worldwide movement for human rights reform. A few received a grudging, or even occasionally a respectful hearing in the state constitutional conventions, especially in Indiana, Minnesota, Ohio, and Wisconsin. In those contentions the delegates who sympathized with antiprejudice, problack, or pro-Indian rights activists struggled mightily against punitive exclusion clauses or other discriminatory provisions. But all of those efforts failed, both in the conventions and even more decisively in the popular ratification votes. Voters rejected the Iowa constitution of 1844 at least in part because of the inclusion of married women's property rights.

Utopian communities such as New Harmony alongside German, Swiss, and English social experiments abounded in Illinois, Indiana, and Iowa, as well as Quaker settlements in Ohio. Many of these communities wrote their own constitutions, and although some conventions permitted radical delegates to speak freely and accepted most reform petitions and referred them to committee consideration, almost no progressive social reforms penetrated the state charters. If anything, the conventions and the ratifying votes actually made it more difficult, even impossible, for legislatures to pass laws that eased discrimination and segregation. The conventions hampered the legislatures with strict term limits, shorter and less frequent sessions, and a great deal of detailed legal code that kept the lawmaking power firmly within the bounds of the popular control.

Modern historians have criticized the proliferation of legal code that has burdened state constitutions – a process they now call "superlegislation": in other words, "legislating for the legislature."[85] That simply means adding constitutional provisions that would probably work better as laws, but are intended to constrain the legislature, or to place some decisions beyond their reach. Nineteenth-century Americans did not use the word "superlegislation," instead frequently referring to the practice of adding extraneous legal code to state constitutions as "loading it with lumber." The framers of state constitutions, according to Stephen Griffin, have less access to built-in elasticity – that is, state constitutions permit less room for interpretation because most such charters do not contain a "necessary and proper" clause. Therefore, contentious problems had to be sorted out in greater detail, especially if the state legislature had already proven itself untrustworthy.[86] In the antebellum northwestern conventions, the delegates were perfectly well aware of the dangers

[85] See John Kincaid, ed., *State Constitutions in a Federal System*, vol. 496 of *Annals of the American Academy of Political and Social Science* (Newbury Park, CA: Sage, 1988); Tarr, *Understanding State Constitutions*; Fritz, *American Sovereigns*.

[86] Griffin, *American Constitutionalism*, 6; Donald S. Lutz, "State Constitutions in Historical Perspective," in *State Constitutions in a Federal System*, 33–42 (definition on 36).

inherent in enshrining detailed legal code in constitutions. Superlegislation had three principal aims: first, to place some reservoirs of power beyond the legislature's reach; for example, to restrict the assembly's ability to plunge the state into debt through deficit spending; second, to take highly charged questions out of the political realm, for example, the salaries of the governor, legislators, and judges; and, third, to reassure the Jacksonian Democratc majority that their demands were being heard and taken seriously, for example, enshrining black exclusion clauses in the constitutions or giving the voters the right to veto corporation charters.[87] Superlegislation may also have been a method for coping with the failed efforts to codify common law rules, by elevating them to the status of constitutional provisions.

Superlegislation certainly ensured the separation of powers. In the 1847 Wisconsin debates, one delegate declared that if the judiciary system they had just constructed at great length were correct (that is, establishing a supreme court that would have original jurisdiction, and that could not be altered by the state legislature), then they ought to "engraft" that system in the state constitution, and not "leave it in the power of the legislature to deprive us of its advantages." He believed in "tying up the legislature so as to confine them to their legitimate business of making laws and in confining each branch of the government within its proper bounds."[88] The voters at home would have agreed, to the extent that the convention actually included (or "grafted," as though the constitution were a living tree, and the superlegislation a way of introducing new varieties without damaging the old stock) the terms they wanted. For example, the Alton, Illinois, *Telegraph* – a staunch Whig newspaper – wanted a provision "ingrafted" that would prevent the legislature from plunging the state into further debt and would allow a majority of the voters to approve or repeal legislation.[89]

Finally, superlegislation could serve as a force for moral uplift. Ohio delegate William Lawrence (Figure 4.1), who always spoke out for temperance reform, found himself deeply disappointed when the convention reversed itself on an earlier provision that would have prevented the state legislature from licensing grog shops. There were "some crimes of so deep a nature," crimes that struck "so strongly at the very foundations of society," he believed, "as to demand the interposition of a remedy in the organic law of the State." A constitutional prohibition would "demolish" the crime of drunkenness because the convention, by passing such an article, declared to the state legislature: "you shall not license [alcohol] and give it a respectability of which it is undeserving."[90]

[87] According to Don Fehrenbacher, this going on in the southern states as well. Don E. Fehrenbacher, *Constitutions and Constitutionalism in the Slaveholding South* (Athens: University of Georgia Press, 1989), 25.

[88] *Journal of the Convention to form a Constitution for the State of Wisconsin, with a Sketch of the Debates Begun and Held at Madison, on the Fifteenth Day of December, 1847* (Madison, WI: 1848), 430.

[89] *Alton* [IL] *Telegraph*, February 5, 1842.

[90] Ohio 1850, 2: 714–15.

FIGURE 4.1. William Lawrence (1814–1895) served in the 1850 Ohio constitutional convention. He served in both the House and Senate in the Ohio Assembly, and later in Congress (1857).

"William Lawrence, Representative from Ohio, Thirty-fifth Congress, half-length portrait."

Source: Digital file from original item. Courtesy of the Library of Congress Prints and Photographs Division, LC-DIG-ppmsca-26748.

Both Whigs and Democrats attempted to "superlegislate," though Democrats were usually much more successful. Provisions that garnered bipartisan support included lawmakers' salaries (proposed by both Democrats and Whigs), instituting school superintendents (primarily Whigs, though supported by Democrats), or instituting twenty-year expirations for bank charters (supported by both parties). Antebellum state constitutions had to serve political and local needs and, above all, had to please an obstreperous public. Both Democratic and Whig delegates were aware of the political dangers and the practical problems associated with superlegislation. Legislative code placed into constitutions removed power from legislatures, strengthened political party authority over policy, and, if delegates were to be believed, undergirded popular sovereignty. Although that idea appears to be paradoxical, Democratic Indiana delegate Robert H. Milroy explained that tight limits on legislative power would leave the people free to prosper, "[and] the narrower ... limits, ... and the fewer [the] powers," he believed, adequate to the maintenance of society and the preservation of order, "the greater ... the amount of liberty left to the people." He put it another way, in a statement redolent of the Anti-Federalists: "*For the more* extended & the *more numerous are the prohibitions and powers of a constitution* the more confined and the fewer will be the powers of the government founded upon that Constitution, and the less will be the burden of that government upon its people."[91] In his inaugural address, Governor Duncan McArthur of Ohio expressed his delight that "but little legislation of a general nature would be necessary, where so much is provided for by the Constitution."[92]

Superlegislation would serve to rationalize the state constitution and to create, in stringently transparent published form, a document that could be read and understood by every citizen, every lawmaker, and every judge. A Republican in the 1857 Minnesota convention observed that the constitution had to be written in such a way that neither Congress nor anyone else could misconstrue any of its provisions.[93] One way to accomplish such a goal – that is, a charter that presented a coherent, standard system of governance – was to flesh out provisions and establish clear parameters for governing bodies. Michigan delegate Calvin Britain, for example, thought that collecting all banking provisions together in the constitution would serve to "secure them all under one system." While he hardly believed that "one wicked or weak Legislature [could] compromise the rights of the people forever," he also thought that tight constitutional provisions would prevent "those at present engaged in banking going against a general banking law in defence of their special interests." More to the point, he believed the voters would respect a constitutional provision more than a regular statute law.[94] Superlegislation also prevented the legislature from

[91] Robert H. Milroy, "Constitutional Convention 1850," manuscript memoir, Robert H. Milroy Papers, Indiana Historical Society, Indianapolis. Emphasis in the original.

[92] Duncan McArthur, "Speech by Duncan McArthur to the Ohio state legislature, upon his election to the Governorship," manuscript speech, December 18, 1830, Duncan McArthur Papers, Library of Congress, Washington, DC.

[93] T. F. Andrews, *Debates and Proceedings of the Constitutional Convention for the Territory of Minnesota, to Form a State Constitution Preparatory to its Admission into the Union as a State* (St. Paul: 1858), 13.

[94] *Report of the Proceedings and Debates in the Convention to Revise the Constitution of State of Michigan, 1850* (Lansing, MI: 1850), 694 (hereafter Michigan 1850).

meddling in matters that could derail state welfare. Legislatures had played fast and loose with education funds, for example, and revenue derived from the sections set aside to fund township schools. In the Michigan 1850 convention, Hezekiah Wells, an educational reform–minded Whig, made a motion resolving that the committee on education be instructed to discuss a constitutional provision that would "forever prevent the Legislature from enacting any law relating to the university and school lands."[95]

For their part, the voters treated such provisions roughly as statute laws. Several letters to convention delegates asked for further explanation of provisions. For example, shortly after the 1846 Wisconsin constitution was submitted to the voters for ratification, one of delegates John Hubbard Tweedy's neighbors asked whether the legislature would be able to add to or diminish the provision. Clearly the constitutional provisions had not been explicit enough; "whilst 40 acres of land would be exempt, the crops raised upon it, household furniture & even wearing apparel would be subject to seizure and ... sale." Would the legislature have the power to "say it shall be less or more, or does not this provision *exclude* all Legislation upon the subject?"[96]

Superlegislation may have been a cumbersome method of calibrating the constitutional "machine," but it was certainly also intended to function as a Democratic Party weapon to limit potential Whig influences. Indiana delegate John Niles's friend James Frazier, a despairing Indiana Whig, loathed the Democrats' attempts to politicize the constitution. "They thus trample upon the very first principle of *true* progression. – to leave the people free to progress." He thought there was simply too much legislation engrafted on the new constitution.[97] Frazier did not "admire much that class of 'Reforms' of 'Friends of Progress' as they soundingly term themselves" who were "irrevocably *fastening* their measures of 'progress' and 'reform' [onto] the constitution." No doubt they imagined that all their "discoveries in the science of government" were the revelations of "superhuman wisdom," and that there could be no "mistake in them and no progress beyond."[98] In the long run, however, the delegates did have to exercise caution in saddling the constitutions with too many controversial provisions. They did not care to risk a popular vote scuttling the charter they had worked so hard to build.

95 Michigan 1850, 60.

96 H. A. Wells to John H. Tweedy, January 9, 1847, John H. Tweedy Papers, Wisconsin Historical Society, Madison.

97 James S. Frazier to John B. Niles, November 6, 1850, John B. Niles papers, Lilly Library, Indiana University, Bloomington.

98 John B. Niles, "Speech on Grand Juries," October 23, 1850, John B. Niles Papers, Lilly Library, Indiana University, Bloomington. Niles had sent a copy of his speech to his friend James S. Frazier. See Indiana 1850, 1: 182.

5

Judges

In a lighthearted aside during one of his convention speeches, Illinois delegate Ezekiel Wright Robbins described his leave taking from one of his constituents: "How long," the old farmer had asked him, "do you expect to be gone to the Convention?" Robbins told his neighbor that he supposed he would be home by the first Monday of August, 1847. "How many lawyers are there in the Convention?" – "About forty," Robbins replied. "Forty lawyers in the Convention," exclaimed the old man; "then farewell, I shall never see you any more!"[1]

Lawyers represented about 26 percent of the northwestern convention delegates; three-quarters of their colleagues were farmers, merchants, and physicians.[2] Yet the lawyers dominated the judiciary committees and ruthlessly controlled every debate that touched on courts, judges, or juries.[3] They did so by deploying both volubility and Latin phrases, which effectively silenced their colleagues. The penchant for lawyerly obscurantism became so annoying that the Ohio convention debated banning Latin terms (not only in the convention,

[1] Excerpted from Ezekiel Wright Robbins' speech, June 14, 1847, in Arthur Charles Cole, ed., *The Constitutional Debates of 1847*, vol. 14 of *Collections of the Illinois State Historical Library* (Springfield: Illinois State Historical Library, 1919), 81 (hereafter Illinois 1847). Robbins was a Democrat, a surveyor, originally from New York (p. 975).

[2] For the breakdown of professions, see Tables 1.5a and 1.5b in Chapter 1, which present the percentage of lawyer delegates in the following conventions: Illinois 1847, Indiana 1850, Iowa 1844, Iowa 1846, Iowa 1857, Michigan 1850, Ohio 1850, Wisconsin 1848.

[3] The older states, particularly those that were revising an earlier constitution, had more lawyer delegates. The newer, more northern states (Michigan, Wisconsin, and Minnesota) had fewer lawyers. Both Caleb Nelson and Kermit Hall observe that in state constitutional conventions throughout the antebellum era lawyers controlled the committees on the judiciary. Caleb Nelson, "A Re-Evaluation of Scholarly Explanations for the Rise of the Elective Judiciary in Antebellum America," *American Journal of Legal History* 37, no. 2 (April 1993): 202; Kermit L. Hall, "The Judiciary on Trial: State Constitutional Reform and the Rise of an Elected Judiciary, 1846–1860," *Historian* 45, no. 3 (May 1983): 342.

but also in the practice of law in the state), a discussion that provoked one of the delegates to suggest "Davy Crockett" as a substitute for one of the Latin phrases, in order to render it "more American."[4]

Good-natured self-mockery aside, the verbal bullying was especially evident among those lawyers who hoped to use the conventions as a springboard to their state's political and judicial arena, and who experienced a powerful desire to impress one another with their knowledge of the language and technology of the law. Above all, they wanted to have a hand in shaping their states' court systems. Naturally they would have to do so with the approval of their constituencies, who were now demanding reforms in all areas of law: both legislative and judicial. Legislatures could be cut down in size, reduced to biennial sessions, and restrained by allowing the voters to weigh in on economic legislation. The judiciary would be much harder to reform, however, for two reasons. First, what the growing region chiefly needed was an expanded, not an economized, judiciary, so the ever-present cry of "retrenchment" would not work. The convention delegates could not cut back the size or diminish the power of the judiciary, as they had with the legislature. As a result, the role, character, and purpose of judges and courts came under careful scrutiny. Nevertheless, some voters believed, rather naively, that these contradictory aims – cutting the costs of the judiciary and speeding up the time to trial – were readily achievable. After all, the delegates had nothing more to do, according to a Democrat Michigan paper, than "cheapening and simplifying legal proceedings, and at the same time protecting the rights and property of the citizen."[5] The more cautions Whigs recognized that the general system of law (taking lawmakers and the judiciary together) had to be worked out carefully – that is, calibrated the way a finely tuned clock would be. An Iowa Whig newspaper explained that it was not to be expected that a code of laws and a well-functioning judiciary could be constructed "at once, to the satisfaction of all parties." The defects of the system would become clear once the "machine" had been set going, after which it would "require alteration and amendment time and again." If, after five years or so, the state succeeded in establishing a judicial system that would "meet the wants of the people, and render justice without delay," then the people of Iowa would have done well indeed.[6]

Second, voters throughout the Northwest were beginning to demand that judges be elected rather than appointed. Most Democrats in the conventions approved of that change, but they faced opposition from those (mostly Whigs) who feared a political judiciary elected by an uneducated Democratic

[4] J. V. Smith, *Report of the Debates and Proceedings of the Convention for the Revision of the Constitution of the State of Ohio, 1850–51* (Columbus, OH: 1851), 1: 588–90 (hereafter Ohio 1850); Ohio 1850, 2: 410, 474. The proposal to ban Latin in legal documents failed. See, John F. Winkler, "The Legal Literature of Ohio," in Michael Les Benedict and John F. Winkler, eds., *The History of Ohio Law* (Athens: Ohio University Press, 2004), 2: 540n100.

[5] *Ypsilanti* [MI] *Sentinel*, September 17, 1845.

[6] *Iowa Standard* (Iowa City), February 6, 1845.

population. To maintain some control over these discussions, and to show off their erudition to their opponents, both Democrat and Whig lawyers brandished their Latin phrases and arcane legal terms. In this way they flouted, perhaps inadvertently, the widely accepted notion that the law ought to be a clear, legible, and comprehensible system that facilitated both justice and community prosperity through the application of straightforward rules and knowledge.[7] As far as the voters were concerned, so long as they had the right to select their own judges, to present their lawsuits before a judge and jury within a reasonable space of time, and to rid themselves of what they considered an outdated and expensive grand jury system, they would be satisfied. As with every other problem of democratic self-governance, northwesterners believed in their capacity – even their duty – to take responsibility for their civic life. This chapter will therefore focus on two of the more salient problems in judiciary organization. First, the delegates had to work out the shift from an appointed to an elected judiciary. Although this transformation was by now widely accepted in the antebellum Northwest, a sustained and articulate opposition forced both delegates and voters to focus deeply on the roles and powers delegated to judges. Second, to a lesser degree, the delegates and their constituencies had to scrutinize judges' (and incidentally, citizens') role in reviewing the rationality and constitutionality of legislation.[8]

These two processes – shifting to an elective judiciary and hammering out the scope and method of reviewing laws for their adherence to the state constitutions – became urgent during the great age of state constitutional revision. In the Northwest the groundwork for aggressive popular intrusions into the judicial process began decades before the territories initiated their bids for statehood. Before the United States government gained control of the Northwest Territory in 1787, the first inhabitants in the Illinois Country and in the early

[7] Rufus King was a journalist deeply interested in education. Men such as Indiana's Alvin Hovey or Ohio's Rufus Ranney weighed in on every topic that interested them. Both Jed H. Shugerman and Caleb Nelson observe that lawyers did most of the talking in state conventions when it came to the reorganization of court systems, or the role and power of judges in northwestern society. Jed H. Shugerman, *The People's Courts: Pursuing Judicial Independence in America* (Cambridge, MA: Harvard University Press, 2012), 115; Nelson, "A Re-Evaluation of Scholarly Explanations for the Rise of the Elective Judiciary in Antebellum America," 190–224. The merchant Charles Reemelin and the blacksmith William Sawyer spoke more than almost any other delegate but did not address questions on the judiciary during the Ohio 1850 convention. Larry D. Kramer explains that the question about which institution has the responsibility of interpreting the fundamental principles of the constitution is one of the most fundamental problems in constitutional theory. For most Americans the answer, he says, is "painfully obvious." The post-*Marbury* Supreme Court has the expertise and power to "say what the law is" despite "variance in skill" and political commitments. Larry D. Kramer, *The People Themselves: Popular Constitutionalism and Judicial Review* (New York: Oxford University Press, 2004), 121–43.

[8] See, Stacy Pratt McDermott, *The Jury in Lincoln's America* (Athens, OH: Ohio University Press, 2012); and David J. Bodenhamer, "Criminal Justice and Democratic Theory in Antebellum America: The Grand Jury Debate in Indiana," *Journal of the Early Republic* 5, no. 4 (Winter 1985): 481–502.

Ohio territory regulated their fur and mining trade relationships with Indians and resolved their conflicts through the aid of British army officers stationed in military outposts.[9] Elizabeth Brown has observed that the courts in the region had already been well established before American settlement, in fact before the British relinquished control over the region.[10] After the Old Northwest became a U.S. possession and under the jurisdiction of the ordinance, the court system consisted of three judges, any two of whom could "form a court" and had common law jurisdiction.[11] These men were to reside in the district, and were granted a freehold estate consisting of five hundred acres of land. They remained in office "during good behavior," meaning that they could serve as long as they wished, and could not be removed for political reasons.[12] The ordinance left it to the territorial assemblies to create the lower court systems.[13] These early governments, which ruled the territory as a temporary colonial arrangement, freely mixed executive, legislative, and judicial functions in the office of the territorial governor. The first northwestern territorial governor – the domineering Arthur St. Clair – appointed the judges, and together with these men was responsible for publishing laws and court decisions.[14] These prosperous, well-educated judges and autocratic

9 Dwight Gaylord McCarty, *The Territorial Governors of the Old Northwest: A Study in Administration* (Iowa City: State Historical Society of Iowa, 1910) 28–32.

10 Elizabeth Gaspar Brown, "Frontier Justice: Wayne County, 1796–1836," *American Journal of Legal History* 6, no. 2 (April 1972): 126.

11 Northwest Ordinance, sec. 4 and art. 2, July 13, 1787 (National Archives Microfilm Publication M332, roll 9); Miscellaneous Papers of the Continental Congress, 1774–1789; Records of the Continental and Confederation Congresses and the Constitutional Convention, 1774–1789, Record Group 360; National Archives and Records Administration, Washington, DC. See also, the reception statute of Virginia of 1776: "And be it further ordained, That the common law of England, all statutes or acts of Parliament made in aid of the common law prior to the fourth year of the reign of King James the first, and which are of a general nature, not local to that kingdom, together with the several acts of the General Assembly of this colony now in force, so far as the same may consist with several ordinances, declarations, and resolutions of the General Convention, shall be the rule of decision, and shall be considered as in full force, until the same shall be altered by the legislative power of this colony." "An Ordinance to Enable the Present Magistrates and Officers to Continue the Administration of Justice, and for Settling the General Mode of Proceedings in Criminal and Other Cases till the Same Can Be More Amply Provided for" (May 1776) Sec. 6, in William Waller Hening, *Hening's Statutes at Large* (Richmond, VA: 1821), 9: 127.

12 In the American colonies that notion translated to mean that supreme court justices should remain in office for a lifetime, so long as they refrained from criminal behavior. Scott Gerber has traced the origins to William Penn. Scott D. Gerber, "William Penn and the Origins of Judicial Tenure during Good Behavior," *The Pennsylvania Magazine of History and Biography* 136, no. 3 (July 2012): 233–51. See also Scott D. Gerber, *A Distinct Judicial Power: The Origins of an Independent Judiciary, 1606–1787* (New York: Oxford University Press, 2011). The phrase "during good behavior" originally derived from the common law notion that judges ought to remain independent of the king, established with the 1701 English Act of Settlement.

13 James E. Pfander and Daniel D. Birk, "Article III and the Scottish Judiciary," *Harvard Law Review* 124, no. 7 (May 2011): 1613–87.

14 Beverley W. Bond, *The Civilization of the Old Northwest: A Study of Political, Social, and Economic Developments, 1788–1812* (New York: MacMillan, 1934), 57–60. See also

governors together made territorial law, but they did so in a constant state of turmoil and in-fighting.[15] The first territorial judges in Ohio, James Mitchell Varnum and Samuel Holden Parsons, both highly trained and experienced lawyers, held considerable sway over the development of law in the Northwest as lawmakers and as judges.[16] After the first northwestern states wrote their constitutions (Ohio in 1802, Indiana in 1816, and Illinois in 1818) and disemboweled the gubernatorial veto, they left legislatures firmly in control of court organization, particularly of lower courts, as well as judges' appointments and salaries. As the first state in the region, Ohio set the precedent for democratizing the state government, and for permitting the state legislature to organize courts. The 1802 Enabling Act had not specified property qualifications for voters, and the first state constitution established a powerful legislature to counter the governor, which resulted in the exponential growth of a highly democratic citizenry that demanded a say in the processes and interpretation of law.

From 1802 through 1857 the legislators and constitutional convention delegates, in concert and antagonistically, rebuilt the familiar court system they knew from their home states. Starting closest to the people, every territory had come into existence with justices of the peace, who presided over small civil cases and minor criminal offenses, issued licenses, and, with the help of local magistrates such as sheriffs, county commissioners, coroners, and county probate clerks, oversaw the day-to-day administration of their counties.[17] Those citizens who disputed larger claims – for example, debts or damages greater than twenty to fifty dollars – hired lawyers and took their cases to a court of common pleas (called district courts after 1830).[18]

In 1851, a Justice of the Peace in Jefferson County, Iowa, sat in judgment over a pair of feuding neighbors. After announcing his decision and forcing

Andrew R. L. Cayton, "Law and Authority in the Northwest Territory," in *History of Ohio Law*, 1: 14.

[15] Michael Les Benedict, "Civil Liberty in Ohio," in Benedict and Winkler, *History of Ohio Law*, 2: 680. See also Andrew Cayton on Varnum and Parsons, in Cayton, "Law and Authority in the Northwest Territory," 1: 23. For further discussion of the St. Clair government, see Jeffrey P. Brown, "Political Culture of Early Ohio," in Jeffrey P. Brown and Andrew R. L. Cayton, eds., *The Pursuit of Public Power: Political Culture in Ohio, 1787–1861* (Kent, OH, and London, England: Kent State University Press, 1994), 1–14. See also Donald J. Ratcliffe, *Party Spirit in a Frontier Republic: Democratic Politics in Ohio 1793–1821* (Columbus: Ohio State University, 1998).

[16] Lawrence Friedman explains that common law judges "made" law, especially since these frontier judges rarely had access to law books or court reports. *A History of American Law*, 3rd rev. ed. (New York: Touchstone, 2005), 118–120.

[17] See Philip Hamburger, *Law and Judicial Duty* (Cambridge, MA: Harvard University Press, 2008). Hamburger explains that in both English and American law, judges had a responsibility to assess the constitutionality not only of statute laws and the acts of the Crown and of governors, but also of customs and corporate bylaws.

[18] Residents hired lawyers for JP cases as well, although they had the option to represent themselves. Most states set the limit around twenty dollars for JP cases. In 1805 the Ohio legislature triggered a controversy by raising the limit to fifty dollars. A judge of the common pleas court

both parties to swear never to bring another suit against one another, he sent them home. The JP secured their agreement by persuading them to "throw in" their court costs and by promising to forgo his own fee. Calling him a model for all other justices, the Iowa *Bellevue Democrat* extolled his wisdom and generosity: Clearly, as an experienced, respectable, and good-humored magistrate who knew his constituents personally, this man ought to be emulated by all others responsible for the welfare of their communities. As the northwestern population grew, the role of JPs became a thorny problem for convention delegates, one that forced them to consider both the abstract role of judicial representation and of popular elections as they struggled to build or reform their court systems.[19]

A justice of the peace, closely tied to his community and respected by his neighbors, did precisely what his title implied: He provided local and accessible justice and safeguarded the peace and stability of his community.[20] The Northwest Ordinance had established the office of "magistrates," a synonym for justices of the peace.[21] In the American colonial past, justices of the peace possessed a great deal of local authority, since they represented the royal governors.[22] In seventeenth-century Massachusetts and Virginia these magistrates wielded wide powers, as their English predecessors had; as a result there was essentially little difference between magistrates and JPs. But in the early Northwest, the settlers had struggled against both patronage and the violation of separation of powers. As soon as they had the requisite population the territories rid themselves of their autocratic governors, and their legislatures passed laws that provided for democratic elections of their justices of the peace. Therefore, some members of the judiciary were elected as early as 1802 in Ohio, 1816 in Indiana, and 1818 in Illinois (see Table 5.1).

subsequently declared that law unconstitutional. David M. Gold, "The General Assembly and Ohio's Constitutional Culture," in *History of Ohio Law*, 1: 92.

[19] *Bellevue* [IA] *Democrat*, May 7, 1851, in "Model Justice," *Annals of Iowa: A Historical Quarterly* 3rd ser., 5, no. 8. (Jan. 1903): 616.

[20] John Wunder in his study of the Pacific Northwest notes the strong link between justices of the peace and their respective communities. John R. Wunder, *Inferior Courts, Superior Justice: A History of the Justices of the Peace on the Northwest Frontier, 1853–1889* (Westport, CT: Greenwood Press, 1979), 19. See also, David F. Forte, "Marbury's Travail: Federalist Politics and William Marbury's Appointment as Justice of the Peace," *Catholic University Law Review* 45, no. 2 (Winter 1996): 349–402; John A. Conley, "Doing It by the Book: Justice of the Peace Manuals and English Law in Eighteenth Century America," *Journal of Legal History* 6, no. 3 (1985): 257–98; Anthony G. Roeber, *Faithful Magistrates and Republican Lawyers: Creators of Virginia Legal Culture, 1680–1810* (Chapel Hill: University of North Carolina Press, 2011). Roeber argues that lawyers, who represented reason and science, were able to take power from JPs, who represented religion and tradition.

[21] Northwest Ordinance, sec. 7; John Bouvier, *A Law Dictionary, Adapted to the Constitution and Laws of the United States of America* (Philadelphia: 1855), 2: 92.

[22] Conley, "Justice of the Peace Manuals and English Law in Eighteenth Century America," 257–98.

TABLE 5.1. *Constitutional provisions for justice of the peace for the original thirteen states (plus Vermont) and the Old Northwest*

State[a]	JPs appointed by government entity[b] (years)	JPs elected by voters (years)
Connecticut		1818+
Delaware	1831+	
Georgia	1798+	
Maryland	1776–1851	1851+
Massachusetts	1780+	
New Hampshire	1784+	
New Jersey	1776–1844	1844+
New York	1821–1846	1846+
North Carolina	1776+	
Pennsylvania	1790–1838	1838+
Rhode Island		1842+
South Carolina	1790+	
Virginia	1776–1851	1851+
Vermont	1793–1850	1850+
Illinois	1818–1848	1848+
Indiana		1816+
Iowa		1844+
Michigan		1835+
Minnesota		1857+
Ohio		1802+
Wisconsin		1846

[a] Summary of data:
Original 13 colonies plus Vermont: Appointed by governor, legislature, or local govt. entity (12): NH, MA, NY (1821–46), NJ (1776–1844), PA (1790–1838), DE, MD (1776–1851), VA (1776–1851), NC, SC, GA, VT (1793–1850). Elected by voters (8): RH, CT, NY (1846+), NJ (1844+), PA (1838+), MD (1851+), VA (1851+), VT (1850+).
Old Northwest: Appointed by governor, legislature, or local govt. entity (2): IL (1818–48), MN. Elected by voters (6): OH, IN, MI, IL (1848+), WI, IA.
Total: Appointed by governor, legislature, or local govt. entity (14): NH, MA, NY (1821–46), NJ (1776–1844), PA (1790–1838), DE, MD (1776–1851), VA (1776–1851), NC, SC, GA, VT (1793–1850), IL (1818–48), MN. Elected by voters (14): RH, CT, NY (1846+), NJ (1844+), PA (1838+), MD (1851+), VA (1851+), VT (1850+), OH, IN, MI, IL (1848+), WI, IA.
[b] Entities included the governor, the legislature, and county courts.

JPs handled local problems such as small claims disputes between neighbors or questioned witnesses and prisoners in minor crimes, such as misdemeanors – essentially any crime punishable by a fine. They also rendered summary judgments over civil matters concerning less than fifty to one hundred dollars and exercised control over immense counties.[23] In practice, therefore, the justices

[23] See, for example, Secretary and Acting Governor Stevens T. Mason, speech, May 2, 1832, in *Journal of the Legislative Council of the Territory of Michigan* (Detroit, 1832), 5: 5–6.

of the peace constituted the first and main justice system for northwestern settlers, in both criminal and civil matters.[24] In early Indiana and Illinois some even presided over six- or twelve-man jury trials.[25] State constitutions left the numbers of JPs and election procedures to the discretion of individual county government.[26] Therefore, JPs shared and overlapped jurisdiction with, or were roughly analogous to, other inferior courts in the territories, such as quarter sessions courts (which eventually became known as criminal courts) or courts of common pleas (eventually called district courts).[27] In 1828, for example, a group of sheepish Ohio Quakers appeared before a justice of the peace, to face an accusation that they had disturbed the peace of a local meeting. Their raucous behavior contravened a law passed in 1816 preventing "low and vulgar" persons from disturbing camp meetings.[28] The plaintiffs had taken the case to a local JP in order to "get one who was familiar with [their] experience." The JP took the evidence from witnesses, but because the defendants had caused a serious disturbance and the law in question was difficult to settle, the case went to a local court of common pleas.[29]

Justices of the peace would petition their territorial or state legislatures to legalize their acts. For other examples of the various roles of JPs see, *Journal of the Senate of the State of Ohio* (Columbus, OH: 1825), 34, 120; Charles A. Beard, *The Office of Justice of the Peace in England in Its Origin and Development*, vol. 20 of *Studies in History, Economics and Public Law* (New York: Columbia University Press, 1904).

[24] Wunder, *Inferior Courts, Superior Justice*, 8–20; John W. W. Loose, "The Courts of Lancaster County: 1729–1791," *Journal of the Lancaster County Historical Society* 92, no. 4 (1989–1990): 102–17.

[25] Harry L. McGurk, "A Pioneer Indiana County Circuit Court," *The American Journal of Legal History* 15, no. 4 (Oct. 1971): 281. See also, "An Act Defining the Powers and Duties of Justices of the Peace," March 23, 1819, *Laws Passed by the First General Assembly of the State of Illinois* (Kaskaskia, IL: 1819), 186.

[26] In both the Indiana (1851) and Ohio (1851) constitutions, the legislature set the number (or set the rules for setting the number), Ohio Const. of 1851, art. IV, sec. 1; Ind. Const. of 1851, art. 7, sec. 1. After a brief investigation of Illinois, in 1826 the legislature gave each county the power to divide itself into from two to eight districts with two JPs elected from each district (so four to sixteen JPs). The county seat district gained an extra JP so the total for each county could be five to seventeen JPs. In 1835, the legislature then gave the county the power to add more JPs to accommodate population increase. The 1848 Illinois Constitution did not change these rules. "An Act to Provide for the Election of Justices of the Peace and Constables," December 30, 1826, *Revised Code of Laws of Illinois* (Vandalia, IL: 1827), 255; "An Act to Amend an Act, entitled 'An Act to Provided for the Election of Justices of the Peace and Constables,'" January 7, 1835, *Laws of the State of Illinois, Passed by the Ninth General Assembly* ... (Vandalia, IL: 1835), 29.

[27] John G. Baker, "The History of the Indiana Trial Court System and Attempts at Renovation," *Indiana Law Review* 30, no. 1 (1997): 240.

[28] Marcus Gould, *Report of the Trial of Friends at Steubenville, Ohio* ... (Philadelphia, 1829), 231. For a general description of the duties of justices of the peace see, John Bouvier, *A Law Dictionary, Adapted to the Constitution and Laws of the United States of American, and of the Several States of the American Union* ... (Philadelphia, 1856), 1: 687–88.

[29] Gould, *Report of the Trial of Friends*, 39.

As the territories joined the Union as states, and as their population continued to grow, the relationship between JPs and regular court sessions required further fine-tuning. The state legislatures began to tinker with the minimum and maximum dollar values of the question under dispute. In Ohio, that problem led to serious disputes over the state supreme court's right to find legislation unconstitutional. Elsewhere, the question of the proper role and sphere of the justice of the peace now became more urgent. Historians often wonder why state convention delegates appeared to become obsessed with minor, finicky points – details of governance or custom that may strike the modern reader as trivial. The debates over JPs in the conventions serve as an excellent case in point of the way such arguments were meant to resolve vital problems in governance. For example, should JPs be considered a part of the justice system, or were they magistrates? That is, the delegates had to figure out whether JPs were to represent the people's interests (in which case they would demand the right to vote for them) or whether they were to remain detached from the political questions of the day. In that case JPs ought to be appointed by the governor or the state legislature. The convention delegates attempted to resolve this problem by ascertaining whether JPs held other offices. In those states where justices of the peace were considered a part of the judiciary, they had to remain independent of state politics. In states where they were considered magistrates (that is, functioned as civil servants) they were permitted to run for a seat in the legislature. That would make it easier, they hoped, to sort out their representative from judicial functions, a distinction that would become a vital question during the debates over elected versus appointed judiciaries. After 1848, every northwestern state constitution provided for elected JPs (see Table 5.1).[30]

The problem of representation raised crucial questions about the role of the judiciary early in northwestern territorial and state legal history, even before most northeastern and southern states had begun thinking about democratically electing judges. In the Michigan Territory, for example, JPs were initially appointed by the territorial governor, a holdover from the Northwest Ordinance days. By the mid-1830s, residents condemned gubernatorial appointments of JPs as an outdated and reactionary arrangement. Justice had to be administered locally, by responsible men who knew the neighborhood. While the 1835–36 Michigan convention was deliberating, a member of the territorial legislature told delegate Lucius Lyon that justices of the peace ought to be elected at local town meetings in order to "divest the executive of the appointing power." The executive (in this case the territorial governor, young Stevens T. Mason) would be unacquainted with their character and abilities.

[30] For example, in the Minnesota 1857 Democratic convention; some delegates demanded that because of the separation of powers, JPs should have been excluded from holding seats in the legislature. Francis H. Smith, *The Debates and Proceedings of the Minnesota Constitutional Convention* ... (St. Paul, MN: 1857), 187–89 (hereafter Minnesota 1857 Democrat).

More to the point: One could trust the people to know who would be their "best servants."[31]

The problem of the selection and the scope of powers of justices of the peace forced northwesterners to think hard about the role of judges in their society. In the early years of northwestern territorial life, the appointments of JPs had served as a rich source of patronage and created conflicts between local communities, who thought JPs ought to respect local laws and customs, and the more repressive regional governors, who recreated the statutes and common law context from the older states. As soon as the northwestern territories rid themselves of their quasi-colonial status and became states they immediately rendered JP offices elective. The counties chose men of standing. Ideally, such men ought to have some legal training, but in the thinly settled areas of the Northwest, finding well-educated, trained lawyers who had achieved a degree of social success proved challenging.[32] Nevertheless, the northwestern counties demanded more and more JPs to fulfill their needs for law and order, for peacekeeping, and for mitigating the long delays in both civil and criminal cases.

At the beginning of their sessions, nineteenth-century circuit courts met and organized their sessions around three distinct divisions of law: common law, chancery, and criminal. The cases would be called one by one on the docket and disposition established. The cases that were expected to go to trial would be scheduled to meet later in the session. Each county circuit court clerk kept circuit xourt records, which reveal that that the typical day in a busy court saw all manner of law cases: common law chancery and criminal (motions, pleas, answers, trials) in rapid succession. There was no separate chancellor; the same judge presided over all three divisions, and the master in chancery was a glorified clerical post, with some authority in making property divisions and executions. The organic law of the Wisconsin Territory, the Iowa Territory (1838), and the 1846 Constitution provided for concurrent common law and chancery proceedings in the supreme court and district courts. In 1851 Iowa also adopted the "Field Code" but did not explicitly abolish chancery proceedings. The 1860 revised code went further in abolishing separate procedure for common law and chancery (but still allowed equity proceedings in certain cases).[33] Finally, Wisconsin's territorial organic laws provided for separate chancery proceedings, which were retained in the 1848 Constitution. The new

[31] H. H. Comstock to Lucius Lyon, May 20, 1835, Lucius Lyon Papers, William L. Clements Library, University of Michigan, Ann Arbor.

[32] John R. Wunder, "Justices of the Peace on the American Frontier, 1787–1853," *Journal of the West* 24, no. 1 (Jan. 1985): 33–38.

[33] For the organic laws, see the 1851 Iowa code (later), pp. 520 (Wisconsin Territory) and 527–28 (Iowa Territory), respectively; Iowa Const. of 1846, art. 6, sec. 4; "Of Courts and the Procedure Therein," February 5, 1851, *The Code of Iowa Passed at the Session of the General Assembly of 1850–51, and approved 5th February, 1851* (Iowa City, 1851), 231–348 (part 3); *Revision of 1860, Containing All the Statutes of a General Nature of the State of Iowa* ... (Des Moines,

constitution also called for a revision of the laws. The revised statutes published in 1849 included a chapter devoted specifically to chancery procedure as part of a larger effort to codify the law.[34]

Most of the early state court systems allowed for some version of chancery, or equity, courts. A chancery court was simply a separate court session that coped with trusts, inheritance cases, and settlements. In the northwestern states, the same judges usually presided over such sessions. Chancery courts were derived from the English court system and were intended to mitigate some of the harsher, less flexible aspects of common law. For example, if the plaintiff was a married woman attempting to retain control over her own property, she could sue in the chancery division of a local court. If she was fortunate enough to have an antenuptial agreement or if her father had instituted a trust, the presiding judge would study the facts of the case and could adjudicate the matter on the basis of documents such as trusts, deeds, or wills; he did not have to follow the common law rule that a wife's property belonged to her husband.[35]

The northwestern state legislatures and constitutional conventions also attempted to reform chancery courts. None ever succeeded in dismantling them, in spite of ongoing criticism about the duplication of effort and the problem of a system in which the same judges sat on both courts.[36] For example, the 1850 Michigan constitution eliminated the office of chancellor (or master in chancery) and gave the power to the legislature to eliminate distinct chancery proceedings. But the legislature apparently never implemented any changes, at least through 1860 and perhaps as late as the 1890s.[37] In Ohio, chancery and circuit courts had already merged before the 1850 constitution, and the new constitution called on the legislature to "revise, reform, simplify and abridge" without reference to distinctions between common law and chancery. The

IA: 1860), 439–43 (part 3, chap. 108); see also: Clifford Powell, "History of the Codes of Iowa Law," *Iowa Journal of History and Politics* 10, no. 1 (Jan. 1912): 54–58.

[34] Wisc. Const. of 1848, art. 7, sec. 2, and sec. 22; "Of the Jurisdiction of Circuit Courts in Chancery, and of Proceedings Therein," *Revised Statutes of the State of Wisconsin* ... (Southport, WI: 1849), 413–28 (chap. 84).

[35] For further discussion of married women's property rights, see Chapter 9. The judge in a chancery court had the latitude to grant injunctive relief – that is, a court order that forces, or prohibits, a specific act such as forcing a husband to maintain a family he had deserted. Common law courts by contrast could only order the payment of damages following specific forms and remedies with very strict rules of evidence.

[36] Debra A. Viles, "Disabilities of Marriage: Gender and Law in Antebellum Michigan," *Michigan Historical Review* 28, no. 1 (March 2002): 1–3; Josiah H. Blackmore II, "Not from Zeus's Head Full-Blown: The Story of Civil Procedure," in *History of Ohio Law*, 1: 444–47.

[37] Mich. Const. of 1850, art. VI, sec. 5; Frank Ravitch, "The Four Michigan Constitutions," in Paul Finkelman and Martin J. Hershock, eds., *The History of Michigan Law* (Athens: Ohio University Press, 2006), 133; Thomas M. Cooley, *The Compiled Law of the State of Michigan* (Lansing, MI: 1857), 2: 1004–32 ("Chapter 115: "Of the Courts of Chancery"); Sanford M. Green, *A Treatise on the Practice of the Circuit Court of the State of Michigan: Embracing Practical Forms of Proceedings Therein* (Detroit, 1860), 2; W. H. H. Russell, "California System of Codes," *Michigan Law Journal* 2, no. 7 (July 1893): 291.

"Field Code" (codification statutes) that the legislature passed in 1852 further melded the two forms by doing away with common law and chancery forms of action and the distinctions between them. This process began with the dismantling of chancery procedure in Ohio – a process that would not end until the unification of common and chancery proceedings in 1838.[38] Illinois and Indiana had equity proceedings in their circuit courts, but after 1852, Indiana copied Ohio's system of unified chancery and common law courts.[39]

Whether in a district, criminal, or chancery court, if plaintiffs or defendants wished to appeal a decision from a lower court, their lawyers took their cases to the state supreme court. This was usually composed of three to five justices. Before 1847, in every northwestern state, these men were to be selected by the legislatures or appointed by the governor. These hardy souls traveled from county to county, along an arduous circuit, sometimes as much as eight hundred miles, twice each year – in spring and fall – remaining for about a week in each town. There they heard both original cases as well as appeals. As the population in the counties grew and the northern areas of the states filled in, their boundaries changed rapidly. Their number also multiplied from eight or ten immense counties to seventy, ninety, and more than a hundred smaller and more densely populated ones, sometimes within a couple of decades.[40]

The new western states provided plenty of opportunities for energetic young men. Stephen A. Douglas, for example, became a lawyer at the age of twenty – shortly after moving to Illinois and beginning his legal studies – an achievement his biographer believed would not have been possible had he remained in his home state of Vermont.[41] By the time the conventions were reorganizing the judiciary system, many of the lawyer delegates were native-born sons of the Northwest, especially in Ohio, Indiana, and Illinois. These men had received a standard legal education: up to seven years of training and apprenticeship, four years of which could include "classical" preparation (usually, college courses

[38] Ohio Const. of 1851, art. XIV, sec. 2; "An Act to Establish a Code of Civil Procedure," March 11, 1853, *Acts of a General Nature Passed by the Fiftieth General Assembly of the State of Ohio* (Columbus, OH: 1853), 51: 57–166; Blackmore, "Not from Zeus's Head Full-Blown," 450–52.

[39] "An Act Declaring What Laws Are in Force in This State," February 4, 1819; and "An Act Regulating the Practice in the Courts of Chancery in This State," March 22, 1819, both in *Laws Passed by the First General Assembly of the State of Illinois* (Kaskaskia, IL: 1819), 1, 170–74; Ill. Const. of 1848, art. V, sec. 8; Ind. Const. 1851, art. VII, sec. 20; "An Act to Revise, Simplify and Abridge the rules, practice, pleadings and forms in civil cases ...," June 18, 1852, *The Revised Statutes of the State of Indiana, Passed at the Thirty-Sixth Session of the General Assembly ...* (Indianapolis, 1852), 2: 27–359.

[40] For changes in number and boundaries of northwestern counties, see the *Atlas of Historical County Boundaries*, Newberry Library, http://publications.newberry.org/ahcbp/index.html (accessed November 16, 2014).

[41] Martin H. Quitt, *Douglas and Antebellum Democracy* (New York: Cambridge University Press, 2012), 65; Maxwell Bloomfield, *American Lawyers in a Changing Society, 1777–1876* (Cambridge, MA: Harvard University Press, 1976), 239–42. See also, Brian Dirck, *Lincoln the Lawyer* (Urbana: University of Illinois Press, 2007), 11–13.

in classical history, philosophy, or logic) as well as three years of apprenticeship with a member of the state bar.[42] The first law school in the Northwest, at Ohio University, began enrolling law students by the early 1820s in the tiny hamlet of Athens, where judges taught among other subjects jurisprudence.[43] Law schools soon appeared throughout Ohio. Indiana University established a law school in 1820.[44]

The historian Elizabeth Brown has argued that these frontier lawyers were meticulous professionals who were deeply familiar with common law pleadings, were careful to follow precedent, and supported their arguments with "lavish citations."[45] In preparing their written and oral arguments they relied on law reports, volumes of published statutes, and law dictionaries; legal treatises by such luminaries as William Blackstone, Joseph Story, and Chancellor Kent; as well as the law digests that were beginning to be published in the early nineteenth century. In their day-to-day professional lives, northwestern lawyers handled a wide variety of cases and clients: Much of their practice concerned debt collection and foreclosure, disputes over boundary issues, land title cases, administering estates (wills, partitions, and dower), broken contract, slander, and common law assault and battery.[46] Lawyers did not specialize – they handled everything from family law to contracts – so they would have been familiar with most of the questions that arose during the conventions. Therefore, because they dominated the convention committees on the judiciary, the constitutional provisions would have been hammered out by men who had a wide array of professional experience, and at least some advanced education, either in eastern or southern colleges or even in law schools.[47]

By the mid-1840s northwestern courts were so overcrowded that judges could barely cope with the caseload. The problem was especially acute in the

42 See William P. LaPiana's section on "Antebellum Legal Education," in *Logic and Experience: The Origin of Modern American Legal Education* (New York: Oxford University Press, 1994), 29–54; Quitt, *Stephen A. Douglas and Antebellum Democracy*, 36–37.

43 Paul D. Carrington, "Teaching Law in the Antebellum Northwest," *University of Toledo Law Review* 23, no. 1 (Fall 1991): 10.

44 Anton-Hermann Chroust, *The Rise of the Legal Profession in America* (Norman: University of Oklahoma Press, 1965), 2: 216.

45 Brown, "Frontier Justice: Wayne County, 1796–1836," 139. See also Roscoe Pound, "The Pioneers and the Common Law," *West Virginia Legal Quarterly and the Bar* 27, no. 1 (Nov. 1920): 1–19; however, Pound also describes the deprofessionalization of lawyers during the antebellum period due to the democratization of state bar entrance requirements. Roscoe Pound, *The Lawyer from Antiquity to Modern Times* (St. Paul, MN: West, 1953), 225–38.

46 For an example of the diversity of legal actions encountered by a typical northwestern lawyer see "The Law Practice of Abraham Lincoln: A Statistical Portrait" ("Legal Actions" subheading) in the reference section of Martha L. Benner and Cullom Davis et al., eds., *The Law Practice of Abraham Lincoln: Complete Documentary Edition*, 2nd ed. (Springfield: Illinois Historic Preservation Agency, 2009), http://www.lawpracticeofabrahamlincoln.org (accessed November 16, 2014).

47 Byron D. Cooper, "Legal Education in Michigan," in *History of Michigan Law*, 256–60.

three older states, whose population had doubled and then quadrupled by the time the states were revising their charters. Because the Ohio constitution required that the supreme court had to sit in each county annually, and the counties had grown in number from eight to eighty-four within the past thirty years, it became urgent to craft a new constitution.[48] Similarly, in Illinois, the rapid expansion of the population (from 55,000 in 1820, two years after statehood, to nearly 480,000 just twenty years later) placed an intense strain on the circuit court judges, who could no longer keep up with the eight hundred miles of traveling.[49] Kermit Hall found that in Indiana civil appeals could take as long as four years to be heard.[50] In Indiana the problem also involved structural issues and duplication of effort. Because of the chronic shortage of trained judges, some had to sit on both local and appeals courts – with the result that (as occurred with a supreme court judge in Indiana, who had earlier served as a circuit judge) they were occasionally forced to overrule themselves.[51]

On the morning of February 11, 1845, the Springfield *Illinois State Register* sarcastically commented that the city's churches had witnessed an en masse attendance by supreme court judges, who were "much more devout than usual." After all, the state legislature was about to vote on the judges' salaries.[52] Yet even though both the lawmakers and constitutional convention delegates possessed some power over salary, tenure, duties, and even the very existence of some of the courts, they also had to find a way to give the people a greater say over all areas of the law. That happened in two ways: first, by rendering appointed judgeships elective, a change that was already taking place throughout the nation; and second, by ensuring that the voters had convenient access to circuit courts, as well as access to reasonably speedy justice. The burning question remained, How much power should lawmakers have over the judiciary? The delegates felt free to criticize the legislators' ineptitude or profligacy, a rhetorical tactic that always played well with their constituents at home. Meanwhile, of course, they were already hedging the lawmakers about with constitutional restrictions. The conventions carefully limited the length of legislatures' terms – indeed fined the legislators if they overstayed their welcome – and removed, at one constitutional blow, both patronage and

[48] Barbara Terzian, "Ohio's Constitutional Conventions and Constitutions," in *History of Ohio Law*, 1: 50–51. According to Terzian, the problems in the 1802 Ohio state constitution caused the call for revision.

[49] Susan Fino observed that the old Michigan constitution was out of harmony with Jacksonian democracy. Susan P. Fino, *The Michigan State Constitution: A Reference Guide* (Westport, CT: Greenwood Press, 1996), 5.

[50] Hall, "Judiciary on Trial," 337–54.

[51] Logan Esarey, *A History of Indiana from Its Exploration to 1850* (Indianapolis: W. K. Stewart, 1915), 226. Esarey does not identify the judge in question. See also Leander J. Monks, Logan Esarey and Ernest V. Shockley, eds., *Courts and Lawyers of Indiana*, 3 vols. (Indianapolis: Federal Publishing Co., 1916).

[52] *Illinois State Register* (Springfield), February 11, 1845.

fiscal power from their grasp. Even so, the lawyers were still willing to leave the organization of the court system and the pay scales to the lawmakers. That was unavoidable. Even the most minutely detailed effort at superlegislation could not predict the needs of the state beyond a decade or so. In spite of repeated assertions that the people knew best – an argument even the most dedicated Whig could hardly avoid making if he wanted to retain some hope of a future political career – those details had to be left to the state legislature.[53]

Yet legislative tinkering failed to resolve the increasingly burdensome caseload for the judges or to relieve the long delays that plagued lawyers and their clients. In 1841 an Illinois lawyer named Junius Hall complained bitterly that last winter the state legislature "among their other acts of folly" had so organized the judiciary as to crowd the court sessions into the spring and fall months, so that the lawyers had "hardly time to breathe during their occurrence." He had been traveling almost incessantly in recent weeks and was now thoroughly exhausted.[54] The circuit judges before whom he argued would have felt similarly fatigued. To cope with the overcrowding and the resultant delays, legislatures throughout the Northwest fidgeted endlessly with the organization of the courts. In addition, the proliferation of counties required shifting the location of the courts at the whim of the residents, who were brawling over the location of county seats. It appeared that the Illinois state legislature could simply not leave the court system alone: sometimes establishing more judgeships, sometimes abolishing the entire circuit court system, and then, in the following year, cobbling it back together.[55] By the time Mr. Hall had written his letter, the Illinois state assembly had already created, destroyed, rebuilt, and expanded the circuit court system, and then repeated the process twice over before 1848. According to the historian Janet Cornelius, the disorganized and inadequate court system was the driving inspiration behind the urge for constitutional reform.[56]

[53] David J. Bodenhamer explains that leaving details to the legislature removed power from judges, in "The Democratic Impulse and Legal Change in the Age of Jackson: The Example of Criminal Juries in Antebellum Indiana," *Historian* 45, no. 2 (Feb. 1983): 216–18. See also Peter Karsen, *Heart versus Head: Judge-Made Law in Nineteenth-Century America* (Chapel Hill: University of North Carolina Press, 1997).

[54] Junius Hall to John Hall, April 20, 1841, Hall Family Correspondence, New York Public Library. The following year Hall bitterly complained about the quality of Illinois courts, noting that "little time is given for the consideration of cases ... everything is hurried." Junius Hall to John Hall, October 22, 1842, Hall Family Correspondence, New York Public Library.

[55] "Court Structure in Antebellum Illinois," in Daniel W. Stowell, et al., eds., *The Papers of Abraham Lincoln: Legal Documents and Cases* (Charlottesville: University of Virginia Press, 2008), 4: 287–98.

[56] See Janet D. Cornelius, *Constitution Making in Illinois, 1818–1970*, rev. ed. (Urbana: University of Illinois Press, 1972); Janet D. Cornelius, "Popular Sovereignty and Constitutional Change in the United States and Illinois Constitutions," *Illinois Historical Journal* 80, no. 4 (Winter 1987): 228–47.

Should lawmakers have the power to rebuild the structure of the courts? Was this not a violation of the first principles of republican government? In the 1850 Michigan convention, for example, the delegates debated whether the constitution ought to leave the legislature free to change the state supreme court later on to meet the needs of a growing population. They had the bitter warning of the Illinois situation before them. If the state's circuit court was to be permanently enshrined in the state's judiciary system – a system that would necessitate establishing new circuits as new counties were created – then the legislature would be forced to organize additional courts. Such an expansion of legislative purview was far more frightening than letting the legislature work out smaller logistical problems of increasing or reorganizing an existing judiciary. The constitutional convention would have to hold the line: to recur to the first principle of strict separation of powers. The Michigan convention left the current structure in place for six years, and set up a basic system roughly analogous to that in all northwestern states, and then permitted the legislature, working within the constitutional parameters, to organize the courts as necessary.[57] In the end this question came down to a pragmatic move: to create as much of the court systems as constitutionally necessary while retaining flexibility for future growth in the hands of the legislature.

Meanwhile, Illinoisans had a distressing habit of choosing "either a fool or a dishonest man" for their governor, according to Judge David Davis. Therefore, gubernatorial appointments of judges were simply "out of the question."[58] Davis wrote that scathing observation while he was serving in the 1847 Illinois state constitutional convention, watching his colleagues struggle to undo the Gordian knot tied by the legislature over the past six or seven years. The truth of the matter, however, was that no Illinois governor had appointed any judge since statehood more than thirty years ago. Davis was making a point about the problem of legislative appointments of judges: not that he thought Illinois citizens were so reliable in the choice of their judges, but that there was simply no reasonable alternative to popular elections. And Davis was a Whig who could be relied upon to oppose most other hard-line Democratic propositions.

His point of view would have harmonized with the wishes expressed by most of the voters: that is, almost all of the Democrats and many of the Whigs. By the time the older northwestern states (Illinois, Indiana, and Ohio) were ready to revise their constitutions and the new territories (Iowa, Michigan, Minnesota, and Wisconsin) were applying for statehood, the tide of national popular opinion had already turned from appointive to elective judiciaries. Beginning in 1832, when Mississippi became the first state to elect judges, state constitutional conventions around the nation watched anxiously to discover

[57] Nelson, "A Re-Evaluation of Scholarly Explanations for the Rise of the Elective Judiciary in Antebellum America," 190–224.

[58] David Davis to Wells Colton, June 25, 1847, David Davis Papers, Chicago History Museum. Davis was a Whig. During Davis's tenure as judge, all but one of the governors (Duncan) had been Democrats, and Duncan was elected as a Democrat.

whether the arrangement worked.[59] In 1846, the New York constitutional convention instituted an elected judiciary, and thirty other states followed suit over the next twenty years. Most historians explain this trend as a result of financial panics and the growing widespread perception that legislators needed more oversight, not only in their legislative function but also in their political and judicial appointments.[60]

Northwesterners certainly viewed both gubernatorial and legislative appointments with deep suspicion. Patronage represented a valuable, if undemocratic, source of political power. Worse, such spoils entailed inevitable corruption and subverted popular sovereignty. Judgeships had to stay out of the hands of political opponents who would sit in judgment over the citizens' economic interests and property rights. But would it be possible to engraft an elective judiciary on a political system that even Jacksonian Democrats – who practically invented the idea of the spoils system – despised as rife with corruption? If one could not reconcile ethics and politics within the legislative framework, then there was only one solution. The whole arrangement had to be reformed constitutionally because neither governors nor legislatures would be likely to curtail their own control over appointments. Where many Whigs thought that the answer was to remove judges from the strife and turmoil of party politics and leave their selection in the hands of elected governing bodies, Democrats thought that the entire structure had to be reformed from the ground up. They wanted to make it impossible for the legislature to fiddle with (without ever truly reforming) the most ethically responsible branch of government. This was especially troubling in questions that touched on the economic welfare of the people.

For die-hard Jacksonians, therefore, the answer was not to keep the power of selecting judges out of the hands of the people, but rather to put the whole problem back on an ethical footing. The influential *Democratic Review* explained that while of course the people would "choose their officers wisely," there was no chance that they would be properly represented so long as political

[59] Benjamin F. Shambaugh, ed., *Fragments of the Debates of the Iowa Constitutional Conventions of 1844 and 1846 along with Press Comments and other Materials* ... (Iowa City: State Historical Society of Iowa, 1900), 61–62 (hereafter Iowa 1844 and Iowa 1846).

[60] Kermit Hall explained that elected judges would be more likely to reform legislation, in "Judiciary on Trial," 337–54. As most scholars do, Hall explains the popular dissatisfaction with elective judiciary as primarily suspicion of legislative patronage. Michael Solimine and Richard Saphire return to the general populism explanation: Elective judiciary was meant to express dissatisfaction with the "decisions of all branches of government," and in order to "empower popular oversight of justice," in "The Selection of Judges in Ohio," *History of Ohio Law*, 1: 214. Caleb Nelson understood the move as a way to limit government in general and to "insulate" the judiciary. He considers that the move toward an elective judiciary in Mississippi was as important as in New York, a point borne out by the fact that an immensely popular letter by a Mississippi judge made the rounds of many state constitutional conventions. Nelson, "A Re-Evaluation of Scholarly Explanations for the Rise of the Elective Judiciary in Antebellum America," 193, 205. For a list of states that had already accomplished the change, see Shugerman, *The People's Courts*, 105.

parties controlled "some four or five thousand lucrative offices" and so long as constitutions permitted "almost unlimited legislative interference with the industry and capital of the state." The *Review* explicitly stated that so long as the legislature retained the power to meddle with the state's economic institutions (referring to state banks, investments in internal improvement projects, and amassing of enormous debts) it would be neither "wise [nor] safe" to elect judges in New York.[61] The point was that judges had to operate in a system that was cleansed of corrupting influences, and the only way to ensure that condition was to allow the people more direct control.

Most Americans would have agreed that politics was a dangerous business.[62] They also understood that there was no other mechanism available to them that would allow them some say over the machinery of state. In his landmark collection of essays, the Ohio legal theorist Frederick Grimke explained that because judges had to decide a thousand private transactions, they were meddling in "things that were political."[63] Illinois delegate Onslow Peters agreed, declaring that the judiciary was the most powerful branch of government because it safeguarded the people's liberties and property.[64] Judges were supposed to be inherently more honorable. Their calling and their role demanded it; their prior education and perhaps the inclination of their character would enable them to discover and stand upon that dividing line between politics and ethical self-government. The Whig *Iowa Standard* defined the judiciary as a type of mechanical power – a power that was at the same time deeply personal because it "[came] home to every man." Every citizen understood that the judicial power, rather than the legislative or executive, was "the instrument" that rendered his possessions secure, "and to which he must resort when his rights are infringed." A weak, ignorant, or dishonest judiciary was the "greatest evil that could befall any people."[65] William P. Bryant, a Whig circuit judge in Indiana originally from Kentucky who had served ten years in the Indiana House and Senate, was well acquainted with the state's political machinery.[66]

[61] "History of Constitutional Reform in the United States," *United States Magazine and Democratic Review* 18, no. 96 (June 1846): 417.

[62] See, for example, Glenn C. Altschuler and Stuart M. Blumin, *Rude Republic: Americans and Their Politics in the Nineteenth Century* (Princeton, NJ: Princeton University Press, 2000); Jean H. Baker, *Affairs of Party: The Political Culture of Northern Democrats in the Mid-Nineteenth Century* (New York: Fordham University Press, 1998); Daniel Walker Howe, *The Political Culture of the American Whigs* (1979; repr., Chicago: University of Chicago Press, 1984), 15–22.

[63] Solimine and Saphire explain that Grimke was not greatly influential in his own time, but his opinions do reflect the effort to sort out ethics with pragmatic concerns. Solimine and Saphire, "The Selection of Judges in Ohio,"1: 214. See Frederick Grimke, *Considerations upon the Nature and Tendency of Free Institutions* (New York, 1856), 407.

[64] Illinois 1847, 449.

[65] *Iowa Standard* (Iowa City), February 20, 1845.

[66] Sidney Teiser, "The First Chief Justice of Oregon Territory: William P. Bryant," *Oregon Historical Quarterly* 48, no. 2 (June 1947): 45–54. 48.

He bitterly opposed the "Locofocos" (an insulting nickname for Democrats), whom he now considered to be in the ascendancy, and he had decided not to run for the judgeship. "I hate as much as you to see the office pass into the hands of some Lousy Devil," he told an Indiana lawyer friend, "but I can not make a second sacrifice of a living practice of the dying rewards of a circuit judgeship."[67]

At least on the surface, there was widespread bipartisan agreement that judges should stay out of politics. At least, no one wanted to be on the record as deliberately advocating having party judges. Even so, the rhetorical tools delegates used in their arguments for and against an elective judiciary remained stubbornly political. This was even true of the Whigs, who claimed fervently that they were nonpartisan. In an editorial titled "Party Judges," a Milwaukee newspaper declared that political caucuses had to keep their fingers off such contests because "party nominations bring *party prejudices, party feelings*, party strife into active and virulent operation, where such influences should not be felt in the slightest degree." Any political pressure on judges, the paper explained, "must be wholly ... evil," even declaring virtuously that by opposing political judges the paper would "gain more real honor for [the Whig] party than by the election of a dozen partisan Whig Judges."[68] A Milwaukee Whig paper went so far as to reprint several so-called Locofoco editorials condemning partisan elections, as proof positive that even staunch Democrats opposed partisan judges.[69] Similarly, the *Iowa Standard*, no doubt in a thinly veiled effort to reassure Democratic readers, complained of ostensible "Whig party tyranny" in the neighboring state of Missouri. Evidently Missouri Whigs had become irate that their Iowa Whig neighbors to the north supported an elective judiciary.[70]

This dislike of party judges was nowhere more evident than in Illinois, where circuit judges had become objects of fear and loathing to lawyers who opposed their politics. A hot debate raged through the Illinois legislature in 1841, which resulted in additional circuit court judges, to be appointed by the (dominantly Democratic) legislature.[71] Cynically observing the debate, the Sangamon County

67 William P. Bryant to Samuel Bernard Judah, February 7, 1845, Judah Mss, Lilly Library, Indiana University, Bloomington. Mark Lause explains that a radical faction of the Democratic Party were called derisively Locofoco, because of their supposed incendiary nature (after recently invented household matches). The nickname quickly spread to the Northwest. Lause, *Young America*, 13.

68 *Daily Sentinel and Gazette* (Milwaukee, WI), July 25, 1848, quoted in Ellen Langill, "Levi Hubbell and the Wisconsin Judiciary: A Dilemma in Legal Ethics and Non-Partisan Judicial Elections," *Marquette Law Review* 81, no. 4 (Summer 1998): 987. Langill examines a scandalous judicial election that took place in 1851. By 1863 the newspaper reversed itself.

69 *Daily Sentinel and Gazette* (Milwaukee, WI), November 25, 1846 (copying the *Albany* [NY] *Argus*).

70 The *Iowa Standard* (Iowa City), January 30, 1845.

71 "An Act Reorganizing the Judiciary of the State of Illinois," February 10, 1841, *Laws of the State of Illinois, Passed by the Twelfth General Assembly* (Springfield, IL: 1841), 173–74.

judge James H. Ralston told a friend that the legislative battles over the elected judiciary had become "vehement & exciting partaking much of party abuse & personal crimination." He worried that if the measure failed, judges whose opinions were "so pliant" (meaning, amenable to political caucus demands) could be expected to "display the malignity of their hearts against all those lawyers who have with manly firmness advocated this bill." He had heard gentlemen "of the first respectability" declare that they could not appear before the supreme court again, unless that court should be reorganized. In fact, he remained convinced that the public could have no confidence in the Illinois Supreme Court.[72] Junius Hall, an Illinois lawyer, complained that the judiciary system was so defective as to constitute a "substantial objection to the practice of law" in the state. In his opinion most of the judges were "mere politicians, who owe their elevation to any thing but fitness for the stations they occupy," and who were utterly unqualified to exercise the high duties of their office. He thought the lawyers had "no confidence in their wisdom & but little in their integrity" and rushed through the "consideration of cases."[73] In the end, northwestern voters resorted to a simple geographic expedient. In the same way they shifted county seats to follow the changing population, they tried to keep judges in line by moving them around various circuits and thus limiting their political influence.[74] One of Indiana delegate Allen Hamilton's friends approved of his actions in "that wrangling body" (meaning, the constitutional convention), especially the resolution on rotation of public officers. In fact he could go further: No present judge ought to be allowed to sit more than one term in his circuit "untill after he has first held one term in each other circuit of the state."[75]

With their past experience of relying on an active and engaged body of justices of the peace, the northwestern inhabitants had already accustomed themselves to the idea of electing their own judges. Moreover, in the Indiana 1816 constitution, Associate Judges and Justices of the Peace were elected; in the 1835 Michigan constitution, only Supreme Court Justices were to be appointed – all others were to be elected. It is safe to say that in the Northwest, despite sustained opposition from the more conservative Whigs, the move from an appointed to an elected judiciary was a foregone conclusion. Wisconsin delegate Gibson told his convention colleagues that no one had ever talked

[72] James H. Ralston to unknown recipient, January 30, 1841, James H. Ralston letters, Abraham Lincoln Presidential Library, Springfield, IL. Ralston had been elected as a justice of the peace and served in the state legislature, where in 1835 he voted for internal improvement schemes that later bankrupted the Illinois economy. Joseph F. Snyder, "Forgotten Statesmen of Illinois: James Harvey Ralston," in *Transactions of the Illinois State Historical Society for the Year 1908* (Springfield, IL: 1908), 219–21.

[73] Junius Hall to John Hall, October 22, 1842, Hall Family Correspondence, New York Public Library.

[74] *Chicago Daily Journal*, November 9, 1844.

[75] Henry Cooper to Allen Hamilton, November 23, 1850, Hamilton Family Papers, Indiana State Library, Indianapolis.

about electing judges in his presence.[76] The shift toward elective judiciaries was so pervasive, in fact, that conservatives did not mount much of an offensive. In the 1847 Illinois convention, Virginia-born judge Richard Servant – a conservative Whig who opposed an elective judiciary – resigned himself to the inevitable. When his fellow Whig Hezekiah Wead proposed that all judicial officers be rendered elective, Servant immediately countered with an opposing amendment. He knew, however, that his cause was hopeless and only wanted his opposition on the public record so that the people at home would know he had stood up against the juggernaut. Even so, if he thought he had the remotest chance of prevailing he would "speak for a month and log roll with every member of the Convention." But he knew better than to waste his time.[77] In the 1850 Indiana convention, in a debate over district elections, Whig Daniel Kelso was fighting with his back against the wall. He told his colleagues that voters who disliked the idea of an elective judiciary would become so angry that they would reject the constitution. He need hardly have worried, however. Northwesterners wanted an elective judiciary and heartily approved this change in their state constitutions.[78]

By the late 1840s and early 1850s, almost all of the northwestern states were busy revising their constitutions, and there was sufficient bipartisan cooperation throughout the region to pass elected judiciaries. The fights in the fractured Minnesota convention always serve as an excellent indicator of political party divisions or agreement in any controversial proposition. Both the Democrat and the Republican bodies (who were meeting in separate chambers) agreed, without much debate, that all judges were to be elected. On the Democratic side, delegate Lafayette Emmet explained that popular sovereignty was the "enlightened view" of government, and more importantly the people wanted an elective judiciary. Therefore it would hardly be safe to put a constitution before the voters that opposed their wishes.[79] The Republican speeches expressed an awkward congeries of both Democratic and old-fashioned Whig doctrine: Frequent exhortations to trust the people jostled against the notion that judges ought to be more knowledgeable and better educated. Yet even on the Republican side of the hall, there was virtually no debate over electing judges.[80] This had an unexpected outcome.

[76] Milo M. Quaife, ed., *The Convention of 1846*, vol. 27 of *Publications of the State Historical Society of Wisconsin* (Madison: State Historical Society of Wisconsin, 1919), 588 (hereafter Wisconsin 1846).

[77] The following conventions discussed elective judiciaries: 1847 Illinois, 1844 and 1846 Iowa, 1835 and 1850 Michigan, 1850 Ohio, and 1846 and 1848 Wisconsin. Illinois 1847, 456. See also Robert M. Ireland, "The Politics of the Elective Judiciary During the Period of Kentucky's Third Constitution," *Register of the Kentucky Historical Society* 93, no. 4 (Autumn 1995): 387–421.

[78] H. Fowler, *Report of the Debates and Proceedings of the Convention for the Revision of the Constitution of the State of Indiana* (Indianapolis, IN: 1850), 2: 1653–54 (hereafter Indiana 1850). Daniel Kelso, a Whig lawyer with occasional Democrat sympathies, had served in both the state House and Senate.

[79] Minnesota 1857 Democrat, 493–95. Lafayette Emmet was a lawyer, who became territorial attorney general at thirty-one and became a judge the year after the convention.

[80] Solimine and Saphire, "The Selection of Judges in Ohio," 1: 214.

Because neither renegade Democrats nor proappointive Whigs hardly dared to gainsay the notion of an elected judiciary, the debates primarily ranged over how judges were to be elected, and by whom. That raised the inevitable problem of political representation: Whom or what did judges represent?

Even the hardiest advocate of popular sovereignty had to admit that the people could exert neither power nor moral righteousness unless they permitted someone to represent them. But judges were a special case: They did not stand for political constituencies. Northwestern judges represented both abstract principles and living citizens: They stood for truth, virtue, and justice, and ideally they represented a truthful, virtuous, and just people. Delegate Edward G. Ryan, a vehemently antibank Democrat in the 1846 Wisconsin convention, argued against an elective judiciary, at least (he averred) in part to combat the popular notion that no Democrat could take such a stance. His explanations reveal that in antebellum northwestern constitutional conventions, ethical principles could transcend and influence even the most deeply held political opinions. Although Ryan firmly believed in popular sovereignty as a "holy human theory" and proclaimed democracy as his "religion," he bitterly opposed the idea of an elective judiciary. "No, sir! No, sir!" he declaimed; "God forever forbid it!" Judges could not represent anything other than abstract ideals. Indeed, judicial interpretation represented "no man, no majority, no people." For Ryan, the judge's "constituencies" were not persons, but rather a triad of abstract principles: truth, right, and justice. "Woe to the land, woe to them who dwell in it," he warned, that when the men who "sat in judgment on all that human beings held dear, ... life, liberty, character, honor, the daily bread man prays for to his God, and the daily peace to eat it – shall represent any voice, save that voice in which God speaks in the consciences of all, their own deep and solemn convictions of right and truth."[81] Throughout the convention Ryan had supported the most radical "Locofoco" (antibank, anti–paper currency, anti–black rights) provisions, so this was a painfully difficult argument for him to make; he felt obliged again and again to avow that he trusted the people, even though he had taken the unpopular position that judges ought to be appointed by the legislature.

This question of representation was equally bewildering for Whigs, who, though conceding that it might be appropriate to elect lower-court judges, insisted that these men only represented the people as agents of justice and integrity, and never as exponents of political platforms. Although staunch Indiana Whig John S. Newman agreed that district court judges ought to be elected by the people, he worried that voters would not have sufficient knowledge of candidates for the judiciary to elect the right men "to represent them."[82]

[81] Wisconsin 1846, 590. The phrase "woe to the land, woe to them who dwell in it" may have been a paraphrase from the Book of Revelations 12: 12 (Authorized King James Version), "woe to the inhabiters of the earth."

[82] Indiana 1850, 2: 1653. Newman was born in Ohio and moved to Indiana as a young child. He was a Quaker and a staunch antislavery Whig. *Biographical Memoirs of Jay County, Indiana* (Chicago: B. F. Bowen, 1901), 319.

Like most Whigs, he was cautious about leaving such important decisions to the people (most of whom were, after all, Democrats). He entertained few illusions about the "purity and uprightness" of representative men, whether they were judges or lawmakers. One did not have to possess the "powers of prophecy" to imagine that that political partisanship and "a few private considerations" could influence both the voters and the judges, instead of "discrimination of legal ability or respect for the administration of the law." In spite of his anxieties, however, the problem of representation forced him to argue for the election of district judges. In any office that affected the people's economic welfare, he believed, the choice "should be made by the constituent body rather than by the representative."[83] Newman's ideas about the judiciary were replete with the logical contradictions that hounded the delegates as they attempted to reform their judicial system. Newman believed that judges could only represent abstract virtues, but agreed that they had to be elected by the people; he worried that the people would be incapable of identifying worthy men, but was equally convinced that such men hardly existed.

Delegates who thought that judges ought to represent both the people and civic virtue confronted a pointed question: How far could one push the Jacksonian representative principle – how much power could one leave in the hands of the people – and still retain a grasp on integrity? Even with the problem of representation settled, the main problem still remained: Who would judge the judges? In the 1848 Wisconsin convention, Judge Edward V. Whiton, who would shortly be elected to the Wisconsin District Court, explained that judges were not supposed to carry out matters of public policy, but instead had to be governed by truth and justice. It was not necessary that their acts "pass in review before the people" as often as those of other government officers.[84] The democratic principle, therefore, stood as the embodiment of modernity. Distributing power among the people (so long as those people took care to educate themselves and hewed to Christian principles) guaranteed a far more just and rational system of governance than leaving it in the hands of the few.

Jacksonian democracy, many northwesterners believed, swept away outdated, irrational Old World hierarchies. The new order had revealed itself, in the United States, as a vast and highly successful experiment in self-government. It stood to reason: Experiments that were proven by numerous examples were mathematically more likely to be correct.[85] Whig Indiana delegate Alexander

[83] *The Iowa Capital Reporter* (Iowa City), November 4, 1844, quoted in Iowa 1844 and 1846, 224.

[84] Milo Milton Quaife, ed., *The Struggle over Ratification, 1846–1847*, vol. 28 of Publications of the State Historical Society of Wisconsin (Madison: State Historical Society of Wisconsin, 1920), 634. Whiton would serve on the Wisconsin Supreme Court for the rest of his life. He was originally from Massachusetts. Parker M. Reed, *The Bench and Bar of Wisconsin: History and Biography* (Milwaukee, 1882), 51–52.

[85] Michael H. Hoeflich, "Law and Geometry: Legal Science from Leibnitz to Langdell," in Steve Sheppard, ed., *The History of Legal Education in the United States: Commentaries and Primary Sources* (Pasadena, CA: Salem Press, 1999), 2: 589–605.

Campbell Stevenson (originally from Kentucky) declared that an elective judiciary was both modern and scientific. Because northwesterners lived in an "age of improvement, not only in the arts and sciences, but in government also," it was time to modernize the justice system as well. And modernization never meant restricting the people, but rather reforming government to allow them "to better govern themselves." In practical terms that meant electing all judges and allowing them to serve only short terms. That would permit the people, through frequent observation and testing, to determine whether the judges were fulfilling their roles honorably.[86]

Men such as Stevenson perceived few practical problems in the notion of submitting the judiciary to popular elections, in spite of the fact that it would be impossible to run any election without the inevitable chicanery and log-rolling. For modern readers, there is an essential logical disjunction here: If politics was a corrupt business, then how could people possibly choose a virtuous judge? Yet Jacksonian confidence always returned to the notion that more democracy was always better and would always, inevitably, produce greater freedom and prosperity. The people would simply have to take responsibility for making a well-informed choice. They would therefore have to educate themselves on the law in order to choose knowledgeable and virtuous judges, and, by extension, the law would have to be accessible to all literate citizens. According to a delegate in the 1850 Michigan convention, enlightened and progressive public opinion had already inspired Michigan voters to "[take] to themselves the power to elect judges."[87] Even people who favored an appointed judiciary in the state supreme court linked scientific government with popular sovereignty. Two Democratic delegates in Minnesota, Henry Setzer (a prosperous lumberman) and Moses Sherburne (an associate judge of the Minnesota Territory Supreme Court), agreed that after only eight years in practice, elective judiciaries were still in an experimental stage and had to be thoroughly tested before a final decision could be reached.[88] Charles Flandrau, a conservative Democrat, who also served on the Minnesota convention judiciary committee, took it a step further. An elective judiciary was certainly "no experiment," but instead, the "settled rule" of every single American state that had recently revised its constitution.[89] Experimentation only clarified, through testing and observation, the core truths. It could not invent new truths, repeal the laws of nature, or abolish biblical injunctions. Economic prosperity, for many northwesterners, constituted proof of a successful experiment and of God's favor.

[86] Indiana 1850, 2: 1080.

[87] *Report of the Proceedings and Debates in the Convention to Revise the Constitution of State of Michigan, 1850* (Lansing, MI: 1850), 115 (hereafter Michigan 1850). The 1835 Michigan constitution provided for election of all judges except supreme court judges, who were still to be appointed.

[88] Minnesota 1857 Democrat, 496–500.

[89] Minnesota 1857 Democrat, 495.

How would the people, however virtuous and intelligent, know whether a candidate for a judgeship had read enough law books? The contemporary focus on law as a science inspired antielective delegates to seek analogies that would support the notion that even the most well-intentioned citizens might not be capable of assessing legal knowledge. Would farmers and merchants be able to choose a "professor of chemistry," for example? In the 1847 Illinois convention, Massachusetts-born Democrat Onslow Peters compared the judges' knowledge of the law to mastery of an "abstruse science." He worried that even "good men" would be unable to assess the learning and character of the men they elected as judges.[90] Peters knew perfectly well that he would be criticized, but still did not think the people wanted to elect judges; nor did he feel capable of flattering his constituency: He doubted that they would be capable of selecting someone who would be the best "expounder of the … science" of the law.[91] In spite of misgivings, northwesterners believed that their democratic experiment had already proven itself a radiant triumph. Any expressions of doubts and fears were at best overcautious Whig hogwash, and at worst unpatriotic carping. Democrat Samuel Bissel dismissed his opponents' arguments as Whig clichés and, as did many of his party colleagues, deliberately linked them to the Anti-Federalist debate that had threatened to scuttle the U.S. Constitution during the ratification debates. As evidence that the system had worked so well, he explained that northwesterners, "while progressing in democratic principles and usages," had developed equally in the "arts, sciences, commerce, agriculture, and manufactures, with a rapidity hitherto unparalleled in the annals of the world." More and more, the people had withdrawn power from their governors and legislators and had taken to themselves all of the decisions they could "conveniently decide … at the ballot box." As a direct result – for Bissel the equation was a mathematical dead certainty – the western part of the country had increased in wealth and happiness "beyond the most sanguine expectations," thus demonstrating that the experiment of popular sovereignty had already succeeded brilliantly.[92]

Arguments like these neglected important factors, such as the land grabs that dispossessed Indians, the chronic discrimination and disfranchisement of black men, and the two catastrophic financial panics that threatened to wreck the western state economies. All Americans were aware of the economic troubles, and many were becoming uncomfortably conscious of sectional and social problems as well. But that did not cast the worth and viability of the American experiment into doubt. The task was simply to find the right balance of reason, truth, and the popular will. Northwesterners always cherished sanguine expectations: If they could hold fast to both Christian and American

[90] Illinois 1847, 458–74. Peters was talking about foreign immigrants who had not yet been granted the right to vote in general elections.

[91] Illinois 1847, 460.

[92] Iowa 1846, 324.

democratic principles, all would be well. Whenever laws flew directly in the face of obvious triumphs, Democratic delegates threatened that the people would simply take power into their own hands, through the "impulses of their own will." Popular rebukes would serve as a cleansing force – a power that intervened in old-fashioned hierarchies by reasserting the will of the people. In the 1846 Wisconsin convention, Charles M. Baker, who served as the chair of the Committee on the Judiciary, exhorted his colleagues to trust the voters. His committee had been keenly mindful of the fact that they had to construct a "popular and useful" judiciary system. The people would undoubtedly elect capable men to the judiciary. Surely sixty years of "happy workings" of a democratic government had by now proved that democracy had been endowed through the "perfectibility of God's Infinite Wisdom" – thus proving that the axioms of reason were united with the principles of religion.[93]

By the 1840s, Jacksonian Democrats had dismissed the belief in an appointed judiciary as an irrational and hidebound adherence to outworn shibboleths. The past was not always a reliable guide to the future; nor was tradition inevitably harmonious with common sense. A *Minnesota Republican* paper made the connection between logic and democracy. Because law was easily "tangled up into knotty points," the common sense of the people [was] quite as likely to "straighten things" as a "perpetual appeal to precedents." One had to steer a middle course between the venerable "wisdom of the past" and a straightforward understanding of the present. "Neither Judges nor people are always right: and so let each be a check upon the other."[94]

For the ever-pragmatic people, that "middle course" had to be unmistakably obvious – that is, it had to be printed in readily available law books and newspaper editorials, and it also had to be plainly visible on the northwestern landscape. Balance required a careful examination of both the hard evidence and the special circumstances surrounding each dispute. While no one doubted that there was a difference between right and wrong, and between just and unjust, a judge would still have to arrive at that truth by explaining the law to juries in a clear and comprehensible manner, and by clarifying the lawyers' arguments. Furthermore, the courts would grant all arguments a fair chance to be heard and render justice both physically and morally available to all citizens. In essence, all of those goals had to be reflected in the placement of judicial districts and the design of courthouses (and incidentally, the selection of county boundaries and capitals, which would determine the location of courts).[95] Nineteenth-century

[93] Wisconsin 1846, 288. Charles M. Baker was a lawyer educated in New York and Vermont. He moved to Wisconsin after being bankrupted during the Panic of 1837, and by 1856 he was a judge. After Wisconsin became a state he served on the committee to codify its laws. Charles M. Baker, "Pioneer History of Walworth County," in Lyman C. Draper, ed., *Report and Collections of the State Historical Society of Wisconsin* (Madison, WI: 1872), 6: 437–38.

[94] "Elected Judiciary vs. Appointed Judiciary," *Minnesota Republican* (Saint Anthony), July 9, 1857, September 7, 1857.

[95] See Chapter 7, "Places."

British and American journals published many articles on the beauty and order of symmetry, which they defined as "heaven's first law."[96] That is, symmetry, balance, and order were the visible manifestations of both democracy and justice. Therefore, when nineteenth-century Americans designed and built their courthouses and state capitals they aimed for a mathematically pleasing symmetry. Their Greek Revival courthouses resembled both temples of democracy and in many cases (because of the presence of a cupola) churches.[97] That same beautiful equilibrium had to be carried through civic institutions. Their courthouses represented equality and justice: the embodiment of antebellum northwestern democracy.[98] Iowa delegate Jonathan Fletcher thought that an elective judiciary would preserve the "beauty and symmetry" of the American justice system; and that popular sovereignty was a healthy and beneficial force that ought not to be divided by giving away any of the people's privileges or powers.[99] The report from the Wisconsin Committee on the Judiciary declared an elective judiciary was not only in accordance with the theory of democratic government; it was "in harmony with its spirit and genius." Confidence in the people and a belief in the "political perfectability of man," the committee chair claimed, were the basis of American institutions because faith in popular sovereignty "emanated from the Deity and [was] founded in the nature and fitness of things."[100]

As predicted, and just like everywhere else in the Union during those decades, every northwestern constitution provided for an elected judiciary.[101]

[96] S. Comfort, "Mental Symmetry," *Ladies' Repository, and Gatherings of the West* 3 (June 1843): 169. See S. Earnshaw, "On the Motion of Luminous Waves in an Elastic Medium, Consisting of a System of Detached Particles, Separated by Finite Intervals," *Philosophical Magazine* 3rd ser., 20 (May 1842): 370.

[97] Marcus Whiffen and Frederick Koeper argue that the presence of a cupola was a conscious design choice of early nineteenth-century architects to remind visitors of the unity of religion and temporal justice. Marcus Whiffen and Frederick Koeper, *American Architecture, 1607–1860* (1981; repr., Cambridge, MA: Massachusetts Institute of Technology, 1996), 1: 164–66. See also Jonathan Rosenbloom, "Social Ideology as Seen through Courtroom and Courthouse Architecture," *Columbia-VLA Journal of Law and the Arts* 22, no. 4 (1998): 463–523. For similar discussions about Old Northwest courthouses, see William E. Firestone, *Grandeur and Grace in the Ohio Country: Building America from the Ground Up, 1784–1860* (Yellow Springs, OH: Red Eft Media, 2009), 4–10, 24; Jon Dilts and Will Counts, *The Magnificent 92 Indiana Courthouses*, rev. ed. (Bloomington: Indiana University Press, 1999).

[98] Stacy McDermott comments on imposing northwestern county courthouses in *The Jury in Lincoln's America*, 4–9. See also William H. Pierson, Jr., *The Colonial and Neoclassical Styles*, vol. 1 of *American Buildings and Their Architects*, (1970; repr., Garden City, NY: Doubleday, 1976).

[99] Iowa 1844, 113.

[100] Charles M. Baker, "Article on the Organization and Functions of the Judiciary," in Wisconsin 1846, 289.

[101] Caleb Nelson, Kermit Hall, and Jed H. Shugerman agree that this was a way of gaining control over legislatures. Nelson, "A Re-Evaluation of Scholarly Explanations for the Rise of the Elective Judiciary in Antebellum America," 203; Hall, "Judiciary on Trial," 339; Shugerman, *People's Courts*, 10, 30–37.

Historians agree that the conventions did this in order to remove the power of patronage from corrupt or inept politicians and executives and to remove judges from political influence. Even so, few Whigs entertained illusions that popular elections would somehow result in a politically neutral judiciary. Whig lawyer Orsamus Cole, who served in the 1848 Wisconsin convention, thought that the whole idea of an elective judiciary was the "most leveling in this leveling age." Such a system would lower the judiciary "down to ordinary meanness and corruption of party strife."[102] Several other delegates warned about the evils of party judges: Such men would be nothing more than "third-rate demagogues."[103] If an elective judiciary were to become a "political question," then Kelso feared they would get men who were "better politicians than judges" and who were nothing better than "babbling politicians." He detested the "strong hints" that his opponents wanted a political party judge.[104] Kelso believed that the only way to avoid having political judges was to set up the districts in the constitutional convention, and not by political party caucuses. According to an Indiana voter, writing to Allen Hamilton, it was high time for Indiana's judges to "mind their business, not sit there to reward their friends or to punish their enemies."[105]

But northwesterners, as with most antebellum Americans, had no other language with which to discuss or manage such a question.[106] All elections had to be organized by political parties, even if those contests ultimately rested in the hands of the people. The Democratic judge William S. Holman told Allen Hamilton on Christmas Day that he was "tired of Indianapolis and of politics," and the only present he wanted that day from the people was a judgeship.[107] In Iowa, a Whig newspaper editorial asked readers casually, "Why Not Elect

[102] *Journal of the Convention to Form a Constitution for the State of Wisconsin*: With a Sketch of the Debates, Begun and Held at Madison, on the Fifteenth Day of December, Eighteen Hundred and Forty-seven (Madison, Wisconsin Territory: Tenney, Smith, and Holt Publishers, 1848.) 693, 798. Hereafter Wisconsin 1848.

[103] Wisconsin 1848, 436, 456. The demagogue quotation was from George W. Lakin, a Whig lawyer from Platteville who would go on to be appointed U.S. attorney of Wisconsin by President Taylor. Reed, *Bench and Bar of Wisconsin*, 215.

[104] Indiana 1850, 2: 1653–54. Daniel Kelso, a Whig lawyer with occasional Democrat sympathies, had served in both the state House and Senate. Charles W. Taylor, *Biographical Sketches and Review of the Bench and Bar of Indiana* (Indianapolis: 1895), 129.

[105] Henry Cooper to Allen Hamilton, November 23, 1850, Hamilton Family Papers, Indiana State Library, Indianapolis.

[106] Caleb Nelson argued that "the appointive system left far more room for the play of partisan politics than the elective system," and the final outcomes were staggered terms, elections by districts rather than statewide, and statewide elections of the highest courts. Nelson, "A Re-Evaluation of Scholarly Explanations for the Rise of the Elective Judiciary in Antebellum America," 194, 196, 198.

[107] William S. Holman to Allen Hamilton on December 25, 1851, William S. Holman mss, Lilly Library, Indiana University, Bloomington. Democrat Holman had been born in Indiana and had served as a probate and common pleas judge and prosecuting attorney during the mid to late 1840s.

a Whig Judge?" Not that the paper wanted to be partisan, but still, so long as the citizens were voting…[108] After the 1851 Ohio constitution went into effect, all judges were nominated by party caucuses. Newspapers frequently indicated that judicial appointments by the legislature served spoils for both sides.[109] The *Milwaukee Courier* explicitly declared that there was "less danger of corruption, of log-rolling, management, and fraud among the people than in the legislature."[110]

Antebellum Americans demanded the right to elect their judges for two principal reasons: to take the appointing power out of the hands of their state legislatures or governors, and to render these men more directly accountable to the citizens and principles over which they would sit in judgment. A judge could only represent an abstract principle if he possessed a highly developed conscience and adequate legal training, and if he remained answerable to the people as a collective whole. Therefore the entire polity had to be able to evaluate whether a judge was doing his job properly. Only the most conservative men (mostly Whigs, but some Democrats as well) fought against this development, worrying that ordinary people would not be able to assess a judge's competence, education, and knowledge. Yet as a British traveler who had seen a judge plowing his own fields and afterward shaking hands with local farmers explained, if judges were neighbors, then surely voters would be able to make an intelligent choice.[111] In the two states where the issue was particularly fraught (Michigan and Ohio) the delegates compromised by having supreme court justices appointed by the legislature and lower court judges elected by local voters. Everywhere else, all judges were to be elected.

Nationwide the development of an elected judiciary, many historians agree, had an unintended consequence: Elected judges felt liberated, not only from the state legislatures, but also from the public will.[112] The historians Caleb Nelson, Morton Horwitz, and Jed Shugerman all concur that there was a significant increase in judicial review after judges began to be elected.[113] Just how

[108] *Fairfield* [IA] *Weekly Ledger*, January 29, 1852.

[109] *Daily Ancient Metropolis* (Chillicothe, OH), March 4, 1850.

[110] *Milwaukee Courier*, July 3, 1846.

[111] Elias Pym Fordham, "Extracts from Letters Written, on a Journey to the Western Parts of the United States, and during a Residence in the Illinois Territory. By an English Farmer," November 15, 1817, manuscript diary, Edward E. Ayer Collection, Newberry Library, Chicago. This entry was written at Shawneetown, Illinois Territory. See also, Elias Pym Fordham, *Personal Narratives of Travels in Virginia, Ohio, Indiana, Kentucky; and of a Residence in the Illinois Territory: 1817–1818*, ed. Frederic A. Ogg (Cleveland: Arthur H. Clark Co., 1906), 128.

[112] Shugerman, *People's Courts*, 123; David Pozen, "Judicial Elections as Popular Constitutionalism," *Columbia Law Review* 110, no. 8 (Dec. 2010): 2047–2134.

[113] Nelson, "A Re-Evaluation of Scholarly Explanations for the Rise of the Elective Judiciary in Antebellum America," 204. See also Shugerman, *People's Courts*, 123–43 (chapter 6, "The Boom in Judicial Review"). For a discussion of the debates over judicial review in state constitutional conventions, see also John J. Dinan, *The American State Constitutional Tradition* (Lawrence: University Press of Kansas, 2009), 123–135.

controversial was this idea that judges could find a law unconstitutional? The idea of judicial review has to be seen as part of a struggle to understand the role of judges in society, and the degree of control and responsibility the citizens were supposed to exert. Northwestern voters, considering themselves to be literate and responsible citizens interested in their state government, experienced not the slightest hesitation in critiquing laws. They might not have used the phrase "judicial review" to explain their behavior.[114] Nevertheless, they saw this problem – specifically, the constitutionality of laws (and perhaps more broadly, the logic, practicality, and ethics of all legal processes) – as open to their judgment and capable of being corrected. Criticizing a law, demanding the right to have a say over some laws, such as charters for corporations that could print money, or even, more radically, to repeal such laws, appeared an eminently reasonable, even a vitally important measure that safeguarded their liberties and their well-being. They understood that judges had primary responsibility for assessing laws, but they retained a firm grasp on their own right to understand and evaluate them.

The notion that judges could scrutinize laws and overturn them dated back to the colonial era.[115] In 1802 the Supreme Court justice John Marshall found some parts of the Judiciary Act unconstitutional. Although his famous opinion in *Madison v. Marbury* was known to Ohio lawyers, the problem of judicial review was clearly still open to debate. In Ohio, where the St. Clair era was still fresh in public memory, the overlap between legislative and judicial powers caused a firestorm between the legislature and the judiciary. As early as 1805, just three years after statehood, and much to the consternation of the Ohio legislature, three state supreme court judges declared a law – the so-called Fifty Dollar Act, which raised the limits of cases that could be heard by justices of the peace to fifty dollars – unconstitutional. That law, according to indignant Ohio citizens, removed the right of a jury trial from anyone bringing an action in an amount less than fifty dollars – a significant amount of money. In 1805, that sum could have purchased twenty-five to forty acres of prime farmland or a horse. This battle resulted in the destruction of several judicial careers. The law was never overturned, and at least one of the judges returned to the bench a decade later. The problem has to be seen as a battle to sort out who had primary responsibility for establishing the limits and reach of justice: Was it the legislature, the judiciary (in its role as a check on the legislature), or the people themselves?[116]

114 I have never found any contemporary instance of the phrase "judicial review" to signify a judge's review of legislation. During the antebellum era, in this context, the phrase always signified a careful or prudent examination.

115 Willi Paul Adams, *First State Constitutions: Republican Ideology and the Making of State Constitutions in the Revolutionary Era*, trans. Rita Kimber and Robert Kimber, expanded ed. (New York: Rowman & Littlefield, 2001), 267.

116 Ratcliffe, *Party Spirit in a Frontier Republic*, 148–150. Ervin H. Pollack, ed., *Ohio Unreported Judicial Decisions Prior to 1823* (Indianapolis: Allen Smith, 1952), 71–105; David M. Gold, *Democracy in Session: A History of the Ohio General Assembly* (Athens: Ohio University

Ohio citizens were less concerned about the constitutionality of the law, which was intended to help relieve the already burdened district courts, and more about the question of separating the judicial and legislative powers of state government. Still stinging from the overbearing St. Clair government, which had freely mixed judicial and executive functions, citizens worried about any encroachment of one branch into another. The *Liberty Hall and Cincinnati Mercury*, for example, worried that the judges were "judging over the heads of the legislature." The writer explicated the problem with some hesitancy, finally deciding that the question of judicial review was far more complicated than simply figuring out the separation of powers. In the early years of the nineteenth century, northwesterners had to sort out the role of the community in assessing the ethics of legal actions, whether by judges, legislators, or the people themselves. Specifically, the editor explained, if legislators or judges misbehaved, then they lost their representative role and became private citizens, liable to the rule of law and accountable to their fellows. That is, when the legislature stepped beyond the bounds set by the constitution, according to the editorial, they acted "without authority." The legislators were no longer representing the commonweal, so their wrongdoing was to be judged exactly as the actions "of any other private man" were judged.[117]

In Ohio the question of the constitutionality of judicial review remained unsettled until the late 1830s. In one of his popular histories of his state, the early Ohio essayist and historian Caleb Atwater declared that the governor should have the power to strike down unconstitutional or unwise laws. Describing the ongoing conflict between the Ohio legislature and the judiciary, he explained that several unconstitutional acts had already been passed and that in all such cases, the governor ought to retain the right to reject such acts as "unconstitutional, as inexpedient, or unnecessary." That would have "saved to the people ... large sums of money."[118] Clearly, in the public mind, the problem of assessing the constitutionally was still in doubt: It did not occur to Atwater that judges could do so. In 1841, Ohio judges once again attempted to strike down a law raising the maximum value of a case to be heard by justices of the peace. An editorial in the *Cleveland Daily Herald* declared these decisions "deeply important" and observed that many citizens considered them "extremely problematical."[119]

Outside Ohio judicial review was not controversial. By the time antebellum conventions were ready to talk about revising their judicial systems, and to

Press, 2009), 33–34; Donald F. Melhorn Jr., *"Lest We Be Marshall'd": Judicial Powers and Politics in Ohio, 1806–1812* (Akron, OH: University of Akron Press, 2003).

117 *Liberty Hall and Cincinnati Mercury*, November 3, 1807. The case is *Rutherford v. McFadden* (1807, unreported), a case of judicial review before the Supreme Court of Ohio.

118 Caleb Atwater, *A History of the State of Ohio, Natural and Civil*, 2nd ed. (Cincinnati: 1838), 171–75.

119 *Cleveland Daily Herald*, January 17, 1842.

join in the national movement of changing from appointed to elected judges, Marshall's famous *Marbury v. Madison* decision had already become widely accepted and was known to most lawyers. Samuel Huntington, the judge who had presided over *Rutherford v. McFadden* in 1807, explicitly stated that the U.S. Supreme Court had already established its power to find legislation unconstitutional. Wisconsin Democrat John L. Doran observed that because Marshall had found the thirteenth section of the Judiciary Act unconstitutional, he wondered whether "other sections could be as well."[120]

In Illinois, citizens had instituted makeshift structures for judicial review, but without marked success. The first Illinois state constitution, ratified in 1818, copied the first (1777) New York state constitution's Council of Revision.[121] This committee, consisting of the governor, chancellor, and judges of the supreme court, were to review bills prior to passage. Any that were inconsistent with the state constitution or contrary to the public good were to be vetoed. Two-thirds of either house could override the veto, and any rejected bills were to be returned within ten days. As might have been imagined, the council quickly became unwieldy and inefficient. Like most contemporary Illinoisans, the early historian Henry Brown severely criticized the council, primarily because the circuit judges also served as members. He considered this an "unfortunate circumstance," because, like most Illinois citizens he considered the council impractical, cumbersome, and, worst of all, thought that it turned all the members into "politicians." Although the legislature had attempted several times to reform the council, all efforts had proved fruitless. The time had come to get rid of the body entirely.[122] A Chicago editorial published under the pseudonym "Justice" demanded a new constitutional convention for the express purpose of reforming the "root of all evil," the current court system, which had to focus on abolishing the "odious" Council of Revision.[123] The council was simply too much of a burden for judges, who

[120] Donald F. Melhorn, Jr., "Jupiter's Sons: Greene County's Citizen Judges and the Sweeping Resolution, 1810–1814," in *History of Ohio Law*, 1: 240; Wisconsin 1848, 412. Other historians argue whether *Marbury* was widely known as a decision that enshrined judicial review. As early as 1914, for example, Edward S. Corwin accepted the idea that judicial review was the "natural outgrowth" of ideas that were "common property" during the *Marbury* era, in "*Marbury v. Madison* and the Doctrine of Judicial Review," *Michigan Law Review* 12, no. 7 (1913–1914): 538–72.

[121] Daniel J. Hulsebosch, *Constituting Empire: New York and the Transformation of Constitutionalism in the Atlantic World, 1664–1830* (Chapel Hill: University of North Carolina Press, 2008), 177–79. The original idea was proposed during the U.S. constitutional convention, in the Virginia Plan, but was never included in the U.S. Constitution.

[122] For a detailed description of the failure of Illinois's Council of Revision, see Robert L. Jones, "Lessons from a Lost Constitution: The Council of Revision, the Bill of Rights, and the Role of the Judiciary in Democratic Governance," *Journal of Law and Politics* 27, no. 3 (Spring 2012): 459–556. See also Henry Brown, *The History of Illinois, from Its First Discovery and Settlement, to the Present Time* (New York, 1844), 352.

[123] *Chicago News*, November 16, 1844; John R. Vile, *The Constitutional Convention of 1787: A Comprehensive Encyclopedia of America's Founding* (Santa Barbara, CA: ABC-Clio,

worked very hard during their circuits and then had to scan hundreds of bills. Most of the delegates in the 1847 Illinois convention agreed that the council had to be disbanded.[124] The state certainly needed an institution or a body of men who would be responsible for judicial review. But the council was cumbersome and undemocratic, and by 1847, the people wanted to take on some responsibility for judicial review in their own right. Three of the conventions (1847 Illinois, 1850 Michigan, and 1850 Ohio) tackled the principles of judicial review.[125] It is safe to say that most northwesterners deemed judges competent to compare legislation to the state and federal constitutions. They also considered themselves equally capable of doing so. And if they were not, then the fault was in the laws and in education, and not in their native ability to assess justice or interpret laws. As we have seen, every convention discussed problems with incompetent or inefficient legislatures; yet they rarely concerned themselves with judicial review of legislation.[126] The delegates were far more concerned with legislative incompetence than with the lawmakers' potential violations of procedural or other rights.[127]

An elected, independent judiciary ought to be able to reverse lower court decisions without fear of political reprisals. According to David M. Gold, by the 1830s lawyers were regularly asking judges to declare statutes unconstitutional, including temperance legislation, laws dealing with taxes or corporation charters, and eminent domain decrees. Citizens wanted to assume control over laws because this was the modern, rational, and moral way to institute

2005), 197; Guy Padula, *Madison v. Marshall: Popular Sovereignty, Natural Law, and the United States Constitution* (Lanham, MD: Lexington Books, 2001), 48–50. According to Max Farrand, Madison was inspired by the New York 1777 Council of Revision and advocated it for the U.S. Constitution. Peter J. Galie, *Ordered Liberty: A Constitutional History of New York* (New York: Fordham University Press, 1996), 54n46. Galie explains that the New York Council of Revision vetoed 169 of 6,500 bills (2.57 percent), one-third of which were overridden by the legislature. The council was abolished in the 1821 constitution (p. 61). See also, Alfred Billings Street, *The Council of Revision of the State of New York ...* (Albany, NY: 1859), 5–7. For the Illinois Territorial Council of Revision, see Illinois Territory, "Minutes of the Council Meetings," Record Series 100.009, Illinois State Archives, Springfield. For the Illinois State Council of Revision, see Council of Revision, "Minutes of Council Proceedings," Record Series 150.001, Illinois State Archives, Springfield; and Ann M. Lousin, *The Illinois State Constitution* (New York: Oxford University Press, 2011), 5.

124 See William Wilson and others (Chief Justice and Associate Justices of the Illinois Supreme Court), "Communication to the Senate and House of Representatives of the State of Illinois," *Reports Made to the Senate and House of Representatives of the State of Illinois* (Springfield: 1845), 198; and N. H. Debel, "The Development of the Veto Power of the Governor of Illinois," *Transactions of the Illinois State Historical Society* 22 (1916): 46.

125 Winkler, "Legal Literature of Ohio," 2: 505.

126 Especially in the 1850 Indiana convention. See Indiana 1850, 2: 1256.

127 Adams, *First American State Constitutions*, 268–69. Lawrence Friedman talks about state legislature oversight, in *History of American Law*, 266–67. Both Friedman and Shugerman discuss the fact that few judges found laws unconstitutional before the mid-1850s, at which point there was an "explosion," as Friedman describes it (p. 403), or a "boom," as Shugerman phrases it in *People's Courts*, 123–43.

popular sovereignty. Judges, therefore, represented both persons and principles. The persons included the people as individual citizens, as property owners, and in the aggregate as a community. Judges also represented legal knowledge, wisdom, civic virtue, and truth. The role of judges was to "expound": to explain, to make clear, to lay bare the facts and logic of the law; and in so doing, to make it possible for citizens to understand and consent to these laws. The *Milwaukee Courier*, a Democratic paper, explained that judicial review would help to define the "length and breadth" of state laws, together with the common law, and that a "well-defined exposition" would lead to a "clear understanding" of the law by the citizens. Clarity remained the central pillar of republican government.[128] Freed from political patronage (and trusting that the people would be able to discern both the expertise and the character of the candidate) judges could, and, as Jed Shugerman has explained, usually did rise above political influences.[129]

All sorts of people – both eligible voters and, even more vehemently, those who thought they ought to have the right to vote – availed themselves of public media in order to criticize the constitutionality of legislation.[130] In 1819, less than a year after Illinois became a state, the *Edwardsville Spectator* published an anonymous letter deploring the injustice and unconstitutionality of the recently enacted road law, which levied a flat tax instead of the constitutionally mandated percentage of property. Local newspapers had published the new state constitution just a few months earlier, and the writer decided to compare the road law against the Illinois state constitution.[131] He found it wrong. Predicting that the legislators of such unconstitutional laws could not long retain the "confidence of a free and republican people," the writer became indignant about the unconstitutionality of a statute, particularly a law that affected the community's economic well-being.[132]

The people believed themselves to be the best judges of legislative malfeasance, and, to a lesser degree, judicial incompetence. In 1834, the *Illinois*

[128] *Milwaukee Courier*, July 31, 1844.

[129] Shugerman explains that in the 1850s elected judges "struck down many more state laws than had their appointed predecessors," and that judges took an increasingly countermajoritarian tack, defending individual rights against … the "misguided zeal" of the voting public. Shugerman, *People's Courts*, 129–132.

[130] According to Larry Kramer, people living during the revolutionary era believed themselves to be responsible for interpreting the content of enacted laws and thus found it customary to "decide what [they thought] the law require[d] or command[ed]." Kramer's definition of judicial supremacy as "an ideological tenet whose whole purpose is to persuade ordinary citizens that, whatever they may think about Justices' constitutional rulings, it is not their place to gainsay the Court. It is a device to deflect and dampen the energy of popular constitutionalism." Kramer, *People Themselves*, 29, 233.

[131] Ill. Const. of 1818, art. 8, sec. 20, "that the mode of levying a tax shall be by valuation, so that every person shall pay a tax in proportion to the value of the property he or she has in his or her possession." On citizens' interest in law see McDermott, *Jury in Lincoln's America*.

[132] *Edwardsville* [IL] *Spectator*, December 14, 1819.

Advocate demanded to know who were the proper "judges of the constitutionality or unconstitutionality of the power" to charter banks? "We answer, the people, – they are parties to the contract, and deeply interested ones." Calling upon every man to search the U.S. Constitution (which had never granted Congress the right to charter a bank) and read it fully to the end, the *Advocate* thought this would be the best way to prevent Whigs from attempting to expand the power of the legislature to charter banks.[133] This specific complaint – legislatures overstepping power – always cropped up whenever northwestern assemblies passed economic legislation, including laws chartering banks, raising taxes, and setting salaries for public officials. Therefore both the citizens and the judges fought to retain the right to restrain power. Clearly, if legislatures acted badly, then lawmakers became individual malcreants, and could no longer function as representatives.

Bad economic laws could have a serious effect on the incomes of residents. When the Illinois legislature passed a law raising land taxes for two or three counties to two cents per acre to build a road there, Calvin Ackley, an early Ohio settler, was positive that the law was unconstitutional "without any regard to valuation of Property and was got up expressly to catch non resident land holders." No doubt the superior court would "set it aside if the matter was brot before it." Comparing the profits in those two years – 1847 and 1848 – would show a striking difference. In that one year the value of the land profits had dropped by about half. In order to understand this for himself, Ackley decided to consult Judge Tilden of Toledo, whom he called "the greatest lawyer in the State."[134] The notion that private citizens could form their own understanding of the law was so widespread that it often became the subject of hilarity. The Minnesota *North-Western Democrat* humorously observed that a "big burly surly gentleman" on one of St. Anthony's streets had declared the Maine law unconstitutional, in spite of whatever Supreme Court Justice Roger B. Taney might have said about it.[135]

Northwesterners evinced so little hesitation in scrutinizing all of the processes and personnel of law that they also felt free to criticize the judges themselves. In 1844, the Michigan Supreme Court found a recently enacted banking law unconstitutional. Democrats in neighboring Ohio, who feared the influx of paper notes, were sharply critical of that ruling. Because the banking law had held investors to strict accountability, the judges' decision to invalidate that law had the practical effect of granting free rein to wildcat banks.[136] The

[133] *Illinois Advocate and State Register* (Vandalia), November 26, 1834, (includes a clipping from an undated issue of the *Detroit Free Press*).

[134] Calvin Ackley to [Gardiner] Greene, October 1, 1849, William P. Greene and Gardiner Greene Papers, New York Public Library. The Greene brothers owned thousands of acres in Mill Creek, Ohio. *North-Western Democrat* (St. Anthony, MN), February 8, 1854.

[135] The *North-Western Democrat* (St. Anthony, MN), February 8, 1854.

[136] "Unconstitutional," *Cleveland Herald*, March 2, 1844. See also the Reverend S. C. Aiken, "The Laws of Ohio in Respect to the Colored People Shown to Be Unequal and Unconstitutional," November 20, 1845 (Cleveland, 1845).

Wisconsin territorial assemblyman William Singer attacked Wisconsin territorial supreme court opinions, which, in his "humble judgment," were "undeserving of respect." In the bitter ratification fight over the 1846 Wisconsin constitution (which was in imminent danger of failing) Singer explained that the territorial judges were attempting to destroy the proposed constitution by claiming, disingenuously, that the new constitution would prohibit the legislature from passing any new laws on such important topics as homestead exemptions or criminal jury trials. This was simply not the case, and it proved that Whig judges were playing a deep game. As a result, if there was any one principle he "heartily desired to see in the constitution it was that of an elective judiciary."[137] In Ohio, the *Cincinnati Daily Chronicle & Atlas* bitterly complained about "man-monkey" judges who exhibited themselves in the public arena, joining the "cock-pit and brawl" of popular elections.[138] And a Republican delegate in the 1857 Minnesota convention argued that the people should have more power than judges, because even the wisest judges could be vitiated by politics, as evidenced by the U.S. Supreme Court justice Roger B. Taney's decision in the *Dred Scott* case.[139]

In their critique of both statute laws and common law traditions, northwesterners were working out real-life problems that concerned them closely. They were primarily interested in safeguarding property and in ensuring that legislatures adhered to the state constitutions in their enactments. Those who were attempting to effect wider reforms – such as the repeal of the odious Black Laws, or guaranteeing married women control over their own property – reached for a much deeper critique of the law. When reform activists scrutinized their state laws, the common law precedent, constitutional provisions, or even unwritten nonlegal codes, they evaluated the entire legal system, not just specific laws or judicial decisions. Members of the 1852 Indiana Women's Rights convention, for example, agreed that "all laws or customs which proscribe Woman do hinder the increase of religion, good morals, and whatever else does vitally interest our race."[140] The abolitionist John G. Britton, who presided over the Convention of the People of Color held in Indiana in1851, explicitly declared that discriminatory legislation violated both the letter and the spirit of the U.S. Constitution.[141]

137 Milo Milton Quaife, ed., *The Struggle over Ratification, 1846–1847*, vol. 28 of Publications of the State Historical Society of Wisconsin (Madison: State Historical Society of Wisconsin, 1920), 281.

138 *Cincinnati* [OH] *Daily Chronicle & Atlas*, January 18, 1850.

139 T. F. Andrews, *Debates and Proceedings of the Constitutional Convention for the Territory of Minnesota, to Form a State Constitution Preparatory to its Admission into the Union as a State* (St. Paul: 1858), 90–91.

140 Indiana Woman's Suffrage Association, Record Book 1851–1886, Folder 1, Indiana Historical Society, Indianapolis.

141 "State Convention of the People of Color of the State of Indiana," in Philip S. Foner and George E. Walker, eds., *Proceedings of the Black State Conventions, 1840–1865* (Philadelphia: Temple

Both black activists and northwestern women's rights reformers broadened their critique to prove that unjust laws would have widespread – even international – consequences, precisely because they were worse than unconstitutional. William Lambert, president of the Michigan State Convention of Colored Citizens, declared that the subject of unjust laws would revolutionize public opinion and was "agitating the world."[142] Radical reformers often declared that unconstitutional laws subverted both justice and virtue. In 1845, the Reverend S. C. Aiken preached a sermon on the unconstitutionality of Ohio's Black Laws, declaring the "Laws of Ohio in Respect to Colored People Shown to Be Unequal, Unjust and Unconstitutional." He critiqued many sections from the state's discriminatory and oppressive laws, condemning them as an "unblushing, legalized denial" of rights of all free citizens of Ohio: both black and white.[143] Finally, a grimly ironic 1856 editorial suggested that the unjust laws of man (the writer was indicting both the Ohio and U.S. Constitutions) railed impotently against the inescapable laws of nature. Declaring that "Jack Frost himself" ought to be indicted for permitting the Ohio River to freeze over, the editorial mocked the "unconstitutionality" of anything that might help free slaves escape. After all, escaping slaves used the ice floes as an "avenue to freedom."[144] These reformers were using conservative arguments against them – specifically, the contention that any interference with slave property, or even agitation against slavery and race prejudice, was unconstitutional. All of these northwesterners, both the ones who possessed a legal right to vote and those who did not, believed they had the right and even the duty to evaluate the legal world in which they lived.

University Press, 1979), 1: 177. For a biography of John G. Britton, see Alton Hornsby Jr., ed., *Black America: A State-by-State Historical Encyclopedia* (Santa Barbara, CA: ABC-CLIO, 2011), 1: 258.

142 "Minutes of the State Convention, of the Colored Citizens of the State of Michigan, ... October 1843," in *Proceedings of the Black State Conventions*, 1: 181–2. For similar views, see "Minutes and Address of the State Convention of the Colored Citizens of Ohio, ... January 1849," in *Proceedings of the Black State Conventions*, 1: 232.

143 *Cleveland Herald*, November 29, 1845.

144 "Unconstitutional," *Ripley* [OH] *Bee*, February 9, 1856, quoting an undated issue of the *Cincinnati Gazette*.

6

Land Rights

Every northwesterner understood, as an undeniable truth, that soil was the source of life. Democrat or Whig, black activist or white farmer, wealthy speculator or poor squatter, wife or husband, all knew that human life could not be sustained without soil. And if life was to be held sacred, as one Illinois newspaper declared, then why should not soil, as the means to support life, "be held sacred also?" This editorial appeared shortly after the 1847 Illinois state constitutional convention had finished its labors and submitted its charter for popular approval – and did so without including a provision protecting family homesteads from foreclosure. Even though Illinois, like every other state in the region, already had laws on its statute books that protected homesteads from debt seizure, citizens believed that this principle should also have been enshrined in the state's organic law. Constitutional protections of rights persisted long after statutes, jury verdicts, or even state supreme court judgments had endured repeal or appeal. The notion that human life was sacred implied that "every human being," according to the editorial writer, possessed "an equal, God-given right" to sufficient soil to feed his family. If the right to life, and a man's right to care for his family, were inalienable, then it followed that the right to own and to cultivate soil had to be inalienable as well and must be protected in state constitutions. In this way, according to the editorial, equal rights to the soil inexorably became the source of equal human rights: a proposition stringently under debate in the legislatures and constitutional conventions in the Old Northwest.[1] Democratic deliberation, particularly when

[1] *Peru* [IL] *Junction Beacon*, October 23, 1847. The *Beacon* copied this editorial from the radical pro–land reform *Columbia* [PA] *Democrat* titled "Land Limitation." The original author was anonymous, but passages such as "Why should a few monopolizing landlords be permitted to seize on and hold all the soil, and by that means reduce the great majority of the human race to the sad and unjust condition of tenants, servants and slaves? Why should the toiling millions be compelled, as they now are, to give to landlords in the shape of rent all that they can raise above

driven by a reckless popular will, forced the question of rights (whether constitutional, statutory, or, more broadly, human) to the forefront.[2] Put simply, when people deliberate, they inevitably talk about their rights. Most of the delegates believed that human rights overlapped with but were not synonymous with civil rights.[3] And because debates over rights had to be based on at least some moral, rather than entirely pragmatic justifications, such fights took place on slippery, expansive, and unpredictable ground.[4]

Only radicals such as abolitionists, black civil rights activists, and reformers concerned about Indian and women's rights attempted to extend the natural right to life to a right to citizenship. Nevertheless, the notion that the soil was a source of basic rights implied, if not the right to own property in land, then at least the right to cultivate the soil for subsistence and to protect one's ownership of those rights. This presented a dilemma for northwestern delegates precisely because antebellum American political and constitutional debates over human and civic rights often relied on conflicting and sometimes entirely contradictory sources. If we trace the origins of that *Peru Junction Beacon* editorial, for example, we find an awkward paradox. This Illinois Whig newspaper had reprinted the letter from a radical Pennsylvania pro–land reform

a subsistence?" appear to be directly derived from such radical reformers as Thomas Devyr or George Henry Evans. Jamie Bronstein points out that Evans and other radical land reformers considered the soil as "the root of all life," though most would not necessarily have equated this right with abolitionism. Jamie Bronstein, *Land Reform and Working-Class Experience in Britain and the United States 1800–1862* (Stanford, CA: Stanford University Press, 1999), 27–31, 66–68.

2 The concept of human rights has a long and complicated historiography, one that lies outside the scope of this book. Perhaps the most helpful bibliographic essay appears in Samuel Moyn, *The Last Utopia: Human Rights in History* (Cambridge, MA: Harvard University Press, 2010), 311–22. Although the specific phrase "human rights" appeared more often in reform literature than in political speeches, northwesterners did employ the idea of general human rights in many other contexts. For example, in 1841, Illinois state representative Ebenezer Peck, serving as chair of the Finance Committee, advocated paying the state debt as a question of human rights because his fellow American citizens depended on the state to honor its obligations. *Reports Made to the Senate and House of Representatives of the State of Illinois ... 1841* (Springfield, IL: 1841), 180.

3 David Jacobson, *Place and Belonging in America* (Baltimore: Johns Hopkins University, 2002), 64.

4 For federal land policy, see John R. Van Atta, *Securing the West: Politics, Public Lands, and the Fate of the Old Republic, 1785–1850* (Baltimore: Johns Hopkins University Press, 2014.) Reeve Huston, *Land and Freedom: Rural Society, Popular Protest, and Party Politics in Antebellum New York* (New York: Oxford University Press, 2000), 139. Huston also emphasizes the antirenters' "borrowing" from reform and political parties to form an "eclectic political style" (p. 108). See also: Jeremy Atack and Fred Bateman, *To Their Own Soil: Agriculture in the Antebellum North* (Ames: Iowa State University Press, 1987), 267–70; Mark Lause, *Young America: Land, Labor, and the Republican Community* (Urbana: University of Illinois Press, 2005), 14–19, 21–27; Dawn Bakken, "'A Full Supply of the Necessaries and Comforts of Life': The Owenite Community of Blue Spring, Indiana," *Indiana Magazine of History* 107, no. 3 (Sept. 2011): 235–49. According to Mark Lause, reformers such as Robert Dale Owen were able to gain a "respectable hearing," which resulted in the founding of a few small "secular socialist communities" such as the one established at Blue Spring, Indiana (p. 10).

"Locofoco" organ.[5] The original anonymous author, who supported the workingmen's rights movement, was not only demanding access to arable land; he was explicitly advocating across-the-board equal rights for all persons. His reference to the right of "any human being" to possess and cultivate the soil implied an unequivocal right to be free from the degrading status of "tenants, servants, and slaves," thus connecting chattel slavery with political oppression in a manner similar to radical revolutionary era pamphleteers such as Thomas Paine. The original author almost certainly opposed slavery and perhaps even discrimination against black people.[6] Midwestern Whigs might have opposed the expansion of slavery, but those moderates who feared a hasty extension of rights for black people would have deplored the writer's more radical notions. The *Beacon*'s editor was using the core argument – the notion that every human being possessed a natural right to life, and therefore, to the soil – to support the idea of homestead exemption from debt seizure, and certainly not to argue for equal rights for black people.[7]

During the tempestuous decades of the 1820s through the 1850s Americans fought bitterly over the meaning and extent of property and human rights, as well as the relationship between property rights and citizenship. This was especially true when property rights conflicted with both party politics and national policy goals (for example, the right to expand the institution of human bondage into territories gained from the Mexican War or the right to take slave property into Illinois).[8] In the long run it would take more than a century of struggle to transform the way Americans made sense of those conflicting and overlapping conceptions of rights. While this chapter investigates the origins of that transformation in the antebellum Northwest, it does not argue that the transformation reached a happy conclusion.

The region serves as a useful laboratory for examining ideas about property rights. Rapid population growth and settlement, combined with easy credit, pushed conflicts over the public lands to the forefront. After 1800, settlement in the Great Lakes and Upper Mississippi region surged from fifty-one thousand to nearly eight million in 1860; these people lived together in an area of 294,000 square miles, nearly the same size as the 340,000 square miles in the original thirteen states.[9] Over the course of the nineteenth century, the federal

5 According to Mark Lause, locofocoism focused on antimonopoly rather than land reform, but in the Northwest, Whigs called any radical Democrats by that nickname. Lause, *Young America*, 13.

6 *Peru* [IL] *Junction Beacon*, October 23, 1847.

7 Jacobson, *Place and Belonging in America*, 62–64, 84. The *Peru* [IL] *Junction Beacon* appeared to be a moderate Whig newspaper. I did not see any references to antislavery or abolitionist sentiment. When black people are mentioned it is often in the form of whimsical anecdotes and stories picked up from out-of-state (upper South) sources.

8 The legality of slave property in the Old Northwest is discussed in Chapter 8.

9 Campbell Gibson and Kay Jung, "Historical Census Statistics on Population Totals by Race, 1790 to 1990, and by Hispanic Origin, 1970 to 1990, for the United States, Regions, Divisions, and States," (working paper 56, Population Division, U.S. Census Bureau, Washington, DC,

government transferred about 871 million acres of land from public to private hands (approximately 279.3 million between 1795 and 1860, and about 592 million until 1923).[10] Moreover, the new constitutions raised discussions over the civil rights of nonwhite men because the Northwest Ordinance of 1787 prohibited slavery in the region, allowing a sharper critique of the institution of human bondage. As a consequence, at least the reformers who settled in the region felt free to critique race prejudice and rights discrimination.

The combination of rapid settlement of diverse populations, the presence of outspoken (if vastly outnumbered) reformers, together with the need to create and then revise governments within a short space of time rendered the process both confusing and exhilarating. Northwesterners' ideas about property rights were built on a similar mix of both concrete and abstract, of pragmatic and principled foundations.[11] That is not to assert that these people were able to articulate a coherent philosophy about the rights of people to land. They cobbled together radical theories (such as the free distribution of land, derived from utopian settlements, land reform societies, or socialist communitarian experiments) with traditional, sometimes even outdated beliefs, such as the discovery doctrine, to justify their acquisition and defense of property.[12] Property rights in land that one had bought (or hoped to be able to buy, which for some amounted to nearly the same thing) were not precisely the same as the right to cultivate soil, but in this bracing context, the distinction could be hard to figure out. As occurred in every other debate over controversial issues, the convention delegates were forced to confront and articulate underlying principles in order to find a common ground for this wild concatenation of ideas about rights and desires.[13]

2002). Information on square miles from John G. Clark, *The Grain Trade in the Old Northwest* (Urbana: University of Illinois Press, 1966), 2. I added Iowa to Clark's calculations.

[10] Gary M. Anderson and Dolores T. Martin, "The Public Domain and Nineteenth Century Transfer Policy," *Cato Journal* 6, no. 3 (Winter 1987): 905–23.

[11] For a discussion of property rights as a mix of things and rights, see Thomas W. Merrill and Henry E. Smith, "What Happened to Property in Law and Economics?" *Yale Law Journal* 111, no. 2 (Nov. 2001): 357–98.

[12] Josiah H. Blackmore II, "Not from Zeus's Head Full-Blown: The Story of Civil Procedure in Ohio," in Michael Les Benedict and John F. Winkler, eds. *The History of Ohio Law* (Athens: Ohio University Press, 2004), 1: 445. See also: Review of *The Government and Laws of Every Country Are the Effect, not the Cause, of the Condition of the People*, by Francis Ocane, *Western Review and Miscellaneous Magazine* 1, no. 1 (Aug. 1819): 18. "The rulers act upon the people, and the people act upon the rulers. Capital, the amount of subsistence, soil, situation, domestic and foreign relations, facilities and disadvantages, existing institutions, all have their influence upon the deliberations and policy of a nation, and will affect the government and the laws; but the government and the laws have their influence in turn upon the condition and relations of a country, and may very rapidly change its aspect, as we ourselves have seen in the United States."

[13] Jacobson argues that natural rights were vested in land and in nature in *Place and Belonging in America*, 64.

Ironically, the original doctrine of discovery, as established by the Spanish philosopher Francisco de Vitoria in 1550, declared that "only voluntary consent" could justify taking Indian land.[14] In British hands, however, that doctrine became a defense of imperial policy toward native peoples. In its most frequent usage, and in spite of the stubborn vigor of the discovery doctrine, the "right to the soil" appeared in nearly every treatise on the aboriginal people's right to live on their ancestral land. Hundreds of such pamphlets explicitly parsed Indians' "right to the soil" (using that precise phrase) as a right that could not be sold or transferred directly to individual owners, but had to be conferred through treaties with the federal government.[15] Judging from the tone of these publications, in spite of widespread race prejudice, there was also a rough-and-ready consensus, at least in theory, that Indian land rights ought to be respected.[16] Yet according to two well-known judgments by the Supreme Court Justice John Marshall in *Fletcher v. Peck* (1810), and *Johnson v. M'Intosh* (1823), Indians did not hold original title and in fact only owned the right to use the soil, but not the soil itself.[17] According to Story the federal government had gained title to Indian land as a result of the British treaties in 1787 and 1795.[18] Together with a third case, these decisions constitute the

[14] Victor M. Salas Jr., "Francisco de Vitoria on the *Jus Gentium* and the American Indios," *Ave Maria Law Review* 10, no 2 (2012): 331–41. For public land policy development and Anglo-American settlement in the Northwest see Paul W. Gates, *History of Public Land Law Development* (Washington, DC: U.S. Government Printing Office, 1968), 33–86; Roger Biles, *Illinois: A History of the Land and Its People* (DeKalb: Northern Illinois University, 2005), 56–82; Mark Wyman, *The Wisconsin Frontier* (Bloomington: Indiana University Press, 1998), 157–84.

[15] Eric Cheyfitz, "Doctrines of Discovery: The Foundation of Colonialism in Federal Indian Law," *Common-Place* 2, no. 1 (Oct. 2001), http://www.common-place.org/vol-02/no-01/cheyfitz/index.shtml (accessed September 22, 2014). Deborah A. Rosen discusses the longevity of the doctrine in *American Indians and State Law: Sovereignty, Race, and Citizenship, 1790–1880* (Lincoln: University of Nebraska Press, 2009), x.

[16] See Rosen, *American Indians and State Law* and Stuart Banner, *How the Indians Lost Their Land: Law and Power on the Frontier* (Cambridge, MA: Harvard University Press, 2005).

[17] Banner, *How the Indians Lost Their Land*, 171–78. In *Fletcher v. Peck*, the state of Georgia had taken 35 million acres of land from the Yazoo, and in an immense fraud, nearly every member of the Georgia legislature had been bribed by four land companies. Although Chief Justice Marshall was disgusted by the fraud, he upheld later purchase agreements because he declared that a state could not impair contracts. Statute laws, even if fraudulently obtained, cannot negate property rights. *Fletcher v. Peck*, 10 U.S. 87 (6 Cranch 87) (1810). In *Johnson v. M'Intosh*, Chief Justice Marshall ruled that Indians could not sell the title to their land to individual purchasers, because only the U.S. government held that title through the right of discovery. *Johnson v. M'Intosh*, 21 U.S. 543 (8 Wheat. 543) (1823). See also William Cronon, *Changes in the Land: Indians, Colonists, and the Ecology of New England* (1983; repr., New York: Hill & Wang, 2003), 178–90. For a discussion of how this case links to the discovery doctrine, see David E. Wilkins, *American Indian Sovereignty and the U.S. Supreme Court: The Masking of Justice* (Austin: University of Texas Press, 1997), 31–35 and Dorothy V. Jones, *License for Empire: Colonialism by Treaty in Early America* (Chicago: University of Chicago Press, 1982).

[18] The Northwest Indians were told that the federal government had acquired all of their land under the Treaty of Paris, 1783. After 1791, the government sought legal means to acquire

famous "Marshall trilogy," a series of decisions that established the relationship between the federal government and Indian nations. Essentially, Indian nations were considered separate and dependent political entities, and only the federal government (that is, neither states nor private individuals) could treat with them about land and property rights.[19]

Justice Marshall had evinced a troubled acceptance of the discovery doctrine in *Johnson v. M'Intosh* He knew it had no moral or ethical grounds but since it was already a fait accompli nothing could be done. In *Worcester v. Georgia*, the final case of the Marshall trilogy, however, he attempted to articulate a more ethical stance. In his opinion in *Cherokee Nation v. Georgia*, Joseph Story dissented, calling the discovery doctrine "excuse but not justification," and declared that because the Indian tribes had inhabited North America "at the time of its discovery," they therefore maintained exclusive possession of the territory as "sovereigns and absolute proprietors of the soil."[20] Moreover, they acknowledged no "subordination to any foreign sovereign whatsoever" and had "ever since asserted this plenary right of dominion, and yielded it up only [to the] superior force of conquest, or transferred by voluntary cession." Story drew an explicit causal link between the unjust usurpation of Indian rights to their own soil and prejudice: According to European conquerors, the "Indians were a savage race, sunk in the depths of ignorance and heathenism," and Story drily concluded that being forced to "yield to the superior genius of Europe" was thought to be ample recompense, indeed "more than an equivalent for [their] every sacrifice and suffering."[21]

Indian land. The 1795 Treaty of Greenville acquired most of the land north of the Ohio River. See: Cronon, *Changes in the Land*; Banner, *How the Indians Lost Their Land*; Dwight La Vern Smith, "Indian Land Cessions in the Old Northwest, 1795–1809" (PhD diss., Indiana University, 1949); Reginald Horsman, "American Indian Policy in the Old Northwest, 1783–1812," *William and Mary Quarterly* 3rd ser., 18, no. 1 (Jan. 1961): 35–53.

19 Banner, *How the Indians Lost Their Land*, 344. See also: Maureen Konkle, "Indigenous Ownership and the Emergence of U.S. Liberal Imperialism," *American Indian Quarterly* 32, no. 3 (Summer 2008): 297–323; Jill Norgren, *The Cherokee Cases: Two Landmark Federal Decisions in the Fight for Sovereignty* (Norman: University of Oklahoma Press, 2004), 212; Lindsay G. Robertson, *Conquest by Law: How the Discovery of America Dispossessed Indigenous Peoples of Their Lands* (New York: Oxford University Press, 2005), 239; Lindsay G. Robertson, "John Marshall as Colonial Historian: Reconsidering the Origins of the Discovery Doctrine," *Journal of Law and Politics* 13, no. 4 (Fall 1997): 759–77; Thomas Flanagan, "The Agricultural Argument and Original Appropriation: Indian Lands and Political Philosophy," *Canadian Journal of Political Science* 22, no. 3 (Sept. 1989): 589–602.

20 Jedediah Purdy, "Property and Empire: The Law of Imperialism in *Johnson v. M'Intosh*," *George Washington Law Review* 75 (2006–2007): 331. See Frank Pommersheim, *Broken Landscape: Indians, Indian Tribes, and the Constitution* (New York: Oxford University Press, 2009), 87–110.

21 Joseph Story, *Commentaries on the Constitution of the United States with a Preliminary Review of the Constitutional History of the Colonies and States before the Adoption of the Constitution* (Boston, 1833), 5–6. I found at least 143 citations in published pamphlets that explicitly used this phrase to support Indian property rights in their ancestral lands from about 1825 through the end of the nineteenth century. For a bibliography, please ask author.

Even the most thoughtful northwesterners, who condemned the discovery doctrine as unchristian and uncivilized, experienced little hesitation in pressing it into service as an explanation for the destruction of Indian land rights.[22] That was a widely shared opinion among northwesterners, though their language might be tinged with regret for race prejudice against aboriginal people.[23] "Indian Hating," according to one anonymous magazine writer, was at the root – however regrettable – of the pioneering urge to "dispute" Indians' legitimate land rights. The author acknowledged that "might [did] not make right." But he also understood the raw reality of the American seizure of Indian land, with or without official government sanctions, with or without recourse to ethical attitudes about respecting the property rights of nonwhite persons. America, he explained, had been settled in an age when the rights of "discovery and conquest" were still considered valid justifications. Yet surely "education, religious training, and civilization" ought to have influenced the actions of the people settling the Northwest. As hard as he tried, he could not reconcile these opposing ideas. The pioneers were unconcerned, he said, with Indians' "right to the soil and the privilege of hunting game." Perhaps the violence was a "regrettable consequence" of the pioneers' yearning for independence, and their "delight in roving uncontrolled in the woods." Employing a Jacksonian metaphor more commonly used to condemn owners of banking corporations and eastern monopolies, the writer denied that either "an Indian [nor] any other man has a right to monopolize" land that pioneers considered "free to all."[24] The Indian, evidently, was trespassing on the pioneer's natural rights.

In the common law tradition, the right to hunt wild animals derived from several sources: first, the Justinianic code, which had been translated into English by 1812, and was available to American lawyers through Blackstone's *Commentaries*. Second, northwestern state laws upheld the Indian property rights as per the Northwest Ordinance:

> The utmost good faith shall always be observed towards the Indians; their lands and property shall never be taken from them without their consent; and, in their property,

[22] Wilbur R. Jacobs, "The Indian and the Frontier in American History: A Need for Revision," *Western Historical Quarterly* 4, no. 1 (Jan. 1973): 43–56; Banner, *How the Indians Lost Their Land*, 112–49; Robert J. Miller, "The Legal Adoption of Discovery in the United States," in *Discovering Indigenous Lands: The Doctrine of Discovery in the English Colonies*, eds. Robert J. Miller et al. (New York: Oxford University Press, 2010), 26–65; Blake A. Watson, "The Doctrine of Discovery and the Elusive Definition of Indian Title," *Lewis & Clark Law Review* 15, no. 4 (Winter 2011): 995–1024. For a theoretical discussion of the abstract rights to own earth, see John G. Sprankling, "Owning the Center of the Earth," *UCLA Law Review* 55, no. 4 (April 2008): 979–1040.

[23] Richard Drinnon, *Facing West: The Metaphysics of Indian-Hating and Empire-Building* (Minneapolis: University of Minnesota Press, 1980; reprint, Norman: University of Oklahoma Press, 1997), 119–91. For Marshall, see Rosen, *American Indians and State Law*, 13.

[24] "Indian Hating," *Western Monthly Magazine, and Literary Journal* 1, no. 2 (Sept. 1833): 403–8. Emphasis in the original.

rights, and liberty, they shall never be invaded or disturbed, unless in just and lawful wars authorized by Congress; but laws founded in justice and humanity, shall from time to time be made for preventing wrongs being done to them, and for preserving peace and friendship with them.[25]

In 1837, shortly after the Choctaw were forced into Oklahoma and less than a year before the Cherokee walked the Trail of Tears, the Democratic *Cleveland Daily Advertiser*, in an editorial titled "The Indians," bemoaned the news of removal. The writer expressed sincere pity for the "original occupier of the soil." Yet because the West had become the "land of the free and home of the stranger," where people from all quarters of the world gathered to "enjoy equally the cool and refreshing shades of the tree of Liberty," the Indian's fate had marked him for an "overwhelming destiny" from which no one could save him. At the same time, however, there was no one who could be blamed, either. "If one was [guilty of trespass], then so were all." Indeed, the editorial suggested, "the Indians themselves may have been trespassers," and their fate was the same as that of every "race of human beings who inhabited this country before."[26]

Jacksonian Democrats may have experienced a nostalgic twinge of culpability in the destruction of Indian rights to the soil or their culture. Western journals (usually Whig productions) were often quite appreciative of some aspects of the Indian nature, which they characterized variously as stoicism, curiosity about white culture, and what they presumed to be a childlike friendliness. By the time these editorials appeared in print, it had become crucial to encourage white settlers to move into the Northwest, so these writers wanted to minimize their potential fears. Indians had by no means vanished, particularly in Wisconsin and Minnesota, but boosters and editors had to maintain that these people had been assimilated into mainstream American culture. That hardly solved the problem for Native Americans in Wisconsin, who as late as the 1840s experienced further destruction of their property rights.

For convention delegates and their constituencies, however, that ethical problem no longer existed. The Indians had been vanquished, removed, or civilized. When western journals talked about Indian land rights, they inevitably referred to their right to hunt or wander over the land – never about their right to raise a subsistence to feed their families. Indians who owned homes had presumably already joined the ranks of property owners and in several states even had the right to vote.

[25] Rosen, *American Indians and State Law*, 58. Northwest Ordinance, July 13, 1787, Art. 4 (National Archives Microfilm Publication M332, roll 9), Miscellaneous Papers of the Continental Congress, 1774–1789, Records of the Continental and Confederation Congresses and the Constitutional Convention, 1774–1789, Record Group 360, National Archives, Washington, DC.

[26] *Cleveland Daily Advertiser*, November 10, 1837.

Outside those instances, northwestern Indian property rights had rarely been protected in law or practice. The first white settlers in the region had arrived without clearly defined property rights, and if they claimed land, they did so illegally. In 1763, George III's royal proclamation protected Indian land rights in the region and prohibited colonial settlement there, but after the Treaty of Paris ended the revolution, the Land Ordinance of 1785 opened the area to white settlers.[27] Although the U.S. government chose to honor many of the land grants given under foreign rule, some previous private land claims were illegitimate.[28] That did not stop migrants from "preempting" Indian land. In this early connotation "preemption" was a euphemism for seizing Indian property that had not yet been sold or ceded.[29] These settlers, therefore, were claiming land to which no one but Indians had any right, trusting that the land would eventually become a U.S. possession. After 1787 the Northwest Ordinance established the grid and township system and mandated surveys in an effort to rationalize settlement patterns. But the concurrent destruction of Indian land rights, together with foreign claims to the governments of France, Spain, and Britain, caused immense problems for local officials.[30] General Anthony Wayne's defeat in 1794 of the Western Indian Alliance at the Battle of Fallen Timbers resulted in vast land cessions – more than 1.5 million acres – that established the Ohio Territory.[31] The Shawnee fought hard to retain their property in Ohio as settlers swarmed into their territory. Even when the federal government concluded treaties, many were fraudulent (that is, the signers were not authorized by their communities) and settlers squatted on Indian lands before their rights had been properly "extinguished."[32] Within five or six years enough white settlers had moved from Virginia, Kentucky, Pennsylvania, and the New England states into the territory to begin the process toward statehood.[33]

[27] For public land policy development and Anglo-American settlement in the Northwest see Gates, *History of Public Land Law Development*, 33–86; Biles, *Illinois: A History of the Land and Its People*, 56–82; Wyman, *Wisconsin Frontier*, 157–84.

[28] Gates, *History of Public Land Law Development*, 59–61, 87–88.

[29] Pommersheim, *Broken Landscape*; Banner, *How the Indians Lost Their Land*, 160–62.

[30] Gates, *History of Public Land Law Development*, 87–88; Pommersheim, *Broken Landscape*, 16–17.

[31] The Indian land cessions included all of the land south of Canada to the western banks of the Mississippi River. Gates, *History of Public Land Law Development*, 72; Patrick Griffin, "Reconsidering the Ideological Origins of Indian Removal: The Case of the Big Bottom 'Massacre,'" in Andrew R. L. Cayton and Stuart D. Hobbs eds., *The Center of a Great Empire: The Ohio Country in the Early American Republic* (Athens: Ohio University Press, 2005), 14–15; Daniel Feller, *Public Lands in Jacksonian Politics* (Madison: University of Wisconsin Press, 1984), 7.

[32] Gates, *History of Public Land Law Development*, 59–60.

[33] See Malcolm Rohrbough, *Land Office Business: The Settlement and Administration of American Public Lands, 1789–1837* (New York: Oxford University Press, 1968); Banner, *How the Indians Lost Their Land*; Reginald Horsman, "American Indian Policy in the Old Northwest, 1783–1812," *William and Mary Quarterly* third series, 18, no. 1 (Jan. 1961): 35–53.

As early as 1800 Secretary of Treasury Albert Gallatin had promoted the sale of public lands to citizens and priced them at $1.25 per acre – an affordable price for any but the poorest settlers. By the late 1810s settlers throughout the American Southwest, from Mississippi to Texas, and in the Northwest, from the Ohio River to the Mississippi, demanded congressional preemption laws that protected their investment of labor in the land. In 1813 Congress passed an act granting preemption rights of a quarter section to every person who had cultivated land "not rightfully claimed by any other person, and who shall not have removed from said territory." The point was to encourage settlement and cultivation of lands, and to discourage large-scale speculation. Meanwhile, settlers had until two weeks before the onset of the sales to make an official application for ownership at the local land office. In 1841 the Missouri senator Thomas Hart Benton first proposed the "log cabin bill," which stipulated that settlers who farmed the land and built a rudimentary dwelling should have the right to purchase it. Within a decade, western and southern representatives developed and supported hundreds of congressional bills that granted squatters the right to purchase, at cheap prices, lands they had settled. Yet the people who preempted these lands considered themselves entrepreneurs, not only subsistence farmers. The material in which they speculated was the soil.

The Northwest had been created from soil, water, timber, minerals, air, and sunlight: not only symbols and guarantees of rights or resources for prosperity, but a divinely bestowed gathering of elements, forces, and blessings. The farmers who moved into the region grew market crops such as wheat and maize; the miners extracted lead, coal, zinc, and salt for the eastern and overseas markets. They were eager to prove to the rest of the world that the American interior could take its place as a contender in the international commodities trade. By 1839, the northwestern territories were growing about one-fourth of the total U.S. wheat crop.[34] During the 1840s and 1850s, the state of Ohio alone outstripped nearly every other state in the United States in grain and beef production.[35] In 1848 alone, lead and zinc miners extracted 21,312 "short tons" of lead in the region.[36] But these agricultural bounties only increased the anxiety over the competitive right to own, farm, mine, or speculate in the soil. Some farmers built their agricultural businesses quickly enough to participate in the transatlantic economy (such as the Indiana delegate Oliver Davis, who shipped his corn and wheat to Ireland during the famine years).[37] Antebellum

[34] Clark, *Grain Trade in the Old Northwest*, 30.

[35] Harry N. Scheiber, ed., *The Old Northwest: Studies in Regional History, 1787–1910* (Lincoln: University of Nebraska Press, 1969), 166.

[36] Selma Langenhan Schubring, "A Statistical Study of Lead and Zinc Mining in Wisconsin," *Transactions of the Wisconsin Academy of Sciences, Arts, and Letters* 22 (1926): exhibit 1. A short ton is a U.S. unit of measurement of two thousand pounds.

[37] Allan G. Bogue, *From Prairie to Corn Belt: Farming on the Illinois and Iowa Prairies in the Nineteenth Century* (Chicago: University of Chicago Press, 1963), 249, 280–81; *Biographical and Historical Record of Vermillion County, Indiana ...* (Chicago: 1888), 261.

American farmers could pick up a handful of soil, or study the wild vegetation on uncultivated land, to understand a great deal about its potential fertility and future profitability.[38]

The Michigan chronicler Jacob Ferris, who wrote a glowing description of what he called the Great West, defined "speculator" as anyone who demanded greater opportunities for "acquiring property." The speculator, "eager to become rich" and willing to risk everything, "hastened impatiently into the wilderness" in search of waterpower and sites for future cities, all the while, paradoxically, "delighting himself in the solitudes, with the prospect of public streets whose lines were blazed trees."[39] Ferris was clearly equating speculators with pioneers, and entrepreneurs with farmers. Such men eagerly studied both scientific sources and published studies of local soils in the Northwest.[40] Those who risked their fortunes on these investments and who desired to keep their families in health and prosperity knew that the rich black soil of Illinois, Iowa, and Wisconsin would yield luxuriantly; many speeches and letters to relatives back east described the land as "inexhaustible."[41] One young Illinois farmer told his brother that the soil

38 We met Oliver Davis in the opening anecdote to Chapter 1. Joseph P. Elliott, *Biographical and Historical Record of Vermillion County, Indiana* (Chicago: 1888), 260–61. Robert E. Mitchell, "Antebellum Farm-Settlement Patterns: A Three-Level Approach to Assessing the Effects of Soils," *Journal of Interdisciplinary History* 41, no. 3 (Winter 2011): 393–420. On the importance of soil, see also Walter Martin Kollmorgen, *The German-Swiss in Franklin County, Tennessee: A Study of the Significance of Cultural Considerations in Farming Enterprises* (Washington, DC: U.S. Bureau of Agricultural Statistics, 1940), 106–7; Douglas Helms, "Soil and Southern History," *Agricultural History* 74, no. 4 (Autumn 2000): 723–58. See also Franklin Thomas, *The Environmental Basis of Society: A Study in the History of Sociological Theory* (New York: Century, 1925), 120–53; Michael Conzen, "The Historical Impulse in Geographical Writing about the United States, 1850–1990," in Michael Conzen, Thomas Rumney, and Graeme Wynn eds., *A Scholar's Guide to Geographical Writing on the American and Canadian Past* (Chicago: University of Chicago Press, 1993), 3–90.

39 Jacob Ferris, *The States and Territories of the Great West ...* (New York: 1856), 14.

40 Allan Bogue notes that after 1840 well-read settlers would have been exposed to scientific analysis of the fertility of northwestern soils. Bogue, *From Prairie to Corn Belt*, 6–7. For the origins of the early conservation movement in the 1840s agricultural reform see, Steven Stoll, *Larding the Lean Earth: Soil and Society in Nineteenth-Century America* (New York: Hill & Wang, 2002), 174–78.

41 The Illinois delegate Campbell spoke of "inexhaustible" soil and minerals in Arthur Charles Cole, ed., *The Constitutional Debates of 1847*, vol. 14 of *Collections of the Illinois State Historical Library* (Springfield: Illinois State Historical Library, 1919), 518 (hereafter Illinois 1847). See other references to delegates' notions of boundless resources in H. Fowler, *Report of the Debates and Proceedings of the Convention for the Revision of the Constitution of the State of Indiana* (Indianapolis, IN: 1850), 1: 720 (hereafter Indiana 1850); Benjamin F. Shambaugh, ed. *Fragments of the Debates of the Iowa Constitutional Conventions of 1844 and 1846 along with Press Comments and other Materials ...* (Iowa City: State Historical Society of Iowa, 1900), 283, 286 (hereafter Iowa 1844); *Report of the Proceedings and Debates in the Convention to Revise the Constitution of State of Michigan, 1850* (Lansing, MI: 1850), 218, 569 (hereafter Michigan 1850); T. F. Andrews, *Debates and Proceedings of the Constitutional Convention for the Territory of Minnesota, to Form a State Constitution Preparatory to Its Admission into the Union as a State* (St. Paul, MN: 1858), 226 (hereafter Minnesota 1857

was "as black as your hat and as mellow as an ash [heap]."[42] Easterners who first glimpsed the treeless northwestern prairies doubted that the land could support family farms, much less market agriculture. But by the 1840s antebellum travelers and farmers began to discover immense possibilities of wealth in undulating prairies and learned how to fence their property with shrubs instead of wood fences.[43] The fortunate settlers who acquired timbered farmlands encountered stands of oak, beech, ash, cherry, walnut, and hickory.[44] Booster literature, such as the immensely popular gazetteers, John M. Peck's widely reprinted emigrant guides, early state histories, and even railroad prospectuses breathlessly eager to resell their land grants at a profit, revealed an intense preoccupation with local soils. They carefully distinguished the northwestern varieties as rich and loamy, as sandy or clay, each with its peculiarities and virtues.[45] An interested gazetteer reader could learn that Indiana's Vigo County possessed "most luxuriant soil," generally ranked as "first rate land, [while] the soil in the high prairies is uniformly a rich loam mixed with sand." Any farmer would have known what rich, loamy, or gravel-mixed soils would be capable of growing.[46] A Michigan history published in 1841 expressed astonishment at the "beautiful variety" of the soil, much of it composed of a "deep vegetable mould sometimes mingled with clay"

Republican); J. V. Smith, *Report of the Debates and Proceedings of the Convention for the Revision of the Constitution of the State of Ohio, 1850–51* (Columbus, OH: 1851), 2: 300–1 (hereafter Ohio 1850). See also many regional gazetteers, emigrant guides, and canal or railroad prospectuses, such as *Charter of the Springfield and Alton Turnpike or Rail-Road Company, Together with the Proceedings Had in Aid of the Objects That Incorporation by the Carlinville Convention, and the Reports of the Engineer and Executive Committee of the Convention upon the Practicability and Advantages of the Undertaking* (Alton, IL: 1835), 17; and the *Territorial Gazette*, quoted in the *Burlington* [IA] *Daily Hawk-Eye*, June 6, 1839; Benjamin F. Shambaugh, *Iowa City: A Contribution to the Early History of Iowa* (Iowa City, 1893), 35–36; Henry H. Sibley, "Speech before the Committee on Elections of the U.S. House of Representatives," December 22, 1848, manuscript speech, Henry H. Sibley Papers, Minnesota Historical Society, St. Paul.

42 Quoted in Allan G. Bogue, "Farming in the Prairie Peninsula, 1830–1890," in *The Old Northwest*, 168; and in Oliver Ellsworth, "Ninety-Eight Years Ago in Bloomington," *Journal of the Illinois State Historical Society* 28, no. 3 (Oct. 1935): 209.

43 Illinois Central Rail-Road Company, *The Illinois Central Rail-Road Company Offers for Sale Over 2,400,000 Acres* ... (New York: 1855), 5–8, reprinted in Paul Gates, ed., *The Fruits of Land Speculation* (New York: Arno Press, 1979)

44 Paul W. Gates, *The Farmer's Age: Agriculture, 1815–1860* (New York: Holt, Rinehart & Winston, 1960), 47.

45 See for example: John M. Peck, *A New Guide for the Emigrant to the West* ... (Boston: 1836), 228. Robert E. Mitchell, "Antebellum Farm-Settlement Patterns: A Three-Level Approach to Assessing the Effects of Soils," 393–420. On importance of soil, see also Kollmorgen, *The German-Swiss in Franklin County Tennessee* (Washington, DC: 1940), 106–7. See also Thomas, *The Environmental Basis of Society* (New York, 1925), 120–53; Conzen, "The Historical Impulse in Geographical Writing about the United States," 3–90; Helms, "Soil and Southern History" *Agricultural History*, 723–58.

46 John Scott, *The Indiana Gazetteer or Topographical Dictionary* ... , 2nd ed. (Indianapolis: 1833), 181.

and capable of producing a "dense and luxuriant vegetation of ... grasses, oats, buckwheat, potatoes, rye, and large crops of corn."[47] In order to understand and take advantage of this prodigal wealth, young farmers would have to educate themselves on the properties of soil and minerals, in addition to climate, the abundance or scarcity of water and timber, and local wildlife. Americans throughout the nation were deeply interested in "natural philosophy," which they defined as a study of every aspect of nature and her powers.

Within two decades of statehood, Columbus, Ohio, established a planetarium, a scientific reading room, and weekly lectures on science.[48] Every midwestern state approved constitutional provisions encouraging agricultural science and education, as well as laws appropriating funds for soil and crop improvements.[49] The English farmer and reformer Morris Birkbeck founded the Illinois Agricultural Society in 1821. The many Farmers' Almanacs published during those years, and magazines like the *Farmer's Weekly* and the *Ohio Cultivator* carried detailed studies of soil chemistry. The *Ohio Cultivator* explicitly stated that most of the young farmers would be able to read and follow the article, since education in soil chemistry was by now fairly widespread.[50] Mechanical innovations swiftly followed soil science and advancements in chemistry. In 1837 John Deere invented the steel plow that could cut the prairie sod, and after 1845 Illinois farmers were eagerly adopting the McCormick reaper. Scientific management and exploitation of the public lands, which included settling, cultivating, "improving," and rendering the soil fruitful, convinced these new westerners that they were fulfilling a national and biblical destiny – and moreover, that they were doing so as modern and enlightened Americans.

Yet we can sense a curious dichotomy between their awed and deeply grateful appreciation of the beauty and grandeur of the West and their hardheaded realism about how best to discipline the splendor into neat, productive farms. Since 1785, when Congress had ratified Thomas Jefferson's land ordinance, the grid pattern that had been imposed on the western landscape without reference to existing topographical features served to commodify the public domain.[51]

47 James H. Lanman, *History of Michigan: From Its Earliest Colonization to the Present Time* (New York: 1841), 18.

48 Charles C. Cole, *A Fragile Capital: Identity and the Early Years of Columbus, Ohio* (Columbus: Ohio State University Press, 2001), 42–44.

49 Paul Salstrom, *From Pioneering to Persevering: Family Farming in Indiana to 1880* (West Lafayette, IN: Purdue University Press, 2007), 119; James Simeone, *Democracy and Slavery in Frontier Illinois: The Bottomland Republic* (DeKalb: Northern Illinois University Press, 2000), 63–67.

50 Daniel Lee, "Improvement of Soils," *Ohio Cultivator* 4, no. 2 (Jan. 15, 1848): 10. The 1841 Farmers Almanac republished a well-known British poem on "digging for gold" in the soil, and asking Science to "lend her kindly aid." Robert Baily Thomas, *The (Old) Farmer's Almanack ... for 1850* (Boston: 1850), 39.

51 For changes in American property rights that served to commodify land, see Lawrence Friedman, *A History of American Law* (1973; repr., New York: Simon & Schuster, 1985), 175. According to Wilma A. Dunaway, the four necessary elements of land commodification

In order to be commodified, then, land first had to be mapped, surveyed, and quantified: that is, rendered intelligible through mathematical and scientific processes. Because science was rational, predictable, and civilized, it also helped to undergird the white settlers' natural right to cultivate the soil and "grow a subsistence," as the anonymous editor of the pro–land reform article put it. Science could become a rationalization for preempting land and for exploiting it to the fullest. Reason became analogous and identical to virtue. Specifically, the process and the knowledge gained from cultivating land, as well as conserving and understanding the soil, helped to build justifications for the right to own and use the soil.[52] Moreover, the commitment to scientific study of the chemical reactions of fertilizers and close study of soil conservation convinced preemptors – those who were actually farming the soil, rather than merely speculating – that it was their duty to salvage and cultivate "waste" ground.[53] Ground could be wasted in two ways: first, by the native people, who might have had a perfectly legal and federally protected right to use their soil, but who were not in fact using it appropriately, according to western settlers – that is, who were not raising market crops or cultivating their land according to modern agricultural practices. Second, speculators wasted ground when they

(particularly land belonging to aboriginal peoples) include displacement of indigenous people, elimination of commons through fencing, modification of land tenure to encourage large land-holdings, and large-scale exploitation of natural resources. Wilma H. Dunaway, *The First American Frontier: Transition to Capitalism in Southern Appalachia, 1700–1860* (Chapel Hill: University of North Carolina Press, 1996), 19. For a study of this process in action in the Northwest, see Brad D. E. Jarvis, "Preserving the Brothertown Nation of Indians: Exploring Relationships amongst Land, Sovereignty, and Identity 1740–1840" (PhD Diss., University of Minnesota, 2006), 196–98. In order to be commodified, land had to be mapped, surveyed, and quantified: that is, rendered intelligible through mathematical and scientific means. Benjamin Davy calls this a "substantial change of territorial value" and likens it to privatization. *Land Policy: Planning and the Spatial Consequences of Property* (Farnham, UK, and Burlington, VT, Ashgate: 2012), 113.

[52] See: Clarence Danhof, *Change in Agriculture: The Northern United States, 1820–1870* (Cambridge, MA: Harvard University Press, 1969); Paul Gates, *Landlords and Tenants on the Prairie Frontier: Studies in American Land Policy* (Ithaca, NY: Cornell University Press, 1973); Robert P. Swierenga, *Pioneers and Profits: Land Speculation on the Iowa Frontier* (Ames: Iowa State University Press, 1968); Donald L. Winters, *Farmers without Farms: Agricultural Tenancy in Nineteenth-Century Iowa* (Westport, CT: Greenwood Press, 1978); Lou Ferleger, ed., *Agriculture and National Development: Views on the Nineteenth Century* (Ames: Iowa State University, Press, 1990); Alan I. Marcus, *Agricultural Science and the Quest for Legitimacy: Farmers, Agricultural Colleges, and the Experiment Stations, 1870–1890* (Ames: Iowa State University Press, 1985); Earl W. Hayter, *The Troubled Farmer, 1850–1900: Rural Adjustment to Industrialism* (DeKalb: Northern Illinois University Press, 1968).

[53] There is an important difference in the idea of "waste" in English and American interpretations of common law. English law considers any damage to existing property, while Americans used the word "waste" to describe underutilized land. For further discussion of the notion of "wasting" soil, see Steven Stoll, *Larding the Lean Earth: Soil and Society in Nineteenth-Century America* (New York: Hill & Wang, 2002), 31.

left it fallow and unproductive while they were waiting to dispose of their investment to the highest bidder.[54]

Eastern or southern emigrants, or Europeans crossing the Atlantic and making their way up the Ohio, Illinois, or Mississippi Rivers, or traveling in the new railroads or canals just beginning to traverse the immense prairies, found the landscape beautiful and overpowering, often describing an ocean of surging grass taller than a man could stand. They found the soil inexhaustibly rich, the mineral and salt deposits promising their own, their region's, and nation's prosperity. The mighty rivers and canals would carry their crops to the East Coast, southward on the Mississippi to New Orleans, and from there across the Atlantic to Europe. Nature was both abundant and powerful, both immeasurably generous and demanding. Yet settlers would have indignantly refuted any suggestion that this splendid state of nature signified that they were primitive or unsophisticated. An uncomfortable paradox inhabited their admiration: An overwhelmingly beautiful nature had to yield quickly to civilizing influences within one generation. Northwesterners could not and would not wait. Towns flowered along canal and rail routes nearly overnight, "as if by magic," as countless booster editorials and pamphlets boasted. Immense profits lay ready to be grasped in the soil, minerals, and water rights.[55] A twenty-one-year-old Stephen A. Douglas, who had recently settled in Jacksonville, Illinois, and was busily studying law, wrote to a friend that he congratulated himself on having settled in the "Paradise of the world." He would spend the rest of his career building a network of railroads and portages from the Great Lakes and the Illinois River.[56]

That paradox was part of a global phenomenon. Mid-nineteenth-century boosters such as newspaper editors, politicians, speculators, and private investors expressed a lofty confidence in the benefits of modern civilization; they might have appreciated the magnificence of natural western landscapes, but it had no place in a developing society. Their rhetoric may have waxed poetic, but their appreciation of natural beauty in no way prevented them from casually advocating the rapid and thorough exploitation of the same resources, even to the destruction of a landscape they admired. Nature had to yield – and very quickly, too – to civilization and progress.[57] The *Iowa Star*, for example, reaffirmed the advantages of Des Moines's hinterlands, which included trade, river

[54] Gates, *Farmer's Age*, 84.

[55] Jeremy Atack and Fred Bateman explain that for farmer-entrepreneurs profit became an "inescapable pursuit." Atack and Bateman, *To Their Own Soil*, 10–12.

[56] Stephen A. Douglas to J. A. Granger, July 13, 1834, Stephen A. Douglas Papers, Special Collections Research Center, Regenstein Library, University of Chicago. See also James C. Scott, *Seeing like a State: How Certain Schemes to Improve the Human Condition Have Failed* (New Haven, CT: Yale University Press, 1998), 35.

[57] David Jacobson describes the Puritan conception about civilizing a howling wilderness (a conception that also appears in contemporary speeches). Land was the "expression of God's presence." Jacobson, *Place and Belonging in America*, 50, 60.

navigation, and building materials, and declared that the great tide of immigration, like a "mighty wave, moving westward," was now transforming the "beautiful Prairies, as if by magic, into highly cultivated farms."[58]

The impatient yearning for modern farms, supported by the history of "preemption" of Indian lands, complemented and exacerbated the driving need for land. At the same time, this concatenation of desires and justifications also muddled the distinction between popular ideas about a human "right to the soil" and a citizen's right to property in land. By the early 1840s, widespread demands for cheap public land for private farmers (that is, explicitly not speculators) appeared in political speeches, legal treatises, judicial opinions and judgments, and newspaper editorials. In 1848 a vocal group of angry Democrats, disgusted and disheartened by their party's unwillingness to confront slavery, stalked out of their party's national convention in Baltimore and formed the Free Soil Party. Along with antislavery activists from the declining Liberty Party and "Conscience Whigs" (New England Whigs who opposed the extension of slavery into the territory, in opposition to southern proslavery "Cotton Whigs"), they gave voice to the rising sense that free white labor would save the nation from the growing slave power. Such reformers used the "Free Soil" slogan to promote the idea of homesteads – primarily for white people – but some also actively fought for civil rights for black people.[59]

A right to the soil, however, was not entirely coterminous with a right to property in land. Congress had dismantled the Northwest Ordinance's property qualifications for voting thirty years earlier. Such restrictions had already disappeared from most of the nation's state constitutions and laws before 1830, at least for white voters. They remained in place for black men and most Indians in every state except Rhode Island.[60] As our anonymous 1847 *Peru Junction Beacon* editorial explained, the soil itself was obliquely analogized as an abstract right – the right to survive, a father's right to feed his family, and the right of inhabitants to make something of themselves. To those people

[58] *Iowa Star* (Des Moines), January 13, 1853. See also, Allan G. Bogue and Margaret Beattie Bogue, "'Profits' and the Frontier Land Speculator," in Vernon Carstensen, ed., *The Public Lands: Studies in the History of the Public Domain* (1963; repr., Madison: University of Wisconsin Press, 1968), 369–94.

[59] The most helpful discussion of the philosophy of the "labor theory of value" appears in James L. Huston, *Securing the Fruits of Labor: The American Concept of Wealth Distribution, 1765–1900* (Baton Rouge: Louisiana State University Press, 1998). See also, Huston, *Calculating the Value of Union: Slavery, Property Rights, and the Economic Origins of the Civil War* (Chapel Hill and London: University of North Carolina Press, 2004), 105–106. Jonathan H. Earle, *Jacksonian Antislavery and the Politics of Free Soil, 1824–1854* (Chapel Hill: University of North Carolina Press, 2004), 68–77; Eric Foner, *Free Soil, Free Labor, Free Men: The Ideology of the Republican Party before the Civil War* (1970; repr., New York: Oxford University Press, 1995), 152–55; Theodore Clark Smith, *The Liberty and Free Soil Parties in the Northwest* (New York: 1897), 48–68.

[60] Alexander Keyssar, *Right to Vote: The Contested History of Democracy in the United States*, rev. ed. (New York: Basic Books, 2009), table A.9, 328–36.

who planted crops; grazed their livestock; mined lead, zinc, or coal; or refined salt, the landscape was the source of life, rights, and prosperity.[61] Arable soil near timber and water was not only a commodity to be marked out by stakes, traded by the hundred-sixty-acre parcel, or amassed, by eastern and European speculators from across the country or even across the Atlantic. It also served as a symbol and a conduit of rights. But that relationship remained complicated and contradictory. An Indian living in the region might have his right to the soil, but his right to his property was under dispute. For nonwhite men the embattled right to claim and farm soil still remained an obstacle (or for some, a threshold) to citizenship.[62] Even so, the recognition of a human right to soil implied other inchoate and incomplete rights, such as the right to remain living in the state. This is true even though the right to soil could mean nothing more than the right to work as a tenant on someone else's farm.

The process of deriving abstract rights from tangible possessions and then attempting to guarantee those rights in a diverse society that drew on multiple property rights theories resulted in unimaginable confusions, particularly for men who were attempting to rush their states' organic law into operation as quickly as possible.[63] In addition to traditional common law rights, constitutionally guaranteed property rights, and the rights guaranteed under the Northwest Ordinance, the delegates casually swept together ideas they found in incongruous sources. Those included radical land reform polemics, biblical and religious justifications regarding both the divine injunction to render lands fruitful, as well as the religious union of husband and wife; and – what was particularly poignant – outdated theories such as the doctrine of discovery.[64]

As they attempted to make sense of the interlocking and contradictory ideas about land and property rights, northwesterners often claimed to possess the "right to the soil," a frequently recurring phrase that appeared in British and

[61] Stanley Lebergott, "'O Pioneers': Land Speculation and the Growth of the Midwest," in David C. Klingaman and Richard K. Vedder, eds. *Essays on the Economy of Old Northwest*, (Athens: Ohio University Press, 1987), 37–57; Gary M. Anderson and Dolores T. Martin, "The Public Domain and Nineteenth Century Transfer Policy," *Cato Journal* 6, no. 3 (Winter 1987): 905–24.

[62] See Dana Weiner, *Race and Rights: Fighting Slavery and Prejudice in the Old Northwest, 1830–1870* (DeKalb: Northern Illinois University, 2013); Stephen Middleton, *The Black Laws: Race and the Legal Process in Early Ohio* (Athens: Ohio University Press, 2005); Leslie Schwalm, *Emancipation's Diaspora: Race and Reconstruction in the Upper Midwest* (Chapel Hill: University of North Carolina Press, 2009); Stacey Robertson, *Hearts Beating for Liberty: Women Abolitionists in the Old Northwest* (Chapel Hill: University of North Carolina Press, 2010).

[63] Charles W. McCurdy, *The Anti-Rent Era in New York Law and Politics 1839–1865* (Chapel Hill: University of North Carolina Press, 2001), 172. For an example of an antimonopoly and antirent polemic see page 1 of this chapter, note 1.

[64] David Jacobson explains the relationship between place, land, soil, and biblical references to "dust." Jacobson, *Place and Belonging in America*, 3. Stuart Banner's discussion of *Johnson v. M'Intosh* makes clear that "some government ... is at the root of all land titles in the United States." Banner, *How the Indians Lost Their Land*, 178.

American editorials, pamphlets, political and constitutional speeches, sermons, and even fiction.[65] The phrase was pressed into service whenever the speaker or writer meant to collect together constitutionally protected rights (such as the right to private property), fundamental rights (the right to life and to care for one's family), with the physical land itself – the handful of soil one could grasp, weigh, and judge. Antebellum northwesterners treated it as a heuristic for parsing conflicting conceptions of property and human rights in the Northwest. In the context of its ideological origin, the notion of a "right to the soil" sometimes harmonized with and sometimes contradicted the common law emphasis on precedent, responsibility to one's neighbors, compensation for harm, and prior ownership (at least, by white settlers claiming land they believed they had a right to preempt).[66] On the surface, antebellum Americans expressed that right as the rough-and-ready idea that every human being possessed a natural right either to the soil itself or at least to the life-sustaining crops, which together with the elements of air, sunlight, and water were the endowments of nature to all humankind.

The idea of a basic human "right to the soil" had its origins in the Roman republic.[67] Among early nineteenth-century Irish land reformers, it referred to the fundamental and unquestionable human right to air, soil, and water.[68] English common law defined soil, air, and water as the necessary components to sustaining human life. Utopian visionaries such as John Harrington wanted to enshrine the idea of a human being's natural right to survive as a permanent part of a society's legal and social structures; in his *Oceana*, published in 1656, he argued that an agrarian law that equalized landownership would prevent monopolies.[69] In 1697 John Locke added firewood to the list of the basic sources of life, though he certainly never intended a reinterpretation of the rights to private property and insisted that the poor be forced to work for

[65] For an example of the phrase in poetry (as part of the New York antirent movement of the 1840s), see Huston, *Land and Freedom*, 114. I did a search in *Making of America* and found 174 hits using the phrase "right to the soil" in quotation marks, http://quod.lib.umich.edu/m/moagrp/.

[66] Morton Horwitz, *The Transformation of American Law, 1780–1860* (Cambridge, MA: Harvard University Press, 1977; repr., New York: Oxford University Press, 1992), 31–34; Friedman, *A History of American Law*, 230–45.

[67] Stephen Hodgson, *Land and Water: The Rights Interface* (Rome: Food and Agriculture Organization of the United Nations, 2004) explains that both Roman and Islamic law hold that running water belongs to the community and cannot be privately owned. According to Hodgson, the Justinianic Code held that air, running water, and wildlife could not be privately owned. For Roman origins of the right to the soil, see Clifford Ando, *Law, Language, and Empire in the Roman Tradition* (Philadelphia: University of Pennsylvania Press, 2011), 19–37.

[68] For an early British land reformer's view of Roman rights, see Henry Schultes, *An Essay on Aquatic Rights ....* (London: 1811), 3.

[69] Bronstein, *Land Reform*, 24–31. Chapter 2 is especially helpful for understanding the intellectual background for British land reform.

their subsistence.[70] Still, his explanation rested on the fundamental rights of the indigent to survive.[71]

Over the coming decades these ideas traveled to the American colonies, where Thomas Jefferson extolled the virtues of an agrarian life in a republic.[72] The historian Laura Scalia has shown how deeply those ideas influenced antebellum state constitutional reform throughout the early years of the republic.[73] The more radical Thomas Paine explicitly demanded an equal distribution of land in a pamphlet titled *Rights of Man*. Paine would become deeply influential to mid-nineteenth-century British land reform activists. Early nineteenth-century English, Irish, and continental radical land reformers frequently quoted from that pamphlet and adopted as a hallmark of their demands the direct link of the notion of the natural right to life with the right to soil. By 1840, British land reform activists began to form associations that demanded access to land. Loosely tied together under the rubric of the Chartist movement, such reformers demanded democratic reforms to the way members of Parliament were chosen and elected. Such reformers were particularly interested in the laws and constitutions of the newer northwestern states, especially Wisconsin, whose state constitution they saw as a nearly ideal exponent of egalitarian self-government. A few hundred British land reformers did make their way to the American Northwest in the ensuing decades, though their inevitable disappointment with the reality – they did not find the utopian society they had sought – soon inspired many to return to England.[74]

In 1821 Robert Owen founded New Harmony in Indiana, a short-lived socialist experiment that nevertheless sparked small communities in Cincinnati, as well as in Michigan and Illinois.[75] His son, Robert Dale Owen, lived in New Harmony after the socialist community disbanded, though he became a Jacksonian Democrat and carved out a brilliant political career for himself

70 Richard Ashcraft, "Lockean Ideas, Poverty, and the Development of Liberal Political Theory," in John Brewer and Susan Staves, eds., *Early Modern Conceptions of Property* (New York: Routledge, 1996), 44–46.

71 See Joseph Story's opinion in *United States v. Harris*, 26 F. 185 (1 Sumn., 21) (D. Mass. 1830), also cited in *Harris et al. v. Elliott*, 35 U.S. 25 (1836).

72 Bronstein, *Land Reform*, 25–26. See Thomas Jefferson, *Notes on the State of Virginia* (1784), in Merrill D. Peterson, ed., *Jefferson: Writings* (New York: Literary Classics of the United States, 1984), 290.

73 Laura J. Scalia, *America's Jeffersonian Experiment: Remaking State Constitutions, 1820–1850* (DeKalb: Northern Illinois University Press, 1999); Bronstein, *Land Reform*, 24–29. See also, Thomas Paine, *Agrarian Justice* (London: 1797), in Philip S. Foner, ed., *The Complete Works of Thomas Paine* (New York: Citadel Press, 1969), 1: 605–23; Philip M. Glick, "The Soil and the Law: Part I," *Journal of Farm Economics* 20, no. 2, (May 1938): 430–47; Philip M. Glick, "The Soil and the Law: Part II," *Journal of Farm Economics* 20, no. 3 (Aug. 1938): 616–40.

74 Bronstein, *Land Reform*, 10–16, 150–59, 234.

75 Lause, *Young America*, 38. For information on Owenite settlements elsewhere, see Bakken, "'Full Supply of the Necessaries and Comforts of Life,'" 235–49. Bakken argues that Owen's ideas received a respectful hearing throughout the Northwest, and particularly in Indiana, in the late 1820s, though none of the Owenite communities survived more than a year.

in Indiana and later in Congress (he eventually joined the Republican Party). Workingmen's movements arose throughout England beginning in the late 1830s. "Chartism" was the catchall name for loosely linked radical reform groups, named after the charter of 1837, which demanded democratic reforms including an equal vote, payment for members of Parliament so that workingmen could serve, a secret vote, annual sessions of Parliament, and equal representation. Although the Chartists did not have a land reform plank, they wanted to democratize land-based voting rights. Chartists, who disliked every trace of government control over their land rights, were attracted by the liberal constitutions of new American states such as Iowa, Michigan, and Wisconsin.[76]

Charles Fourier's ideas may not have flourished in France, but cooperative societies called "phalanxes" experienced some success in Massachusetts and a few short-lived groups in Ohio.[77] Both Horace Greeley, who popularized Charles Fourier's ideas in America, and George Henry Evans, founder of the reform newspaper named the *Working Man's Advocate* in 1829, argued that all adults were entitled to equal property and "all mankind to equal privileges."[78] Greeley and Evans both ran into the same conundrum: One could not distribute lands already owned by private individuals, and public lands were being grasped by speculators. Public lands ought to be open to the workingmen, and the federal government ought to prohibit land speculation and monopolies. Freedom to settle on public lands would emancipate labor from "thraldom and misery," though like most American radicals, Greeley added a careful caveat, "to a reasonable amount." According to the historian Mark Lause, both Greeley and Evans understood that it would be hard to convince Americans of the benefits of handing out free land.[79] Jamie Bronstein explains that by the time of the Homestead Act in 1862 the land reform movement's radical roots in Chartism and Fourierism were long forgotten.[80] The British reformer

[76] See Malcolm Chase, *Chartism: A New History* (Manchester: Manchester University Press, 2007). For the experiences of Chartists who immigrated to the Old Northwest, see Ray Boston, *British Chartists in America 1839–1900* (Manchester: Manchester University Press, 1971), 29–30.

[77] See Charles Fourier, *The Utopian Vision of Charles Fourier: Selected Texts on Work, Love, and Passionate Attraction*, ed. and trans., Jonathan Beecher and Richard Bienvenu (Boston: Beacon Press, 1971), 1–75; and Carl J. Guarneri, *The Utopian Alternative: Fourierism in Nineteenth-Century America* (Ithaca, NY: Cornell University Press, 1991). There was also a short-lived phalanx in Sangamon County, Illinois, see: Kelley Boston, "A Phalanx Disintegrated: Socialism in Sangamon County, Illinois," *Journal of Illinois History* 8 (Autumn 2005): 209–26. Guarneri's map on p. 418 shows phalanxes sprinkled throughout the Northwest: Ohio, Indiana, Michigan, Illinois, Wisconsin, and Iowa.

[78] Evans quoted in, John R. Commons, "Horace Greeley and the Working Class Origins of the Republican Party," *Political Science Quarterly* 24, no. 3 (Sept. 1909): 478.

[79] Mark Lause says that the National Reform movement had some success in Wisconsin, Illinois, and Ohio, as well as with urban craftsmen in cities including Cincinnati, Milwaukee, and Chicago – though he explains that this attitude was more based on Free Soil politics. Lause, *Young America*, chapter 8.

[80] Bronstein, *Land Reform*, 8.

Evans George Henry had moved to the United States and in New York in 1839 founded the National Reform Association, which preached free availability of land as the only salvation for the nation. Evans edited *Young America*, a newspaper that served as the main organ for the National Reform Association, and which supported workingmen's rights, free land, and abolitionism.[81]

Historians have debated how much influence the National Reform Association and socialist movements wielded in the Northwest.[82] Transatlantic socialist land reform advocates including Evans, Frances Wright, and Robert Dale Owen had some success in the Old Northwest, but their ideas were adopted only piecemeal and rarely interfered with traditional racial or gender hierarchies. Even so, radical delegates were elected to the conventions by their own like-minded communities. For example, an antislavery activist Quaker named William Savery Bates in Ohio, elected by his community, and Ceresco, a Fourierist Phalanx in Fond du Lac, Wisconsin, sent Warren Chase (Figure 6.1) to both the 1844 and 1846 conventions. Still, most of those radicals ran under a Democrat ticket, which ensured that they would be placed on important committees in the conventions. By the time he entered politics, Robert Dale Owen, son of the utopian reformer Robert Owen, had transformed himself into a Jacksonian Democrat without jettisoning his more radical ideas. In spite of his unconventional socialist antecedents and his shocking notions about the equality of the marital relationship, Owen was treated with respect, even if a few delegates occasionally criticized his more radical notions about women's equality. That said, there is no question that even some highly conservative Democrats, such as Wisconsin's William Singer, also subscribed to land reform principles. Because such views married natural rights with Jacksonian acquisitiveness, they could appeal to anyone from socialist radicals to ultraconservatives; from Jacksonian Democrats who thought black people had no right to enter their states, to Free Soilers who considered granting them, if not the vote, then at least their basic right to their own land. William Singer, who throughout the convention would bitterly oppose black men's suffrage, nevertheless declared roundly that all men possessed an equal and indivisible "right to the soil as well as to the elements of air and water." Those rights must be protected "to the amount that is necessary to the subsistence of himself and family." He never addressed this paradox, but it would become a nearly insuperable logical conundrum for his colleagues when they reconvened in the following year.[83]

There were of course significant differences in the way northwesterners and European reformers understood the relationship between democratic

[81] Earle, *Jacksonian Antislavery*, 27–28.

[82] See Lause, *Young America*; Bronstein, *Land Reform*; Earle, *Jacksonian Antislavery*; Feller, *Public Lands in Jacksonian Politics*.

[83] Milo M. Quaife, ed., *The Struggle over Ratification, 1846–1847*, vol. 28 of *Publications of the State Historical Society of Wisconsin* (Madison: State Historical Society of Wisconsin, 1919), 281. He was a member of the territorial legislature.

WARREN CHASE

FIGURE 6.1. Warren Chase (1813–1891) served in the 1844 and the 1846 Wisconsin conventions. He belonged to a Fourierist Phalanx in Wisconsin, and later became a member of the Wisconsin state senate.

Source: Joseph Schafer, "Editorial Comment: The Wisconsin Phalanx," *Wisconsin Magazine of History*, Volume 19, No. 4, June 1936. Courtesy of the Wisconsin Historical Society.

self-governance and the rights of property ownership, particularly the right to own land. The northwestern constitutional delegates and their constituencies focused on the ever-present Jacksonian rage against "aristocratic" speculators, the eastern banking interests, and corporations.[84] In England and in Ireland, by contrast, reform movements aimed at distributing private landed property to the common people. American convention delegates would have dismissed such notions as rankest anarchy.[85] Northwesterners had no trouble appropriating

[84] Bronstein, *Land Reform*, 160–62.

[85] During the 1830s and 1840s, radical British pamphlets demanded redistribution of English and Irish landholdings. See Richard Oastler, *The Right of the Poor to Liberty and Life* (London: 1838);

the arguments of reform societies (even very radical ones) when those notions suited their needs, but they never strayed far from the common law principle that a man's property was his own, that he could do what he liked with it to the degree that his decisions were more or less in line with community welfare, and that he retained the right to protect his possessions through an adversarial and fair judicial system.[86] William Cronon, Jonathan Earle, and Reeve Huston have explained that most antebellum Americans believed that they possessed a natural "right to the soil," that indeed this right belonged to all white people, and they experienced no hesitation in articulating this right in their petitions to state governments and Congress.[87] Briefly, the rights of settlers to their homesteads were changing from a focus on individual and highly localized property rights, firmly tied to the race, gender, and marital status of the owner, to a gradual conception of community welfare that was based on, and ultimately redefined by, fundamental constitutional rights. Over time that change would result in the rights of married women to their own property, and the rights of black families to live on and farm their own soil (though not until the twentieth century). That painful and protracted struggle was taking place throughout the nation and would require more than a century to come to fruition in practice as well as in law, but it is possible to trace the fragile and tender roots of that transformation in the antebellum Northwest.

In 1851, the Wisconsin legislature did vote on Greeley's notion that land inheritance should not exceed 160 or 320 acres. The vote failed. A year later, in Congress, Speaker of the House Galusha Grow proposed a bill that guaranteed homestead rights, published under the title "Man's Right to the Soil."[88] He asserted that human beings possessed a natural right to air, water, and soil. Once again support for these measures arose from a wide diversity of viewpoints, some radically contradictory: For example, eastern land reformers such

and John Noakes, *The Right of the Aristocracy to Soil Considered* (London: 1848). In Noakes's radical pamphlet he claimed that all land was stolen and discussed the North American Indians' right to the soil. He indicated that American Indians had no right to sell land to William Penn because they possessed only a life interest (p. 7). For a later generation, the American reformer Henry George discussed man's "inalienable right to the soil," in *Progress and Poverty: An Inquiry into the Cause of Industrial Depressions, and of Increase of Want with Increase of Wealth. The Remedy*, 4th ed. (New York: 1881), 349. See also: E. Springs Steele, "Henry George on Chattel and Wage Slavery: The American Social Philosopher Condemned Both Forms as Immoral, Irrational Denials of Equality," *American Journal of Economics and Sociology* 46, no. 3 (July 1987): 369–78.

86 Bronstein, *Land Reform*, 33–34.

87 Cronon, *Changes in the Land*, 56–57; Earle, *Jacksonian Antislavery*, 59; L. C. Green and Olive P. Dickason, *The Law of Nations and the New World* (Edmonton: University of Alberta Press, 1989), 4, 17; Huston, *Land and Freedom*, 138; Bruce Elliott Johansen and Barry M. Pritzker, eds., *Encyclopedia of American Indian History* (Santa Barbara, CA: ABC-CLIO, 2008), 1: 146, 208–10, 2: 526–27; David E. Wilkins and K. Tsianina Lomawaima, *Uneven Ground: American Indian Sovereignty and Federal Law* (Norman: University of Oklahoma Press, 2001), 19–22.

88 Robert D. Ilisevitch, *Galusha A. Grow: The People's Candidate* (Pittsburgh: University of Pittsburgh Press, 1988), 73–90.

as George Henry Evans and Horace Greeley believed in the rights of laborers to own land, while southerners and westerners wanted to have access to the best land and to keep it out of the hands of wealthy speculators. The agrarian alliance of the 1830s and 1840s therefore accommodated a range of radical viewpoints and resulted in success for the 1841 Preemption Act.[89]

In the long run, even though a few radicals and freethinkers managed to win seats in northwestern constitutional conventions, none were able to persuade their colleagues to tinker with private property rights, at least not beyond homestead exemptions and bankruptcy provisions.[90] The Indiana delegate Thomas Smith, like Owen, another die-hard Jacksonian Democrat, but without Owens's socialist leanings, asked his fellow delegates whether they did not all have an equal "right to live, the right to breathe the pure atmosphere of heaven, the right to pursue happiness, the right to enjoy it, and the right to obtain it?" God had created the earth "for all that live and breathe." These were unexpectedly liberal attitudes for a mid-nineteenth-century Jacksonian Democrat. But the next part of Smith's speech revealed the conundrum he was facing in attempting to understand natural rights to soil in light of unwritten, but deeply entrenched social customs. Natural rights to soil may have been God-given; they may have struck deep roots in American revolutionary history; but in the Northwest, they had to bow to local desires and prejudices. Declaring that he respected "conventional rights as well as natural rights," he remained willing to "set up these different barriers between castes in society if necessary." By conventional rights he meant the rights of white people to live in a racially segregated community. In his case, black people's natural right to life could not trump the rights of white people to a traditionally ordered society.[91]

Few northwesterners lost sleep over this logical inconsistency. Many Democrats (and some Whigs) reconciled entirely contradictory schools of thought to justify their demands for access to soil. They believed they had a right not only to survive, but to prosper. Ethical considerations remained, at best, idealistic or "visionary" goals for the future. Even so, they could not easily silence the impassioned reformers or even the pro–black rights Free Soilers. There is little doubt, judging from sarcastic remarks that occasionally enlivened the convention debates, that the delegates were fully aware of the utopian, socialist, or communalistic experimenters in their midst.[92] But most northwesterners had no interest in sharing their own land, whether they squatted and dug a temporary sod house they had no intention of improving, borrowed loans they might never be able to repay, or invested in town lots that would

[89] Roy Marvin Robbins, "Horace Greeley: Land Reform and Unemployment, 1837–1862," *Agricultural History* 7, no. 1 (Jan. 1933): 18–41.

[90] See, for example, an irate criticism of Robert Dale Owen's socialism and a condemnation of his egalitarian marriage vows, discussed in Chapter 2.

[91] Indiana 1850, 1: 968–69.

[92] See Chapter 2.

only become valuable through chicanery or fraud. Whigs and Democrats alike loathed the absentee speculators who tyrannized homesteaders by purchasing immense tracts of land and then reselling them at exorbitant prices. Inflammatory newspaper editorials lumped creditors and speculators together. The historian Daniel Feller has best described the myth, which he calls the "false dichotomy" of the "archetype" of the honest settler versus the swindling speculator.[93] Feller explains that everyone speculated, even if only on a small scale. According to Malcolm Rohrbough, the sale of public lands triggered rampant speculation, a roaring trade in "platting, buying, selling of non-existent future cities." As soon as the Michigan Territory opened for the land office business, settlers rushed in, and within three years, there were funds to the tune of $5,241,228.70 in the land bank.[94]

This conflation condemned local lenders unjustly and in any case, everyone speculated.[95] Most people living in the Northwest (particularly those who had borrowed money to buy more land than they could cultivate) would have been acutely aware of the difference between an eastern absentee speculator and a local prosperous farmer. Most creditors were local businessmen or farmers who had enough laid by to lend to their neighbors. Although absentee land speculators rented their claims to cash-strapped farmers, they preferred to use the land as an investment or to sell it outright.[96] Information on tenancy is incomplete before the 1880 census, but some historians suggest that by the 1850s, about a third of young men in Illinois had become agricultural laborers, and land tenancy quadrupled.[97]

Honest creditors who had loaned money to farmers certainly deserved protection of property rights; yet popular diatribes, such as the one that appeared in the *Muncietonian*, likened them to "vampires," who drained the life blood of farm families. Proponents of homestead exemptions equated debt seizure to "old world cruelties" and "a more desperate slavery" than suffered by "our African slaves." Wealthy absentee East Coast speculators, with their millions of acres of land – land that lay fallow and uncultivated – were features of an undemocratic

93 Feller, *Public Lands in Jacksonian Politics*, 29. Gates, *Landlords and Tenants on the Prairie Frontier*, 22.

94 Rohrbough, *Land Office Business*, 243–48.

95 Gates, *Farmer's Age*, 81.

96 Allan Bogue shows the intersections of lending, borrowing, and homesteading in "Land Credit for Northern Farmers, 1789–1940," *Agricultural History* 50, no. 1 (Jan. 1976): 68–100.

97 Jeremy Atack, Fred Bateman, and William N. Parker explain that tenancy information is unavailable before 1880, but also suggest that by then about 20 percent of homesteads in the Northwest were tenant farms, in "Northern Agriculture and the Westward Movement," in Stanley L. Engerman and Robert E. Gallman, eds., *Cambridge Economic History of the United States* (Cambridge: Cambridge University Press, 2000), 316. For Illinois tenancy, see James E. Davis, *Frontier Illinois* (Bloomington: Indiana University Press, 1998) 406. For tenancy in Indiana, see Paul W. Gates, "Land Policy and Tenancy in the Prairie Counties of Indiana," *Indiana Magazine of History* 35 (March 1939): 1–26.

society.[98] Nevertheless, the funds farmers had borrowed from creditors were legitimate property and therefore ought to be protected under the U.S. and state constitutions. Wisconsin delegate Horace D. Patch, an ardent Democrat in the 1846 convention, tried to reconcile the notion of state protection of debtors against creditors. While he fully supported legal protections for creditors' property rights, he would not beggar the debtor nor "erect over him a petty monarchy" (in the shape of a creditor) to "trample upon him with impunity.... Home is an endearing word," he told his colleagues, and human nature, he explained, demanded the right to homestead exemption.[99] His colleague agreed: There were "poor creditors" to be protected as well as "poor debtors" and it was always the "middle class" who suffered most.[100] Commenting on the 1850 Indiana convention's refusal to pass a homestead exemption, an editorial letter published in the *Muncietonian*, a Whig Indiana newspaper, complained that the Indiana constitution allowed any "land-monger" who could pay the "pittance" asked by the federal government to seize "all God's footstool ... regardless of the numbers who may be entitled by the fact of their existence to a certain portion." If it was true that God had granted human beings the right to life, then that right must be protected by also granting "that which sustains life." Human beings naturally drew their subsistence from the soil, so it was inevitable that access to enough soil for a family's survival was an inalienable right. Every "landmonger who [ground] the face of the poor" and "extracted their sweat" could rob them of their most sacred rights. The state became a willing partner to the robbery and corruption, protecting the "strong against the weak."[101]

"Squatting" and "preemption" had slightly different, but overlapping meanings that had to be resolved both in statute law and in constitutions. During the eighteenth century British subjects in the American colonies defined the word "squatting" (or its slightly more euphemistic analogue, "preemption") simply as claiming land for which one had not yet paid, and to which the settler might

[98] *Muncietonian* [IN], April 27, 1850. The epithet "vampires" was a popular antebellum American insult for creditors, banks, and tariffs. See, for example, *The War on the Bank of the United States; or, a Review of the Measures of the Administration against That Institution and the Prosperity of the Country* (Philadelphia: 1834), 155; "Usury Laws of the United States," *The Banker's Magazine and Statistical Register* 5, no. 10 (April 1856), 759; Nathan Appleton, "Speech on the Bill to Reduce and Otherwise alter the Duties on Imports," Delivered in U. S. House of Representatives, Washington DC, January 23, 1833, 13 in Nathan Appleton, *Correspondence between Nathan Appleton and John A. Lowell in Relation to the Early History of the City of Lowell* (Boston, 1848); John Agg, *Proceedings and Debates of the Convention of the Commonwealth of Pennsylvania, to Propose Amendments to the Constitution, Commenced at Harrisburg May 2, 1838* (Harrisburg, PA: 1838), 6: 201; for a poem, see M. Deavenport, *Humbuggiana: A Poem* (Nashville, TN: 1842), 21–22.

[99] December 4, 1846. Milo M. Quaife, ed. *The Convention of 1846*, vol. 27 of *Publications of the State Historical Society of Wisconsin* (Madison: State Historical Society of Wisconsin, 1919), 634 (hereafter Wisconsin, 1846).

[100] Wisconsin 1846, 879.

[101] *Muncietonian*, April 27, 1850.

not even have a legal right. Therefore, "preemption" could mean simply asserting the right to take Indian lands before their rights to their land had been extinguished. By the early nineteenth century, the definition of squatting was beginning to take on an additional meaning: Preemption could also mean the right to settle on public lands before they had been surveyed.[102] Some people swarmed in; squatted on lands that they improved minimally, quickly roughing in a temporary shelter; sold their "claims" to someone else (perhaps another speculator); and then made off, farther west or farther north, to begin the process again.[103] Others, who intended to stay, had to squat if they had not accumulated enough capital to purchase their land outright, if they had trouble arranging loans, or if there were other practical problems, such as delays in issuing patents or in settling prior private land claims. Surveyors could not keep up with the pressure of rapidly expanding populations, and the constantly changing land laws that had to be phased in as the territories were applying for statehood[104]

Statutes prescribed protections and procedures to carry out the provisions of the constitution. Common law precedents protected property rights and established roughly equivalent guidelines for handling similar disputes. State constitutions were meant to tie all of these legal rules together in a rational, and ideally permanent fashion. The citizens themselves had set into motion constitutional change, and they demanded a say over common law interpretations of property rights, and even some statute laws. Every northwestern state, even those whose constitutional conventions had not included homestead provisions, passed exemption laws.[105] There was virtually no opposition to the idea of exemptions in principle. The few opponents in state constitutional conventions believed that such provisions belonged to the purview of the legislature, which would ensure the proper safeguards and could work out the details of precisely the types of property that ought to be included in homestead exemptions. Indiana delegate James E. Blythe, for example, was sure that the legislature would pass such laws because the notion of exemption was popular throughout the state, indeed throughout the nation. But he was equally convinced that such provisions did not belong in constitutions.[106] On

[102] See: Pommersheim, *Broken Landscape*; Banner, *How the Indians Lost Their Land*; and Rosen, *American Indians and State Law*.

[103] Rohrbough, *Land Office Business*, 162.

[104] Rohrbough, *Land Office Business*, 87.

[105] For dates of legislation, see the table on page 472, in Paul Goodman, "The Emergence of Homestead Exemption in the United States: Accommodation and Resistance to the Market Revolution, 1840–1880," *Journal of American History* 80, no. 2 (Sept. 1993): 470–98.

[106] Indiana 1850, 1: 721. Robert Dale Owen agreed with him. He believed that homestead exemptions ought to safeguard married women's property rights but believed that women's rights should be enshrined in the Indiana state constitution, while homestead exemptions should be handled by the state legislature. Indiana 1850, 1: 763. J. G. Read, a Democrat originally from Kentucky, and a powerful advocate for married women's property rights, stated that married women's property protection was "the true homestead law." Indiana 1850, 1: 533. Similarly, the Minnesota Republican Balcombe also favored homestead exemptions but

the other hand, Democrats were more insistent on constitutional provisions in addition to state laws. In its coverage of the 1846 convention, a Democrat paper in Madison, Wisconsin, reminded the delegates that "friends in different sections of the territory" were now making their will known to the delegates. The editor was positive that if "the will of every man, woman, and child from the Lake to the River could be heard, it would sound as the voice of strong men compared to an infant's cry, and would strike as a death knell upon the ear of the cold hearted oppressor." Indeed, so universal was the Wisconsin settlers' desire for a homestead exemption that "however obnoxious the constitution may be made upon other points we do not doubt that a homestead exemption ... will carry it by an almost unanimous vote over any opposition."[107]

A much more serious problem was that homestead exemptions, land preemptions, and impossibly large loans could subvert northwestern morals. Some delegates (even many of those who supported homestead exemptions) feared that if exemptions were enshrined as constitutional grants to the soil, such provisions would tempt citizens to fraud and dishonesty. In the 1850 Ohio convention, Democrat D. P. Leadbetter worried that exemptions permitted poor men "without energy, without industry or morals" to be artificially elevated to become "owners of the soil."[108] In response to such arguments, another Wisconsin Democrat, William Singer, argued that no one need fear deception or fraud; families could be trusted. The homestead exemption provision was nothing but "a good intent, a benevolent design, and a principle of human justice." It was clearly the duty of the legislature to carry out the popular will. Indeed, protecting homesteads was for the benefit of community welfare and would obviate a need for poor relief. "Every man must have a home somewhere," he observed, and depriving a family of their homestead condemned them to be "thrown upon the community to be furnished at the expense of the community with a home."[109]

Yet legislatures were not completely reliable. Enough people worried that the legislature could continue to tinker with extant homestead laws, or that consideration for creditors would overwhelm sympathy for debtors, that they wanted the provisions removed from the purview of lawmakers. One of Wisconsin delegate John Hubbard Tweedy's constituents asked whether the legislature would be able to change the forty-acre minimum homestead provision under the new constitution. "If not, whilst 40 acres of land would be exempt, the crops raised upon it, household furniture & even wearing apparel would be subject to seizure and ... sale."[110] The most pragmatic argument

thought the convention should "leave something for the legislature to do," Minnesota 1857 Republican, 107.

[107] *Madison* [WI] *Democrat* October 31, 1846, editorial titled, "The Exemption," 130–31, quoted in Quaife, *Struggle over Ratification*, 131.

[108] Ohio 1850, 2: 473.

[109] "Remarks of Mr. Singer, February 6, 1847," in Quaife, *Struggle over Ratification*, 281.

[110] H. A. Wells to John Hubbard Tweedy, January 9, 1847, John Hubbard Tweedy Papers, Wisconsin Historical Society, Madison.

against homestead exemptions was that most families in Indiana owned, on average, about eight hundred dollars; the five-hundred-dollar limitation therefore amounted to a de facto bankruptcy law. Such delegates opposed the exemption simply because they thought it would be unpopular in their counties and might endanger ratification of the state constitution. In response, land reformers such as the socialist Robert Dale Owen thought the exemption was based on such a fundamental principle (retaining a home and the right to livelihood for a family) that it ought to be permanently enshrined in the state constitution.[111]

The Ohio constitution never provided for free land to settlers. A disappointed resident wrote an editorial letter to an unidentified Ohio minister, asking that his ideas be published in his newsletter. He thought it was time to let go of the dream of becoming prosperous in Ohio, and "12 young men should put $100 together & go to Oregon." After half a century of statehood, everyone knew that "Land monopolisers" had robbed freeborn Americans of their birthright. Every landless man should have been given at least a quarter section, but instead, matters stood as they always had: "Thus Lord the poor do keep down but raise the rich to high renown Thus takeing away the rights of man & giving the publick property to the few & so upholding Aristocrasy."[112]

Settlers throughout the new territories in the Southwest and Northwest demanded state constitutional provisions as well as statute and congressional laws protecting their squatter rights. By the 1830s hundreds of congressional bills granted squatters the right to purchase, at cheap prices, lands they had settled.[113] Indian land rights had first to be "extinguished" in treaties with the federal government, and those lands had to be surveyed and paid for properly. But settlers rarely waited. The moment Native people lost their land in the early 1830s (for instance, Sacs and Foxes, after the brutal Black Hawk War, or the Kickapoo, after they were forced out of Iowa), white settlers overran the territorial boundaries. Squatters swarmed over the land preempting the best acres, fought off legitimate purchasers, and formed vigilante Claims Clubs that resorted to violence and intimidation to protect their stakes.[114] Squatting was essentially speculation: These were entrepreneurs who possessed raw energy and a considerable

111 Indiana 1850, 1: 786.

112 I. L. Peselm to Reverend (unknown), 1852, Edward E. Ayer Manuscript Collection, Newberry Library, Chicago.

113 Robert W. McCluggage, "The Pioneer Squatter," *Illinois Historical Journal* 82, no. 1 (Spring 1989): 47–54; Allan G. Bogue, "The Iowa Claims Clubs: Symbol and Substance," *The Mississippi Valley Historical Review* 45, no. 2 (Sept. 1958): 231–53; John R. Van Atta, "'A Lawless Rabble': Henry Clay and the Cultural Politics of Squatters' Rights, 1832–1841," *Journal of the Early Republic* 28, no. 3 (Fall 2008): 337–78; Richard White, "Outlaw Gangs of the Middle Border: American Social Bandits," *Western Historical Quarterly* 12, no. 4 (Oct. 1981): 387–408.

114 Ilia Murtazashvili, "The Political Economy of Claim Clubs: Squatters, Presumptive Rights, and the Origins of Legal Title on the American Frontier" (PhD diss., University of Wisconsin-Madison, 2009).

store of courage, but no capital.[115] Complicating matters further, the federal government did not distinguish among purchasers, but rather granted to everyone, whether citizen, absentee investor, European or British immigrant, or free black family, the right to purchase public land. Even so, black families who were able to acquire homesteads in the Northwest endured vigilante violence, disfranchisement, and expulsion.[116] All of these legal, quasi-legal, and illegal processes rendered the transfer of public lands to individual and corporate investors highly volatile.[117]

The heart and soul of every northwestern community – the place where all these conflicting desires converged – was the family homestead. An article published in 1856 declared that even the poorest father who found himself unable to cope with "the wants of a growing family" could move westward. If he and his family were willing to endure the privations and hardships of the first few lean years, they could create a decent life for themselves. But the point was not just to subsist: Husbands and fathers, "cheered by the certainty of securing a competence to [their] children," could look confidently to a prosperous future. Even a small amount of capital could speedily "accumulate into a fortune without having to wait upon the slow processes of industry."[118]

In this way a right to the soil (to feed and protect a family) was transformed into a right to prosperity. Land reformers and proexemption advocates began to employ the phrase "right to the soil" to support the notion of the natural right to survive, to cultivate the land, and to take care of their families. For nonwhite men, a homestead provided at least the fundamental human right to protect and support their wives and children.[119] English common law did not explicitly define the word "homestead," though nineteenth-century legal treatises considered a

[115] Gates, *Landlords and Tenants on the Prairie Frontier*, 282–85. Craig Thompson Friend wrote a thoughtful article arguing that subsistence itself was never the main point for squatters. Craig Thompson Friend, "Liberty Is Pioneering: An American Birthright," *OAH Magazine of History* 19, no. 3, (May 2005): 16–20.

[116] Anna-Lisa Grace Cox, "The Unjust Manacles of the Free," David Brodnax Sr., "'A Freeholder and Taxpayer': The Black Iowan Struggle for Equal Citizenship through Home Ownership, 1830–1868," and Jérémie Nathan-Brink, "Prairie Routes to a Black Republic: An 1823 Passage of African American Settlers from Illinois to Haiti" (papers presented at the annual meeting for the Society for Historians of the Early American Republic, St. Louis, MO, July 18–21, 2013).

[117] Rohrbough, *Land Office Business*, 157–79. Both John W. Hall, in *Uncommon Defense: Indian Allies in the Black Hawk War* (Cambridge, MA: Harvard University Press, 2009), 6, and Kerry Trask, in *Black Hawk: The Battle for the Heart of America* (New York: Henry Holt, 2006), 72, argue that the Black Hawk War was a turning point in the northwestern land grab.

[118] Jacob Ferris, *The States and Territories of the Great West* (New York: 1856), 14.

[119] Irving Mark discusses the fights for public land donations to citizens, but mainly focuses on the post-1860 period in "The Homestead Ideal and Conservation of the Public Doman," *American Journal of Economics and Sociology* 22, no. 2 (April 1963): 263–78. Paul W. Gates explains developments after the Civil War in "The Homestead Law in an Incongruous Land System," *The American Historical Review* 41, no. 4 (July 1936): 652–81. This author argues that home-stead laws did not get rid of speculators.

homestead "a home, owned and occupied, by the family," where the husband and wife provided "mutual care for their children."[120] State laws listed specific acres, buildings, and household tools as exempt from seizure but curiously did not specify the race or even the gender of the homeowner.[121] John Crain, a Democratic delegate in the 1847 Illinois constitutional convention (originally from Tennessee), proposed a homestead exemption protecting the "cultivator of the soil," whether "male or female."[122] In this context the "right to the soil" should be understood as a general right to the necessities that supported a decent life. This right preserved women's private property in direct contravention of traditional common law coverture, which granted wives' personal property to their husbands. For example, Illinois exempted a milk cow, clothing, two spinning wheels, and a loom – usually, the dowry that most young women took with them when they married.[123] Iowa exempted a Bible, family portraits, wool shorn from five sheep, and any spinning wheels and looms "put up and ready for use."[124] Also exempted were a mechanic's tools, a physician's surgical implements, a lawyer's library, and a schoolmaster's astronomical instruments. By 1850 Wisconsin, Indiana, and Michigan framed constitutional provisions that protected families from eviction and debt seizure, and every other state in the Northwest passed laws that protected family homesteads.[125] Twenty years later every state in the region had passed laws

[120] Neither Chancellor Kent nor William Blackstone defined homestead. A late-nineteenth-century law journal defined it as "a right retained by a wife after the death or even the divorce of her husband." "Weekly Digest of all the Current Opinions of all the State and Territorial Courts of Last Resort ...," *Central Law Journal* 33 (July–Dec. 1891): 136.

[121] For a summary of laws regarding homestead exemptions in Illinois and Iowa see Delos White Beadle, *The American Lawyer, and Business-Man's Form-Book* ... (New York: 1851), 312, 321; Eric H. Miller, "Florida's Constitutional Property Exemptions: Changed Intent of Unchanged Text," *Florida Historical Quarterly* 91, no. 2 (Fall 2012): 181–211; Timothy S. Huebner, "Judge John Hemphill, the Homestead Exemption, and the 'Taming' of the Texas Frontier," *Western Legal History: The Journal of the Ninth Judicial Circuit Historical Society* 11, no. 1 (Winter/Spring 1998): 65–85; Paul Goodman, "The Emergence of Homestead Exemption in the United States: Accommodation and Resistance to the Market Revolution, 1840–1880," *Journal of American History* 80, no. 2 (Sept. 1993): 470–98.

[122] *Journal of the Convention, Assembled at Springfield, June 7, 1847, ... for the Purpose of Altering, Amending, or Revising the Constitution of the State of Illinois* (Springfield: 1847), 309. The debate occurred on August 11, 1847.

[123] Young brides in the rural Northwest contributed spinning wheels and looms to the family property. See the speech of Robert Dale Owen, who fought for married women's property rights, Indiana 1850, 1: 530.

[124] "Put up and ready for use" indicates that the wife was actively working on textile production. Beadle, *American Lawyer, and Business-Man's Form Book*, 321.

[125] See Alison Morantz, "There's No Place like Home: Homestead Exemption and Judicial Constructions of Family in Nineteenth-Century America," *Law and History Review* 24, no. 2 (Summer 2006): 245–95; Lena London, "Homestead Exemption in the Wisconsin Constitution," *Wisconsin Magazine of History* 32, no. 2 (Dec., 1948): 176–84; Paul W. Gates, "The Homestead Law in Iowa," *Agricultural History* 38, no. 2 (April 1964): 67–78; Gates, "Homestead Law in an Incongruous Land System," 652–81; Rufus Waples, *A Treatise on Homestead and Exemption* (Chicago, 1892). In Illinois, the 1870 constitution provided that

granting married women control over their personal property and profits from their real estate.[126]

The right to acquire land – and perhaps more important, particularly in the case of free black families, the right to own the value earned by one's backbreaking labor – conferred membership in the community, if not political rights. True, in every northwestern state, the political rights of black persons and most Indians were disputed or entirely disregarded. Nevertheless, at least for some of these contested populations, land-ownership would move their status as citizens to the forefront of constitutional debate. As we shall see in a later chapter, the mere fact of land-ownership did not automatically grant citizenship rights, but it did force white northwesterners to confront the notion of every man's unquestioned right, regardless of his ancestry or appearance, to feed his family.[127] For all these reasons, homesteads represented, among other rights, a family's survival; white (and some nonwhite) citizens' property rights (and by extension, their right to protect their property in courts); the health and prosperity of the community; and above all a dwelling place for decency and virtue.[128]

For the delegates to the northwestern state constitutional conventions, working out the difference between citizenship and inhabitancy proved a difficult challenge, one that would not be resolved until after the Civil War. For nonwhite men, inhabitancy implied, at the very least, the right to be present in the state with one's family. By contrast, citizenship could include a man's right to vote, as well as his duty of paying taxes, helping with road building, and serving in the state militia. Yet nonwhite husbands and fathers, whether of African or Indian descent, and white Europeans who were not yet citizens retained a legal right to buy acres of land. The U.S. government maintained exclusive power to dispose of the soil. Indian land rights were still in dispute or in the process of being dismantled, from Iowa in the late 1830s to Minnesota through the late 1850s, and both free black families as well as European immigrants

the legislature "shall pass a liberal homestead law." Indiana had no homestead statute law, but the 1850 constitution did provide for a homestead exemption. Iowa, Michigan, and Ohio had homestead laws. Waples, *Treatise on Homestead and Exemption*, 959–61, 963–64, 970.

[126] Samuel P. Orth, *Readings on the Relation of Government to Property and Industry* (Boston: Ginn, 1915), 439. This provision would be interpreted as a right to a cost-of-living wage. The earliest mention of the phrase appears in Richard Allestree, *The Art of Contentment* (Oxford: 1677). For a discussion of the household as a "miniature version of society," see Christopher Clark, *Social Change in America: From the Revolution through the Civil War* (Chicago: Ivan R. Dee, 2006), 5. For a discussion of the nineteenth century family as a basis for society, particularly in Illinois, see Don Harrison Doyle, *The Social Order of a Frontier Community: Jacksonville, Illinois, 1825–70* (Urbana: University of Illinois Press, 1978), 110.

[127] Miller, "Florida's Constitutional Property Exemptions," 181–211; Huebner, "Judge John Hemphill," 65–85; Goodman, "Emergence of Homestead Exemption in the United States," 470–98.

[128] Beadle, *American Lawyer*, 309, 321.

could purchase land directly from the federal government.[129] Homesteads protected families' rights. But the predicament was much more serious than simply owing for the land and the improvements. There was also an ineluctable moral component to the problem of protecting homesteads that all decent citizens had to confront: the inability, or, worse, the unwillingness to pay for what one has taken.

To the modern reader the word "squatting" connotes a trespass on both charity and property rights: cheating, dissolute poverty, grasping what one has no right to take. Nineteenth-century writers, particularly those who composed celebratory county histories, memoirs, poems, and even fiction, portrayed squatters as heroic pioneers.[130] An 1832 short story by William Leggett, a "Locofoco" newspaper editor and fiction writer then living in Edwardsville, Illinois, captured the widespread northwestern sympathy for squatters. The hero, a young farmer named William Wilson (often simply identified in the story as "The Squatter"), lived with his family amid a vast flower-strewn prairie. His log house was surrounded by profound solitude, life-giving sunshine, a silvery brook, and a landscape blessed with peace and quiet. Although the villain of the piece – a land lawyer trying to drum up business – used the term "squatter" as an insult, the author's description of the family reveals both admiration for the farmer and undisguised abhorrence of speculators:

> "Snug cabin you have got here, Mr Wilson" said [the lawyer], "very snug cabin for a squatter." A blush mounted to the forehead of William Wilson at being thus uncourteously addressed by the appellation which he knew was generally applied, in the language of the country, to persons who, like himself, had settled without permission on public lands.[131]

Mr. Wilson personified the hardworking young farmer, supporting a wife and two children. As did many of his compatriots he had to face up to the idea that he did not yet have the capacity to pay cash for his homestead. He told the lawyer that it had taken him seven years of arduous labor to create his homestead and still had to endure the pejorative appellation of "squatter"; yet it was clear, from the description of the family and the homestead, that he had an indisputable right to his land. The plot takes the squatter and lawyer into other directions, but the family would certainly have had to find a way to legitimize

129 Banner, *How the Indians Lost Their Land*, 222–24, Rosen, *American Indians and State Law*, 67; Bogue, *From Prairie to Corn Belt*, 17.

130 Stephen Aron, *How the West Was Lost: The Transformation of Kentucky from Daniel Boone to Henry Clay* (Baltimore: Johns Hopkins University Press, 1992) talks about the respectability of squatters and their transformation into speculators.

131 Mary Russell Mitford, ed., *Lights and Shadows of American Life* (London: 1832), 1: 140–41. The English author Mary Russell Mitford collected anonymous short stories by early nineteenth-century American "folk" authors. The author of this one, titled "The Squatter," is unknown.

their homestead property, and their rights as property owners and as citizens would have to be worked out in both state constitutions and laws.[132]

The purpose of preserving homesteads under the law was to safeguard the well-being of families, who represented the core of the state's well-being. Communities could not exist without families, and families could not survive without homesteads. And every state in the region passed statute laws that protected family homesteads from debt seizure, ranging from forty acres to about one thousand dollars total value.[133] Three northwestern state constitutions (in Wisconsin, Indiana, and Michigan) included explicit provisions that protected families from eviction and debt seizure. The issue was so important to voters that in several states, including Wisconsin, convention delegates had run for election on the homestead exemption issue.[134] The 1851 Indiana constitution included a homestead exemption in the Bill of Rights, which the convention copied verbatim from the Wisconsin constitution. Both charters guaranteed "necessary comforts of life." That phrase may have been directly taken from Chartist and NRA land reform pamphlets and newspapers, and in any case appears to have been in the common parlance, and dates back at least to the early eighteenth century. Specifically, debtors were to retain the "privilege ... to enjoy the necessary comforts of life," and the state legislature was to support that privilege by passing "wholesome laws, exempting a reasonable amount of property from seizure, or sale for the payment of any debt." In both constitutions the "necessary comforts of life" provision also did away with imprisonment for debt, by now considered a barbaric remnant of European law. In the antebellum Northwest, only the Indiana and Wisconsin constitutions included the specific phrase "necessary comforts of life," but by the end of the nineteenth century many western state constitutions provided for necessary comforts, including Minnesota, Montana, Nevada, as well as North and South Dakota.[135]

[132] Brendan McConville, *These Daring Disturbers of the Public Peace: The Struggle for Property and Power in Early New Jersey* (Ithaca, NY: Cornell University Press, 1999); Huston, *Land and Freedom*; Irving Mark, *Agrarian Conflicts in Colonial New York, 1711–1775*, 2nd ed. (Port Washington, NY: I. J. Friedman, 1965); Alan Taylor, *Liberty Men and Great Proprietors: The Revolutionary Settlement on the Maine Frontier, 1760–1820* (Chapel Hill: University of North Carolina Press, 1990). Richard White explains that "claims of legality, extra-legality, and illegality became quite confusing," in "Outlaw Gangs of the Middle Border," 388.

[133] Irving Mark discusses fights for public land donations to citizens, but mainly discusses the post-1860 period, in "The Homestead Ideal and Conservation of Public Doman," 263–78. This is important for tracing the history of "right to land soil" idea (land to actual settlers, men with plows). In Illinois, the 1870 constitution provided that the legislature "shall pass a liberal homestead law." Indiana had no homestead statute law, but the 1850 constitution did provide for a homestead exemption. Iowa had homestead laws. Waples, *Homestead Exemption*, 959–61, 963–64, 970. See also: Morantz, "There's No Place Like Home: Homestead Exemption and Judicial Constructions of Family in Nineteenth-Century America," 245–95.

[134] Wisconsin 1846, 130–31. This is an editorial titled "The Exemption."

[135] Orth, *Readings on the Relation of Government to Property and Industry*, 439.

The multiple origins of ideas about the very right to own or at least cultivate the soil – as contradictory as the sources might have seemed – resulted in practical gains for many white families, and some nonwhite ones as well. Every state passed a homestead exemption law that protected families from debt seizure; technically, these exemptions would have protected black families as well.[136] Even though black families and so-called 'uncivilized' Indians received no explicit protection in any northwestern state constitution, the natural law ideas about a right to survive, at least on the most basic level of growing food, could never be entirely silenced. Once such arguments arose to support a broader interpretation of the human right to life, they created immense difficulties for those delegates who, as did John Marshall, experienced an uncomfortable realization that unwritten prejudices could gainsay unwritten rights.

[136] Augustus Wattles, "Communications," *Philanthropist* (Cincinnati, OH), August 4, 1837, 2, 25; Joan E. Cashin, "Black Families in the Old Northwest." *Journal of the Early Republic* 15, no. 3 (Fall 1995): 449.

7

Places

A Democratic delegate to the 1850 Indiana convention described the "civil polity" as the "sum total of ancient laws," while an Ohio delegate used the same phrase, in the same year, to designate townships and counties as entities with rights.[1] Scholars now variously define the word "polity" as a system of authority in a defined physical space, or as a body of geographically connected citizens who have a say in their government.[2] In nineteenth-century

[1] H. Fowler, *Report of the Debates and Proceedings of the Convention for the Revision of the Constitution of the State of Indiana* (Indianapolis, IN: 1850), 2: 1370 (hereafter, Indiana 1850); J. V. Smith, *Report of the Debates and Proceedings of the Convention for the Revision of the Constitution of the State of Ohio, 1850–51* (Columbus, OH: 1851), 1: 150 (hereafter Ohio 1850). Indiana delegate Gordon referred in his speech to the "ancient custom" of grand jury indictments, which he believed was outdated and ought to be destroyed. Ohio delegate Taylor referred in his speech to reform of electoral canvass. Other conventions in the country frequently referred to "polity." See, for example, the 1837 Pennsylvania constitutional convention debates in which polity referred to the people and to republican government, interchangeably and together. John Agg, ed., *Proceedings and Debates of the Convention of the Commonwealth of Pennsylvania to Propose Amendments to the Constitution ...* (Harrisburg, PA: 1837), 4: 146, 324, 342. See also, Henry Brown, *The History of Illinois from Its First Discovery and Settlement to the Present Time* (New York: 1844), 344; and *The Revised Statutes of the State of Wisconsin, Passed at the Second Session of the Legislature* (Kenosha, WI: 1849), iii.

[2] The term "polity" has been defined by sociologists and modern political commentators, particularly those writing on global issues, but few historians have attempted to interpret antebellum conceptions of "polity." Mathew Frye Jacobson is closest to articulating a theory of American polity in *Whiteness of a Different Color: European Immigrants and the Alchemy of Race* (Cambridge, MA: Harvard University Press, 1998), 15–28. Jacobson explains that race (particularly whiteness) is the organizing principle in the development of the modern concept of polity. For modern struggles to define the concept of polity, especially in global studies, see Yale H. Ferguson and Richard W. Mansbach, *A World of Polities: Essays on Global Politics* (New York: Routledge, 2008), 61. Ferguson and Mansbach define polities as those collective entities, with a defined identity, organization, and hierarchy, that wield power by promising and to some degree delivering material advantages, which in turn legitimizes that power. Craig L. Carr defines "polity" as an identifiable group of citizens committed to an ideological framework, as in "the liberal

American political texts, however, the term encompassed a wider and looser meaning that embodied, in addition, principles, statutes, and the physical state. For example, in 1846, the Illinois lawyer Henry Brown explained that the Northwest Ordinance embodied "the best maxims of our civil polity." And when the first Wisconsin state legislature published its laws in 1848, the section that described county boundaries, the structure of the state administration, and the method for electing state officials was titled "Civil Polity." The definition of "polity," therefore, could embrace an array of philosophical, geographic, flesh-and-blood, and parchment entities: the body of statutes, republican and democratic principles, the land, those persons empowered to elect representatives, and, finally, foundational American documents such as the Declaration of Independence, the Northwest Ordinance, the U.S. Constitution, and the Bill of Rights. This chapter connects the places to the people of the northwestern states, in much the same way our convention delegates would have done. This was especially crucial because both the places and the people faced conflicts that had to be worked out in the state constitutional conventions.

David Jacobson and David Glassberg have written about the power of "place" in historical movements and actors: the notion that where something happens is integral to the story and to the motivations of the people who live through these events.[3] Antebellum northwesterners perceived deep connections among their region, people, homesteads, soil, and rights. They declared to the world that they had now become westerners and that this new identity lent them a sturdy character, a sense of adventurousness, a friendly egalitarianism toward all white people, and, above all, new opportunities for becoming prosperous and independent. They had chosen to settle in a region gifted to them by Divine Providence, and they now intended to exploit their new home to the fullest. Consequently both black and white settlers defined their western identity in three principal ways: first, as a symbol of an abstract right tied to the natural right to life; second, as a physical location that – together with the people who lived there – defined the polity; and third, as an entity (again together with the people who lived there) with its own rights, for example, as a town,

polity," working toward a just society. Craig L. Carr, *Polity: Political Culture and the Nature of Politics* (Lanham, MD: Rowman & Littlefield, 2007), 124. Paul Ricoeur defines polity as a body of rational decisions, involving "analysis of current situations and decisions projecting future probabilities," in *History and Truth*, trans. Charles A. Kelbley (Evanston, IL: Northwestern University Press, 1965), 255. Sylbia Walby defines polity as "an entity which has authority over a specific social group or territory or set of institutions [with] some degree of internal coherence, ... centralized control ... the ability to enforce sanctions against those members who break its rules." *Globalization and Inequalities: Complexity and Contested Modernities* (London: Sage, 2009), 158.

[3] David Jacobson, *Place and Belonging in America* (Baltimore: Johns Hopkins University Press, 2002), 1–4, 197n1; David Glassberg, *Sense of History: The Place of the Past in American Life* (Amherst: University of Massachusetts Press, 2001). To define "place" Jacobson cited Steven Grosby, "Territoriality: The Transcendental, Primordial Feature of Modern Societies," *Nations and Nationalism* 1, no.2 (1995): 150.

a county, a state, or a region. People moved rapidly into, around, and out of the region. While statistics for westward migration are scarce before 1840, we know that the migration into the West was part of one of the greatest American population movements of the nineteenth century, both to the western territories and within the region.[4] As a result, counties could change their boundaries drastically. That meant that they had to move their capitals and courthouses, too. Rivers could change their courses through erosion or through the buildup of snags, and if a state boundary was marked by that river, then the people living there could suddenly find themselves dispossessed of expensive harbor and river improvements. Therefore, a "place" could be variously defined as an individual family's guarantee of survival or as a community's access to trade routes, as well as to centers of justice and government. These places became the sites of battles between neighboring states and counties over advantageous boundaries and resources.

The Northwest Ordinance decreed that there would be no fewer than three, nor more than five states formed from the region; and because most northwestern settlers assumed that the vast tracts of northernmost land were uninhabitable, too raw and wild to govern, few of the states worried about the extent of their territory.[5] What they wanted, principally, was to retain hold of rich mineral lands, advantageous waterways, harbors, any internal improvements such as roads or canals they had paid to build, as well as the fertile lands that would attract both settlers and investors. The Minneapolis *North-Western Democrat* denounced convention delegate Joseph Rolette's modest plan for the state boundaries. "We have the elements here to make Minnesota one of the greatest States of the Union," the paper trumpeted. The new state had to demand the "three great resources of Agriculture, Lumber and Mineral," as

4 Daniel Feller refers to the post–War of 1812 influx into the Northwest as a "Great Migration," in *The Public Lands in Jacksonian Politics* (Madison: University of Wisconsin Press, 1984), 15; Jeremy Atack and Fred Bateman, *To Their Own Soil: Agriculture in the Antebellum North* (Ames: Iowa State University Press, 1987), 71; Steven Stoll, explains contemporary warnings against heedless exploitation and Malthusian references in *Larding the Lean Earth: Soil and Society in Nineteenth-Century America* (New York: Hill & Wang, 2002), 23; Joseph P. Ferrie, "Internal Migration," in *Historical Statistics of the United States*, Millennial ed. (New York: Cambridge University Press, 2006); Russell Thornton, "Population History of Native North American Populations," in Michael Haines and Richard Steckel eds. *A Population History of North America* (New York: Cambridge University Press, 2000), 9. See also Kenneth J. Winkle, *The Politics of Community: Migration and Politics in Antebellum Ohio* (New York: Cambridge University Press, 1988); Peter D. McClelland and Richard J. Zeckhauser, *Demographic Dimensions of the New Republic: American Interregional Migration, Vital Statistics, and Manumissions, 1800–1860* (New York: Cambridge University Press, 1982); James W. Oberly, "Westward Who? Estimates of Native White Interstate Migration after the War of 1812," *Journal of Economic History* 46, no. 2 (June 1986): 431–40.

5 Northwest Ordinance, July 13, 1787 (National Archives Microfilm Publication M332, roll 9); Miscellaneous Papers of the Continental Congress, 1774–1789; Records of the Continental and Confederation Congresses and the Constitutional Convention, 1774–1789, Record Group 360; National Archives, Washington, DC (hereafter Northwest Ordinance).

well as "the great harbor on Lake Superior, and the Mississippi with all its tributaries, for the purposes of commerce." These resources would make the state "at once great and powerful."[6]

The previous chapter described the natural rights of individual persons to soil, air, and water. Let us now turn to the rights of northwestern communities: the towns, counties, territories, and states that also fought for land and water rights. When communities tried to assert their property rights, however, they faced much more powerful opponents: the federal Department of the Interior, the congressional committee on western territories, the U.S. president, and the Supreme Court. And these national institutions had to consider national problems. The United States was experiencing severe sectional disputes throughout this era, from the 1830s through the late 1850s, so the new territories asking for entry into the Union had to be balanced against the southern and southwestern states. During the crises over Missouri's admission, the tariffs, and later the Mexican cessions, some of the slave states even began to threaten disunion. Popular sovereignty, at least the way northwestern Democrats defined it, could not solve this problem. As we have seen, northwesterners demanded tight control over political power (rendering their judiciary elective) and suffrage (depriving black men and most Indians of the right to vote). But geographic fights had to be carefully negotiated, just as political battles over economic or legal issues did. And when those battles occurred in a larger arena, for example, between states, they had to be solved by Congress, the Supreme Court, or even the president. Fights over geographic objectives were of such crucial importance that they sometimes escalated into violence, such as in the famous western "county seat wars" or in armed conflicts over state boundaries. James Schellenberg argues, for example, that Iowa had one of the most violent and contentious histories in the annals of American county seat wars.[7]

How and why did these fights over geography become a state constitutional problem? To begin with, state legislatures could not set their own states' boundaries. When the territorial assemblies passed enabling statutes, they had to pay attention to the rough boundaries depicted in the Northwest Ordinance. No matter how angry the settlers might become over disagreements with

[6] *North-Western Democrat* (Minneapolis, MN), editorial copied from the *Daily Minnesotian* (Saint Paul). For the Minnesota boundary dispute, see Theodore, C. Blegen, *Minnesota: A History of the State* (Minneapolis: University of Minnesota Press, 1963).

[7] Daniel J. Boorstin, *The Americans: The National Experience* (New York: Vintage, 1965), 164–66; James A. Schellenberg, "County Seat Wars: A Preliminary Analysis," *Journal of Conflict Resolution* 14, no. 3 (Sept. 1970): 345–52. For later Kansas county seat wars that became much more violent, see Robert K. DeArment, *Ballots and Bullets: The Bloody County Seat Wars of Kansas* (Norman: University of Oklahoma Press, 2006). For a discussion of controversial county boundary fights in early Ohio, see Jeffrey P. Brown, "Political Culture of Early Ohio, in Jeffrey P. Brown and Andrew R. L. Cayton, eds., *The Pursuit of Public Power: Political Culture in Ohio, 1787–1861* (Kent, Ohio, and London: Kent State University Press, 1994), 2.

neighboring territories or states, they could not resort to violence with impunity. Otherwise they would risk losing their bid for statehood. Judging from the intensity with which newspaper editors and local boosters battled with one another over such issues, these fights became immensely important to settlers. Internally, the state constitutions laid out the correct size and population for counties, and they often intervened in the fights over the placement of state and county capitals. In any case, the political fights over all such geographic battles were so fraught that legislatures preferred to leave the solutions and negotiations to the constitutional conventions. When conventions favored one district over another, however, a spate of angry newspaper editorials ensued.

Every state in the region, and indeed most of the states in the nation, became embroiled in a fracas over boundaries. Most of these fights came down to land and water grabs. Some of them were in direct contravention of the provisions laid out by the Northwest Ordinance, existing state boundaries by older states (which, granted, were rarely surveyed accurately), and explicit congressional mandates. Indiana had disregarded the provisions of the Northwest Ordinance that its northern boundary must be drawn through the southern end of Lake Michigan. Before the Michigan Territory became a state, the Indiana legislature moved their state's boundary ten miles northward, thus casually appropriating forty-five extra miles of shoreline on the lake.[8] The Michigan Territorial Assembly complained to Congress, but their protest was largely ignored: The committee on the interior decided that Michigan had no jurisdiction over the area claimed by Indiana (which, after all, had been a state since 1818). Michigan also brawled with Ohio (Map 2); the so-called Toledo Strip, a narrow band of land between the two states, became the source of a bitter dispute in 1835. Illinois copied Indiana in drafting its statehood bill in 1817, and it also extended its northern boundary by ten miles. In April 1818, as Congress prepared to act on the bill, the Illinois territorial delegate Nathaniel Pope extended the northern boundary even farther, almost sixty miles north of the lake's end, to the line 42 degrees, 30 minutes. Pope's goal was to gain more lake shoreline and an outlet for the Illinois and Michigan Canal that would run from the Illinois River to Lake Michigan. Congress accepted the new boundary in granting statehood to Illinois and created the Wisconsin Territory from the remainder of the old Illinois Territory.[9]

In the northwestern territories, debates over the location of capitals, internal improvements, and other geographic advantages rested on two unshakable assumptions. First, political equality had to be represented on the landscape. The boundaries between states and between counties had to be adjudicated fairly, and internal improvements and public institutions had to be apportioned

[8] See George Pence and Nellie C. Armstrong, *Indiana Boundaries: Territory, State, and County*, vol. 19 of *Indiana Historical Collections* (Indianapolis: Indiana Historical Bureau, 1933).

[9] Don Faber, *The Toledo War: The First Michigan-Ohio Rivalry* (Ann Arbor: University of Michigan Press, 2008).

MAP 2. Michigan-Ohio boundary dispute.

to benefit the people living on both sides. The second widespread assumption was that most of these compromises and negotiations had to be written into the new states' founding documents. Even in the strongly Democratic northwestern settlements, such decisions were rarely left to state legislatures or to popular referendum. They had to be written into the constitutions, partly in order to prevent future fights over the capital cities, and partly to enshrine the idea of central access in the document that framed the state's character and destiny. In the first constitutions drafted by new territories, the problem of state boundaries also had to win congressional approval. And the problem proved to be particularly thorny for several young states fighting for what they believed were their territorial rights.

Northwestern territories used "squatting" or "preemption" rights and arguments in precisely the way individual settlers had used them: without so much as a glancing reference to potential legal questions about property rights. Improvements, cultivation, and hard work rendered a place as good as a legal possession. Roads, canals, and harbors became analogous to a squatter's improvements, and settlers demanded a right to the property upon which they had expended energy and money to improve. During the Michigan-Ohio boundary battle, one of the most fractious issues was the placement of a canal that Ohio had begun to build. That canal might end up in the Michigan Territory if Congress decided to favor Michigan. The Ohio judge Benjamin Tappan worried that a canal terminus would result in the creation of a large city, and "this concentrated capital brought together at our expense *must* pay its contributions into the treasury of that power by which it has been created."[10] Therefore, he, as did most northwesterners, believed that internal improvements should determine boundary lines. Similarly, one of Wisconsin delegate John Hubbard Tweedy's constituents observed that the congressional boundary for Wisconsin would cut right across a contemplated railroad line. That line, he believed, should be either farther east or west, so that one or the other state should have the ground on which to build the road. Naturally, he deemed it of "vast importance for *us* to [retain] it."[11] What was at stake: the state's identity, and, as a consequence, the state's future prosperity. Larger, more abundantly wealthy states would inevitably attract more settlers and investors. Michigan 1835 convention delegate John Norvell demanded to know whether no one was concerned about maintaining the integrity of the state's territorial limits. If the boundaries were not worth preserving, then Michigan was "not worth a conversion into a state." He was prepared to resign from the convention in protest if his colleagues surrendered to Ohio.[12]

Political organizations and loyalties played a significant role, primarily to mobilize local action, but they were more fluid in the antebellum Midwest than in the more established regions. For example, support for internal improvements remained an important plank of the Whig national political platform. But northwesterners of all political stripes understood the importance of building transportation networks, aimed at improving and extending markets and communication both within the state and with the eastern states. Still, the most explicit arguments for the fact that capital site location would yield internal improvements appeared in Whig papers, while Democrat papers, always more fractious, rather stressed the local fights for these improvements. But because of their adherence to the importance of the centrality of geographic advantages as the best guarantor of democratic justice, both Whig and Democrat papers agreed that the precise location of internal improvements ought to be determined before the state became fully settled. That would ensure that roads would lead to the capital, which would inevitably become the radiating center

[10] Benjamin Tappan to Mr. Vinton, December 16, 1834, Benjamin Tappan Papers, Ohio Historical Society, Columbus.

[11] Unknown to John Hubbard Tweedy, December 11, 1847, John H. Tweedy Papers, Wisconsin Historical Society, Madison; Alice E. Smith, *From Exploration to Statehood*, vol. 1 of *The History of Wisconsin* (1973; repr., Madison: State Historical Society of Wisconsin, 1985), 678–79.

[12] Harold M. Dorr, ed., *The Michigan Constitutional Conventions of 1835–36: Debates and Proceedings* (Ann Arbor: University of Michigan Press, 1940), 83 (hereafter Michigan 1835). John Norvell was a Jeffersonian Democratic-Republican (founder of the *Philadelphia Inquirer*), while John Biddle was a Philadelphia Whig.

for future transportation networks. The Whig *Oskaloosa Herald* stressed that the current state capital's present location was inconvenient to "north, south and west, while the unsurpassed increase of population in the south and west, render it anything but equitable in its location to them." The capital should be removed as soon as possible because the location of the permanent site would determine the "locating of Railroads, Plank roads &c., because it is desirable to have the question definitely settled as soon as practicable." This sentiment was so pervasive that it was expressed with equal vehemence by both Democrat and Whig newspaper editorials, even though traditional Democrats – those outside the western territories – usually opposed massive internal improvement projects, deeming them unconstitutional.

Western Democrats (some of whom were members of the "Young America" faction of the Democratic Party) supported river, harbor, and road improvements, however. For example, the Democratic *Iowa Star* declared that the sooner the capital was located where it would be permanent, "so that the works of internal improvements, roads, mail routes, ... can be made in reference to it," the better it would be for the whole state.[13] The debates for and against internal improvements can be difficult to reconcile with national or regional party platforms, but it remains clear that the commitment to centrality and geographic justice often outranked national party commitments.[14]

The Department of the Interior, and sometimes even the U.S. president, stepped in to negotiate compromises, just as they did in sectional battles over the control of western territories. Unfortunately, the territories themselves never had the political clout or wielded the backing of established states. That was particularly true in fights with states that possessed a powerful political machine, such as Ohio. As a result the younger territories had to be satisfied with a congressional solution. During the Michigan fight with Ohio, for example, the *Constantine Democrat*, a paper that supported a negotiated boundary, exhorted its readers to let go of the 650 square miles they had been demanding. The real question in this battle was whether they would refuse the federal government's offer of 20,000 square miles of lakefront territory on Lake Superior, with immense additional land and water rights that included profitable fisheries, navigable streams, mineral rights, "large and deep forests of pine and other valuable timber," and the potential of "nearly half a million of the surplus revenue in the national treasury." Did it really make sense to fight on for a southern boundary, remain out of the Union, and risk losing the "new territory, lands, money character, and all?"[15]

[13] *Iowa Star* (Des Moines), November 7, 1850.

[14] Yonatan Eyal, "'Rift in the Democracy': Young America, River and Harbor Improvements, and the Old Northwest" (paper presented at a special conference of the British American Nineteenth Century Historians, Edgefield, SC: March 2005).

[15] *Constantine* [MI] *Democrat*, August 24, 1836.

There was no choice; Michigan could, at most, refuse to enter the Union, but even so, there was never any chance that the state could renegotiate a more advantageous boundary with Ohio. President Jackson had already thrown the full weight of his office behind the outcome, and since Michigan had to join with Arkansas in the traditional north-south pairing of new states, the state dared not risk further delay. And in Wisconsin, Rufus King, a delegate to the 1848 Wisconsin convention, told John Hubbard Tweedy, who had been a member of the 1846 convention, "We shall, of course, accept the Boundaries proposed by Congress." But he felt that even though the shortened boundaries were a foregone conclusion, the people of Michigan should still express their "wish for a different line." In a similar fight twelve years later, Minnesotans understood that if they did not accept the congressional boundaries, they might not join as a state at all.[16] In struggles over geographic advantages, as in demands for civic rights, combatants ought not to bow too easily to foregone conclusions.[17]

Yet even if they had no control over the final outcome of boundary disputes, communities still insisted on rights within those geographic and legal parameters – rights that echoed individual notions of ethical property divisions. They demanded those rights using familiar natural rights arguments, but had to rely on a different meaning of the word "natural"; instead of as inborn or innate, they defined it in a geographical or environmental sense. That is, they defined it as the opposite of artificial or contrived. Illinois lawyer Elihu B. Washburne told Senator Stephen A. Douglas that he disapproved of Wisconsin's new state boundary and disliked all of the other proposals for settling it – because they all depended on small bodies of water to define state boundaries. Rivers and streams, he believed, were notoriously unreliable as boundaries, because of their changeable nature, and especially because they divided "settlements and villages" and so made "the worst kind of boundaries between States or nations." Dividing Wisconsin along a northern river boundary would leave the leftover land as an "unnatural appendage to any other State or Territory." Now turning to the nature of the people – that is, defining "natural" as kinship – Washburne argued that a St. Croix River boundary would divide people "whose interests and pursuits are the same" into different jurisdictions and would produce "endless disputes and interminable litigation." It would be unjust to the "inhabitants up there to attach them to a State in opposition to all their feelings and interests and from which they would, from their situation be almost entirely isolated."[18] Similarly, in 1828, Galena lead

[16] See, for example. the debate in the Republican Minnesota 1857 convention. T. F. Andrews, *Debates and Proceedings of the Constitutional Convention for the Territory of Minnesota, to Form a State Constitution Preparatory to Its Admission into the Union as a State* (St. Paul: 1858), 419.

[17] Rufus King to John Hubbard Tweedy, January 4, 1848, John H. Tweedy Papers, Wisconsin Historical Society, Madison.

[18] Elihu Washburne to Stephen A. Douglas, March 17, 1848, Stephen A. Douglas Papers, Special Collections Research Center, Regenstein Library, University of Chicago. Washburne was serving

miners in northern Illinois petitioned Congress for the creation of a separate territory. They declared they were not well represented in Illinois, where the majority of the population consisted of farmers and were much closer to the state capital (then Vandalia, in the southwestern corner of the state). They based their petition on the 1787 Ordinance, arguing that they had a right to expect that their district, north of the 1787 line, "would remain together."[19]

In order to make their address more appealing (they hoped) to a wider audience, some delegates explicitly relied on the language of the Declaration of Independence. The members of the Constitutional Convention of Michigan, feeling cornered and outgunned, decided to publish an appeal to all of the "People of the United States," reminding them that conflicts between smaller and larger states were of national significance. The Michiganians declared that they understood that geographic limits – what they called the "nature of the country" – meant that the state would have to remain small. A loss of 650 square miles would be serious. It would be wrong for the territory to be wrested from Michigan's citizens by a powerful southern neighbor (no doubt an oblique reference to the growing sectional conflict), who was "in the same case, party, judge, and executioner." Resorting to the typical "slippery slope" logical fallacy, the convention delegates went so far as to predict that all the small states would fall in succession if Michigan lost any of its territory.

Frustrated territorial citizens who felt they were not being heard became downright martial. Protesting that Congress had no right to contravene the Northwest Ordinance, the Michigan delegates declared that granting Maumee Bay and River to Ohio would "add power to the powerful, and would take from the weak, without the slightest justifiable necessity." Such a tone and temper found "a parallel only in the language of the Emperor Napoleon, in the days of his most dazzling success and splendor, towards the abject German principalities, overrun and subdued by his [millions] of soldiers." This martial tone found inspiration in revolutionary language: Michigan expected "civil war," and if Ohio refused to wait until the matter was properly adjudicated, then the people of Michigan would fight for their rights "with all the energy which a just cause, and their own unexampled union, can inspire."[20] In a speech to the territorial citizens, Michigan's "Boy Governor," Stevens T. Mason, reminded voters that the rights and privileges of both citizens and corporations were guaranteed to them by law and "held sacred and inviolable." Were not the political rights of communities of free men to be equally protected? Invoking natural rights

on the Committee on Appropriations, and Douglas chaired the Congressional Committee on Territories.

19 Louis P. Cain, "Carving the Northwest Territory into States," in Joel Mokyr, ed., *The Vital One: Essays in Honor of Jonathan R. T. Hughes*, Research in Economic History 6 (Greenwich, CT: JAI Press, 1991), 163.

20 John Biddle, Charles W. Whipple, and Marshall J. Bacon, *Appeal, by the Convention of Michigan, to the People of the United States; with Other Documents, in Relation to the Boundary Question, between Michigan and Ohio*, Broadside (Detroit, 1835).

language, Mason worried that the "privileges of self government derived from nature and secured by compact" might now be denied to Michigan. In that case, faith in the compact, respect for laws, and affection for the government were all endangered. Mason never threatened rebellion or violence, and since the next section of the speech expressed the need to ask for federal treaties with the "unfortunate" Indians who remained in the path of settlement, he must have been uncomfortably aware that the federal government remained the sole authority in these matters.[21] As a protégé of Andrew Jackson, Mason had been appointed as territorial governor at the tender age of twenty-two, but his unwillingness to back down over the Toledo Strip boundary temporarily cost him his position – even a presidential favorite could not stand against national political negotiations.[22]

Meanwhile, however, in April 1836, more than a hundred Michigan citizens sent a Remonstrance to Congress that revealed their underlying constitutional philosophy: community welfare as individual rights. The new boundaries would be "robbing the poor and feeble to aggrandize the rich and powerful." The citizens complained that Ohio "with its million of freemen" possessed immense territory and rich resources, while Michigan had a population of "little more than one hundred thousand with one half her Territory sterile and positively worthless." These citizens had left their homes in other parts of the United States because they wanted to be in Michigan; more to the point, they had bought their land from offices in Michigan, and not in Ohio. They also pointed out that they had ratified the state constitution and had never delegated any power to Congress to alter it, nor to "curtail the bounds of Michigan." They were not willing to "sell their Birth right for a mess of Pottage, for the frozen and sterile shores of Lake Superior which are not naturally connected with Michigan, and could be of no use to her or part of her state." Yet all was for naught. In territorial disputes between northwestern states, the older, more powerful, and more politically influential polity always won. The freshly minted northwestern states might have been pawns in a national political negotiation that kept southern states cooperative, and most western politicians were capable of discerning the future greatness of their role. But before the states joined the Union, they would have to be carefully controlled. Their constitutions might render their own citizens sovereign, but they could not stand up against the overwhelming power of the national government.[23]

[21] Stevens T. Mason, manuscript speech to the State Legislature of Michigan, February 1, 1836, Stevens Thomson Mason Papers, Bentley Historical Library, University of Michigan, Ann Arbor. Mason served as acting governor in 1834–35, and as governor from 1835 to 1840.

[22] Don Faber, *The Boy Governor Stevens T. Mason and the Birth of Michigan Politics* (Ann Arbor: University of Michigan Press, 2012), 48–75.

[23] Cain, "Carving the Northwest Territory into States," 163; R. Carlyle Buley, *The Old Northwest: Pioneer Period, 1815–1840*, 2nd ed. (Bloomington: Indiana University Press, 1978), 2: 190–203. United States Congress, *House Documents, Otherwise Publ. as Executive Documents*: 13th Congress, 2d Session-49th Congress, 1st Session, 164.

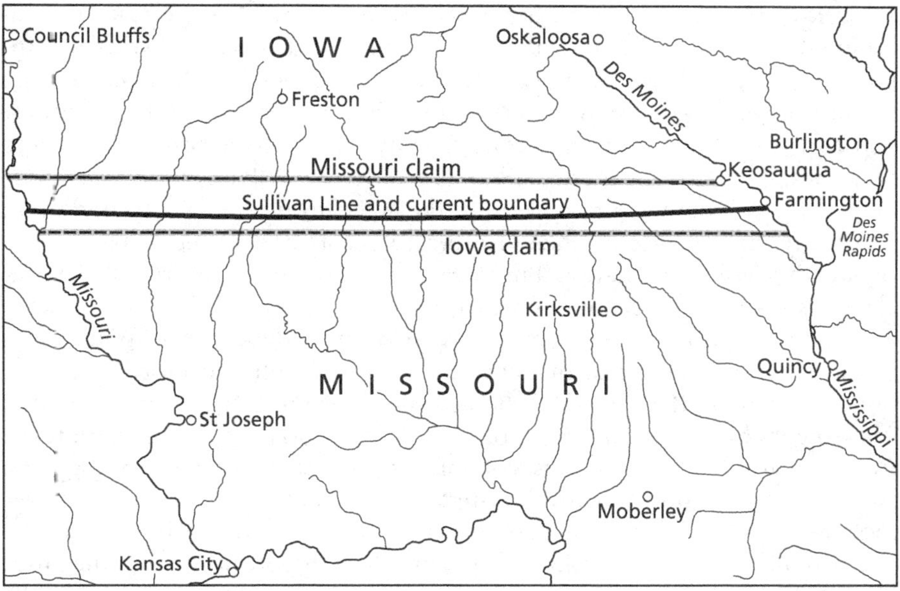

MAP 3. Iowa-Missouri boundary dispute.

Such struggles may strike us as mildly comical; a few of the so-called boundary wars (Map 3) certainly contained elements of high farce. When angry Missouri tax collectors chopped down Iowa farmers' bee skeps (in order to collect the honey in lieu of tax payments), the conflict eventually took on the grandiose name of the Honey War.[24] Yet even if they occasionally expressed a mild embarrassment, northwestern citizens took these boundary issues seriously. Territorial and state newspapers printed reams of angry commentary about the efforts of upstart neighbors endangering the property rights of political communities. The loss of significant water rights or rich farmlands could have long-term economic repercussions. Moreover, people who had settled in a county believing that they would be part of a like-minded community protested vigorously if they were moved against their will into a different county or state.[25] The Galena lead miners, for example, had asserted that political sovereignty over them had been transferred to Illinois without their knowledge or consent. Congress did not act on the Galena petition, and the issue remained dormant until Wisconsin applied for statehood. Indeed, none of these disputes remained active after any northwestern state joined the Union; that probably helps explain the frantic efforts to determine the outcomes while there remained any chance of obtaining a favorable resolution.

[24] See Dorothy Schwieder, *Iowa: The Middle Land* (Ames: Iowa State University Press, 1996).
[25] Robert P. Howard, *Illinois: A History of the Prairie State* (Grand Rapids, MI: William B. Eerdmans, 1972), 234.

Even if states or territories could not prevail against Congress, intramural geographic negotiations inside the states – that is, fights between smaller communities, such as towns, counties, or even unincorporated districts sparring for advantages – were far more successful. White settlers in the Old Northwest Territory forced such fights into state constitutional debates primarily because they considered their state and county capitals to be visible symbols of democracy and equal representation. Most of the newly formed territories and states eventually moved their capitals in order to accommodate the demands of a rapidly expanding population. But these "removals," as they were called, never came easily or quietly. Because state capitals also represented economic, social, and cultural opportunity, any promising town near the center of population, or the geographic center of the territory or state, fought hard for the distinction of becoming the capital of the new state (or the seat of a new county). These fights broke out in many arenas – the territorial and state legislatures, state constitutional conventions, columns of partisan newspapers, and private parlors and hotel rooms. Local boosters, settlers, and investors used whatever tools came to hand, including personal connections and friendships, as well as political alliances. Their methods may have been opportunistic, but they usually resulted in a democratic decision that moved the capital city closer to the center of their state, as the population expanded. This agreement that important civic institutions had to be equally accessible to all citizens was so vital to settlers that it could beat all other arguments – even highly self-interested ones. Centrality was justice; few northwesterners cared to argue for their personal advantages if they contravened the idea that public institutions, capital cities, or transportation networks were to be roughly equidistant (or at least, equally accessible) to all citizens. The location of a capital city in the middle of a state or territory promoted fair access to representation in more sparsely populated counties, expedited travel to the capital for delegates from all parts of the territory or state, and made courts equally available to most residents.[26]

Dennis Pennington, the Indiana farmer who had designed, financed, and helped build the courthouse at Corydon, and who served as a delegate in the first Indiana constitutional convention in 1816, decided to exert his considerable force of will on the location of county and state capitals (Figure 2.1). Attaining the honor of becoming a seat of justice, or – if the town was reasonably close to the center of the territory – even the state capital, ensured the future health and prosperity of the town. A county or state capital would inevitably become a terminus for roads, canals, and, later, railroads. Town lot prices

[26] The historian Rosemarie Zagarri argued that the choice of state capitals in the colonial Northeast provided a physical representation that was not yet in place in colonial governments. Rosemarie Zagarri, "Representation and the Removal of State Capitals, 1776–1812," *Journal of American History* 74, no. 4 (March 1988): 1239–56. See also, David Ralph Meyer, "A Dynamic Model of the Integration of Frontier Urban Places into the United States System of Cities," *Economic Geography* 56, no. 2 (April 1980): 120–40.

would appreciate almost overnight (and in cases when the politician and investor was the same man, as soon as this gentleman won an election). In 1815 – a few months before the territorial legislature was to call for a constitutional convention – Pennington told his friend Colonel John Paul that "party sperrit" must indeed be running high if the Jefferson County citizens could imagine that they had the right to move their seat of justice without consulting the wishes of the rest of the county, particularly those in Madison, who would sustain considerable "Dammage." He had learned that the town of Salem intended to take the state capital "up on [wheels] as soon as the Legislature meets and [bear] it off." But he trusted that the county capital would be moved "for the good of the community at large and not for a few individuals," and if he had anything to say about it, then "Salem never shall enjoy it." He had no intention of "humouring them," because they were nothing but "Children," and that was the way he proposed to treat them.[27]

Much more important, the Indiana Territory would soon become a state, and Pennington knew that the constitutional convention would "undoubtedly ... have it in their power" to decide where the state capital would be located. Pennington's handsome courthouse would greatly increase the chance that the town would become the state capital. A man with enough ambition could influence decisions about the placement of capitals, particularly if, as did Dennis Pennington, he had the knack of making people listen to and follow him. Convention delegates deliberated over the size of counties and handled hundreds – perhaps thousands – of petitions from counties asking for an adjustment or increase of their boundaries, but they left the decision about the location of the county seats to popular elections. A state capital, however, had to be explicitly assigned in the state constitutions.[28] This was such a difficult prize to negotiate that moving the capital had to be taken out of the hands of the legislature. In the new western territories, the competition could become so intense that the legislatures often chose a completely undeveloped site close to the center of the state. That action not only resolved a potentially destabilizing issue, but also ensured that settlers would flock to and populate new areas (that is, away from the southern or eastern borders) and that transportation networks would quickly reach the center of the state. When the internal fights over territorial capitals became too bitter, some states (for example, Iowa and Indiana) created entirely new cities as state capitals.[29]

Towns and cities – like individual farmers in the northwest – gambled with investments and hoped for the best. In 1820 the *Edwardsville Spectator*

[27] Dennis Pennington to John Paul, November 3, 1815, in John W. Ray, "A Recollection of Dennis Pennington," *Indiana Magazine of History* 3, no. 1 (March 1907): 29–30. See also, Matilda Gresham, *Life of Walter Quintin Gresham 1832–1895* (Chicago: Rand McNally, 1919), 25.

[28] Every northwestern state except Wisconsin explicitly named the capital in the state constitution.

[29] See Edward T. Price, "The Central Courthouse Square in the American County Seat," in Dell Upton and John Michael Vlach, eds. *Common Places: Readings in American Vernacular Architecture* (Athens: University of Georgia Press, 1986), 128.

published an enthusiastic description of the countryside surrounding Vandalia, which at that time was the Illinois state capital. "The lands are good, and, being in the neighborhood of the capital of the state, hold out inducements to emigrants [as] no other part of the country does." Mechanics would surely settle there, particularly brick makers and carpenters; best of all the prospective "great national road" would undoubtedly pass through the city.[30] Illinois had joined the Union in 1818 as the second state carved from the Old Northwest Territory. In the new western states, any young town that won the honor of being named the state capital gained valuable commodities: skilled immigrants, prosperous investors, and, perhaps most crucial for their future success, a place on vital transportation routes. As it happened, the *Spectator* was partly right; the National Road did eventually reach Vandalia in 1850.[31] But that was fifteen years too late. By the mid-1830s so many settlers had moved to Illinois that it became necessary to move the capital closer to the center of the state. Vandalia sank into relative obscurity, and the competition for the new state capital soon sparked vehement debates in the state assembly and among all the towns in central Illinois.

Local parties functioned as organized coalitions to mobilize votes for sympathetic candidates, gather petition signatures, and collect funds to finance public buildings. For example, according to Abraham Lincoln's biographers John G. Nicolay and John Hay, when Lincoln was serving as Whig state representative he and his friends worked to move the capital from Vandalia to Springfield in the mid-1830s. Meanwhile, however, "every city in the state, and several which existed only on paper, demanded to be made the capital."[32] The most serious Democratic opponent to the capital removal, Usher Linder, tried to link Springfield to abolitionist agitation in order to defeat the city's bid to become state capital, and when that failed, proposed to divide Sangamon County in half. Lincoln skillfully negotiated these maneuvers by galvanizing political friendships in the legislature, and crushed the competition by inserting a provision in the removal law that the victorious city would have to donate land and funds for a capitol building.[33]

Westerners' debates over these issues reveal a highly participatory form of democratic self-government. Their rhetoric mixed raw opportunism and creative experimentation with traditional political ideals and tools. In spite of the unbridled self-interest evident in these encounters, most of the fights over capitals and institutions had to give way to a rough-and-ready justice. Private citizens could affect these decisions by banding together to raise money and

30 *Edwardsville* [IL] *Spectator*, June 20, 1820.

31 Gregory S. Rose, "Extending the Road West," in Karl B. Raitz ed., *The National Road* (Baltimore: Johns Hopkins University Press, 1996), 165.

32 John G. Nicolay and John Hay, *Abraham Lincoln: A History*, (New York: Century Co., 1909), 1: 137–38.

33 David Herbert Donald, *Lincoln* (New York: Simon & Schuster, 1995), 62–63.

collect signatures. Local boosters, investors, and politicians fought tooth and nail to win these contests. The stakes for the competing towns and counties were high. The winners gained the prestige of being chosen as capital; they secured greater access to political influence, and their property values increased. Defeated towns lost income, residents, and status – and sometimes disappeared altogether.

The new western territories had to establish basic institutions (a legislative body and a circuit court) in order to move through the territorial phases and apply for admission to the Union. Rosemarie Zagarri examined eighteenth-century relocations of capital cities in the eastern states and has explained that there was widespread agreement that capitals ought to be located near the center.[34] Similarly, no new territory could establish a government or call together an assembly without first deciding where the members would meet. Until the capital site was chosen no decisions could be made about the permanent location of internal improvements such as paved roads or railroads. Normally the territorial governor chose the site of the first capital. For example, in 1836 the Wisconsin territorial governor, James Doty, located the capital at a rural village named Belmont. He immediately purchased one thousand acres of land there, to the vehement complaints of Wisconsin settlers. Belmont remained the capital for about six weeks. Most territorial legislatures passed a law stipulating that the capital city site was to be reexamined, either when the territory became a state, or when the population grew to sufficient size. The governor or the legislature then appointed a commission (anywhere from one to five men) whose task was to select a capital site near the geographic center. Wisconsin settlers, with the possible exception of those who lived in the existing capital, expressed little popular disagreement over the question of removal. The conflicts broke out when the selection was opened to fresh competition – and some of these contests could become violent, especially if fueled by political antagonisms. When the Federalist faction of Ohio threatened to move the territorial capital from Chillicothe to Cincinnati in 1801, for example, an armed mob of Democrats marched through the streets, until the territorial governor, Thomas Worthington, threatened its leader with death.[35]

A town was a mark of advancing civilization and the spread of modern American democracy. For this reason it was important that towns should make a positive impression on travelers, and that meant that individual citizens had to develop civic pride in their hometowns. The Sigourney newspaper *Life in the West*, a proud western booster publication, declared that "to build such a town requires sound judgment, good taste, an enterprising spirit, and liberal outlays of labor and money." The editor was particularly incensed about the

34 Zagarri, "Representation and the Removal of State Capitals," 1239–56.

35 Alfred Mathews, *Ohio and Her Western Reserve* ... (New York: D. Appleton & Co., 1902), 225. The capital moved from Chillicothe to Zanesville, then back again, and finally, in 1812, to Columbus at the center of the state, which was at that time a deep forest.

unappealing messes in Sigourney's streets: "When a stranger arrives and sees your streets encumbered with wood-piles, old wagons, buggies, sleds, plows, etc.," as well as "drunk men and other filth and nuisances" it was no wonder that other towns moved ahead in the race for institutional advantages.[36]

Such editorials revealed awareness that a town required the personal commitments of its residents, investment by speculators, and the constant in-migration of travelers and new emigrants. After all, the civil polity was defined as both a collective body of citizens and a place with a distinctive identity. As a result, there was also a tension between the recognition that growing towns contained dangerous corrupting elements, and the notion that the very newness of the place – its recent creation – could lend a lively originality and inventiveness to the enterprise of building a town and its public institutions. For example, doubts about the moral influences of city life arose several times in the 1857 Iowa constitutional convention, especially during deliberations about the future location of the state university and its several branches. Some constitutional convention delegates recognized that parents would not wish their children to be exposed to the moral menace posed by urban life. The temperance activist Lewis Todhunter of Warren County, for example, observed that many people traveled to Iowa City "because the State Capitol was located here." Questionable people had been drwn to Iowa City "by the inducements [of] ... state offices, and things of that nature." They were perhaps "not the best class of persons among whom to locate the State University." Hiram D. Gibson of Jefferson County agreed; he believed that Monroe City was a better choice for the state university because of its handsome, more central location, as well as its "high, dry, rolling hills." Moreover, the newness of the place not only bestowed natural virtues but also encouraged greater innovation in designing and building public institutions. According to Gibson, Monroe City was "an entirely new place" and if the state university were located there, its architecture and landscaping could be designed creatively to suit its educational purposes. Further, Gibson explained that an educational institution "ought not to be located in a commercial or manufacturing city, but should be located in a quiet, rural place, where those influences felt in large cities would not be brought to bear upon the students." He added hastily that he did not mean to say "a word against Iowa City," but it must be clear to all that the city possessed influences to which parents would not care to expose their children.[37]

[36] *Life in the West* (Sigourney, IA), June 11, 1857. David Hamer has commented on mid-nineteenth-century travelers stopping at all towns and cities and writing extensive reports for booster publications. See David Allan Hamer, *New Towns in the New World: Images and Perceptions of the Nineteenth Century Urban Frontier* (New York: Columbia University Press, 1990), 41–49; see also William Cronon, *Nature's Metropolis: Chicago and the Great West* (New York: Norton, 1991), 31–41.

[37] W. Blair Lord, *The Debates of the Constitutional Convention; of the State of Iowa, Assembled at Iowa City, Monday, January 19, 1857* (Davenport, IA: 1857), 2: 840 (hereafter Iowa 1857).

Michigan became a state in 1835 with Detroit as the capital, at which time the legislature ruled that the question of the capital location would be revisited in 1847. According to a Methodist circuit minister, every town in central Michigan clamored to become the capital, offering real estate, building materials, and money.[38] Finally, after bitter debates, the legislature chose Lansing (in the middle of a forest) as a "truce measure."[39] An attorney named Levi Bishop, who was present during the legislative session, claimed that those who were interested in lands around Lansing "saw the game" and rushed there to invest in building lots. Those who could not afford to travel to the wilderness to purchase town lots denounced the selection of Lansing as a "great mistake" and a "gigantic fraud and iniquity."[40] Still, the location was a roaring success. Within two years, a new road from Detroit to the Grand River reached Lansing, and the town boasted grocery stores, sawmills, and a four-story hotel.

American territories and states could please themselves when they selected their new capital cities. So long as the town was somewhere near the center of settlement (and, once the state had achieved its final borders, near the geographic center) all towns were more or less equally in the running. The capital cities in early nineteenth-century British possessions or colonies such as Australia, New Zealand, or Canada, by contrast, had to be decided with the permission and guidance of Parliament and the Board of Trade.[41] In the American territories, however, all important towns possessed an equal chance of becoming the state capital – and enjoying the prosperity that capital status would surely generate. More to the point, many of the towns platted by speculators vanished or were abandoned after a few years, so the battle over capital city status could become a fight for survival.[42]

In the debates over the location of state capitals or other geographic advantages such as transportation networks and civic or educational institutions, one

[38] The Reverend F. A. Blades, "Driving the First Stake for the Capitol at Lansing," in *Michigan Historical Collections* (Lansing, MI: Michigan Pioneer and Historical Society, 1904), 33: 17.

[39] "A Brief Bit of History about the Location of the Old Capitol," in *Michigan Historical Collections* (Lansing, MI: Pioneers Society of the State of Michigan, 1884), 6: 292; Theophilus C. Abbot, "The Michigan State Agricultural College: The Earlier History of the College up to Its Reorganization in 1861," in *Michigan Historical Collections*, 6: 123.

[40] Levi Bishop, "Recollections," in *Michigan Historical Collections*, 2nd ed. (Lansing: Pioneer Society of the State of Michigan, 1900), 1: 514–15.

[41] For comparison with European capital cities, see David R. Ringrose, "Capital Cities, Urbanization, and Modernization in Early Modern Europe," *Journal of Urban History* 24, no. 2 (Jan. 1998): 155–83.

[42] Glenn R. Carroll and John W. Meyer, "Capital Cities in the American Urban System: The Impact of State Expansion," *American Journal of Sociology* 88, no. 3 (Nov. 1982): 565–78. See, for example, Alabama's early state capitals, two of which became "ghost towns" in the early nineteenth century, discussed in Sam Earle Hobbs, "History of Early Cahaba, Alabama's First State Capital," *Alabama Historical Quarterly* 31, nos. 3 and 4 (Fall and Winter 1969): 155–81; and Nan Fairley, "The Lost Capitals of St. Stephens and Cahawba," *Alabama Heritage* 48 (Spring 1998): 18–31.

finds frequent use of the word "sectionalism."[43] This had no relation to national political contests. In those contexts they used the word "sectional" to describe enmities between eastern and western, or northern and southern settlements. In contrast to the national sectional conflict, the territorial and state debates were purely concerned with geography, not ideology. For example, Iowa Whig William Penn Clarke was sure that statehood had been sacrificed to local "sectional" jealousies and conspiracies against northern Iowa. The southern part of the territory, he asserted, had manifested an "increasing hostility to the North" (by which he meant the northern part of the state). He was convinced that the "South" wanted the shorter boundaries for no other reason than to steal the capital away from Iowa City. That is, since all agreed that the capital had to be situated near the center of the territory, those shorter boundaries would force Iowans to move their capital. Those who voted for the ratification of the state constitution, then, would do so with the "moral certainty" that they would lose their prestigious identity as the state capital.[44]

Such local "sectional" quarrels echoed many of the characteristics of national sectionalism: attempts at negotiation and compromise, as well as threats and sometimes even outbreaks of violence. However, regional issues were easier to settle. The fierce local loyalties, often expressed in the mid-nineteenth century by the word "jealousy," were usually resolved in deals cut in the lower house of the General Assembly. Negotiation, conciliation, and compromise were, after all, the hallmarks of the American democratic process. No town was willing to concede advantages without gaining something in return, such as the fair distribution of roads or railroads, or public institutions such as universities, asylums, or prisons. For example, the University of Iowa had been established at Iowa City in 1847, and there was some discussion in the 1844 and 1846 constitutional conventions about relocating the university as well as the capital. Iowa City was determined to hold on to the university at all costs, however, especially as the new western counties became more vocal about the relocation of the capital.[45]

When northwestern towns vied with one another for county and state capitals, they had to take into account features such as waterways or the relative

[43] See also, for example, D. Duff McKee, "'The People vs. Caleb Lyon and Others': The Capital Relocation Case Revisited," *Idaho Yesterdays* 36, no. 2 (Summer 1992): 2–18; Stephanie D. Moussalli, "Choosing Capitals in Antebellum Southern Frontier Constitutions," *Southwestern Historical Quarterly* 101, no. 1 (July 1997): 58–75; James B. Potts, "The Nebraska Capital Controversy, 1854–59," *Great Plains Quarterly* 8, no. 3 (Summer 1988): 172–82; Paul E. Stroble, "The Vandalia Statehouse and the Relocation to Springfield," *Illinois Heritage* 2, nos. 3 and 4 (Spring–Summer 2000): 12–19; Neil B. Thompson, "A Half Century of Capital Conflict: How St. Paul Kept the Seat of Government," *Minnesota History* 43, no. 7 (Fall 1973): 238–54.

[44] Benjamin F. Shambaugh, ed., *Fragments of the Debates of the Iowa Constitutional Conventions of 1844 and 1846 along with Press Comments and other Materials ...* (Iowa City: State Historical Society of Iowa, 1900), 286, 361–64.

[45] The 1857 Iowa Constitution placed the university at Iowa City. Iowa Const. of 1857, art. 11, sec. 8.

centrality of the town vis-à-vis a growing population, over which they had little control. The state constitution would eventually fix those decisions in the organic law. Meanwhile, town leaders and boosters tried to exploit every negotiable instrument in their town's arsenal. As a result towns also competed for civic and educational institutions, which were within the gift of constitutional conventions and would certainly yield jobs and attract travelers, emigrants, and investors. John Edwards, a Republican delegate to the 1857 Iowa constitutional convention, thought that Iowa State University should have been constitutionally located at Monroe City, rather than at Iowa City. If the matter were submitted to the people, Edwards asserted, there would be "half a dozen contestants for each of these institutions," and it would take another "ten years" to settle the question.[46] Another Republican, Rufus L. Clarke, commented on the sharp battle now being waged over the insane asylum among the town leaders of Fairfield, Oskaloosa, Mount Pleasant, and Keokuk. Such an institution would draw state money and jobs. "We all understand perfectly well," he declared, "how local interests operate in such cases; how compromises … spring up."[47] And that is what happened. In exchange for moving the Iowa state capital from Iowa City to Des Moines, the university remained at Iowa City; the penitentiary was built near Fort Madison in southeastern Iowa; and Mount Pleasant, one of the most serious contenders for the capital, eventually received the insane asylum in 1861.[48] Similarly, when St. Paul became the state capital of Minnesota in 1849, St. Anthony received the university and Stillwater the prison. The St. Anthony legislators had to accept this bargain or risk losing the university but proposed to rename the law that carried this negotiation into effect "A bill to provide for carrying out a magnificent scheme of log rolling."[49]

The economic value of American or Canadian frontier town lots and the surrounding farmlands depended on the investments and contributions of private speculators. By comparison, similar settlements in other developing societies or in Europe either were already populated or had farmlands that were more fully developed. Urban historians have commented on the importance of hinterlands in the growth and vitality of European cities. American speculators and settlers certainly understood that without rich surrounding farmlands a city could not succeed. The situation in the American Midwest was more precarious because hinterlands could not be improved without the labor and investment of "the right kind" of settlers, who would be attracted by the goods and services available in developing towns. This was one of the most vital elements in the fight

46 Iowa 1857, 2: 932.

47 Iowa 1857, 2: 926. See also Robert R. Dykstra, *Bright Radical Star: Black Freedom and White Supremacy on the Hawkeye Frontier* (Cambridge, MA: Harvard University Press, 1993).

48 Charles R. Tuttle and Daniel S. Durrie, *An Illustrated History of the State of Iowa …* (Chicago, 1876), 112.

49 William P. Murray, "Recollections of Early Territorial Days and Legislation," in *Collections of the Minnesota Historical Society* (St. Paul: Minnesota Historical Society, 1908), 12: 115–16.

for a capital city: The status, prestige, and centrality of future transportation networks would attract teachers, lawyers, and other professionals, not to mention the kinds of emigrants who would know how to cultivate the soil. The *Iowa Star*, for example, in boasting about surplus grain crops, explained that this could be attributed to the fact that Fort Des Moines was "attracting the best people."[50] The Whig *Des Moines Courier* also commented that while their city was "not exactly in the centre of the State," it was close enough to roads and waterways to make it easily accessible to emigrants – a consideration they considered "of the utmost importance."[51] Moreover, Des Moines had an abundant supply of water, which was "indispensable to the growth and security of cities." Whig papers, especially, were sharply aware of the necessity of developing hinterlands in new towns. For example, the Whig *Oskaloosa Herald* explicitly stated that the prosperity of new towns "depended altogether upon the natural resources of their respective counties." According to the *Herald*, Oskaloosa had always been "backed up by the immense riches of Mahaska County," and had now "moved onto wealth and distinction." In comparison, Fort Des Moines was nothing but a "moon-struck village" that did not deserve the honor of being chosen the state capital.[52]

Nineteenth-century Americans, especially those who understood farming or who had some experience in the territories, were good judges of the health, fertility, and prospective prosperity of the land. But they sometimes made mistakes, usually born of overconfidence. Few American settlers feared the overdevelopment of cities or towns, as did their European counterparts. But they were certainly aware of the dangers of overextension, which in their minds were often linked to corruption and speculation. The Democrat *Iowa Star*, for example, deplored the fact that every town in Iowa "seems determined to be the metropolis of this rich and beautiful State. But each of them will not succeed in their praiseworthy efforts.... Those that fail, will do so ... with a heavy debt hanging over them which will be like a mill stone upon the neck of their anticipated prosperity and growth."[53] The Whig editor of the *Fairfield Weekly Ledger* once again cautioned his readers that removal was premature and sincerely hoped that the "good sense of the present legislature will not permit a few hot-headed speculators to lead them off upon any such wild goose chase."[54] Iowa settlers, boosters, and politicians may have been wise to be cautious. Hasty investments, speculation in town lots, and overconfidence in the establishment of a county or state capital could ruin the prospects of a new town.[55]

[50] The *Iowa Star* carried many editorials on this subject. See, for example, *Iowa Star* (Des Moines), May 15, 1851.

[51] *Des Moines Courier*, January 6, 1853.

[52] *Oskaloosa* [IA] *Herald*, February 6, 1857.

[53] *Iowa Star* (Des Moines), May 15, 1851.

[54] *Fairfield* [IA] *Weekly Ledger*, December 23, 1852.

[55] James H. Madison observes that Indiana towns that lost the struggle to become the county seat often failed. James H. Madison, *Hoosiers: A New History of Indiana* (Bloomington: Indiana University Press, 2014), 94.

So far we have seen newspaper editors, politicians, and candidates for political office weigh in on the debate. Private citizens, especially businessmen and speculators, also played an important role. Democracy in the Northwest – particularly in the new territories – was highly participatory and demanded personal action and investment. Whenever the question of removing the capital arose in the assembly, or in the calls for constitutional conventions, investors in the contending towns immediately made offers of town lots, funding and materials for the construction of public buildings, or rent-free accommodations. In 1836, leading Vandalia citizens invested their own funds in the destruction of the current state capitol building and the construction of a new one. That investment failed: The Illinois assembly, and a brilliantly successful fund-raising effort by state representative Abraham Lincoln, voted to move the capital to Springfield. That move so enraged Vandalia businessmen that the victorious Springfield faction had to face serious charges of corruption.[56] Similarly, in 1839 Walter Butler, a prominent Iowa City businessman, had donated the first wood frame capitol building while the beautiful stone capitol was being constructed. Similarly, in the early 1850s, when the town of Des Moines had become a viable contestant, its boosters would vie with one another to offer valuable town lots for the construction of the state capitol there. In the northwestern capital city contests, such offers were, in effect, shrewd investments by entrepreneurs who had already bought property in the hinterlands surrounding these towns. For the hard-strapped western state governments, such donations were a crucial, even indispensable element in determining the site for a capital city. In early 1852, for example, a capital relocation bill passed by the Iowa Assembly provided that commissioners empowered to examine contending towns must "take into the account ... the amount of donations proposed to be given to the State for the erection of public Buildings."[57] Reliance on private donations, however, could lead to fraudulent dealings and influence peddling. Robert Gower, a delegate to the 1857 constitutional convention, bitterly complained that corruption and bribery had been used to force the removal from Iowa City. He quoted from a letter written by one of the representatives of the General Assembly, who had been the recipient of gifts and entertainment and who declared his intention to "remove to Fort Des Moines" after purchasing town lots there at a low price, because, he observed, property there would become "very valuable" as soon as the removal act became law. According to Gower, the removal had been accomplished "through the application of money, town lots, and oyster suppers" – that is, the typical inducements that boosters and investors used to achieve their ends.[58]

[56] Ida M. Tarbell, *The Life of Abraham Lincoln* (New York: Cosimo, 2008), 132–39. For fund-raising and charges of corruption, see Allen C. Guelzo, *Abraham Lincoln: Redeemer President* (Grand Rapids, MI: Eerdmans), 80–82.

[57] *Des Moines Courier*, December 9, 1852, and January 6, 1853.

[58] Iowa 1857, 2: 923–24. James H. Gower was the delegate from Cedar County.

Constitutional convention delegates, particularly those who were forming the first constitutions for their states, confronted an immense task: They had to frame governments, delineate and protect rights, and organize their physical states into functioning, prosperous, and respected polities. Every state boundary in the Union had required some negotiation (at best), but the ones in the Northwest were particularly contentious.[59] Problems in surveying private property lines, state boundaries, the difficulties of determining the centers of waterways, and arguments over who owned the profits from canals and roads, all contributed to a lively conversation about the rights of states. This happened principally because the legal and moral constraints – constraints even the most go-ahead Jacksonian Democrats recognized – could hardly hold back the tide of in-migration, the relentless hunger for land, or the ferocious determination to grasp hold of as much of the state as possible. Those constraints would have included both legal prohibitions against taking private property (including private property from Indians without a federal treaty or "extinguishment") as well as the private property of creditors, which had been lent to white settlers. Other constraints included the simple right of all human beings to remain alive, to feed their families, and to have access to the source of all life: soil, air, and water.

For the modern reader, those legal and ethical constraints carry more weight when applied to the protection of human rights than when used to shore up the potential wealth and status of a community. The fights over state boundaries and the location of northwestern capital cities were relatively easy to settle, once all the contending parties accepted the outcomes. The antebellum white settlers used the same arguments in all of those fights: a mix of traditional natural rights philosophy, callous disregard of legal and moral constraints, and radical land reform ideas. All of these components of the fight for "places" would create such profound conflicts (particularly when applied to the human right of survival) that they required constitutional intervention. Northwesterners blended simple geographic justice, a shamefaced (and ultimately weak) compassion for nonwhite people suffering from prejudice or dispossession of their homelands, a rejection of slavery and murder, together with a relentless and nearly insuperable race prejudice. But the overarching idea that justice had to be achieved through a recognition of fundamental human rights, through equal access to government and transportation, and through a care for one's descendants, always had to do battle against a willingness to grab land one had no right to, indeed land one could never pay for or even cultivate.

[59] For boundary fights between other American states, see Benjamin F. Shearer, *The Uniting States: The Story of Statehood for the Fifty United States* (Westport, CT: Greenwood, 2004).

8

Citizens

In early spring 1851 William Savery Bates, a Quaker doctor from Smithfield, a tiny eastern Ohio farming village, wrestled painfully with his own conscience. His congregation had elected him to the state constitutional convention to fight for the rights of free black people. As one of the leading lights of Ohio's antislavery community, he had been sped on his way with the well-wishes of both his black and white neighbors. He had left home firmly convinced that Ohio's free black residents were entitled to "all the common rights of humanity."[1] Indeed, Bates had been committed to abolitionism almost from the moment of his birth: His parents had named him after William Savery, a famous antislavery orator.[2] As an idealistic young physician Bates had left western Virginia in 1840 with a group of fellow Quakers and several free black families, determined to make a new home in Ohio where all could live in dignity and freedom. But when he took his seat in the constitutional convention ten years later he discovered that his ideas about human rights – and the pledges he had made to his black friends – could not withstand the battering meted out by his political opponents. While protesting a constitutional provision that would exclude black people from Ohio, he suddenly found himself calumniating his neighbors and repudiating many of his principles: He condemned free black people as a "nuisance" and declared himself unwilling to invite more of them into his state.[3] That statement was, at its heart, a falsehood.

[1] J. V. Smith, *Report of the Debates and Proceedings of the Convention for the Revision of the Constitution of the State of Ohio, 1850–1851* (Columbus, OH: 1851), 1: 600 (hereafter Ohio 1850).

[2] Francis R. Taylor, *Life of William Savery of Philadelphia 1750–1804* (New York: Macmillan, 1925). Bates belonged to the Ohio Yearly Meeting, a Quaker meeting that did not advocate immediate abolition of slavery, which caused disagreements and disaffection with other members of the congregation, some of whom supported immediate emancipation. See Enoch Lewis, ed., *Friends' Review: A Religious, Literary, and Miscellaneous Journal* 4, no. 1 (Sept. 21, 1850), 9.

[3] The word "nuisance" appeared frequently in the convention and public discussions about free black people. The word's legal connotation meant "injurious to the public good and morals";

He knew his neighbors to be decent, responsible people; more to the point, he had *already* invited black families into Ohio. For a Quaker, this kind of untruth was tantamount to a breach of ethics. Bates's internal struggle exemplified western reformers' questions about nonwhite human beings: their inborn qualities, their potential, and the role they were to play in the new states. More poignantly, it illustrates the moral failure of northwestern reformers and politicians who recognized the humanity and rights of their nonwhite neighbors, yet could not bring themselves to argue for their equality.[4]

From the 1830s through the late 1850s, the Great Lakes region experienced rapid expansion and population growth in the midst of rising sectional tensions. The delegates to the northwestern conventions faced a difficult task: They had to establish their governments and define citizenship within a short period, without much prior experience in state building and in the presence of a highly diverse society – a society that also reflected national sectional divisions.[5] Originally settled by upland southerners, the region soon drew emigrants from New England and the Mid-Atlantic states: first to Ohio, then Michigan, Wisconsin, and Minnesota. The influx of antislavery activists and social reformers ensured that debates over nonwhite people's rights remained at the forefront of all discussions over political rights.[6] Because most delegates had little prior political or oratorical experience (two-thirds were farmers or merchants and not lawyers) they were forced to reach deep into their early training in revolutionary ideology and Christian ethics to make sense of the complicated subjects confronting them. As they traveled to their state capitals to participate in their conventions, most delegates may have believed that they knew their own minds; however, they would soon find that the debates challenged their most profound beliefs about human nature and about the limits and reach of the rights guaranteed in a democratic republic. Although this chapter focuses on suffrage rights as a fundamental component of democratic citizenship, it should be noted that northwesterners did not necessarily organize their thinking about nonwhite people in such a neat or straightforward fashion. In some of the states – particularly Illinois and Indiana – the question

therefore, a nuisance could be abated (mitigated) without prejudice, even before the injury had taken place. John Bouvier, *A Law Dictionary; Adapted to the Constitution and Laws of the United States of America …* (Philadelphia: 1854), 1: 597.

[4] Ohio 1850, 600; Hugh Barbour, *The Quakers* (Westport, CT: Friends United Press, 1994); Thomas D. Hamm, *The Transformation of American Quakerism Orthodox Friends, 1800–1907* (Bloomington: Indiana University Press, 1988). The provision lost, 72 to 26, Ohio 1850, 2: 605.

[5] For important and valuable new insights into the borderland between free and slave states, particularly along the Ohio River, see Matthew Salafia, *Slavery's Borderland: Freedom and Bondage along the Ohio River* (Philadelphia: University of Pennsylvania Press, 2013).

[6] Eugene H. Berwanger, *The Frontier against Slavery: Western Anti-Negro Prejudice and the Slavery Extension Controversy* (Urbana: University of Illinois Press, 1967); Stephen Middleton, *The Black Laws in the Old Northwest: A Documentary History* (Westport, CT: Greenwood Press, 1993); Dana Weiner, *Race and Rights: Fighting Slavery and Prejudice in the Old Northwest 1830–1870* (DeKalb: Northern Illinois University Press, 2013).

of civic rights for black men never even reached the final draft of the constitution. The principal issue there, as far as the white voters were concerned, was the right of black persons to migrate into the state. As a result, both the public and convention debates over black people's rights became a referendum on racial prejudice, and not (or not only) on citizenship, let alone voting rights.

One primary task the delegates confronted was to decide which persons would constitute the polity and which ones were to be excluded. Those delegates intent on keeping citizenship strictly confined to its present limits focused their efforts on two goals: to restrict the franchise to white men older than twenty-one and to prevent more black people from entering their states (while encouraging more white foreigners to move into the region). In the antebellum Northwest provisions depriving black men of the right to vote must have seemed to be foregone conclusions. These states contained large majorities of Democratic voters, many of whom had migrated from southern states, who could be depended on to support restrictive provisions. Nevertheless, debates over that issue took up more space in the printed journals than any other topic, including banks, legislatures, or married women's property rights. Indeed, most conventions had to adjourn without reaching a final decision on the issue of black people's rights: Most of them submitted discriminatory provisions in a separate referendum. All told, this represented an immense amount of official attention on a debate where the outcome was essentially predetermined.

Why, then, were these provisions considered so controversial that they had to be submitted as separate referenda? There were several factors at work. First, although radicals (defined here as pro–black rights activists) were such a tiny minority, they kept the debates alive, and their opponents had no choice but to engage with them. The architecture of democratic constitutional conventions made it impossible to suppress even the most radical reformers. There was simply no way to silence an articulate enemy, especially when that enemy's weapons included revolutionary ideology and Christian ethics – abstract ideals that even the most die-hard Democrat ignored at his peril. The prospect of the expansion of personhood and the concurrent expansion of rights frightened some people, heartened a few others, and made those in the middle uncomfortable. This chapter will argue that radical reformers held fast to their underlying principles and employed every rhetorical, moral, constitutional, and logical device to prove that racial prejudice undermined those ideals. They used these weapons to launch persistent assaults on what they deemed theological or scientific misconceptions, with a stubborn insistence on the first principles of American political ideologies. And when all else failed, they mocked their opponents' ideas as bigoted and castigated their speeches as hateful.

Every American state constitutional convention, dating back to the 1770s and 1780s, had to define the constituency: For most, that meant sane, white, property-owning men. After 1790, eastern and southern states that had previously permitted black people to vote began to rescind those rights in state constitutions and passed increasingly restrictive discriminatory laws.[7] By 1820 black men possessed the right to vote only in five New England states. They never had the right to vote in the other twenty-five states admitted before the Civil War.[8] The New England and Mid-Atlantic states counted black men as citizens, but after the 1820s free black people could not become citizens in many southern slaveholding states. At the same time none of the states outside the Northwest mentioned Indians as citizens, presumably because they were not yet considered U.S. citizens.[9] In 1832 U.S. Chief Justice Marshall wrote the decision that decreed Indian tribes to be domestic dependent nations; throughout the nineteenth century Indians' citizenship status was usually determined in state constitutions and based on abrogation of their tribal affiliations.[10] All sorts of Americans – black people and white ones, women and men, Whigs and Democrats, Free Soilers and Republicans, reformers and conservatives – struggled to make sense of the contradictory goals of constructing a just, democratic society that carried forward their revolutionary heritage and simultaneously holding diverse, conflicting, often unjust, and occasionally even hateful convictions about their fellow inhabitants. While these battles usually occurred between delegates belonging to different parties, they sometimes raged within a single soul.

Classifying delegates as radicals, moderates, or conservatives – while a useful tool for explaining diverging viewpoints – can be difficult. For example, Benjamin Bond, an Illinois Whig who served at the 1847 convention and would later become an antislavery Republican, authored the infamous exclusion clause that condemned black Illinoisans to decades of discrimination. Alvin Hovey, an antislavery Whig who evidently had befriended or employed a black man named Isaac, refused to argue for the removal of the word "white" from the election law. He told the convention that he thought most people in Indiana were "satisfied with the law" as it stood. While Hovey was serving in the convention, Isaac occasionally wrote a few lines to him, which he asked Mary Ann to include in her letters.[11] Charles Flandrau, a conservative

7 Delaware did so in 1792, Kentucky in 1799, Maryland in 1809, Connecticut in 1818, New Jersey in 1820, and Pennsylvania in 1838. Kirk Harold Porter, *A History of Suffrage in the United States* (Chicago: University of Chicago Press, 1918), 90.

8 Leon F. Litwack, *North of Slavery: The Negro in the Free States, 1790–1860* (Chicago: University of Chicago Press, 1965), 31.

9 Alexander Keyssar, *The Right to Vote: The Contested History of Democracy in the United States* (New York: Basic Books, 2000), 165–66.

10 Indians were not defined as U.S. citizens until 1924, when Congress passed the Indian Citizenship Act. Before 1924, Indians who were members of tribal groups were not U.S. citizens or citizens of any state. Frank Pommersheim, *Broken Landscape: Indians, Indian Tribes, and the Constitution* (New York: Oxford University Press, 2009), 87–125.

11 See, for example, Mary Ann Hovey to Alvin Hovey, January 19, 1851, Hovey MSS, Lilly Library, Indiana University, Bloomington. Indiana 1850, 2: 1292. I found no specific reference to a black person named Isaac living in the Hovey household. I found a twenty-year old man named Isaac James who lived in Mt. Vernon Township, but the 1850 census did not indicate his race. Mary

Democrat, fought hard to obtain citizenship status for Indians in Minnesota. The fact that equivocal men such as Ohio's Dr. William Bates would have been considered radicals in their own time renders contemporary classifications particularly difficult to parse. That said, this chapter defines radicals as those delegates who supported political equality for nonwhite men (and a few, even for women). They comprised the smallest and the most vocal group: perhaps 5 percent of all northwestern convention delegates. They included black and white abolitionists, a few Whigs, and later, radical Republicans. They battled widespread racial prejudice and encountered severe political antagonism. It should be said that while this chapter focuses primarily on the question of nonwhite men as citizens – because few convention delegates took the notion of women voters seriously – all discussions of citizenship must confront the fact that black women were, at best, ignored in the state conventions. Black women did participate in the Ohio and Indiana Colored Citizens Conventions but were rarely able to prevail on their male colleagues to allow them a voice. The 1850 Colored Citizens Convention that took place in Columbus sent delegates to meet with sympathetic state constitutional convention delegates. Evidently some of the women who participated in the convention protested their exclusion from the debates and threatened to walk out if they were not granted the right to address the convention. That right was granted, but there is no record of any speeches by the women. When the women attempted to gain the same privilege in the following convention, the men voted a resolution to refuse permission. Some black women attended the Ohio women's rights convention, and Sojourner Truth famously addressed the 1851 meeting in Ohio with her "Aren't I a Woman" speech.[12] State constitutional convention delegates in the Northwest never talked about black women at all, except in one scurrilous suggestion, made by the ultraconservative Wisconsin Democrat Edward Ryan, that all black men were thieves and all black women "far worse" (meaning, essentially, that they were prostitutes).[13]

The most disparaging racially prejudiced comments always raised protests, but on the whole, especially as the sectional conflict intensified, antislavery, prorights activism became increasingly controversial. The men who

Ann observed in her letter that she thought Isaac "[felt] his position in the community, ... [and] ought to go to Liberia when circumstances will admit."

12 Stacey Robertson explains that black women participated in black reform conventions into the 1850s, *Hearts Beating for Liberty: Women Abolitionists in the Old Northwest* (Chapel Hill: University of North Carolina Press, 2010), 47; see also, Shirley J. Yee, *Black Women Abolitionists: A Study in Activism, 1828–1860* (Knoxville: University of Tennessee Press, 1992); Dana Weiner, *Race and Rights*.

13 Milo M. Quaife, ed., *The Convention of 1846*, vol. 27 of Publications of the State Historical Society of Wisconsin (Madison: State Historical Society of Wisconsin, 1920), 214–15 (hereafter Wisconsin 1846). The 1846 Wisconsin convention did not publish a journal, so the speeches were compiled from newspaper reports. It is unclear that anyone rejected the observation about black women.

opposed racial equality construed any agitation against slavery or for black people's rights as disruptive and even dangerous to national unity. The best way to combat such arguments, activists found, was to redefine the terms of the debate. The radical reformers deliberately shifted the focus to prejudice, and not activism, as the core threat to the republic. They stressed that republicanism, Christian ethics, and democracy formed one inviolable whole – a favorite nineteenth-century rhetorical strategy. Prejudice, they argued, threatened all three. To weaken or remove any part of that triad would imperil the integrity of American self-government.[14] Perhaps one of the best examples of this style of reasoning can be found in a speech given by an unknown activist at a "Colored Citizens Convention" held in Columbus, Ohio, in January 1851. The organizers scheduled their meeting at the same time and in the same city as the state constitutional convention. Several of the delegates addressed the members of the state constitutional convention in order to demonstrate how race prejudice subverted republican goals. They invoked both revolutionary principles and Christian ethics in envisioning the democratic republic as framed by a spiritual, rational, and universal body of laws. Quoting John Adams, an anonymous speaker declared that the "greatest good to the whole and *not to the greatest number*, was the end of all righteous legislation." He then cited William H. Seward's claim that every law must be "a re-enactment of the law of God," and finally, the abolitionist William Goodell's declaration that the law found its home and definition "nowhere but in the bonds of an universal brotherhood" and that "equality, and inherent and inalienable rights ... [were] identical with the principles of democracy and the genius of the Christian religion." Race prejudice, he concluded, was destructive not only because it oppressed black people but because it subverted and annihilated the "great principles [of] equal rights to all men ... laid down in our organic law, as the foundation of our political institutions."[15] In each of these examples, the

[14] The notion that opening any discussion of voter qualification was dangerous, and would result in a rapid and undesirable extension of suffrage to unsuitable persons such as women and children, has a long history. John Adams explained in 1776 that such discussions were a "fruitful source of controversy," and that inevitably "women will demand the vote; lads from twelve to twenty-one will think their rights not enough attended to; and every man who has not a farthing, will demand an equal voice with any other. ... It tends to confound and destroy all distinctions, and prostrate all ranks to one common level." Quoted in Keyssar, *Right to Vote*, 1.

[15] Unidentified speaker quoted in Philip S. Foner and George E. Walker, eds., *Proceedings of the Black State Conventions*, 1840–1865 (Philadelphia: Temple University Press, 1979), 269–70. The quotation from John Adams is from "Thoughts on Government," Apr. 1776, in Robert J. Taylor, Gregg L. Lint, and Celeste Walker, eds., *Papers of John Adams* (Cambridge, MA: Harvard University Press, 1979), 4: 86. Note that in this speech, the author misattributed the quotation that every law must be "a re-enactment of the law of God" to Daniel Webster. Webster's famous speech on the Fugitive Slave Bill, which he gave in the Senate on March 7, 1850, made a similar assertion, that it was not necessary to "reaffirm an ordinance of Nature, nor to re-enact the will of God," but the intended meaning was somewhat different. The unknown speaker intended to quote William Henry Seward's speech on March 11, 1850, which was reported in the *American Review* 11, April 1850, 434. The abolitionist William Goodell also argued that religion and

speaker demonstrated the deep nineteenth-century American faith in analogies involving religion, democracy, and law.

Similarly, radical constitutional convention delegates reminded their colleagues that their creator endowed them with inalienable rights; rights that – as a gift of God – had to be perfect and perdurable. Indeed, Thomas Jefferson had explained in 1809 that the "best principles" of the republic secured "to all its citizens a perfect equality of rights."[16] In defining the equality of rights, Jefferson's generation had defined the word "all" as all free white men. As the nation expanded westward and new people demanded rights, however, the word "all" had to expand as well, with or without the consent of the white settlers. In the western territories free black families could acquire small homesteads, Indians could assume the habiliments of white men, and women could become politically active as temperance or antislavery reformers.[17] Reformers sought to broaden the meaning of the word "all" by casting doubt on the assertion that ideas about race (or, for the most radical, even about gender) were based on science or theology. Both sides of the struggle, therefore, emphasized purity, wholeness, and inviolability: qualities that extended rights infinitely (for reformers) or preserved hierarchies indefinitely (for conservatives).[18] In the 1850s, for example, radical northwestern newspapers demanded a new democracy untainted by prejudice. A Minnesota editorial insisted that the convention "present to the people a constitution instinct with the spirit of freedom, and as broad as the rights of man." Such a constitution would not "falter before these terrible influences which have long been consuming the vitals of American liberty."[19] Another stated boldly that Indians, black people, and all the citizens of a republic constituted one coherent polity and declared that true republicanism ignored "all distinctions founded upon color, caste or condition [and gave] every a man a chance to become the equal of his fellow."[20]

In this way, reformers expanded the belief, expressed by both Jefferson and Adams (neither of whom would have taken this notion to its logical conclusion), that a true republic guaranteed all rights to all white men. The more radical northwestern antiprejudice activists enlarged that idea to the proposition

democracy were "indissolubly joined" and explained that because of mankind's common origin, there was an "Essential Unity and Equality of Mankind," in William Goodell, *The Democracy of Christianity* (New York, 1849), 1: 34.

16 Thomas Jefferson: Reply to the Citizens of Wilmington, 1809, quoted in *The Writings of Thomas Jefferson: Memorial Edition* (Washington, DC: Thomas Jefferson Memorial Association, 1903), 16: 336.

17 Berwanger, *Frontier against Slavery*, 30–59.

18 This conflict would not be resolved before the ratification of the Fourteenth Amendment. Lincoln adverts to this fundamental paradox in his house divided speech. Harry V. Jaffa, *Crisis of the House Divided: An Interpretation in the Issues of the Lincoln-Douglas Debates* (Chicago: University of Chicago Press, 1973), 232–38; Eric Foner, *The Fiery Trial: Abraham Lincoln and American Slavery* (New York: Norton, 2010), 82–131.

19 *Faribault* [MN] *Herald*, July 1, 1857.

20 *Winona* [MN] *Republican*, July 14, 1857.

that it protected all rights of all human beings. The diminution of rights for anyone would shake the foundations that supported everyone. In 1857 an Iowa Republican delegate declared that because the constitutional rights of "life, liberty, and property" were guaranteed to all, "it followed that *every* person was entitled to these rights, *or none*." Refusal to grant basic political rights to black people risked destroying them for white people. "Shall we deny ourselves air," he demanded, "because negroes will be benefited by the breathing of it?"[21] According to a delegate in the Minnesota convention held the same year, the principle had to be held true across the board. Any departure from principles meant that there would be "no principle we can depend upon for a moment by which to vindicate our own rights." Therefore, inserting the word "white ... would take from a large portion of our fellow citizens the rights we claim for ourselves."[22]

If radicals were arguing for a unity of rights, then their conservative opponents battled for a unity of the polity. Conservatives condemned the presence of nonwhite people as destructive of republicanism and as damaging to society. "A true patriot," declared a Wisconsin newspaper in 1846, would seek to "improve his countrymen – physically, intellectually, and morally, as well as politically," and would therefore "never think of introducing among them an inferior race."[23] Conservative Democrats dominated the northwestern state conventions; they are defined here as stringently opposed to any changes in suffrage rights and as advocates of black exclusion provisions. According to nineteenth-century natural philosophers, traits such as hair texture, skin color, the weight of the brain, or the shape of the skull signaled innate intellectual and moral abilities. These physical characteristics marked nonwhite persons as inherently incapable of appreciating or participating in republicanism, which required intelligence and moral discernment.[24] Divine Providence had bestowed physical differences such as the mark of Cain, as a guide for Christians to help them understand how to assess and treat their inferiors.[25]

[21] Emphasis in original. W. Blair Lord, *The Debates of the Constitutional Convention; of the State of Iowa, Assembled at Iowa City, Monday, January 19, 1857* (Davenport, IA: 1857), 1: 220–21, 651–67 (hereafter, Iowa 1857).

[22] T. F. Andrews, ed., *Debates and Proceedings of the Constitutional Convention for the Territory of Minnesota, ...* (Saint Paul, MN 1858), 348 (hereafter Minnesota 1857 Republican). This was the journal of the Republican side of the convention. The Democratic side published its own journal under a different title.

[23] *Milwaukee Courier*, September 9, 1846.

[24] John Carson, *The Measure of Merit: Talents, Intelligence, and Inequality in the French and American Republics, 1750–1940* (Princeton, NJ: Princeton University Press, 2007), 53–77.

[25] See Audrey Smedley, *Race in North America: Origin and Evolution of a World View* (Boulder, CO: Westview Press, 1999), especially the chapter titled "A Different Order of Being." Smedley describes Dr. Samuel G. Morton's study of skulls that found Native Americans inherently savage (p. 230) and Dr. Josiah Nott's polygenist theory (p. 233). Thomas Gossett, *Race: The History of an Idea in America* (New York: Oxford University Press, 1997), 73–76. Barbara J. Fields argues that debates over emancipation gave rise to sharper prejudice everywhere in the nation, in

Therefore, conservatives were building their own comprehensive and seamless republic, in which visible variations between human beings indicated the unchangeable truth of inferiority and resulted in an inevitable denial of political rights. Ohio German Democrats petitioned the 1850 constitutional convention to demand that the delegates "protect the purity of Caucasian blood" from the "moral, physical, intellectual and material degradation" inflicted by the presence of black people. While the signers thought the state government should not "wantonly injure" Ohio's black people or deprive them of their basic human rights, the petitioners still recommended removing black families by force if they did not leave willingly. And that would be easy to accomplish. After all, the petitioners reminded the convention, "we have already removed the Indians."[26]

Like radicals, conservatives wanted to build a just democratic republic. But they had to do so in a diverse society where nonwhite men and women clamored for rights – rights that even some die-hards were (however reluctantly) beginning to concede belonged to all. A Democratic Wisconsin newspaper editorial, for example, explained that the principle that "all men are born free and equal" was sacred, indeed "universal and world-wide in its application." Therefore, if the abolitionist principle "that the negro is a *man*, in the widest and broadest sense" was correct; if it were true that "his origin, his destiny, his intellectual and moral organization are the same as ours, and that the one common Parent has stamped his image upon him, as he has upon the white man," then would it not be equally true that "he be entitled to the civil and political privileges of the white man?" There was simply no getting around this; if a black man "is entitled to any, he is entitled to all the rights and principles ... in this Republic." Even the smallest right denied him would constitute the "veriest robbery and the directest cruelty." On the other hand, it was clearly impossible "in the nature of things" (presumably, the naturalness of racial prejudice) that a black man would ever receive political or legal rights. Presaging the *Dred Scott* decision, the *Courier* declared this proved conclusively that he was entitled to none in the United States, because the nation was "not his home."[27] In this way, race prejudice – a "natural" sentiment – trumped historic or religious principles. Similarly, Francis Gehon, a Democratic delegate to the 1846 Iowa convention, acknowledged, and but dismissed for more pragmatic reasons, the rights of black persons. He declared that "the negro was entitled to as much freedom as the white man." Nevertheless, he voted against receiving petitions

"Ideology and Race In American History," in J. Morgan Kousser and James M. McPherson, eds., *Region, Race, and Reconstruction: Essays in Honor of C. Vann Woodward* (New York: Oxford University Press, 1982), 143–177.

[26] The petition was not published in the convention journal, rather in the *Cincinnati Daily Enquirer*, July 9, 1850.

[27] *Milwaukee Courier*, September 9, 1846; *Milwaukee Courier*, June 10, 1846.

presented on behalf of the rights of free black people, because he feared they would become "divisive" and might endanger ratification.[28]

If republican rights could not be diluted without destroying the whole principle, and if (at the same time) racial categories remained immutable, then what were the delegates' options? Only the most intransigent bigots, such as Illinois delegate Andrew McCallen or Indiana's James Rariden recommended "a war of extermination."[29] Other conservatives were resigned to the idea of universal rights, but prescribed a limited geographic sphere for Divine Providence. Ohio delegate William Sawyer declared that because God had "designed the United States for the Anglo Saxon race alone," the Declaration of Independence was meant only for black people in Liberia, and "not here."[30] For Sawyer, the Declaration of Independence was applicable, in the abstract, to all human beings. But that worked only if "inferior" persons were removed to a safe distance. If they remained in proximity, then the notion of universal and comprehensive rights raised intense fears of social equality. Iowa Democrat Jonathan Hall declared that the right to vote was far more than "a mere badge of equality of rights. It is a guarantee of social, political, and personal equality." Hall explained that all rights were equally sacred to black persons as to white ones, at least "so far as nature [was] concerned." But he was quick to point out that this was nothing more than "an abstract proposition" without practical application. To render this point logically unassailable, he reminded his colleagues that females submitted to disfranchisement "without complaint or murmur," and no one (in his view) sympathized with them "in their deprivation."[31]

Moderates, as always trapped in the moral and political middle, were by far the most numerous in the conventions and among the voters, and by far the most perplexed. They believed in the republican project, but they also considered prejudice a matter of popular will, just as they deemed slavery a matter of popular sovereignty. Therefore, published laws and written constitutions (and by extension, republican principles) always had to bow to unwritten individual beliefs and preferences. And that made for some awkward ethical dilemmas. As early as 1827, a Chillicothe, Ohio, newspaper admitted that discriminatory legislation was unjust. In describing a meeting of black men to obtain relief

[28] Benjamin F. Shambaugh, ed., *Fragments of the Debates of the Iowa Constitutional Conventions of 1844 and 1846 ...* (Iowa City: State Historical Society of Iowa, 1900), 123 (hereafter Iowa 1844 and 1846); Emma Lou Thornbrough, *The Negro in Indiana, the Study of a Minority* (Indianapolis: Indiana Historical Bureau, 1957), 120. For an extended discussion of Gehon's speech, see Robert R. Dykstra, *Bright Radical Star: Black Freedom and White Supremacy on the Hawkeye Frontier* (Cambridge, MA: Harvard University Press, 1993), 59.

[29] Arthur Charles Cole, ed., *The Constitutional Debates of 1847*, vol. 14 of Collections of the State Historical Library (Springfield: Illinois State Historical Library, 1919), 860 (hereafter Illinois 1847); H. Fowler, Report of the Debates and Proceedings of the Convention of the Revision of the Constitution of the State of Indiana (Indianapolis, IN: 1850), 1: 651 (hereafter Indiana 1850).

[30] Ohio 1850, 1: 56.

[31] Iowa 1857, 2: 650.

from such laws, the writer found their speeches full of "good sense, sound forcible arguments, justice and humanity." These speeches, he felt, expressed articulate arguments against the "degradation imposed upon the blacks by law and custom." Yet he still believed that black people could "never commune with white society" and feared that most Americans felt "an unconquerable repugnancy to any association with them." He admitted frankly that he could not resolve this conundrum and hoped that colonization would be given a fair trial.[32] The writer clearly perceived the immoral and unjust character of Ohio's black laws but could not propose a solution that accommodated justice and Christian charity with prejudice.

For some moderates, the inability to harmonize prejudice with republicanism, justice, and particularly compassion resulted in wild circumlocutions. In the 1847 Illinois convention Whig Benjamin Bond – who originated the notorious constitutional provision excluding black people from the state – whipsawed back and forth between the conflicting goals of compassion, the rule of law, natural rights, and the notion that a true republic must extend all rights to every person. First, he assured his colleagues that there was "no one who had a greater desire to do justice to that class of unfortunate individuals, called free negroes." At the same time, like Ohio's Dr. Bates, the ambivalent Quaker physician, Bond was convinced that they had already become a "nuisance" to the people of Illinois. Then again, while he believed it was his duty to protect the legal property rights of slave owners, he would refrain from fastening "more tightly the bonds by which these people were held in slavery." He would certainly never unlock a man's stable and steal his horse, but neither would he stop a slave in his flight. But not to Illinois: That would create an impossible paradox because, he believed, free black people in Illinois would then have to have all of the rights of "freemen and citizens of a free republic," including the vote.[33] Similarly, Ohio's William Savery Bates refused to extend his principles as far as political equality for black people. While he implored his colleagues not to increase the "bitterness of the sufferings" of the victims of slavery and race prejudice by forcing them to leave their homes, he also remained convinced that a "wide difference" existed between granting them human rights, which included "a home upon our soil and the means of mental and moral improvement," and political rights for which "they may not be prepared."[34] Moderates such as Illinois's Bond and Ohio's Bates (with his unimpeachable

[32] *Evening Chronicle* (Chillicothe, OH), November 3, 1827.

[33] Benjamin Bond was a Whig but later became a Republican. Historians frequently cite this incident as the beginning of exclusion in Illinois, but the story is more complicated. For example, see Berwanger, *Frontier against Slavery*; Arvarh E. Strickland, "The Illinois Background of Lincoln's Attitude toward Slavery and the Negro," *Journal of the Illinois State Historical Society* 56 (Autumn 1964), 474–94; Illinois 1847, 202. In the mid-1840s Benjamin Bond edited the moderately Whiggish *Carlyle Truth Teller*, which (judging by surviving editions) never advocated black rights or editorialized against slavery.

[34] Ohio 1850, 2: 600.

antislavery credentials) had snared themselves in a moral dilemma: they recognized the essential humanity of the victims of prejudice, they believed that a republic guaranteed all rights to all persons, but they could not bring themselves to advocate for those rights.

One Democratic Indiana delegate dismissed compassion as an irrelevancy – and then wrestled unsuccessfully with the resulting logical problem. John Pettit (Figure 8.1) recognized the validity of republican rights for black people and still resolutely rejected the claims of humanity. He demanded that the situation should be viewed "without any mawkish sentiment of compassion." Indeed, black people and their descendants ought to have the right to own land. If one deprived them of the inducement to become "good and peaceable citizen[s]," and if those black people who were already present were to be allowed to remain, then they ought to have the right to acquire property. Landownership would give them "an interest in the country." Men who had no say in their community would have no concern for its "harmony, well-being, and prosperity." Because such men contributed nothing to the coffers of the state, had no stake in the country, and had nothing to lose, then "fires may rage in your towns and villages" without any effort, on their part, to save their white neighbors' property. They would rather "rejoice and chuckle."[35] Yet throughout the time he spent in the convention Pettit vehemently opposed extending the right to vote, let alone any move toward social or political equality.[36] Most delegates simply refused or were unwilling to extend the notion of natural rights (interpreted as the right to life and to support life through landownership) and the right to participate in one's political community in some way, even if that did not include the right of suffrage.

Therefore the first priority for radicals was to change their opponents' minds about both the validity of prejudice and the permanency of racial inferiority. They did so by pointing out logical inconsistencies, exceptions, and possible evasions and, always, by hammering home the insurmountable contradiction that a just society could permit exclusion and discrimination.[37] These arguments enjoyed some slight success, in that conservatives began to accept the notion that they were working with opinions, not scientific or theological facts. They still claimed, in response, that such sentiments, and the laws that enshrined them. were mainly a matter of popular sovereignty. This

[35] Indiana 1850, 1: 461–62. Pettit explicitly stated that he would vote against extending suffrage to black men and for excluding them from Indiana (1: 462).

[36] John Pettit had served three terms in the U.S. House of Representatives and would become famous, during the Kansas-Nebraska congressional debates, for calling the Declaration of Independence a "self-evident lie." For Abraham Lincoln's reaction to Pettit's remark, see Allen Jayne, *Lincoln and the American Manifesto* (Amherst, NY: Prometheus Books, 2007), 150, 184.

[37] For the national political context of exclusion of persons from states, see Christopher Clark, *Social Change in America: From the Revolution through the Civil War* (Chicago: Ivan R. Dee, 2006), 112–114.

FIGURE 8.1. John Pettit (1807–1877) served three terms in the U.S. House of Representatives, was a member in the 1850 Indiana convention, and later served in the U.S. Senate (1853–1855.) He would become famous, during the Kansas-Nebraska congressional debates, for calling the Declaration of Independence a "self-evident lie."
"John U. Pettit, Representative from Indiana, Thirty-fifth Congress, half-length portrait." *Source*: Vannerson, Julian, 1827-, photographer. Courtesy of the Library of Congress Prints and Photographs Division, LC-DIG-ppmsca-26790.

was the essential conundrum for people who were working out democratic self-government: They hoped that popular sovereignty would rest on principles but found that it could sometimes be swept along on the tide of feeling. Democratic deliberation brought to light ideas – even some highly progressive ones – that were already current in society, but nevertheless did not yet have the power to persuade everyone.[38]

Still, the most conservative westerners (those who remained unconvinced by radical arguments that prejudice was irrational) experienced no qualms about perceiving, and acting upon, racial differences. They considered such attitudes scientific and religious truths.[39] In Illinois and Indiana, whose southern counties had been settled by people from Virginia and Kentucky, the convention debates resounded with aggressive expressions of racial hatred. Despite the fact that he was a Whig "of the Henry Clay school," Indiana delegate James Rariden, who loathed black people and often shocked his peers with his intemperate speeches, declared that it would be "better to kill them off at once," since there was no other way of getting rid of them. While he admitted that Indiana had not yet "come to that point" with black people, he reminded his colleagues that this is precisely what "Puritans did with indians who were infinitely more magnanimous and less impudent than this colored race."[40]

Because they were building a democratic republic, the constitution builders had to be guided both by immutable principles and by the popular will. Unfortunately, however, people were far from perfect, so the expression of popular desires could sometimes caricature, misrepresent, or truncate principles – even those the people hold closest to their hearts. Northwestern reformers understood that they would continually have to remind their more cautious brethren that selfish, shortsighted aims threatened both the people and the principles that made up their polity. Categorical beliefs about race would have to be worn away, belief by belief, prejudice by prejudice, until nothing was left but the essential truth. Most historians who have studied the role of race prejudice in the long tradition of discrimination and segregation in the Northwest have shown that prejudice arose from a belief in the inborn permanent inferiority of nonwhite people. In spite of its apparent durability, however, race prejudice was beginning to erode in the region. Stacey Robertson, Leslie Schwalm, and Dana Weiner have explained that in spite of bitter opposition, both black

[38] For an excellent treatment of antiprejudice activism in the Northwest, see Dana Weiner, *Race and Rights: Fighting Slavery and Prejudice in the Old Northwest, 1830–1870* (DeKalb: Northern Illinois University Press, 2013).

[39] Eighteenth- and nineteenth-century people defined prejudice as an opinion without judgment, that is, a strong attachment or belief not based on conclusions drawn from evidence. For example, Voltaire defined prejudice as to "prepossess with unexamined opinions," though he considered some prejudices necessary and virtuous, such as the belief in God. François Marie Arouet [François Voltaire], *Philosophical Dictionary*, trans. Theodore Besterman (New York: Penguin, 2004), 165–92; Johnson's dictionary also explains that prejudice is "not necessarily a bad thing although it is generally construed so," John Walker, ed., *Johnson's Dictionary of the English Language* (London: 1839), 725. Noah Webster associated negative legal connotations with prejudice, including "loss," "damage," "hurt." and unfair "favoritism" in *A Dictionary of the English Language* (Hartford, CT: 1817), 94, 1245, 193.

[40] Indiana 1850, 1: 574.

and white reformers engaged in determined antiprejudice activism, spanning a forty-year period and reaching into every remote village and county.[41]

Antebellum Americans believed that petitions were the lifeblood of democratic deliberation: This is especially true in a swiftly changing and growing society; and the northwestern population was composed of diverse human beings clamoring for their rights.[42] Petitions circulate the polity's desires to the deliberants, even when some of those claims are so controversial that they threaten the health of the community. Because the right to petition was a fundamental civil liberty guaranteed by the U.S. Constitution, the delegates could not ignore the petitions, however much they may have wished to do so.[43] This was true even though petitions expanded the polity in frightening ways – that is, from flesh-and-blood white men, to anyone capable of signing her or his name to a demand for justice. As nonwhite people and activist women pushed their way into the discussions about rights they also, obliquely, entered the body politic. Petitions proved that the borders could not be held firm. The black lawyer and abolitionist John Mercer Langston (see Figure 8.2), for example, presented fifteen hundred signatures in petitions for black rights to the Ohio 1850 convention.[44] Petitions therefore became a powerful factor in eroding the notion that nonwhite people and women should not, and by implication could not, participate.[45]

From the mid-1820s through the beginning of the Civil War, proslavery men argued that congressional debates over slavery endangered national unity because antislavery petitions had besieged free state legislatures and Congress since the early 1830s. Antislavery activists (many of whom were women) collected more than three million signatures for their cause and created a furor; their opponents demanded that because these petitions were divisive and wasted the legislature's time, they had to be tabled without further discussion.[46]

[41] Robertson, *Hearts Beating for Liberty*, 27–28; Leslie M. Schwalm, *Emancipation's Diaspora: Race and Reconstruction in the Upper Midwest* (Chapel Hill: University of North Carolina Press, 2009), 29–34; Weiner, *Race and Rights*.

[42] The right to petition, and the role of petitions in state constitutional conventions, is discussed at length in Chapter 1, "Delegates." There I argue that petitioning in state constitutional conventions represented direct democratic action, influencing both the structural and normative aspects of the constitutions; a deliberative move that sought to force delegates to broaden the scope of popular intrusion into governmental and legal affairs; and the physical (i.e., paper and ink) expression of the people's desire to participate in democratic action, which in turn served as a form of popular sovereignty. This is in direct contrast to petitioning Congress, where the right to petition has been traditionally interpreted as subsumed by the right of free speech, not as a right to admonish, control, instruct, or rebuke legislative bodies.

[43] U.S. Const. Amend. I.

[44] William Cheek and Aimee Lee Cheek, *John Mercer Langston and the Fight for Black Freedom* (Champaign-Urbana: University of Illinois Press, 1996), 160.

[45] Susan Zaeske argues that petitions became a subversive activity and changed from redress of grievances to "collective persuasion," in *Signatures of Citizenship: Petitioning, Antislavery, and Women's Political Identity* (Chapel Hill: University of North Carolina Press, 2003), 13.

[46] Zaeske, *Signatures of Citizenship*, 5.

FIGURE 8.2. John Mercer Langston (1829–1897) was an Oberlin-educated Ohio lawyer, activist, and abolitionist, who later served in the U.S. Congress and Senate. "John Mercer Langston, 1849."
Source: Unknown daguerreotype artist. Courtesy of the Oberlin College Archives.

By 1836, the U.S. House of Representatives passed resolutions that automatically tabled petitions submitted to Congress. Northwestern state legislatures also tussled over the right to present (let alone discuss) antislavery or pro–black rights petitions. These "gag rules" generated intense anger in the free states, as well as in most northern state legislatures and among voters – even among people who loathed abolitionist agitation. Limiting the rights of any white man to express his views, even if those views were politically dangerous, endangered the foundations of all civil liberties. Northwestern state legislatures and constitutional conventions debated bitterly over petitions: Were these documents so divisive that they constituted a threat to the civil order? Would it not therefore be constitutional to silence them? In 1839, for example, Ohio legislators passed a law whose purpose was, according to one state senator, to "close [black peoples'] mouths for good."[47] In the 1844 Iowa convention, Francis Gehon condemned the practice of presenting black peoples' petitions to the territorial legislature as an evil "to be choked off," because it consumed too much time and caused too much strife, and "had come nearer severing the Union than any other thing."[48]

Every antebellum Northwest constitutional convention received petitions from free black people and from their white supporters. Most of these documents must have been consigned to the fires in committee rooms or in the convention halls: Almost none have been preserved in state archives. Therefore, it is difficult to judge the number of black persons or women who signed or even the number of petitions that reached the convention (since many were not reported in the published journals). In a few cases petitions were reported in newspapers, but most have been lost to the historic record.[49] Severe opposition to black rights meant that any effort to present such a petition took courage.[50] On May 13, 1850, a group of black men from southwestern Ohio

[47] Quoted in Frank Uriah Quillin, *The Color Line in Ohio: A History of Race Prejudice in a Typical Northern State* (Ann Arbor: University of Michigan, 1913), 52.

[48] Iowa 1844, 123.

[49] Most state historical societies and archives preserve petitions to constitutional conventions, but almost all are petitions for enlarging county boundaries, moving a county capital, or setting up new judicial districts. Petitions by and on behalf of black people or Indians are scarce in archival collections. Illinois 1847 (Arthur C. Cole's compilation of newspaper reportage) indicates that there were at least three petitions for black rights, all of which were referred to committees; also at least one petition demanded that the "destructive hordes" of free black people be kept out of the state. Indiana 1850 had at least five pro–black rights petitions and several discussions of allowing women to petition the legislature, but only for temperance legislation. The Iowa 1844 and Iowa 1846 conventions both had three or four, but there is no accurate record because neither convention published its proceedings. There were no petitions mentioned in the 1857 convention. Michigan 1835 had three or four; Michigan 1850 had one petition asking to use the hall for black civil rights speakers. Minnesota 1857 Republican engaged in a discussion about one petition; the Minnesota 1857 Democrat convention had none. In Ohio 1850, Frank Quillin found twenty-nine petitions. In Wisconsin, there is one record, contained in the archival file titled Wisconsin Petitions, proposing suffrage for black citizens, "We the undersigned inhabitants of the Town of Prairieville in Waukesha County – do hereby respectfully petition that in adopting a Constitution for the future State of Wisconsin – you will provide that the elective Franchise of its citizens may be enjoyed without any distinction grounded upon color. Dated at Prairieville October 17th A.D. 1846." This petition contained eighty-five signatures. Delegate Burchard presented this petition on November 21, 1846. It was referred to committee.

[50] In the 1850 Indiana convention a fight broke out over whether Congregational Friends should have a right to present a petition proposing equal rights for black people, or whether they were respectable enough. Schuyler Colfax questioned the wisdom of those delegates who suppressed petitions of constituents who differed "from us in opinion we will disrespectfully and contemptuously lay on or under the table? Is this republican sir? Is this the true policy to adopt in a free State like this or in any State.... This memorial is couched in the most respectful terms; and, although I shall vote against adopting a Constitutional provision extending the right of suffrage to negroes as I told the people of my district before they sent me here, a constituency as deeply imbued with free-soil sentiments as the constituency of any other delegate on this floor, I shall cheerfully vote for its reception and reference. I shall vote for the reception of this petition as

asked their convention delegate to present their petition for equal political rights. Whig John Milton Williams (later one of the founders of the Republican Party in Ohio) presented the petition, but nervously disclosed that it had been signed "exclusively" by black persons – he wanted to be sure that his colleagues would not be "deceived" as to their race – and apologized in advance for any potential breach of protocol.[51] One of his Democratic colleagues from Cincinnati (home to thousands of free black people and an active pro–black rights community) immediately objected, not only to the content, but even to the reading of the petition.[52] He claimed that there were some things (that is, black rights) for which "even a white man" could not petition.[53] The recurring phrases "close their mouths," "gag," and "choke off" suggest that black activists, and the white people who spoke for them in legislatures and conventions, could not be silenced – at least, not permanently. Indeed, their determination to enter the deliberations appeared to require throttling, as though words were tools with the power to wreck careful arrangements and hierarchies of partial rights.[54] Northwestern delegates – both those who supported, and even most of those who opposed nonwhite citizenship rights – agreed that petitions had to be heard. In the end, despite conservative opposition, every convention permitted the reading of the rights petitions, whether by black people, Indians, or women. Every convention voted to submit these petitions to the appropriate

I shall vote for the reception of all other petitions, couched in respectful language, from the people of this State." To act otherwise he would "justly forfeit the esteem and respect of every lover of free speech and free discussion." Indiana 1850, 1: 78.

[51] Antebellum Congresses were consistently hostile to emancipation petitions. See Stephen A. Higginson, "A Short History of the Right to Petition Government for the Redress of Grievances," *Yale Law Journal* 96, no. 1 (Nov. 1986): 142–66. For congressional gag rules regarding antislavery petitions see William Lee Miller, *Arguing about Slavery: The Great Battle in the United States Congress* (New York: A. A. Knopf, 1996). See also, Anita Hodgkiss, "Petitioning and the Empowerment Theory of Practice," *Yale Law Journal* 96, no. 3 (Jan. 1987): 569–92. None of the conventions debated women's right to vote. Although every convention debated married women's property rights, those discussions were rarely linked to political rights (only in Indiana, by Robert Dale Owen, and in Ohio, by Townsend, and the Ohio discussions were excised from the convention journals). In Michigan, women's voting rights were raised as a joke; delegate Robertson explicitly separated women's right of voting from property rights. *Report of the Proceedings and Debates in the Convention to revise the Constitution of the State of Michigan, 1850* (Lansing, MI: 1850), 851 (hereafter, Michigan 1850). In Indiana, white women's right to petition was even proposed as a constitutional provision exhorting the legislature but was linked to temperance provisions. Indiana 1850, 1: 51.

[52] The Ohio convention voted to receive the petition, 76 to 26. Ohio 1850, 1: 59. Ohio's free black community had been petitioning the state legislature regularly since 1839 and had to fight to have their petitions received. The historian Frank Quillin found twenty-nine petitions in the Ohio convention, signed by fifteen hundred people, for black votes and political rights. Despite chronic objections to these petitions, the Ohio convention – as did every other convention – received the petitions.

[53] Quillin, *The Color Line of Ohio*, 62.

[54] Iowa 1857, 78.

committees; it was simply not constitutional to table them, and no one prevailed in the effort to silence petitions from nonwhite persons.

Northwestern Indians had an easier time getting the ear of the convention, particularly in the three northernmost (and youngest) states: Michigan, Minnesota, and Wisconsin. All three of those states had a significant Indian population, which had been trading and intermarrying with white settlers for decades. In all three states, the Democratic Party was more supportive of Indian citizenship rights, both in state legislatures and in constitutional conventions, while the Whig (and later Republican) parties opposed political rights for Indians, unless it could be proven that these men had thoroughly assimilated to mainstream white culture. Therefore, Indian petitions generated little controversy in northwestern conventions. Far fewer Indians presented petitions or wrote to constitutional delegates. Petitioning was usually left to Indian political leaders, who were fully literate in English, possessed some white ancestry, and had experience in dealing with U.S. or state governmental officials. James R. Godfrey, for example, who was a leader of the Miami in Fort Wayne, charted what he understood to be the requirements for citizenship: landownership and tax payment. Asserting that he and his people had met these requirements, he wrote to Allen Hamilton, a Whig member of the Indiana 1850 convention, asking for the rights of citizenship. Many Miamis owned "land property" and paid taxes, so they ought to have the "same privileg as the white People ... so why is the reason we cannot have the same privilege & we would be very glad for you to report this."[55] Indians lived in every state in the Northwest, contrary to the beliefs of contemporary writers who lamented or celebrated their disappearance. In the older northwestern states (Illinois, Indiana, and Ohio) delegates rarely discussed the rights of Indians, believing them to be no longer an issue: Those who had not been driven out, or died of malnutrition or disease, had become, according to popular belief, "civilized" landowners. The Illinois and Indiana constitutions denied Indians the right to serve in militias but did not include provisions either guaranteeing or denying them citizenship, other than to limit the right of suffrage to white men (Table 8.1).[56]

[55] James R. Godfrey (also as Godfroy or Godefroi) to Allen Hamilton, December 7, 1850, Hamilton Family Papers, Indiana State Library. He married one of Jean Baptiste Richardville's granddaughters and was a leader of the Miamis. B. J. (Bert Joseph) Griswold, *The Pictorial History of Fort Wayne, Indiana: A Review of two Centuries of Occupation of the Region about the Head of the Maumee River* (Chicago: Robert O. Law, 1917), 381. For further petitions see also, Michigan 1850, 93, which includes Memorial of Wm M. Johnston in Behalf of Sundry Civilized Indians Praying the Rights of American Citizenship Referred to Committee on the Government and Judicial Policy of the Upper Peninsula. There is no record that Hamilton made any such resolution. The Indiana 1850 constitution contained no provisions concerning Indian rights (8.2).

[56] See, for example, the editorial, James Hall, "Indian Hating," *Western Monthly Magazine* 1 (Sept. 1833): 403–8, which details the regrettable, though "entirely understandable," prejudice against

TABLE 8.1. *Northwest population totals by race*

Illinois

Year	Total	White	Total black population	Free	Slave
1860	1,711,951	1,704,291	7,628	7,628	–
1850	851,470	846,034	5,436	5,436	–
1840	476,183	472,254	3,929	3,598	331
1830	157,445	155,061	2,384	1,637	747
1820	55,211	53,837	1,374	457	917
1810	12,282	11,501	781	613	168
1800	2,458	2,275	183	76	107

Indiana

Year	Total	White	Total black population	Free	Slave
1860	1,350,428	1,338,710	11,428	11,428	–
1850	988,416	977,154	11,262	11,262	–
1840	685,866	678,698	7,168	7,165	3
1830	343,031	339,399	3,632	3,629	3
1820	147,178	145,758	1,420	1,230	190
1810	24,520	23,890	630	393	237
1800	2,632	2,517	115	87	28

Iowa

Year	Total	White	Total black population	Free	Slave
1860	674,913	673,779	1,069	1,069	–
1850	192,214	191,881	333	333	–
1840	43,112	42,924	188	172	16
1830					
1820					
1810					
1800					

Michigan

Year	Total	White	Total black population	Free	Slave
1860	749,113	736,142	6,799	6,799	–
1850	397,654	395,071	2,583	2,583	–
1840	212,267	211,560	707	707	–
1830	28,004	27,775	229	228	1
1820	7,452	7,295	157	157	–
1810	4,762	4,618	144	120	24
1800	3,757	3,618	139	139	–

Minnesota

Year	Total	White	Total black population	Free	Slave
1860	172,023	169,395	259	259	–
1850	6,077	6,038	39	39	–
1840					
1830					
1820					
1810					
1800					

Ohio

Year	Total	White	Total black population	Free	Slave
1860	2,339,511	2,302,808	36,673	36,673	–
1850	1,980,329	1,955,050	25,279	25,279	–
1840	1,519,467	1,502,122	17,345	17,342	3
1830	937,903	928,329	9,574	9,568	6
1820	581,434	576,711	4,723	4,723	–
1810	230,760	228,861	1,899	1,899	–
1800	42,159	41,961	198	198	–

Wisconsin

Year	Total	White	Total black population	Free	Slave
1860	775,881	773,693	1,171	1,171	–
1850	305,391	304,756	635	635	–
1840	30,945	30,749	196	185	11
1830	3,635	3,571	64	33	31
1820	1,444	1,427	17	17	–
1810					
1800					

Source: Campbell Gibson and Kay Jung, Population Division, U. S. Census Bureau Washington, DC 20233. September 2002. Working Paper Series No. 56: http://www.census.gov/population/www/documentation/twps0076/twps0076.html.

Indians. Henry Brown explained that while the "correctness and humanity" of claiming Indian lands were not "readily apparent," no important discussion was worthwhile because "it was always thus with Anglo Saxons." Henry Brown, *The History of Illinois, from its First Discovery and Settlement, to the Present Time* (New York, 1844), 405. See also: "Rights of the Aborigines of Our Country," *Western Review and Miscellaneous Magazine* 4 (June 1821): 292–300; *Monmouth* [IL] *Atlas*, February 5, 1847; and Stuart Banner, *How the Indians Lost Their Land: Law and Power on the Frontier* (Cambridge, MA: Harvard University Press, 2005).

Black convention members had emphasized democratic and republican principles and highlighted the sobriety and literacy of their constituencies as proof that they were fit for citizenship. Indians' petitions, by contrast, were less emphatic about republicanism, and more concerned about the role of land in protecting citizenship (and vice versa). Democratic Minnesota delegate Charles E. Flandrau, who had been appointed agent to the Sioux the previous year, presented a petition signed by Dakota Indians who had "become civilized." The petition explained that many of the signers were literate, dressed the way white men did, and were promoting "civilization, education, and the religion of the Bible" among their people, suggesting that civilization, not race, was to be the operative criterion. Flandrau explained that he knew every person who had signed the petition. These men had separated themselves from their tribe, had established a "neat little church," and had adopted a well-organized, formal, and regular system of government with a written constitution. The signers, a man named Paul Mazakutemani (see Figure 8.3) and eleven other Minnesota Indians, asked that "all who are civilized and educated among the Indians whether part or full blood may be recognized by the Constitution as citizens of the State of Minnesota and be entitled to all the immunities and privileges of the same." The Minnesota constitutional convention was so severely divided that the Republicans (who, paradoxically, opposed sweeping political rights for Indians) and Democrats (who supported Indian rights, primarily because they represented fur traders who had intermarried with Indians) occupied rooms at opposite ends of the state capitol. In spite of the intense political divisions, Paul Mazakutemani's petition, and indeed his fame, had already garnered widespread bipartisan approval.[57] No one on the Democratic side of the convention contested Flandrau's right to present the petition, and even the diehard Republican *Winona Advertiser* commented that "Ma-za-ku-te-ma-ni and his friends [deserved] all the rights of citizenship."[58]

The delegates in the East Coast, Mid-Atlantic, or southern state constitutional conventions, such as those in Massachusetts, New York, Kentucky, or Virginia,

[57] Francis H. Smith, *The Debates and Proceedings of the Minnesota Constitutional Convention ...* (St. Paul, MN: 1857), 430–31 (hereafter Minnesota 1857 Democrat). The Democratic convention voted to submit the petition to the committee on rights. Paul Mazakutemani became president of the Hazelwood People and later played a significant role in the 1862 Dakota War. Charles E. Flandrau had been appointed Indian agent by President Pierce. In 1862 he would lead expedition against the Sioux during the Dakota War. Rossiter Johnson and John Howard Brown, eds., *The Twentieth Century Biographical Dictionary of Notable Americans* (Boston: Biographical Society, 1904), 4: n.p. ("Flandrau"); Marion D. Shutter and J. S. McLain, eds., *Progressive Men of Minnesota. Biographical Sketches and Portraits of the Leaders in Business, Politics and the Professions ...* (Minneapolis, MN: 1897), 121–22; William H. C. Folsom, *Fifty Years in the Northwest*, ed. E. E. Edwards (St. Paul, MN: 1888), 576–77.

[58] The *Winona Republican* described Ma-za-ku-te-mani (translating his name as The Man Who Shoots Metal as He Walks) as a "most benevolent appearing Indian, ... dressed entirely in civilized habiliments. He cultivates his ground, lives in a house, and has adopted the Christian faith. He is moreover President of the Dakota Republic – a government formed by civilized Indians on the Dakota Reservation."

FIGURE 8.3. Paul Mazakutemani (1806–1887) was the son of a Wahpeton woman and a Mdewakanton man. He converted to Christianity, became a farmer, and helped to found the Hazelwood Republic.
"Paul Maza Ku-te Ma-ni" (He that shoots metal walking)."
Source: Unknown photographer. Courtesy of the Gilcrease Museum.

never compared Indians to black people, or nonwhite persons to European foreigners.[59] By contrast, every convention in the Northwest mixed these people

[59] For example, the New Jersey 1844 constitutional convention never discussed the rights of foreigners. Delegate Vanarsdale presented a petition requesting that no distinctions be made among

together in their speeches, often in the same breath. No one – not the most aggressive reactionary, not the most visionary radical – could escape the tangled mess of rights, principles, and people that resulted from the effort to sort out the status of black people, métis Indians, and Europeans who had not yet declared their intention to become citizens. If a delegate wished to exclude free black people, for example, then by logical extension that delegate would have to agree that all other delegates possessed an equal right to exclude persons. Republicanism and democracy could not exist comfortably in the realm of idiosyncratic exceptions, isolated cases, and shifting boundaries. Northwestern delegates experienced this as a painful dilemma because they found themselves at a turning point in the creation of a frontier American democracy. There were simply too many different kinds of people demanding too many different kinds of rights at once.

Both Democrats and Whigs protested against political exclusions. Where Democrats demanded full political rights for foreign immigrants, Whigs called for at least some limited rights for black people. Both sides sought to undermine their political opponents' criteria and authority for exclusion. Therefore both sides were (inadvertently) establishing the precept that exclusions were wrong per se. It followed, therefore, that one had to recognize the injustice of exclusion as a general principle, and not as an idiosyncratic rule. An 1845 editorial in the Democratic *Wisconsin Argus* demanded to know, "is it our prerogative to say that any man who has come here to make Wisconsin his home, shall be excluded? If so, where is the standard? Who had made it, and by what authority?"[60] This new idea shook the foundations of the authority to keep people out of the state. Indeed, it proved that both sides of the political aisle now attacked the belief that political bodies possessed the right to exclude an entire "class" of people. If one arrogated to oneself the right to classify undesirable populations and limit their rights, then the opposition would immediately claim the same right (classifying different types of people, of course). Speaking in the Wisconsin legislature, Democratic state representative Benjamin

citizens, and that men of foreign birth be considered eligible for holding office, but the motion was laid on the table and never discussed. *Journal of the Proceedings of the Convention to form a Constitution for the Government of the State of New Jersey* ... (Trenton, NJ: 1844), 88. Kentucky (a western slave state) debated foreigners more stringently, but did not discuss them alongside black people or Indians. One Kentucky delegate described foreigners as the "natural foe of slavery." *Report of the Debates and Proceedings of the Convention for the Revision of the Constitution of the State of Kentucky, 1849* (Frankfort, KY: 1849), 1004, 1017. In Louisiana delegates debated whether foreigners would ever be able to love the country, but there were no comparisons to persons of other races. *Journal of the Proceedings of the Convention of the State of Louisiana* ... (New Orleans, LA: 1845), 63–68. A delegate in the New York 1846 convention talked about black people in the same breath as Russian serfs, but did not debate their rights alongside those of other nonwhite persons or foreigners. Another New York delegate discussed the testimony rights of "black or white, female or male, negro or Indian," but only in the context of "sacrificing rights of white people for the benefit of black people." New York 1846, 184, 272, 298.

[60] The *Wisconsin Argus* (Madison), February 18, 1845.

H. Mooers objected to a law that prohibited foreigners from voting for delegates to the forthcoming constitutional convention. Such limits were "incompatible with the fundamental principles of our institutions ... as set forth in the preamble to the declaration of Independence of 1776." According to Mooers, the legislature had no authority to keep out "any man who has come here to make Wisconsin his home."[61]

State Representative Mooers would certainly have excluded black men from his definition of "any man," but he had to state his objection as a general principle in order to legitimize it to the opposition: Otherwise his argument would not be based upon a principle but rather on an idiosyncratic and, by extension, an undemocratic preference. At the opposite end of the political spectrum, the radical abolitionist Jacob Lybrand made a similar argument. He bitterly protested against discrimination to the 1846 Wisconsin convention. As a leading citizen, indeed as the founder and one of the wealthiest landowners of Monroe County, Lybrand had run for a slot as convention delegate. He had lost that election, no doubt because of his radical abolitionist views. In a letter addressed to the convention, he declared that "in a Democratic, Republican Government, there should be no grades in reality, as well as in profession, among the Inhabitants, some being acknowledged full Citizens, others partly so, while others are entirely debarred of the Right." He implored the convention that the "Article defining Citizens" ought to make no distinction "on account of Color, Sex or Nation, recognising all the Inhabitants of the State of Wisconsin, ... on a perfect Equality one with another."[62]

Rhetorical analogies to oppressed peoples, such as Greek slaves or the Israelites under the rule of Egypt, had long served as stirring metaphors during the revolutionary era, and later for antislavery activists.[63] In 1855 abolitionist Frederick Douglass denounced the injustice of "limiting the Negro in the right to vote, when within a reasonable length of time full suffrage was granted to foreigners."[64] European comparisons were so popular that a black Cuyahoga physician named H. F. Douglass (no relation to Frederick Douglass), who

[61] "Remarks of Hon. Mr. Mooers: In the House of Representatives, Jan. 27, 1845 on the Bill to Repeal the Act Relating to the Qualification of Voters on the Question of State Government, &c.," speech reprinted in the *Wisconsin Argus* (Madison), February 18, 1845.

[62] Jacob Lybrand to Delegates of Constitutional Convention, October 17, 1846, Constitution file, Wisconsin Historical Society, Madison. The petition was read into the record and laid on the table, Wisconsin 1846, 271.

[63] Eighteenth- and nineteenth-century political rhetoric often relied on comparisons to explain, ornament, strengthen an argument. George Campbell, *The Philosophy of Rhetoric*, 7th ed., (London: 1823), 90–91. Campbell quotes Quintilian, explaining that "a comparison hath almost the effect of an example." Hugh Blair called a rhetorical comparison a "sparkling ornament that could either explain or embellish," in *Abridgement of the Lectures on Rhetoric* (Carlisle: 1808), devoted an entire chapter to the function of comparisons in persuasive rhetoric, 116–23, esp. 121.

[64] Quoted in Howard Holman Bell, *A Survey of the Negro Convention Movement, 1830–1861* (1953; repr., New York: Arno Press, 1960), 19.

frequently spoke in the Ohio Colored Citizens Conventions, described himself as an "American Hungarian" suffering a worse despotism than that inflicted by the Austrian Empire.[65] For their part, conservatives also relied on comparisons, though usually invidious ones, to argue against the rights of black people. Iowa Democrat Jonathan C. Hall defended foreigners, particularly Catholics, in order to derogate free black people. He simply could not understand how it was possible to discriminate against foreigners, "in consequence of the peculiar religion in which he was nurtured," and at the same time argue for "citizenship of the negro and advocate the doctrine of inviting negroes to become citizens of this state."[66] Similarly, the Whig *Muncietonian* published a letter to the editor on the convention debates, calling homestead debt "a more desperate slavery than our African slaves are subjected to!" and comparing it to "old world cruelties."[67] And Iowa Republican Harvey J. Skiff compared Indians to black people. While he did not wish to exclude Indians, he believed that they did not "care about the privilege of voting" and "would rather have the wild prairie to roam over, and be a wild man, than engage in the arts of civilization, and become a civilized person." That, however, was "not the character of the negro," who presumably needed to protect his private property rights and his family's welfare.[68] In 1844 the Democratic *Wisconsin Argus* compared the battle over Indian citizenship to the struggle for immigrants' rights. In a recent election, the *Argus* complained, "it was contended, zealously, and certainly with ability, by the whigs ... that the law of Congress in relation to the Brothertown Indians" made them citizens, but "*did not make them voters*." The Whigs fought to keep Indians "under the same bonds and restrictions, as they would now confine upon our foreign friends, to wit: *the right and privilege of paying taxes, without the right of voting*."[69] When conservatives compared black people, Indians, and European immigrants, they were – however unintentionally – mingling them in the minds of their colleagues and blurring the boundaries of identity and citizenship.

While conservatives would have blasted any suggestion that this opened the door for black equality, their comparisons and analogies made it difficult to generalize about people who apparently shared some characteristics. And that confusion opened the door for reformers to assail race prejudice. Michigan Whig delegate Dewitt Clinton Leach explained, for example, that he had often heard that black people's "immorality and intellectual inferiority" disqualified

[65] *Minutes of the State Convention of the Colored Citizens of Ohio, Convened at Columbus, Jan. 15th, 16th, 17th, and 18th, 1851*. (Columbus, OH: 1851), 9.

[66] Iowa 1857, 2: 693, 828.

[67] *Muncietonian* [IN], April 27, 1850.

[68] Iowa 1857, 1: 665; Indiana 1850, 1: 588.

[69] The *Wisconsin Argus* (Madison), September 5, 1844. The editor was in error. The Brothertowns were granted federal citizenship. Ronald H. Lambert, *History of the Brothertown Indians of Wisconsin* (Bloomington, IN: Author House, 2010), 160.

them from being citizens. "Now of some colored men this is unquestionably true," he admitted, but he also observed, in an effort to show that men of his own race were similarly difficult to categorize, that it was "equally true of some white men." Did that mean that the "whole class" should be denied the right to vote? Cleverly insinuating a comparison to the protégés of Michigan Democrats, he wondered whether the "unfortunate Irishman" who has sought freedom in the United States be deprived of his rights simply because "he had not yet learned to read?" Leach declared that he had "yet to learn that our colored population as a class are more immoral than those of a lighter color."[70] Similarly, in the Ohio 1850 convention, antislavery judge Sherlock Andrews denounced the idea of excluding an entire "class" because of a few irresponsible individuals. He knew that some felt that black people were "too ignorant and degraded" to exercise citizenship rights. The question depended not on individual qualities, but rather on "their condition as a class." Comparing the rights of black people with those of foreigners, Andrews explained that foreign immigrants had been granted the right to vote "not because are all qualified to vote, but because as a class, there is sufficient intelligence among them to make it safe to admit them to citizenship, and because the elective franchise is itself, an important means, to their elevation." He was judging the general population, and not the individual, and he relied on intelligence, and not on color, as the operative criterion. More important, voting rights would improve foreigners, and so he was suggesting that the exercise of republican principles endowed people with virtue. Both intelligence and virtue were capable of elevation and therefore not permanent.[71]

When thinking about human capabilities, mid-nineteenth-century Americans relied on rough-and-ready measures of intelligence. Late eighteenth-century scientists had begun to assess intelligence, which they defined as the ability to think, reason, and learn, by measuring physical features such as the circumference of the cranium and the weight of the brain.[72] Intelligence was not an abstract, fluid quality, but a feature linked to the corporal being. Most western delegates, along with their constituents, remained firmly convinced of the permanent intellectual inferiority of all nonwhite people, and of women to men. At the same time, however, the democratic focus on widespread common school education and the rise of literacy rendered ideas about intelligence slightly more egalitarian, or at least shook what had previously appeared to be perdurable convictions-.[73] Education was being offered to girls, as well as to people with disabilities: indeed, even to girls with disabilities, such as Miss

[70] Michigan 1850, 286–87. Leach became one of the founders of the Republican Party in 1854.
[71] Ohio 1850, 2: 637.
[72] Carson, *Measure of Merit*, 77.
[73] Rush Welter, *Popular Education and Democratic Thought in America* (New York: Columbia University Press, 1965), 25–26.

Orchard, a young deaf girl who performed, in sign language, a speech for the 1850 Indiana convention delegates to great acclaim.[74]

Intelligence, then, not color ought to serve as a guide to humanity and personal worth. Like most mid-nineteenth-century Americans, Judge Andrews defined "intelligence" as virtuous common sense, coupled with the ability and the will to make good judgments based on experience.[75] Whether Democrats were extolling Germans, or Whigs defending the rights of black people, most referred to their protégés as "intelligent." The problem for conservatives, however, was that some Americans were beginning to believe that intelligence could be improved, however slightly, by religious training, education, and participation in the rights and duties of citizenship. Andrews's observations suggest that at least for some reformers definitions of race, human capabilities, and human rights were shifting from unalterable God-given categories to a dynamic potential of improvement and elevation. It became possible to foresee (or dread) a future in which nonwhite persons, simply by virtue of literacy and respectability, could participate in democratic government. For reformers, then, education was to be the new standard: not inborn appearance. A Minnesota voter explained that because the state was "laying her platform of human rights" it should take a step forward. Would that be too much to expect? "Cannot our Constitution recognize as citizens Indians who dress like white people and read and write their own language? Cannot we have education ... as the *sine qua non* of citizenship?"[76]

For all these reasons, black activists and those Indian leaders who wanted a voice in state government agreed that education was an essential step toward citizenship. The 1851 Ohio black convention recommended founding literary societies for free black people in the Northwest and quoted at length from the Ohio secretary of state's speech praising the many "moral and intelligent" black teachers working in the state.[77] For white traditionalists, the problem of educated and "intelligent" black people raised an inevitable and painful dilemma: what to do with the black people who were already present and clamoring for the right to educate their children? Would it not be dangerous to improve them? On the contrary: All but the most intransigent advocated educating black children to render them as responsible as possible. Even the most racially prejudiced Americans had begun to believe that it was possible to improve black people somewhat, through evangelizing and training. Anti–black rights Iowa Democrat Jonathan C. Hall, for example, believed that nonwhite people were inferior. But he still desired to improve black children. "If the

[74] Several delegates to the Indiana 1850 convention wrote home about Miss Orchard. Her performance and the convention's responses are discussed in Chapter 1.

[75] Carson, *Measure of Merit*, 53–77.

[76] S. R. Riggs to Martin McLeod, February 27, 1857, Martin McLeod Papers, Minnesota Historical Society, St. Paul.

[77] *Minutes of the State Convention of the Colored Citizens of Ohio*, 17.

negroes and Indians are permitted to live and settle in Iowa," he argued, "the first thing ... is to ... educate them. I would force education upon them because they are not fit to be here without some education. I would be the tyrant over them in that respect." Nevertheless, he would never "insert in our Constitution anything by which that class of people could force themselves into schools designed exclusively for the education of white people."[78] Similarly, in 1850, the Free Soil *Indiana True Democrat*, while strenuously opposing voting rights for black men in their "present ignorant and degraded condition," still declared that "justice to that long enslaved and deeply injured race" required that white Indianans had a duty to "elevate their moral and intellectual condition."[79] If these Democrats were beginning to argue that black people and Indians could be (and should be) improved and educated, then reformers would have an easier time convincing conservatives of the mutability of human characteristics.

Therefore, if virtue, ability, and personal worth existed on a continuum – or if such excellent qualities could at least be glimpsed in a few isolated cases – then surely prejudice could be shown to be irrational, even unchristian. Intelligence could be raised through education, and virtue elevated through participation in a republic or through religious conversion. Minnesota Republican delegate Colburn claimed that both Indians and black people were uplifted by the right to vote; his colleague Andrews went so far as to argue that extending the right to vote would elevate *everyone*.[80] In Wisconsin, the Democratic (and foreign-born) delegate Dr. Francis Huebschmann declared that even if some foreigners were as "ignorant as the rest of our population," that was no reason to make them wait. On the contrary, the right to vote would "elevate them in their own and in the estimation of the community." Giving them political responsibility would impel them to "investigate the political questions of the day." They would thus "gain and pursue an enlightened political course."[81] Republicanism raised both intelligence and virtue; therefore, external attributes or birth on foreign soil could no longer serve as a foolproof guide for the correct distribution of rights.

Ironically, every argument against extending rights forced conservative speakers to make their arguments universal and comprehensive.[82] If one single black man, or one particular Indian, could be considered acceptable as a citizen, did that mean that others could become responsible through training, Christian missionary work, and education? For conservatives, however,

[78] Iowa 1857, 2: 693, 835.

[79] *Indiana True Democrat* (Centreville), June 26, 1850; quoting from an unknown newspaper partially titled the *Whig*, June 5, 1850.

[80] Minnesota 1857 Republican, 397.

[81] Milo Milton Quaife, ed., *The Struggle over Ratification, 1846–1847* (Madison: Wisconsin Historical Society, 1920), 234–36; Dr. Francis Huebschmann was born in the Duchy of Weimar, settled in Milwaukee in 1842, and served on the suffrage committee in the 1846 convention. David Atwood, *Memorial Record of the Fathers of Wisconsin* (Madison, 1880), 95–96.

[82] Iowa 1857, 2: 693; Michigan 1850, 294.

"isolated cases" such as wealthy churchgoing Indians or articulate black men served as the exceptions that proved the existence of legitimate differences between people. In the 1850 Michigan convention, for example, Democrat Calvin Brittain admitted that some black people were industrious, sober, and "regular," and that the right of suffrage might be safely entrusted to them. Yet most, he believed, were not, and so it was in the best interest of the state to deny the right to vote to all of them.

After all, in a society where all men were entitled to all rights regardless of their ancestry, "isolated cases" would be meaningless. Isolated cases illustrated and denoted the boundary line between white and nonwhite, between civilization and barbarity, between human rights and political rights. Therefore, isolated cases had to be firmly constrained within the boundaries of noncitizenship. Otherwise undesirable people would overflow their proper spheres, into one's local government offices, one's home, or one's daughter's marriage bed. Laws could not "adapt themselves to isolated cases," according to Michigan 1850 delegate Judge Joseph H. Bagg. "Colored people, negroes, and Indians should not be allowed to bear arms with us," because Bagg maintained that they would make that a pretext "to get into other circles," which would be a disaster, "believing them to be a species at least one link beneath us." What particularly frightened Bagg was that "the moment you let them into political circle you open the social and other circle[s]." He admitted that there might be "isolated cases" of individuals to whom he would extend more liberality than to others, but that meant nothing. Constitutions, he declared, must be written on general principles, and must therefore "never leave out the word white."[83] Foundational ideas (such as the separation of races) had to remain impervious to idiosyncratic exceptions, and so had to be inscribed into constitutions. But that was precisely the philosophical ground occupied by Whigs and Free Soil reformers, who always argued for higher law interpretations of constitutional rights. The result was simply not sustainable in logic or ethics: Either the principles were general, in which case all citizens ought to have all rights, or they were not, in which case, one would have to resort to undemocratic differentiations between people who might be intellectually equal or at least capable of moral elevation.

In response to Bagg, Whig William McLeod, a Presbyterian minister, angrily rose from his seat protesting that black people were now "thrown almost out of the protection of our laws." Was it not bad enough to deprive them of the vote? After all, they were distinguished from legitimate voters only "by the mere accident of color." He knew many Indian and black men "who in point of

[83] Michigan 1850, 62–63. Bagg was a surgeon originally from Oneida, New York. He accompanied an expedition of Indians who had been forced off their lands. Bagg was a moderate Democrat who launched the temperance provision in the 1850 Michigan constitution and later supported Abraham Lincoln in the 1860 election. F. A. Barnard, *American Biographical History of Eminent and Self-Made Men ... Michigan Volume* (Cincinnati: 1878), 4–5).

intelligence, virtue, and personal appearance, in all that elevates the man above the brute, are at least equal to [Mr. Bagg]." As if to highlight the absurdity of the whole conversation, delegate Williams then chimed in, to the hilarity of all, to inquire whether the convention "would not allow the women to defend themselves." His quip was ignored. Northwestern convention delegates never seriously debated citizenship rights for women. Although there was a discussion on women's suffrage in the 1850 Ohio convention, the debate was deemed distracting and irrelevant and was later excised from the journal.[84]

Radical pro–black and Indian rights activists were sharply aware of these logical and moral disjunctions and used them to their full advantage. Men who based their arguments on abstract ideas, such as republican principles, revolutionary ideologies, or Christian faith, wielded an impressive arsenal of rhetorical tools: devices that included irony, satire, and logic. By contrast, delegates who relied on social traditions had to resort to blunt assertions that what had occurred before ought to remain so. And that specific argument was growing less congenial in the region. Those who focused on physical characteristics resorted to crude racial epithets or else had to argue that changeable and unreliable attitudes such as dislike or prejudice could govern a democratic state. Therefore, claims based on tradition or emotion, rather than on logic, now elicited scorn. A Republican delegate in the Minnesota 1857 convention, for example, objected to the word "white" because he felt it simply made the convention "ridiculous." How could this criterion help determine legitimate voters? What was to be the standard? "There are as many shades of complexion as there are differences in the contour of countenances. There are as many shades of color of the hair, of the eyes, of the skin, as there are individuals in the world." Just how much whiteness was necessary, and just how much blackness was bearable, he demanded to know, to allow election judges to reject, "legally and constitutionally," a man who went to the polls?[85] According to reformers, then, physical features and long-standing social traditions were unreliable as criteria for citizenship because they could resolve themselves into a thousand variations.[86] Ohio delegate Townshend presented a petition for equal rights signed by a person he described as "an educated constituent who happened to have some negro blood in his veins but was nearer white than black." Radical activists would have deplored his focus on skin color. Edward B. Woodbury, the

[84] Michigan 1850, 62–63. William Norman McLeod, a former Presbyterian minister from Pittsburg, was considered a brilliant, "thrilling" speaker. George H. Hazelton, "Reminiscences of Seventeen Years Residence in Michigan, 1836–1853," *Michigan Historical Collections*, vol. 21:, 399–400; Hezekiah Well's "A Sketch of the Members of the Constitutional Conventions of 1335 and 1850," Michigan Historical Collections, 3: 40. Nancy Isenberg, *Sex and Citizenship in Antebellum America* (Chapel Hill: University of North Carolina Press, 1998), 214.

[85] Minnesota 1857 Republican, 359.

[86] Irony and satire as rhetorical devices had a long history and were discussed in every textbook on rhetoric and oratory. Joseph H. Hull, *English Grammar, by Lectures* (Maysville, KY: 1833), 134; Henry Copée, *Elements of Rhetoric: Designed as a Manual of Instruction* (Philadelphia: 1859), 101–3.

youngest member of the Ohio convention, objected to the word "white" because it was ambiguous and subject to infinite gradations. Exposing the logical difficulty of calibrating differences in color, he focused on the central truth of personhood. "Humanity does not consist in the color of the hair or eyes or skin or where a person may have been born or what his origin or capacity." He asserted that "these peculiarities" were subject to "indefinite change," but "a man is a man for all that."[87] A speaker at the 1850 Colored Citizens Convention of Ohio declared that nothing was required of a citizen but "arriving at the right age & fulfilling conditions equal to all, so that no accident of hair texture, skin color, or shape of the nose should have any power in reference to rights."[88] Black activists made this point again and again: They were human beings, and all their individual dissimilarities merely served to prove that point beyond dispute. In 1849 black activist John Mercer Langston quoted the second-century BCE playwright Terence, a North African who had arrived in Rome as a slave, included a famous quotation from his play, "I am a man, I consider nothing that is human alien to me."[89]

Reformers enjoyed mining conservative ideas about racial differences for logical inconsistencies. After the 1846 Wisconsin convention granted equal rights to Indians, but not to black people, a Whig newspaper explicitly assailed the irony of Democrats' linking the name of their party with their avowed principles. "So it seems the equal rights of Democracy belong to the whites, half breeds, and Indians, while those of little darker shade have no part ... in the matter," even though, according to the author, there were plenty of people in Iowa willing to extend those rights. There had been "able and strong speeches" in the convention against exclusion and in favor of a practical application of "those principles of Democracy which its loud mouthed devotees so noisily profess but utterly disregard."[90] In 1857, Iowa Republican delegate William Penn Clarke found it amusing to observe the convoluted workings of recent northwestern state constitutions. Some of them were so suspicious of "negroes, and negro blood, wherever they could find it circulating with Saxon mixture in any human being [that they] have provided in their constitutions that no negro or mulatto should be allowed to vote." He pointed out that the New York state constitution considered any propertied black man capable of being a citizen and a "stake-holding member of the community." Indeed, it turned out that black New Yorkers voted just like "white folks," and he was willing to bet that even the Democrats would not be able to "smell the difference."[91]

Expressions of panic about intimacy arose in many conventions. In response to one such speech, black activist John Mercer Langston invited the men of

[87] Ohio 1850, 1: 8, 2: 550.

[88] "Minutes of the State Convention, of the Colored Citizens of Ohio, convened at Columbus ..." quoted in Philip S. Foner and George E. Walker, eds., *Proceedings of the Black State Conventions, 1840–1865* (Philadelphia: Temple University Press, 1979), 1: 241–56.

[89] Quoted in Cheek and Cheer, *John Mercer Langston*, 118. This quotation was from Terence's play *Heauton Timorumenos* (The Self-Tormentor).

[90] Iowa 1844, 74.

[91] Iowa 1857, 2: 671.

Ohio to introduce their "good-looking, intelligent, refined" daughters to him.[92] Prorights delegates were particularly biting about hypocrisy over intimate contacts. Iowa Republican James Thorington called Iowa Democrats the "nigger breeding party," by which he meant the party that supported slavery and sexual exploitation of slave women. Republicans observed that black and white people were already interacting in an intimate fashion. When a Democrat delegate in the Iowa 1857 convention expressed his distaste for associating with black people, Republican Rufus Clarke pointed out an essential irony: evidently his opponent "would not object to allowing [a black barber] to put a handkerchief about his neck, set him in the right position upon an easy chair, take him by the nose and remove from his face the exuberance of his beard." Clarke observed that it was hardly necessary for him to expatiate because, as his opponent had already taken pains to inform him, there was "only one person of that race in his entire county."[93]

Anxiety about intimate contacts, whether in ordinary day to day intercourse or visible in the troubling presence of mixed-race people, became especially poignant. Since the seventeenth century, state laws throughout the nation had sought to minimize such difficulties by defining persons with even "one drop" of African ancestry as black.[94] Mixed race people were never considered white, but the so-called one-drop rule did not have much force in the Great Lakes region. According to Jeff Brown mixed race men could vote informally throughout the region, at least in local elections, and state laws were unevenly enforced in most northwestern states.[95] The U.S. Constitution did not define either race or race-based citizenship. Therefore, states included provisions in their constitutions specifying who could vote. Legislatures then enacted these provisions, and election judges were responsible for carrying out those laws. Presumably their task would not be difficult: It should be easy enough to tell the difference between a man and a woman, between a black man and a white one, between an Indian wearing his traditional garb and a gentleman sporting a woolen suit. In the Northwest, however, particularly in Michigan, Minnesota, and Wisconsin, the issue of mixed race was even more complicated when persons with parentage of two or three races became wealthy, prominent members of the community (see Table 8.2).[96]

92 Cheek and Cheek, *John Mercer Langston*, 1.

93 Iowa 1857, 2: 829.

94 Christine B. Hickman, "The Devil and the One Drop Rule," in Kevin R. Johnson, ed., *Mixed Race America and the Law: A Reader* (New York: New York University Press, 2003), 105.

95 Jeffrey Paul Brown and Andrew R. L. Cayton, eds., *In Pursuit of Public Power: Political Culture in Ohio, 1787–1861* (Kent, OH: Kent State University Press, 1994), 180–81.

96 Martha Hodes, "The Mercurial Nature and Abiding Power of Race: A Transnational Family Story," *American Historical Review* 108, no. 1 (Feb. 2003): 84–118; see also Deborah A. Rosen, *American Indians and State Law: Sovereignty, State, and Citizenship 1790–1880* (Lincoln: University of Nebraska Press, 2007), 140–42; Thomas N. Ingersoll, *To Intermix with Our White Brothers: Indian Mixed Bloods in the United States from Earliest Times to the Indian Removals* (Albuquerque: University of New Mexico Press, 2005), 239–46.

TABLE 8.2. *Constitutional convention votes and popular referenda on the rights of black people in the northwestern states 1802–1857*

State	Convention	Majority party in convention	Will black men vote?	Remove "white" from suffrage requirement?
Illinois	1818	N/A[a]	No convention vote	Voted to keep "white," but votes not enumerated in journal (likely 17 to keep "white" and 14 to remove it)
	1847	Democrat	51 For, 60 Against	8 For, 137 Against
Indiana	1816	N/A[b]	No convention vote	N/A
	1850	Democrat	1 For, 122 against	N/A
Iowa	1844	Democrat	Are blacks & mulattoes citizens? 32 For, 35 against	19 For, 51 against
	1846[c]	Democrat	Unavailable[d]	Unavailable
	1857	Republican	No convention vote	Submitted to the people 24 For, 10 against
Michigan	1835		No votes recorded[e]	–
	1850	Democrat	N/A	13 For, 46 against
Minnesota	1857	Democrat	N/A	N/A
	1857	Republican	N/A	17 For, 34 against
Ohio	1802	Democratic-Republican	N/A	14 For, 19 against
	1850	Democrat	13 For, 75 against	N/A
Wisconsin	1846	Democrat	Submitted to people	47 For, 51 against
	1848	Likely Democrat	21 For, 45 against	29 For, 37 against

[a] The Illinois 1818 convention delegates were not elected by political party affiliation, but they can be roughly divided into three categories: proslavery, antislavery, and compromisers. According to the historians Richard V. Carpenter and J. W. Kitchell, there were about four antislavery men in the convention, about ten proslavery men, and the rest they identified as "compromisers," in "The Illinois Constitutional Convention of 1818," *Journal of the Illinois State Historical Society*, Vol. 6, No. 3 (Oct. 1913), 327–424.

[b] The Indiana 1816 convention was not elected along political party lines. According to James H. Madison, "all but nine" of theforty-three delegates were from below the Mason-Dixon line. *The Indiana Way: A State History* (Indianapolis: 1986), 51.

[c] The Iowa 1846 constitution failed in the popular vote.

Submit black voting rights to a popular vote?	Popular vote on black voting rights	Submit black in-migration rights to popular vote?	Popular vote on black in-migration
No	N/A	N/A	N/A
No	N/A	Yes	60,585 For, 15,903 against (legislature banned black migration in 1853 45 to 23
No	N/A	N/A	N/A
N/A	N/A	82/54	113,828 For, 21,873 against
Passed but does not enumerate votes	No votes recorded	Convention voted against exclusion 33 For, 35 against	N/A
Unavailable	Unavailable	Convention voted against exclusion 8 For 12 Against	N/A
24 For, 10 against	Voted down, only 1/5 who voted supported black suffrage	Convention voted against exclusion 8 For, 20 against	N/A
No	–	–	–
21 For, 59 against	N/A	N/A	N/A
N/A	N/A	N/A	N/A
N/A	N/A	N/A	N/A
N/A	N/A	N/A	N/A
N/A	N/A	N/A	N/A
49 Yeas, 24 nays	7,664 For, 14,615 against	N/A	N/A
N/A	N/A	N/A	N/A

[d] The Iowa 1846 constitutional convention debates were not recorded or published, except in contemporary newspaper editorials. See Milo Milton Quaife, *Fragments of the Debates of the Constitutional Conventions of 1844 and 1846* (Iowa City: 1900).

[e] The Michigan 1835 convention did not publish its votes. No precise record of party affiliation exists, but the convention was "overwhelmingly Democratic," according to Harold M. Dorr, *The Michigan Constitutional Conventions of 1835–36: Debates and Proceedings* (Ann Arbor: 1940), 17.

For all these reasons, northwestern Indians, especially those who had intermarried and had children with black or white people, created a special problem for convention delegates. Although no one considered them white, the Democratic delegates in the three newest states (Michigan in 1835, Wisconsin in 1848, and Minnesota in 1857) viewed their citizenship rights with equanimity, though always with the proviso that they adopt mainstream American culture, literacy, and dress. For the Indians themselves, however, American citizenship remained a two-edged blade: It incurred the abandonment of their own culture and could involve them in lawsuits and state government seizure of land. Whigs, and later Republicans, paradoxically, were more suspicious of Indians' capability of citizenship and often cautioned against trusting that their assimilation was both sincere and lasting.[97] Nevertheless, 1835 Michigan convention delegates still had to wrestle with the interrelated categories of color and civilization.[98] John McDonell observed that because Indians were copper-colored and not black, they could fall under the category of "white." On the other hand, Democrat John Norvell thought that the word "alien" should not be used for white people if it was "tainted" by referring to both black *and* Indian persons.[99] Wisconsin delegate Democrat James D. Reymert demanded that the word "white" be removed because Indians were not white, yet should be allowed to vote. His motion was struck down, no doubt because his opponents feared that Reymert's argument might expand the right to vote to black men.[100]

Ohio case law had already established some accommodations to mixed race voters. In *Polly Gray v. State of Ohio*, the Ohio Supreme Court decided that a person "nearer white than black" had the right to vote.[101] The Supreme Court judge[102] expatiated on the practical difficulties and potential injustice to a white person who *appeared* to have a slightly darker complexion: "We believe a man of a race, nearer white than a mulatto, is admissible as a witness, and should partake in the privileges of whites," partly because the court was unwilling to extend legal disabilities of the statute "further than this letter requires," and "partly from the difficulty of defining and of ascertaining the degree of duskiness which renders a person liable to such disabilities." Similarly, in 1842 the supreme court held that "nearly white" persons of Indian descent could vote

97 For an extended discussion of assumptions about Indian race and rights in the Northwest, see Deborah Rosen, *Indians and State Law*, especially 117, 272–73.

98 Table A4, in Keyssar, *Right to Vote*, 59.

99 Harold M. Dorr, ed., *The Michigan Constitutional Conventions of 1835–1836: Debates and Proceedings* (Ann Arbor: University of Michigan Press, 1940), 246 (hereafter Michigan 1835).

100 Quaife, *Struggle for Ratification*, 393.

101 *Polly Gray v. Ohio* 4 Ohio 353(1831); *Jeffries* v. *Ankeny*, (1842); Stephen Middleton, *The Black Laws: Race and the Legal Process in Early Ohio* (Athens: University of Ohio Press, 2005), 130–132; Nikki Taylor, *Frontiers of Freedom: Cincinnati's Black Community, 1802–1868* (Athens: Ohio University Press, 2005), 117; Clement Bates, ed., *The Annotated Revised Statutes of the State of Ohio* (Cincinnati: 1897), 3: 3494.

102 The name of the judge is unknown.

if they appeared more white than Indian.[103] In 1858 the Ohio state legislature attempted to resolve this problem in a particularly baroque manner, by means of a law that graded and assessed rights for persons whose physical appearance revealed a "visible admixture" of black ancestry.[104] Radical reformers considered the notion of "suitable whiteness" a halfhearted and exasperating criterion.[105]

The debates over Indian citizenship in Michigan and Wisconsin and the "visible admixture" decisions in Ohio suggest that the hitherto perdurable "one-drop" rule was dissolving in the Northwest, and racial divisions were becoming permeable, slippery, and difficult to hold straight. Some nonwhite people now mocked the almost supernatural characteristic of racial identity. Clearly, their status as persons and as potential citizens slid this way and that, depending on who was looking at them. Three leaders of the Stockbridge Indians – a community that was severely internally divided on the issue of acquiring state citizenship – debated the question of remaining Indians, evidently believing that it was not possible to be both. They were asking that patents be issued according to the Act of 1843 in order to "terminate, as soon as possible, the difficulties and political dissensions" that had plagued "the Stockbridge people." If the present internal divisions were to continue, these men foresaw "no other prospect before us but the entire ruin of our people." In an attempt to explain the "very peculiar situation" under which the Stockbridges labored, the writers explained that an 1843 law had indisputably established citizenship; but "an Act was subsequently passed by the same body, in 1846 which attempts to transmogrify them again into Indians."[106] Similarly, four years after Ohio revised its constitution, John Mercer Langston – the first black man to be admitted to the Ohio Bar – appeared before the judge who would decide his status. Asked to stand, Langston complied while the judge looked him over and determined that he was white enough to pass the bar, a process that Langston called a "beautiful hocus pocus" that "construed him into a white man."[107]

While dark skin could only be lightened over generations through sexual relationships between persons of different races, civilization could be assumed and discarded like a costume. In Minnesota and Wisconsin, many so-called civilized Indians retained some part of their traditional clothing, even when they adopted woolen suits, linen shirts, "neat little churches," or bicameral

[103] Newspaper clipping from the *Cincinnati Enquirer* "May Colored Persons Vote in Ohio," September 26, 1852, collected in the James Family Papers, Ohio Historical Society, Columbus.

[104] Charles W. Wadelington, "Ohio's Visible Admixture Principle, 1802–1870" (MA thesis, Miami University, 1977); Franklin Johnson, *The Development of State Legislation Concerning the Free Negro* (1919; repr., Westport, CT: Greenwood Press, 1979), 71–72, 163–64.

[105] Brown and Cayton, *Pursuit of Public Power*, 181; George H. Porter, *Ohio Politics during the Civil War* (New York, 1911), 22; Taylor, *Frontiers of Freedom*, 136.

[106] John Chicks, John Abrams, and Joseph Chicks to John H. Tweedy, February 16, 1848. John Hubbard Tweedy Papers, Wisconsin Historical Society, Madison.

[107] September 13, 1854; quoted in Cheek and Cheek, *John Mercer Langston*, 233–34.

governments.[108] Convention delegates expressed anxieties about the incompleteness of this transformation. When Charles Flandrau pressed the Dakotas' claims to citizenship, his protégés interpreted his description as a tentative and partial concession to justice. Nevertheless, anxiety about this kind of deliberate manipulation highlighted the difficulty of discerning the degree of civilization. Flandrau described them as "men of intelligence, possessing knowledge of all the lesser branches of education"; it seemed to him that the least his colleagues could do would be to encourage the Indians. Like all northwestern moderates, however, he added an inevitable caveat: "with safety to ourselves." While he considered it "just and right" that Indians should be accorded these privileges, he added a caution. Wisconsin citizens had to be careful not to jeopardize their own rights. Leaving the matter to election judges in remote frontier settlements was hardly a solution. If an unscrupulous politician wanted to manufacture votes, all he had to do was to find a "wild Indian, dress him up, bring him in and pass him off as having adopted the habits and customs of civilized life." After the vote had been fraudulently obtained, the Indian could "strip off his clothes" and return to his tribe. Similarly, Democrat delegate Gould Curtis vehemently denied that "hoeing a hill of corn, and wearing pantaloons" constituted "all the habits and customs of civilization." Visual inspection was simply not enough. It would be "necessary to have a tribunal" that would ascertain "whether these barbarians ha[d] become civilized."[109]

In both the Wisconsin and Minnesota conventions, Democrats argued that persons of mixed Indian and white descent should have full voting rights, so long as they had become "civilized," and no one expressed opposition in either convention.[110] Moreover, the fact that so many progressives demanded that black people should be treated "like Indians" suggests that conservatives viewed the idea of Indian citizenship with some tolerance, if not equanimity.[111] Only the 1835 Michigan convention discussed the potential citizenship for Indians at length. The last two northwestern states that entered the Union, Wisconsin in 1848 and Minnesota in 1857, included provisions for Indian citizenship rights in the state constitution.[112] These were newer states with younger delegates, many of whom had personal and business dealings with Indians.[113] And at least

[108] Jean Baptiste Richardville, for example, who was the son of an aristocratic French fur trader and a Miami woman, wore the traditional métis garb. Bradley J. Birzer, "Entangling Empires, Fracturing Frontiers: Jean Baptiste Richardville and the Quest for Miami Autonomy, 1760–1841" (PhD Diss., Indiana University, 1998).

[109] Minnesota 1857 Democrat, 429, 431. The 1857 Minnesota convention Democrats met in a separate room in the capitol and published their debates under a different title from the Republican version.

[110] Bruce M. White, "The Power of Whiteness, or the Life and Times of Joseph Rolette, Jr." in Anne R. Kaplan and Marilyn Ziebarth, ed., *Making Minnesota Territory, 1849–1859*, (St. Paul: Minnesota Historical Society Press, 1999), 41–42.

[111] For example, see also Indiana 1850, 1: 580.

[112] Only in Minnesota and Wisconsin.

[113] William Wall, "Shab-eh-nay: Cultural Survival and Preservation in the Old Northwest, 1812–1860," *Native Studies Review* 19, no. 2 (2010): 59–93.

FIGURE 8.4. Joseph Rolette (1820–1871), a fur trader and member of the Territorial Legislature, served as a delegate in the Minnesota constitutional convention.
"The Hon. Joe Rolette who saved the Capital to St. Paul by running away with the Bill removing it to St. Pete in 1856."
Source: Unknown photographer. Courtesy of the Minnesota Historical Society.

three of the Democrats in Minnesota were related to Indians; Joseph Renshaw Brown's wife, Susan Freniére, was a member of the Sisseton Dakota tribe, and Henry Bailly's mother, Lucy Ann Faribault, was the daughter of an Ottawa woman and a French fur trader. Delegate Joseph Rolette (Figure 8.4) was also distantly related to the Ottawa.[114] None of the other convention journals

[114] According to George Warner, Bailly was Ottawa on both sides of his family and had some Sioux heritage. *History of Dakota County and the City of Hastings* (Minneapolis, 1881), 93, 262.

mentioned petitions by or about Indian political rights aside from the one presented by Flandrau in the Minnesota Democratic convention.

When the subject of European immigrants was raised for discussion in the conventions, the delegates relied on similar arguments: Democrats exalted their usefulness and intelligence, while Whigs (and later Republicans) expressed the usual fears about election fraud. None of the conventions seriously debated European immigrants' political rights, however, and every convention voted to grant them suffrage. This suggests that structural and institutional rules were relatively easy to circumvent when the population in question was white, and therefore considered desirable. In 1849 the Minnesota territorial governor, Alexander Ramsey, praised the "constant in-pouring tide of foreign immigration" as "excellent, beyond dispute." Advertisements, gazetteers, and emigrants' guides lured land-hungry Europeans to the Northwest. White foreigners brought hard cash, and their improvements increased land values, which in turn encouraged investors to run rail lines, canals, and roads into the new settlements.[115] Although the Native American Party found a foothold in the Old Northwest during the 1840s, it was a conservative fusion movement that focused on resolving sectional issues and was less vocal about its anti-Catholic and antiimmigrant notions than its eastern chapters.[116] Even some members of the Know Nothing Party were willing to grant rights to foreign immigrants. In the Iowa 1857 convention, for example, Rufus Clarke explained that even though he still clung to American Party principles, he had left the Know Nothing Party the moment he realized that they targeted foreign persons, rather than the political evils generated by the demagogues who duped them. Foreigners, he proclaimed, were not the danger. The polity (neither the principles nor the people) would never be harmed by foreigners.[117]

All state conventions showed bipartisan support for white foreign voters. The only question that remained was not whether, but when, foreign immigrants would be allowed to vote. Robert Dale Owen explained that the new liberal constitution, which allowed foreigners to vote after they had been in residence for six months and had made a declaration to naturalize, would undoubtedly increase the "wealth and population of [the] State, by attracting emigrants towards it."[118] His Democrat colleague James W. Borden, a merchant and judge, agreed that harsh naturalization laws would drive foreigners into

[115] Alexander Ramsey, *Message from the Governor of the Territory of Minnesota, to the First Legislative Assembly. September 4, 1849* (Saint Paul, MN: 1849), 11.

[116] Robert P. Swieringa, "The Settlement of the Old Northwest: Ethnic Pluralism in a Featureless Plain," *Journal of the Early Republic* 9, no. 1 (Spring 1989): 73–105. See also, John P. Senning, "The Know-Nothing Movement in Illinois, 1854–56," *Illinois State Historical Society Journal* 7 (1914): 18–21; Evangeline Thomas, *Nativism in the Old Northwest 1850–1860* (Washington, DC: Catholic University Of America, 1936).

[117] Iowa 1857, 2: 862.

[118] Indiana 1850, 1: 965.

other states, and "thus [divert] capital and labor ... from our State."[119] When foreign settlers received voting rights in the constitutions, few regretted the outcome. They possessed, or could acquire, all the right ingredients: white skin, intelligence, the willingness to learn republican principles, and the strength and wit to contribute "capital and labor." Every state convention voted to grant foreign immigrants full suffrage rights if they had resided in their state for either six months or a year.

By 1857, every northwestern constitution denied political rights to black men, and some denied the right of in-migration to all black people. The 1848 Wisconsin constitution left the door open for later reconsideration of black citizenship, by stating that the legislature could later "extend, by law, the right of suffrage to persons not herein enumerated" (meaning, black men). Still, no such law could ever take force until and unless the white citizens agreed in a separate referendum.[120]

Most recognized, or ignored, the political rights of assimilated Indians, and all granted the vote to European immigrants after a relatively short residency. Would a delegate to any of the northwestern conventions have been able to predict that result?[121] Indiana delegate Allen Hamilton's correspondence suggests that even delegates who represented a fairly united polity – in his case, a northeastern, antislavery Indiana county – would have been profoundly uncertain about the popular opinion on nonwhite people's rights. Hamilton was a man of abolitionist convictions, but he felt unsure enough about the final decision to conduct an informal public opinion poll.[122] Yet even though his Fort Wayne constituency had largely emigrated from New England, he received no clear consensus, certainly nothing that would have hinted at the 84 percent popular vote against black people's rights in Indiana. One of his friends implored Hamilton to "let the poor negroes alone," adding, "this earth is made for them as well as for us, and the liberty that does not profit to *all*, is not worth the name."[123] Others were more uncertain. B. W. Oakly, for example, told Hamilton that most of the community opposed exclusion and disfranchisement and would refuse to ratify a constitution that was "so injust and oppresive [sic] against any of our people even the negro." Nevertheless, he understood it was a tricky, and potentially dangerous question. "When the publick mind is disturbed, and divisions are springing up among our people,

[119] Indiana 1850, 2: 1297.

[120] Wisc. Const. of 1848, art. 3, sec. 1, sub-sec. 4.

[121] Chapter 1 discusses the interactions between delegates and their constituencies in detail. That chapter argues that many voters were deeply interested and involved in the convention proceedings and wrote detailed letters, petitions, and newspaper editorials and had "indignation meetings" to make their wishes plain.

[122] Iowa 1857, 2: 651–67. For example, in a debate on the Bill of Rights, Rufus Clarke explained that there was no consensus in the committee so they had to submit separate reports.

[123] I. Benoit to Allen Hamilton, December 6, 1850, Hamilton Family Papers, Indiana Historical Society, Indianapolis.

and North & South agitated" responsible men had to do their utmost "to quiet the publick mind."[124]

Some of Hamilton's constituents were concerned about the influx of more free black people. P. Hoagland understood perfectly well that this was a painful question nationally and particularly in his state. Because Indiana bordered a slave state, he feared that the "slave owners of Kentucky and other States, when the labor of their aged and super-annuated Slaves ceased to be profitable to them, would gladly free them and send them over to our State, to become a charge on our free population in their old age or suffer for the want of necessaries of life." He believed, therefore, that free black people ought to be kept out, or if permitted into the state, ought to be forced to post a bond.[125] Hoagland's view would eventually prevail in Indiana, and indeed throughout the Northwest: No state in the region extended the suffrage to black men, and several instituted harsh exclusion provisions. The palpable relief expressed by some revealed that even the most conservative voters and newspaper editors had experienced private doubts. One Ohio newspaper, for example, could hardly "forbear to express the hope" that the state's black population would now be satisfied, as they were well represented in the Convention, by men of "high integrity and undoubted abilities." Their claims had been urged by articulate supporters, and they had a "fair, and patient, and respectful hearing in the convention; which, by an overwhelming vote," had decreed that they would have no rights. Because the vote was not in the form of a resolution or statute, but rather as a provision in the state constitution, black persons "ought to realize that it was final." In this case the popular will resulted in, and perhaps even engendered a constitutional provision, which the *Enquirer* correctly assumed carried more weight than a statute law or a judicial decision. They hoped that this was a "permanent solution": as final as the perceived inferiority of the people whose rights had now been lastingly limited in the state's constitution.[126]

Exclusion provisions that were submitted to the popular vote received overwhelming support. Those that were decided by convention delegates passed by a two-to-one margin, thus proving the power of an entrenched commitment to racial discrimination. The interchange between the delegates and the white voters brought to light the people's deepest fears and desires. But the debates could not easily accommodate the delicate shades of meaning involved in such a difficult subject as defining humanity. While delegates wrestled to understand the competing problems of race and rights, as they teased and mocked and

[124] B. W. Oakly to Allen Hamilton, December 13, 1850. Hamilton Family Papers, Indiana State Library, Indianapolis. For a similar point of view, see also Samuel Brenton to Allen Hamilton, December 27, 1850, Hamilton Family Papers, Indiana State Library, Indianapolis.

[125] P. Hoagland to Allen Hamilton, December 6, 1850. For a similar view, see also John H. Browning to Allen Hamilton, November 30, 1850, all in Hamilton Family Papers, Indiana Historical Society, Indianapolis.

[126] *Cincinnati Daily Enquirer*, March 27, 1851.

exhorted one another all the tinges of meaning were lost. Controversial constitutional provisions simply would not withstand popular sovereignty. Hence, deliberation over rights boiled down to a simple yes-or-no vote in the conventions and the popular referenda. Reform-minded delegates who might otherwise have supported the rights of black people understood that such provisions would be unpopular with their constituents. Even if they supported the idea of black rights, they were afraid to endanger the constitutions that had taken them months to craft. In the 1847 convention in Illinois, the Whig the Reverend Henry Palmer, for example, thought it unfair to prohibit free black people from entering the state but declared that he would still vote for exclusion because it was what his constituents wanted.[127]

Popular sovereignty flattened out the nuances of a lively, promising debate on human rights. Perhaps the greatest tragedy was that even people like Ohio's Dr. William Bates succumbed to (and perhaps even helped to strengthen) racial prejudice, and that well-meaning Whigs such as Benjamin Bond bequeathed the legacy of discrimination to generations of Illinoisans. In this case popular sovereignty worked to the detriment of a commitment of democratic deliberation of underlying republican principles. Even a self-proclaimed "staunch Democrat" newspaper wrestled with the problem of creating a new state with the old contradictions still in place, especially at a time of growing sectional enmity. The *Michigan City News* criticized the 1850 Michigan constitutional convention for not rising above "miserable prejudice, unworthy of intelligent men." The editorial condemned the provisions that denied basic rights to Michigan's free black people as a "perfect caricature of [revolutionary] principles." Such laws were nothing but a contradiction of fundamental rights and truths. Even so, the writer assumed that a large majority of the citizens would oppose black suffrage, and that mere discussion of the subject would "aggravate existing prejudices against colored men."[128]

Nevertheless, in spite of the disheartening outcome, the antebellum northwestern debates revealed slight progress. First, the principles of common law decreed, and all but the most conservative delegates agreed, that every adult man who lived in the territory, regardless of his race or ethnicity, had a right to his own soil, whether he owned it or only cultivated it. Second, northwestern state legislatures had already begun passing laws that granted liberty to slaves taken inside their borders. Even in Illinois – a state that consistently passed the harshest antiblack laws in the region – slaves would be automatically freed if they remained in the state for more than six months.[129] The language of the

[127] Illinois 1847, 857. This incident was reported in the *St. Louis Republican* on August 26, 1847.

[128] *Lafayette* [IN] *Daily Courier*, November 22, 1850, initially reported in the *Michigan Daily News* (unknown date). The *Lafayette Daily Courier* was a Free Soil newspaper. I have not been able to determine the political affiliation of the *Michigan Daily News*.

[129] Charles R. McKirdy, *Lincoln Apostate: The Matson Slave Case* (Jackson: University Press of Mississippi, 2011), 67.

law explicitly referred to the slave's foot's touching the soil of Illinois. For white northwesterners, this was an acceptable compromise of principle and pragmatism: Slaves would be freed if they remained on the soil of Illinois for half a year, but new free black people would be refused entry. Abolitionist Frederick Douglass, however, condemned this solution as the very abrogation of one's obligations to – worse, even one's membership in – the human race. In a stinging attack on the 1848 exclusion law Douglass condemned Illinoisans as ravening wolves or tigers and doubted whether they had even been "born and nursed of women."[130]

Ultimately, white northwestern reformers' vacillating, halfhearted efforts toward inclusion failed, and prejudice triumphed. After the passage of Indiana's 1851 black exclusion provision, one voter crowed that the state would not be "cracked in color – degraded in literature, nor contaminated in morals by association with niggars after this."[131] The radicals' hope of creating a just new republic ran aground, but the conservatives' hope of a pure white community failed as well. They simply could not remove all nonwhite people, although they did manage to limit the percentage of the black population and to deny them political rights for generations.[132] Moderates may have been more successful in achieving their aims; they were able to witness the birth of their young states and to keep racial hierarchies intact. Still, the discriminatory provisions were controversial enough that four conventions submitted them for a popular vote. In spite of the fact that both the conventions and the popular votes swept away black people's rights, one can see the fragile tendrils of change in the way northwesterners were beginning to think about human and political rights. These provisions deprived black people of their rights for generations. Northwestern states did not grant the vote to black men until after the Civil War, and kept legal segregation on the books for another century.[133] Within a decade or two of their state constitutional conventions, westerners would discover that a nation founded on the principles of liberty could not long endure with the injustice of slavery still in place, or, to paraphrase Abraham Lincoln, half dedicated to democratic republicanism and half given over to a prejudice that was increasingly understood as irrational, immoral, and unconstitutional.

130 "The Black Law of Illinois," *Frederick Douglass' Paper*, March 18, 1853, quoted in Matthew Norman, "The Other Lincoln-Douglas Debate: The Race Issue in a Comparative Context," *Journal of the Abraham Lincoln Association* 31, no. 1 (Winter 2010): 1–21.

131 Amos Dudley Seward to John W. Seward, August 11, 1851, John W. Seward Papers, Indiana Historical Society, Indianapolis.

132 Table 8.1 shows that although the black population in the Northwest did increase throughout this period, the actual percentage of black people vis-à-vis white people decreased.

133 Schwalm, *Emancipation's Diaspora*, 175–218.

9

Wives

Could anyone still believe, an anonymous Ohio lady demanded, that a woman's mind was "a soil from which no perennial flowers [could] spring?" Had modern ideas about education and women's intellectual capabilities completely bypassed the western states? In her magazine article on the benefits of a scientific education for women, a writer identified only as "Z" defended women's capacity for learning, particularly in the realm of science. The widespread belief that women were incapable of being educated beyond their sphere, she declared, was nothing but narrow-minded prejudice. Such outdated ideas, according to "Z," were based on unwritten, irrational laws – man-made, idiosyncratic decrees, certainly not legitimate ones like statutes or the "laws of nature." Unfortunately those illegitimate laws still possessed enough power in the western territories to confine women in a "prison of ignorance." Although "Z" made no explicit claims about northwestern women's legal or political status, her arguments combined all the common elements of antebellum northwestern reform: the rhetorical reliance on science and reason, the natural metaphors that reminded readers of divine creation, and, just as in the struggles against racial intolerance, the hard battle that logic always had to fight against outdated and unreasonable prejudices. "Z" implied that nature had endowed women with rich intellectual resources. Therefore women possessed a natural right, and in fact the duty, to develop their potential. Yet man-made laws – both in the form of legitimate ones promulgated by legislatures, judges, and constitutional conventions, and in the form of illegitimate ones like prejudices – deprived women of those rights.[1] Worse, those irrational laws interfered with a

[1] Z. ("A Lady"), "The Destiny of Woman," *Western Monthly Magazine* 3 (March 1834): 135–40, quotations on 136 and 139. The editor, the Philadelphia-born judge and prolific author James Hall, was a protemperance Whig. See Wendy Jean Katz, *Regionalism and Reform: Art and Class Formation in Antebellum Cincinnati* (Columbus: Ohio State University Press, 2002).

woman's duty to develop her moral and intellectual qualities, to the detriment of American society.

Because "Z" concealed her identity under a pseudonym, it is difficult to know whether she was an activist. Whig periodicals such as the *Western Monthly Magazine* frequently published essays sympathetic to women, and an active and vocal women's rights community flourished in Ohio at the time she wrote her article. Activists also kept the question of women's rights squarely before their legislatures and constitutional conventions, primarily in the form of petitions. In response, as always, the delegates confronted what they thought would be a straightforward question: whether state constitutions should provide protections for married women's separate property rights. Although the outcome was fairly predictable (only one of the seven states included such a provision), the debates reveal considerable ambivalence about women's private lives and inner development. The effort to understand and regulate women's property rights became more troubling than the delegates anticipated because this process combined a pragmatic need to harmonize statutes, constitutional provisions, and judicial decisions with cultural attitudes and religious beliefs.

Conservative northwesterners would have disagreed passionately with "Z" that only "unwritten, manmade" laws kept women in their intellectually inferior position. Just as they said when confronted with arguments for racial equality, such men responded that nature had endowed different types of people with different capabilities. It was nature, acting through God's intelligent design and through Divine Providence, that had assigned women subordinate roles in the family, in matters of the mind, and in public life.[2] This question of nature's laws stood at the crux of debates over the rights of people who were neither white nor men (or both). Were their civic limitations supported by natural inborn differences, fashioned by a wise author of creation in order to regulate a harmonious world? Or were these differences merely the product of idiosyncratic and outworn prejudices masquerading as legitimate laws? For reformers, natural law dismissed the outward physical differences between people as irrelevancies. For traditionalists, such differences were the whole point.[3]

"Z" may well have been right: Most Northwesterners would not have considered an advanced scientific education necessary or even beneficial to females, at least not for those living and working on rural homesteads. Even so, for the

[2] Norma Basch, *In the Eyes of the Law: Women, Marriage, and Property in Nineteenth-Century New York* (Ithaca, NY: Cornell University Press, 1982), 19.

[3] See John Carson, *The Measure of Merit: Talents, Intelligence, and Inequality in the French and American Republics, 1750–1940* (Princeton, NJ: Princeton University Press, 2007); H. Robert Baker, *The Rescue of Joshua Glover: A Fugitive Slave, the Constitution, and the Coming of the Civil War* (Athens: Ohio University Press, 2006); Audrey Smedley, *Race in North America: Origin and Evolution of a World View* (Boulder, CO: Westview Press, 1999); and Thomas Gossett, *Race: The History of an Idea in America*, new ed. (New York: Oxford University Press, 1997), 73–76.

daughters of more prosperous families (who would include the children of almost all of the delegates), a cultural shift had already begun – a change that encouraged girls and women to immerse themselves in the study of mathematics and science. Young ladies' academies offered basic courses in mathematics, chemistry, "natural philosophy" (botany and zoology), and astronomy.[4] Popular women's magazines like *Godey's Lady's Book* and *Peterson's* frequently carried articles on scientific subjects.[5] Moreover, most Democrats would have agreed that so long as girls and women remained within their proper spheres and became responsible wives and mothers, they should be educated to full literacy, basic numeracy, and a decent grasp of American civic life.[6] And few doubted that girls and women had to develop their inner lives through religious training, particularly in reading and understanding the Bible. As we saw in an earlier chapter, the convention debates over the civil rights of nonwhite men demonstrated that social prejudice did indeed serve as a type of "man-made law." In those discussions delegates acknowledged that a republic guaranteed many rights to property-owning husbands and fathers, whether they were white, black, or Indian. The delegates who opposed married women's property rights also believed, however, that personal prejudice against nonwhite people could (and for some, should) defeat fundamental constitutional and common-law guarantees. For example, even though the common law protected the rights of property owners to defend their claims in courts, the northwestern Black Codes prohibited black persons from suing or giving testimony against white people.[7] In this way, according to reformers, prejudice

[4] In the early 1840s, the Monticello Female Seminary in central Illinois, for example, offered courses in algebra, geometry, botany, physiology, natural history, chemistry, geography, and astronomy alongside traditional women's education in domestic economy, moral philosophy, and Bible study. Barbara J. Mitchell, "'O Fairest Monticello': Monticello Female Seminary," *Journal of the Illinois State Historical Society* 93, no. 3 (Autumn 2000): 255. Margaret Rossiter explains that colleges began educating women scientists in the mid-1800s and hired them as teachers for the next generation. Margaret W. Rossiter, *Women Scientists in America: Struggles and Strategies to 1940* (Baltimore, MD: John Hopkins University Press, 1982), 1–28. Barbara Miller Solomon discusses the Protestant view of the disconnection between women's personal development and their domestic roles in, *In the Company of Educated Women: A History of Women and Higher Education* (New Haven, CT: Yale University Press, 1985), 16. Solomon is careful to distinguish between the daughters of middle-class or professional parents, who educated their daughters in academies, and the children of farmers, who attended rural district schools for a few years.

[5] This is discussed at length in Chapter 2. See also, Mary Kelley, *Learning to Stand and Speak: Women, Education, and Public Life in America's Republic* (Chapel Hill: University of North Carolina Press, 2008), 21–23, 39, 71–75.

[6] I found no references to the education of girls in the northwestern convention journals, but delegates did frequently refer to "children" when discussing common schools, and "young men" when referring to academies or colleges.

[7] See Stephen Middleton, *The Black Laws: Race and the Legal Process in Early Ohio* (Athens: Ohio University Press, 2005); and Stephen Middleton, *The Black Laws in the Old Northwest: A Documentary History* (Westport, CT: Greenwood, 1993).

acted as a powerful force for stasis – a process that was even more evident in the debates over married women's property rights.[8]

Antebellum Americans were governed by three overlapping legal systems, and, if we take cultural and religious norms into account, by nonlegal systems as well. Constitutions framed the government and delineated rights; statutes codified and amplified those provisions; the common law set the precedent for resolving conflicts and protected traditional relationships. In addition to these legal frameworks, religious and cultural laws regulated daily lives and behavior. Many Americans believed that the Almighty had assigned specific roles to persons of different races and genders, so their beliefs about nonwhite people and about women, especially those who were married, were deeply interwoven with their religious faith.

Under the common law rule of coverture, a married woman's legal existence was suspended and "covered" by her husband, who had full rights over her personal possessions. That property included her clothing, money, household goods, livestock, and any wages she earned. He also possessed rights to all profits and rents from any land she took into the marriage.[9] She could not make contracts or sue on her own behalf, and when she did business with tradesmen, she did so only as an agent of her husband. In contrast to many other aspects of common law, which were adapted to suit the new American context, the practice of coverture passed almost unchanged into the American legal system. Even when states (however briefly) repealed their reception statutes, and even when lawyers and lawmakers complained about the outdated, hidebound, and undemocratic elements of the English common law, they adopted the system of coverture wholesale.[10] This was true throughout the nation. British colonies in North America had adopted the common law provisions on women's property rights in their entirety, but without the structures of English courts that mitigated some of the harsher aspects of the doctrine of coverture. The English legal system had a separate chancery court, which was under the direction of the Crown. The lawyers who argued cases in chancery had been trained in universities and understood both civil and common law: They were therefore well versed in trusts, wills, and other legal instruments that protected married

[8] For conflicts among common law, statute law, and constitutional provisions, particularly codification of common law coverture, see Peggy A. Rabkin, "The Origins of Law Reform: The Social Significance of the Nineteenth-Century Codification Movement and Its Contribution to the Passage of the Early Married Women's Property Acts," *Buffalo Law Review* 24, no. 3 (Spring 1975): 683–760.

[9] See William Blackstone, *Commentaries on the Laws of England* (London: 1765–1769), 1: 430–31. For reception of the English common law of marriage in American states, see also Richard H. Chused, "Late Nineteenth Century Married Women's Property Law: Reception of the Early Married Women's Property Acts by Courts and Legislatures," *American Journal of Legal History* 29, no. 1 (Jan. 1985): 3–35.

[10] See Hendrik Hartog, *Man and Wife in America: A History* (Cambridge, MA: Harvard University Press, 2000), 116; and Basch, *In the Eyes of the Law.*

women's rights.[11] Most American states did not establish separate chancery courts, however.[12] In the antebellum Northwest, only Iowa and Wisconsin briefly instituted such courts, and the judges were often the same men who presided over lower courts.[13]

Perhaps the greatest difference that distinguished the American common law on marriage from its British origins was in the way Americans interpreted the religious roots of coverture. Every American state legislature had passed laws that confirmed women's common law status alongside her biblical identity as "one flesh" with her husband.[14] By contrast, the English common law tradition of coverture was originally intended to clarify problems of inheritance and succession. Most historians agree, therefore, that in England the notion of legal and matrimonial unity between husband and wife was intended as a legal fiction.[15] True, English marriages, like American ones, were both civil and religious unions.[16] Ecclesiastical courts adjudicated matters of marriage, succession to property, separation, and legitimacy.[17] The English common law traditions about marriage (calling banns, defining marriage as between one man and one woman, impossibility of divorce, and coverture) remained almost unchanged in American state law until the last quarter of the nineteenth century. In the United States the common law remained deeply linked to biblical injunctions about wives and husbands becoming "one flesh," but without the protections offered by ecclesiastical courts.[18] Most antebellum northwesterners never separated the notion of the

[11] Lee Holcombe, *Wives and Property: Reform of the Married Women's Property Law in Nineteenth Century England* (Toronto: University of Toronto Press, 1983), 11–13, 64.

[12] Carol Elizabeth Jenson, "The Equity Jurisdiction and Married Women's Property in Ante-Bellum America: A Revisionist View," *International Journal of Women's Studies* 2, no. 2 (March–April 1979): 144–54; William H. Nelson, *The Americanization of the Common Law: The Impact of Legal Change on Massachusetts Society, 1760–1830* (Cambridge, MA: Harvard University Press, 1975), 46; Kathleen S. Sullivan, *Constitutional Context: Women and Rights Discourse in Nineteenth-Century America* (Baltimore: Johns Hopkins University Press, 2007), 67–93.

[13] For a discussion of court systems see Chapter 5.

[14] Linda K. Kerber, *No Constitutional Right to Be Ladies: Women and the Obligations of Citizenship* (New York: Hill & Wang, 1998), 11–12; Dianne Avery and Alfred S. Konefsky, "The Daughters of Job: Property Rights and Women's Lives in Mid-Nineteenth Century Massachusetts," *Law & History Review* 10, no. 2 (Autumn 1992): 323–35

[15] Hartog, *Man and Wife*, 104. Hartog went so far as to assert that no one would have been "insane enough" to believe in the physical truth of this idea.

[16] Homer H. Clark Jr., *The Law of Domestic Relations in the United States*, 2nd ed. (St. Paul, MN: West, 1988), 21–31. Clark maintains that state laws had power to regulate marriages until at least 1965. The biblical injunction for a married couple to become "one flesh" appears in both the Old and New Testaments: Gen. 2: 24 and Mark 10: 8 (Authorized King James Version).

[17] Hendrik Hartog explains that seventeenth- and eighteenth-century English ecclesiastical courts instituted these rules to regulate dowries, inheritance, and betrothals. Hartog, *Man and Wife*, 116.

[18] William Blackstone explained that a woman could sue her husband in an ecclesiastical court. He understood this as part of the civil law tradition: "In the civil law the husband and the wife are considered as two distinct persons, and may have separate estates, contracts, debts, and injuries; and therefore in our ecclesiastical courts, a woman may sue and be sued without her husband."

sacredness of matrimony from the common law definition of marriage, and they did not believe that women's status could or should be changed by legislatures or constitutional conventions.[19]

That said, most delegates believed that a transformation was necessary. The catastrophic panics and increasingly complicated (and vague) statute laws about property forced legislatures to consider making small changes to married women's property rights. By the turn of the eighteenth to the nineteenth century, several New England states had already begun to pass statute laws to protect some property assets for women who had lost their husbands through desertion, divorce, or death.[20] Connecticut passed a law as early as 1809, for example, permitting women to write their own wills. In 1823, the Maine legislature protected the property of deserted wives; a year later, an Ohio statute permitted divorced women to recover some of their property. By the mid-1830s several other states, such as Massachusetts in 1835 and Indiana in 1837, had followed suit with similar laws.[21] The first states to pass statutes explicitly granting married women the right to control their own property were Arkansas in 1834 and Mississippi in 1837. Those measures secured a woman's right to retain slaves willed to her by her father.[22] State laws on married women's property rights were primarily pragmatic efforts to mitigate the effects of economic change, but the fact that they were necessary at all suggests that married women's property rights were becoming more complicated, particularly in the unstable economies where speculation and paper money were wreaking havoc with traditional notions of property rights.

Similar changes were beginning to occur in the Northwest. In 1835 the Ohio legislature provided that when a wife acknowledged a deed she should be bound by it. Because that law rendered a wife individually liable to legal proceedings, it obliquely weakened marital unity. In 1837, when Robert Dale Owen (Figure 3.1) was serving as a representative in the Indiana assembly, he proposed a bill that would have protected and expanded widows' dower rights: that is, permitted widows to inherit two-thirds, rather than the one-third law portion she would

Blackstone, *Commentaries on the Laws of England*, 1: 432. Women had a greater chance of divorcing their husbands in equity courts (something that was not possible in most American states until the 1830s). R. B. Outhwaite, *The Rise and Fall of the English Ecclesiastical Courts, 1500–1860* (New York: Cambridge University Press, 2006), 51–52, 163. For a discussion of the equity courts and married women's property rights in England, see Holcombe, *Wives and Property*, 9–11, 23.

[19] Hendrik Hartog, *Man and Wife*, 120; Basch, *In the Eyes of the Law*, 154; Norma Basch, "Invisible Women: The Legal Fiction of Marital Unity in Nineteenth-Century America," *Feminist Studies* 5, no. 2 (Summer 1979): 346–66; Kerber, *No Constitutional Right to Be Ladies*, xiii.

[20] See Chused, "Late Nineteenth-Century Married Women's Property Law."

[21] See Joan Hoff, *Law, Gender, and Injustice: A Legal History of U.S. Women* (New York: New York University Press, 1991).

[22] See Michael B. Dougan, "The Arkansas Married Women's Property Law," *Arkansas Historical Quarterly* 46, no. 1 (Spring 1987): 3–26.

have received under the common law.[23] In spite of bitter opposition the bill passed in 1838, though the legislature repealed it six years later.[24] Meanwhile, northwesterners watched the New York Legislature carefully. When that body began to pass legislation to protect widows, conservative northwesterners worried that these changes would have unpredictable and deleterious moral effects. A New York law granting to widows the entirety of life insurance premiums upon the death of their husbands raised fears, and the Ohio *Scioto Gazette* expressed doubts as to the widows' moral strength to resist the lure of inheritance with a sardonic "What a temptation to Jezebels!"[25] This may have been intended as a joke, but it does reflect anxiety over the profound changes in the husbands' relationships with their wives.

As with all questions about contested rights, such issues raised both pragmatic concerns (such as the need to harmonize common law precedent with statutes, or to protect families from homelessness) and ideological ones (such as the imperative to coordinate Christian and republican principles with the popular will). Because the delegates were already engaged in a scrutiny and reform of the law, the need to harmonize the contradictions in statutes and in judicial decisions rendered it obvious that these confusions had to be addressed and resolved. In the Ohio convention, for example, Simeon Nash, a Whig judge, explained that the court decisions on women's deeds were so confused and contradictory that the matter had to be settled in the state constitution.[26] Another Ohio delegate, Whig lawyer Benjamin Stanton, complained that "thousands of deeds" had been filed without any "examinations of the wife's understanding or consent," contrary to common law doctrine.[27] Those who opposed any change in women's status were convinced that statute laws,

[23] For a discussion of dower rights and community property, see Carole Shammas, Marylynn Salmon, and Michael Dahlin, eds., *Inheritance in America from Colonial Times to the Present* (New Brunswick, NJ: Rutgers University Press, 1987).

[24] Robert Dale Owen's biographer believed this was done out of spite. Richard W. Leopold, *Robert Dale Owen: A Biography* (Cambridge, MA: Harvard University Press, 1940). For rights of northwestern widows, see Christopher A. Schnell, "Wives, Widows, and Will Makers: Women and the Law of Property," in Daniel W. Stowell, ed., *In Tender Consideration: Women, Families, and the Law in Abraham Lincoln's Illinois* (Urbana: University of Illinois Press, 2002), 129–60.

[25] *Scioto Gazette* (Chillicothe, OH), April 16, 1840. In the case of the wife's death, her insurance would be payable to her children.

[26] J. V. Smith, *Report of the Debates and Proceedings of the Convention for the Revision of the Constitution of the State of Ohio, 1850–51* (Columbus, OH: 1851), 1: 270 (hereafter Ohio 1850).

[27] Ohio 1850, 2: 241. Stanton was not talking about married women's property provisions but rather "curative laws," essentially a legislative device allowing assemblies to fix problems without resorting to constitutional revision. See also, Alison D. Morantz, "There's No Place like Home: Homestead Exemption and Judicial Constructions of Family in Nineteenth-Century America," *Law & History Review* 24, no. 2 (Summer 2006): 245–95; Debra A Viles, "Disabilities of Marriage: Gender and Law in Antebellum Michigan," *Michigan Historical Review* 28, no. 1 (Spring 2002): 1–31; Sara L. Zeigler, "Uniformity and Conformity: Regionalism and the Adjudication of the Married Women's Property Acts," *Polity* 28, no. 4 (Summer 1996): 467–95.

court decisions, common law precedent, and constitutions had to harmonize. That did not mean that constitutions had to reform women's rights or roles – quite the reverse. Benjamin Stanton explicitly stated that he was not asking for changes to common law married women's property rights. He was only asking that the "old law," which he "liked best," be reinstated in order to coordinate statute laws with the common law principle of coverture.[28] Clarifying, codifying, or harmonizing laws by no means meant reforming them, but the process did bring inconsistencies to light.

Wisconsin delegate Marshall Mason Strong, for example, fought bitterly against the provisions granting married women separate property rights. That proposal, he explained, functioned as "civil legislation." Worse, because it was "wholly inconsistent" with the common law, it rendered the constitution illegitimate. Worse, constitutional interference with common law precedent would uproot all rules of "pleading practice, evidence, domestic relations, and indeed throw confusion into every branch." Strong had supported political equality for black men but was deeply concerned about the encroachment of laws into improper spheres. Constitutions ought to serve as "palladia" to guard the political and civic rights of all men, but surely that task ought not to extend to a private home. He feared that this disjunction would generate endless appeals on the married women's property rights provision. Worst of all, the constitutional provision that guaranteed married women control over their personal property struck "deep among first principles."[29] The phrase "first principles" usually referred to revolutionary era tenets such as the separation of powers, but Strong was explicitly connecting marriage (a sacred, biblically sanctioned relationship) with the foundations of constitutional government. True: Everyone knew that there were bad husbands who mistreated their wives, who drank too much and shirked their responsibilities as providers, or who speculated away their families' homesteads. Men like Marshall Mason Strong, who revered the matrimonial tie as both a religious and a legal institution, believed that husbands who failed in their duty ought to be punished by law enforcement. The problem did not belong in state constitutions: an attitude held by many moderate delegates as well. Such questions should be left to criminal courts, to civil suits (by a woman's father or brothers), or to the chancery courts.

But what happened when families suffered through an act of God or as a consequence of economic disasters? In times of economic instability, individual husbands could not always manage the family's welfare successfully. The financial panics exposed structural problems in governance: When families starved, the government was clearly not serving the community. Historians usually point to the antebellum American economic panics as an explanation for the age of widespread constitutional revision in the 1820s through the late

[28] 1850 Ohio, 2: 241, 597.

[29] Milo M. Quaife, ed., *The Struggle over Ratification, 1846–1847*, vol. 28 of *Publications of the State Historical Society of Wisconsin* (Madison: State Historical Society of Wisconsin, 1920), 241.

1850s.[30] Protections for married women's property rights, they explain, were primarily intended to protect homes and lands from debt seizure.[31] During the terrible years of the early 1840s political leaders realized that the old common law rules that granted women's personal property to the main provider caused problems when that provider, through misfortune or profligacy, plunged his family into debt. Therefore it became necessary to set off some property to safeguard it from seizure.[32]

That narrative leaves several questions unanswered. First, why not simply use homestead exemptions to safeguard family survival? As Raquel Fernandez has observed, the antebellum panics alone could not explain why legislatures throughout the nation expanded married women's property rights later in the nineteenth and into the early twentieth centuries, after the state economies had recovered from the devastating financial failures.[33] Considering the opposition in the conventions, why did all of the northwestern state legislatures pass laws that protected married women's property rights within the next twenty years? Part of the answer lies in the widespread belief that even though homestead provisions and laws did obliquely overturn some common law principles, constitutions were not supposed to rearrange family or community customs, but should instead support biblically sanctioned relationships. Part must be sought in the vocal, if ultimately unsuccessful efforts of reformers to advocate a constitutional reconsideration of human rights as the core of community welfare.

Dana Weiner has called northwestern women activists a "grass-roots, homegrown" body of reformers.[34] These people began fighting against slavery and racial prejudice in the early 1830s and, as both Weiner and Stacey Robertson have shown, were part of an energetic and cooperative antiprejudice community.[35] Many of these women and men participated in both the antislavery

[30] See Chused, "Late Nineteenth Century Married Women's Property Law," 3–35.

[31] See Viles, "Disabilities of Marriage," 1–31; and Chused, "Late Nineteenth Century Married Women's Property Law," 3–35.

[32] Historians have argued about this considerably over the past thirty years. Until the mid-1970s most explained married women's property statutes as primarily a protective measure against homestead seizure. See, for example, Ellen Dannin, "Marriage and Law Reform: Lessons from the Nineteenth-Century Michigan Married Women's Property Acts," *Texas Journal of Women and the Law* 20, no. 1 (Fall 2010): 1–54; and Joseph A. Custer, "The Three Waves of Married Women's Property Acts, with a Focus on Mississippi, New York, and Oregon," *Ohio Northern University Law Review* 40 (2013–2014): 395–440. Ellen Dannin and Norma Basch both suggest that none of the laws had much practical effect.

[33] Raquel Fernández, "Women's Rights and Development," (working paper 15355, National Bureau of Economic Research, Cambridge, MA, 2009), 6.

[34] Dana Weiner, *Race and Rights: Fighting Slavery and Prejudice in the Old Northwest 1830–1870* (DeKalb: Northern Illinois University Press, 2013), 73. Stacey M. Robertson devotes a chapter on grassroots antislavery activism among northwestern women, in *Hearts Beating for Liberty: Women Abolitionists in the Old Northwest* (Chapel Hill: University of North Carolina Press, 2010), chap. 1.

[35] See Stacey M. Robertson, *Betsy Mix Cowles: Champion of Equality* (Boulder, CO: Westview Press, 2014); and Susan Zaeske, *Signatures of Citizenship: Petitioning, Antislavery, and Women's Political Identity* (Chapel Hill: University of North Carolina Press, 2003).

and pro–women's rights movements, and in the course of their advocacy, held meetings and gathered thousands of petition signatures, some of which they sent to the state constitutional conventions. It is difficult to know to what degree these activist women represented their less outspoken sisters. Newspaper editorials, letters between delegates and their families, and a few hints in speeches and essays by women writers suggest that there was a persistent, if limited movement to expand women's sphere. This endeavor encompassed the efforts of female and male reformers and certainly reached educated women outside reform circles, judging from the prevalence of petitions sent to northwestern constitutional conventions.[36]

Those women's rights activists who had cut their teeth as antislavery reformers had learned how best to broadcast their ideas and how to persuade their more reluctant neighbors. The two most powerful and well-publicized weapons in their arsenal were the same ones wielded by African American civil rights groups: state, regional, and national rights conventions, especially in Ohio and Indiana, and petition drives in all of the other northwestern states. Moreover, in both Salem, Ohio, in 1850, and Richmond, Indiana, a year later, antiprejudice activists tried to schedule their conventions to coincide with the state constitutional conventions. Because of logistical problems, the Indiana convention could not finalize its arrangements until after the state constitutional convention had already adjourned.[37] The women's rights activists faced serious pragmatic difficulties as they struggled to organize their meetings, which resulted in delays and in reduced participation. The Ohio women's rights conventions in Salem (1850) and in Akron (1851) drew the majority of their membership from the antislavery movement, not from an organized women's rights community. They had only one newspaper, the *Antislavery Bugle*, in which to announce their meetings or recruit participants. In Indiana, the *Free Labor Advocate and Anti-Slavery Chronicle* served that purpose.[38] Northwestern newspapers sometimes published editorial letters by women, but they rarely publicized their reform meetings.[39] By contrast, African American activists, both women and men, had already been meeting for more than a decade and had established a widespread and diverse network. They were able to depend on church groups, schools, local civic organizations, and business associates. Women's rights activists were only able to draw on antislavery groups reliably and consistently, though they did have some success in local church groups. This was especially

[36] This chapter identifies as "activists" those women who struggled for married women's full control over their property and for political and civic equality.

[37] Indiana Woman's Suffrage Association Record Book 1851–1886, Indiana Historical Society, Indianapolis.

[38] Weiner, *Race and Rights*, 34–36.

[39] Media participation is discussed extensively in Sylvia D. Hoffert, *When Hens Crow: The Women's Rights Movements in Antebellum America* (Bloomington: Indiana University Press, 1995). For northwestern newspaper participation, see Weiner, *Race and Rights*, and Robertson, *Hearts Beating for Liberty*.

true in areas dominated by Whigs, such as Ohio's Western Reserve, or Robert Dale Owen's Posey County (a Whig stronghold in Indiana), and in Michigan.[40]

Black women attended and may have addressed the Colored Citizens' Convention held in Columbus, Ohio, in 1850. The officers of that convention seated women delegates but at first did not permit them to speak. When the women protested and threatened to leave, the male delegates consented. Unfortunately there is no record of what the women said.[41] And in subsequent meetings, it is likely that the male delegates changed their minds and reneged on their earlier permission. Although women were present at the 1851 and 1852 Ohio meetings and may again have demanded the right to speak, they were rebuffed by a resolution that "certain members" of the convention were forbidden to address the floor.[42] It is unknown whether these women carried out their earlier determination to leave the convention. Some black women did participate in reform societies and fairs, as well as in the 1851 Akron, Ohio, women's rights convention, where Sojourner Truth (see Figure 9.1) made her famous antislavery and pro–women's rights speech.[43] White constitutional convention delegates rarely discussed black women in any of the conventions; or if so, only in ugly accusations of immorality.[44]

No matter how radical the women activists might have been, they encountered two insurmountable obstacles. The first was the categorical opposition to women's political and economic equality, and the fact that few northwestern women had personal experience addressing lawmaking bodies. The African American men who gathered in northwestern civil rights conventions were able to exploit one significant advantage: As ministers, teachers, and lawyers, they already had some experience addressing large groups and speaking to state officials. They were also agitating for political and civic equality, goals that had somewhat more support (at least, in progressive reform circles) than

[40] For example, the ladies of Lawrenceburg, Indiana, met in the basement of a local Methodist Episcopal church on December 16, 1850, to discuss the "propriety of inserting a clause in the new Constitution more effectually to secure the property rights of married women." H. Fowler, *Report of the Debates and Proceedings of the Convention for the Revision of the Constitution of the State of Indiana* (Indianapolis, IN: 1850), 2: 1184 (hereafter Indiana 1850).

[41] The proceedings were published and contained detailed notes on some of the speeches but did not record the women's contributions. "Report of a Meeting of the Colored Citizens of Indiana, January 17, 1842," in Philip S. Foner and George E. Walker, eds., *Proceedings of the Black State Conventions, 1840–1865* (Philadelphia: Temple University Press, 1979), 1: 173–75; "State Convention of the People of Color of the State of Indiana, August 9, 1851," in *Proceedings of the Black State Conventions*, 1: 176–77.

[42] See Chapter 7.

[43] Robertson, *Hearts Beating for Liberty*, 97–98.

[44] For example in the 1846 Wisconsin convention, Edward G. Ryan stated that "every negro was a thief, and every negro woman far worse," implying that all black women were prostitutes. Milo M. Quaife, ed., *The Convention of 1846*, vol. 27 of *Publications of the State Historical Society of Wisconsin* (Madison: State Historical Society of Wisconsin, 1919), 215 (hereafter Wisconsin 1848). I found no other references to black women in any other convention journal.

FIGURE 9.1. Sojourner Truth (1797?–1883), was born into slavery in New York. She became an abolitionist and women's rights activist, and spoke at the 1851 Akron, Oho women's rights convention. Original caption: "I sell the shadow to support the substance. Sojourner Truth."

"Sojourner Truth, three-quarter length portrait, standing, wearing spectacles, shawl, and peaked cap, right hand resting on cane."

Source: Detroit, 1864. Courtesy of the Library of Congress Manuscript Division, LC-USZ62–119343.

women's suffrage. African American convention delegates were able to schedule a meeting with Ohio constitutional convention delegates. By contrast, although the Salem, Ohio, women's rights convention explicitly denied men the right to speak – a rather daring move for 1850 – none of the women delegates was able to steel herself for the ordeal of meeting with the state constitutional convention delegates. Speakers at the women's convention expressed profound disappointment that in spite of several calls exhorting the participants to volunteer for such a meeting, none of the women stepped forward.[45] This suggests that even activist women confronted immense personal difficulties in attempting to cross customary boundaries, even when they held deep convictions about their right and duty to do so.

Northwestern women activists were determined to expand the categories that defined women's rights and roles. Because their opponents based their arguments on women's natural submission to men, women's rights activists rendered their conception of women's roles as both natural and rational. The women's conventions (like the black rights conventions) broadened their analysis far beyond economic and political demands. The Salem, Ohio, women delegates condemned all "class legislation," which they defined as all statute laws that singled out any group of human beings for discriminatory treatment, as unjust. Nineteenth-century activists, deeply influenced by and reliant on Baconian scientific methods, eagerly exploited the scientific tools of classification. Treating naturally occurring elements and creatures in the wrong category was fundamentally illogical and would result in incorrect conclusions. In a society that purported to be governed by democratic constitutions, such errors would result in unjust laws. And because the close observation of nature was a distinctly Christian and moral endeavor, unjust laws based on irrational conclusions were by extension also unethical laws.[46]

The logical inference, then, was that such laws would harm society in every area of the human experience. Where the state constitutional conventions kept the topic of women's rights contracted around a narrow sphere – primarily focusing on married women's property – the women activists contemplated a broad range of human endeavor. The 1851 Richmond, Indiana, women's rights convention declared that laws that distinguished between men and women were "politically, pecuniarily, ecclesiastically, and socially" in direct contradiction of the "inalienable and self-evident truth" that God had gifted to every human being both understanding and the capacity to discern right from wrong. Further, such laws contravened God's will that all human beings make full use of such gifts.[47] Both the 1850 Ohio and the 1852 Indiana women's conventions echoed the widespread liberal belief that self-evident facts about the world were

[45] Mercy L. Holmes to "Women's Convention assembled in Salem," April 12, 1850, in Robert W. Audretsch, ed., *The Salem, Ohio 1850 Women's Rights Convention Proceedings* (Salem, OH: Salem Area Bicentennial Committee and Salem Public Library, 1976), 29–30. Holmes offered to serve as a member of the delegation but must have reneged, since the convention minutes expressed regret that no one (in the end) stepped forward when the time came. She wrote from Selma, Ohio, which was reputedly a stop on the underground railroad. *History of Clark County, Ohio* (Chicago: 1881), 767–68.

[46] Audretsch, *Salem, Ohio 1850 Women's Rights Convention*, 17.

[47] "Richmond, Indiana women's rights meeting minutes, 1851," Indiana Woman's Suffrage Association, Record Book 1851–1886, Indiana Historical Society Library, Indianapolis (hereafter Indiana Women's Rights Minutes).

available to every individual through the senses. Individual self-development was the core duty of any virtuous person. The opening call for the Ohio women's convention, for example, explicitly declared that the American woman had been denied the right to expand "her immortal nature" under the present state constitution. The women were called to "come and inquire" whether their current position in society had been "designed by wisdom, and designed to secure the best interests of the human race."[48] That kind of sustained inquiry required an inborn ability to examine one's circumstances closely, and the training to make thoughtful judgments about them.

Sylvia Hoffert has explained that eastern women reformers were influenced by the Scottish Enlightenment philosophers, whose works were read in every college in antebellum America. Judging from the signatures appended to the Indiana and Ohio women's convention minutes, most of the leadership were well-educated women from prominent political and reform-minded families and would undoubtedly have encountered these ideas in their educational careers.[49] For all these reasons, in the Northwest these ideas took on a strongly communitarian tinge that linked personal duty to the greater good of the human family.[50] Every human being, whether male or female, was individually responsible to God, so it was destructive of societal mores to hinder women's individual rights or their ability to qualify themselves, both mentally and morally, to act as responsible citizens.[51] The Ohio women explained that the "odious distinctions" that deprived women of their rights harmed the entire community because they threatened the state's prosperity. Moreover, because the doctrine of rights was "dictated by God Himself," unjust statutes and constitutional provisions had to be considered "null and void."[52] They considered such laws as illegitimate as the unwritten laws of prejudice.

How widespread were these ideas? Participation in women's rights meetings is difficult to gauge. Historians of the 1850 Salem, Ohio, convention assume that about four hundred women attended. Many more wrote letters regretting their inability to participate; such women simply did not have the time or means to attend, even when they yearned to be there. We have to measure

48 Audretsch, *Salem, Ohio 1850 Women's Rights Convention*, 17.

49 Hoffert, *When Hens Crow*, 19–21. See also, Daniel Walker Howe, *Making the American Self: Jonathan Edwards to Abraham Lincoln* (New York: Oxford University Press, 2009), 63–77. Members of the Hayes, Giddings, and Tilden families attended these conventions in Ohio and Indiana.

50 Stacey Robertson explains, in *Hearts Beating for Liberty*, that the antislavery activists in the region demonstrated a strong cooperationist impulse, 10–13. I argue that this is borne out in their communitarian rhetoric.

51 Indiana Women's Rights Minutes. Sylvia Hoffert discusses this at length in *When Hens Crow*, 45–49. For William Paley (who she explains was the best-known and most widely read of the Scottish Enlightenment philosophers) social custom and prejudices would have constituted the core of any individual's moral sense: He contended that there was no such thing as an innate moral sense.

52 Audretsch, *Salem, Ohio 1850 Women's Rights Convention*, 20, 23.

northwestern women's participation, and more specifically their desire to participate, through petition signatures, private letters, and newspaper editorials. Newspapers – particularly those that espoused Whig views – did carry editorial letters by female readers, as well as reports of charitable events, church meetings, and women teachers' speeches at academy commencement exercises.[53] Midwestern manuscript collections contain far fewer letters by women than by men. Whether the women's letters did not survive, were not collected, or were never written is impossible to determine. Scarcity of documentary evidence is at best a rough guide. Nevertheless, the surviving evidence suggests that while mainstream women were not completely silent on the question of their rights, their more militant sisters' complaints that northwesterners were simply not interested in women's issues may be justified.[54]

In 1837 an Illinois lady who identified herself as "E" wrote a biting editorial for the *Alton Telegraph*, one of the state's most powerful Whig organs. The writer was aware that women had not asserted their rights. She considered that silence "entirely natural," since women had always been taught to consider themselves inferior and had allowed themselves to be convinced that it was "just, right, and proper" that they should be "subordinate to, and entirely dependent" upon men.[55] Fifteen years later, the Ohio educator Maria Boyton was able to publish a similar speech she presented at a school exhibition. Boyton declared that women were "too listless and inactive on the important subject of their rights." That was not their fault: As did "E," Boyton believed that women had been trained "from their very infancy to remain ignorant of affairs which should occupy a good portion of their time and talents." She was particularly irritated when she heard girls say that they did not want to be seen going to an election and "voting for a pack of rowdies." What, she demanded, would happen if their future husbands became ill or died?[56]

These editorials and speeches, while hardly representative of conventional northwestern views on women's roles, nevertheless formed a persistent backdrop during the great age of constitutional revision in the region. Judging from published newspaper editorials, even in the Democratic press, the more outspoken or more daring women did have some outlet for their views. Still, there is no question that the decision to write pro–women's rights editorials required some courage. Even "E," who minced no words about her contempt for those who styled themselves "God's noblest work" (she meant men), admitted that

[53] A group of women met in Indiana and implored the convention to consider women's rights, but I never found any record of this meeting other than a comment R. D. Owen made during the convention. See n. 40. Sylvia Hoffert has discussed the use of print media in detail, in *When Hens Crow*.

[54] There is a lively historiographic debate about whether women had the ability and/or desire to speak in public or to express political views. See Ann Russo and Cheris Kramarae, eds., *The Radical Women's Press of the 1850s* (New York: Routledge, 1991).

[55] *Alton* [IL] *Telegraph*, June 28, 1837.

[56] *Western Reserve Transcript and Whig* (Warren, OH), April 8, 1852.

she knew she had not chosen a "very popular, nor yet very agreeable subject."[57] Yet a close look at the unfavorable responses suggests that these women were not criticized for expressing their opinions, but rather for attacking men. Even the angriest Democrat rejoinders appeared to be bemused or annoyed, but contained hints that women had a right to publish their ideas, at least within the limits of proper behavior and respect for men. For example, one young Indiana lady who called herself Clotilda, after a sixth-century Catholic saint, declared that no respectable man would dare to argue that women should not have "at least *half* the say in the formation and regulation of the society." Her editorial stressed men's morality and sobriety rather than women's political rights. Perhaps for that reason her letter reaped several sharp rebukes. Male readers castigated her for her criticism, though not for writing in the first place. "I would advise 'Clotilda'," one such respondent recommended, that instead of writing "inflammatory articles against the young men," to employ her talent "in the production of articles that may be admired for their propriety and female modesty, more than for their dictatorial and haughty character." He thought she would gain more admiration that way, rather than "by all the lashing her fair hand may do."[58] A week later a wag who called himself "Bill Twotle" published a much rougher response, written in a typical antebellum comical dialect, but clearly linking Clotilda's behavior to Whig politics rather than to women's rights activism. Addressing his response "Too Klotildee," the author mocked her for "singin such funny Whig songs" and made fun of women who "hollered and hurraed so," and who abused any "feller that didn't jine" in the proceedings.[59] These responses suggest that women were not expected to disappear entirely from the public scene, merely that they ought to refrain from criticizing men.

Whig and Free Soil newspapers were usually more sympathetic. For example, when a letter appeared in the Free Soil *Indiana True Democrat* condemning activists who transgressed Old Testament injunctions, the editorial – written by an anonymous critic who styled himself "one of the "B'hoys" – reaped a series of blistering responses from both men and women.[60] For reform-minded women, however, familiarity with the Old and New Testaments engendered an ability to apply biblical exegesis to their opponents' arguments. One such letter mocked the original writer for having "raked together" Old Testament, "might-makes-right," and many other conflicting sources to prove that women were inferior and should not gain additional rights. The anonymous author, signing herself "One of the G'hirls," rebutted his editorial through a careful

57 *Alton* [IL] *Telegraph*, June 28, 1837.

58 *Delaware County Democrat* (Muncie, IN), May 10, 1845; see also May 31, 1845. She may have chosen Clotilda because of the saint's instrumentality in converting her husband to Christianity.

59 *Delaware County Democrat* (Muncie, IN), May 17, 1845.

60 The pseudonyms are not an infallible guide to the gender of the writers, but internal evidence suggests that "One of the G'hirls" was probably a woman.

scriptural analysis and then showed that because women needed food, clothing, and shelter and because they had the "same capacities and wants, were born with the same mental organs (as Phrenology testifies)" as men, the apparent difference was attributable to nothing more than a lack of educational opportunities for girls.[61] Those categories – self-improvement versus traditional spheres – were not mutually exclusive, even in the eyes of highly conservative people. As northwestern men considered the roles and rights of women, they often admitted that a degree of self-development was necessary in order to allow a woman to mature into an ideal wife.[62]

This back-and-forth about women's rights and abilities was part of an ongoing conversation about two overarching questions, both of which would affect women's legal status in the coming decades. The first theme revolved around women's natural and traditional roles in the family and in society, and the second, their right to develop their inborn abilities. Certainly no one argued that women should not attend to their moral and, to some degree, intellectual improvement. But the idea that a woman ought to develop her soul, character, and mind inevitably raised awkward questions about her capacity to handle her expanding civic role. If women were good, competent, and intelligent, then politicians had to admit that some of their contributions might be valuable, at least in Whig circles.

One way to understand this conundrum is to examine antebellum northwestern women's participation in party politics, as opposed to their contributions to reform activism. These two fields of activity overlapped, but they were not identical. Female reformers participated in the civil arena as much as they were able, mostly through petition drives, church meetings, and private exhortation to their friends and neighbors. Women who were active in the antislavery and women's rights movements, however, were less welcome to participate in conventional party politics. Mainstream political party leaders usually shied away from radical reform agendas. On the other hand, if the northwestern wives and daughters of party members wished to participate, they could sometimes create such an opportunity. Historians have explained that Whig women were more likely to become interested, and perhaps even involved, in politics than Democrat women.[63] The Whig *Ypsilanti* [Michigan] *Sentinel*, for example,

[61] *Indiana True Democrat* (Centreville), May 8, 1850. These are the same arguments used by anti-prejudice activists who fought against Black Laws. Several anonymous writers, evidently both men and women, responded to a humorous attack on women's rights, and all were published in the Free Soil *Indiana True Democrat* from May 8 through May 22, 1850. In the same issue, a Quaker lady named Lucy Haughton argued that Old Testament scripture was far more flexible on women's rights.

[62] For the growth of the "ideal of self-improvement," see Howe, *Making the American Self*, 109–113.

[63] Daniel Walker Howe, *What Hath God Wrought: The Transformation of America, 1815–1848* (New York: Oxford University Press, 2007), 606. See also Paula Baker, "The Domestication of Politics: Women and American Political Society, 1780–1920," *American Historical Review* 89, no. 3 (June 1984): 620–47.

roundly condemned those unenlightened "Loco-Focos" who bragged that no women and boys were present at their political rallies. The *Sentinel* declared that Whigs were proud to have *all* the women and boys on their side to "attend their meetings, make banners, march in their processions, and perform any other becoming duty that will cheer on the voting Whigs to the full performance of their duty."[64]

Even so, Democrat women and girls sometimes joined in too, or were at least expected to support Democratic Party ideas. Humorous slogans by some of the Indiana convention delegates, which they published in their convention's biographical chart, casually assumed that their children espoused political views, either harmonizing with or even contradicting their own.[65] Robert Work announced that he had seven sons and one daughter, all "Democrats of the first water," and Jacob Wunderlich boasted about his "five girls and one boy, all Democrats."[66] Democrat George A. Gordon proudly declared that he had two Democratic boys and two Whig girls. At least one Wisconsin Democrat lady, who made no apologies for her political involvement and justified her boldness on the basis of natural rights, wrote a forthright letter to the territorial delegate John Hubbard Tweedy. Mrs. Howe knew that she ought to apologize for addressing Mr. Tweedy – ladies rarely wrote to gentlemen they did not know – but stated she could "give or offer no apology for this address as a female – other than the free republic in which we live & the right which a generous nature has given us all." She was asking Tweedy, who had served as one of the few Whigs in the 1846 constitutional convention, for his influence in obtaining the local post office for her husband. She trusted Tweedy as a man of integrity, but felt that she had to come clean about her politics. "I cannot or will not disguise my principles, or personal feelings so far as regards yourself," she told him bluntly. Moreover, both Mrs. Howe and her husband were "educated democrats," so it would be both "folly & a great deception" to say that she had "aided" Tweedy's election. The truth was, she would be happier if the Wisconsin Territory were represented by an "honest smart democrat." Her letter made it clear that she had strong political opinions and that she considered herself capable of making a contribution to a political contest. She experienced little hesitation in expressing the plain facts of her political allegiance, though she reassured Mr. Tweedy that she and her husband had no objection to him "as a Whig."[67]

Some northwestern women deliberately challenged their husbands' or fiancés' political views, though generally with a tinge of humor or under the

[64] *Ypsilanti* [MI] *Sentinel*, June 20, 1844.

[65] This is a large embellished pink silk chart published by the convention, which shows the name, county, residence, political affiliation, marital status, and humorous personal slogan for each delegate. Constitutional file, Indiana State Historical Society, Indianapolis.

[66] Several of the single delegates announced themselves to be "candidates for Matrimony."

[67] Mrs. W. H. Howe to John Hubbard Tweedy, January 8, 1848, John H. Tweedy Papers, Wisconsin Historical Society, Madison.

shroud of anonymity. The lady who wrote the editorial on women's rights (who had called herself "One of the G'hirls") jokingly confessed, at the end of her letter, that she had to close because her husband "wanted his fixin's" so that he could go off and vote against the homestead exemption, an act that, she presumed, would leave her and her children destitute and homeless in the event of a catastrophe.[68] A young up-and-coming Minnesota Democrat named William Pitt Murray, who would shortly be elected to the state constitutional convention, exchanged lighthearted political correspondence with his Indiana fiancée. She had become rather taken up with Whig activities and confessed sheepishly that she had talked of nothing but politics in the past two months. She worried that William would say she was "quite out of [her] sphere." Yet she also told him she was having "a great deal of fun," and because all her friends were Democrats, was "almost tempted" to change her politics.[69] William did not appear to be unduly concerned, at least not about her political activism. Although he admitted that he felt half inclined "*out of pure spite*" to oppose the idea of ladies "talking politics," that was only because they had never consulted him or elected him as an "honourary member of any of their associations, for the advancement of their 'Rights.' " But because he had an "abiding faith in the success of *lady politicians,*" then so long as Carrie would consider changing her politics (as she had already hinted she might be ready to do) he would be happy to have her "assist [him] to election" in Minnesota. He did observe later that he thought wives should follow their husbands in politics, but that in their turn, husbands should join their wives' religion.[70] Taken together, these letters and editorials suggest that even in a society that objected to women's participation in the public sphere, there was still a degree of toleration for women's contributing to political contests and developing their own ideas.

Of course none of that toleration was ever strong enough to engender approval, let alone sympathy, for women's suffrage rights in the antebellum northwestern state constitutional conventions. If the regional culture was indeed beginning to expand women's public and intellectual sphere, however slightly, that expansion did not reach the convention debates. Constitutions were simply not the place to inscribe shifts in conventional family life. Yet it is possible to observe some slight symptoms of change in the way the constitutional conventions chose to categorize discussions about women's property rights. The delegates always referred to married women's property as a question of "rights," even though they refused to include them in discussions of civic rights, or in conversations about the Bills of Rights. As a result, considerable awkwardness surrounded the problem of assigning the topic to committees.

[68] *Indiana True Democrat* (Centreville), March 6, 1850.

[69] Carrie (Caroline) Conwell to William P. Murray, November 17, 1850, William Pitt Murray and Family Papers, Minnesota Historical Society, St. Paul.

[70] William P. Murray to Carrie (Caroline) Conwell, December 15, 1850, William Pitt Murray and Family Papers, Minnesota Historical Society, St. Paul.

Where the radical reformers wanted to broaden both categories, and perhaps even extend them indefinitely, conservatives wanted such discussions to be strictly limited. They believed that rights had to be sifted and apportioned precisely so that suffrage, court testimony, the right to hold office, and other important privileges would not be extended to persons unworthy or incapable of exercising them properly. Therefore, the state constitutional conventions addressed black men's civil rights in the committees on suffrage and on the Bill of Rights. By contrast, women's property rights were generally subsumed under other discussions, such as homestead exemptions or "miscellaneous subjects." Antebellum American women were citizens of the United States and citizens of their own states, but unlike black or Indian men (especially those whose mixed racial heritage rendered them putatively white), women had no voting rights anywhere after 1807.[71]

Many of the state conventions classified married women as part of the family, and not as separate individuals.[72] This classified the topic as a discussion of constitutional rights (which is what Robert Dale Owen wanted) and not as a traditional, biblically ordained, or common law relationship.[73] But even that failed to resolve the problem satisfactorily. The 1847 Illinois convention charged the Committee on Revenue with the exemption topic, generating further confusion: The committee reported a provision that made each citizen liable for taxes on "his or her property," which complicated married women's common law status. The Committee on Miscellaneous Subjects also proposed that widows should have the right to dispose of all property and should never be deprived of it to pay their late husbands' debts without their consent – but that countermanded the common law rule that widows should inherit one-third of the husband's estate. The Illinois convention did not pass either provision, though the constitution did exempt the "household and kitchen furniture of every house keeper in the state," thereby obliquely protecting women's private property.[74] The 1850 Michigan convention was the only one that explicitly

71 New Jersey women possessed the right to vote between 1797 and 1807. Wyoming passed a state law in 1869 granting women suffrage. See Alexander Keyssar, *The Right to Vote: The Contested History of Democracy in the United States* (New York: Basic Books, 2000), especially chap. 3.

72 The 1850 Michigan, the 1848 Wisconsin, and the Republican side of the 1857 Minnesota conventions considered married women's property rights in their homestead committees. No convention established a separate standing committee on married women's rights. The 1847 Illinois convention, the Democratic chamber of the 1857 Minnesota, and the 1848 Wisconsin, 1844 and 1846 Iowa, and 1850 Ohio conventions discussed married women's property rights in the "miscellaneous subjects" committee. The 1857 Iowa convention did not debate married women's property rights because the state had already passed laws protecting them.

73 Owen fought to have the subject placed under the rights committee, of which he was a member. He believed that married women's property rights ought to be included under the Bill of Rights. He was able to win his point, but in the long run the Indiana convention chose not to include married women's property rights in the constitution. Indiana 1850, 1: 56–57.

74 *Journal of the Convention, Assembled at Springfield, June 7, 1847 ... for the Purpose of Altering, Amending, or Revising the Constitution of the State of Illinois* (Springfield, IL: 1847), 79, 315.

mentioned the subject in a standing committee, titled "Exemptions, Real and Personal, and the Rights of Married Women."[75] This question about committee assignments may appear to be a minor point of taxonomy, but it reveals the principal difficulty these men encountered as they were attempting to make sense of women's rights and roles, and by extension, all northwesterners' rights and duties. The problem about categorizing this specific topic highlights the difficulties of negotiating the conflicting legal and nonlegal codes that governed the lives of northwestern women.

Meanwhile, few newspapers engaged with the subject of married women's property rights in any sustained fashion; nor did many voters write about the issue to their delegates. Inside the conventions this topic only exercised the men at the extremes of the question: that is, the most radical, who advocated both property and civic rights for women, and the most conservative, who vehemently opposed such provisions.[76] Democrats usually dismissed such proposals with anger or with a crude jest. In the 1846 Wisconsin convention, for example, one delegate commented sarcastically that the delegates who supported married women's property rights should go home and attend to the rights of married women there.[77] The moderates thought the question ought to be handled in state legislatures, which is precisely what was happening elsewhere in the nation. Nevertheless, perhaps because of the deeply personal nature of such topics, as in all other debates over controversial subjects, political lines became blurred. Robert Dale Owen, a die-hard Jacksonian Democrat in spite of his radical socialist roots, was the most ardent proponent of women's property rights in all of the northwestern conventions. Wisconsin's Marshall Mason Strong, an anti-slavery Free Soiler committed to black men's political equality, bitterly protested the inclusion of the married women's property rights provision in the 1846 constitution. He loathed that provision so

Judging from the titles of almanacs and guidebooks for young married women, the term "house keeper" referred to women. The vote on the women's property exemption is on page 91 of the *Journal*.

[75] *Report of the Proceedings and Debates in the Convention to Revise the Constitution of State of Michigan, 1850* (Lansing, MI: 1850), 7 (hereafter Michigan 1850). The 1850 Michigan Constitution is also the only one that contains an explicit provision protecting the rights of married women.

[76] A study of the recorded votes in state government documents reveals that the subject engaged rather more discussion than might be inferred from the convention journals and from the capital city newspapers that published the debates. The documentary record on the debates over women's rights, particularly their civic rights, was redacted by both antebellum and mid–twentieth century editors and is therefore incomplete. It appears at first glance that the 1847 Illinois convention never discussed women's rights at all, but the published record of motions and votes in the journal reveals that the committee on homestead exemptions considered the subject, and that there must have been at least some support for women's separate property among Whigs. In 1919 Arthur Chester Cole compiled a detailed record of the 1847 Illinois convention from newspaper sources but decided for unexplained reasons to cut all references to the women's rights debates.

[77] Quaife, *Struggle over Ratification*, 62.

much that he resigned from the convention in a fit of rage and then worked tirelessly to defeat the constitution. Only radical reformers such as Indiana's Robert Dale Owen, Wisconsin's Warren Chase (Figure 6.1), and Ohio's Norton Strange Townshend (Figure 1.2), all of them abolitionists and women's suffrage activists, proposed women's property rights provisions. And as radical reformers did everywhere, they phrased their arguments in natural rights language. Owen, for example, declared women's rights "natural, inherent, inalienable," and bitterly criticized the fact that rights were withheld from half the citizens of Indiana. Women were not represented in the legislature and had "no voice in selecting those who [made] laws and Constitutions for them." Owen wished he had as much confidence as his more conservative colleagues that husbands would be fair to their wives and "careful of their rights," but he was sure that only political equality would protect women's welfare.[78]

Moderate pro–women's property rights delegates – that is, all but the most "visionary" radicals – talked about women's property as a benefit for the whole family. They focused on the homestead as the family's most important asset, and the one that would guarantee the family's survival. They seldom talked about women's property as an abstract right, let alone as the potential for a woman's future wealth. According to most convention delegates, then, married women's property rights belonged in legislation and not in constitutions. The finer details could be worked out as statutes without permanently altering the relationship between men and their wives. For example, Ohio delegate George Holt reported several petitions of "sundry females" from his county asking for state constitutional protections of the rights of married women. Holt – who opposed married women's property rights – explained that because the subject had recently been debated in the Ohio General Assembly and (more to the point) because the legislature would almost certainly shortly pass laws granting to married women the power to dispose of their own property, the committee ought to be discharged from the further consideration of the subject. The legislature would be capable of handling the subject "without jeopardising the unity and mutuality of feeling, affection, and interest, which should always be cherished in the relation of husband and wife."[79]

Because many of the delegates treated the question of women's suffrage rights as a joke (at best) or a social and moral catastrophe (at worst), the reformers never found it an easy topic to navigate. Norton Strange Townshend, an ardent abolitionist, also supported women's rights. His second wife, Margaret (Figure 1.3), was a gifted mathematician and teacher who worked hard to educate herself. It must have been a constant struggle for people such as

[78] Indiana 1850, 1: 462.

[79] Ohio 1850, 1: 338. Almost all of Townshend's pro–women's rights speeches were excised. He did propose an amendment that removed the words "white" and "male" in the description of legal voters. None of the newspaper editorials collected by Milo Milton Quaife details any of Warren Chase's speeches in Wisconsin.

Owen, Chase, and Townshend to keep women's property rights strictly bounded and away from political rights. Even the most ardent supporters of radical reform resigned themselves to the fact that women would never be granted suffrage. They knew they could not win that battle, so they rarely pursued it beyond a simple statement that women ought to have the right to vote for their representatives.[80] Indiana delegate William F. Sherrod, who supported women's property rights but had no remote intention of extending the suffrage to women, humorously reassured his colleagues on other points. He told them not to worry – women would neither vote nor join the state militia:[81]

Delegates who opposed married women's property rights based their arguments on a triad of traditional ideas about women's role in a marriage: first, the biblical unity of the wife and husband; second, the wife's economic and spiritual dependence upon and subservience to her husband; and third, her sexual virtue and attractiveness as legitimate possessions of her spouse. Many worried that granting women any control over their own property would catapult them into a sordid world of trade, lawsuits, and perhaps even financial double dealing: an open invitation to loose virtue and even debauchery. The most explicit such arguments, which arose from Free Soiler and abolitionist Marshall Mason Strong, shocked and dismayed pro–women's rights delegates in Wisconsin. Strong openly declared that granting women any control over their property would instantly turn them into adulteresses and even prostitutes.[82] The most passionate anti–women's rights arguments immediately went to extremes, and the most shocking of those extremes focused on white women's sexuality, a rhetorical strategy also employed in the discussions over black men's voting rights.[83] Strong (Figure 9.2) (who in other contexts could never be considered a traditionalist) stretched the argument to a degree that horrified some of his colleagues. A married woman who controlled her own property, he warned, would be able to make contracts and partnerships promiscuously, "at any hour or place and with anybody."[84]

Strong thus relied heavily on the "slippery slope" logical fallacy – the notion that some small action is dangerous because it might lead to far graver consequences.[85] That said, he based his core argument on the common law right to

80 The subject was probably discussed at length in the 1850 Ohio convention, but because the journal entries for all those debates have been redacted, we have no record of specific speeches.

81 Indiana 1850, 1: 512.

82 This occurred about a year after he tragically lost his wife and children in a fire. See Eugene Walter Leach, "Marshall M. Strong, Racine Pioneer," *Wisconsin Magazine of History* 5, no. 4 (June 1922): 6–7. Speech of Marshall M. Strong, February 5, 1847, in Quaife, *Struggle over Ratification*, 235–39.

83 For a helpful discussion of the emotional nature of conversations about families, see Martha Albertson Fineman, *The Illusion of Equality: The Rhetoric and Reality of Divorce Reform* (Chicago: University of Chicago Press, 1991), 17.

84 Quaife, *Struggle over Ratification*, 239–40.

85 Few of the delegates would have encountered the basic principles of logic in their academy or even college educational careers. American colleges were not teaching courses in logic at this time,

FIGURE 9.2. Marshall Mason Strong (1813–1864), lawyer and newspaper editor, served in the 1844 Wisconsin constitutional convention.
Source: Billings, Racine, Wisconsin. Courtesy of the Wisconsin Historical Society, image number Whi-2445.

protect one's property and one's contracts. Give a married woman the right to control her own property, Strong argued, and she would have to protect that property; that meant, of course, that she had to have access to courts and could sue anyone infringing on her property rights, including her husband. The common law rule of coverture had to remain in place, therefore, in order to prevent women from employing common law rights of protecting private property.

though college-educated men might have read John Stuart Mill, *System of Logic: Ratiocinative and Inductive* (London: 1843), which was widely published in the U.S.

That was precisely the problem. By an odd contrast, it fell to the Virginia-born Indiana delegate William R. Haddon – a conservative Democrat – to discover links among the expansion of property rights, women's intellectual capacities, and their potential civil rights. In his mind, if a constitution were to establish the principle that the "pecuniary interest of women [was] separate and distinct from that of men," then the same constitution inevitably had to establish the right of representation and suffrage. Just as anti-black-rights Democrat delegates had conceded when they denied black men the right to vote, property ownership technically ought to confer civic rights. But they feared that extending civil rights to black men would have deleterious consequences. They also argued that most black men were not ready for such responsibilities. Haddon agreed that it was a simple matter of justice that married women's "separate interest should be represented." But because women had never been adequately prepared, and lacked experience or "leisure" to acquaint themselves with legislative matters or qualifications, they would undoubtedly elect an incompetent legislature. Women reformers made exactly the same claim: Women were only kept in the shadows because they had been denied education and participation. Haddon was, in fact, inadvertently preparing the way for an argument that could open the door for the political and intellectual equality of women. For the moment, these political paradoxes – delegates such as Strong and Haddon, who had such different backgrounds and who held stringently opposite ideas about black rights, but reached similar conclusions on women's property rights – suggest that these thorny issues were becoming more complicated and confused, not amenable to resolution through common law or constitutions. Therefore such arguments would eventually have to come down to personal convictions, passions, and sentiment.[86]

True, women's rights were protected by their fathers and after marriage by virtuous husbands. Yet all acknowledged that some husbands were far from virtuous (just as, by contrast, all acknowledged that some black men were far from worthless). The problem was not to adulterate women's sacred marital ties or to expand black men's civil rights. For conservatives, the mandate was rather to hold bad husbands accountable under the law, and to ensure that responsible black men had whatever rights decency and humanity could grant them, within the boundaries of racial segregation and discrimination. If one extended citizenship rights to any person who was not a white man, one risked wrecking the careful balances and restrictions that kept the family – and society as a whole – functioning properly. Men who argued for black exclusion did so because they feared the "taint" to their white communities. In a similar way, married women's separate property was an especially troubling idea for men who believed that their wives were of one flesh with them. A wife's moral transgressions would inevitably reflect on her husband, so it was of the first importance not to shake the foundations on which traditional marriages were built.

[86] Indiana 1850, 1: 469.

Their opponents bitterly rejected the imputation that northwestern women, if granted control over their property, would succumb to the lure of immorality. The reformers' anger over the insults to northwestern women was not just a chivalrous move to protect the reputations of their wives, sisters, and daughters. In any republic, they believed, individual morality formed the foundation for good government. Both the men and the women who argued for married women's property rights had to find a way to connect individual self-development to individual rights. They did so by focusing on education and religion. The reformers' counterarguments used similar reasoning to the logic they employed in the fight for black suffrage. Wisconsin representative William Singer, one of Marshall Mason Strong's most vehement opponents in the battle over the doomed state constitution, condemned his diatribe as "pernicious." Singer angrily denied that northwestern women were "prone to go astray and to prostitution." Was there nothing that could restrain a good woman within her proper sphere, or that could preserve her chastity from "pollution's soiling embrace but the husband's absolute control over her property?"[87] Employing the methods of legal reasoning, Singer contended that Strong had given no proof of any kind and had not "adduced anything like reason, argument, or common sense in support of his declarations." He clinched this line of reasoning by hinting that Strong's ideas bordered on obscenity: His ugly "declarations," Singer asserted, stood forth "in naked absurdity and deformity without even the gossamer of sophistry to veil their nudity."[88]

For traditionalists such as Strong and Haddon, not only in Wisconsin but also in the other northwestern conventions, the most serious moral problem was that married women's separate property rights conflicted with Protestant Christianity. And as we have seen, many directly identified Christianity with the principles of common law as the only moral foundation for an American state constitution. Now that the reformers had forced the married women's property provision into the Wisconsin state constitution, Strong argued, the charter directly countermanded the biblical injunction "that woman shall leave father and mother and cleave unto her husband and they twain shall be one flesh."[89] Similarly, after the Indiana convention (temporarily) passed a married women's property rights provision, Whig Othniel Clark declared that the provision not only assailed, but sought "by a constitutional enactment" to eradicate, a fundamental idea of Christianity. "The sacred ordinance of marriage and the relations arising out of it ought not to be ... disturbed." In other words, constitutions and statutes should not countermand biblical "ordinances," because

[87] This interchange appeared in the legislative reports after the 1846 Wisconsin convention ended. Quaife, *Struggle over Ratification*, 280.

[88] Quaife, *Struggle over Ratification*, 277. William Singer, who was a state legislator, not a convention delegate, made this speech in response to Marshall Mason Strong. He was referring to the city of Corinth in ancient Greece, where women prostituted themselves at the temple of Aphrodite.

[89] See Hartog, *Man and Wife*. The Scripture quotation is from Matthew 19: 5.

that would be directly counter to the natural order of family life and would only result in the destruction of society.[90] Both activists and traditionalists, then, agreed that changes in married women's property rights would have a powerful and lasting impact on all of northwestern society. Both realized that the battle would have to be fought on a constitutional terrain.

Conservatives who opposed the in-migration of black people had explicitly stated that white citizens possessed an inalienable, if unwritten, right to live in a homogeneous, racially segregated community. In the same way, traditional northwestern husbands believed that they had a right to a well-regulated family life and a submissive, virtuous, cheerful wife. For Indiana delegate James Rariden, women, or at least their physical attractions and their smiles, were a species of property. Women had been divinely bestowed on men to aid in their moral improvement and to supply the adulation necessary to accomplish their civic duties: "Woman was given to man," he explained to his colleagues, to "make up for his deficiencies, to constitute the complement of his existence, to teach him to love everything around him, and to give to everything around him a comely aspect that he may love it." Every husband had an undisputed right of possession to his wife's correct behavior. According to Rariden, men experienced an "absorbing passion" for women's praise and "approving smiles." Indeed, women's disapproval was essentially emasculating. Take away female applause and men had to "lay down their bayonets" and would inevitably become "dispirited and powerless." Farewell, then, to all mighty deeds of daring and high achievement! He explicitly stated that women's smiles and beauty were man's reward in the "great tournament of life."[91]

What did the women think about these arguments? Ladies were present throughout the time this debate was going on in the 1850 Indiana convention. They left no record of their reaction, but evidently they caused a sensation. Some delegates thought that their presence generated "excitement" – even accusing one another of playing to the ladies in the galleries.[92] As far as we know, however, women did not attend any of the other northwestern conventions. Illinois delegate David Davis told his wife that no ladies attended his convention, and there is no indication that women attended any other convention besides the one in Indiana, or ever succeeded in speaking to any of the delegates.[93] At least one lady discussed women's rights privately. Emerine J. Hamilton (Figure 9.3),

[90] Indiana 1850, 1: 469. Dr. Othniel Clark of Tippecanoe was a Whig and later became a Republican; according to his biography, he was briefly interested in the Episcopalian faith but never joined any church. *Biographical Record and Portrait Album of Tippecanoe County, Indiana* (Chicago, 1888), 681–82.

[91] Indiana 1850, 1: 476. See Hartog's discussion of "Wives as Things," in *Man and Wife*, 24.

[92] Indiana 1850, 1: 475. See letter from John Barron Niles to Mary Niles, November 3, 1850, Niles MSS, Lilly Library, Indiana University, Bloomington.

[93] David Davis to Sarah Davis, June 19, 1847, David Davis Papers, Chicago History Museum. I found no evidence in any of the state archives, newspaper editorial columns, or private correspondence that women opposed separate property ownership.

FIGURE 9.3. Emerine J. Hamilton (1810–1889) was a women's rights activist and philanthropist, who founded a public reading room in Fort Wayne, Indiana.
Source: Unknown engraving. Use by permission from the Allen County (IN) Public Library Community Album.

a well-known Indiana activist who fought for both temperance and women's suffrage, evidently discussed the subject with both her husband and her brother. Allen J. Hamilton (Figure 9.4), a delegate to the 1850 Indiana convention was her husband, and William Steele Holman, who also served in the convention, was her brother. Shortly after the 1851 constitution was ratified, both Allen Hamilton and Holman were back in the state assembly. Holman felt obliged to apologize to his sister for his opposition to the married women's property law. He worried that legislation concerning the property of married women could become a "wedge for a separation of the husband & wife's interests in property." In that case, he requested that Allen "pleas say to Mrs. Hamilton I shall be obliged with much regret on her account, to oppose it."[94]

[94] William S. Holman to Allen Hamilton, December 25, 1851, William S. Holman MSS, Lilly Library, Indiana University, Bloomington. Unfortunately the collections do not contain any of Emerine J. Hamilton's letters. Holman did vote for married women's property rights in the convention. Indiana 1850, 2: 1183.

FIGURE 9.4. Allen Hamilton (1798–1864), with his wife, Emerine J. Hamilton, helped to found Fort Wayne, Indiana. Hamilton served as a delegate in the 1850–51 Indiana constitutional convention.

Source: Unknown engraving. Courtesy of the Allen County Public Library Community Album.

Few of the other delegates' wives commented on any of the discussions related to women's rights. The delegates' wives wrote letters that kept their husbands informed of the doings at home, encouraged them in their work, scolded them for not writing, and told them how much they missed them. But they rarely adverted to the political nature of their husbands' work or asked for more information on the constitutional provisions – not even the provisions on women's rights. John Niles's wife, Mary, explicitly asked him for his speeches on women's property rights and thanked him for sending them "under her own name," which suggests that he took the trouble of addressing the pamphlet directly to her rather than to the household. However, beyond praising the speech as "*very* good," and admitting that she found some others "not bad," Mary did not comment on its contents. Nevertheless, of all her surviving letters, this one said more about Niles's activities in the convention than any other she wrote to him while he was away.[95] The American women Tocqueville met, many of whom were the daughters of lawyers, appeared not to dispute or even resent their subordinate position and, according to him, took pride in their submission to their husbands.[96] Judging from the surviving documentation, it is likely that many northwestern women hesitated to express views on the married women's property rights question and might even have agreed with Tocqueville's informants. Indiana conservative James Rariden was positive that women had no remote wish to manage their own property. There was simply no point in endangering the sacred union of marriage for the sake of a reform that "no sane woman" even wanted.[97]

Even so, there must have been at least some mainstream support for women's rights in the Northwest. Women's rights reformers such as L. Maria Giddings (Figure 9.5), daughter of the abolitionist Joshua Giddings, or Betsy Mix Cowles (Figure 9.6) were able to gather a significant number of signatures. Three thousand people signed the petition the Salem convention presented to the state constitutional convention; at that time, Ohio had a population of nearly two million. These petitions serve as the best surviving evidence of mainstream interest in and support for married women's property rights. Just as with pro–black rights petitions, most of the conventions sent the women's rights petitions to committees and rejected a few out of hand. For example, when residents of Stilwell, Ohio, presented a petition from fifteen people that white women older than age eighteen ought to have all the privileges and immunities "enjoyed by the opposite sex," the petition was laid on the table without discussion or referral.[98] On the other hand, the petition from the Salem, Ohio, women's rights conference demanding political equality bore eight thousand signatures. Their petition was referred to committee, perhaps because of the large number of signatures.[99] Although the women's petitions did not receive the opprobrium meted out to petitions for black people's rights, they often

[95] Mary Niles to John B. Niles, January 5, 1851, John Barron Niles MSS, Lilly Library, Indiana University, Bloomington. Niles always voted with Robert Dale Owen on any question or amendment relating to the property rights of married women.

[96] Alexis de Tocqueville, *Democracy in America*, ed. and trans. Harvey Mansfield and Delba Winthrop (Chicago: University of Chicago Press, 2000), 563–77.

[97] Indiana 1850, 1: 474–75.

[98] Ohio 1850, 1: 59.

[99] D. C. Shilling, "Woman's Suffrage in the Constitutional Convention of Ohio," *Ohio Archaeological and Historical Society Publications* 25 (1916): 167–70. See also Nancy Isenberg, *Sex and Citizenship in Antebellum America* (Chapel Hill: University of North Carolina Press, 1998). The *Anti-Slavery Bugle* (Salem, OH), March 30, 1850, announced the Women's Convention. Audretsch, *Salem, Ohio 1850 Women's Rights Convention*, 19.

FIGURE 9.5. L. Maria Giddings (1825–1871) was an antislavery and women's rights activist in Ohio.
"L. Maria Giddings, daughter of Joshua Giddings."
Source: Photograph Image: 9 cm x 5.7 cm; whole page (visible in large image): 22.5 cm x 15.4 cm. Courtesy of the Massachusetts Historical Society.

became the subject of rude hilarity.[100] More petitions appeared in the 1850 Ohio convention, or at least more were entered into the record there, than in

[100] For example, in the 1850 Ohio convention delegate Stilwell presented a petition from fifteen people asking for white women's suffrage rights. Delegate Cook also presented two petitions seeking to liberalize the franchise, one for all people "color or race," and another without regard for sex or color. Yet another petition was referred to committee. Ohio 1850, 1: 59, 75, 164. In response to these petitions one Ohio delegate joked that he did not care whether

FIGURE 9.6. Betsy Mix Cowles (1810–1876), a leader in the abolitionist and women's rights movements, especially in Ohio, where she founded schools and later served as superintendent of the Painesville, Ohio, school system.
"Button with photograph of Betsy Mix Cowles, "Cleveland Society of Ashtabula County People, 11th Annual Picnic, August 27, 1904.""
Source: Campaign Button. Courtesy of the Kent State University Archives.

any other northwestern convention.[101] There was only one petition (assuming the record is correct and complete) in Illinois; none in the 1835 Michigan convention; and Minnesota and Wisconsin did not keep a record of petitions.[102]

the women voted, so long as no black people did. Another delegate joked about whether the legislature should be elected by the people, since, after all, colored people, women, and children were all people. Ohio 1850, 1: 138, 385. Thirty-three women of Clermont County, Ohio, petitioned for married women's property rights, but there is no record of what happened to the petition. Another asking for the same rights was referred to the committee assigned to handle miscellaneous subjects. Ohio 1850, 2: 232. See also, a memorial by a man at Ohio 1850, 2: 556.

101 Ohio 1850, 2: 232.

102 Neither the Minnesota Republican nor the Democrat conventions recorded details of petitions, though members of both conventions mentioned petitions regarding boundaries (1857 Minnesota Republican, 278) and, in the Republican convention, a petition regarding Sabbath breaking (87, 259). In both conventions, various citizens petitioned their side of the convention to expel members of the other side.

After the 1846 Wisconsin convention adjourned, rumors began to circulate that the married women's property provision was causing dissatisfaction among voters. taunch Democrat Edward G. Ryan told newspaper editor Horace A. Tenney that he feared the constitution would fail and that he hoped Tenney would stand by the charter.[103] He knew perfectly well that the "real opposition, although nominally directed against exemptions, married women's rights etc.," was purely motivated by the rather radical antibank provisions.[104] The 1846 constitution would have prohibited state-chartered banks, and Ryan was undoubtedly right; the radical bank provision was the main reason for the failure of the constitution. But granting women property rights was the final nail in the coffin, and Whig Marshall Mason Strong spared no effort to ensure that the constitution would fail in the popular vote. No northwestern state ever instituted explicit constitutional protections for married women's property rights, either before or after the failure of the Wisconsin constitution. Delegates in several subsequent state conventions took the Wisconsin rejection seriously and warned their colleagues that a similar fate would befall them.[105]

Whatever inferences we draw from the delegates' decision to exclude married women's property rights, and to dismiss women's political rights as a tasteless joke, we should not conclude that they considered women social ciphers, intellectually weak, or lacking in decisiveness of character. Private letters reveal a rather nuanced portrait of the relationships between delegates and their wives, or between young midwestern men and their future spouses, whether real or only dreamed of. Above all else, white northwestern men (particularly those in their twenties) wanted good-hearted, useful, pious, "conversable" wives. In 1835 an Indianan confided to his diary that he hoped to meet and marry a lady who was virtuous "to a fault," but well educated and well read. She should be able to understand "Locke & Stewart," for example, and ought to enjoy biographies and works of foreign travels. At the same time, she should raise her children well and be able to regulate servants. But God preserve him from "a woman who makes notes on metaphisics."[106] When a young Democrat named William Conway, then serving as the secretary of the Iowa Territory, wrote to his fiancée, Charity Anne, he thanked her for her "very pretty letter," and complimented her on what a good woman she was. He told her that the only thing lacking in her character was that she had to learn to think for herself and be independent while he was away.[107] The twenty-one-year-old

[103] Alice E. Smith, *From Exploration to Statehood*, vol. 1of *The History of Wisconsin* (Madison: State Historical Society of Wisconsin, 1973), 665–66.

[104] G. Ryan to Horace A. Tenney, February 17, 1847, Horace A. Tenney Papers, Wisconsin Historical Society, Madison.

[105] Illinois 1847, 255, 461, 554.

[106] George A. Bicknell diary entry, February 3, 1835, manuscript diary, George Augustus Bicknell Mss, Lilly Library, Indiana University, Bloomington.

[107] William B. Conway to Charity Anne Kinney, January 4, 1839, William B. Conway Collection, State Historical Society of Iowa, Iowa City. For biographical information, see T. S. Parvin, "The

Ohio schoolteacher Cyrus Clay Carpenter, who was about to move to the Iowa frontier, gave his brother – already living in the territory – an assignment to find a wife for him. He told his brother to "take turns a-courting some half dozen sweet-singing, high-minded, good-natured poverty-stricken pretty [girls]," and have one ready to marry upon his arrival, when he would take her off his brother's hands and "make her [his] companion in arms all the time."[108] Although these men did not explicitly say so, their musings about the ideal wife suggest that such women would have taken the time and effort to develop their characters and talents. Moreover, there was no question that such women would be morally weak or likely to succumb to easy temptation.[109] A wife's virtue, then, included a range of capabilities and qualities beyond her chastity or her religious piety.[110] And as we have seen, when young men dreamed of their ideal wives, they rarely foregrounded their personal attractions. Indeed, some writers expressed suspicion of physical beauty. The Whig *Western Monthly Review* explicitly condemned physical attraction as a basis for marriage because the spouses would soon tire of one another and become "disgusted." Worst of all, such couples would likely suffer incompatible and discordant unions, which the *Monthly* described as "the most insupportable of all human miseries." Which quality would be the more highly regarded in a wife three weeks after marriage: Was it her beauty, or was it her "knowledge, amiability and good sense?"[111]

Women were supposed to pay attention to their qualities of character: not to an artificial physical beauty or even a listless virtue. Both Democrat and Whig newspapers observed that an ideal wife would be natural, sensible, and honest, as to both her personal character and her appearance. The Democrat (later Free Soil) *Muncietonian* carried a humorous story that made it clear that a

Quarrel between Governor Lucas and Secretary Conway," *Annals Of Iowa* 3rd ser., 2, nos. 2–3 (July–Oct. 1895): 221–24.

[108] Cyrus Clay Carpenter to Frederick D. Carpenter, June 2, 1850, Cyrus Clay Carpenter Papers, Historical Society of Iowa, Iowa City. Cyrus Carpenter was probably a Whig in the 1850s. He became the eighth governor of Iowa (Republican). Rick L. Woten, "Carpenter, Cyrus Clay," in David Hudson, Marvin Bergman, and Loren Horton, eds., *The Biographical Dictionary of Iowa* (Iowa City: University of Iowa Press, 2008), 73–74.

[109] There is a significant historiography on the growth of companionate marriage during the eighteenth and nineteenth centuries. For recent works, see Priscilla Pope-Levison, "Separate Spheres and Complementarianism in American Christianity: A Century's Perspective," in Priscilla Pope-Levison and John R. Levison, eds., *Sex, Gender, and Christianity* (Eugene, OR: Wipf and Stock, 2012), 58–79; Lucia MacMahon, *Mere Equals: The Paradox of Educated Women in the Early American Republic* (Ithaca, NY: Cornell University Press, 2012), 116–38; Anthony J. Guerra, *Family Matters: the Role of Christianity in the Formation of the Western Family* (St. Paul, MN: Paragon, 2002), 25–49.

[110] Ruth H. Bloch has explained the shift to personal virtue at the end of the eighteenth century, in *Gender and Morality in Anglo-American Culture, 1650–1800* (Berkeley: University of California Press, 2003). For a discussion of the role of educated wives in marriage, see Solomon, *Company of Educated Women*, 37–39.

[111] "Cincinnati Female Institution," *Western Monthly Review* 3 (April 1830): 508.

man had to talk to a woman in order to discern her personal qualities. One writer declared that he could never learn "so much of woman's character by dancing with her, as by conversing with her at home," where he could observe her behavior "at the table, at the fireside, and in all the trying circumstances of domestic life."[112] A young Minnesotan named Richard Washington told his father about his engagement to Ellen Center, a young lady who was "in education, refinement, and association surpassed by no one." He was taken by her accomplishments, not by her physical appearance. "To me," he explained, "she is of course beautiful, but her beauty is not such as I think the world would particularly admire. She is pious & a most consistant [sic] member of the church. I love her with all the intensity of my nature."[113]

As we saw in an earlier chapter, many of the delegates commented in their letters home that they wanted their wives to cheer up, to be happy, to remain even-tempered. This quality of cheerful sweetness in women was important to northwestern men of all political stripes. While he was working in the convention, Michigan delegate Alpheus Felch often exchanged letters with his wife. He found some of them rather cheerless. Although he was a staunch Democrat, as did many Whigs he blamed her education, particularly the dreary sermons she was hearing in church. He worried that his "dear wife" was not fully appreciating the great gifts bestowed on them by a loving providence, and he exhorted her to be stronger. Should they not rejoice in their health and the "means of gratifying our moral and intellectual powers?"[114] Evidently he expected her to join him in this satisfying endeavor. At least one young northwestern woman defended herself from an accusation of cheerlessness and explained that the changes in her character were due to growth in experience and wisdom. When William Pitt Murray worried that his Carrie had become somber and that her "smiling face, and joyous laugh" had given way to "a more serious countenance, and a less lively disposition," Carrie explained that if she was changed, then it was for the better. She had taken up new duties and faced new challenges (in this case, the death of a friend) and had matured as a result. It had been two years since he last saw her, and he could not expect her "to be the same." Carrie believed that her character remained her own responsibility.[115] A few months later, William apologized for teasing and

[112] *Muncietonian* [IN], May 4, 1850. He was paraphrasing the eighteenth-century British poet William Cowper. William Cowper to Reverend Hurdis, June 13, 1791, in *Life and Letters of William Cowper*, ed. William Hayley, new ed. (London: 1835), 433.

[113] Richard Washington to Lawrence Washington, November 9, 1858, Richard Washington Letters, Minnesota Historical Society, St. Paul. Little is known about Richard Washington's political affiliations; in a different letter to his father he mocked both Democrats and Republicans in the 1857 convention equally, calling both sides together "rather a rare specimen." Richard Washington to Lawrence Washington, August 9, 1857, Richard Washington Letters, Minnesota Historical Society, St. Paul.

[114] Alpheus Felch to Lucretia W. Felch, November 27, 1842, Alpheus Felch Papers, Bentley Historical Library, University of Michigan, Ann Arbor.

[115] William P. Murray to Caroline Conwell, October 13, 1850; Caroline Conwell to William P. Murray, November 17, 1850, both in William Pitt Murray and Family Papers, Minnesota

scolding her, which he felt had occurred on both sides. He readily accepted her "offer of neutrality in regard to *scolding*," providing she agreed to add "some penalty for the one who first violates to pay." But surely she must have misunderstood him, "for it was certainly not [his] intention to dictate or advise." He "most positively disown[ed] any thing of the kind."[116]

Since so little women's correspondence has been preserved, it requires some speculation to parse the cause for this constant call for cheerfulness. Some of these exhortations expressed a hope that the wife would grow emotionally; some sounded a call to self-sacrifice to keep the peace in the home; and some were a rejection of selfish (perhaps undemocratic) languor. Even highly traditional exhortations to wives contained an occasional hint that women could be the equal to men in the intellectual realm. For example, a Democrat Wisconsin newspaper explicitly told women that they had to submit even to an abusive, wicked husband, and that they ought never to raise a differing opinion, "even if they were the equal" intellectually.[117] A Democrat Michigan paper could not quite go so far, but minimized the differences: The editor allowed that women had only "one fibre more in the heart, and a cell less in the brain, than men."[118] Most, however, did expect girls and women to take responsibility for their mental and moral development. The *Michigan Farmer* described the "industrious and happy girl" as useful and buoyant, never idle, nor afraid to "soil her hands or dirty her apron. Such girls would always be loved and respected, the writer told his young readers, whether they were found in "a palace or a hovel." Flirts and "bustle-bound girls" were good for nothing "but to look at; and that is rather disgusting."[119] Democratic Michigan Supreme Court judge Warner Wing frequently wrote to his fifteen-year-old daughter May while she was away at school in Massachusetts, warning her to focus on her education and to refrain from copying the affectations of some "silly girls." She had recently cultivated a "drawling" sound in her speaking that annoyed him. Of all things, he told her, an "affected mouthing girl or woman" was the most "contemptible and repulsive." He hoped that her strength of mind would help her "resist the temptation to display her dress or figure," and he exhorted her to cultivate her mind.[120]

Historical Society, St. Paul. Alvin Hovey often told his wife that she should try to be more cheerful. See, for example, Alvin Hovey to Mary Hovey, October 18, 1850, Hovey Mss, Lilly Library, Indiana University, Bloomington.

116 William P. Murray to Caroline Conwell, February 12, 1852, in William Pitt Murray and Family Papers, Minnesota Historical Society, St. Paul.

117 *Green Bay Intelligencer*, October 31, 1835.

118 *Newark Daily Advertiser* [MI], June 10, 1846. The editorial goes on to explain that the "dew lies longest and produces most fertility ... in the shade."

119 *Michigan Farmer, A Semi-Monthly Journal Devoted to Agriculture* ... 7, no. 1 (April, 1849): 109. This article was widely reprinted throughout the northwest,

120 Warner Wing to May Wing, November 27, 1847, Warner Wing Papers, Bentley Historical Library, University of Michigan, Ann Arbor. May was probably a student at the Young Ladies Institute in Pittsfield, Massachusetts, evidently a fairly conservative school, judging from a commencement address given by a prominent local attorney, James R. Spalding, in 1855, whose

It would have been impossible to educate females, or even render them useful to northwestern society, without considering their moral and intellectual self-development. Northwestern females had a right, even a republican duty to become educated and rational. Academies for the daughters of the prosperous farmers and lawyers, such as the delegates who staffed the constitutional conventions, were now offering, among the more conventional subjects such as deportment, music, and needlework, courses in geography, physics, advanced mathematics, and literature. Northwestern women were meant to be refined – that is, literate, educated, cultured, and neatly turned out, but without succumbing to the lure of antirepublican luxury.

Whig newspapers were more likely to emphasize a woman's inner life, and at least one editorial directly linked the idea of self-development with the notion of "something of her own," hinting at a link to her property rights. The Whig *Alton Telegraph* observed that because a lovely woman could endure great suffering when the time arrived to "lay down her beauty," she needed to find something else to take up.[121] Clearly, this "something else" was meant to be a worthwhile pursuit of knowledge, piety, or skill that would help the lady overcome her sorrow at losing her youthful beauty. Even so, northwestern women and girls had to tread a delicate line between familial competence and personal development. John Barron Niles's wife, Mary, told him that their daughter Leafy was doing so well that she received a "pocket book" at school, but she would still keep her home next term because the tuition was so high and she needed Leafy to help out at home.[122] Most northwesterners, particularly Democrats, still firmly believed that even an educated woman had to stay strictly within her sphere. A Democratic Cincinnati paper, excerpting a speech at the Ohio Female College at Pleasant Hill, declared that the "essential quality" of even an educated woman was that she would refuse to "wrest authority from her husband."[123] Similarly, the Whig *Indiana Signal* praised female orators who presented speeches at a recent exhibition of the Ladies of the Calliopean Society, and declared that their "education should justly fit them for the duties of a wife." Moreover, because their independence was "modestly expressed," they won applause from the audience.[124] Even "Z," the lady who opened this chapter, claimed that women would be happiest within their appropriate spheres. Attitudes about women's capacities were slowly beginning to change, but the notion of enshrining that change in constitutions simply went too far for most northwesterners.

"very soul was sickened at the antagonistic spirit so often displayed in upholding what are called the rights of woman," in *The True Idea of Female Education: An Address Delivered at … The Young Ladies' Institute* (New York: 1855), 4.

[121] *Alton* [IL] *Telegraph*, February 21, 1838.

[122] Mary Niles to John Barron Niles, December 6, 1850, John Barron Niles Mss, Lilly Library, Indiana University, Bloomington.

[123] *Central Christian Herald* (Cincinnati), November 16, 1849.

[124] *Indiana Signal* (Muncie), August 1, 1849.

In the short run, neither side won. The 1850 Michigan constitution was the only one that included a provision that protected married women's property rights, which disappointed the reformers.[125] But within a few years – by 1879 – every northwestern state legislature passed married women's protections, as well as laws that granted them the right to their own earnings.[126] And that annoyed the conservatives.[127] There is an essential contradiction in all this that probably irritates the modern reader: the notion that an adult woman can be recognized as intelligent, virtuous, and competent, but still not be granted control over her own property, let alone the right to vote. These men liked, admired, wanted, and respected women. This was not simply a matter of grandiloquent Fourth of July toasts declaring women's purported and largely fictitious power over men. When the delegates wrote home to their wives, or begged women to marry them, or worried about their daughters' education, they made it clear that they thought women ought to be sensible, intelligent, literate, "conversable," and capable of exercising prudent judgment. The reluctance to redefine family life in state constitutions suggests that changes in the most intimate connections in northwestern society – marriage and parenthood – could not easily be accommodated within such a framework. Still, the traditional links among the common law, Christian convictions about matrimony, and conventional beliefs about women's roles in the household appeared to have loosened somewhat: at least enough to allow northwestern lawmakers to inscribe married women's property rights in their statute books within a decade or two after they refused to do so in their constitutions.

[125] 1850 Mich. Const. of 1850, art. XVI, Exemptions, sec 5. The real and personal estate of every female, acquired before marriage, and all property to which she may afterwards become entitled, by gift, grant, inheritance or devise, shall be and remain the estate and property of such female, and shall not be liable for the debts, obligations or engagements of her husband, and may be devised or bequeathed by her as if she were unmarried.

[126] Hoff, *Law, Gender, and Injustice*, 380 (appendix one: "Married Women's Property Acts, 1800–1900").

[127] Most historians agree that this was primarily a pragmatic move, meant to protect homesteads from debt seizure. The changes occurred incrementally, and, according to Debra Viles and Raquel Fernandez, did little to overturn husbands' control over their wives' personal property. Viles, "Disabilities of Marriage"; Fernández, "Women's Rights and Development"; see also Carole Shammas, "Reassessing the Married Women's Property Acts," *Journal of Women's History* 5, no. 1 (Spring 1994): 9–30.

10

Banks

In 1833, a year after Black Hawk's defeat forced the Sac and Fox to cede 6 million acres near the eastern border of the Iowa Territory, the first trading posts opened along the Upper Mississippi River. Within a few months, young white Indiana farmers rushed in to seize the rich timbered soil for their homesteads. They did so illegally. In their haste to grasp as many acres as they could, they ignored federal land legislation that prohibited squatting on public lands until they had been properly surveyed. More to the point: No money exchanged hands. And because these settlers had no legal right to their homesteads, they risked losing everything, especially if they could not raise the purchase price by the time the federal government was ready to sell the acres to legitimate purchasers.[1] Cash-poor families quickly had to find money to finance their farms, so they borrowed from neighbors, sold their furniture and cooking pots, and even pledged their homes to raise the purchase price. That left them deep in debt to one another, to local merchants, and to speculators.

During the 1820s through the 1850s, as the federal government began to open public lands to white settlement, similar scenes occurred throughout the Northwest. The fertile, cheap public lands drew settlers who hoped to establish prosperous farms and communities and dreamed of participating in national and international cash crop markets. Reports of rich lead and iron deposits attracted mining investors to Illinois, Iowa, and Wisconsin. But the new states lacked the economic or political infrastructure to support these projects.[2] Even

[1] Eastern Iowa was temporarily under the jurisdiction of Michigan Territory (1834–36); then under Wisconsin Territory (1836–38). The Iowa Territory came into existence in 1838. Max Farrand, *The Legislation of Congress for the Government of the Organized Territories of the United States, 1789–1895* (Newark, NJ: 1896).

[2] Malcolm Rohrbough, *The Land Office Business: The Settlement and Administration of American Public Lands, 1789–1837* (New York: Oxford University Press, 1968), 39–45; and Allan G. Bogue, *From Prairie to Corn Belt: Farming on the Illinois and Iowa Prairies in the Nineteenth Century* (Chicago: University of Chicago Press, 1963), 32.

more troubling to the northwestern territories were the two devastating financial panics (1819 and 1837) that occurred just as they were beginning to build their governments and apply for statehood. The resulting economic upheavals forced white settlers and their political representatives to search for practical solutions. Settlers blamed the financial troubles on their inexperienced and profligate territorial and state legislatures, which, they believed, had succumbed to the lure of the powerful international credit and banking systems. These fears compelled the citizens to demand fundamental reforms that would bypass irresponsible legislatures and thwart undemocratic financial institutions in the Northwest. These economic challenges raised a central question in popular sovereignty that hinted at a nascent midwestern populism: Should citizens, acting together and relying on traditional republican values such as representative government, civic virtue, and constitutionalism, have the power to direct their legislators in matters that affected their economic well-being?

Banks and paper money were ferociously divisive topics, which arose in every political arena. They were particularly significant in the conventions that framed state constitutions in the Great Lakes and Upper Mississippi region – an area that combined rapid settlement with a powerful drive to establish modern transportation and market infrastructure. An examination of these state constitutional conventions, and the passionate popular engagement with them, reveals two key developments in the region's commitment to democratic constitutionalism. First, because many northwesterners condemned both banking and paper money as financial, moral, and political failures, they believed that the problem required a constitutional solution. Second, because the problem struck at the heart of northwesterners' conception of themselves as virtuous, self-reliant, independent farmers, they believed they could best judge what would work for them, both ethically and economically. They demanded a say over their political representatives' actions. Such a profound structural change could only be accomplished in the states' constitutions.[3]

As early as 1821, in Bond County, Illinois, a "large and respectable assembly" of angry farmers met at the home of the Revolutionary War veteran Thomas White to foment their own revolution; they had gathered to protest the legislature's pending bill to establish a state bank. Illinois was only three years old, and its economy was already in serious trouble. In the aftermath of the Panic of 1819, every bank in the young state – indeed, most banks throughout the region – had failed. And now, much to the ire of the farmers, the Illinois legislature had decided to establish a new state bank, to be capitalized at the staggering sum of $3 million. How would the nearly bankrupt state treasury raise the capital? The farmers were convinced that because the proposed bank would be "founded on nothing" it would inevitably fail. The

[3] For a discussion of the importance of democratic wealth distribution in antebellum America, see James L. Huston, *Securing the Fruits of Labor: The American Concept of Wealth Distribution, 1765–1900* (Baton Rouge: Louisiana State University Press, 1998).

risk was too great; failure would endanger their livelihoods as well as ruin the state's financial reputation. The Illinois legislature had determined that a state bank was necessary to attract eastern and foreign investors and fund roads and river improvements. According to the voters, however, the lawmakers were overstepping their responsibilities. Taking matters into their own hands, the Bond County citizens drafted resolutions that reminded the Illinois assembly of the privilege and duty of citizens to protest any measure that threatened their rights or welfare. And an unreliable bank, even if owned and controlled by the state, threatened the well-being of every Illinois citizen.[4]

Most scholars have treated the history of private and state banks as economic or political history rather than as constitutional history. Historians of banking, particularly in the Northwest, have reexamined the master narrative about the unreliability of antebellum banks and bank notes. Jill M. Hendrickson and Howard Bodenhorn have challenged the traditional focus on bank failures and panics in the Northwest and stressed the positive role banks played in economic development.[5] Although historians agree that banks failed throughout the nation – particularly in the Northwest – during the antebellum decades, they also point out that banks fulfilled their basic functions of monetizing the economy and encouraging development and investments. Recent studies have shown that wildcat banking and unstable paper currency largely disappeared after state legislatures passed laws making establishing legitimate banks easier.[6] Still, the widespread loathing of speculators, banks, and paper notes engendered bitter political fights throughout the region until the early twentieth century. Robert C. McMath Jr. and Jeffrey Ostler have observed that the mistrust of banks would have a long life in the Northwest, and it formed the basis for later cooperative agricultural movements such as the Grange and the Farmers'

[4] *Edwardsville* [IL] *Spectator*, February 13, 1821; Benjamin J. Klebaner, *American Commercial Banking: A History* (Frederick, MD: Beard Books, 2005), 49–51; and Hubert Schmidt, "Farming in Illinois a Century Ago as Illustrated in Bond County," *Journal of the Illinois State Historical Society* 31 (June 1938): 155–58.

[5] Jill M. Hendrickson, *Regulation and Instability in U.S. Commercial Banking: A History of Crises* (New York: Palgrave Macmillan, 2011), 21–25 and Howard Bodenhorn, *A History of Banking in Antebellum America: Financial Markets and Economic Development in an Era of Nation-Building* (New York: Cambridge University Press, 2000), 12, 16–19. For mixed feelings on banks in early Ohio, see Donald J. Ratcliffe, *Party Spirit in a Frontier Republic: Democratic Politics in Ohio 1793–1821* (Columbus: Ohio State University, 1998), 221–23.

[6] John A. Dove, Gary M. Pecquet, and Clifford F. Thies, "The Michigan Free Bank Experience: Wild Cat Banking or Interference with Contract?" (paper presented at the Annual Meeting of the Economic and Business History Society, Grand Rapids, MI, April 2009); Bray Hammond, *Banks and Politics in America from the Revolution to the Civil War* (Princeton, NJ: Princeton University Press, 1957), 249–64; Hugh Rockoff, "American Free Banking before the Civil War: A Re-Examination," *Journal of Economic History* 32 (March 1972): 417–20; Arthur J. Rolnick and Warren E. Weber, "Inherent Instability in Banking: The Free Banking Experience," *Cato Journal* 5 (Winter 1996): 877–90; John Joseph Wallis, "The National Era," in Price Fishback, ed., *Government and the American Economy: A New History*, (Chicago: University of Chicago Press, 2007), 148–87.

Alliance. Midwestern farmers feared that monopolies threatened traditional independence and democracy.[7] The purpose of this chapter, however, is not to engage in an analysis of the potentially destructive nature of banks and paper money but rather to discover the long-term impact these fears had on ideas about good government and virtuous citizenship.

After 1800 settlement in the Great Lakes and Upper Mississippi region surged from 51,007 in 1800 to 1,470,018 in 1830. The region's population doubled to 2,924,728 in 1840, then expanded to 4,523,260 in 1850. Rapid settlement outran both laws and infrastructure. Farmers, speculators, and mining entrepreneurs grabbed millions of acres before the federal government had "extinguished" Indian land rights or established local land offices, much less a territorial government. Fur trading became well established in the region from 1816 to 1832, but after Indians were forced westward, the fur trade lost its dominant place in the northwestern economy. In the first quarter of the nineteenth century, territorial and state legislatures had to charter every bank through a private law (a law that concerned a specific individual or corporation, rather than a statute aimed at the public's general welfare). Private laws supposedly gave the legislature the power to oversee and control banks, but because lawmakers could be bribed or persuaded by special interests, citizens began to believe that private laws encouraged monopolies and conferred "aristocratic" privileges on wealthy speculators.[8] And because many of those speculators and investors lived a thousand miles to the east, or even overseas, they were mistrusted as much as they were courted.

Privately chartered banks (owned by private individuals and corporations) and state banks (chartered though not owned by states) served to monetize the local economy by printing "notes" and lending money to investors or speculators. Paper notes functioned as a medium of exchange but were not legal currency and could not be used to pay taxes. Still, a farmer could not purchase a mule, let alone thousands of acres of timbered farmland, without some kind of circulating medium. Metallic currency was scarce; the first communities managed on a barter economy. But barter could not pay for land or build roads. Farmers, fur traders, miners, merchants, and mill owners demanded access to banks and money in order to build their businesses; buy plows, livestock, and seed; and borrow more money to buy more land. Investors and their agents

[7] John M. McFaul, *The Politics of Jacksonian Finance* (Ithaca, NY: Cornell University Press, 1972), 211; Daniel Feller, *The Jacksonian Promise: America, 1815–1840* (Baltimore: Johns Hopkins Uinversity Press, 1995), 40–43; Robert C. McMath Jr., *American Populism: A Social History 1877–1898* (New York: Hill & Wang, 1993), 19–49; and Jeffrey Ostler, *Prairie Populism: The Fate of Agrarian Radicalism in Kansas, Nebraska, and Iowa, 1880–1892* (Lawrence: University Press of Kansas, 1993), 1–2.

[8] John D. Haeger, *The Investment Frontier: New York Businessmen and the Economic Development of the Old Northwest* (Albany: State University of New York Press, 1981), 62; and Robert M. Ireland, "The Problem of Local, Private, and Special Legislation in the Nineteenth-Century United States," *American Journal of Legal History* 46 (July 2004): 271–99.

needed access to money to build canals and railroads to move goods and mail down the river, to the eastern states, or across the Atlantic Ocean.[9]

Early northwestern territorial legislatures authorized a few legitimate banks, as well as private corporations such as fire insurance companies, that carried on banking functions. State oversight was minimal, and most of the early banks disappeared within a few years. In 1811, just as public lands came on the market, the charter of the Bank of the United States expired. Federalists fought hard to recharter the bank, but they did not succeed until 1816. During those years, neither the federal government nor territorial assemblies exercised much control over the privately owned banks that jumped up in the new territories. Ohio, Indiana, and Illinois boasted a few state-chartered banks, which were authorized to print notes, take deposits, and grant real estate loans. Early territorial and state laws provided for basic oversight and established regulations for banks, such as minimum capitalization, boards of overseers, and individual liability. But legislatures found it nearly impossible to police private banks and few banks could show that they owned enough metallic currency to pay on demand. The 1819 panic destroyed banks throughout the region, in turn causing widespread foreclosures and inflation.[10]

As the region began to recover from the panic by the early 1820s, white settlers, northwestern state legislatures, mining entrepreneurs, and eastern investors threw themselves headlong into reckless overspending – on land, on investments in canals, and on chimerical towns that came and went only on paper. The spirit of speculation encouraged land-hungry, overconfident settlers. Henry Howe deplored the "defaults of people who bought too much land" and could not manage their vast holdings. The land sales and importation of goods from the eastern states and overseas "constituted an immense and an eternal drain of the circulating medium, across the mountains." The new states lacked money, financial institutions, manufacturers, and interstate commerce. The northwestern economy had not yet been sufficiently developed to put sound money back into circulation. "Ours was a population of buyers," Howe lamented. And the chronic demand for money generated more local banks.[11]

9 Matthew Jaremski, "Free Bank Failures: Risky Bonds versus Undiversified Portfolios," *Journal of Money, Credit and Banking* 42 (Dec. 2010): 1567; and Edward Pessen, *Jacksonian America: Society, Personality, and Politics*, rev. ed. (Urbana, IL: Illini Books, 1985), 122–48; and Hammond, *Banks and Politics*, 93, 272.

10 Jerry W. Markham, *From Christopher Columbus to the Robber Barons (1492–1900)*, vol. 1 of *A Financial History of the United States* (Armonk, NY: M. E. Sharpe, 2002), 126–29; Hammond, *Banks and Politics*, 605–11; McFaul, *Jacksonian Finance*, 22; Bodenhorn, *History of Banking*, 40–44; Murray N. Rothbard, *The Panic of 1819: Reactions and Policies* (New York: Columbia University Press, 1962; repr., Auburn, AL: Ludwig von Mises Institute, 2007), 19–24; and Arthur J. Rolnick and Warren E. Weber, "Banking Instability and Regulation in the U.S. Free Banking Era," *Quarterly Review* 9 (Summer 1985): 3.

11 Donald R. Adams, "The Role of Banks in the Economic Development of the Old Northwest," in David C. Klingaman and Richard K. Vedder, eds., *Essays in Nineteenth Century Economic History: The Old Northwest*, (Athens: Ohio University Press, 1975), 218 and Henry Howe,

The demand for money also – paradoxically – triggered a willingness to take immense risks. Two brothers wrote to the *Iowa Standard* in November 1840, calling themselves "Poor Richard and His Brother." The letter may have been written by Lott Thornton and his younger brother, Err, both of whom had settled in Muscatine around 1834.[12] Explaining that they had no way of raising funds, the brothers had to borrow money at 25 to 75 percent interest and pledge everything they owned to repay the debt. They had taken immense risks. But they remained confident that Iowa's productive farmland would some day become valuable, especially since their acres lay so near the Mississippi River. Muscatine County had been a depot for steamships since 1836, so they would easily be able to move their wheat, corn, oats, and flax to market.[13] But for now they had hazarded their livelihoods on their future wealth and were barely surviving.[14] Iowa land was among the cheapest and most fertile in the Old Northwest, but because the young pioneers were considered a poor credit risk, speculators sold the land at exorbitantly high interest rates, ranging upward from 40 percent – the highest in the nation.[15] And as did many other settlers in the Old Northwest, the Thorntons had pledged themselves to buy far too much land. If they had only had time to render their acres productive – that is, if they could have raised the crops quickly enough, shipped them downriver to other Iowa settlements, St. Louis, or even New Orleans, then they could have become prosperous beyond the dreams of most western settlers. But they could not afford to wait. If they wished to retain their footing in the territory, they would have to sell off enough land to pay their debts in order to "keep off the sheriff."[16] For men like Lott and Err Thornton, however, who would have been in their late teens or early twenties during the 1819 Panic, the answer was not to flinch from risk. By the time they reached Iowa around 1834, the national economy was experiencing a financial resurgence. With their beautiful fertile lands, so close to the Mississippi, confidence in the new western territories ran high. True, the new settlements were still far too raw to allow the farmers to make good on their investments. But the abundance of cheap land, even at exorbitant interest rates, swept away caution.

Historical Collections of the Great West, Containing Narratives of the Most Important and Interesting Events in Western History ... (Cincinnati: 1854), 257.

[12] According to the 1836 Wisconsin territorial census, Lott and Err Thornton were the only two adult brothers who settled in Muscatine County, Iowa Territory, before 1840. Eleanor B. McCleary, Wisconsin Territorial Census Transcription, State Historical Society of Wisconsin Archives Division, Microfilm reel 1, p. 1.

[13] Irving B. Richman, ed., *The History of Muscatine County Iowa, from the Earliest Settlements to the Present Time* (Chicago: S. J. Clarke Publishing, 1911), 1: 235–36.

[14] Bogue, *From Prairie to Corn Belt*, 29, 33.

[15] Stanley Lebergott, "'O' Pioneers': Land Speculation and the Growth of the Midwest," in *Essays on the Economy of the Old Northwest*, 44–50.

[16] Howard H. Preston, *History of Banking in Iowa* (Iowa City: State Historical Society of Iowa, 1922), 3; *Iowa Standard* (Iowa City), November 27, 1840.

From the 1810s through the mid-1850s, so-called wildcat banks (quasi-legitimate, often unchartered banks) set up shop throughout the western states, usually near trading posts. The nickname referred both to the remote location (near wildcats) and to their dangerous, even rapacious nature. Some were so unsound they were little better than counterfeiters. Indeed, some counterfeit bank notes were more stable than those backed only by debts and insufficient or even fraudulent capitalization.[17] Frank Allen, a prosperous western merchant who dealt in everything from a "silk dress to a goose yoke," explained that after the Iowa assembly prohibited banks in 1848, the territory became a dumping ground for "all sorts of stump tail red dog wildcat notes issued by anybody who could get them engraved and printed ... issued from some isolated inaccessible place and sent for circulation as far away as possible." He remembered visiting one of those banks in a logging camp in the thick woods near the eastern shore of Lake Michigan. "It was about eight feet square, eight feet high, made of rough boards, flat roof, with one small sliding window, a plain board shelf on which the notes were signed, [and] a small door over which in red chalk was the name of the bank."[18] The proprietors of such banks traveled to the backcountry, and, with whatever capital they had taken along, immediately bought up as much public land as they could, and then resold it to settlers, merchants, or traders, at a considerable profit – at whatever interest they could charge – often at least 25, or 40, sometimes as high as 70 percent.[19] Legitimate banks, by contrast, were chartered by legislative action and were usually subject to some oversight, at least in the larger towns. Some state banks functioned responsibly and served their communities well for decades.[20]

At first the settlers snatched up the paper notes, but as the money depreciated, it drove the most trustworthy currency (Mexican silver dollars or secure notes from New York or Pennsylvania banks) out of circulation. Bank debts were added to land debts. Reprehensibly, bankers then used these debts as collateral to finance more loans and investments, thus destabilizing the value of both land and money. Indeed, the practice of using debts as collateral, which would continue to plague the northwestern states for decades, became one of the principal reasons convention delegates sought to control privately chartered banks and their unstable paper notes. Michigan Democrat John D. Pierce, a convention delegate, roundly condemned collateralized debts as a means "to rob labor of its reward,

[17] Stephen Mihm, *A Nation of Counterfeiters: Capitalism, Con Men, and the Making of the United States* (Cambridge, MA: Harvard University Press, 2007), 160.

[18] Quoted in Lorenzo F. Andrews, *Pioneers of Polk County, Iowa and Reminiscences of Early Days* (Des Moines, IA: Baker-Trisler Co., 1908), 1: 57; Larry Allen, *The Global Financial System, 1750–2000* (London: Reaktion Books, 2001), 103.

[19] See John Jay Knox, *History of Banking in the United States* (New York: Bradford Rhodes & Co., 1903).

[20] See Bodenhorn, *History of Banking*, chap. 2.

by enabling persons to bank on a debt and nothing but a debt." A legitimate basis, he proclaimed, "it has none."[21]

By the mid-1830s, selling land and platting new towns were in full swing in Ohio, Indiana, and Illinois; immigrants were pouring in and investors vied to fund canals, roads, and railroads. The economic future of the Northwest seemed assured. Still, Democratic opposition to the Bank of the United States and the high failure rate of local banks in the region combined to create a profound suspicion of all corporations, especially those that had the right to print paper money and lend to speculators. In July 1836, President Andrew Jackson launched his war against the Second Bank of the United States (the first B.U.S. had expired in 1811 and was rechartered in 1816), directing Secretary of the Treasury Levi Woodbury to issue the Specie Circular forbidding the sale of public lands for paper notes (or paper not backed by specie); a month later, Jackson removed the federal deposits from the bank. The resulting devaluation of paper money triggered widespread inflation. Wheat, corn, and hog prices whirled out of control. Vital transportation projects such as canals, plank roads, and river improvements lost funding and became hopelessly stalled. As a result, crops rotted in barns. Settlers who had hazarded their possessions for a chance to become prosperous landowners found themselves, within a few years, at the brink of bankruptcy.[22]

The 1837 panic hit particularly hard in the northwestern territories. Eastern and overseas investors – who had recently fallen over each other to invest in land, transportation projects, fictional towns, and mortgages for farms that could never be cultivated, let alone paid for – called in loans or attempted to cash in their paper notes. Banks throughout the nation suspended specie payment (that is, refused to cash in paper notes for metal coins), thereby demolishing the value of paper money everywhere. By the 1840s, every bank in Illinois, Michigan, and Wisconsin had failed. During those difficult years, northwesterners lost their remaining confidence in banks and paper money. They now expressed profound indignation against the systems that had seduced them into overspending and overborrowing. And because legislatures chartered these banks through private legislation rather than public laws that would benefit the entire community, northwesterners considered the financial catastrophe a violation of their fundamental rights as American citizens.[23]

[21] John D. Pierce quoted in *Report of the Proceedings and Debates in the Convention to Revise the Constitution of the State of Michigan, 1850* (Lansing, MI: 1850), 560 (hereafter Michigan 1850) and Warren E. Weber, "Banknote Exchange Rates in the Antebellum United States," (working paper 623, Research Department, Federal Reserve Bank of Minneapolis, MN, 2002), 3.

[22] James Roger Sharp, *The Jacksonians versus the Banks: Politics in the States after the Panic of 1837* (New York: Columbia University Press, 1970), 46–54. For a discussion of the role of agricultural depletion and economic panics, see Steven Stoll, *Larding the Lean Earth: Soil and Society in Nineteenth-Century America* (New York: Hill & Wang, 2002), 41–49.

[23] Carter H. Golembe, "State Banks and the Economic Development of the West, 1830–44" (PhD diss., Columbia University, 1952), 4; Sharp, *Jacksonians versus the Banks*, 18.

What rendered this breach of trust especially odious, however, was that from the mid-1820s through the early 1840s, northwestern legislatures had become infatuated with colossal transportation projects. The widespread enthusiasm for new technology, the boundless energy for growth, and the confidence that they would become the principal suppliers to eastern and transatlantic markets for corn, wheat, and pork created a concatenation of risks. Although most state budgets were severely constrained, the members of the state assemblies, just like the people they represented, had taken immense financial gambles. Indiana's 1836 Mammoth Internal Improvement Act increased the state debt by $10 million. Northwestern state debt soared from a few million dollars in 1820 to more than $200 million in 1841.[24] State budgets, which lacked cash flow, had to fund internal improvements through a combination of federal land grants, loans from New York and Pennsylvania banks, and European investments. The British investment firm and bank Baring Brothers & Co. was primarily responsible for British investments in transportation networks in the northwestern territories and states. By 1832 Baring had established an office in Liverpool to finance American cotton trading and transportation projects; four years later, the firm owned more than $2 million in railroad stocks in the Baltimore and Ohio Railroad Company alone. According to Augustus J. Veenendaal, billions of dollars of gold from France, the Netherlands, and Germany flowed into the northwestern American states to fund early railway systems. If the northwestern states repudiated their debts, European and East Coast investors would refuse to invest further funds. The repeated threats of debt repudiation exacerbated the popular perception that legislatures were not fulfilling their ethical obligations to their citizens.[25] And now, as the region was on the brink of entering international markets, the states would need a modern, efficient transportation infrastructure and sound relationships with foreign investors. This was not the time to imperil the region's ethical reputation.

Northwesterners recognized that they stood at the crossroads of a modern, enlightened, prosperous America; indeed, the region's well-being would play a central role in driving the national economy. After Andrew Jackson, who opposed federally funded transportation measures, left office in 1836, Congress supported northwestern transportation projects through land grants. Those grants were only available to states that had already initiated road,

24 Wallis, "National Era," 177; and John Joseph Wallis, "Constitutions, Corporations, and Corruption: American States and Constitutional Change, 1842 to 1852," *Journal of Economic History* 65 (March 2005): 216.

25 See Philip Ziegler, *The Sixth Great Power: A History of One of the Greatest of All Banking Families, the House of Barings 1762–1929* (New York: Knopf, 1988); Francis W. Hirst, *The Credit of Nations: With Special Reference to the Debts of Great Britain, Germany, France, and the United States*, 61st Cong., 2nd sess., 1910, S. Doc. 579, 172; Augustus J. Veenendaal, "European Investment in American Railways," in Ralf Roth and Günter Dinhobl, eds., *Across the Borders: Financing the World's Railways in the Nineteenth and Twentieth Centuries* (Burlington, VT: Ashgate, 2008), 165; and Bodenhorn, *History of Banking*, 44.

canal, and river improvement projects, payable from their own treasuries. In 1844, Illinois Whig William S. Wait feared that the loss of transportation networks would prevent the state's economic recovery. The legislature's undertaking risky investments in canals and railroads did not mean that all internal improvements were dangerous. Wait dismissed such fears as "totally fallacious." But if Democrats refused to permit legislatures to establish banking corporations and finish canal and railroad projects, then all hope of repaying the crushing state debts would have to be abandoned.[26]

Whigs knew that banks were necessary to economic development. But they also recognized the inadequacy of laws regulating their functions and note issue. For Democrats, economic institutions such as banks and corporations appeared to assault traditional republican values directly and conspired to deprive farmers of their rights. Private charters had given the state legislature some supervisory function and power, but because legislatures possessed no real authority over law-enforcement personnel (who were scarce at best), the charters were hard to enforce and carried the taint of bribery and corruption. Matthew Jaremski has argued that private bank charters depended equally on political influence and personal resources. Taking risks was necessary, but the dividing line between risk and ethics became increasingly harder to discern. Privately chartered banks, owned by a corporation of stockholders, were supposed to retain a percentage of metal coins to cash in their paper notes on demand. But because of insufficient capitalization, most early banks could rarely redeem all their notes. As a result, the value of bank notes often varied wildly from one county to the next.[27] This instability and lack of control were nerve-wracking for farmers who needed a supple money supply.

Any circulating medium, while necessary to moving goods and funding transportation projects, would have to be monitored and controlled by the people who held the deepest stake in the region's economy. Commercial newspapers carried weekly reports on the value of bank notes, and businessmen in northwestern towns met – usually on Mondays – to evaluate paper money. The farther a bank note traveled from its point of origin, the harder it was to assess. In the popular perception, volatile paper currency created rich pickings for money brokers far from commercial centers. Brokers principally purchased bank notes or other paper that could be used as a circulating medium. The notes would then be loaned – usually out of state – or cashed in at their point of origin, always at a profit to the broker. In cities such as Chicago, men who discounted (assessed the value of) paper notes consulted weekly monetary

[26] Carter Goodrich, *Government Promotion of American Canals and Railroads, 1800–1890* (New York: Columbia University Press, 1960), 178; Laurence J. Malone, *Opening the West: Federal Internal Improvements before 1860* (Westport, CT: Greenwood Press, 1998), 4–6; and William S. Wait to James B. Woollard, December 17, 1844, James B. Woollard Papers, Abraham Lincoln Presidential Library, Springfield, IL.

[27] McMath, *American Populism*, 8–10; Jaremski, "Free Bank Failures," 1565–87; and Weber, "Banknote Exchange Rates," 1–3.

bulletins called "note reporters" and kept the value of paper notes on a stable footing. But in rural areas, especially in the new northwestern states, settlers feared and hated note brokers.[28] Backwoods "discount brokers" who assessed, and inevitably reduced, the face value of paper notes operated without any vestige of financial backing. Surviving on the fringes of the region's economy, rural note brokers rarely consulted the real worth of bank notes in other states, or even in adjacent counties; their shortsighted and irresponsible exploits could undermine the financial well-being of a local community. According to Warren E. Weber, after 1837, when states began to pass general banking laws that permitted private entrepreneurs to establish banks without state charters, wildcat banks no longer posed a serious threat. But because brokers evidently decided the value of bank notes – which they never priced at face value – at whim, they were nevertheless perceived as the most destructive players in the northwestern economy. The Indianapolis judge Napoleon B. Taylor condemned brokers as "those vultures and jackals of the monetary world, who leave the purses of the poor unfortunates who fall into their hands as clean as do the aforesaid birds and beasts of pray [sic], the bones of the unburied slain on a forsaken battle field." Since even the best state money was not worth "more than ... 50 or 85 cents to the dollar," the brokers reaped an abundant harvest. They could buy the paper for a song and leave the farmers, mechanics, and artisans to foot the bill. Taylor considered the entire system dishonest. And ineffectual state law meant that instead of its being a "terror to evil-doers," the evildoers had become a "terror to the law." Because brokers could dismantle their businesses and disappear quickly, state governments were powerless to restrain them.[29]

Still, even the riskiest paper money was vital to buying, selling, borrowing, and lending. Many northwesterners considered short-term, accessible paper notes relatively safe for face-to-face interactions. The best way to cope with paper money was to rid oneself of bad notes as quickly as possible. This morally questionable practice also led to overspending and overcommitting: for example, using dubious money to pay for or claim more land than a family could cultivate. The Ohio congressman Elisha Whittlesey worried that a "feverish excitement" pervaded every kind of business and "caused overtrading ... and overdoing" throughout the Northwest. Indeed, Whittlesey believed that "a burning desire to get rich at once, by a splendid dash, [was] one of the

[28] Gary Gorton, "Reputation Formation in Early Bank Note Markets," *Journal of Political Economy* 104 (April 1996): 355 and Don M. Daily, "The Early Development of the Note-Brokerage Business in Chicago," *Journal of Political Economy* 46 (April 1938): 202–17.

[29] Warren E. Weber, "Banknote Prices in the United States Prior to 1860" (working paper 629, Research Department, Federal Reserve Bank of Minneapolis, MN, 2003), 1–3; Dove, Pecquet, and Thies, "Michigan Free Bank Experience," 18–23; G. S. Callender, "The Early Transportation and Banking Enterprises in the States in Relation to the Growth of Corporations," *Quarterly Journal of Economics* 17 (November 1902): 145; and Napoleon B. Taylor to Laurel Summers, December 25, 1854, Laurel Summers Papers, State Historical Society of Iowa, Des Moines.

demoralizing evils of the day."[30] The problem extended beyond ineffective laws and lack of enforcement resources. Northwestern citizens now recognized that they would have to take matters into their own hands and tell their state legislatures, as the Bond County citizens had, precisely what kind of legislative interference they would tolerate and what went too far.

Northwestern debts had spiraled out of control, driven by the availability of abundant, fertile land as well as the discovery of lead, iron, and salt deposits. By the early 1840s, overwhelming debts permeated every level of society. Families owed for their households and land, banks were in debt to creditors, and state treasuries had borrowed from eastern and overseas investors. The combination of debts, crop failures, deficit spending in state legislatures, the collapse of cotton prices on the international commodities market, and the British economic problems proved disastrous. Eight states and the Florida Territory defaulted in the mid-1840s. The list included three Old Northwest states: Indiana, Illinois, and Michigan. After 1836, following Jackson's lead, hard-money (gold or silver), antibank Democrats took a radical line not only against the Second Bank of the United States but against state-chartered banks as well. And everyone – even probank Whigs – feared and mistrusted unstable, poorly capitalized wildcat banks.[31] Ethical democratic self-government, northwesterners feared, was now in its death throes. It would not withstand the external threat from corrupt economic systems and the internal threat of moral recklessness. If individual citizens failed to honor the rule of law, their freewheeling, enthusiastic, energetic society would go off the rails. The people had to find a way to balance courageous risk taking with moral self-control – on their own farms, in their businesses, and in their state governments.

State constitutional conventions that deliberated during the 1830s to the mid-1850s fought bitterly over paper money, banks, and the private charters that brought these hated institutions into existence. Because of the widespread mistrust of money-printing corporations, delegates who opposed all banks had the easiest time gaining the floor of the convention hall. They bounced up from their seats the moment a convention opened or interrupted other discussions, in order to let the voters know that their interests were being represented. But a coalition of moderate Democrats and Whigs outnumbered them. Despite the parties' profound political differences, and despite internal Democratic Party divisions, the constitutional convention debates revealed a clear moral consensus: Constitutions had to shore up the citizens' reverence, as one Ohio voter told his delegate, "for the government and for law & order." Respect for government, he believed, had been severely tested by the abundance of worthless money, which tempted decent citizens to engage in questionable financial practices. On a more pragmatic level, governments also had to defend citizens

[30] Elisha Whittlesey to Roger M. Sherman, November 15, 1836, Isaac Bronson Papers, New York Public Library.

[31] Sharp, *Jacksonians versus the Banks*, 25–27.

from the onslaught of disreputable business practices and flimsy out-of-state paper money. Hard-money Democrats may have believed that destroying banks would be good for the northwestern soul, but most were also forced to admit that removing banks would leave the territories and states helpless in the storm of paper notes from neighboring states. John Edwards, a Whig delegate to the 1857 Iowa constitutional convention, explained that even though it was illegal to print money in Iowa, there were just as many paper notes in the state as anywhere else. He reminded his colleagues that prohibition simply encouraged disrespect for the law. A sound circulating medium, carefully supervised and controlled, would "drive out ... this worthless trash that we now have among us."[32] Likewise, the Wisconsin Democrat Joseph Bowker observed that in spite of his lifelong opposition to banks and paper money, he did not see how citizens living near state borders could avoid taking "foreign" (out-of-state) money. If one wished to participate in interstate and interregional trade, one would have to erect a "[Chinese] wall of separation." Even worse, banning all paper money would invite deliberate contravention of state laws. When settlers trampled upon such dead-letter laws, they would "bring the whole constitution into contempt."[33]

This core dilemma plagued northwestern farmers and miners: Popular sovereignty, which required agricultural and economic independence, could also undermine law and order. Respect for laws was more than setting up regulations and ensuring that they would be followed; it was a restoration of simple republican virtue. Foreshadowing the late nineteenth-century Populist Movement in the region, northwesterners considered nonproducing aristocrats who became wealthy at the expense of the plain folk the worst offenders. Bankers who flouted the public trust were not just criminals – they were sinners. The loathed Miners' Bank of Dubuque, Iowa – an institution that garnered national infamy for its defalcations and its presumed oppression of hardworking Iowa lead miners – became a byword for the moral corruption of citizens by a monopolistic corporation.

Lead miners had arrived in northwestern Iowa by the early 1830s, and the territorial legislature had chartered the Miners' Bank in 1836 to serve the zinc and lead mining business in Dubuque. The bank languished in a precarious state for much of its existence. By 1845 two die-hard Democrats in the territorial council watched its lingering end with interest. H. M. Shelby told his

32 McFaul, *Jacksonian Finance*, 57–58; William Trimble to John A. Smith, January 11, 1843, John Armstrong Smith Papers, 1816–1893, Ohio Historical Society, Columbus; and John Edwards quoted in W. Blair Lord, *The Debates of the Constitutional Convention of the State of Iowa, assembled at Iowa City, Monday, January 19, 1857* (Davenport, IA: 1857), 1: 351, 355 (hereafter Iowa 1857).

33 Joseph Bowker quoted in Milo M. Quaife, ed., *The Convention of 1846*, vol. 27 of *Collections of the State Historical Society of Wisconsin* (Madison: State Historical Society of Wisconsin, 1919), 692–95 (hereafter Wisconsin 1846). The 1846 Wisconsin Constitution was rejected in the subsequent popular ballot.

colleague Laurel Summers that the "starved hungry swindling loafers who have got possession of the stinking carcass of this filthy concern have set up a terrible howl at its death[,] poor fellows." After all, "great sinners," Shelby believed, "are apt to be loath to give up the Ghost." The lazy, well-dressed confidence men who cheated the hardworking miners had bathed too long "in Widows tears and fattened on orphans bread." Perhaps these "parasites" could learn a lesson from brawny Dubuque miners. If they lost their fraudulent livelihood, no doubt some of the real miners could "put them in the way of making an honest living." When the territorial assembly revoked the bank's charter after an investigation, finding that it had been fraudulently capitalized, the corporation finally closed its doors, by which time its notes had depreciated to forty cents on the dollar.[34]

Colorful reports from investigations around the Northwest underscored the difficulty of regulating local banks. In 1838, when an Iowa bank commissioner inspected the Jackson County Bank, he discovered more than a thousand dollars worth of gold and silver coins "loose in a drawer." But when the teller exhibited additional strongboxes under the counter, claiming they contained similar amounts of specie, the inspectors decided to open the first box – only to discover that it contained a superficial layer of silver "while the remaining portion consisted of lead and ten-penny nails." The rest of the boxes presented similar contents, "with a single exception, in which the substratum was window-glass broken into small pieces."[35] Whether these banks were all similarly corrupt is unlikely. Clearly, people living in the Northwest were trying to make sense of a money market controlled by distant institutions that appeared to be tied to powerful international economic systems and that had trapped them in debt and instability and – worst of all – rendered them complicit in moral corruption. By the mid-1840s, northwestern Locofoco (radical Democrats opposed to banks and paper money) opposition to banking rose to a fever pitch.

The most pressing danger – indeed, the main reason banks had to be controlled through constitutional prohibitions rather than legislation – was that fraudulent corporations had hoodwinked both legislators and private citizens. The voters of Verona, a town in southwestern Wisconsin, sent resolutions to the 1848 constitutional convention declaring that the entire system of banking was rotten and intended to "mislead and defraud the public mind." Because no system of banking could serve everyone, it must "therefore be confined entirely to the wealthy and ... speculating classes." Its benefits excluded the industrious

[34] Robert F. Klein, *Dubuque during the California Gold Rush: When the Midwest Went West* (Charleston, SC: History Press, 2011), 19–23; H. M. Shelby to Laurel Summers, August 6, 1845, Laurel Summers Papers, State Historical Society of Iowa, Des Moines; Ivan L. Pollock, *History of Economic Legislation in Iowa* (Iowa City: 1918), 171–72; and Preston, *Banking in Iowa*, 22.

[35] Preston, *Banking in Iowa*, 16.

poor. The Verona assembly instructed the convention to deny the legislature the right to authorize any bank or any corporation having banking privileges.[36]

The Verona assembly represented the popular will, but the people would have to wield greater power in order to accomplish that end. The legislature could not diminish its own authority, so citizens would have to force a fundamental change. And that could only happen through constitutional revision. By the late 1840s, several states in the region (as did most states throughout the nation) demanded constitutional revision, primarily to remove power from state legislatures they thought had overstepped their authority. Five Northwest states revised their original constitutions during those decades: Illinois in 1847; Indiana, Ohio, and Michigan in 1850 to 1851; and Iowa in 1857. The two new states that entered the Union – Wisconsin in 1848 and Minnesota in 1857 – paid careful attention to the economic clauses of their sister states' constitutions.[37]

Brass bands, young ladies' academies, railroads, canals, and banks – indeed, all nonpublic enterprises and associations – required private laws to bring them into existence: That is, in order to create such entities, state legislatures had to pass laws that named specific individuals, as opposed to public laws intended for general benefit. Private laws had enjoyed a long history, both in Congress and in states. Their main purpose was to resolve matters that could not be handled through general laws or courts. In the first half of the nineteenth century, there was no other way of granting divorces, bringing private associations into existence, and chartering corporations.[38] Traditionally, private legislation was meant to address personal or individual problems (such as a land grant for a soldier or a pension for his widow). Ironically, however, by the 1820s and 1830s, private laws became a drain on the state budget. According to Robert Irelan, most laws in the states were private, rather than public laws; indeed, in the 1830s, two-thirds of all Indiana statutes were special laws. By the mid-1840s, the ratio stood at three to one. During those two decades, Indiana

[36] Resolutions, March 4, 1848, Verona Assembly and Verona Lyceum records, Wisconsin Historical Society, Madison.

[37] For example, the 1857 Minnesota constitution copied elements from the 1848 Illinois constitution, such as individual stockholder liability. See William Anderson and Albert James Lobb, *A History of the Constitution of Minnesota* (Minneapolis: University of Minnesota, 1921), 125–27. Wisconsin borrowed its banking provisions from the Illinois 1848 and the Iowa 1846 constitutions. See Jack Stark, *The Wisconsin State Constitution: A Reference Guide* (Westport, CT: Greenwood Press, 1997), 4–5.

[38] See House Committee on the Judiciary, *A History of the Committee on the Judiciary 1813–2006*, 109th Cong., 1st sess., 2007, H. Doc. 109–53; Matthew Mantel, "Private Bills and Private Laws," *Law Library Journal* 99 (Winter 2007): 87–100; Francis Newton Thorpe, "Recent Constitution-Making in the United States. North Dakota, South Dakota, Montana, Washington," *Annals of the American Academy of Political and Social Science* 2 (Sept. 1891): 1–57; and Charles Chauncey Binney, "Restrictions upon Local and Special Legislation in the United States," *The American Law Register and Review*, 1st ser., 41, no. 12 (Dec. 1893): 1109–61. Note that the Indiana 1851 constitution forbade all private legislation unless "otherwise declared in the statute itself," Ind. Const. of 1851, art. 4, sec. 27.

passed more than four hundred private charters.[39] The sheer volume of such private laws, and the necessity to trade favors, a practice called "logrolling," was an undemocratic waste of time, and (because of printing and salary costs) far too expensive for the budgets of the new assemblies.[40]

For fast-thinking bank, canal, railroad, or plank road entrepreneurs, private laws became a direct route to a monopoly. If investors could persuade the legislature to charter their businesses first, they gained an exclusive right to crowd out similar businesses or grasp special privileges before legitimate competitors could appear. Westerners therefore deemed private legislation undemocratic. Legislators were too easily swayed by wealthy corporations, or by the lure of future wealth. Western settlers feared that their legislators accepted bribes to support private laws chartering banks, granting corporations the right to issue paper notes, or giving them exclusive control over roads, canals, or river improvements.[41]

Worse, private legislation favored those who lived in the capital cities or who had the means to travel to the state capital, stay in hotels, and lobby legislators. The hardworking miners, mechanics, and artisans, or even the more prosperous farmers, who were yoked to their seasonal chores, had limited access to the state assembly. As a result, private charters quickly became synonymous with corruption, fiscal recklessness, and aristocratic monopolies. Private corporations, especially those that possessed banking privileges, were often directed by spurious personnel – for example, men who did not own stock in the corporation and who could not be held answerable for defalcations. Therefore, it was often difficult to identify specific individuals who were responsible, and could be held liable. This is precisely why state legislations and constitutional conventions enacted provisions to corporate charters that held individuals liable.[42]

Therefore, when canal fever burned across the nation in the 1820s and early 1830s, western state legislatures passed thousands of private laws to support new transportation networks and nearly bankrupted their new states with debts. Just as their voters did, the state senators and representatives plunged

[39] W. W. Thornton, "The Laws of Indiana as Affected by the Present Constitution," *Indiana Quarterly Magazine of History* 1, no. 1 (1905): 27–32.

[40] Robert M. Ireland, "The Problem of Local, Private, and Special Legislation in the Nineteenth-Century United States," *American Journal of Legal History* 46, no. 3 (July 2004): 271–99.

[41] Simon Sterne, "Crude Methods of Legislation," *North American Review* 137, no. 321 (Aug. 1883): 163.

[42] See House Committee on the Judiciary, *A History of the Committee on the Judiciary 1813–2006*, 109th Cong., 1st sess., 2007, H. Doc. 109–153; Andrew J. Theising, *Made in USA: East St. Louis, the Rise and Fall of an Industrial River Town* (St. Louis, MO: Virginia, 2003), 66. Theising discusses problems arising from private legislation in Illinois after 1867, which he blameson the inability of the "unpopular" 1848 constitution to address the needs of the growing state. See also, *The Indiana Gazetteer: or Topographical Dictionary of the State of Indiana*, 3rd ed. (Indianapolis, IN: 1849), 122–23, for a contemporary discussion of problems with private legislation focusing on fraud and divorce.

into risky ventures, with insufficient backing, but with the great hope that their gamble would pay off. So they extended charters to anyone who could propose a scheme for building a canal or railroad – which almost always included a charter to permit banking operations – including, of course, the right to print paper notes.

Throughout the first half of the nineteenth century, the U.S. Supreme Court protected privately legislated contracts, invalidating state interference with corporate charters. For example, in *Fletcher v. Peck*, 1810, the Court found that the state legislatures had to uphold even illegally obtained land contracts. In *Dartmouth College v. Woodward* (1819), Chief Justice John Marshall ruled that the original college charter was to be held sacred, and that the New Hampshire legislature could not transfer the control of trustee appointments to the state. Public outcry against such decisions in the 1820s and 1830s – primarily because they were deemed undemocratic and a violation of state sovereignty – led to a national movement for reform of state constitutions to grant state assemblies the right to alter or revoke private charters. Ironically, during those decades, the surfeit of private legislation, particularly those charters that granted banking privileges, now forced a reassessment in western states. Private laws were now condemned as unfair and undemocratic, and constitutional reform demanded that legislatures be deprived of the power to grant such charters.[43]

"Whoever heard of the legislature or the constitution creating an individual?" In the Wisconsin 1846 convention, Democrat William Smith mocked (with subtle ribaldry) the notion that a political body could "create" an individual, an act that, he claimed, could only be accomplished by human beings. Corporations were not persons. Therefore, they possessed as little real substance as paper money; both could be fiddled into existence at a whim and disappear just as quickly.[44] The problem was that corporations were dependent upon political representative entities for their creation. Therefore, they were (by virtue of that relationship) "clothed with exclusive powers and privileges." According to Horace Butler, a radical antibank Democrat in the 1847 Illinois convention, they were therefore contrary to the "spirit and fundamental principles of our republican institutions, oppressive to the best interests of the people at large, and tend to unequal, unjust, and oppressive monopolies." Such bodies could control the flow of commodities and therefore enslave the "truly worthy and deserving" farmers, millers, miners, and trappers – "making the rich richer and the poor poorer." That meant that wealth would predominate over merit, virtue, and integrity. Therefore, the state legislature ought to be prohibited from creating any companies, associations, or corporations by special

43 *Fletcher v. Peck*, 10 U.S. (6 Cranch) 87 (1810); *Trustees of Dartmouth College v. Woodward*, 17 U.S. (4 Wheat.) 518 (1819); R. Kent Newmyer, *John Marshall and Heroic Age of the Supreme Court* (2001; repr., Baton Rouge: Louisiana State University Press, 2007), 222–53.

44 William R. Smith, "Banks and Banking" (speech), October 15, 1846, in Wisconsin 1846, 159.

laws. The convention adopted this resolution, and similar provisions appeared in all of the state constitutions.[45]

It went without saying that party politics would never be able to resolve the problem of corporate fiscal ethics. The two main political parties "differed chiefly on commercial subjects," as an 1840 Indiana Democratic Party pamphlet explained.[46] The Whig Party supported a national transportation and communication network that bound the Union together in a glorious, progressive nation. Whigs also believed in a central bank that could control the money supply, tariffs to protect American manufactures, and federal funding for transportation projects. Democrats supported some internal improvements but opposed federal interference, believed that tariffs were destructive to farmers, loathed paper money, and excoriated the national bank. Both nationally and within the western states, however, the Democratic Party split into two main factions: moderate, forward-thinking Democrats, sometimes called "Young America," who supported banks (with proper restrictions) and internal improvements. They fought against the so-called Old Hunkers (a nickname for conservative elderly people) or, more commonly in the West, the "Locofocos" (after the new wooden matches that could ignite instantly). The Locofocos became the most conservative branch of the party. They supported metallic currency, opposed all banks wholesale, and championed Jackson's bank war. Until the mid-1830s, Democrats dominated western state legislatures. By 1836, the Whigs emerged as a political force in the Old Northwest, and within four years, during the 1840 presidential election, Indiana, Michigan, and Ohio went for the Whig western territorial governor William Henry Harrison.[47]

Economic concerns such as paper money, banks, and corporate charters caused deep divisions among western Democrats. The more moderate among them understood the necessity of a fluid circulating medium and demanded progress on transportation networks. The national Democratic Party platform looked askance at large federal involvement in internal improvement projects. However, mid-nineteenth-century party distinctions broke down in the western states, primarily over the government's role in promoting internal improvements and banks.[48] As moderate Democrats, especially the businessmen and capitalists

[45] Arthur Charles Cole, ed., *The Constitutional Debates of 1847*, vol. 14 of *Collections of the Illinois State Historical Library* (Springfield: Illinois State Historical Library, 1919), 64–67, 120 (hereafter Illinois 1847). See Howard Schweber, *The Creation of American Common Law, 1850–1880: Technology, Politics, and the Construction of Citizenship* (Cambridge: Cambridge University Press, 2004), 52.

[46] *Address of the Democratic Convention of 1840. Together with an Abstract of the Proceedings* (Indianapolis, IN: 1840), 4.

[47] Yonatan Eyal, *The Young America Movement and the Transformation of the Democratic Party 1828–1861* (New York: Cambridge University Press, 2007), 27–38; Jean H. Baker, *Affairs of Party: The Political Culture of Northern Democrats in the Mid-Nineteenth Century* (New York: Fordham University Press, 1998), 210; Daniel Walker Howe, *The Political Culture of the American Whigs* (Chicago: University of Chicago Press, 1979) 17, 48.

[48] Michael F. Holt, *The Rise and Decline of the American Whig Party: Jacksonian Politics and the Onset of the Civil War* (New York: Oxford University Press, 1999), 684–88; John Joseph

who invested in western transportation and building projects, began to lean toward banking, the conservative wing of the party became increasingly radicalized. Antibank, hard-money Democrats wanted to use state constitutions as weapons in the war against banks. They feared their more moderate colleagues in the state assemblies, who were being lured by the promise of profits at the cost of private property rights. They saw banking as a wicked system that threatened the very foundations of American liberty. Constitutions were the only bulwark against such aristocratic, undemocratic privilege. Andrew Jackson understood this as early as 1834. He wrote to Robert M. Burton, a member of the Tennessee state constitutional convention, demanding that he speak out against the "Whore of Babylon," whose oppressive powers, according to Jackson, "the Government cannot controle, [sic] or relieve the people from." Although Jackson believed that that power ought never to have existed, he now felt that the people "by main force" would "never permit [it] to exist again."[49] Constitutions had to go to war, and the people's "virtue and will" would have to provide the armaments, against a corrupt, elite, powerful institution.

Wisconsin delegate Moses M. Strong received a letter from one of his hard-money constituents admitting that there was some difference of opinion on banks among the Democrats of Milwaukee.[50] Western Democrats such as Stephen A. Douglas, for example, considered themselves hard-money, antibank men. But they still recognized the profits to be earned from successful banks and real estate loans. In 1835, Douglas observed that capitalists were "rushing in from all quarters to take our Bank stock which it is supposed will be very proffitable." He hastened to assert that he was "no friend to the Banking System," but instead considered himself a "real Bentonian *Shiner*" – in other words, a Democrat who, like the long-term Missouri senator Thomas Hart Benton, trusted only gold and silver coins. Still, if Illinois wished to defend itself against worthless paper notes from other states, and to be capable of handling deposits from public land sales, then a state bank would have to be endured. The following year, President Jackson won his war against the U.S. Bank and forced through his Specie Circular, which would force moderates such as Douglas to take an even softer line on banks and paper money.[51]

Wallis, "State Constitution Reforms in the 1840s and 1850s and the Relationship of American Government and the Economy" (working paper, National Bureau of Economic Research/Development of the American Economy, July 2001). For further information on the transformation of rural culture because of the market revolution, and the role of party politics in that transformation, see Donald J. Ratcliffe, "The Market Revolution and Party Alightments in Ohio, 1828–1840," in Jeffrey P. Brown and Andrew R. L. Cayton, eds., *The Pursuit of Public Power: Political Culture in Ohio, 1787–1861* (Kent, Ohio, and London: Kent State University Press, 1994), 99–116.

49 Andrew Jackson to Robert M. Burton, April 27, 1834, Andrew Jackson Letters, St. Louis Mercantile Library, University of Missouri-St. Louis.

50 J. W. Helfenstein to Moses M. Strong, December 2, 1846, Moses M. Strong Papers, Wisconsin Historical Society, Madison.

51 Stephen A. Douglas to J. A. Granger, April 25, 1835, Stephen A. Douglas Papers, Special Collections Research Center, University of Chicago Regenstein Library.

Moderate Democrats were willing to recognize the necessity of at least some viable paper money and of keeping local banks alive. As early as 1837, as another international financial panic overwhelmed the nation, even some of those Democrats who detested banks began to argue for their continued existence. For example, the *Constantine Republican*, a staunch Democratic Michigan newspaper, denied that Jackson's Specie Circular, and his removal of deposits from the federal bank, had caused the bank failures in the West. If so, what should the public do about the current economic disaster? Why, sustain the banks, in order to prevent further bank closures. And what did the public and banks owe each other? Banks had to be moderate and safe. The editor hastened to explain that he was describing state and local banks. National banks had too much power, whether in the United States or overseas. Citing the Bank of England as a cautionary example, the *Argus* made it clear that a national bank would not be able to "preserve its people from blighting effects of present revulsion." During the 1830s, the Bank of England funded the Crown's debts by passing interest on the national debt to its shareholders. The U.S. Bank would soon control the western money market, entirely to the benefit of wealthy eastern investors. The entire system – what the *Argus* called "ordinary banking principles" – was at war with American democratic ideals.[52]

In spite of these dangers, however, most western Democrats understood the banks were necessary to modernize the west. In the late 1830s and early 1840s, Democratic editorials on banking always began with dire depictions of the instability and inevitable collapse of state banks, and often ended with grudging admissions that banks served vital economic functions. In 1838, for example, the national *Democratic Review* criticized corporations that could "spring up from a fertile soil with all the ease and quickness ... of the wild rice or prairie grass." Meantime, every street and lane was "haunted with the ghosts of broken banks, stalking dismally amid the scenes of former speculation!" Nevertheless, the *Review*'s editor maintained that he remained friendly to banks. It was simply that they had to be used correctly, as did all modern tools. Indeed, they were the "labor-saving machines in the transactions of commerce, and of the general business of society." While the editor deplored the abuses of "vicious" principles, he was persuaded that safe, responsible banking would produce capital and legitimate credit for the convenience of commerce and industry.[53] Moderate Democrats – particularly those who occupied state government positions – were fully alive to the importance of national transportation networks. Stephens T. Mason, the so-called Boy Governor of Michigan,

[52] *Constantine* [MI] *Republican*, May 31, 1837; *Albany* [NY] *Argus*, June 7, 1837. See Richard Sylla, "Comparing the UK and US Financial Systems, 1790–1830," in Jeremy Atack and Larry Neal, eds., *The Origins and Development of Financial Markets and Institutions, from the Seventeenth Century to the Present* (Cambridge: Cambridge University Press, 2009), 209–40.

[53] "The Banks and the Currency," *United States Magazine and Democratic Review* 2, no. 5 (April 1838): 7.

who had been appointed by Andrew Jackson at the tender age of nineteen, insisted that the national importance of railroads could not be overstated. He was positive that the state treasury could borrow enough money (by offering a small commission to eastern banking houses) to begin building the railroads that would connect Lake Michigan with the East – and so effect a union "among all the great internal improvements of the country."[54]

Convention delegates received one unambiguous mandate from all their constituencies, regardless of party affiliation: Retrench and reform. The delegates were keenly aware that a failure to tighten restrictions on corporations, or to set up safeguards and provisions for strict oversight, could result in a failure of the constitution. The 1847 Illinois constitutional convention passed a provision that provided a small sales tax (two-hundredths of a penny) whose purpose was to defray the state debt. And most western settlers accepted responsibility for their actions in bringing about the financial disasters that engulfed them. An article entitled "Commercial Delusions" that appeared in the *American Whig Review* in 1845 viewed the financial woes connected with banking with a touch of rueful humor. Shrugging off some of the more violent suggestions put forth by the "duped," the Whig observed that "hanging and quartering is a poor method of revenge in any case; it will never insure a profit out of a bad speculation, nor transform a fancy stock into a safe commodity." Americans who had been "bitten" were too honest, and too wise, to waste their time in loud complaints and lamentations. They regarded their speculative losses as nothing more than a business transaction, "in which he who wins may laugh, and he who loses learns the necessity of being doubly careful thereafter, and endeavors to console himself with the idea that the lesson is a quid pro quo."[55] Experience was hard-won; rather than grumbling, perhaps it was better to erect safeguards to preventing the problems from recurring.

The moral crisis at the heart of this problem was the pervasive lack of accountability at every level of society. Daniel Solomon, a Democratic delegate to the 1857 Iowa convention, feared that an uncontrolled banking "system" would destroy the morals and standing of their state. This system generated its own corrupt creations (such as monopolistic corporations, legislative malversation, and unsound paper money), which were essentially un-American. Worse, this powerful system tempted otherwise virtuous citizens into wrongdoing. Solomon regarded banking as "nothing more or less than a series of tricks of adroit swindlers, invented by ingenious financiers, to rob the laboring man of the fruits of his labor." Any state that "gives her aid and credit in breathing … life into the nostrils [of] such monsters as this" had already lost

[54] Stevens T. Mason, "Message to the Legislature," February 1, 1836, Stevens Thomson Mason Papers, Bentley Historical Library, University of Michigan, Ann Arbor.

[55] "'Commercial Delusions'–Speculations," *American Review: A Whig Journal of Politics, Literature, Art and Science* 2, no. 4 (Oct. 1845): 341.

its honor.[56] Northwesterners could not allow their fresh young states to be degraded before they had even begun to flourish.

Republican constitutionalism, radically reinterpreted in the Northwest as a rough-and-tumble popular sovereignty that ruled lawmakers (and to a degree, judges), would have to stand as the bulwark that repelled the juggernaut of banking, paper money, and monopolistic corporations. In grappling with the burdensome issue of banks, delegates in the Northwest forged a new understanding of democratic participation and civic virtue. State constitutions were the foundation of an ethical system that supported individual responsibility and self-restraint. They also instituted a greater reliance on the citizens' ability to judge what was best for their young economies. Citizens would have to be placed at the center of – indeed, in control of – economic aspects of the political process. Provisions that established direct democratic control over economic issues enjoyed widespread bipartisan support in the region. Even Whigs and, after 1854, Republicans demanded strict constitutional provisions regulating banking corporations and agreed to place control over bank charters directly into the hands of citizens. Delegates responded to the demands from constituents in two ways. First, they removed power from the state assemblies by inserting provisions in their constitutions that restricted their ability to charter corporations with banking privileges. The second and far more innovative method was to grant citizens the direct authority to veto state legislation. Provisions that gave voters the final say over bank and corporation charters, for example, forced a clear distinction between the powers of the legislature (to propose and enact legislation) and the final authority of the people (to deny the right of the legislature to risk the people's welfare by chartering too many banks, for example).[57]

If laws supposedly safeguarded citizens' right to a stable economy, and if, at the same time, profligate legislatures wrote laws, then who would guard the guardians?[58] Democratically elected legislatures could be voted out of office, but the next crop of lawmakers – who were, after all, drawn from and elected by the people – might not comport themselves any more wisely than their predecessors or, for that matter, their constituents. In a report widely circulated in northwestern newspapers, New York Whig congressman James Tallmadge explicitly declared the need to protect the tangible value of American property in state constitutions – not in state legislatures. He explained that legislatures across the nation had granted private charters to thousands of bank directors, who now possessed complete control over the "value of all property." Even

[56] Iowa 1857, 1: 350.

[57] See table 10.1. Five state constitutions in the Old Northwest permitted citizens to veto bank charters: those of Illinois, Iowa, Michigan, Ohio, and Wisconsin.

[58] He was quoting from Juvenal: "Who would guard the guards themselves?" *Quis custodiet ipsos custodes?* For a contemporary translation, see, for example, the Reverend Martin Madan, *A New and Literal Translation of Juvenal and Persius* (London, 1829), 2: 195.

a die-hard Whig such as Tallmadge condemned the corporate control of the value of property as undemocratic. Legislatures could do little to protect the free market from corporate encroachments. Banks were morally dangerous precisely because they had taken "deep root in the hearts" of state legislators – the very men who were to guard the "portals" of their state constitution. Corporations that possessed the right to print and decide the value of paper notes could destroy the "measure" of property by making it impossible to standardize the value of money and thus "made a lottery of all private property."[59] Northwesterners still believed that paper money represented real worth only if it were redeemable by precious metals at face value. Conservative Democrats feared that as representations of money – particularly those that possessed no value in and of themselves – replaced metal currency, the value of all property would plummet.[60]

Unsound paper money encroached on the homesteads, mills, and workshops of the very people whose labor raised the value of the land. The federal government controlled all legal tender coinage and did not print paper money until 1862, so paper money was not legal tender for tax payments. Therefore, state legislatures were responsible for chartering corporations that issued bank notes; they also operated state banks funded by private and state money. Paper money and privately chartered banks, many Democrats believed, worked as a disease envenoming the character of American property rights. William Allen, a speaker at the Ohio Democratic convention, complained that banks could determine, "at their own pleasure," the value of both property and labor. In this way, banks retained a "strangle-hold on the credit of the nation." The most horrifying aspect of this power was its contamination of "the whole frame of society" through the circulation of paper money. Nineteenth-century northwesterners believed that moral worth was tangible and predictable.[61]

Constitutions fixed institutional structures, guaranteed rights, and established basic equality for white men, but a system that jeopardized property rights and subverted the democratic ethos fundamentally threatened these purposes. An 1846 Ohio Democratic convention opposed all paper currency and resolved that the state ought to return to the "constitutional currency of gold and silver." Although this hardly realistic demand received no serious hearing

[59] James Tallmadge, "Letter from General Tallmadge," *Niles' Weekly Register* 51 (Dec. 3, 1836): 220. See also, William M. Gouge, *A Short History of Paper Money and Banking in the United States … to Which Is Prefixed an Inquiry into the Principles of the System …* (Philadelphia: 1833), 79. Tallmadge served in the 1821 and 1846 New York constitutional conventions.

[60] James L. Huston, *Securing the Fruits of Labor: The American Concept of Wealth Distribution, 1765–1900* (Baton Rouge: Louisiana State University, 1998), 356–57.

[61] Hammond, *Banks and Politics*, 98; William Allen, *Speech Delivered at the Great Democratic Festival, held at Lancaster, Ohio, on the 19th Day of August, 1837* (Lancaster, OH: 1837), 6; and Edward S. Cutler, *Recovering the New: Transatlantic Roots of Modernism* (Lebanon, NH: University Press of New England, 2003), 32–34.

in the region's state constitutional conventions, it does reveal the depth of northwesterners' concern for how diminished property values affected their self-worth, their children's inheritance, and the very nature of democratic self-government. Because privately chartered corporations possessed the right to meddle with monetary value, delegates regarded them as destructive to equality and hostile to free institutions.[62] Similarly, when the rights of corporations came up for debate in the 1847 Illinois convention, Democratic delegate George W. Armstrong offered a resolution that linked the moral problems of paper money directly to private corporations and their threat to American democracy. Because paper money was a protean, malleable substance, those in power would always be able to manage it to their own benefit. Paper money was "but the representative and not the reality – a shadow or promise of the substance on which no reliance can be placed." Armstrong especially deplored the fact that the value of money solely depended on the caprice of unscrupulous wastrels who produced nothing of any real value. Farmers, miners, and mechanics could be swindled – especially if they lacked the self-control to withstand temptation.[63]

Northwestern settlers would have to take a hard look at their own ethical shortcomings. As they scrutinized the fundamental causes of economic disasters, they demanded a new society purified of undemocratic inequities – one capable of guiding its citizens back to a path of moral righteousness and fiscal probity. This recognition crossed party lines. For example, the Michigan *Constantine Republican*, a radical antibank Democrat newspaper, wondered who was to blame for the present "unparalleled distress" in the United States and Europe. There could be only one answer: The international economic depression had been caused by the "great and almost universal CUPIDITY of the American and English people, which has increased the worst of all systems, called the BANKING SYSTEM." The most culpable offenders were the great banking house managers – incompetent, poorly educated men "whom the God of Nature intended for pop beer and ginger-bread makers." These malefactors had reneged on their fiscal obligations and, worse, had extended loans to those who "were not deserving credit, and cannot now pay ten cents on a dollar!" But the plain, hardworking people were at least partially responsible for their distressed situation. They had erred in overbuying, pledging their credit for farms they would never be able to purchase or cultivate, using unstable currency, borrowing from unreliable sources, and electing irresponsible

[62] *Resolutions of the Democratic Convention Held in 1846* quoted in Samuel Medary to Alpheus Felch, January 28, 1846, Alpheus Felch Papers, Bentley Historical Library, University of Michigan, Ann Arbor.

[63] George Armstrong quoted in *Journal of the Convention, Assembled at Springfield, June, 7 1847 ... for the Purpose of Altering, Amending, or Revising the Constitution of the State of Illinois* (Springfield IL: 1847), 199.

legislatures. The time had come to acknowledge their mistakes and take up their ethical responsibilities.[64]

Since the 1810s, the whole region – from farmers to bankers and businessmen to legislatures, with the complicity of eastern and foreign investors – had plunged into chancy ventures. The nineteenth-century word for such large-scale economic gambles was "speculation." That word often carried a sense of moral opprobrium but could also convey optimism and daring. Several contemporary sources declared that without the spirit of enterprise, and without a willingness to speculate, economies would stagnate. In 1835 the French traveler Michel Chevalier observed that in the United States "every body is speculating, and every thing has become an object of speculation," especially "cotton, land, city and town lots, banks, railroads." Similarly, in 1840 the economist and historian Richard Hildreth asserted that successful speculation, "however wild it may have appeared in the beginning," was always considered "an excellent thing, and ... commended as *enterprise*; it is only when unsuccessful that it furnishes occasion for ridicule and complaint, and is stigmatized as a *bubble* or a *humbug*."[65]

That enterprising spirit drove the northwestern economy – and threatened the northwestern soul. The Democratic State Convention of 1840, held in Indianapolis, alerted voters to the dangers of their state's "recklessly extended credit" system. At the same time, the convention reassured the voters, "far be it from us to discourage the spirit of enterprise, or to undervalue its beneficial effects." But "good also brings evil," and it was time to explain the state's financial difficulties. If the answer did not lie in Jackson's war against the Bank of the United States or the withdrawal of federal deposits, then perhaps the cause lay closer to home. Indeed, Indiana Democrats had "ransacked the whole world" for an answer and found only one cause: "EXTRAVAGANT SPECULATION, by States and by individuals," which resulted in widespread and long-range debt. Worse, the hopeless debts of the present generation would inevitably descend, "as hereditary burdens, to the next." But most deleterious to the state's future was the injury to people's morals caused by their habit of "carelessly incurring debts, on remote and uncertain chances of finally discharging them." Only one solution remained: fundamental political reform. The author reminded his readers that revisions to the Indiana State Constitution could be voted on every twelve years. The time had arrived. Nothing less than a "constitutional check can effectually restrain the giant strides of the modern State funding System." The problems of financing vast internal improvement projects, and in restraining reckless speculation by the state assembly, required a "fixed barrier against improvident public loans." In 1850, at the very next

64 *Constantine* [MI] *Republican*, July 12, 1837. Emphasis in the original.

65 Michel Chevalier, *Society, Manners, and Politics in the United States: Being a Series of Letters on North America* (Boston: 1839), 305; and Richard Hildreth, *Banks, Banking, and Paper Currencies* (Boston: 1840), 160 (italics in original).

opportunity, the Democratic Party in Indiana succeeded in its call for constitutional reform.[66]

The delegates who framed or revised the region's state constitutions during those decades understood that if they did not heed the demand for popular control over economic legislation, the voters would reject the constitutions out of hand, wasting all of the conventions' hard work. Morgan L. Martin, a delegate at the 1848 Wisconsin convention, explained that the principal object of the convention had been to draft a "popular" constitution, and this could only be accomplished by "allowing the people to fight over such questions of policy among themselves."[67] Five of the constitutions (all but Indiana's and Minnesota's) contained explicit provisions for removing the power to charter banks from legislatures and handing it directly to the people. In the Michigan 1850 convention, Daniel Goodwin explained that the people had been scourged by banks and had a right to decide whether they should be chartered. If banks were necessary and beneficial, then the people would establish them through general laws.[68] Petitions and "indignation meetings" regularly rebuked the delegates throughout the conventions. An angry group of Ohio Democrats sent a resolution to the 1850 constitutional convention declaring that they opposed "granting power to the Legislature to create an unlimited State debt" and demanding that the "new Constitution shall protect the people against the use of such a power." A few months later, a Democratic newspaper editorial demanded that the Ohio constitution prevent an increase of debt "without consent of the people."[69] Incorporating legislative codes (specifically, provisions that would establish strict supervision and liability clauses) in state constitutions would restrict the lawmakers' ability to hazard the general welfare and to charter risky, undemocratic monopolies. Such economic protections were necessary in constitutions, because legislators had proven themselves unreliable. But mid-nineteenth-century westerners demanded a far greater say in the political process. Simply establishing legislative limits was not enough. The voters insisted that they had the right to supervise, rebuke, challenge, and even veto the lawmakers' actions.

In response to pressure from voters, delegates devised solutions to fulfill three objectives: prohibit legislatures from chartering corporations that

66 *Address of the Democratic Convention of 1840, Together with an Abstract of the Proceedings* (Indianapolis, IN: 1840), 14–15.

67 "Narrative of Morgan L. Martin: and Interview with the Editor," in Reuben G. Thwaites, ed., *Collections of the State Historical Society of Wisconsin*, (Madison, WI: 1888), 11: 409.

68 Daniel Goodwin quoted in Michigan 1850, 560–63.

69 Eleanor von Ende and Thomas Weiss, "Consumption of Farm Output and Economic Growth in the Old Northwest, 1800–1860," *Journal of Economic History* 53, no. 2 (June 1993): 308–18; E. Gale, S. W. Andrews, and A. Jackson Morgan, "Resolutions of Columbus Democrats," March 30, 1849, *New Constitution* 1, no. 1 (May 5, 1849): 5; [Samuel Medary], "Debts of the State – Prohibition of Its Increase without the Assent of the People," *New Constitution* 1, no. 8 (June 23, 1849): 113–14.

possessed the power to print and lend money, legitimize popular sovereignty over important financial decisions, and, despite widespread mistrust of banks, grant legislatures the right to pass general banking laws. Coalitions of moderate Democrat and Whig delegates defeated hard-money conservatives in order to fulfill all three aims. Most state constitutions instituted strict oversight over banks, placed the will of the people squarely in control over the legislature's economic decisions, and, in spite of powerful, conservative Democratic opposition, permitted some form of banking.

With the single exception of Illinois, every northwestern state constitution written or revised before the Civil War allowed state legislatures to establish state banks. The Illinois restriction became so problematic during the war, however, that the legislature found it impossible to float the loans and bonds necessary to raise state regiments. As a result, Illinois revised its constitution again in 1862. The Republican-dominated 1857 Iowa convention, following the lead of most other constitutional conventions in the Northwest, permitted both state and private banking. Democrat Henry O'Connor wrote an angry letter to his delegate, William Penn Clarke, demanding to know what the "convention [met] for?" Were there "no interests in the state to be cared for but the interests of the Rail Road and Banking corporations?"[70]

Considering the widespread popular mistrust of legislatures, the fact that delegates permitted legislatures to charter state (rather than private) banks may be somewhat surprising. True, in their day-to-day functions, state banks did not differ markedly from banks owned by private individuals or corporations. But the legislatures could at least regulate the percentage of capitalization required to establish the bank, the number and kinds of notes the bank was allowed to print, and the obligations to note holders. The convention delegates believed that state banks would be safe so long as legislatures could not grant new private charters to any corporations with banking or money-printing powers. And legislatures ought not / should not handle money. The Indiana and Iowa legislatures were not permitted to own stock in any private banks. No state was permitted to grant private charters to corporations, and all charters previously granted would expire in twenty years.

Did these tight restrictions kill banking? Those who recognized the importance of stable financial institutions certainly feared that they would. At the 1848 Wisconsin convention, Whig judge Edward V. Whiton, who chaired the banking committee, drew up a restrictive set of provisions controlling banking and corporate charters. None of the Whigs at the convention, according to his colleague Almerin M. Carter, believed that banks could henceforth come into existence. Nevertheless, the moment the new constitutions were ratified, every state except Illinois immediately passed general banking laws. Banks funded

[70] Dan Du, "Illinois Free Banks, 1851–1865," *Business and Economic History* 8 (2010): 21; Henry O'Connor to William Penn Clarke, February 18, 1857, William Penn Clarke Papers, State Historical Society of Iowa, Des Moines.

under these laws required stockholders to show that they had enough specie on hand to cover a percentage of their paper notes. Stockholders also had to assume personal liability in the case of bank failures. They also had to submit their charter for public scrutiny.[71]

This outcome bitterly disappointed the most radical northwestern hard-money Democrats; they had hoped that all corporations with the power to print paper bank notes would be outlawed and that the economy would henceforth return to a gold and silver basis. By the late 1850s, however, with the nation exporting $150 million in cash crops overseas annually, antibank, hard-money Democrats had been left behind. Investments in railroads, canals, and town lots had paid off: Thirty thousand miles of railroad tracks connected the Atlantic Ocean to the Ohio River Valley and the Great Lakes. The region's population had grown to nearly 5 million. Despite another panic in 1857, per capita income in the Northwest grew by a steady 2 percent every year. The states and territories at the economic and geographic heart of the nation required modern financial infrastructures. They also needed to attract eastern and foreign investors. Because so many citizens considered banks and corporations dangerous to their flourishing young republics, however, they had to find ways of retaining control over their legislatures' and their own voracious appetite for land and profits. Territorial and state legislatures, they believed, proved incapable of controlling the economic chaos or leading by example. And so northwesterners found constitutional solutions.[72]

The debates over banks highlight an essential American constitutional paradox: how to leave people free to pursue economic opportunities and build a modern, technologically advanced nation that could participate in international trade, while safeguarding an ethical democracy that rested on traditional republican principles. State constitutional provisions (Table 10.1) had granted voters a say over private laws chartering banks, but in the face of subsequent widespread banking legislation in the region, those provisions were probably meaningless. True, citizens had argued for – and won – control over economic legislation and safeguards over banks and currency. Equally true, the region's banks encouraged investors to fund transportation projects, large-scale

[71] Almerin M. Carter, "An Account of the Adoption of Our State Constitution," 1896, typescript recollection, Wisconsin Historical Society, Madison; Rockoff, "American Free Banking," 418.

[72] John G. Clark, *The Grain Trade in the Old Northwest* (Urbana: University of Illinois Press, 1966), 172–75; Richard Vedder and Lowell Gallaway, "Economic Growth and Decline in the Old Northwest," in, *Essays on the Economy of the Old Northwest*, 299–303; Morton Rothstein, "Antebellum Wheat and Cotton Exports: A Contrast in Marketing Organization and Economic Development," *Agricultural History* 40, no. 2 (April 1966): 91–100; Willard W. Cochrane, *The Development of American Agriculture: A Historical Analysis*, 2nd ed. (Minneapolis: University of Minnesota Press, 1993), 218; William G. Thomas, *The Iron Way: Railroads, the Civil War, and the Making of Modern America* (New Haven, CT: Yale University Press, 2011), 2.

TABLE 10.1. *Northwestern state constitutional provisions on banking, paper money, and corporations*

State	Date of constitution	Does the state constitution allow new banks?	State banks?	Private charters permitted?	Submission to voters?	Stockholder liability	Specie redemption
Illinois	1818	No; only those already in existence	Permits state bank with 6 branches	No new banks chartered by private laws, no renewals			
	1848	No new banks without popular consent	No state banks permitted	No charters renewed hereafter	Yes	Stockholders individually liable	
Indiana	1816	No new banks, only those already chartered	Permits state bank with 3 branches			Stockholders individually liable	
	1851	Yes	Yes, but state may not be a stockholder in any private bank	No recharter permitted; all charters end in 20 years.		Stockholders individually liable	All paper notes redeemable by gold or silver; first priority to note holders
Iowa	1846	No	Yes, but state may not be a stockholder in any private bank	Only nonbank corporation charters			
	1857	Yes	Yes	By general laws only, no private laws	Yes	Individual liability	Paper notes redeemable by specie
Michigan	1836				Yes		
	1850	Yes			Yes	Individual liability	Priority of note holders; no suspension of specie payments

(*continued*)

TABLE 10.1 (*continued*)

State	Date of constitution	Does the state constitution allow new banks?	State banks?	Private charters permitted?	Submission to voters?	Stockholder liability	Specie redemption
Minnesota	1857	Yes		Only nonbank corporation charters		Individual liability	Priority of bill holders; no suspension of specie payments
Ohio	1802	No mention of banks					
	1851		No mention of state banks	Legislature not permitted to pass private laws conferring charters	Yes	Individual liability only for unpaid stocks	
Wisconsin	1848	Yes		No private charters, no private laws	Yes		

agriculture, and mines that generated the region's national and international exports. Four years after Minnesota entered the Union as the last northwestern state, civil warfare broke out. The region experienced tremendous prosperity as their wheat, corn, hogs, cattle, lumber, lead, iron, and zinc sustained the U.S. Army's war effort.[73]

[73] Von Ende and Weiss, "Consumption of Farm Output and Economic Growth in the Old Northwest," 308–18; Vedder and Gallsway, "Economic Growth and Decline in the Old Northwest," 301–4; Clark, *Grain Trade in the Old Northwest*, chaps. 11 and 12.

Epilogue

By the time the 1850–51 Indiana constitutional convention had concluded its labors, three of the Whig delegates were fast friends. They had spent many pleasant evenings together talking over the day's proceedings at Mrs. Dill's boarding house, where all three were rooming while serving in the convention. As middle-aged antislavery Whigs, Melchert Helmer, William Winans Thomas, and Dr. Henry G. Todd had more in common with one another than they did with the young Jacksonian Democrats with whom they had been contending and against whom they had lost so many important battles.[1] After he returned home to his medical practice in Fayette, Todd wrote to Thomas, redeeming his promise to stay in touch. Looking back on his work in the convention, he sometimes worried that he had been "patching up" rather than "revising and amending" the Indiana constitution, which left so many important social reforms unrealized. Even so, Todd had thoroughly enjoyed his work and had learned a great deal. He could not resist laughing a bit at their less experienced selves, when they had first begun their labors in Indianapolis. Looking back on their high hopes, Todd gently mocked their naïve aspirations as "noble? and awkward." Yet there were still "many pleasing associations connected with [the] slow progress" of the convention, memories he would long cherish. Chief among those were the "hours spent in social *Table Talk* with newly acquired friends." Todd ended his letter to Thomas with a plaintive quotation: "When shall we three meet again?"[2]

[1] Melchert Helmer, forty-nine at the time of the convention, born in New York State, had moved to Louisville but soon moved his family to Indiana because of his opposition to slavery. Dr. Henry G. Todd, a Whig from Kentucky, was thirty-nine. William W. Thomas, originally from New York, was fifty.

[2] Henry G. Todd to William W. Thomas, April 23, 1851, William W. Thomas Papers, Indiana Historical Society, Indianapolis. He was a doctor, an elder in the Presbyterian Church, Whig, later Republican; originally from Kentucky. It is unknown whether any of the friends ever met

We do not know whether they ever did meet again. After Melchert and his friends returned home and took up their farms and professions, Thomas became ambassador to Sweden and Norway, and Todd served in the Indiana State Legislature for several years. A decade later many of their colleagues, both in Indiana and in the other northwestern states, would lead regiments for the United States Army in the Civil War. No matter how wearisome they had found their duties in the conventions, many of the delegates later took up local, state, and, in many cases, national political offices. Most of the delegates for whom we have biographical information spent the rest of their lives in their states; perhaps their role in crafting their state governments had given them a solid stake in their communities. In any event, most of them seemed willing to forget their antagonisms after they concluded their labors. At the end of the Illinois convention in August 1847, for example, the delegates relieved their pent-up tensions by throwing paper balls at each other, resulting in a scene of great hilarity.[3] And several of the conventions held reunions twenty or thirty years later to reminisce about their achievements.

Of the eleven constitutions examined in this book, only two failed in the popular vote: the 1844 Iowa and the 1846 Wisconsin. Those defeats must have been bitter blows to the delegates who had sacrificed so much of their time and effort, and who had remained apart from their families, farms, and offices for months. Moreover, both of those constitutions, if successful, would have taken their territories to statehood. Yet the voters were willing to delay entry into the Union and to bear the costs for a second convention rather than to live under what they believed to be the wrong kind of government. For white people living in the antebellum Northwest, this question of the "wrong" kind of government involved two crucial matters: the physical shape and size of their new states (together with the rich resources located in disputed territory) and the extent and reach of popular sovereignty.

The main objection to the 1844 Iowa constitution had been the disputed Iowa-Missouri state boundary. Congress had redrawn the state's contours slightly, giving Missouri a few hundred square miles of contested borderland. The Iowa citizens, enraged about what they saw as robbery, rejected their state constitution 7,019 to 6,023 and agreed to wait for statehood. Two years later, the next convention rewrote the constitution, which, in fact, closely resembled the earlier one. By that time the state boundaries had been adjudicated (though not to the benefit of the Iowans) and the new constitution passed, by a little more than 400 votes.[4] By contrast, the rejected 1846 Wisconsin state constitution contained more problematic elements – provisions that the

again. Thomas's correspondence contains a few letters from Todd. The quotation is from William Shakespeare's *Macbeth*, act i, scene 1.

3 Hezekiah Wead manuscript diary, August 28, 1847, Abraham Lincoln Presidential Library, Springfield, IL.

4 Jack Stark explains, for example, that the subsequent constitutions – the one written in 1846, which admitted Iowa into the Union, and the one in 1857, which revised the initial state

voters found too radical, and that suffered a resounding defeat at the polls. Those included a strong homestead exemption provision, a radical prohibition of privately owned banks, and an article guaranteeing married women's property rights.[5] The next Wisconsin convention, held less than two years later, rewrote the homestead exemption, permitted some banking, and ignored married women's property rights entirely. These two rejected constitutions in Iowa and Wisconsin, together with the hundreds of thousands of indignant petition signatures for and against controversial provisions in other states, suggest that popular sovereignty strongly influenced constitution building in the antebellum Northwest. Constitutions framed the physical and legal boundaries of the state much more permanently than legislation. No new constitution could come into being if those provisions went beyond the line of what people were willing to accept.

If pressed, white northwesterners would have defined any constitution as satisfactory so long as that document allowed the people to retain sovereignty over the legislature and the laws, especially those laws that touched them most closely: in their homes, their family lives, their property rights, and their communities. Put plainly, what these people wanted from their constitutions was the right to supervise the lawmaking process and, if necessary, to veto legislation that threatened their livelihoods. They also demanded the right to say who should serve on the judiciary. Above all, they wanted constitutions that did not materially alter their existing familial and social arrangements. The voters were less concerned with the notion of constitutional longevity, since most assumed that charters could be and should be rewritten to suit the changing times. Indiana's state constitution, for example, mandated a popular referendum every twelfth year. From the point of view of the white people living in the antebellum Northwest during those tumultuous years, then, it could be said that most of those eleven constitutions set up governments and delineated, or restricted, the inhabitants' rights precisely the way the voters expected and desired.

The state constitutions that survived the ratification votes embodied Jacksonian democracy. All of them shortened legislative sessions, rendered political offices and the judiciary elective, and set up populist safeguards to prevent both lawmakers and financial corporations from wreaking havoc with the state economies. On the social front, too, there were few surprises – neither from the point of view of antebellum northwesterners, nor from that of the modern historians who have studied the antebellum Northwest. Black people suffered intense discrimination as constitutions provided for their continued

constitution, made only slight changes. *The Iowa State Constitution: A Reference Guide* (Westport, CT: Greenwood Press, 1998), 3. It was a close vote: 9,492 to 9,036.

[5] Jack Start, *The Wisconsin State Constitution: A Reference Guide* (Westport, CT: Greenwood Press, 1997), 4.

disfranchisement and exclusion – provisions that perpetuated grave injustices in their lives, and in the lives of their descendants, for generations.

What does this tell us? As has been frequently observed throughout this book, it would be a mistake to search for a coherent political and constitutional philosophy in the way these young men set up their state governments. True, the delegates certainly assumed that their spiritual, political, and rational worlds were part of a single harmonious whole. They also believed that their own political commitments (of whichever party) were more in line with that harmonious whole than were those of the opposition. They believed that the American democratic experiment, blessed by a Divine Providence, had already been amply proven as a success by numerous historic examples and through rational observation. Any serious problems, such as the national panics or the looming sectional conflict, were the result of deviations from the democratic ideal and of failure to heed popular sovereignty and could be corrected by reverting to first principles.

Yet somehow this handsome architecture – the religious, scientific, and historic elements that they believed formed the foundation of their state constitutions – failed to join together as neatly as Northwesterners had hoped. The antebellum tendency to think in logical extremes – their "all or nothing" habit of thought – may have made perfect sense when contemplating a constitutional structure that embodied abstract ethical, rational, and historical elements. But given northwesterners' concurrent reliance on the "unwritten" laws of prejudice, on old-fashioned legal and nonlegal codes, and given the rapidly shifting antebellum cultural attitudes toward nonwhite people and women, it was simply not possible to build constitutions that enshrined both of those worldviews. Either constitutions would be founded on a unified political and spiritual philosophy, or else they would be based on personal, idiosyncratic feelings and thoughts. The antebellum American tendency to press conclusions to logical extremes seemed to render the goal of achieving both ends difficult, even impossible. If a democratic constitution protected rights, and if the diminution of any right threatened all rights, then how did one justify undemocratic provisions such as the disfranchisement of property owners – even property owners who did not belong to the legitimate polity?

The delegates' work in the conventions was clearly aimed at finding a way to harmonize both of those worldviews into a cohesive framework, but the delegates could only innovate so far. They adhered to the standard design of republican government based on popular sovereignty, divided into two chambers and three separate powers, and as representative of the polity as they could manage, in terms of both population distribution and geography. These people framed governments that respected the fundamental political rights for white people. But something troubling remained in all of these agreements. If human beings could be trusted to discern right from wrong – if nature, or nature's God, had endowed people with the innate ability to govern themselves in a moral and rational manner – then how was it still possible to frame inequitable constitutions? Antebellum northwesterners, at least all but the most intransigent, wrestled sorely with this conundrum, even if they were rarely able to find a workable solution during their service in the conventions.

Many of the bitterly fought-over provisions were overturned, some within twenty years. The constitutional prohibitions that prevented black families from migrating into Illinois and Indiana, and that deprived black men of the franchise everywhere in the region, were all gone (at least from the state constitutions) by the early 1870s.[6] After the Civil War, partly as a result of the massive economic demands of recruiting, arming, and equipping state regiments, legislatures had to return to annual sessions, and tight restrictions on banks had to be modified to allow for both state-controlled banks and out-of-state paper money. Almost all of the antebellum northwestern constitutions omitted married women's property rights from their charters, but every state legislature passed such protections within two decades. Finally, every state charter rendered appointive judiciaries elective, and the judges responded by rendering decisions that often collided with the popular will. It is difficult to know whether all of those economic, social, political, and judicial changes would have occurred as quickly had the nation not plunged into the national calamity of civil warfare in 1861. The rough-and-ready popular sovereignty that forced (or even encouraged) the delegates to leave hard moral questions to the voters in separate ratification ballots was swept away with the aftermath of Reconstruction. The Thirteenth, Fourteenth, and Fifteenth Amendments forced northwestern legislatures to rescind state constitutional discrimination against black people, at least on paper.

The constitutional conversations allow insights into the essential dilemma inherent in democratic deliberation. Even when people meet together with prior agreements about justice, fair representation, and constitutionally protected rights, they can still fail to live up to those ideals. In the antebellum Northwest, the intrusion of selfish, shortsighted, and even bigoted motives

[6] Every northwestern state rescinded discriminatory constitutional provisions by 1870. Illinois deleted the word "white" in the 1870 constitution, but the convention first waited to be certain that the Fifteenth Amendment to the U.S. Constitution would pass. Indiana struck down black exclusion and disfranchisement in 1866. Iowa struck out the word "white" from voter qualifications in 1868; Michigan in 1869 (by a very small margin, and after numerous votes to maintain disfranchisement). Minnesota voters once again voted against black voting rights in 1865 and in 1867 but finally granted voting rights to black men in 1868. Ohio ratified the Fifteenth Amendment in 1870 (by one vote), effectively negating the state constitutional disfranchisement of black men. Pursuant to a provision in the 1848 Wisconsin state constitution, the legislature attempted to pass black voting rights laws in 1849, 1857, and 1865, but all laws failed in popular elections. In 1866, *Gillespie v. Palmer*, a Wisconsin Supreme Court decision, finally granted black men the right to vote. Eugene H. Berwanger, *The Frontier against Slavery: Western Anti-Negro Prejudice and the Slavery Extension Controversy* (Urbana: University of Illinois Press, 1967); Stephen Middleton, *The Black Laws in the Old Northwest: A Documentary History* (Westport, CT: Greenwood Press, 1993); Dana Weiner, *Race and Rights: Fighting Slavery and Prejudice in the Old Northwest 1830–1870* (DeKalb: Northern Illinois University Press, 2013).

resulted in tragic disappointments. Black families who had been granted a grudging right to their own land, for example, were still deprived of the rights of citizenship. These conventions, and the urgent popular conversations that engaged with them, tested the possibilities and risks of democratic deliberation on a frontier landscape. The delegates had left the most controversial issues to the voters, a process that built injustices right into the state constitutions. The only way to repair the damage caused by those popular referendum votes (and of course by the convention votes as well) would have been to amend the constitutions, a difficult process in most states, requiring several legislative enactments and popular ratification. The stormy relationship between the delegates and their constituencies, combined with the notorious failure of the 1846 Wisconsin constitution, may have contributed to the delegates' unwillingness to take a stance on morally fraught issues. Perhaps without meaning to, they built a northwestern style of democratic deliberation, which combined traditional parliamentary procedure with wild intrusions of the popular will. Even given their ingrained cultural beliefs, and their reluctance to incur the wrath of their constituencies, however, the convention delegates rarely flinched from even the most difficult questions.

Index